DEAD GOD RISING

RELIGION AND SCIENCE IN
THE UNIVERSAL LIFE-SYSTEM

Graeme Donald Snooks

IGDS

Institute of Global Dynamic Systems Books
Canberra

First published 2010
by **IGDS Books**
Canberra

© Graeme Donald Snooks, 2010

Printed in the United States of America by CreateSpace

National Library of Australia cataloguing-in-publication data
Snooks, G.D. (Graeme Donald)
Dead God Rising
Bibliography.
    1.   Religion and science
    2.   Economic transition
    3.   General dynamic theory
    4.   Strategic *logos*

ISBN: 978-0-9808394-1-8

Dedicated to

The illustrious "strategic gardian" Thoth (Djehuty)

3000 BC–400 AD

Discoverer and interpreter of the universal laws of *maat* (or life)

Contents

List of Figures

List of Tables

Preface

The purpose of this book, which was researched and written between July 2005 and July 2008, is to explore the origin, development, nature, role, and future of religion in human society. While the subject matter is unremarkable, particularly during a time of religious fundamentalism and atheistic revival, the method employed is innovative, and the conclusions challenge the conventional wisdom. But even more importantly, this exploration of religion and science has led to the discovery of the hidden materialist life-system that I have called the **strategic** *logos*. The discovery of this remarkable life-system, which provides the key to understanding the success of human society – indeed, of life itself – in a hostile physical world, together with the nature of religion and "god", was only possible by the employment of a novel general dynamic theory, which I have been developing over the past two decades. This "dynamic-strategy" theory has already provided major reinterpretations of a wide range of social, behavioral, and biological issues during that time.

As this book is the outcome of a period of solitary reading, thinking, and writing, my main debts are due to my family for their generous indulgence. I would also like to thank Debbie Phillips for cheerfully and expertly transforming my handwritten manuscript into a readable typescript, and Julie Hamilton for preparing the typescript for publication and for designing the cover. The costs of typing, formatting, and copyediting were financed privately and not by any educational or governmental institution. Publication was delayed for almost two years by a scholarly publishing industry that has lost its way in the internet era. In contrast, IGDS Books has embraced the challenges of the twenty-first century.

As usual in my books, words and phrases bolded in the text are explained in the "Glossary of New Terms and Concepts".

GDS of Sevenoaks

Prologue: In the Beginning

*It must be written. Words have to be found. To leave a record. To provide
an account for those who are to follow. To have lived so long and seen
so much; to have acquired wisdom; only to die alone without passing
it on. Otherwise future generations will need to start again. I have
translated these words of mine, which are marks and pictures on the
cave wall before me, in an imaginative rather than a literal way.*

*There are many mysteries. Where does the sun go at night? Why
does the moon wax and wane? What is the meaning of the lights in the
night sky? Where do the winds come from, and go to? What is the source
of the great rivers and what is their end? Why are there four seasons?
But even greater than these: what accounts for the way we come into
this world, the way we grow into adulthood, the way we are able to hunt,
gather food, tell stories, make love, have children, mature, grow old,
die, and go to be with our ancestors. What explains this cycle of life and
death? And what prevents it breaking down? This cycle – this mandala –
of life is the greatest mystery of all. The mystery of mysteries.*

*To understand the mystery of mysteries would grant us some
influence over it. To ensure that everything functions as it should. To
ensure that the seasons come and go on time. To ensure the rains return
when they should, and in abundance. To ensure there is a plethora of
animals to hunt and plants to gather. To ensure our families multiply,
our children and grandchildren live into adulthood to give us pleasure
and security, and our old people enjoy their final years and go to be
with their ancestors at the right time. There is a way of understanding
and influencing this mysterious life-system. Nothing is more important.
Nothing more profound.*

*All hunters know that every outcome has a cause. That
all causes are connected. What is the source of these causes? The
answer seems obvious, yet it is difficult. According to the shaman,
our life-system is shaped by the spirits – supernatural beings from the
Otherworld. A world we cannot see, but which is a shadow of this one.
What the Shadow World looks like we do not know. What the Spirits are
like we do not know. Perhaps they are the spirits of our ancestors, or
the spirits of animals on which our lives depend. Where do the Spirits
live? From my experience of this world there are two possibilities.
Some Spirits reside in the heavens, because some great power must be
responsible for the lights in the night sky and their regular pattern of
journeying. Perhaps the sun and moon are ancestral Spirits who have*

changed shape to become these great beacons of light and heat, which are essential to power our mysterious life-system. Perhaps some Spirits have become stars – those eternal lights in the night sky that guide us on our journeys and determine our destinies. Other Spirits, of a darker kind, probably live in the underworld, that great repository of the dead. Spirits that can guide us to our ancestors after death.

To discover where the Spirits are is only half the journey. We need to devise ways of gaining access to these realms, and to return with hope for our people. Access to the underworld is straightforward. Entry points can be found in great caves like this one, which reach deep into the Earth. They are dark, mysterious, and terrible places that only the bravest and most prepared dare enter. Some who have penetrated their dark depths have never returned. Surely they passed over to the underworld and decided to stay, or were unable to persuade the Spirits to let them return. Perhaps they remain to argue a case on our behalf. Journeying to the heavens is more difficult. But there are tall trees, hills, and mountains that take us closer. Our wisemen visit these places, and return with news from the Spirits. Some even fly like eagles – or so it is said.

While we need the ancestral Spirits to sustain our life-system, they have little need of us. We have to persuade them to act as guardians of our way of life. We have to convince them to sustain our well-being. We have to treat them with respect through sacred ritual, acceptable sacrifice, living by their values, and taking good care of the land. They are the Guardians of our world, which would fall into ruin if we failed to please them.

But will the people listen? Perhaps my words – my marks and pictures on this cave wall – will never be understood. How can they possibly communicate the turmoil of thoughts in my mind.

In the beginning was the strategic *logos* – the mandala and meaning of life.

Chapter 1
The Mystery of Mysteries

There are many mysteries in life, which are gradually being driven back by modern science. Some of these mysteries are more important to us than others. What we have never been able to comprehend, and what is infinitely more important to us than any other mystery, is the nature of the universal life-system that enables us to survive and prosper. In this book I will argue that the supreme, yet unsuccessful, attempt by mankind to understand the universal life-system has been responsible for the world's great myths and religions. Religion is the instrument employed by mankind to understand and manipulate this great mystery of mysteries.

THE HIDDEN LIFE-SYSTEM AND ITS MYTHS

Mankind has always been aware that their lives are the outcome of a hidden system of forces. But because it is hidden, we have, until now, not been able to understand it in a rational manner. And this lack of understanding has led to a concern that this vital system might break down, leading to the destruction of our society, even our species. Hence, our greatest priority throughout the history of human society has been to understand the universal life-system, gain access to the forces controlling it, and to exert some influence over its functioning. The underlying fear that has driven this great quest has been fuelled by the evidence all around us of human societies that have failed. Yet despite the failure of individual societies, the human race has prospered, owing to the underlying robustness of the universal life-system, which I call the **strategic *logos*.**

As the strategic *logos* has remained a mystery throughout human history – as it has resisted rational exploration – the only way in which it could be accessed was through myth – through the exercise of our story-making imagination. Karen Armstrong in her small book entitled *A Short History of Myth* (2005) also eloquently makes this point. She tells us that:

> Myth is about the unknown; it is about that for which initially we have no words. Myth therefore looks into the heart of a great silence ... all mythology speaks of another plane that exists alongside our own world, and that in some sense supports it. Belief in this invisible but more powerful reality, sometimes called the world of the gods, is a basic theme of mythology ...

> ... mythology is an art form that points beyond history to what is timeless in human existence, helping us to get beyond the chaotic flux of random events, and glimpse the core of reality.[1]

Myth, of course, is not truth. It is the imaginative equivalent of truth in a fictional parallel world. It may encourage us to think that we are approaching the "core of reality" and, thereby, are able to exert some mystical influence over it, but to really understand and shape the strategic *logos* we must employ science not myth. We must operate within the real world not a virtual parallel world.

The original authors of these sacred myths understood what they were attempting to do. They knew they were groping for an understanding of their life-system through the use of metaphor rather than reason. Their "gods" were ephemeral **strategic guardians** of their particular *logos*, not eternal lords of the cosmos. It was only much later that generations of professional **priestly philosophers** turned these founding strategic myths into what we understand today as religion. And, as we shall see, this was the outcome of persistent **strategic failure** followed by intense and prolonged **strategic frustration**. In the process, the early strategic guardians were transformed into "gods". Rather than treating the early strategic myths as metaphor, the priestly philosophers – or metaphysicians – employed them as factual statements about reality. For this reason, any discussion of the role of religion in society is really an exploration of man's vision of the hidden strategic *logos*.

Contemporary commentators on ancient religions, however, fail to understand the origin of these mythologies as metaphors for the hidden life-system. Here is what an otherwise perceptive Egyptologist, Erik Hornung, in *Conceptions of God in Ancient Egypt* (1996) has said of this issue:

> Of course we no longer attempt to 'explain' gods – the farther we penetrate into the world of these ancient images the less we can explain what a god is.[2]

Scholars have, in the main, abandoned the attempt to explain the origin of gods and religion because, like the priestly philosophers, they have no understanding of the strategic *logos* in either rational or mythical terms. Religion is seen merely as a reflection of the cultural attainment of the society that give rise to it. In contrast, explaining what gods *are* is the very purpose of *Dead God Rising*.

MAN'S EXISTENTIAL ANXIETY

Man has an intense desire to understand, manipulate, and sustain his life-system. This is an outcome of the need to survive and, having survived, to prosper. Prosperity, at its most basic, is insurance against future crises. The driving force in this process is what I've called **strategic desire**. It is a concept discussed in detail in my earlier books *The Collapse of Darwinism* (2003) and *The Selfcreating Mind* (2006). There are two dimensions to this basic need of mankind that are central to our exploration of the nature and role of religion. The first and most important is the desire of the entire society to understand the mystery of mysteries to ensure its longevity and prosperity; and the second is the longing of the individual within this society for peace and security.

Mankind, as shown in later chapters, has always been concerned about the viability of its societies. Human society is a fragile and ephemeral entity.[3] Hear what the Anglo-Saxon poet had to say on this matter:

> Where has gone the steed? Where has gone the man? Where has gone the giver of treasure? Where has gone the place of the banquets? Where are the pleasures of

the hall? Alas, the gleaming chalice; alas, the armoured warrior; alas the majesty of the prince! Truly, that time has passed away, has grown dark under the helm of night as though it had never been ... Here wealth is ephemeral; here a friend is ephemeral; here man is ephemeral; here kinsman is ephemeral; all this foundation of the earth will become desolate.[4]

Such ephemerality has always been obvious to mankind as the evidence of failed societies lies all round. We need only reflect on the haunting lines of Percy Bysshe Shelley's (1792–1822) well-known poem "Ozymandias" (a reference to Ramesses II):

I met a traveller from an antique land,
Who said – "two vast and trunkless legs of stone
Stand in the desert ... near them, on the sand,
Half sunk a shattered visage lies, whose frown,
And wrinkled lips, and sneer of cold command,
Tell that its sculptor well those passions read
Which yet survive, stamped on those lifeless things,
The hand that mocked them, and the heart that fed;
And on the pedestal these words appear:
My name is Ozymandias, King of Kings,
Look on my Works ye Mighty, and despair!
Nothing beside remains. Round the decay
Of that colossal Wreck, boundless and bare
The lone and level sands stretch far away."

In the past, the very greatest of societies – such as Egypt, Greece, and Rome – arose from and eventually returned to obscurity over long periods of time, whereas lesser societies only briefly made their mark before being engulfed by oblivion. Even today, in living memory, well-established empires like Britain and the USSR have suddenly collapsed after giving impressions of permanence, while lesser ones like Nazi Germany and Imperial Japan have emerged and collapsed in a handful of years. Smaller societies in the Pacific, Southeast Asia, the Middle East, and south-eastern Europe are forever forming and foundering. Even the superpower of today, the United States of America, will be eclipsed this century.

Why this is so has always been a great mystery for the leaders, citizens, and scholars of the many societies of man, both past and present. This widespread and profound failure to understand the sources of the emergence, the expansion, and the collapse of societies has generated an intense anxiety in the breast of man. It is an anxiety that leads to an overwhelming need to achieve order and balance (or equilibrium) in human society. In the past, ancient societies like Egypt judged the living and the dead by their contribution to the mystical *maat*, or worldly and cosmic order; and today we are fixated with the desire to achieve economic equilibrium through the equally irrational "war on inflation", or, alternatively, to intervene massively in order to "fix" global recession and climate change. Irrational because inflation plays a vital and positive role in the dynamic processes of the strategic *logos,* and massive interventions disrupt and distort this *logos*.[5]

In the past, the priestly philosophers were regarded by their societies as the experts concerning the mystery of mysteries – concerning the life-systems underlying the prosperity of their societies. In today's modern world these experts are considered to be the worldly philosophers or economists. Both groups of so-called experts have focused their attention upon the same objective – order and equilibrium. Interestingly, today's worldly philosophers, who are inadvertently attacking the very dynamic mechanism that underlies their society's strategic success, are no closer to understanding the mystery of mysteries than were the priestly philosophers of the past.

In the past, this great anxiety about whether order and stability would emerge from the mystery of mysteries led to the creation of comforting myths about strategic guardians – myths that were ultimately turned into religions about creator gods, even a supreme creator God of the Universe. The vast number of gods – tens or hundreds of thousands – and their associated religions, together with the massive investment of time and material surpluses required to maintain them, is testament to the great anxiety of mankind in the face of the mystery of mysteries. In the contemporary world this anxiety has led to the creation of a body of metaphysical knowledge called neoclassical economics, which is attended to by a "priestly" class of experts called economists, who have captured the ears of politicians throughout the Western world. These economists are responsible for creating new myths about the mystery of mysteries in order to assuage our existential anxiety. And more recently our fear of future chaos has led to the new science of climate change, and to the metaphysics of climate mitigation conjured up by the worldly philosophers – see my new book *The Coming Eclipse* (Snooks 2010).

Existential anxiety is not just a collective experience. Individuals in any society also harbor intense personal fears about the future. If their society is uncertain, how can they, as individuals, hope to survive and prosper. As our study of history shows, individuals also look to the strategic guardians or gods of their society to soothe their primeval anxiety. Initially, the strategic guardians were called upon by a society's wisemen or shamans for the benefit of the entire community. But, later, in the hands of the professional priestly philosophers, these strategic guardians were transformed into creator gods that could be sought out by individuals, as well as by communities through their kings and priests. This "democratization" of access to the gods was an outcome of the ever-present pressure in human society for the masses to partake of the privileges of their leaders.

Transformation of strategic guardians into personal gods, however, had an ironic twist. Initially, as I have suggested, the strategic guardians were required to ensure the material success of their society. But in the course of this successful **strategic pursuit**, individual members of a given society were required to do things that their rational faculties told them were wrong. The source of this problem – as I show in *The Selfcreating Mind* (2006) – is that individuals are composed of a body, driven by strategic desire, and its facilitating strategic instrument, the mind, ruled by reason. What the body craves, the mind both facilitates and, sometimes, questions. This problem has led to a compartmentalization in the personal lives of human beings – a separation of what we do on a daily basis to survive, from what we believe we should do. In *The Dynamic Society* (1996) I called this compartmentalization, **existential schizophrenia**.[6]

In some people, existential schizophrenia works quite well. They are able to participate fully in the strategic pursuit – which involves, at least, intense competition with others and, at worst, systematic killing – and still regard themselves as morally upright and entirely justified in what they need to do to survive and prosper. Sanity is retained by refusing to integrate reality with their distorted perception of themselves. Other individuals, however, are not so "fortunate". In some of these, as I show in *The Selfcreating Mind*, existential schizophrenia leads to pathological schizophrenia,[7] while in others the only resolution of this fundamental dilemma of life is forgiveness from a supernatural being. What these guilt-stricken people cannot forgive in themselves, requires forgiveness from the gods. This is where the ironical twist comes in. These individuals are led to call on gods, which arose from the need to ensure strategic success, in order to obtain forgiveness for actions committed in the course of achieving that strategic success. Perhaps it is fortunate they are unaware of the origin of their gods.

EMERGENCE AND TRANSFORMATION OF THE GODS

In this book I will argue that it was man's attempt to penetrate the mystery of mysteries and to come to grips with the life-system underlying everyday activities that led to the emergence of strategic guardians in paleolithic societies. The recognition of these strategic guardians, and the attempt by shamans to contact and influence them, enabled these early hunter-gatherer societies to participate in the strategic pursuit with greater confidence. While they did not rationally understand how their life-system, or strategic *logos,* worked, they did achieve a sense of *rapprochement* with it by employing a simple **strategic ideology**, or mythological explanation.

With the neolithic technological paradigm shift (or agricultural revolution) beginning about 10,600 years ago in the Old World and about 7,700 years ago in the New World, surpluses were generated that could be used to support a professional class of priests and priestly philosophers, and to invest in great temples and pyramids as working models of the mystery of mysteries. Over several millennia, simple ideas about strategic guardians were reworked into complex myths about the gods – whereby the **G**uardians **O**f **D**ynamic **S**trategy, or **GODS**, were transformed into "gods" – which provided a protective shield under which the society could progress strategically. This was the work of the priestly philosophers, who responded to strategic demand generated by the *logos* of neolithic communities – such as Egypt and Mesopotamia – for a more sophisticated strategic ideology. In this transformational process, the ritual of the strategic ideology because more elaborate, and responsibility for it was assumed by the strategic leader, or king, the ruling social elite, and the professional class of specially trained and educated priests. This elaborate system of strategic ideology in support of the *logos* was the outcome of strategic success in the ancient world. As seen through the eyes of ancient neolithic man, the great strategic success of Egypt and Mesopotamia was a reflection of the power of their gods and the efficacy of their strategic ideologies in eliciting the support of these strategic guardians.

The transformation of neolithic strategic ideologies – centered on a multiplicity of gods – into what we would recognize as modern religion – centered on a single divine being – was a product not of strategic success, but of strategic failure. In the ancient world, the most difficult region to build a successful strategic society was the land of Canaan – what we know today as Palestine and Syria – lying between the superpowers of Egypt in the south and Mesopotamia in the north and east. Canaan was a land dominated by these superpowers. The small societies in this rich corridor of commerce – the reason it was so attractive to the superpowers of the ancient world – only prospered on the rare occasions that both superpowers were otherwise distracted. In the absence of superpower attention, small Palestinian or Syrian states quickly expanded. But never quickly enough, because the returning superpowers just swept them away and imposed their hegemony on the local peoples. This geopolitical reality generated a depressing sequence of long periods of oppression and exploitation, followed by short periods of liberation and prosperity, followed in turn by long periods of oppression and exploitation. This vicious cycle generated intense and prolonged strategic frustration – a type of individual and collective neurosis – as discussed in *The Selfcreating Mind*.[8]

In the eighth century BC, Josiah, king of the small society of Judah, attempted to take advantage of the temporary absence of the superpowers, by developing plans to expand his kingdom into northern Palestine and Syria under the protection of the strategic guardian YHWH. To this end, Josiah's priestly philosophers reworked the local myths of YHWH into a sophisticated strategic ideology, later revised and called the Hebrew Scriptures (or, to Christians, the Old Testament). But even before his plans were executed, Josiah was captured and killed by the Egyptians returning to control this commerce corridor. The subsequent destruction of Judah by the Babylonians, the fall of Jerusalem, and the Exile in Babylon, led the captive priestly philosophers to transform Josiah's strategic ideology of conquest (under the conquest strategic guardian, YHWH) into a religion – a spiritual (nonstrategic) rather than a materialist (strategic) ideology – later known as Judaism. This transformation was an outcome of strategic failure and intense strategic frustration. In the subsequent three centuries of superpower oppression by the Mesopotamians and Macedonians (586–301BC), the Egyptians (301–200BC), and the Mesopotamians again (200–107BC), Judaism could only survive as a religion – a *spiritual* ideology – as there was no scope for the exercise of an independent *strategic* ideology.

With the revolt of the Maccabees in 167 BC at a time of superpower withdrawal, the Jews experienced a rare period of independence. For about a century Judaism was employed both as a religion and a strategic ideology for a short-lived conquest strategy that led to the Hasmoneans occupying all of Palestine. Predictably, however, this period of independence and prosperity was brought to a sudden and final end in 63 BC by the expansion of the Roman Empire under Pompey. Once again the people of Palestine experienced deep existential frustration arising from this strategic failure. The response was varied. Some Palestinians attempted to accommodate themselves to Roman occupation, others looked to apocalyptic prophets, others rebelled, and yet others attempted to construct a new *nonstrategic* community within their oppressed land. The latter was the path chosen by Jesus of Nazareth and his followers – a path determined by strategic frustration. In the hands of the priestly philosophers in the centuries after Jesus' death, however, this new nonstrategic ideology was transformed into a new monotheistic religion called Christianity.

Ironically, Christianity, with its *nonstrategic* origins was later adopted by the Roman emperor Constantine as a new *strategic* ideology. Owing to the exhaustion of Rome's conquest strategy in the late second century AD, the old gods of war had lost favor and the empire was desperate to find a new strategic ideology and a new strategic guardian. Constantine, who attempted to revive the flagging fortunes of the empire, adopted the Christian God to lead his conquest strategy and Christianity as the new strategic ideology. Christianity also served as the new religion of Roman citizens. With the collapse of Rome in the early fifth century, Western European societies, employing the conquest strategy, continued the use of Christianity as both strategic ideology and state religion.

The other great monotheistic religion, Islam, also emerged in the borderlands between superpowers, this time – in the early seventh century AD – comprising the Eastern Roman empire (later called Byzantium) and the Persian empire. Like the Palestinians of earlier times, the Arabs had long experienced strategic failure, intertribal warfare, and intense strategic frustration. With the examples of Zoroastrianism (Persia), Judaism, and Christianity (Roman empire) surrounding him, Muhammad wanted to fashion a monotheistic strategic ideology that would unite his people and enable them to succeed and prosper like the surrounding superpowers. Owing to fortunate timing – the Roman and Persian empires had fought each other to a standstill – the Arabs were remarkably successful. Within the space of a generation, they had conquered the Persian Empire and made themselves and their Islamic ideology masters of Egypt, Palestine, Arabia, Mesopotamia, and Iran. Islamic forces even went on to challenge the survival of the West with its Christian strategic ideology – a challenge that was only finally eliminated by the industrial technological paradigm-shift effected by Western Europe in the nineteenth century.

The Industrial Revolution, beginning in the late eighteenth century, marked the end not only of the Islamic challenge but also, ironically, of Christianity as a strategic ideology, if not a religion, in the most advanced societies. The underlying reason is that the new technological strategy was based on science rather than religious mysticism. The advanced Western societies in both the Old and New Worlds looked to technology and science to sustain their strategic *logoi*, rather than to the old metaphysical mythology – a belief in the power of science to ensure mankind's survival and prosperity. In these circumstances Christianity as a strategic ideology became irrelevant, leading intellectuals like Friedrich Nietzsche (1844–1900) to proclaim, in the last quarter of the nineteenth century, "God is dead". Even as a religion Christianity has been declining in strategically advanced societies and, like Islam, has only made new converts in the Third World. The new ideology in the industrialized world is "scientism". This ideology has also taken a spiritual trajectory in the form of environmentalism and the cult of Gala, and has become a new religion for some.

The new priestly philosophers of scientism initially believed that, armed with their new strategic ideology, they would be able to finally penetrate the mystery of mysteries where their religious predecessors had failed. But this has not been the case. The reason is that once they leave the realms of the natural sciences the priestly philosophers of scientism – including orthodox economists – approach human society with metaphysical reasoning (deduction) rather than **strategic thinking** (induction). A breakthrough in this respect had to wait until the more difficult inductive methodology could be successfully employed in the realm of human and other living systems. The results of that breakthrough in understanding the strategic *logos* can be found in part III of this book. Yet, even in the era of science and technology, religion, in the form of scientism, has re-emerged, owning to the persistence of metaphysical thinking. For as long as there are priestly philosophers and materially frustrated citizens, there will be religion of some kind or another. Yet this need not worry us as it clearly worries the new atheists, such as Richard Dawkins. It is essential to remember that it is material rather than spiritual issues that determine human motivation. As my work clearly shows: desires drive, while ideas, whether religious or otherwise, merely facilitate those desires.

WHAT IS TO COME?

Owing to the immense amount of material on myths and religion, *Dead God Rising* focuses on a number of important and representative case studies. The unifying aspect of these case studies is that most are located in regions of technological transformation – the Fertile Crescent following the Neolithic Revolution, and Western Europe following the Industrial Revolution. During the neolithic era we focus on Egypt, the Levant, Mesopotamia, and Arabia; and during the industrial era we focus on Western Europe and its New World translocations. This theme is less helpful in the paleolithic era, where we focus on Neanderthal society and Aboriginal Australia for more practical reasons.

Part I – The Old Strategic Gods – develops the argument that in the beginning the gods were no more than strategic guardians called upon by paleolithic society to sustain the hunting-gathering life-system. Sacred art and ritual was the manner in which these societies, through their wisemen, attempted to enter into the presence of the guardians in order to persuade them to continue providing protection. And the sacred stories and myths contributed to the strategic ideology of these societies. The case studies of Neanderthal society in Western Europe and Aboriginal society in Australia – dealt with in Chapter 2 – are placed in the wider context of the worldwide paleolithic society. This era saw the birth of the gods.

Chapter 3 is concerned with the era following the Neolithic Revolution – an era when the early gods were transformed from simple strategic guardians of the *logos* into creator gods of the cosmos. The argument is that this transformation took place in response to the new strategic demand generated by the neolithic *logos* for a more sophisticated strategic ideology in order to pursue the dynamic strategy of conquest or commerce. The resources to fund this new ideology, together with its supporting institutions and priestly philosophers, were generated by the new neolithic technological paradigm of settled agriculture. It was, in other words, an outcome of strategic success by the Old World's superpowers. The case studies, once again placed in a wider context of the Old World, are Egypt (a commerce society) and Mesopotamia (a plethora of conquest kingdoms).

Chapters 4 and 5 focus on the emergence of a monotheistic strategic ideology – the triumph of the One God of Zoroastrianism, Judaism, Christianity, and Islam. The argument is that this final stage in the transformation of the old strategic guardians into a cosmic God was initiated by strategic failure of small societies eking out a living in the borderlands of the Fertile Crescent's superpowers. Religion, as opposed to strategic ideology, was the invention of small societies wracked with strategic frustration and psychic anguish. Yet, despite his amazing success in presiding over the competing conquest strategies of the Old World for almost two millennia, this One God suddenly died. In Chapter 6 it is argued that this was the outcome of paradigmatic exhaustion – the "god-breaker" – in Western Europe during the eighteenth century. This was a process that saw the replacement of the exhausted neolithic technological paradigm with the new industrial technological paradigm.

Part II – The New Strategic Gods – accounts for the rise and consolidation of the new strategic guardian of science. It is an analysis of "dead god rising".

While the exhaustion of the old neolithic technological paradigm led to the death of the old God, its replacement by the industrial technological paradigm led to the rise of a new, more powerful god of science and a new strategic ideology of scientism. Chapter 7 is an account of the industrial technological paradigm shift – the "god maker" – and the rise of science and its attendant ideology of scientism – of dead god rising. In Chapter 8 – A Science of Religion? – I chronicle the unsuccessful attempts of neo-Darwinists of various types to explain religion scientifically as a "superorganism" (Edward Wilson), an "evil virus" (Richard Dawkins), and as the outcome of a "God gene" (Dean Hamer). And in Chapter 9 – A Religion of Science – I show how some scientists have attempted to use their craft to construct a religion of the "living" Earth – Gaia – and even of the "living" cosmos – the Biocosm.

Part III – The Universal Life-System – provides the first ever rational insight into the strategic *logos* of humanity. That hidden vehicle of life that has enabled mankind to make the transition in the space of just two million years from an insignificant species numbering no more than a few thousand in southern and eastern Africa, to the dominant global species numbering almost seven billion. This unveiling of the mystery of mysteries is the very climax of the book. Chapter 10 – Life's Great Odyssey – analyses the pathway taken by the transformation of life in general and human society in particular. It lays bare the patterns of biological and technological paradigmatic change. Chapter 11 presents a general dynamic theory – the dynamic-strategy theory – to explain these patterns of biological and technological transformation. It is a realist theory of life, which has at its core the dynamics of selfcreation. In the process, the alternative theories of Darwinism and complexity are rejected. In Chapter 12, the strategic *logos* – the mystery of mysteries – is, for the first time, constructed from life's patterns and our general dynamic theory with its laws of life and history.

Finally, in the epilogue – Dead Gods Also Rise – I consider what the discoveries in this book enable us to conclude about the existence of a Creator God. Is there any substance to the new atheism, or is it just the mythology of another group of priestly philosophers? While part III is the climax of the book, there may be some readers who wish to begin there, and then focus on parts I and II in that order. Like life, reading a work of this nature is a matter of personal preference.

PART I
THE OLD STRATEGIC GODS

Chapter 2
Birth of the Gods

The birth of the gods was a momentous event, but an event that occurred many times in the early society of mankind. Even so these events are lost in the mists of time. By the time we were able to make out the images of these gods, they had gone through a process of transmutation that had carried them far from their origins. In these new forms they would have been unrecognizable to the men and women who had attended their birth, just as the descendants of these people would not have recognized the origin of their gods. There was no permanent record in these preliterate times. In this chapter we are concerned with the birth of the gods – those guardians of the strategic *logos* – and in the next with the transmutation process by which these early guardians became unrecognizable to the first civilized societies.

Life is a great mystery. We understand its precariousness well enough, but not the forces and laws that determine its operations, successes, and failures. It is not surprising, therefore, that mankind has always felt the need for assistance from superior beings in negotiating life's difficulties. This chapter will attempt to establish that the life of early man was so precarious that they desperately believed the survival of their society required assistance from "guardians" – superior beings who could ensure the success of their way of life; of their dynamic strategy of hunting and gathering; of their life-system. These superior beings can be thought of as the Guardians Of Dynamic Strategy, the acronym of which is **GODS**.

The guardians, or GODS, of early hunter–gatherer societies were all closely related to the essential requirements – the animals, plants, rivers, hunting grounds, weather – of the dynamic strategy they had adopted. To ensure these GODS continued to support their life-system – or strategic *logos* – it was vital that the wisemen be able to attract and please these supernatural beings by displaying the correct attitude, by conducting proper ceremonies, and by providing acceptable offerings. In the beginning, therefore, the guardians, or GODS, were very closely associated with a society's dynamic strategy. Yet, while the GODS were born out of strategic necessity, they were soon associated with the wider cosmos in a metaphysical way.

ORIGIN OF THE GODS: THE PALEOLITHIC ERA SURVEYED

Early religious beliefs and rituals can be reconstructed from the evidence left by paleolithic societies on the walls of caves and rock shelters. But these sacred sites provide only a glimpse of a religious activity that included dance, song, and rites of various kinds. These religious activities can be found in all societies of modern humans (*Homo sapiens*); and there are even tantalizing suggestions in the archeological record that they were performed by *Homo neanderthalensis*

(0.3 myrs ago) and possibly even *Homo erectus/ergaster* (1.2 myrs ago).

What is the nature of the evidence for sacred art in these early societies? The reason some scholars believe that art – and, hence, "religious" activity – begins with *H. erectus/ergaster*, is that a few lumps of unused ochre have been found along with stone tools in Olduvai Gorge in Tanzania that have been dated to 1.2 myrs BP (Leakey 1958); and that "deliberately collected" lumps of ochre and hematite have been found in "many other lower palaeolithic sites in Africa, Europe and India".[1] The earliest known used and striated pigment lumps, dated to about 250,000 years BP, have been found in Becov in the former Czechoslovakia, in Hunsgi in southern India, and Nice in France.[2] In addition, intentionally engraved animal bones have been uncovered in sites dated as early as 300,000 BP in the Pech de l'Aze cave in France, and to about 250,000 BP at Bilzingsleben in Germany. All of these discoveries point to art activities being undertaken by *H. erectus/ergaster*.

Art activity is also associated with *H. neanderthalensis*. Engraved bones and rocks, as well as pendant beads with bored holes, have been discovered in European sites that were active during the long period 100,000 to 35,000 years BP.[3] The Neanderthals are also known to have conducted their burials with ritual. Some scholars, such as Randall White, are convinced that the Neanderthals only engaged in art activities after coming in contact with modern humans, because they believe our early cousins had the capacity to copy art but not the wit or desire to initiate it. When we come to consider the Neanderthals in more detail, I will argue that this perception is mistaken.

While *H. erectus/ergaster* and *H. neanderthalensis* appear to have employed art for religious purposes, it is not until about 40,000 BP that we have any detailed information about the nature, role, and significance of these activities. The oldest, most detailed, and continuous stream of evidence for sacred art concerns Aboriginal Australia, where an unbroken tradition has existed for over 30,000 years. This ancient culture is of particular significance as it has been directly observed and interrogated by our own age. While Western European cave paintings can also be dated back to over 30,000 BP, we know considerably less about the culture that produced it. In Eastern Europe and Siberia, art objects – including ceramics, textiles, and ivory sculptures – can be dated back to 26,000 BP, and personal ornaments to 42,000 BP.[4]

While there are many prehistoric art sites in Africa – some 30,000 sites in the Republic of South Africa alone – dating back to more than 10,000 BP, few have been adequately examined and studied. Art objects, such as ostrich egg-shell beads, have been dated to 35,000 years of age, with some, such as cross-hatched lumps of hematite, being dated "controversially" to 77,000 BP. Painted religious symbols on rock shelters throughout southern Africa are at least 28,000 years old; and some of these can, as in the Kalahari and in Australia, be discussed with the direct descendants of the prehistoric artists. Much of this art is thought to be associated with shamanism.[5]

In the Americas, Californian rock paintings have been dated conservatively to 9,300 BP, and petroglyphs (or rock engravings) controversially to 19,000 BP. Much of this symbolic representation is thought to be "shamanic in origin and nature".[6] Brazil posses rock paintings that are about 12,000 years old; and in Alaska, representational objects have been dated to over 3,000 years.

While considerably more evidence will undoubtedly be unearthed in the future, it is clear that symbolic art has been created in all paleolithic societies across the globe, and that it was deeply embedded in the functioning and history of those societies. Of particular interest is the fact that the sacred art of all these societies had many features, and, it will be argued, purposes in common. In the geometric art genre, the "track and line" style could probably be regarded as a world style, even though those societies were rarely, if at all, in contact with each other.[7] Similarly, much of the later figurative art, representing major hunting animals and guardian spirits, can be read in a similar way throughout the world. In order to draw out the nature and role of this prehistoric, or paleolithic, art, I will focus in this chapter in more detail on Europe and Aboriginal Australia.

STONE-AGE WESTERN EUROPE 300,000–11,000 BP

Stone-age settlement in Western Europe can be traced with increasing attention to detail from about 300,000 to 11,000 years ago, before the Neolithic Revolution transformed their life-system and their religion. The majority (about 90 percent) of this vast period of time was dominated by a version of mankind – namely *Homo neanderthalensis* – that disappeared from the archaeological record about 28,000 years ago, which was some 12,000 years after *Homo sapiens* invaded Western Europe. While there are some notable exceptions, such as Francesco d'Errico, it is usually claimed that modern man at this time was intellectually and culturally superior to Neanderthal man. In view of the undisputed fact that the first inhabitants of this region were able to compete with the invaders for a period of time that exceeds the entire history of human civilization, we should be cautious about branding the Neanderthals as inferior in any respect. In this section, the nature and achievement of Neanderthal society and culture will be discussed in terms of my general dynamic theory. Some novel and unexpected conclusions will emerge.

Conventionally, the cultural and technological history of this long period of human settlement is divided into the following phases of artifact-making activity:

Mousterian (Neanderthal) — 300,000–40,000 BP

Châtelperronian (Neanderthal) — 38,000–28,000 BP

Aurignacian (modern) — 40,000–28,000 BP

Gravettian (modern) — 28,000–22,000 BP

Solutrean (modern) (south-west only) — 22,000–18,000 BP

Magdalenian (modern) — 18,000–11,000 BP.

The Mousterian covers more than a quarter of a million years, when the Neanderthals enjoyed a monopoly over Western Europe, which was in the grip of a mighty ice age; while the Châtelperronian is the period of Neanderthal culture in which increasing competition for scarce resources slowly but finally pushed these first settlers to extinction. The other four cultural phases belong to modern man who finally had Western Europe to itself. Unlike the sacred art of Aboriginal Australia (discussed below), the cultural artifacts of Western Europe can be interpreted only from the outside. The cultural tradition we are concerned with here was totally destroyed by the Neolithic Revolution that began in the Fertile Crescent about 10,600 years ago and reached Western Europe some 6,000 years later.

Neanderthal man 300,000–28,000 BP

The very limited amount of information available concerning Neanderthal man – the great competitor of Cro-Magnon man – has enabled some scholars to give free rein to their imaginations. I will review some of these interpretations and show why they provide a distorted picture of one of the great contributors to human history. By employing a general dynamic theory, such as my dynamic-strategy model, it is possible to make some sense of the incomplete available evidence and to suggest which of the existing interpretations is most realistic.

Neanderthal settlements and society

So far, archaeologists have discovered several hundred Neanderthal sites, which contain carefully collected fossil shells and a range of skillfully constructed stone tools. While the shells have not been modified for ornamental use (no holes have been bored), they are enough to demonstrate that the Neanderthals possessed a relatively sophisticated aesthetic sensibility. Randall White, an expert in prehistoric art, assures us that these artifacts:

> clearly reflect an interest in form and color, and may well imply that Western European Neanderthals had all the cognitive hardware necessary for aesthetic judgement and symbolic action. However, such action seems to have been nonmaterial, or at such a low level as to be virtually invisible in the several hundred Mousterian sites excavated. The purposely altered symbolic objects found to date in the Mousterian of Western Europe can be counted on the fingers of one hand, and these generally come from turn-of-the-century excavations where mixtures with later deposits are likely.[8]

It is important not to equate absence of evidence with absence of cultural structures and religious rituals. There are, for example, a number of sites, particularly in the caves of Pech de l'Aze, that contain specimens of "worked" – that is, objects scraped with stone tools – manganese dioxide nodules.[9] This suggests that powdered minerals were used to make pigments, perhaps for body painting and/or the painting of objects and rock surfaces that either have faded with time or, as I argue here, were deliberately removed, destroyed, or reworked by Cro-Magnon man. Also it is likely that, as with many Australian societies that employed sand "paintings" in their religious ceremonies, the Neanderthals practiced ephemeral art forms, together with singing and dancing.[10]

It is important to realize that while only a few representational objects have been found in Mousterian sites, they do constitute evidence that Neanderthal man was capable of symbolic thought. What are these candidates for representational art? First, there is the Berekhat Ram figurine, found in a 250,000-year-old site in Israel, which suggests a female form.[11] Second, there is the bone "flute" recovered from a 50,000–35,000-year-old site in the Divje Babe Cave in Slovenia, which displays two complete holes and, at the broken ends, two partial holes.[12] As even most modern flutes are wooden, we can see why the musical instruments of Neanderthal man would not have survived. Third, there are several incised and pierced bone objects from a 300,000-year-old site at Bilzingsleben in Germany, of which at least one has been interpreted as displaying symbolic markings.[13] And finally, there are a small number of other deliberately marked objects, which are thought by some to be of a representational nature.[14] Admittedly, this doesn't amount to a great deal of evidence, and there are some who assert that even this shows the hand not of sophisticated minds, but of the mocking indifference of nature.[15] But, as we shall see, some of these scholars clearly possess conflicts of interest.

The most persuasive evidence of symbolic thought displayed by the Neanderthals is to be found in the Châtelperronian period between 38,000–28,000 years ago. Yet even then, there are only a couple of sites that contain representational objects. The most important of these was discovered in the limestone caves near the village of Arcy-sur-Cure, east of Paris. These finds include Neanderthal bones, residential structures constructed from mammoth bones and tusks, and about thirty personal ornaments (with bored holes) made from marine fossils and animal teeth.

But even these finds have been dismissed by some scholars as the result of mindless imitation by Neanderthals of objects introduced by modern man. Randall White tells us:

> It seems then, that the late Neanderthals were quite capable of manufacturing such objects, but that *they did so in their own way* and only after they had come in contact with Aurignacian culture.[16]

It is interesting that White is ready to dismiss any similarity between Neanderthal and Cro-Magnon artifacts as mere imitation even when "they did so in their own way", which suggests, at worst, an integration of outside ideas into their own culture, just as we do in our own culture today. He also notes that "there are substantial differences in form and technique" between the artifacts of both human species.

This theme of mindless imitation is a persistent one among those determined to draw a sharp distinction between the intellectual achievements of Neanderthal man and modern man. The prehistorian Steven Mithen, for example, argues that change in Neanderthal technology and culture in the later Châtelperronian around 35,000–30,000 BP, was out of character for a society that had been largely static for 250,000 years. We are told that:

> So my view is that the final Neanderthals in Europe were imitating the symbol-using modern humans without understanding the power of symbols. Imitation was, after all, at the center of Neanderthal culture as the key means by which tool-making traditions were passed on from one generation to the next.[17]

There are four major problems with this interpretation. First, Mithen treats a 5,000 year period of change as if it were insignificant in duration. Just reflect on how much human civilization has changed in the past 5,000 years in comparison with the previous 150,000 years over which modern humans have existed. Should we dismiss these "final years" as being out of character with the earlier years? The idea that long-established species/societies can be *either* static *or* dynamic and are unable to change their "character" is totally without foundation. No doubt the explanation behind this idea is that the "character" of a species/society is fixed by genetic inheritance. This is an example of the fatally flawed supply-side approach. The dynamic-strategy theory – a demand-side theory – shows that all long-established species/societies are flexible and opportunistic, adopting the dynamic strategy that they believe will maximize the probability of their survival and prosperity. In the absence of external competition (as in the Mousterian) a society will strive for dynamic equilibrium (which is not the same as stasis), whereas in the presence of external competition (as in the Châtelperronian) it will strive for varying degrees of dynamism. It has nothing to do with supply-side acquired genetics, as suggested by neo-Darwinian theory.

Second, and even more importantly, Mithen fails to realize that imitation – what I call **strategic imitation**, a key component of the dynamic-strategy theory – is "at the centre" of the dynamics of *all* animal and human societies, especially of the most advanced societies in the world today. Strategic imitation is the key process by which the ideas and strategies of successful individuals (either internal or external) permeate entire societies. Rather than being a sign of intellectual and cultural backwardness, it is a sign of advanced thinking and social development. Third, why would the Neanderthals have wasted valuable effort – effort badly needed to survive in ice-age Europe – in imitating the manufacture of objects for which there was no strategic demand in Neanderthal society? It is an absurd idea. Ice-age man could not afford to be economically irrational.

Neanderthal cognitive ability

In order to determine whether the Neanderthals adopted religious practices, we need to evaluate their intellectual sophistication. A brief comparison of the origins and cognitive equipment of Neanderthal man and modern man is a useful starting point. Both *H. neanderthalensis* and *H. sapiens* can trace their ancestry back to *H. ergaster*, who existed about 1.9 to 1.0 myrs ago. While they probably shared a common ancestor *H. heidelbergensis* – who lived from about 0.7 to 0.3 myrs ago – *H. neanderthalensis* developed in Europe and Western Asia, and *H. sapiens* emerged in Africa. By the time they saw each other again, at about 100,000 years ago in the Levant and 40,000 years ago in Western Europe, they had, on average, different physical characteristics but similar sized brains, and *similar dynamic strategies*. As we shall see, it is the latter – the dynamic strategies they pursued – that will play the key role in our story.

In terms of brain size it would appear, at least at first glance, that Neanderthal man had a slight advantage over Cro-Magnon man. While the average brain size for Cro-Magnons was about 1340 ml, that for the Neanderthals was about 1520 ml.[18] One Neanderthal skull, recovered from the Amud Cave in the Levant, suggests a brain size as large as 1750 ml. On average, however, Neanderthal man had a brain-size advantage of 13 percent. Of course, this doesn't take into account differences in body mass – if, indeed, it should be taken into account for this comparison.

While Cro-Magnon man was relatively tall (178 cm for the average male) and long-limbed, Neanderthal man was relatively short (166 cm for the average male) and thickset, with a large barrel chest, heavy bones, large muscle sets, and shortish arms and legs.[19] These differences in physical structure were reflected in differences in body mass. It has been estimated that the average Neanderthal male weighed 77 kg and the average Cro-Magnon male weighed 65 kg. Needless to say, these estimates of physical structure and body mass are only very approximate owing to the small number of complete skeletons that have been recovered.

Not daunted by this, John Kappelman has attempted to calculate the encephalization quotient (EQ) – the degree to which brain size of a given species exceeds the brain/body ratio for mammals as a whole – for hominids over the past 3 myrs.[20] This quotient is supposed to tell us that although brain size might increase, if EQ remains the same owing to an offsetting increase in body mass, then cognitive ability also remains the same. The underlying assumption of this statistical procedure, of course, is the existence of a fixed relationship in a given species between brain size, body mass, and cognitive ability. Kappelman's data suggests that in the period of overlap in Europe between Neanderthal man and Cro-Magnon man – 40,000 to 28,000 years ago – the average EQs were 4.6 and 5.2 respectively – a 13 percent difference in favor of Cro-Magnon man.

The important questions here are: do these EQ estimates reflect a real difference between the two species or merely a statistical aberration; and, if real, is it meaningful for the debate about religious practice? In short, owing to the overwhelming problems of estimation, I believe it is a statistical aberration. But we need to consider the matter in more detail. First, the sample size – two specimens for each species – for the 12,000 years of competition between them is far too small to enable us to draw any statistically significant conclusions. Second, there are a number of ways in which EQs can be estimated, and no consensus as to which is the most appropriate. Third, in order to estimate sensible EQs we need solid data on body mass as well as brain size. Our problem here is that as extant skulls rarely have bodies attached, Kappelman has attempted to *estimate* body mass from cranial characteristics, such as the size of the orbital area (or eye socket). Clearly, such estimates of body mass can be no more than very approximate. Owing to these daunting estimation problems, it is highly risky at this time to base any conclusions about the relative cerebral ability of Neanderthals and Cro-Magnons on EQ estimates. But the exercise is interesting and demonstrates how we might proceed if more data becomes available.

But would a statistically significant difference in EQ between these two competing species really translate into a meaningful difference in cognitive ability? The short answer, in the light of my dynamic-strategy theory, is no! The main reason is that the underlying assumption of a fixed relationship between brain size, body mass, and cognitive ability is incorrect. Kappelman, for example, believes that a more rapid increase in body mass relative to brain size (as in Neanderthal man) will lead to a reduction in cognitive ability; and, conversely, that a fall in body mass while maintaining a given brain size (as in modern man) will lead to an increase in cognitive ability.[21] He also suggests that body mass was the driving force in these changes. This assumption is based on the theory of Darwinian adaptation.

In reality, rather than in Darwinian theory, both body and brain respond independently and flexibly to *different* aspects of strategic demand generated by the unfolding dynamic strategy of family multiplication. For Neanderthals, a larger brain was driven not by the demands of a larger body – the difference in body mass *between* species was no greater than gender differences *within* species – but by the need to supervise a meat-and-marrow version of the dynamic strategy of family multiplication in a demanding ice-age environment. Larger bodies, on the other hand, were required to tackle the large mammals, such as wild cattle, woolly mammoths, and woolly rhinos. As the Cro-Magnons employed a similar dynamic strategy, they also required large brains; but as they targeted smaller mammals (reindeer) and salmon, they didn't require such robust bodies. In other words, in these competing species of the genus *Homo*, body and brain could respond *differently and flexibly* to the *different* requirements of strategic demand without causing an offsetting change in cerebral activity. Clearly, in reality there was no fixed relationship between these three variables.

Also it should be noted that, as recent studies of nutrition and human stature show, it is possible to maintain a large brain with declining but adequate nutrition, by reducing body size.[22] This, however, does not lead to an increase in cerebral activity. Conversely, these studies show that with improved nutrition in the modern world, body mass has increased, without reducing cerebral ability.

Once gain real-world evidence demonstrates there is no fixed relationship between these three EQ variables. The larger body of Neanderthal man, therefore, cannot be taken as a measure of his inferior cerebral ability or as the basis for claiming that this species was not involved in religious activities.

Neanderthal inferiority or just bad luck?

The key to any discussion of the relative success between groups of competing humans is the dynamic strategies they pursue. In *The Ephemeral Civilization* (1997) I was able to demonstrate this for the different societies of modern man, and in this book I extend the dynamic-strategy argument to the great struggle between Neanderthals and modern humans. While the Neanderthals in Western Europe hunted a range of large mammals, from mammoths to wild cattle, using spears, modern humans targeted reindeer and salmon using a wider range of weapons.[23] Both species also gathered plants and fruit to supplement their diets. With these very similar versions (meat-and-marrow) of the same family-multiplication strategy (of procreation and migration), neither species possessed an obvious advantage over the other. It is possible – and this can only be recognized in retrospect – that the version employed by modern humans was a more general and flexible instrument in the pursuit of survival and prosperity. But any advantage was so small that it took 12,000 years before modern humans finally triumphed over the Neanderthals. In contrast, the seemingly equally matched struggle for control of the Western Mediterranean in ancient history – called the Punic Wars – saw Rome completely destroy Carthage in merely a century.

Nor were the Neanderthals technologically backward. Before the arrival of modern humans in Western Europe, the Neanderthals employed an advanced form of stone-age technology. Using the Levallois technique they were able to produce long stone flakes of a predetermined shape and size, which would be used as spear blades without further working. This technique, which can be traced back to 300,000 BP in Neanderthal Europe, required considerable intellectual and physical skill in the manufacturing process, but also considerable imagination in the conception and design phases.[24] Some scholars, who are convinced that the Neanderthals lacked the necessary cognitive skills, argue unconvincingly that these tool-making skills were the result of "selecting from a repertoire of tried and tested tool-making methods".[25] This viewpoint totally overlooks the imagination required to generate that tool-making repertoire in the first place – an imagination that the Neanderthals must have shared because they (as did modern man) inherited both from their ancestor *H. heidelbergensis*.

While they were as technologically advanced as modern humans[26], the Neanderthals are often denigrated for their lack of specialized weapons and tools. This criticism is, however, misplaced. The range of weapons and tools developed in any human society is a product not of the DNA of its members but of the strategic demand generated by its unfolding dynamic strategy. Hence,

the decision concerning whether to adopt a general hunting weapon or a range
of more specialized weapons will depend on the requirements of the particular
hunting strategy adopted. The failure to realize this is the outcome of employing
– even implicitly – a supply-side rather than a demand-side theory of societal
dynamics.

Similarly, the many denigrators of the Neanderthals are keen to highlight
the cultural differences between these competing species, which, they assert,
reflect fundamental cognitive differences.[27] But, as argued above, both species
of mankind appear to have possessed similar intellectual capabilities, similar
technologies, similar dynamic strategies and, hence, similar strategic *logoi*.
Similar strategic *logoi* in turn will produce similar cultures at the fundamental
level, which is consistent with significant variation at the superficial level
owing to different histories and influences. Could the cultural differences that
are usually highlighted between these two species of mankind exist merely at
the superficial level?

The main difficulty in answering this question is that we just don't have
enough information about Neanderthal culture. But why is this the case? Not
because the relatively sophisticated culture required to support an extremely
successful dynamic strategy in one of the world's most hostile environments
did not exist; not even because it finally came to an end as long as 28,000 years
ago; but, I will argue, because our ancestors systematically destroyed and/or
reused all known Neanderthal sites and cultural artifacts. Why? Because the
struggle by our ancestors for access to Neanderthal land – a struggle not just for
individual survival, but also for the survival of our species – had been very long,
very drawn out, very harsh, and very bitter. In victory, piece by hard-fought
piece, our ancestors attempted very successfully to destroy all evidence of the
world's greatest act of genocide – an act of genocide that could have gone either
way. It was, in my opinion, a very close-run thing, as evidenced by the length
of time taken to accomplish it – 12,000 years. If the circumstances had been
only slightly different, the writer and readers of this book could very well have
been the direct descendents of Neanderthals. And if so, there would be little or
no evidence of the material culture of *Homo sapiens* – those intellectually and
culturally inferior cousins of the sole surviving species of humanity!

If the reader thinks that the systematic destruction of all evidence of a savagely
exterminated human society is farfetched, consider the way this has occurred in
all subsequent phases of the history of modern humanity. Consider the way the
emerging Roman empire completely destroyed Carthaginian civilization once
it had finally won the last of the deadly Punic wars in 146 BC. Not only did the
Romans attempt to kill every man, woman, and child in Carthage, but they set
fire to the city, razed all buildings to the ground, and even sowed salt into the
Carthaginian fields to prevent them from being used productively again. Not
surprisingly, we know very little about Carthaginian culture. Consider also the
way that the invading Spaniards in the early sixteenth century systematically

destroyed the once mighty Aztec and Incan civilizations. Aztec Mexico, for example, was completely leveled and built over, and all evidence of Aztec culture was systematically destroyed.

Surely it would have been so much easier for Cro-Magnon man to systematically destroy all evidence of Neanderthal culture as they ever-so-slowly drove their arch-rival to the brink of extinction. All European settlements of this period were small and ephemeral and, hence, easily dismantled and extinguished. And modern man had, as we have seen, ample time to dispose of the evidence. Our ancestors also had an excellent reason for doing so – to prevent the Neanderthals from regrouping, reoccupying their old cultural and economic sites, and, most important of all, re-establishing contact with their strategic guardians. **Modern man was determined to destroy the Neanderthal strategic *logos* together with its guardians.** But, of course, even the most systematic attempt at genocide and cultural obliteration will leave traces of defeated societies, as we know from the determined work of archaeologists in Tunisia and Mexico, as well as in the limestone caves of Western Europe. And from these traces, a variety of strange stories will inevitably be told.

Some evidence of Neanderthal religious beliefs certainly has survived. It is well-known that they buried their dead – or at least their most important dead – perhaps as early as 400,000 years ago in Spain and 250,000 years ago in Wales.[28] And in these graves, Neanderthals deposited interesting "found" objects.[29] Also, from at least 120,000 years ago, Neanderthal dead were accorded special treatment, such as ritual defleshing, which some scholars think was done in preparing the deceased for admission into the presence of their ancestors who were treated as strategic guardians.[30] It has even been suggested that "the development of mortuary rites by Neanderthals, combined with their apparently heightened interest in caves, is suggestive of a latent and burgeoning cosmological perception".[31]

It is quite clear from the available evidence that the Neanderthals conducted religious ceremonies. As they had a very similar dynamic strategy – and, hence, strategic *logos* – to modern humans, it is highly likely that their religious ideas and rituals were also similar. This would not have been as a result of imitation of the invaders (as the invasion was still in the future) but a response to a similar strategic demand. As we shall see in the case studies of Cro-Magnon man and of Australian Aboriginals, this involves attempting to understand and influencing their strategic *logos* through their guardians, who took the forms of human ancestors and animal "helpers".

The bizarre neo-Darwinian interpretation

My interpretation of the great paradox of Neanderthal society – the contradiction between technological/existential success and representational/symbolic "failure" – may appear speculative, but it is entirely consistent with both my general dynamic theory and with later historical evidence. Some other influential attempts to explain this paradox are ahistorical, lack any real theoretical justification, and are downright bizarre. I have in mind the so-called neo-Darwinian explanation favored by the well-known prehistorian Steven Mithen. While Mithen's work leans heavily on the unconvincing explanations of evolutionary psychology, it is also influenced by the historical work of Paul Mellars (1996), Clive Gamble (1999), and David Lewis-Williams (2002).

In a recent book entitled *The Singing Neanderthals* (2006), Mithen develops the hypothesis that Neanderthals failed to develop language as we know it. Instead, he claims, they employed a form of signing without words. The matter of language is seen as central to the larger issue of Neanderthal man's ability to think symbolically and, hence, to engage in representational art forms and in religious thought and practice. Language is also seen by some, including Mithen, as the driving force in the enlargement of the brain of modern man. Without any hard evidence, Mithen asserts that:

> the Neanderthals used their [large] brains for a sophisticated communication system that was Holistic, manipulative, multi-modal, musical, and mimetic in characters: Hmmmmm. While this was also the case for their immediate ancestor and relatives, such as *Homo ergaster* and *Homo heidelbergensis*, the Neanderthals took this communication system to an extreme …[32]

Mithen's task in establishing this hypothesis is extremely difficult for a large number of reasons. We have already seen that the Neanderthals had a brain capacity at least as large as that of modern man; they developed a highly successful society that flourished for 300,000 years (twice as long as the entire history of modern man to this point); they employed state-of-the-art technology; they pursued a similar dynamic strategy to modern man; and they shared a common ancestor as recently as 500,000 BP.

But there is more. Mithen is forced to admit that Neanderthal man had the same vocal and auditory capacity as modern man. These common features include the hyoid bone, which is attached to the cartilage of the larynx in order to anchor the muscles required for speech; the hypoglossal canal that carries nerves from brain to tongue; the thoracic vertebrae, through which pass the nerves that control the diaphragm and breathing; and the bones of the inner ear that enable man to perceive sound. Mithen concludes:

> Although the Neanderthal vocal tract may have been unable to produce exactly the same range of sounds as a modern human, they would certainly have been sufficiently diverse to enable speech if the neural circuitry for language was present in the Neanderthal brain.[33]

Despite all the evidence suggesting that Neanderthal man had the cerebral and physical attributes required for symbolic thought, including language, Mithen continues to insist that:

> While the evolution of language would conveniently explain the large Neanderthal brain, the vocal tract, auditory capacity, and motor control over the tongue and breathing, *there is nonetheless overwhelming evidence that language had not yet*

evolved within this lineage of the Homo *genus.* So we must look to an advanced
form of "Hmmmmm" to explain these anatomical developments and cultural
achievements.[34]

Mithen, as we shall discover, requires more than "overwhelming" evidence
– he also requires a realignment of reality. These two issues are dealt with
separately.

The assertion that hominid brain development was the outcome initially of
"singing without words" and later, in the case of modern humans, language,
has no realist-theoretic underpinning. It is merely the outcome of guesswork,
because supply-side theorists lack a general dynamic theory of human society
and life. It contrast, the dynamic-strategy theory shows that the development
of the hominid brain, together with the emergence of the need and physical
attributes for language, were both interactive responses to the unfolding
hominid dynamic strategy of family multiplication (hunting-gathering version)
expressed through strategic demand. As I show in *The Selfcreating Mind* (2006),
the hominid hunting-gathering strategy generated a growing demand for the
following groups of *combined* inputs into the strategic process: improved
hunting weapons and tools; improved biological systems of navigation; more
effective economic and social organization; better means of communication
for conducting economic and social activities; "strategic thinking", involving
pattern-recognition and generalization; and tactical thinking, involving social
interaction.[35] These *combined* strategic inputs could only be supplied if the
hominid brain developed as a general and flexible instrument rather than as
an aggregation of domain-specific modules as the evolutionary psychologists
claim. It is essential to realize that these inputs required by the hominid strategic
pursuit were not separate and autonomous adaptations, but rather *simultaneous*
and *integrated* changes in response to changes in overall strategic demand.
This was a selfcreating, or autogenous, process because strategic demand was
an outcome of individuals actively exploring strategic opportunities. This is
why the idea that the Neanderthal brain consisted of the usual set of domain-
specific modules *minus* an "integrative module" – the one thing that made the
Neanderthals less than human – is patently ridiculous, as the following endnote
explains.[36] Neanderthal man was just as intellectually capable of a religious
response as modern man.

We can now turn to the "evidence" that Mithen calls upon to support
his assertions about the lack of symbolic language and, hence, religious
practice in Neanderthal society. He nominates three sets of "compelling" and
"overwhelming" arguments: namely that "Neanderthals lived in small socially
intimate communities" and, therefore, didn't require language; that the absence
of symbolic artifacts means they also lacked language; and that the "immense
cultural stability" of Neanderthal society reflects the absence of language,
which is *assumed* to be "a force of change".[37]

The first argument is extremely weak and cannot be regarded as evidence at all, let alone "compelling" or "overwhelming". *All* hunter-gatherer and hunter-herder societies operating under harsh climatic conditions do so in small, socially intimate communities. Such societies of modern man include the Inuit of North America, the Aboriginals of Australia, and the San People of southern African. And *all* of these societies have complex languages.

Mithen's second argument is that "the absence of symbolic objects must imply the absence of symbolic thought, and hence of symbolic utterances".[38] If this argument is to have any validity, it is essential that not a single Neanderthal object be interpreted as symbolic in nature. Just one symbolic object would demonstrate that Neanderthal man possessed a mind capable of symbolic thought and, hence, language. This is why Mithen is forced to deny the symbolic nature of *each and every* artifact that many other scholars regard as representational. Even at the best of times it is dangerous to argue the absence of action in the past from the absence of evidence. In this case his evidence is underwhelming rather than overwhelming.

The third argument proposed by Mithen is that the "immense cultural stability" of Neanderthal society – in contrast to the cultural dynamics of modern humans – is the outcome of a lack of language, which he claims is the driving force in human society. He insists that "the tools they made and the way of life they adopted at around 250,000 years ago were effectively no different from those current at the moment of their extinction, just after 30,000 years ago".[39] There are at least three empirical difficulties with this claim, which in turn are dwarfed by an insurmountable existential problem. First, we have virtually no information about the Neanderthal way of life 250,000 years ago; second, the final 12,000 years of the Neanderthal's time on Earth were marked by considerable cultural change, which some see as the outcome of Neanderthal innovation that predated the arrival of modern humans[40]; and third, Neanderthal technology was the equal of modern man's and, while the Neanderthal toolkit may have been different, it was no less effective, because it was a rational response to their version of the human hunting strategy.

The most important difficulty with Mithen's stability thesis, however, is that it runs counter to what we now know about the dynamics of living systems. Mithen regards the "immense cultural stability" as the outcome of Neanderthal man's alleged cerebral deficiency – the outcome of a people both "primitive" and "lacking in intelligence" when it came to cultural issues, despite their ability to make complex stone tools and to survive for so long in a harsh climate. Mithen views this alleged dichotomy as the Neanderthal "paradox". We need to evaluate this stability thesis.

Before we begin, it must be made clear that no society is ever static over the long, or very long, term. Under competitive conditions, societies are either actively dynamic or in the process of collapse, and under isolated conditions they either achieve a *dynamic* equilibrium or they collapse. While a society in dynamic equilibrium is constantly responding in a dynamic way to changing circumstances, the competitive pressures are insufficient to cause it to undergo any major transformations. Accordingly, this dynamic state, which is often confused with stasis, is both a rational and intelligent response to total isolation from external competition. There is nothing "primitive" about it at all. Rather it is one of a range of responses – to what I called the "global scale of competitiveness" in *The Dynamic Society* (1996) – that both the Neanderthals and modern humans display.

Australian Aboriginal society, for example, also experienced "immense cultural stability" over a vast period of 60,000 years, owing to its similar ice-age isolation – from external competition. Clearly these peoples – whose religious practices are discussed later in this chapter – are undeniably part of the family of modern mankind. Yet, any scholar adopting the "immense cultural stability" thesis, and also valuing intellectual consistency, would have to conclude that Australian Aboriginal society was also "primitive" and "lacking in intelligence" in cultural matters. This, of course, would be a totally false conclusion and, no doubt, such scholars would hasten to distance themselves from it. But, if so, where would this leave Mithen's thesis about Neanderthal man?

This is an intellectual trap into which scholars employing supply-side theories inevitably fall. While not always realizing it, supply-side theorists always imply that human culture is the outcome of the particular and inflexible genetic structure of the human mind. Evolutionary psychologists and their followers are, of course, completely aware of this implication, as it is a central article of their intellectual faith. Essentially, supply-side theorists like Mithen view the relative performance of societies (such as that of the Neanderthals and moderns) as the outcome of their different genetic characteristics. In contrast, demand-side theorists (such as myself) view relative societal performance as the outcome of different dynamic strategies (or different versions of the same basic dynamic strategy) that call forth, via strategic demand, different individual and group responses. It has nothing to do with alleged genetic differences – and, hence, racial differences – at all. No doubt it will come as a great shock to scholars to learn that, at bottom, their supply-side theories are racist in nature, no matter how unintentional that may be. While supply-side theorists – and evolutionary psychology is a supply-side theory – can still get away with this approach to the Neanderthals, the wheels start to fall off when it is applied to modern hunter-gatherer societies.

It has already been suggested that the reason Neanderthal Europe and Aboriginal Australia experienced similar states of dynamic equilibrium is that they were both effectively isolated from the rest of the world by ice-age conditions. Also, it is significant that neither society was located in, what in *The Dynamic Society* (1996) I called a **funnel of transition** – a competitive corridor such as the Fertile Crescent in the Old World or the Mesoamerican isthmus in the New World. While both isolated societies responded in a dynamic way to changing local conditions of a societal and environmental kind, they were free from the life-transforming pressures of external competition for vast periods of time.

Only when external competition confronted Europe and Australia did the native populations have any need to significantly change their systems. In Western Europe after 40,000 – or, at least, 36,500 – years ago, the Neanderthals needed to take action, because the new competitive pressure applied by modern humans changed the Neanderthal life-system (or strategic *logos*) and the strategic demand it generated. And the Neanderthals responded in their *own* way to their *own* changing *logos*. No doubt this had a major impact on the Neanderthals view of their strategic guardians and their strategic ideology. This was not a matter of mindless imitation but of *creative* responses to their *own* unfolding dynamic strategy. Clearly this creative response was remarkably successful, as the Neanderthals were able to participate effectively in this life-and-death **strategic struggle**, and to resist the invaders, for some 12,000 years.

Modern humans, therefore, possessed only the smallest of advantages – advantages that could not have been predicted in the year 40,000 BP – which suggests that the Neanderthals were not at all culturally "primitive", were far from "lacking in intelligence", and had not been standing still for the past 250,000 years while modern humans surpassed them. In Australia the outcome was very different and it was swiftly determined. The strategic *logos* and the guardians of the invaders from Western Europe had, under the pressure of external competition, been transformed by two great technological paradigm shifts (the first agricultural, and the second industrial) and, therefore, provided a marked strategic advantage over that of the isolated locals. The Antipodean strategic struggle, unlike that in stone-age Europe, was massively one-sided.

Hence, there is no paradox. Neanderthal man possessed both the technological *and* imaginative/symbolic capacity to compete with modern man. Neanderthal strategic guardians and religious ritual would have been seen as effective as those of modern humans. Which is why our ancestors systematically destroyed all Neanderthal sacred sites. As much as many scholars would like to think differently, the final triumph of our ancestors in Western Europe about 28,000 years ago was a very close-run thing. And it was the outcome of a great strategic struggle – involving a clash between competing GODS – not climatic factors as some like d'Errico have suggested.[41]

There can be no doubt that the Neanderthals possessed a highly successful strategic *logos* that enabled them to survive in a very harsh environment for a period twice as long as modern man has so far managed. They were also highly intelligent, and able to employ and modify state-of-the-art technology and to construct complex social relationships. Like all intelligent communities, the Neanderthals would have been concerned to understand and influence the mysterious life-system that enabled them to survive in such difficult conditions. Hence they – like even the early societies of modern mankind – would have sought the assistance of ancestral and animal guardians. The religious ideas and practices of the early societies of modern man between 40,000 and 11,000 BP (to be discussed in the next section of this chapter) could be regarded as providing a rough guide to those of the Neanderthals, especially during the long period of overlap between these two societies in Western Europe. Why? Because of the shaping influence of a strategic *logos* very much like our own.

The fact that very little evidence of these religious or – as I prefer to think of them – strategic practices have been discovered is probably the result of the systematic destruction of Neanderthal material remains and sacred sites by their desperate competitors. The great tragedy of the triumph of our species is that we can no longer converse with our highly intelligent cousins, as we most surely once did.

Modern man 40,000 – 11,000 BP

While the changing nature of the material art – the mirror of religious ideas and practices – of modern man in Western Europe can be clearly outlined, it is more difficult to interpret this work. The reason, as mentioned earlier, is that we are unable to interrogate the society that created this sacred art – unlike the case of Aboriginal Australia. Accordingly, interpretations of European prehistoric art tend to be more speculative and controversial.

There is, however, a solution to this problem. By discarding the usual supply-side theories – which, as we have seen, usually generate bizarre interpretations – and embracing a workable demand-side perspective (such as the dynamic-strategy theory) more realistic interpretations can be made. Fanciful interpretations will, in this demand-side framework, identify themselves.

All societies possessing very similar strategic *logoi* – in this case the generic paleolithic *logos* of hunting and gathering – will also have, at the basic functional level, very similar cultural institutions (rules), organizations (social networks), and rituals. There will, of course, be superficial differences of form, reflecting their different histories and geographies. This is most obvious in post-paleolithic societies, which were and are capable of generating surpluses that can be employed to indulge the human passion for elaborate detail of expression. But in paleolithic societies there are no such surpluses and, as a result, the scope for elaboration of artistic and societal detail is more limited. paleolithic society is, as a result of material circumstance, pared back to functional necessity. Hence, we would expect the purpose and meaning of prehistoric art (dealt with here) to be very similar to Australian Aboriginal art (in the next section). But, of course, our interpretation must be true to the empirical detail of each paleolithic society.

The prehistoric art of Europe

The prehistoric art of Western Europe is usually divided into four phases, of which only three – the Aurignacian, Gravettian, and Magdalenian – were experienced throughout the region. The Solutrean was restricted to Spain, western France and Belgium. It is important to adopt a realistic perspective when evaluating the nature of these periods of changing technology and culture. Experts in prehistoric art use words like "revolution", "tidal wave", "veritable explosion", for changes of a fairly modest kind that took place over very long periods of 6,000 to 12,000 years. If we attempted to calculate the implied annual rates of change of these ideas, techniques, and of output per capita, we would produce tables with lots of zeros in front of any real numbers. This is just common sense because if the technical and cultural ideas under consideration had undergone change that could truly be described as "revolutionary", then these stone-age people would have enjoyed living standards much higher than they in fact did.

The tribes of modern man that invaded Western Europe from the Fertile Crescent beginning around 40,000 years ago, were accustomed to greater competition than the locals, together with a more extensive exchange of objects embodying the ideas of technology, religion, and ornamental fashion. The land from which they came was a great forcing ground for change in the period 100,000 to 40,000 BP, just as it was to be in the later neolithic period from 11,000 to 6,000 BP. The reason, as explained in *The Dynamic Society* (1996), is that its geography created one of the great "funnels of transformation". Also, as these peoples came from warmer and more productive climates – driven by their dynamic strategy of family multiplication – they had sufficient leisure to elaborate the details of their life-system. Hence, any comparison of the superficial aspects of both Neanderthal and Cro-Magnon culture in the period 40,000 to 28,000 BP would reflect these differences of circumstance and history. At the fundamental level, however, the commitment these societies had to understanding and influencing their strategic *logos* would have been the same.

Experts in prehistoric art tell us that between 40,000 and 35,000 BP:

> the Aurignacian culture hit Western Europe like a tidal wave. In comparison to the Mousterian everything was different: new stone-, bone-, antler-, and ivory-working techniques; deadly new hunting weaponry; new social transformations; long-distance exchange of raw materials; great numbers of painted, engraved, and sculptured images that varied from one region to another; and large quantities of personal ornaments.[42]

This "tidal wave", however, was more apparent than real. The invaders certainly brought with them a different, and a wider, range of weapons owing to their adoption of a different variant of the common hunting strategy. Also they probably possessed more richly elaborated social/religious rituals, owing to the greater competition and greater exchange of objects and ideas that had existed in the Fertile Crescent. But even those differences appear more stark and important today than they were at the time because, as already argued, the victors systematically destroyed or reused most of the Neanderthal artifacts over thousands of years. Had the contrast between these two societies been as great as is usually suggested – had it really been a "tidal wave" of technological and cultural change – the invaders would have pushed the locals to extinction in a fraction of the time actually taken. **A "tidal wave" would hardly take 12,000 years to pass through Western Europe.** Hence, it is *not* correct to say that the Aurignacian amounted to "a *revolution* in human cultural *evolution*"[43] – even if that is not a contradiction of terms!

The art of the Aurignacian (40,000–28,000 BP) consists of geometric designs – dots, notches, and incisions – on bone and stone, small sculptures in the round, rock paintings and engravings, musical instruments (flutes), and personal ornaments. Some of the rock art, which can be dated back to at least 33,000 years ago, is similar to that of Aboriginal Australia created around the same time. This was a period of intense competition with the Neanderthals, which would have led to changes in Cro-Magnon as well as Neanderthal religious practices.

The Gravettian (28,000–22,000 BP) saw the introduction of new technology, new tools and weapons, and new representational art forms. Over these 6,000 years, the range and detail of geometric design, and the representation of animals and humans, increased. Of the new motifs, the most striking were the large number of human images, almost entirely of pregnant women, and of human handprints. The fertility symbols are consistent with a more rapid unfolding of the dynamic strategy of family multiplication – of procreation and migration – now that the great Neanderthal resistance had been completely eliminated.

While a new cultural phase, the Solutrean (22,000–18,000 BP) can be detected in Spain, western France, and Belgium, the Gravettian continued elsewhere in Western Europe at this time. The Solutrean innovations included the use of heat and pressure rather than percussion in stone working, the introduction of the spear-thrower, eyed needles and the rapid expansion of large-scale bas-relief sculpture. In the rest of Western Europe it was pretty much life as usual until the *relatively* rapid change of the Magdalenian.

The Magdalenian cultural era (18,000–11,000 BP) saw "a veritable explosion of symbolic representation, accompanied by quite dramatic and continual changes through time in projectile weaponry, stone tool technology, and human demography."[44] As the number of known settlement sites increased three-fold during this era, it is clear that population density increased *relatively* rapidly prior to the end of the ice age and the retreat of the polar ice cap. Hence, the technological and cultural changes that took place can be interpreted as an attempt by the Europeans to gain more intensive access to existing natural resources. In this period, our ancestors depended heavily on reindeer hunting.

In view of the more rapid expansion of population during the Magdalenian, it is hardly surprising that more representational objects and images have been found for this 7,000-year period than for all the preceding periods combined. So far, some 300 sites containing 10,000 portable representational objects, and thousands of engraved or painted rock surfaces, have been discovered. The geometrically designed objects and images, which are "superabundant" in this era, are said to "constitute coherent elements of an iconographic system" but that their meaning remains obscure.[45] Art techniques, ranging from the preparation of pigments to the working of bas-relief friezes, were relatively highly sophisticated. There is even evidence of the creation of shape-changing images (from human to animal), which suggest shamanistic activity.

A new strategic interpretation

How is it possible to interpret these art activities when we are unable to interview the people who participated in them or their cultural descendents? The usual responses to this question are:

- we can only categorize and describe the surviving artifacts;
- we can go further and draw comparisons with the continuous artistic traditions in Australia, South Africa, and South America;
- we can employ various cultural theories to hypothesize about the artistic record.

The first of these approaches has the appearance of objectivity, but it can tell us little about the meaning and role of prehistoric art. It constitutes the study of art for art's sake, which is certainly not the reason it was created. While the second approach can be useful in extending our knowledge of a particular society, the depth of insight provided is usually limited by the investigator's understanding of the dynamics of contemporary hunting societies. And the third approach, as seen in the case of the Neanderthals, can lead us wildly astray if we employ unrealistic *deductive* theories.

The most fruitful way of interpreting European prehistoric art is, in my opinion, by employing a well-tested, realist theory of the dynamics of human society – a truly general dynamic theory of complex living systems, such as my dynamic-strategy theory. This general theory has proven successful in analyzing the dynamics of human societies of all types – prehistoric, ancient, medieval, and modern – as well as of life in general. Before using the dynamic-strategy theory, we need to survey existing interpretations.

One of the earliest interpretations of Western European prehistoric art is that it was a form of hunting magic. To support his view, it is claimed that geometric motifs near to or superimposed on animal images should be interpreted as weapons, traps, and even wounds. Some, like Randall White, interested more in the aesthetics than the sociology of these images, is highly critical of this "old tradition".[46] He argues that "less than 10 percent of animal images are directly associated with such signs", and that 99 percent of these are not "even remotely convincing". He also claims that:

> Another observation that would seem to refute hunting magic as an explanation for deep cave paintings (and portable representations as well) is that animals are

almost never seen in postures of pain and suffering. Indeed there is an almost total absence of violence and clear acts of hunting. When it occurs, it is truly the exception...[47]

White favors a complex, multi-faceted cultural explanation of prehistorical art, which he claims can't be clearly defined, because there is insufficient evidence about motivation.

It is odd that White, as an eminent historian of prehistoric art, overlooks the fact that "increase" art and ritual – certainly as practiced by Australian Aboriginals – is not about pain and suffering, merely about ensuring abundant supplies of hunting animals. While stone-age man was confident about his hunting abilities, he felt deep anxiety concerning the continued supply of animals to hunt. It was, therefore, to ensure normal supplies of game that these expert hunters looked to the guardians of their strategic *logos*. In the same way, contemporary mankind is confident about their technological ability, but feels deeply anxious about the future of climate change. So today we look to our strategic guardian – the spirit of science – to ensure that climate change doesn't accelerate out of control. In the light of this strategic interpretation, neither the supporters of the "old tradition" nor of White's revisionism is correct.

Other scholars, such as Miranda and Stephen Aldhouse-Green, are willing to use observation of contemporary hunting societies to shape their interpretation of prehistoric European art. The Aldhouse-Greens have been strongly influenced by their professional experiences in southern Chile with the *Machi* or Mapuche shamans, "who travel in a multi-layered cosmos and who use drums, marked with these layers, to call up the spirits". They go on to say:

> The glimpse we have had of the Mapuche sacred cosmos and its shamans contains strong resonances with the world of the ancient ritualists with whom this book is concerned. It has been a rare privilege for us to have encountered living shamanism in a wild, remote, beautiful and enchanted landscape which, although far removed in space and time from our chosen area, nonetheless serves to convince us that "shamanism", in its broadest sense, is and has been endemic to rural communities in much of the ancient and modern world. Our quest ... is to identify the "shamans' footprint".[48]

In other words, their view of stone-age European art and religion is strongly influenced by what they found in simple rural communities in South America.

Shamanism, however, has its critics. Randall White, for example, regards the view that Western European caves were visited and painted by shamans in order to "encounter and have visions of a parallel spiritual universe" to be "a quite new and provocative interpretation".[49] He points out that "perhaps ten percent of Paleolithic cave images lend themselves to this kind of shamanistic interpretation", and warns that "the shamanism hypothesis risks falling into the same trap as the hunting-magic hypothesis". Basically, White is critical of any attempt "to explain all Paleolithic cave art as being the product of a single motivation and purpose". He reminds us that "we are dealing with complex humans, capable of juggling a multiplicity of meanings and motivations at one and the same time", and suggests that in view of the "enormous time span ... it would not be surprising ... if religious beliefs and practices transformed themselves again and again".

With this warning ringing in our ears, let's consider some views about shamanism in prehistoric Europe. In my strategic view, shamanism was an attempt by simple, pre-scientific societies to engage with the mystery of life. Owing to the ordered way in which the natural world operated, according to principles that could not be observed, it was believed by paleolithic societies that there was an invisible reality beyond this world that could only be accessed by supernatural means. It was further believed that specially talented individuals could, through a long and difficult process of training, discover those places where the natural and supernatural worlds intersected, and master the mystical techniques of ecstasy to pass from one to the other. The main aim in doing so was to enter into the presence of the supernatural beings – spirits or guardians – in order to negotiate about the critical issues of life – survival and prosperity.

In confirmation of this strategic interpretation, the Aldhouse-Greens tell us:

> In a trance state, an altered state of awareness, shamans may visit other worlds to negotiate with the spirits on behalf of their communities in order to avert or cure disease; they may intervene to prevent or stop famine, failure of herds or pestilence; and intercede with the supernatural world to promote their people's prosperity and success.[50]

Hence, while the means employed by the shamans were supernatural – because their life-system, or strategic *logos*, was a great mystery – the objective of their profession was to promote material success in the natural world. In particular, shamanism is said to have been closely related to the economic activity of hunting:

> Shamanism is generally regarded as having been endemic to hunter-gatherer societies because of the importance of its role in hunting. Hunter-gatherer societies enjoy a close relationship with game animals ... Shamanism is above all a hunter's cosmology.[51]

What then were the methods and practices employed by shamans to seek out the guardian spirits of the otherworld and to negotiate with them? Mircea Eliade provides the following formula, which is at once both a definition of the shaman and of his method:

> the shaman, and he alone, is the great master of ecstasy. A first definition of this complex phenomenon, and perhaps the least hazardous will be: shamanism = *technique of ecstasy*.[52]

To pass from this world to the otherworld, shamans selected "liminal" (or threshold) places to conduct their ecstatic rituals. These transition places included caves, bogs, sacred pools, rapids, estuaries, mountains and islands. At these "spiritual" (in reality, "strategic") sites, paintings and engravings were made, ceremonies were conducted, sacrifices and offerings were presented, and graves were constructed. Shamans painted their bodies (as Neanderthals probably did), wore animal costumes and headdresses, played musical instruments (drums, percussion instruments, rattles, gongs and bells), and invoked ecstatic trances in order to enter into the otherworld and negotiate with the guardian spirits.[53]

The Aldhouse-Greens tell us that:

animals are usually crucial to shamanistic systems: thus, in hunter-gatherer and hunter-herder communities, a particular beast, often the one on which the group's survival depends, may be perceived as an animal-helper, a creature that aids the shaman in transgressing between worlds and paving the way for negotiation with the spirits.[54]

In other words, as animals are central to the strategic *logos* of hunting society, the shamans believed it would help negotiations with the guardians to take on the appearance of animals – hence the term "shape-changing" – and to employ animals as helpers in this critical task. A critical task on which the survival of the entire society was thought to depend. It was this "helper" role that accounts for the lack of violence to animals in cave-wall paintings. Who would want to offend one's helpers in this critically important task?

Shamanism provides a stone-age model of the hunting life-system. In order to visit the otherworld and negotiate with their guardians, the shaman had to know the spiritual territory through which he needed to pass. We are told that "in visiting the spirit-world, the shaman must be able to control his/her trance and possess a mental map or chart of the cosmos".[55] Shamanistic cultures usually thought of the "cosmos" as a three-tiered structure, with an upperworld inhabited by spirits or guardians, a middle world consisting of normal people and animals, and an underworld occupied by the dead. The forces of evil (which could cause natural crises) and disease that periodically afflicted the world of people and animals, came from the underworld. Yet, paleolithic societies were not just the playthings of the cosmos, as they had some influence over their destiny. The shamans could gain mystical access to the upperworld and negotiate with the guardians of their dynamic strategy – with the GODS. Accordingly, the fluctuating fortunes of paleolithic societies were seen by their intellectuals as the outcome of complex interactions between the various spheres of their three-tiered life-systems. This is a very early model of the strategic *logos*.

Although shamanistic society was primarily concerned to explain and influence the system of forces that determined the favorable and unfavorable outcomes of their hunting way of life, they extrapolated their philosophical system onto the observed Universe – onto the heavens, the Earth, and the feared realm below the Earth. In other words, while they were primarily concerned with their materialist way of life – their strategic *logos* – paleolithic thinkers conflated this with the cosmos. In this way, the *logos* and the cosmos became one. This was the beginning of the confusion in men's minds between strategic and religious issues. It was the beginning of the deductive intellectual process by which the **Guardians Of Dynamic Strategy** – the **GODS** of the *logos* – became gods in the cosmos.

My strategic interpretation of the religious artifacts of paleolithic society in Western Europe, therefore, is that they were part of the attempt to explain and influence the guardians of their strategic *logos*. This is not to say that stone-age art performed no other function – such as training the new generation, sharing life's experiences, as a library of hunting knowledge, or even a form of entertainment – just that all other functions were subordinated to the vitally important need to sustain their strategic *logos*. Also it was probably the case that ordinary members of the community, watching from a distance and with imperfect understanding, drew upon the strategic ideology of their society to obtain personal support from the guardians in their individual struggle against the rigors of life. This is clearly the case in neolithic societies, where influential individuals left behind evidence of their personal lives.

Finally, while shamans may have played an important role in the "religion" (or, more accurately, the strategic ideology) of prehistoric Europe, that ideology was *logos*-centered rather than shaman-centered. While the shaman was a "religious" (ideological) leader, and his/her methods of making contact with the guardian spirits were an important part of stone-age "religion", the focus of paleolithic thinking was the viability of their *logos* not the shamanistic instruments by which it might be achieved. Today, it would be like interpreting catholicism as priest-centered rather than Christ-centered. Some scholars have focused on the instrument rather than the substantive mystery.

ABORIGINAL AUSTRALIA 65,000–200 BP

What is highly significant about the sacred art of Aboriginal Australia is that it can be observed from the inside as well as the outside. At the time of the European invasion of Australia in 1788, Aboriginal culture was a viable, living culture, and it has been directly interrogated by scholars of our own time. For this reason, a study of stone-age Australian sacred art can expect to see intimately from the inside what could only be imputed from the outside with stone-age European forms.

The current evidence and dating techniques suggest that the Australian continent was first settled by modern humans about 65,000 to 60,000 years ago. As these new arrivals faced an abundant supply of natural resources, together with a relatively moderate climate, it is reasonable to expect that geographical expansion via the family-multiplication strategy would have reached the maximum rate possible for a paleolithic society. Hence, the main phase of population growth and settlement would have occurred during the first half of this long period of Aboriginal occupation, rather than the last few millennia as some have claimed.[56] Certainly the archaeological evidence suggests that by

30,000 to 20,000 BP all parts of Australia had been fully occupied. Habitation sites in southern Tasmania (Warreen Cave) have been dated to 35,000 BP, and in the glacial uplands to at least 20,000 BP.[57] Hence, by about 20,000 years ago, the natural resources of Australia were probably fully exploited by the Aboriginal strategic *logos*.

As Australia was effectively isolated from external competition, particularly from 15,000 to 5,000 BP, the Aboriginal *logos* was able to achieve the rare state of dynamic equilibrium through Aboriginal abandonment of the family-multiplication strategy in favor of population control. This was achieved by controlling both their mortality rates through abortion and infanticide, and their fertility rates through simple forms of contraception. At this time the population would have been roughly the same size as in early 1788, and the system of land use would have stabilized but been subject to variation owing to climate and societal changes. My estimate of the changes in Aboriginal population over the past 60,000 years are presented in Figure 2.1; and the detailed methods and explanations are contained in my paper "Dynamics Downunder" (2006b). From the very beginning, Aboriginal Australians were engaged in artistic activities. We will survey those activities and suggest how they were reflective of attempts to understand the operation, and to influence the outcomes, of their strategic *logos*.

Figure 2.1 **Australian Aboriginal population, 60,000BP – AD 1788**

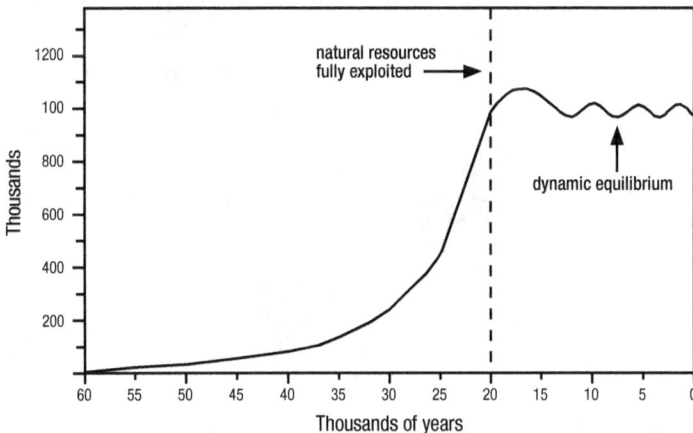

Source: Snooks 2006b (author's estimates)

Cave paintings and markings

At the top end of the Northern Territory, known as Kakadu, a large piece of striated, non-local hematite (the source of red pigment) has been discovered in a campsite dated to 60,000 BP.[58] Also, evidence of rock paintings dating back to 40,000 BP have been discovered in the Kimberley at Carpenter's Gap[59]; and to between 35,000–30,000 BP in a number of sites on Cape York Peninsula.[60]

Indeed, ancient rock art has been discovered throughout the northern half of Western Australia, the Northern Territory, and New South Wales; and in western Victoria, and eastern South Australia – see Figure 2.2. But, although there are more than 100,000 sites throughout Australia, owing to the ephemeral nature of this form of human activity, the "vast majority belong to the last few hundred or, at most, the last few thousand years".[61]

Figure 2.2 **Australian Aboriginal archeological sites**

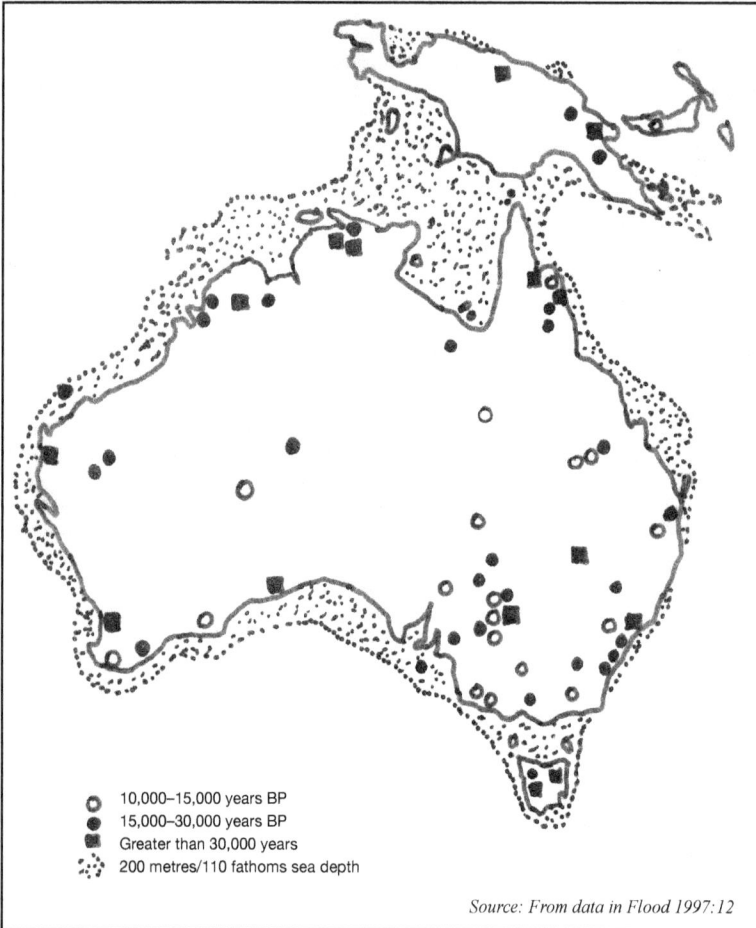

○	10,000–15,000 years BP
●	15,000–30,000 years BP
▧	Greater than 30,000 years
⸬⸱	200 metres/110 fathoms sea depth

Source: From data in Flood 1997:12

Of particular interest is that some of these engraved lines lead into, or possibly emerge from, narrow crevices in cave walls or ceilings, as if the rock face is merely a veil between us and another world – a veil that can be penetrated by "religious" (read strategic) ritual – like the false doors in Egyptian tombs. As shown above, this has a counterpoint in European cave art; as does the genre of finger flutings. The religious/strategic significance of many of these sites is also attested to by the apparently deliberate placements of kangaroo bones on prominent stones and in cave-wall niches, as well as the ordered arrangement of stones in cairns that some scholars interpret as "proto-sculpture".[62] This rock art has been professionally interpreted as follows:

> The weight of the evidence and balance of probabilities seem to me to suggest that the motivation to enter and make marks in these deep, dark, remote places was primarily religious, rather than simply casual or utilitarian.[63]

There can be little doubt that the many limestone caves in southern Australia, which were deep and dark, had special religious/strategic significance.

Open-air rock engravings

In the absence of deep caves in the arid regions of Australia, Aboriginal clans created what are know as "open-air rock engravings". This ancient form of rock art, which was created during the Pleistocene (or ice age), is known as the "Panaramitee style". This term, coined by Lesley Maynard, has stimulated considerable controversy.[64] Some scholars claim that it is really part of an international style, which should be called the "track and line genre".[65] As Randall White shows, this style of rock engraving is commonly found in global paleolithic rock sites, such as those in the Americas, Africa, and Europe.[66] Whatever it is called, this rock art consists of a limited range of widely distributed motifs, mainly consisting of the tracks of birds and macropods (kangaroos and emus) and circles. A typical composition, taken from 1,826 engravings at Karolta (formerly called Mannahill) north of Adelaide, involves 35 percent circles, 28 percent tracks, 16 percent "dots" (or cupules), 13 percent abraded grooves, 7 percent lines, and 1 percent more complex designs.[67] In other words, circles and tracks account for two-thirds of this sample of open-air rock engravings.

Although the subject of debate, rock engravings in the Olary region north of Adelaide are thought to have been made during the 38,500 years between 40,000 and 1,500 BP. Not only does this place them amongst the oldest rock engravings in the world, but they are also the most enduring style and technique of stone-age art. In commenting on this remarkable longevity of style and technique, Josephine Flood has written:

> It seems that both the technique, subject matter and manner of engraving remained remarkably constant over 40,000 years or 1,600 human generations. Such continuity is at first mind-boggling, but our perspective is deeply colored by the incredible rate of change in the modern world. Perhaps, the norm in hunter-gatherer societies was continuity? Environmental change at the end of the ice age was far less dramatic in Australia than in the northern hemisphere, and even after the demise of the megafauna, there were still kangaroos and emus to hunt, and their tracks to replicate with stone hammers.[68]

For a scholar who accepts the Darwinian idea that species adapt to environmental change, the evidence of technological and institutional (religious at least) continuity and stability over 40 millennia must be more than a little embarrassing. It is not surprising, therefore, that Flood attempts to downplay the extent of environmental change induced by the ending of the last ice age. In fact, the impact of that major environmental event was considerable. First, it led to a rise in sea levels by about 130 meters between 18,000 and 5,000 BP (see Figure 2.3), resulting in the flooding of large stretches of coastal land. In the north these flooded lands extended to New Guinea and two-thirds of the way to Timor, and in the south they separated Tasmania from the mainland. Second, the ending of the ice age caused increasing aridity throughout central Australia, as well as growing lushness of coastal regions in the north and east, which in turn led to the large-scale migration of animals and people in Australia. And this was not a once-only change, as sea levels (see Figure 2.3) and, hence, climate, vegetation, and animal life, fluctuated widely throughout the entire 60,000 years or so of Aboriginal occupation of Australia. Despite these significant changes in environmental conditions, Aboriginal rock engravings remained highly stable in terms of subject matter and technique. This confounds Darwinian theory! The real explanation, of course, is that the Aboriginal strategic *logos* and, hence the resulting strategic demand for technology and cultural institutions – including religious/strategic ones – remained largely unchanged.

Figure 2.3 **Fluctuating sea levels: Australia, past 140,000 years**

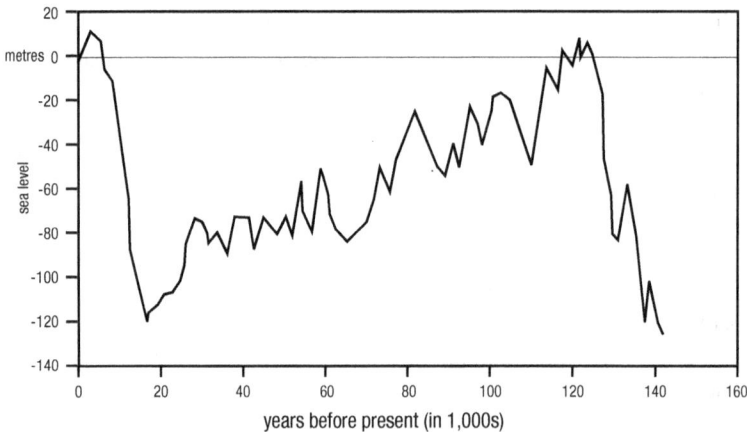

Source: From data in Chappell (1994).

The contrast to what was happening in the Fertile Crescent – where technology and cultural institutions were changing relatively rapidly – could not be more stark. In this highly open and competitive region, the old paleolithic technological paradigm was being exhausted and a new neolithic technological paradigm was, around 11,000–10,600 BP, being explored. This transforming strategic process involved the replacement of the old hunting-gathering dynamic strategy with the new agricultural-pastoral strategy. Owing to these changes the strategic *logoi* of the societies of the Fertile Crescent – in Mesopotamia, the Levant, and Egypt – were transformed, and the new and dynamic strategic demand for technology, institutions, and organizations forged new religious/strategic ideas and practices – including sacred art. These economic, social and cultural changes – which will be examined in Chapter 3 – had absolutely nothing to do with environmental change. Nothing to do with Darwinian adaptation.

In order to gain some insight concerning Aboriginal religious/strategic ideas and practices, we need to consider the meaning and function of open-air rock engravings. Circles are the most widespread motif in rock art in Australia and around the globe, despite being one of the most difficult to draw and engrave with any precision. In Aboriginal Australia, concentric circles were and are, normally employed to represent Ancestral Beings; and adjacent concentric circles linked by lines represent the passage of these beings through the landscape. The intention was (and is in modern canvas paintings) to create "mythological landscapes". While noting that some scholars have speculated that the circle motif may have derived from the corroboree circle, female breasts, waterholes, or even the sun, moon, and stars, Flood admits that: "'Why circles?' is a question to which I have, as yet, found no satisfactory answer".[69]

For those willing to speculate about this subject, the following strategic interpretation may be of interest. Perhaps all early societies of mankind had an intuitive awareness of the circular nature of their life-system – of the strategic *logos*. As can be seen from Figure 12.1, the dynamic-strategy theory suggests that the *logos* consists of a set of concentric circles that represent the hidden circular forces of the universal life-system. The strategic *logos,* therefore, can be thought of as a complex mandala. Hence, the circle in sacred art can be thought of as representing the mystery that is the strategic *logos*, in the never-ending attempt to sustain life. It is a symbol that emerges in most, if not all, human societies.

Engraved tracks are more easily, if less interestingly, interpreted. They clearly represent the passage of birds and macropods as viewed from above. Hunters searching for prey always look down at tracks rather than out at objects, at least until they have found the moving objects of interest. Killing their prey was the easy part, finding it was more difficult and required special skills. It is generally accepted that the track motif was employed as "hunting magic" in "food-increase" ceremonies. In other words, this motif was part of a sacred art employed to sustain their dynamic strategy of hunting.

What of "dots" (or cupules) and lines (or abraded grooves) in Aboriginal rock art? These motifs are usually, but not exclusively, found on vertical rock surfaces and were formed by repeated pounding or rubbing over very long periods of time. They make up the earliest Aboriginal (and global) rock art, and were the outcome of a concern not with making images as such, but with ritual activity. Certainly these motifs are not of a utilitarian nature – not, for example, grinding holes for grass seeds and roots. Instead they are associated with "increase" rituals – rituals designed to increase future animal and other food stocks – and with rain making at special totemic sites. In other words, these motifs resulted from sacred activity required to release the "life essence" of a totem (such as the goanna, kangaroo, or emu), or to "bring out the power" of a sacred rock that was known to be permeated with the spirit of an Ancestral Being. Flood tells us that:

> Ancestral Beings are credited with retaining control of all power and functions such as maintaining an adequate food supply and the continuity of seasons and the human race. Performance of rituals such as rain-making or food-increase ceremonies is believed to activate or release the inherent power of the Creative Spirits. Rituals are religious enactments prescribed by tradition, and through ritual action individuals believe that they can contact the supernatural world.[70]

Ronald and Catherine Berndt explain how this religious belief came about in the Dreamtime – the ancestral past and mythological era of creation when "the patterns and cycles of life and nature were initiated"[71]:

> The mythological era, then, is regarded as setting a precedent for all human behavior from that time on. It was the period when *patterns of living were established, and laws laid down for human beings to follow*. This was the past, the sacred past; but it was not the past in the sense of something that is over and done with. The creative beings who lived on earth at that time did perform certain actions then, and will not repeat them: but their influence is still present, and can be drawn on by people who repeat those actions in the appropriate way, or perform others about which they left instructions. This attitude is summarized in the expression 'the Eternal Dreamtime', which underlies the belief that the mythological past is vital and relevant in the present, and in the future ... The mythical characters themselves are not dead. *They continue to live, although in different forms and in different places ... as long as men obey their instructions, and act in ways laid down for them at the beginning*. The 'life' of these beings, and the life of the Aborigines as a group or constellation of groups distinct from others, are linked together, the one depending on the other. *In other words, there is a close relationship between the religious life and the rest of the social life in general.*[72]

More specifically they explain that in the Kimberley "the Wondjina are mythical beings, male and female, the great creators and *guardians responsible for the continuing welfare of the local Aborigines".*[73]

These explanations of the "religious" activities of Australian Aboriginals support my argument about the *logos* and its strategic guardians. Aboriginal society – like all societies – was vitally concerned to sustain its life-system – its "patterns of living" – and they attempted to do this by calling upon the power of the creator/guardians, who were believed to determine the fortunes of their life-system. Hence, Aboriginal sacred rituals were, in fact, *strategic* rituals and their "religion" – so-called by modern observers who have a very different conception of the nature and role of religion – was a *logos*-affirming social activity.

Stylistic change – figurative paintings

It would be a mistake to conclude that Aboriginal religious/strategic art and ritual were entirely static. Although the Panaramitee (or track and line) style spread throughout the continent where it was to dominate for much of the 60,000 years of Aboriginal occupation, greater regional diversity began to appear about 13,000 BP and flourished after about 5,000 BP. Not surprisingly, this change in artistic style coincided with a change in stone technology.[74] Yet this change in art style did not reflect a change in "religious" belief, merely a change in the way those beliefs were expressed. These stylistic changes were due to the unfolding of the Aboriginal dynamic strategy, which took place within the context of an untransformed strategic *logos*.

Broadly speaking, the Panaramitee style of geometric art persisted, with some changes in emphasis, in the central regions, while a figurative style emerge in the coastal periphery. We will first consider the changes taking place in the traditional geometric style. In western New South Wales over the past 40,000 years, circles, lines and dots as a group remained fairly constant in the range 39 to 34 percent of all motifs in the sample, while "tracks" declined from about 57 to 4 percent, and silhouettes increased from about 5 to 62 percent.[75] Hence, within the traditional geometric style of the Australian central regions, the way in which animals and humans were depicted changed gradually from a depiction of their tracks to their silhouettes. In the coastal periphery this new focus on silhouettes of both animals and humans came to dominate the geometric style, particularly around Sydney where it replaced other geometric motifs completely.

Figurative paintings, particularly those in the less European-settled parts of Australia, provide the opportunity to explore the meaning of Aboriginal rock art. The reason is that this more recent art is still understood by the local Aboriginal inhabitants, whereas they regard the ancient geometric rock engravings as mysterious. Owing to the relatively densely settled nature of the coastal regions of southern Australia, the most easily interrogated figurative art is to be found in northern Australia. This northern figurative art, which dates back to 13,000 BP, includes: the Quinkans, or evil spirits that live in rock crevices, on Cape York Peninsula; the x-ray figures created by "clever men", who can see through objects, and the dramatic Dynamic Figures (earliest known narrative painting in the world) of Arnhem Land; the Bradshaw Figures and the Ancestral Beings (Wandjina) in the Kimberley; and the Lightening Brothers in the Wardaman area (between Katherine and Victoria River) in the Northern Territory.

We can do no more here than focus briefly on a few of these fascinating groups of figurative art. The first of these is the Wandjina of the Kimberley, which are Ancestral Beings that assume human form. They are the spirits of the clouds; makers of land, sea and humans; spirits of lightening, thunder and rain; controllers of fertility and regenerators of all life; and they are the upholders of law, who punish law-breakers with natural disasters such as cyclones, destructive lightening, and floods. Josephine Flood explains:

> Wandjina sites in the Kimberley were focal sites for totemic clans exercising territorial rights over the surrounding country … each clan has a totemic relationship with a particular Wandjina hero, its founding ancestor. Paintings were retouched at annual ceremonies at the Wandjina sites, *in order to propagate the clan's totemic [food] species on behalf of the wider community.*[76]

In other words, the Wandjina were the creator/guardians of the strategic *logos* of these peoples, and the purpose of their sacred art and associated rituals was to protect and sustain their clan and the clan's dynamic strategies.

Wardaman country in the Northern Territory is the site of the Dreaming Beings or Creator Beings, who are either Traveling Beings, such as the Rainbow Serpent, or Local Beings associated with aspects of the landscape. Pictures of these Beings are called *buwarraja* or "Dreaming pictures", and they are sacred pictures believed to have been made by Creator Beings in the Dreamtime. In other words, these Beings – these guardians of the *logos* – are said to have painted themselves in the places they finally ended their journeys, after changing themselves into different parts of the surrounding landscape. These sacred *buwarraja* are distinguished from the *bulawula*, which are secular pictures acknowledged as being made by the local Aboriginal people.

Interestingly, these Northern Territory clans "do not have specific names for themselves, and their estates are not identified by clear boundaries but rather by focal Dreaming sites". And their sacred art "is an expression of the Dreaming … [and] serves to reinforce tribal and clan identity and affiliation with particular tracts of land".[77] In other words, these clans identify themselves primarily in terms of the creator/guardians of their life-system, and their sacred/strategic art serves to make contact with these guardians in order to sustain their life-system. Quite correctly, in their eyes, they and their *logos* are one.

The Lightening Brothers – a pair of very large striped figures – are believed to have painted themselves on a rock wall in the Wardaman area after a fight with each other over an issue of moral injustice. It was a violent fight attending by lightening, rain, and the Rainbow Serpent (Gorrondolmi). As these figures, known as Jabirringgi and Yagjagbula, were in fact painted after European settlement of this region, archaeologists have interpreted them as follows:

> paintings of the Lightening Brothers resulted from the dislocation of traditional peoples following initial European incursions … In response, local people painted the land's identity in rock shelters, both as a re-affirmation of that identity and as a means to strengthen their rightful links to the land.[78]

This conclusion needs to be revised in the light of the dynamic-strategy theory presented in this book. These impressive figures were painted by the Wardaman people to invoke the support of the Creative beings, as guardians of their strategic *logos*, to reinstate and protect their strategic pursuit. Some "spirit figures" were even painted over a droving scene at one site (Wirhugunyang) in a desperate attempt not merely to assert their rights over the land but, more importantly, to ensure the dominance of their *logos* over that of the invaders. It is the *logos* rather than the land that was vital to the local Aboriginal people. The land was merely a strategic input demanded by a successful *logos*. Today, Aboriginal emphasis is placed solely on the land because their *logos* has been destroyed. In the case of the Wardaman people, the struggle was between a stone-age *logos* and an industrial *logos;* and as such there could be only one outcome. The rock paintings depicting the Lightening Brothers were a final and unsuccessful appeal to the guardians of their dynamic strategy – an appeal to their GODS.

Interpreting Aboriginal sacred art

In this section we survey the traditional interpretation of the meaning of Aboriginal sacred art, and of the forces that have sustained and modified the styles of this art. Not surprisingly, these two issues are closely interconnected. The dynamic-strategy theory gives rise to an entirely new interpretation of these matters.

The meaning of sacred art

Sacred art is, as suggested above, an important part of religious ritual that also includes singing/chanting, dancing, retouching ancient rock paintings, pounding cupules, and rubbing rock grooves. All of these activities are associated with drawing on the powers of mythological and totemic characters. The Berndts tell us:

> The general idea in all these rites is to get in touch with these [ancestral] beings, to draw on their power to achieve the particular goal the performers have in mind ... Beliefs of this kind are not isolated, or haphazard, but part of a coherent system – for nearly all ritual and ceremonial expression in Aboriginal Australia is concerned with defining and establishing or sustaining man's relationship with his environment.[79]

They stress that "Aboriginal religious systems are economically based – not simply in terms of immediate aims (e.g. increase and fertility), but in relation to their organization ... [as well as being] a powerful factor in social control".[80]

These "increase" rites concerned not only food sources, but also rain, calm weather, normal seasons, and the "regular operation of various natural phenomena like the sun, moon, stars, wind and rain".[81] Aboriginal societies were primarily concerned, therefore, to ensure the operation of *normal* conditions that would enable them to survive and prosper, rather than to be recipients of some unnatural windfall gain. Once again the Berndts explain that "the Aborigines did not try to go contrary to nature, to alter or disturb its course, but simply to keep it going in a normal way".[82]

What was the nature of this relationship with the environment, as expressed through sacred ritual? The Berndts tell us that:

Their [the rituals'] main concern is with matters in which human beings are most vulnerable: issues of life and death, fertility, and the relations between man and other aspects of nature. We have seen that the Aborigines have a subsistence economy. They are, or were, directly dependent on the earth and what it produces, and on the animals and fish and other creatures which share that earth and its waters with them. There are no human or mechanical intermediaries, except of the most elementary kind, to qualify this dependence or to act as a buffer between them and crises or disasters in their natural environment ... In such a situation it is no less than a matter of life and death that the seasons should continue in an orderly, predictable way, that the supply of animal and vegetable food should not diminish.[83]

This is all fairly clear. Sacred ritual was *strategic* ritual directed towards sustaining the normal Aboriginal life-system, and this life-system was the strategic *logos*, which effectively operated to ensure their survival and, within the limited means of paleolithic society, prosperity. But, owing to a deep anxiety about the mysterious *logos*, this could only be achieved with the supernatural assistance of the guardians.

We also need to know something about those responsible for these sacred/ strategic rituals. While Aboriginal society was fairly democratic – as were all paleolithic societies[84] – with all initiated members of the community being involved in totemic and increase rituals, religious leaders did possess some information not know to others in the clan. These religious/strategic leaders were the "clever men" or "native doctors", who possessed exceptional intellectual abilities. In preparation for this important strategic role in society, a religious leader received special instruction, such as having his totem "sung into him", and learning songs that would "release it from his body in times of need"; he learnt to "fly"; he underwent a symbolic process of death and rebirth; he was introduced to shape-changing Creator Beings, which were sometimes human, sometimes animal (such as goanna, possum, emu, mallee-hen).[85] All these skills were required to seek out and negotiate with the guardians, as well as to undertake other functions.

The role of the native doctor has been described by the Berndts as follows:

He may be the oracle of his group, foretelling coming events, offering advice, curing patients, making rain, divining the 'murderer' after a death, and countering alien magic ... He may be believed to have hypnotic power, supernormal abilities like thought transference, clairvoyance and mindreading; produce a magical cord [for climbing] ...; be able to see and speak with the spirits and ghosts; create illusions; fly or travel at an unnaturally fast pace; become invisible, or change into a puff of smoke, a breath of wind, or a reptile.[86]

As we have seen, these special abilities and activities were typical of shamans, who claimed to be able to gain access to, and exert influence over, the guardians of their *logos*, in hunter-gather societies around the globe. Aboriginal native doctors practiced a mix of religious ritual – a strategic activity required to support their life-system – and magic arts – in part a destructive antistrategic activity including "bone-pointing". But overall, their activities were part of

> a religion which focuses attention on *life rather than death, on earthly wellbeing rather than on a hypothetical future state*, and on the continuity and persistence of the human spirit, the issues of sexual satisfaction and relations between persons, not to mention *the maintenance of the food supply*.[87]

Quite clearly, Aboriginal "religion" was concerned with sustaining their earthly life-system rather than with the spiritual issues we moderns associate with that institution.

Like all successful societies – and Aboriginal society survived longer than any other on Earth – the focus was on life rather than death, even when performing mortuary rituals. The experts tell us that

> through the appropriate [mortuary] rites the participants express their united antagonism toward death as such, and the way it disrupts the ordinary course of events. They reaffirm, collectively, their own status: the living are more important than the dead. The elaborate and extended mortuary rituals ... express not a preoccupation with death but an emphasis on life.

> The immediate practical concern, then, is to sever connections with the spirit and to send it on its way ... A disgruntled and unsatisfied spirit can do harm to near kin and to others.[88]

It is for this reason that bodies of the dead were tied up, just as in European hunting societies they were sometimes either bound tightly or weighted down with large rocks.[89] Even in death, the focus was on the viability of their life-system.

These expert interpretations support my strategic argument that sacred ritual was primarily employed to attract the attention of, and exert influence over, the Creative Beings in order to protect and sustain the life-system of which the "clever men" were custodians. While anthropologists emphasize the relationship with the natural environment, it is the strategic *logos* that Aboriginal society was concerned to protect and sustain, because it is the *logos* that is required to extract from natural resources (including the land) the surplus required for survival and prosperity. Without a viable *logos*, even abundant natural resources cannot be exploited; but conversely, a viable *logos* can always be transformed through the introduction of new ideas to exploit a changing natural environment, even if the latter involves major climate change.

Perhaps it would help to spell out this idea more fully. While the natural environment is the source of resources that the strategic *logos* needs to work with, it is the character of that *logos*, both in technological-paradigmatic and strategic-dynamic terms, that determines the way the environment will be exploited. What this means is that the Aboriginal (or paleolithic) *logos* is no more special in its relationship to the natural environment (or "the land") than any other type of *logos* – just more direct. The neolithic *logos*, for example, is also closely environment-dependent, but has a distancing element provided by the storage of surplus agricultural output. Hence, it is the *logos*-type not the natural environment that is the source of this difference. And it is the *logos*, not the natural environment, that determines issues of survival and prosperity. The natural environment is a given, over which we have little control; whereas we can and do influence the strategic *logos*. And the guardians are supposed to intervene to the same end.

The conclusion of this argument is that in early human societies, such as Aboriginal Australia, so-called "sacred" art and ritual – or art as ritual – was really *strategic* ritual and art. The objective was to sustain the success of the strategic *logos* by approaching this mystery of mysteries through the Creator Beings or guardians. As they were supernatural beings this could be done only through supernatural means. Yet while the means were supernatural the objective was material, and was seen to be material by Aboriginal society. Hence, it is misleading to call this strategic activity "religious", because we normally employ that term in reference to spiritual rather than material objectives.

Before leaving this topic, something could be said about the role of strategic art in the emergence of the visual and performing arts. Strategic art provided a visual and physical vocabulary that was subsequently employed by the entertainment industry. In other words, the origin of secular art is to be found in the attempt to attract the attention of, and exert itself over, the guardians of the *logos*. We can conclude, therefore, that strategic art – the highest form of art – has been concerned with giving shape and meaning to the strategic *logos*, the ultimate reality; whereas secular art has shaped the entertainment industry, which provides the means of escape from that ultimate reality. Because of the harshness of life, both forms of art are required.

The dynamics of sacred art

What is the nature of the dynamics of sacred art in Aboriginal Australia? How can we account for the development of a pan-Australia style of art – the "track-and-line" style – that had much in common with paleolithic art around the globe? How can we account for the remarkable stability of this dominant style over a period of 40,000 years? How can we explain the late emergence of regional diversity in the form of figurative art around the coastal periphery, while the central inland core maintained much of its old traditions? Questions of this type have been raised, and tentative answers provided by a number of anthropologists, most recently by Josephine Flood.

In the first place, we need to explain the emergence of a remarkably persistent pan-Australian style of sacred/strategic art. Traditionally, anthropologists have claimed that, owing to the marked similarity of the track-and-line style to the early geometric style in India and southeast Asia, it is highly likely the first waves of Aboriginal migration carried this mainland style to Australia, and subsequent waves swept it throughout the Great South Land. A more recent argument is that it springs from universal subconscious images (called "phosphenes") generated by mankind's "common neural circuitry".[90] This is, of course, a species of the Darwinian brain-module argument, which is popular with evolutionary psychiatrists, Darwinian sociobiologists, and some philosophers of the mind. I discuss and refute this idea in general in *The Selfcreating Mind* (2006) and in relation to Neanderthal man above.[91]

Josephine Flood, however, is unimpressed by any of these earlier hypotheses. Instead she opts for a "resources crash" argument, which she constructs on the basis of the totally mistaken Malthusian notions of Tim Flannery (1994) about cycles of population boom and bust. She argues that waves of Aboriginal immigration led to rapid overexploitation of the existing megafauna, which collapsed "some time before 40,000 years ago". The subsequent stress on the Aboriginal lifestyle led to the adoption of practices and beliefs designed to sustain supplies of surviving natural species. In turn this led to the emergence of the pan-Australian track-and-line style.[92]

Second, how do traditional scholars account for the great stability of the track-and-line style over such a long time period? Most anthropologists appear to favor a Darwinian/Malthusian approach, by which Aboriginal society adapts to changes in the natural environment in a lagged fashion. This thesis runs into an obvious difficulty, because cultural stability should, in a Darwinian world, reflect environmental stability. In fact, over these 40,000 years, as one would expect, there was considerable change in climate, vegetation and animal types. These changes can be briefly surveyed.

The early Aboriginal migrations to Australia are thought to have occurred during the early part of the last great ice age, between 80,000 and 65,000 BP when sea levels (Figure 2.3) fell to 80 meters below the present level. After a warmer period between 60,000 and 45,000 BP, when sea levels rose to 60 meters below present levels, the ice age reasserted itself, reaching a peak around 18,000 BP, when sea levels were 130 meters below present levels. Then, just as suddenly (relatively speaking!) from 18,000 to 5,000 BP, the ice age ended and the sea rose to its present level. The wide fluctuations in climate underlying these changes in sea levels had a considerable impact on Australia's natural environment. The colder periods were also drier and the vegetation and wildlife were sparser; while in the warmer periods rainfall increased and vegetation and wildlife became more abundant.

The Darwinian/Malthusian adaptationist thesis predicts that changes in art style will change during each of the phases of dramatic climatic/vegetation/ species change as Aboriginal societies struggled to adapt. Yet, as we know, the track-and-line style prevailed throughout the entire period in the continental core, and only began to change in the periphery after 13,000 BP. Quite clearly, the Darwinian adaptation thesis is not an adequate explanation of the dynamics of Aboriginal sacred art and religion.

We are still left with the question of why figurative art developed in the periphery, while geometric art continued to dominate the continent's central core, even after 13,000 BP. Some anthropologists find it convenient to ignore the first 50,000 years of Aboriginal history and focus on the last 13,000 years to provide proof for the Darwinian/Malthusian adaptation thesis. Flood, for example, argues that the continued aridity of the continent's center at a time when the periphery was becoming more hospitable, led to an outward shift of population, which generated "stress" and the need for local populations in the periphery "to assert their ownership of land to refugees from the arid central deserts".[93] This stress, she claims, would have been exacerbated by rising seas that steadily flooded coastal territories, particularly in the north.

There are at least two matters that completely undermine this argument. First, climate change, sea-level rises, and land-flooding, occurred over a relatively long period of ten thousand years. For us today, this is like looking back on the whole history of human civilization. How stressful could such a perspective have been for specific groups in Aboriginal society, either in the center or the periphery? Second, if Flood is concerned with long swings in climate change, what about the 50,000 years before 13,000 BP? The reason these earlier long swings are ignored is that they were not associated with any significant cultural change. Third, it is rather strange that in the arid central regions, where the people apparently felt stressed enough to migrate to the diminishing coastal regions, religious practices did not change significantly after 13,000 BP. Flood is silent on this clear failure of her "use of images as visual markers of social identity at times of stress" argument.[94]

In the face of obvious difficulties with existing explanations, we need to ask whether there is a better, more consistent, more comprehensive, more general explanation of the origin, role, and dynamics of Aboriginal religious practices. Needless to say, I believe there is, and that it centers on my discovery of the strategic *logos*. The origin of "sacred" art, together with other forms of "religious" ritual, can be found in the urgent desire of Aboriginal Australia to understand and influence their mysterious life-system, so as to ensure the success of their strategic pursuit. Given the strategic structure of the human mind (see *The Selfcreating Mind*), the type of ritual developed in any human society is determined by the nature and requirements of the strategic *logos* as communicated to its members via strategic demand. This is true for all cultural characteristics, including all forms of institutions (societal rules), organizations (societal networks), and ideas, both genetic and technological. And the nature of the *logos* at any point in time is a function of the technological paradigm under which it operates, the dynamic strategy being pursued, and the degree to which they have unfolded. This is why paleolithic societies throughout the world are so similar in their social arrangements.

Around 65,000 years ago, the first migrants came to Australia from societies that operated within the paleolithic technological paradigm that had first emerged about 1.9 myrs BP and would finally exhaust itself in the Fertile Crescent about 11,000 BP. Hence, the Aboriginal *logos* was the product of a mature technological paradigm. Within this paradigmatic context, Aboriginal societies were pursuing an active dynamic strategy of family multiplication (procreation and migration), which in southeast Asia was also approaching exhaustion. Only by migrating to Australia could this mature dynamic strategy be given a new lease of life for tens of thousands of years, owing to the vast supplies of unused resources. And this new lease on life was to be extended even further by the almost complete isolation of Australia created by the ending of the ice age after 18,000 BP, and the rising of sea levels by 130 meters. In their isolated Dreaming, the Aboriginal *logos* achieved a dynamic equilibrium, cut off from the external competition that forged a neolithic revolution in southeast Asia.[95] At least until 1788.

The implications of my strategic *logos* theory are, first, that "sacred" art and "religious" ritual were required by the first migrants to Australia to ensure the success of their strategic pursuit – to maximize the probability of survival and prosperity. To achieve this they needed the assistance of the **G**uardians **O**f **D**ynamic **S**trategy – of the GODS. Second, my theory suggests that Australian religious ritual would be influenced by that of the societies in southeast Asia from which they came owing to their very similar strategic *logoi*; and that it would be communicated to social groups via a very similar strategic demand. Third, any unusual "stress" from whatever source would merely increase the intensity of interest in *existing* religious ritual rather than change it significantly or radically. This could be thought of as similar in the modern world to increased church attendance in *existing* religions at times of crisis, such as world war, depression, or terrorist attack. Radical change in religious (and other) institutions only occurs when an old dynamic strategy (say family multiplication) is exhausted and replaced by a new dynamic strategy (conquest or commerce). Prior to the European invasions this could not happen in Aboriginal Australia because of its almost complete isolation, and after 1788 it was too late. It is the relative stability of the strategic *logos* over 60,000 years that accounts for the relative stability of religious ritual, art, technology, and all other forms of institutional and organizational arrangements. While the strategic *logos* was relatively stable – in dynamic equilibrium owing to an absence of external competition – it didn't matter how much the natural environment changed. This analysis exposes the fatal flaw in the Darwinian/ Malthusian hypothesis and demonstrates the strength of the strategic *logos* theory.

Fourth, our new theory can also explain the late flourishing of a new "sacred" art style in Aboriginal Australia. It must be emphasized at the start that the shift from geometric to figurative art in the periphery should not be regarded as a radical change in religious activity, merely the shift to a new style *within the old religious structure*. A radical change could only have come about as a result of a neolithic (agricultural) technological paradigm shift, as shown in Chapter 3. This stylistic change, in contrast, was merely the outcome of the unfolding of the family-multiplication strategy; an unfolding process that also led to a marginal change in stone-tool technology. This was the high point of the Australian paleolithic technological paradigm. But, why only in the periphery? Because the more abundant resources enabled the higher level of prosperity and the greater leisure required to develop more sophisticated forms of religious expression. It is like comparing the pyramids of Egypt (2,650–1,540 BC) with Stonehenge in England (2,800–1,400 BC) – while both were products of the neolithic technological paradigm, Egypt had access to a greater abundance of agricultural resources through large-scale irrigation than did England. But, of course, both the pyramids and Stonehenge were expressions of a religiosity (neolithic) *radically* different from that (paleolithic) expressed by Aboriginal figurative art. Hence, for the first time, the strategic *logos* theory provides a radical and comprehensive explanation for the dynamics of Aboriginal art style for the entire period (65,000 years) of their occupation of the Great South Land.

CONCLUSIONS

The stone-age societies of both Western Europe and Australia have, at their deepest levels, much in common. They both employed the dynamic strategy of family multiplication – of procreation and migration to gain greater access to natural resources – which was expressed through hunting and gathering. They were both isolated for vast periods of time – 300,000 years during the Neanderthal Mousterian, and 60,000 years during the Aboriginal Dreaming – during which they expanded geographically to exploit the animal and plant resources of these unoccupied lands using advanced stone-age technology. Once they had fully occupied and exploited the natural resources of these lands at opposite ends of the globe, they both achieved states of dynamic equilibrium. They both attempted to understand and influence their mysterious life-systems, or strategic *logoi* – in order to survive and prosper – by devising strategic rituals. In this way they were able to penetrate these mysteries so as to negotiate with the **G**uardians **O**f their **D**ynamic **S**trategies. They both gave birth to the **GODS**. And they both extrapolated an understanding of their hidden life-systems onto the visible physical Universe. In this way the *logos* and the cosmos – the strategic and the religious – became one.

This chapter also provides a clearer interpretation of the nature and achievement of the much maligned Neanderthals. The conventional wisdom – despite the scholarship of a dissident few – is that Neanderthal man lacked the higher intellectual, imaginative, and innovative capabilities of modern man. In particular, the Neanderthals are said to have been incapable of symbolic thinking, representational art, and religious ritual. Using the theory of the strategic *logos*, I have been able to show that this conventional wisdom is totally incorrect. This new approach validates the claims of the dissenting few, and refutes the absurdities of Darwinian evolutionary psychology. There can be no reasonable doubt that the Neanderthals possessed a highly successful strategic *logos*, which they too attempted to understand and influence through sacred/strategic rituals. Early modern man, therefore, is not unique in inventing and serving the guardians of the strategic *logos* – in giving birth to the GODS of prehistory.

Chapter 3
The Gods Transformed

With the great economic transition from hunting to agriculture came an equally significant transformation of the strategic guardians into metaphysical beings. In this transformational process, by which early ideas about the strategic *logos* were projected onto the cosmos, the **G**uardians **O**f **D**ynamic Strategy – or **GODS** – became the gods of all creation. It was the era of ancient civilization that witnessed the gods transformed.

In this chapter consideration is given both to the mechanism of transformation, and to the way it worked itself out in the early agricultural societies of the Fertile Crescent. While surveying developments throughout this pivotal region in the transformation of Old World society, we focus primarily on ancient Egypt as a case study. For it was ancient Egypt that came closest of all societies in the Fertile Crescent to understanding the strategic reality underlying their mythological models of the cosmos. This had much to do with the remarkable material success and unusual longevity of Egyptian civilization.

THE MECHANISM OF DIVINE TRANSFORMATION

Divine transformation was an outcome of fundamental changes in the strategic *logoi* of newly emerging agricultural societies. The central dynamic mechanism within the strategic *logos* was an interaction between strategic demand and supply-side forces, which I call **strategic exchange**. A more sophisticated life-system — or strategic *logos* – that emerged in the wake of the neolithic agricultural revolution, generated a growing demand for more complex systems of guardian surveillance and security. In turn this led to the emergence of **priestly philosophers**, who substituted a new deductive (metaphysical) thinking for the old inductive (strategic) thinking of the shamans. This new class of professional priestly philosophers was financed from the growing agricultural surpluses of these neolithic societies. These metaphysicians were responsible for transforming the old guardians of the *logos* into the new gods of the cosmos. Essentially, therefore, divine transformation was a predictable response to a major change in the strategic *logos* of mankind.

The strategic *logoi* of major societies in the Fertile Crescent began to change in fundamental ways around 8,000 BC owing to the impact of the **neolithic technological paradigm shift**, which I have analyzed in *The Dynamic Society* (1996).[1] This great agricultural revolution began in the Old World about 10,600 years ago owing to the exhaustion of the old hunting paradigm that had existed for almost 2 myrs. The development of dryland farming and herding in favored regions of the Fertile Crescent led to the production and storage of grain; to the development of walled towns and, later, cities; and to the emergence of specialized and highly trained groups of professionals in the military, craft, legal, political and religious spheres of urban life. This was in response to changes in strategic demand on the one hand, and to the growing agricultural surpluses on the other, both generated by an increasingly sophisticated strategic *logos*.[2] The supply response, which influenced the more superficial forms taken by new cultural institutions and organizations, depended on the nature of the physical environment, the degree and nature of competition with neighboring societies, and their historical experiences.

The professional priestly classes were called forth to create and sustain a more complex and sophisticated life-system. They were educated in the various arts of history, mythology, reading, writing, mathematics, science, and logical thought. This was the beginning of formalized deductive thinking. Prior to the emergence of civilization, the society of mankind was dominated by **strategic thinking**, which involved the recognition and systematic observation of patterns in nature and society. This observation formed the basis for inductive generalization. The nature of strategic thinking is discussed in detail in my recent book *The Selfcreating Mind* (2006).[3] While strategic thinking dominated human society for nearly 2 myrs, the neolithic revolution created a demand for more abstract and precise thinking in order to build cities; to develop great religious temples and monuments (such as the pyramids in Egypt); and to invent and construct military machines. Deductive thinking was required for the development of engineering and science. When applied to science, great advances could be made, but when used for speculations about the great mysteries of life, fanciful mythologies were created.

The greatest mystery of all was the hidden dynamic system that sustained urban life in the wealthy Fertile Crescent: urban life throughout the Nile Valley, along the Levantine coast, and on the floodplain between the Euphrates and Tigris rivers. It was to explain this great mystery that the priestly philosophers employed their relatively new formalized deductive thinking. The only problem is that this great mystery – the hidden strategic *logos* – could not be accessed by the new deductive thinking, only by the much despised old strategic thinking – the thinking of formally uneducated people in uncivilized, nomadic societies. Unable to penetrate the mystery of the *logos*, the priestly philosophers employed metaphor and myth to construct fictional stories that they *could* understand, and from which they could derive a sense of security. They constructed mythical models rather than realistic models about their life-system.

In this way, the priestly philosophers transformed the existential strategic *logos* of their paleolithic forefathers into a new metaphysical cosmos, and the guardians of a material *logos* into the gods of a spiritual universe. By projecting the *logos* onto the cosmos, the priestly philosophers were able to develop a theology and a religion of which they were the unchallenged custodians. And by holding the mythological keys to the afterlife, these authors of metaphysical fantasy were able to extract a sizeable proportion of the material surplus generated by this life. All this in the name of sustaining a precariously balance strategic *logos*, which they understood less completely than their forefathers.

THE GODS OF EARLY AGRICULTURAL SOCIETIES

Before focusing on ancient Egypt as our case study in the transformation of the gods, a brief survey of religion in the Fertile Crescent will provide a wider perspective. As will become clear, the agricultural revolution in this region was the driving force for changes in the perception of the gods.

The first efforts in "agriculture" appeared in Syria and Lebanon, with Natufian hunter-gatherers harvesting wild cereals by 10,500 BC. By 9,000 BC villagers were cultivating "domesticated" – unable to survive without human intervention – wheat and barley using dry-farming techniques throughout the Middle East.[4] In Egypt, farming along the Nile did not begin until about 5,000 BC, some three millennia later. To facilitate the development of these farming communities, long-distance trade emerged in the Fertile Crescent in the eighth millennium BC. Eventually, a number of these agricultural societies adopted commerce as a dynamic strategy that would lift their standards of living far above the levels that existing agricultural technology could support. Others adopted conquest.

Not until the development of large-scale irrigation techniques around 5,500 BC did Near Eastern farmers move from the foothills of the Zagros Mountains (that form a natural border between Iraq and Iran) onto the rainless plains of Mesopotamia. Together with the invention of the plough around 4,500 BC, large-scale irrigation enabled, for the first time, urban civilization to emerge and flourish. Many vibrant city states – such as Eridu, Ur, Uruk, Nippur, Lagash, Umma, Kish, Agade – emerged on the rich alluvial plains between the Tigris and Euphrates rivers. They formed the land of Sumer (non-semitic) in the south and Akkad (semetic) in the north, and created a new form of strategic *logos*. In these walled cities – fortifications were essential to protect their new wealth from raiding nomads – all the essential instruments of civilization were soon developed. This included: writing by 3,400 BC (cuneiform by 2,900 BC); the measurement of time; advanced mathematics (and other deductive thinking); the invention of bronze (particularly for weapons); the development of specialized professions (military, political, legal, religious) and crafts; and, most important of all, the construction of temples as "homes" for the guardians of their new strategic *logos*.

Between 4,300 and 2,334 BC, the world's first civilization, the Sumerian, flourished and provided an example for the rest of the Old World. At its base was a highly productive agricultural system. But the greater wealth of cities like Uruk – which by 2,900 BC had a population of about 50,000 people – was generated by the dynamic strategies of commerce and, increasingly, conquest.[5] In a climate of escalating competition for, and conflict over, control of commerce, one city leader, King Lugalzagesi of Umma, conquered all of Sumer, for the first time, in 2,350 BC. Yet this was soon followed – just sixteen years later – by the assault of the Akkadian king of Kish, who not only conquered Sumer but fashioned the world's first empire that extended from the Persian Gulf to the Mediterranean Sea. Political stability was to be an elusive goal in the Near East, as the subsequent ancient history of Mesopotamia consisted of relatively short-lived empires of conquest, dominated successively by Ur, Assyria, Babylon, the Hittites, the Kassites, Neo-Assyria, Neo-Babylonia, the Persians, and finally the Macedonians.

Figure 3.1 **The Fertile Crescent, 1300 BC**

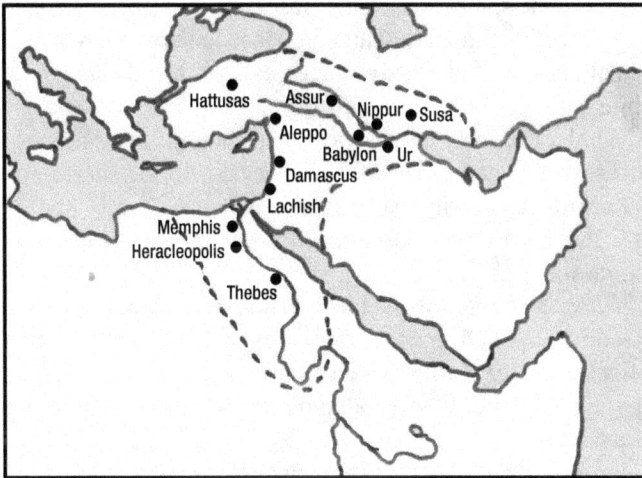

Egypt took a different strategic path. Once the various agriculturally based "confederacies" along the Nile had been forged militarily into a unified kingdom – probably by King Narmer around 2,900 BC – Egypt pursued the dynamic strategy of commerce rather than conquest. Military action was used only to extend and defend the highly lucrative commerce strategy, or to reunify Egypt as a commerce society after periods of chaos – the so-called "intermediate" periods.

How do we account for these very different dynamic strategies at either end of the Fertile Crescent? The hypothesis in this book is that it was the outcome of different degrees of external competition. The Nile valley was effectively isolated from other competing societies by deserts in the west; deserts, mountains, and the Red Sea in the east; deserts and cataracts in the south; and the delta marshes in the north. In addition, the Levant, which did not have the natural resources to match Egypt, provided a buffer between it and the other powerful riverine civilization of Mesopotamia. The geographical circumstances not only provided defensive advantages, they also raised the costs of conquest that might have been pursued by the Egyptians. All of this made the alternative dynamic strategy of commerce more economical. Also, Egypt occupied a key position in the long-distance trading network between central and eastern Africa on the one hand, and the Near East and the Aegean on the other. A key position that could be fully exploited by any king who could eliminate the voracious middlemen by unifying the many regional communities along the Nile.

In contrast, the city-states of Mesopotamia were constantly faced with intense competition, not only from each other but also from neighboring societies in and beyond the Zagros Mountains to the east; Elam on the north-eastern side of the Persian Gulf; Parsa (homeland of the Persians) on the mid-eastern side of the Persian Gulf; Media to the south-west of the Caspian Sea; Hatti in Turkey; Mitanni on the headwaters of the Euphrates; and the Macedonians in far-eastern Europe. It was a situation that held disadvantages as well as advantages. A good military machine was not only essential for survival, but also enabled successful states to conquer the many nearby wealthy societies. It was not only a matter of conquer or be conquered, but of realizing that, in the short term, conquest was a more profitable activity than commerce.

Our interest in this book concerns the implications of these very different dynamic strategies for a society's world view and religious outlook. As I show in *The Ephemeral Civilization* (1997), while the dynamic strategy of commerce generates a more optimistic and uplifting world view expressed in both religion and the arts, that of conquest leads to a more pessimistic and darker view of life.[6] Commerce-Egypt and conquest-Mesopotamia are not exceptions to this universal strategic rule.

In Egyptian religion, the relationship between man and the gods was one of enlightened cooperation in the great task of defeating the forces of chaos in both this life and the next. After death, those who could be "justified" by the way they had participated in this great struggle would join the gods in paradise, known as the Field of Reeds or the Elysian Fields. In contrast the Mesopotamians saw the gods as capricious aristocrats who, tired of the hard work of providing for themselves, created men to act as their slaves. The gods even maliciously inflicted unjustified suffering on mankind, in the form of pestilence, the Great Flood (because the gods had been disturbed by the unceasing din made by humans), drought, and war. It was Mesopotamia that invented the concept of the "righteous sufferer" – a concept unknown in Egypt – later adopted by other religions such as Judaism (The Book of Job).

After a lifetime of providing for the gods, and assisting in the eternal struggle against chaos, even the most deserving and loyal Mesopotamian found himself in a hellish underworld, living a "ghostly half-life".[7] This world of the dead had prison-like walls, monstrous guards, and was ruled over by the forbidding goddess Ereshkigal ("the great below"). Perhaps they thought it an inevitable and fitting end for a people like themselves who spent their lives killing, raping, and plundering for a living; while the Egyptians were more satisfied about their strategic path through life and about their just desserts in the next. In reality, neither society had any real choice in their dynamic strategy if they wished to survive and prosper in an indifferent world. Only the true saints – the nonstrategists – exercised a real choice and, thereby, perished.

While these contrasting agricultural societies had very different worldviews, their ideas about the role of gods were very similar. Both societies viewed the gods as the guardians of their dynamic life-system, and as allies (no matter how capricious) in the great battle between the forces of order and chaos. These similar religious/strategic ideas need to be briefly reviewed.

Both societies had a similar story to tell about the nature of the cosmos before the creation of gods and man. It was thought to consist of primeval waters or a watery chaos, which constituted an undifferentiated oneness. This view had a long history and is also found in Jewish scriptures. From these primeval waters, called Tiamet/Aspu in Sumer and Nun in Egypt, the selfcreating creators emerged to bring forth land from the waters, to separate the heavens from the Earth, and to create all living things, particularly mankind. This emergence of existence from non-existence was part of the great struggle between the forces of order and chaos. In the Babylonian creation story, we are told about a mighty war between the forces of chaos, represented by Tiamet, the goddess of saltwater, and those of order, represented by Marduk, the god of thunderstorms, who rose to be "Lord of the gods". Marduk wins this battle, slays Tiamet, and uses her body to create the heavens and the Earth. The Egyptian creation myth, in contrast, is much less war-like, befitting a commerce society.

In both societies the gods were responsible for the survival and prosperity of their patronized city or society. To ensure the continued presence of their patron god – and, hence, of his/her protective influence – it was the responsibility of mankind to construct divine dwelling places or temples (called Ziggurats in Mesopotamia), to provide suitable offerings and to generally make the gods welcome and content. In Egypt these temple offerings were made in gratitude for the services the gods gave of their own volition, whereas in Mesopotamia their more capricious gods had to be wooed. While the presence and beneficial influence of the gods – as guardians of the strategic *logos* – could never be taken for granted, this was particularly so in Mesopotamia where the gods might act irrationally and maliciously.

Whenever ill fortune fell on either society, it was said that the gods had "withdrawn" from the city or the empire. A Sumerian text called "The Curse of Agade", tells how Agade, capital of the Akkadian empire in the third millennium, prospered because of the presence of the gods – particularly Inana – but later declined and eventually collapsed when the gods departed.[8] Further, we were told by Mesopotamian scholars that

> lamentations over destroyed cities became a genre of Sumerian literature ... The underlying theme ... is that cities, dynasties and states are part of an ongoing ebb and flow of destruction and rebirth.[9]

And the gods were responsible for this rise and fall. They were the guardians of the *logos* of mankind.

Central to maintaining the divine presence and protection was the role of the king in both Egypt and Mesopotamia. In Mesopotamian society the king was the "supreme mediator between the gods and the people", owing to the "fact" that he was "chosen by the gods" for this purpose.[10] Indeed, in Sumer, "kingship" was known as "Enlilship", after Enlil, the god of air, patron of Nippur, and the most important god of southern Mesopotamia in the third millennium BC.

The kings of both societies were responsible, with the assistance of priests, for conducting temple rituals and other festivals celebrating the presence and protection of the gods. While modern commentators usually draw a distinction between the secular and religious functions of kings, these strategic leaders would not have recognized this distinction. Seeking the protection and assistance of the gods – the guardians of dynamic strategy – was an integral part of strategic leadership. It was no different in kind to exercising military or commercial leadership. Indeed, temples in which the kings officiated, rather than palaces where they merely lived, were the epicenters of Mesopotamian cities and empires. For example, we are told that, in the vicinity of the temple

> where heaven and earth were connected, where gods hovered in elevated security above the city, the hub of the state could be contemplated as a cosmic pillar assuring continuity and renewal.[11]

Here then is a metaphor for the Mesopotamian *logos*. A major difference between these two societies was the view that after death the Egyptian king joined the other gods in their continued struggle against the demons of chaos, whereas the Mesopotamian king was, like all other citizens, engulfed by a hellish half-life. Protecting the Mesopotamian *logos* was the job of the living.

How were the gods viewed by Mesopotamian and Egyptian priestly philosophers? Both societies had thousands of gods. Of these, the main ones were associated with various aspects of their dynamic life-systems. In Mesopotamia, Inana, goddess of fertility and war, represented both the "primal drive"[12] in their life-system, as well as the dominant dynamic strategy of conquest, which was responsible for the Ur's great wealth and prosperity. Other major gods included An (Anu), god of heaven and supreme creator god, responsible for the cyclical nature of seasons; Utu, the sun god, who was judge of the gods and responsible for the eternal recurrence of day and night; Enlil (Ellil) of Nippur, god of winds and agriculture, who invented the hoe, and was responsible for the prosperity and abundance of his chosen city in war and peace (but who could also be highly destructive if displeased, as in the Great Flood); Enki (Ea) of Eridu, god of wisdom and sweet water of the life-giving rivers, who was a creator god engaged in the primordial battle between good and evil, was god of artists and craftsmen, and was responsible for the well-being of the natural world; Marduk who, under the Babylonians, replaced An and Enlil as the chief deity and leader of the forces against chaos; and Assur, who was the national deity of the Assyrians, replaced Marduk as the hero god.

As the social structure of Mesopotamia changed from a collection of competing city-states to a conquest empire – owing to the unfolding of the Mesopotamian **strategic sequence** – the roles of the gods and the relationships between them changed as suggested above. At first, the various patron gods of the city-states were regarded as equals; but when Nippur built its empire, Enlil became the supreme god of Sumer – later superseded by the Babylonian god Marduk and then the Assyrian god Assur – and the Sumerian pantheon was reorganized. In other words, the gods, in their role as guardians of the dynamic strategies, were responsive to changes in the Mesopotamian *logos*. But, at the same time, the material success of the *logos* provided the priestly philosophers with the freedom to employ their imaginations to reshape their stories about the gods and to indulge in ever more elaborate religious ritual. Over time, these metaphysicians, in response to the emergence of empire, elevated one of the many city gods to be the chief amongst his peers, clearing the way, as will be shown in the next chapter, for the chief god to become the one and only God of all creation.

Like the gods of Mesopotamia, the Egyptian deities were regarded as representatives of the major characteristics and dynamic forces of their life-system. Indeed, Egyptian ideas about their gods contain the most elegant and complete mythological analysis of the strategic *logos*. This was largely the outcome of a strategic system that remained intact for three millennia – a strategic system that was subjected to close scrutiny by an intellectual class that remained faithful to its dictates and resisted the temptation to divorce the idea of their gods from the reality of the strategic *logos* of which they were the custodians.

THE EGYPTIAN *LOGOS* AND ITS GUARDIANS

Historical background

Prehistorical era

The foundation upon which Egyptian history and civilization was based is the mighty Nile river, which has its main source in a series of large lakes fed by melting glaciers from the "Mountains of the Moon" (mentioned by Ptolemy) in the Ruwenzori Range. These lakes – which include Victoria, the largest, Albert, Edward, and George – had their origins in the great depressions that formed about 1 myrs ago. After filling gradually, Lake Victoria finally spilled out of its geological depression about 12,500 years ago, flowed into Lake Albert, which in turn gave rise to the White Nile in Uganda. Flowing through Sudan, the White Nile joined forces with the Blue Nile at Khartoum and the Atbara River – both rising in the Ethiopian highlands – and finally found its way through a series of marshes into the south-eastern corner of the Mediterranean.

The remarkable regularity and control of the flood cycle in the Nile is the outcome of regular monsoonal precipitation along the Ruwenzori Range, the summer melting of its glaciers, and the surrounding rainforest that, together with the massive size of its lakes of origin, act as a great water-release regulating mechanism. Each year the Nile begins to rise in summer, and by August (at least, before the construction of dams in the twentieth century) bursts its banks and inundates the floodplain. The flood reaches its zenith in September and then, in October, subsides. As it recedes, the Nile leaves deposits of rich, dark-colored silt on the floodplain (the "Black Land"), which contrasts with the red sands of the engulfing desert (the "Red Land"). It is this regular flooding that made the Nile Valley so fertile in ancient times, resulting in wheat yields comparable to those in modern wheat-producing countries. Surely such a regular and beneficial system could only be given and sustained by the gods?

Yet the surrounding "Red Land" did not always consist of parched deserts sparsely dotted with oases. Before 9,000 BP, North Africa enjoyed a higher and more regular rainfall, which produced extensive savannah and endless grasslands rather than the rainless deserts of modern times.[13] During the seventh and sixth millennia BC, however, this region became steadily drier and hotter, and the grasslands gradually turned to desert. The scattered northeast-African population of hunter-gatherers and cattle herders gradually moved into the Nile Valley, where they lived by hunting in the marshes, fishing in the river, and raising livestock on the alluvial river flats. By the fifth millennium BC, these Nile settlements were turning to farming – growing emmer wheat, barley, flax and a variety of fruit and vegetables; and raising domesticated cattle, sheep, goats and donkeys. These agricultural commodities, together with craft goods (particularly pottery, stoneware and fabrics) produced in the growing villages, were traded throughout the Nile Valley and along the Mediterranean and Red Sea costs. The dynamic strategy that generated this economic expansion was family multiplication – procreation and migration – that increasingly drew the resources of the Nile Valley into the process of production. It was a strategy that dominated Egyptian prehistory until, given the technology of that era, the Nile's resources were fully exploited.

Why did this burst of agricultural development occur a few thousand years later than that in the upper Fertile Crescent? For two main reasons. The first, discussed earlier, was the relative isolation of this end of the Fertile Crescent. Second, and more importantly, is the fact that at the time the neolithic revolution was occurring in the Levant and Mesopotamia, the moister climate of north-east Africa did not provide any pressure to relocate to and concentrate in what I call (in *The Dynamic Society* (1996)), a **funnel of transformation**;[14] instead it permitted the migration over an endless grassy plain. Only after 7,000 BC did the nomadic peoples of this region begin to concentrate their cattle-herding and agricultural activities in the Nile Valley as the rainfall diminished and became less reliable. Hence, rather than undermining human society, climatic change actually promoted it, with the Nile settlements eventually being forged into one of the most brilliant and enduring civilizations in human history. There is an important lesson here: the flexibility of human beings and their strategic *logoi* enable them not only to overcome but even to exploit climatic change (see Snooks, *The Coming Eclipse*, 2010).

By 4,000 BC the peoples of the Nile Valley had fashioned a prosperous material culture known as "Nagada", after the southern Egyptian town where a distinctive "black-topped" style of pottery has been unearthed (see Figure 3.2). The first evidence of these people calling on the powers of strategic guardians has been discovered in their grave goods, which, in addition to utilitarian pottery, include female and bearded male idols.

Figure 3.2 **Ancient Egypt and Nubia**

During the 500 years prior to the emergence of the first Egyptian dynasty – about 2,900 BC – strong and prosperous government was exercised in "confederations", or proto-kingdoms, dominated by towns such as Abydos, Nagada (Nubt), and Hierakonpolis (see Figure 3.2), where large brick tombs were built by the ruling elite. Cults of the deities Horus, Seth, and Neith appear to have been widespread in this later Nagada, or pre-dynastic, period. It is probably from the struggle between the leaders of these proto-kingdoms in upper (or southern) Egypt that the first king of all Egypt – known as Narmer – emerged around 2,900 BC. Based in Hierakonpolis in the Confederacy of Nekhen, king Narmer waged a series of successful campaigns as far south as the second cataract near Buhen (22° north) and as far north as the Nile delta (32° north). Quite clearly, the driving force in the Nile Valley at this formative time was the dynamic strategy of conquest, although the longer term objective was to gain a monopoly over trade goods and trade routes, in order ultimately to pursue the dynamic strategy of commerce. Both strategies were capable of generating far greater wealth for military and commerce elites than could be achieved from agricultural pursuits alone.

The dynastic era: 2,900–337 BC

The early dynastic period (2,900–2,650 BC) witnessed the emergence of the Egyptian nation-state. During this time – Dynasties 1 and 2 – the rulers from upper Egypt successfully forged not only the institutions of a powerful state, but also a national consciousness in a land consisting formerly of a large number of regional societies possessing strongly held local customs. This period also saw a shift in the country's economic and political center from upper to lower Egypt – from Thinis to Memphis. From the middle of the third millennium BC, therefore, Egypt was in a position to begin the first phase of its material expansion as a highly unified nation-state by pursuing the extremely lucrative commerce strategy.

The main "orderly" phases of the entire dynastic period are conventionally categorized as the Old Kingdom, Middle Kingdom, New Kingdom, and Late Period; and they varied from 440 to 500 years in duration. Each of the "orderly" phases were separated by more "chaotic", or "intermediate", periods, ranging from 70 to 290 years. Each of these kingdoms and intermediate periods covered a varying number of dynasties that in turn comprised the reigns of associated Egyptian kings or pharaohs.

Table 3.1 **Egyptian Kingdoms, Dynasties, and Great Waves of Expansion, 2650–337 BC**

Kingdoms		Dynasties	Dates (BC)	Duration	Great Waves
I	Old	3–6	2,650–2,150	500	350
II	Middle	11–13	2,080–1,641	439	320
III	New	18–20	1,539–1,069	470	334
IV	Late	25–30	780–337	443	NA

Intermediates		Dynasties	Dates (BC)	Duration
1	First	8–10	2,150–2,080	70
2	Second	14–17	1,641–1,539	102
3	Third	21–24	1,069–780	289

Notes:

(i) These dates are only approximate, and vary slightly as between sources. They are taken from Manley (1996: 132–35).

(ii) The "Great Waves" are my estimates of the phases of continuous economic expansion. The Late Period is not included as it was a time of periodic invasion and foreign occupation.

According to the ancient Egyptians, this pattern – summarized in Table 3.1 – of "orderly" and "chaotic" periods was the outcome of the struggle between the forces of order (*maat*) and chaos (*isfet*) – a struggle between kings and gods on one side, and the chaos monsters (particularly Apophis the "Great Rebel" or the "Evil One") on the other. When the king and gods triumphed, the kingdom flourished. But when the king was a "usurper" and the gods withdrew, chaos, which was always near, overwhelmed Egypt. As during the intermediate periods when central authority declined, foreigners (who inhabited the kingdom of chaos)[15] invaded Egypt, and the monopoly over commerce was lost.

While this is a fascinating interpretation – which was common to most ancient societies – it is metaphorical rather than scientific. This pattern of order and chaos – which I call the **great waves of economic change** (see final column of Table 3.1) – can only be satisfactorily explained by employing a general dynamic theory. My dynamic-strategy theory suggests that these great waves of just over 300 years in duration – similar to the great-wave pattern in all successful dynamic societies in the ancient world[16] – can be explained as the outcome of the adoption, exploitation, and exhaustion of dynamic strategies of either conquest or commerce. It was suggested earlier that the main dynamic strategy employed in Mesopotamia was conquest and in Egypt was commerce.

Egypt's first great wave

During Egypt's first great wave of economic expansion from 2,650 to 2,150 BC, economic and political growth was generated by the exploitation and exhaustion of the dynamic strategy of commerce. While agriculture provided a surplus that could be invested in a "higher" dynamic strategy, it did not form the basis of dynastic expansion. Once the agricultural resources of the Nile were fully employed, the economic system ceased to grow, at a relatively low level of GDP per capita and of city size. While agriculture continued to support an annual cycle of economic activity, it could no longer generate linear economic growth of Egyptian city centers. Further growth of income, living standards, and city size could only be achieved through the adoption of the dynamic strategy of either conquest or commerce. Owing to the relative isolation of Egypt from other wealthy and competitive societies, that dynamic strategy had to be commerce.

Commerce provided a strong incentive for the political elite to attempt to unify the various independent proto-kingdoms throughout the Nile Valley. Whoever controlled the Nile controlled the lucrative trade between central and eastern Africa at one extreme and the Mediterranean and Fertile Crescent at the other. If this control was divided between a large number of independent Egyptian proto-kingdoms (at least sixteen in the pre-dynastic era[17]), the returns to commerce would be much diluted. But if one of proto-kingdoms, or confederacies, could unify the whole of Egypt, they would gain a monopoly over the very considerable returns flowing from the pursuit of the commerce strategy.

In this light it becomes clear that the military expansion of the Confederacy of Nekhen (or Hierakonpolis) was undertaken to gain complete control of the commerce strategy (including its mining interests) of Egypt rather than as the start of a large-scale conquest strategy. But, of course, in the short-term, conquest was also highly remunerative for the first successful warlords of Nekhen. The existing literature supports this dynamic-strategy hypothesis. We are told that "the issue was not the conquest of foreign territory, but the assertion of Egypt's economic interests and trade"[18]; and "military actions were also frequently undertaken to secure trade interests".[19] Military action also had to be undertaken against the Bedouin in the Sinai and Nubian deserts to protect trade routes and mining interests, particularly towards the end of the Sixth Dynasty.

While direct Egyptian rule during the Old Kingdom extended only as far as Elephantine (Abu) at the first cataract, their commercial and mining (gold and diorite) interests extended throughout Nubian territory to Buhen at the second cataract and beyond. The Nubian trade in incense, oils, ivory, gold, ebony and animal skins was conducted not only along the Nile (which could be traversed in three weeks by sailing boats) but also by caravans via the oases in the Western Desert (taking a longer three months). Egypt also traded with societies along the coasts of the Mediterranean (Palestine, Syria, Turkey and the Aegean) and Red Sea (the fabled land of Punt, located either in Eritrea or Somalia), particularly for timber, resins, spices, minerals, wine, opium, and craft goods in exchange for grain, natron (soda), gold, gemstones and malachite.

This commercial activity was undertaken by the leading Egyptian institutions, including the monarchy and religious temples. At the highest level, the king's diplomats arranged for the exchange of commodities require by the royal court; while other trade was conducted by priests, who administered Egypt's leading temple complexes. The temples employed agents and operated fleets of commercial ships to conduct trade in the vast array of commodities they required to serve the interests of the gods – the guardians of the Egyptian *logos*. At the height of empire in the New Kingdom, the temple of Amun employed a fleet of 83 ships.[20]

So successful was the commerce strategy of the Old Kingdom that it enabled the pharaohs to build the great pyramids with which Egyptian civilization is so closely associated. King Netjerykhet (Djoser) (2,630–2,610 BC) built the first stepped pyramid at Sakhara near Memphis; while Khufu (2,551–2,528 BC) and Khaefra (2,520–2,494 BC) built the great pyramids at Giza. All told, some twenty-three pyramids were built in lower Egypt during the Old Kingdom. Pyramid construction on this scale was a huge and extremely expensive task, which required the most advanced organizational, planning, mathematical, engineering, and craft skills.

Khufu's pyramid, for example, took approximately 113,500 man-years to build, over a period of fourteen years, with a workforce (including those in the quarries and on the construction site) beginning with 24,000 men in the first year, and declining to about 4,000 men in the final year. In addition, the domestic community required to support this workforce would have been at least equal to these numbers.[21] At this time the total population of Egypt was no more than 1.6 million, so that the construction of Khufu's pyramid may have occupied about 10–11 percent of the Egyptian workforce.[22] The difficulty of the task, and the skill of execution, is reflected in the fact that during just fourteen years of construction, a total of over two million blocks of sandstone, each weighing about 2.5 tons, were quarried, dressed, transported, and put in place (with a precision that would be difficult to achieve today) in a massive structure that has a base of 230.35 meters on all sides, a height of 146.71 meters and a volume of 2.6 million cubic meters. Just imagine, during the first year of construction it would have been necessary to cement into place some five 2.5 ton limestone blocks every two minutes for every working day.[23] Clearly, this momentous "non-productive" activity absorbed a significant proportion of Egyptian national income – perhaps in the vicinity of 10 percent in the first year, declining to 1.5 percent in the final year. This is a large burden for a neolithic society dependent upon agricultural and commerce surpluses. In the contemporary world, even leading countries like the USA spend only about 7–8 percent of GDP on the infrastructure of science, technology, and knowledge (OECD 2003); which is the modern equivalent of the pyramids. It also begs the question of how it can be accounted for. While no one has been able to satisfactorily explain this large "non-productive" expenditure, the dynamic-strategy theory provides, for the first time, a persuasive strategic hypothesis, which is discussed below.

Despite the heights reached by this first great wave of prosperity, the end was in sight by the beginning of the Sixth (and last) Dynasty of the Old Kingdom, around 2,300 BC. Certainly by the remarkably long reign of 96 years by Pepy II, royal authority had been greatly diminished, and provincial cult centers – such as Abydos, Coptos, and Thebes – had become increasingly important. By this time the dynamic strategy of commerce had exhausted itself, as all possible sources of trade had been fully exploited.[24] And as the unifying influence of the commerce strategy weakened, the Egyptian kingdom began to fragment. Just as the Egyptians always feared, the forces of chaos, at least temporarily, finally triumphed over those of order.

The collapsing great wave of Egyptian prosperity began in the Sixth Dynasty and reached its lowest point during the Eight to Eleventh Dynasties (2,150–2,007 BC), known to scholars as the First Intermediate Period. During this time of chaos, the Old Kingdom establishment was swept away by the governors of Hierakonpolis, who styled themselves as rulers of the Ninth and Tenth Dynasties. Despite this show of authority, their influence was limited to the northern half of the country, as the south was firmly under the control of the governors of Thinis, Thebes and Hierakonpolis. At this time no great monuments were built, famine was experienced, internal conflicts broke out, and Egypt was subject to invasions from both north and south. Fear and uncertainty prevailed throughout the land, the old values were increasingly ignored, and many royal tombs were plundered.

The ancients viewed the Ninth and Tenth Dynasties as a period when the gods – like the commerce strategy – withdrew from Egypt, and *isfet* triumphed over *maat*. In "The laments of Khakheperrasonb" we are told of this time that

> The ways of the gods are violated, and their offerings are neglected. The land is in distress and there is mourning everywhere. Towns and districts are sorrowful, and all alike are weighed down with iniquities.[25]

Surprising as it may seem, this ancient explanation is far closer to the mark than modern ones concerning the senility of Pepy II or the sudden and coincidental emergence of regional strongmen. I will argue that the exhaustion of the dynamic strategy of commerce prior to the reign of Pepy II disrupted the operation of the strategic *logos* of Egypt that was responsible for the orderly dynamics, which the ancients called *maat*. To say that the gods – the guardians of their dynamic life-system – had withdrawn from Egypt was a shorthand, if mythological, way of saying that the strategic *logos* was in crisis, and there was no one, either in this world or the next, who could lend a helping hand.

Egypt's second great wave
The second great wave of economic expansion and prosperity, know as the Middle Kingdom, began in Thebes under the strategic leadership of Nebhepetre

Montjuhotep, who came from a family of hereditary governors of that province. He inherited a military struggle between Thebes and its neighbors, which he prosecuted with great skill and vigor. By 1986 BC, now grandly styled Montjuhotep II (2007–1956 BC), he ruled over a reunited Egypt that stretched from the Mediterranean in the north to Buhen at the second cataract in the south.

The second great wave of economic expansion began around 1986 BC and continued for about 320 years until the generation before the end of the Thirteenth Dynasty in 1641 BC. Like the first phase of expansion, this was a great wave of fairly typical duration, and it too was driven by the dynamic strategy of commerce. As soon as the new regime had concluded its wars of unification, it got down to the serious business of exploiting Egypt's commercial advantages. The Middle Kingdom showed little interest in conquest beyond its own borders. As one historian has observed: "The pharaoh's interests at this period [the Middle Kingdom] regarding the Syro-Palestinian area concentrated primarily on the maintenance of trade routes".[26] The high point of this great wave of prosperity was the Twelfth Dynasty (1937–1759 BC), which presided over a efflorescence of the arts, particularly architecture, painting and literature – as commerce is always a great patron of the arts.[27] It was also a time of growing centralization of administrative and religious power, and a diminution in the role of regionally located governors, gods, and clergy.

Egypt's commerce strategy, as noted earlier, was the outcome of its key position on the trade routes between central Africa and both the Mediterranean and Near East. This second great wave was made possible by a central Egyptian authority re-establishing and re-exploiting these commercial links. As in the Old Kingdom, Egypt acted as the middleman in the lucrative flow of timber, resin, lapis lazuli, copper, malachite, galena and opium from the Mediterranean and Near East; and of spices, gold, and African trade goods from the south. Egypt added to this flow of much demanded commodities by supplying its own wheat, barley, craft goods, gold, natron, quartzite and alabaster.

To facilitate this trade, Egypt re-established trading centers in southern towns such as Buhen, and forts along the river and in the Nubian desert to control the southern caravan routes and to protect Egyptian mining (gold and copper) interests. Eventually, Egyptian armies under Senusret III (1836–1817 BC), for the first time in history, extended the southern border beyond the second cataract as far as Semna, in order to trade directly with the kingdom of Kush. Egypt also re-opened trading links with the fabled Punt via the Red Sea route. In the north they re-established trading links with Palestine by caravan, with Lebanon (particularly Byblos) and Syria (Ugarit) – and thereby with Babylonia – by sea, and with the Greek world both by sea and overland through Turkey. This northern trade was facilitated by diplomatic relations with Egypt's northern neighbors, by providing a home for refugees from Palestine (echoes of which can be heard in the Bible), and by establishing fortified outputs along the coastal route (the "Ways of Horus") between the eastern delta and Palestine to control the caravan trade. The return on this investment in the commerce strategy was well worth the expenditure.

But, as before, after about 300 years, the dynamic strategy of commerce finally exhausted itself. This occurred once all new sources of tradable goods had been fully exploited. And the predictable outcomes were economic stagnation, and political fragmentation as the material reason for unification evaporated. Egypt's strategic *logos* was in crisis once more. This failure of order and the triumph of chaos is known as the Second Intermediate Period, and it lasted for about a century – see Table 3.1. One historian has commented that "the short reigns of the last kings of the Twelfth Dynasty and those of the Thirteenth Dynasty … suggest that there were violent conflicts over control of Egypt".[28] This was associated with the infiltration of peoples from Palestine and Syria, which led to the emergence of Hyksos kings, known as the Fifteenth Dynasty, who ruled in the delta. At the same time, Egypt lost control of Nubia in the south to the kingdom of Kush. Once again the gods had withdrawn from Egypt and taken *maat* with them.

While the Hyksos kings, who were recognized as Egyptian pharaohs, established their courts at Avaris in the eastern delta, the descendants of the old Memphite rulers retreated further south. The Seventeenth Dynasty established itself at Thebes in defiance of the Hyksos kings in the contemporaneous Fifteenth Dynasty, and began to arm themselves in secret. Eventually this action led to open hostilities with the kingdoms of Avaris in the north and Kush in the south. This new drive for Egyptian unity began with Senakhtenra Taa (1560 BC), who was killed in a campaign against the Hyksos, and was continued by his sons Kamose (1541–1539 BC) and the victorious Ahmose (1539–1514 BC). Ahmose defeated the Hyksos rulers and reunited Egypt under Theban leadership, thereby founding the Eighteenth Dynasty, which was the beginning of the New Kingdom.

Egypt's third great wave
While Ahmose re-united Egypt through force of arms, his intention, and that of his brother and father before him, was to re-establish the old Egyptian *logos* under the strategic guardian Amun by restarting the dynamic strategy of commerce – not to embark on a strategy of conquest. Hence, after crushing the Hyksos Palestinian fort and trade center at Sharuhen in 1518 BC, the new pharaoh made it clear he wanted to trade with, not occupy, major cities and towns in Palestine and Syria. Nevertheless, life for Ahmose continued to be turbulent, with rebellions in Nubia and even in Egypt (led by the little-known figure Tetian). Lucrative dynamic strategies are always keenly contested. But by the time his son Amenhotep I (1514–1493 BC) came to the throne, the stage was set for the full resumption of commercial expansion.

Egypt's third great wave of economic expansion lasted for 334 years (see Table 3.1), and, as before, was based on commerce. The vast mineral resources, particularly gold, of Nubia provided a major foundation stone in the rebuilding of Egypt's commerce strategy. Gold facilitated trade with both the African and Mediterranean–Middle East worlds. But it was not an easily won resource. Considerable military effort was required to annex large tracts of Nubia as far south as the third cataract, to extend Egyptian influence to the fifth cataract – further south than the Middle Kingdom had ever ventured – and to suppress periodic Nubian rebellions. The New Kingdom kings were so determined to retain control of this vast and rich mineral-producing region that they even granted the indigenous chiefs the same status as high-ranking Egyptian court officials, and arranged for the education of their sons in the Egyptian court (no doubt both for indoctrination and ransom purposes), provided they kept the peace in their own lands.

Egypt's relationships with its northern neighbors were very different. As there were no rich mineral resources to covet in Palestine or Syria, Egypt had no desire to occupy this territory – at least not in the beginning. Egypt only became militarily involved once its commercial interests were endangered. Any threat to the Levantine ports that dominated the sea trade, or the Palestinian and Syrian towns that controlled the caravan routes, led to a quick Egyptian military response. Such military responses occurred during the reigns of the Eighteenth Dynasty kings Thutmose I (1493–1481 BC), Thutmose III (1479–1425 BC), and Amenhotep II (1427–1392 BC). After these military operations, Egypt was able to "dominate" the coastal region of Palestine from the delta to Byblos and Sumur, and to "influence" Syrian towns as far north as Aleppo near the headwaters of the Euphrates. This, however, was merely part of its strategy of commerce, not of conquest.

As one historian has written: "New Kingdom Egypt was no imperial war machine: she was a self-confident, cultural and commercial giant, linking the highways of Africa to Europe and the Near East"[29]; and another concurs: "This can at best be described as imperialism geared to the exploitation of raw materials and the control of trade routes".[30] Even the large tribute extracted by Egypt from defeated neighbors both in the north and south should be thought of as compensation for the large cost of having to take direct action to protect its trade network. This was the high point of Egyptian prosperity and, hence, cultural flowering.

The New Kingdom, however, provides an excellent illustration of how the strategic *logos* can be endangered by a failure of leadership at the very height of strategic success. During the reign (1344–1328 BC) of Amenhotep IV (later called Akhenaten), coinciding with the New Kingdom's most prosperous phase, Egypt lost sight of the main game and indulged in highly risky *antistrategic* activities. Akhenaten attempted to overthrow the strategic guardian Amun – who had enabled Ahmose to restore the Egyptian *logos* – together with his priestly retinue at Karnak. The intention was to replace Amun and all other gods with the one and only god Aten, the sun disk or, more meaningfully, the divinity associated with the power of the midday sun. This religious revolution extended to all aspects of Egyptian governance. The court was moved from Thebes to an entirely new capital called Akhetaten ("horizon of Aten"), and Akhenaten vowed "never to leave the boundaries of the city" and to devote himself entirely to religious activities. Many commentators are puzzled by this apparent emergence of "monotheism", which was the first and only time this happened in three thousand years of Egyptian history. I argue later in this chapter that it was a case not of monotheism, but of the strategic leader identifying himself with the strategic guardian of Egypt – a rejection of the strategic *logos* in favor of the megalomaniacal pursuit of self-aggrandizement and self-love.[31] A modern equivalent is the self-promoted cult of Mao Tse-Tung that was equally disastrous for the modern Chinese economy.

There was considerable disquiet throughout the kingdom at Akhenaten's decision to abandon the traditional gods – the guardians of the Egyptian *logos* – and, in particular, to refuse to serve the goddess *maat* so as to maintain worldly order. Needless to say, the unemployed priests of Amun and the other gods were particularly annoyed and plotted against their pharaoh. And outside the kingdom, the Hittites used this opportunity to increase their influence in Syria and Palestine, while Kadesh rebelled against Egyptian control. There are suggestions that toward the end of this reign, Akhenaten realized his mistake in ignoring the strategic *logos* and its dynamic strategy of commerce, and attempted to reverse the growing chaos in internal and external affairs.[32] A sense of this growing chaos is encapsulated in a contemporary description of the state of affairs in his father's reign carved on Tutankhamun's "Restoration Stela". It reads:

> At the time when his majesty [Tutankhamun] was crowned as king, the temples of the gods and goddesses beginning in Elephantine and ending in the marshes of the delta … had fallen into ruin. Their shrines had fallen into decay having become mounds and teaming with weeds. Their sanctuaries were like that which did not exist. Their domains were footpaths. The land was in distress; *the gods had abandoned this land.*
>
> If an army was sent to Djahi (Syria-Palestine) in order to widen the boundaries of Egypt, they could not succeed. If one petitioned to a god in order to take counsel from him, he did not come at all. If one prayed to a goddess likewise, she did not come at all. (Quoted in Darnell and Manassa 2007:50. My emphasis.)

At the end of his reign, the only strategic guardian left to Akhenaten was the glorified image he had created of himself. Possibly, in his dying days, Akhenaten finally realized why earlier pharaohs had sought help in maintaining *maat* from supernatural beings.

It was too late for Akhenaten and his descendents, because the internal and external difficulties led to the emergence of military strongmen, who looked to the old gods for support in these critical times. Following the sudden deaths of both Akhenaten (1328 BC) and his young son Tutankhamun (1318 BC) a succession of powerful generals declared themselves king. These included Akhenaten's courtier and general Ay (1318–1315 BC) – who had advised Tutankhamun to return to the old god Amun and who began the systematic removal of the name of the heretic Akhenaten from the historical record – the army's commander-in-chief Horemheb (1315–1295 BC), and finally the latter's military deputy, Ramesses I (1295–1294 BC), who began the Nineteenth Dynasty. But it was Ramesses II (1279–1213 BC) who, by 1270 BC, finally defeated the Hittites together with rebellions in Palestine, Syria and Kadesh. These incursions and rebellions had seriously disrupted commerce – the life-blood of Egyptian civilization – which could only resume once Ramesses II had overcome the chaos unleashed by the antistrategic pharaoh Akhenaten. Ramesses II – or Ozymandias – might well claim, in the words of Percy Shelley, to be the "King of Kings" — and without the poetic irony.

This re-imposition of *maat*, or order, also involved a return of the court to the old capital and the old gods, and to the total removal of all memory of the antistrategists Akhenaten – called the "criminal of Akhetaten"[33] — his family and immediate successors, including the famously beautiful Nefertiti, together with Smenkhkare, Tutankhamun, and Ay. This included being chiseled from stone monuments and omitted from the official list of kings, which jumped from Amenhotep III to Horemheb – leaving a gap of 29 years. As one historian has noted, this official omission was "the dreaded 'Second Death'; total obliteration from which there could be no return".[34] There was no greater sin in Egyptian – or, indeed, in any – society than for a strategic leader to turn his back on the *logos* and its guardians in order to become an antistrategic ("criminal") megalomaniac. Only by imposing the greatest penalty, the "Second Death", could Egypt's new leaders hope to encourage the old guardians to return to their temple homes. Which they did — for a season.

Egypt's problems, however, were not at an end. Merenptah (1213–1203 BC), the son of Ramesses II, had to contend with a civil war between the northern and southern regions of the country, together with incursions from the mysterious Sea Peoples – who disrupted trade routes in Asia Minor, Cyprus, and Palestine – and from the Libyans from the west. While these problems continued down to the time of Ramesses III (1184–1153 BC) of the new Twentieth Dynasty, victory was finally secured during his reign. While the booty from Ramesses III's victories in Palestine was very considerable, this region and its trade were gradually taken over by the Philistines, who were originally from the Greek world. Despite these problems, over a period of one-and-a-half centuries, the commerce strategy generated great wealth in Egypt, which is reflected in the monumental building during the Nineteenth and early Twentieth Dynasties, particularly by Ramesses II.

But the end of Ramesses III's reign marked the beginning of economic decline, owing to the final exhaustion of the commerce strategy of the new kingdom. This decline was marked by the gradual loss of upper Egypt by succeeding kings (who enjoyed only very short periods in office) and of serious strikes by workers in Thebes. By the time of Ramesses XI (1099–1069 BC) – the last king of the Twentieth Dynasty – Thebes had become a theocracy under Herihor, General of the Armies and High Priest of Amun; and Nubia regained control of the southern territories – together with its gold mines and trade routes – that had been under Egyptian control for almost half a millennium. The loss of revenues during the reign of Ramesses XI led to official asset-stripping of the extremely rich royal tombs in the fabled Valley of the Kings.[35] This marked the collapse of the commerce strategy and the beginning of the period of chaos known as the Third Intermediate Period (1069–780 BC), which lasted an unprecedented three centuries. It was a period not only of economic and political fragmentation, but also of rule by kings – the Twenty-Second Dynasty – of Libyan origin. The guardians had deserted, and the Egyptians had lost control of their *logos*.

The rest of ancient Egyptian history – the Late Period (780–337 BC) and beyond (337 BC – AD 395) – was the outcome of a largely unsuccessful struggle by the locals against foreign powers to regain and retain control of their own commerce strategy and *logos*. The foreign takeovers included those by Kush (the Twenty-Fifth Dynasty, 780–656 BC); Assyria (670s and 660s BC); the Persians (Twenty-Seventh Dynasty, 525–404 BC; and Thirty-First Dynasty, 340–323 BC); Libya (Twenty-Eighth Dynasty, 404–397 BC); Macedonia (332–30 BC); and, finally, the Romans (30 BC – AD 395). Between these foreign dynasties, short-lived native Egyptian dynasties were formed, including the Twenty-Sixth (672–525 BC), the Twenty-Ninth (397–378 BC), and the Thirtieth (378–337 BC). Throughout these years, the native Egyptian *logos* and dynamic strategy of commerce were under attack, until they were finally extinguished by the Romans, who made Egypt a colony of Rome — a sad end to a glorious history.

In the Late Period and beyond, the Egyptian gods of commerce were in retreat from the foreign gods of conquest until they were finally banished by the greatest god of them all – Augustus. Finally there was no Egyptian *logos* for the commerce gods to protect and sustain. Even the memory of these once great gods – the greatest in the ancient world – was extinguished when the Christian God became sole guardian of the eastern Roman empire. A memory only revived by scholars during the past two centuries.[36]

The Egyptian *logos* of commerce

It is time to draw these historical details together to show how Egypt's commerce *logos* worked. This is the key to understanding Egyptian religion, theology, and myth. As is discussed in detail in Chapter 12, the strategic *logos* – or universal life-system – is the vehicle of life. It provides a protective yet invisible receptacle in which life flourishes despite the hostility of the outside world. It consists of a series of interacting dynamic forces that generate material improvement in conjunction with sociopolitical and cultural change. Yet, as we have seen, it can be endangered by uncontrollable internal and external forces that cause the *logos* to malfunction and even collapse.

Egypt's commerce *logos* – like all strategic *logoi* – was driven by **strategic desire** and governed by the **strategic cerebrum**. The Egyptian expression of strategic desire, which was used whenever a king's name was mentioned, was "life! prosperity! health!"[37] In order to satisfy strategic desire – to survive and prosper – the peoples of Egypt adopted the most effective available dynamic strategy, which, in the beginning, was family multiplication to bring all the agricultural/pastoral resources of the Nile Valley into the process of production. Once these land resources had been fully utilized with the available agricultural technology, there emerged an intense competition between regional strongmen to unify the large number of independent communities stretched out along the Nile, so as to take full advantage of the key position that region held in the trading networks between Africa and the Mediterranean/Middle East. The fabulous returns from exploiting this commercial monopoly outweighed those that could have been generated by the alternative dynamic strategy of conquest, owing to Egypt's isolation from other major societies. Not to grasp this commercial potential would have led to economic and social stagnation that would have made Egypt rife for a takeover by other societies.

The unfolding dynamic strategy of commerce generated a changing **strategic demand** for a wide range of inputs required by Egypt's burgeoning *logos*. The resulting **strategic demand-response mechanism** – which is a circular process of interaction (see Figure 12.1) – led to the emergence of commercial infrastructure, tradable commodities, commercial institutions, commercial ideas (such as writing and mathematics), and religious/strategic ideas.

Strategic infrastructure was required to facilitate the commerce strategy. This involved the investment of agricultural surpluses in ships, docks, warehouses, donkey trains, markets, together with an effective navy and army to protect and extend this lucrative dynamic strategy. Strategic defense was assisted both by Egypt's geographical isolation, which was enhanced by flanking deserts and, in the east, hills and sea; and by having considerably less wealthy neighbors in Libya to the west and Palestine, Lebanon and Syria in the east, owing to the lower productivity of dryland, compared to floodplain, farming. The return on this investment in infrastructure was very considerable, owing to Egypt's monopoly position in international trading networks; a fact that permitted them to construct one of the most dazzling civilizations the world has ever known.

The unfolding commerce strategy of Egypt also required the availability of tradable commodities. This demand generated a growing need for greater grain surpluses that could be exported to foreign countries. Hence, commerce was the driving force behind the growing investment in agricultural technology, particularly in agricultural dams and irrigation works. Also the unfolding commerce strategy generated a growing demand for an expanding manufacturing sector, producing not only ships and other forms of transport and storage equipment, but also craft goods including pottery, stoneware, jewelry, furniture, textiles, and paper as trade goods. But, of course, central to Egypt's highly profitable commercial strategy was its access to mineral deposits, particularly gold, at sites in both the Eastern and Nubian deserts. It was the buying power of gold that made Egypt's commerce strategy so lucrative and that provided the driving force behind Egypt's southward expansion.

Technological change was also a response to the needs of Egypt's commerce *logos*. Egypt produced major inventions in the fields of agriculture, shipping, navigation, recording, accounting, and military equipment.[38] In the field of agriculture, the Egyptians invented artificial canals (4000–3000 BC); the water mill, complex lifting and force pumps (300–200 BC); and the processes of large-scale wine making (3000 BC). In shipping and navigation, they invented plank ships (3000 BC); sailing ships (3100 BC); the sounding pole (2000 BC); the complex harbor, including a combination of quays, jetties, cargo-handling equipment and facilities, warehouses, food and water supply systems, and ship-building facilities (300 BC); the lighthouse at Pharos, one of the "seven wonders of the world" (250 BC); and maps (1160 BC). In the field of recording and accounting, the Egyptians invented an advanced writing system (3250 BC); together with the 365-day calendar, mathematical tables and problems (2000–1000 BC); and an effective weighing system (4000–3000 BC). And in the military sphere, they invented battering rams (1900 BC); war chariots (1600–1500 BC); and cavalry (1400 BC). Clearly, Egyptian technological ideas were largely associated with trade: accounting for trade, the means of trade, tradable commodities, and the defense and expansion of trade. Commerce was the life-blood of Egypt.

The commerce strategy also required the development of facilitating institutions and organizations – sociopolitical structures that gave Egyptian civilization its distinctive culture. The political structure of Egypt reflected that strategic reality. In particular, Egypt could only reap the full benefits of its key trading position if the communities of the Nile Valley were united under a single political regime. And to prevent the society fragmenting into its natural regional parts, that regime had to be highly centralized. In view of this imperative, it is hardly surprising that Egypt developed an absolute form of monarchy, or that the country fragmented whenever the unifying commerce strategy was disrupted or naturally exhausted itself. **Strategic crisis** always led to the power of the king being challenge by regional strongmen – as they no longer had anything to gain by supporting the central government – and to the fragmentation of Egyptian society. An interesting implication of this strategic argument is that the nature of Egypt's political institutions was *not* the outcome of large-scale irrigated agriculture as many scholars have argued, rather that both were responses to the dynamic strategic demand generated by the unfolding commerce strategy.

The monarchy was responsible not only for the unity of the country – when accepting the crown, each king promised to unify upper and lower Egypt – but for maintaining both worldly and cosmic order, or *maat*. In effect this meant sustaining the dynamic life-system that gave rise to order out of chaos. This was the very foundation stone of Egyptian "religion" – the attempt to understand and to sustain their strategic *logos*. The king and his advisors – the priestly philosophers – were acutely aware of the vulnerability of this life-system. Not only was it in peril each evening when the sun disappeared below the horizon, but, they believed, the *logos* would eventually collapse and the primeval chaos would finally and irrevocably reassert itself. Egyptian religion, therefore, was a direct response to the fundamental needs of the strategic *logos* of commerce.

So seriously did the king take his role as custodian of the *logos* that he committed a large proportion of national income – and a huge proportion of the national surplus after basic living requirements had been met – to be invested in the material machinery of ensuring this outcome. He invested heavily in temples to the gods, in the economic support of large numbers of priests, and in funerary complexes such as the great pyramids of Giza and the elaborate tombs in the Valley of the Kings. This massive investment should not be regarded as "unproductive". Certainly, neither the king, priests, nor people thought that it was. Indeed they believed it was the most productive form of investment they could possibly undertake, because it was investment in sustaining *maat*, or the worldly and cosmic order on which the very survival and prosperity of Egypt depended. Without *maat* all the rest mattered not one iota. Expenditure on so-called "religious" institutions and monuments, was actually investment in the Egyptian strategic *logos*. And for three millennia it appears to have worked! Will Western civilization be able to say the same?

Egyptian construction of the cosmos

Cosmic order

The key condition of life aspired to by the political and intellectual elite of Egypt throughout its very long history, as we have seen, was *maat*, or worldly and cosmic order. It was to the sustenance of *maat* that each incoming king dedicated himself and that the huge investment in temples, funerary complexes, and priestly activity was directed. "Living with *maat*" was the kingly responsibility.

What was *maat*? To the ancient Egyptians it was the opposite of *isfet*, or chaos, a state of non-being from which the cosmos emerged and to which the cosmos would eventually return. Life, according to this view, is a constant struggle between the forces of both order and chaos, between being and non-being, between complexity and oneness. In this sense, the ancient Egyptian concept of *maat* is similar to the modern concept of entropy – namely that the "closed" cosmos is involved in a one-way trip towards thermodynamic equilibrium, molecular disorder, or heat death. While that may be the very long-run fate of the entire cosmos, there are systems within it that have found ways of decreasing their entropy – or increasing their order and complexity – by converting energy from external sources into work and releasing heat. This is what all life forms are able to accomplish through their strategic *logoi*, and what the Egyptians rationalized through their fascinating philosophy of life. The "temporary" reversal of entropy is what the strategic *logos* is all about.

Driven by a desire to survive and prosper, the ancient Egyptians harnessed the energy of the sun, wind, and the Nile to grow, extract, create and transport commodities that could be traded with other societies at very favorable rates of exchange. They created, in other words, a dynamic life-system that was capable of offering some respite against the wider process of entropy in the cosmos. What this implies is that order is the outcome of systematic change and not of stasis. Whenever the dynamic life-system broke down, chaos triumphed over order, thereby frustrating the desire to survive and prosper. Egyptian society also diverted some of the energy it harnessed to develop material structures, religious ideas, and religious rituals to explain and sustain their *logos*. While this was a very persuasive mythological system of thought and practice, it confused "cosmic" order with "worldly" order, and the "cosmos" with the "strategic *logos*". This confusion arose from their belief that Egypt was at the very center of the Universe.

In Egyptian philosophy, *maat* was so important it was personified by a goddess of the same name, Maat, who was the "beloved daughter of Re", the creator sun god, or ultimate source of energy. Maat, the goddess, was "identified with the basis of life: air to breathe, bread to eat, and beer to drink".[39] In other words, Maat was identified with the fruits of the strategic *logos*. While *maat* was created in the beginning by the sun god Re, Maat's presence was considered vital to Re's daily regeneration.

The symbols of *maat* included the ostrich feather worn by the goddess Maat; the winged goddess who could revive the dead with air generated from her beating wings; and the "plinth sign" used to write Maat's name (the plinth sign is shown in Egyptian pictures beneath the thrones of deities who act as divine judges). The feather of Maat, which was identified with truth, justice, righteousness, order and balance, has particular significance. It is well known from the Book of the Dead, where it plays a central role in judging the lives of the recently dead. By balancing the soul of a person, who is on the threshold of the afterlife, against the feather of Maat, it was possible for the gods to determine whether that person had "*maat* in his heart" or had "sinned against *maat*".

In terms of the dynamic-strategy theory, I interpret this as determining whether the recently deceased person had contributed to or detracted from the strategic *logos* – whether they were strategists or antistrategists. My concept of an antistrategist is equivalent to the Egyptian concept of a *maat* "criminal" – like Akhenaten – who deserved to experience the dreaded "Second Death" or total obliteration. Only life-long strategists, who had been "true" to *maat*, could possibly join Re in his daily struggle against the monster of chaos (Apophis). Also it is interesting that the plinth of *maat* is found beneath the thrones of divine judges, who were the custodians of the Egyptian life-system.

Maat was an outcome that both gods and men deeply desired, and a pursuit in which they both cooperatively participated. Possibly the best exposition of this aspect of Egyptian thought is by Erik Hornung:

> *Maat*, which came from the gods at creation, returns to them from the hands of men; it symbolizes the partnership of god and man which is brought to fruition in Egyptian religion ... Through creation gods and men acquire a common task: to maintain their existence, which has an end, against the unending nonexistence [chaos] and together build a living order that allows space for creative breath and does not become atrophied.[40]

In terms of my schema, *maat*, or worldly order, emerges from the selfcreating *logos*, which, once men understand, enables them to dispense with the fiction about gods.

The one who interceded with the creator sun god Re in support of *maat* was the king. As the strategic leader it was his job to "make the country flourish as in primeval times by means of the designs of Maat".[41] Kings, who were expected to "do *maat*", or to "live with *maat*", were frequently depicted offering a miniature figure of the goddess Maat to the chief deity of the temple. In doing so, the king reaffirmed his coronation oath to uphold *maat* by interceding daily with Re, the creator guardian of the Egyptian life-system. Similarly, judges and high officials wore images of the goddess Maat "to signify that they were enforcing her laws" – in effect, the laws of the strategic *logos*. They were required to live "righteous lives" and to support "truth and justice". By "living in accordance with *maat*" these Egyptian elite were "adhering to *factual* truth".[42] What was essential to the Egyptians in sustaining their dynamic life-system was *factual* truth – the truth of the strategic *logos* – not *metaphysical* truth – the truth of the priestly philosophers.

In the light of my schema, a "righteous" life should be regarded as a strategic life, lived according to the laws of the Egyptian *logos*. It is an interpretation that receives indirect support from other commentators. J.A. Wilson, for example, has said of *maat*:

> If we render it 'order' it was the order of created things, physical and spiritual, established at the beginning and valid for all time. If we render it 'justice' it was not simply justice in terms of legal administration; it was the just and proper relationship of cosmic phenomena, including the relationship of the rulers and the ruled. If we render it 'truth' we must remember that, to the ancient, things were true not because they were susceptible of ... verification but because they were ... in their true and proper places in the order created and maintained by the gods ...[43]

The king could find support in his duty to "do *maat*" from the selfcreating deity Thoth who, as the impartial judge of wisdom and knowledge, was charged with upholding cosmic order. Thoth was the ibis-headed god depicted in the

Book of the Dead, who judged whether the recently deceased was "true of voice", and who recorded the resulting judgment. Those who could not be "justified" were fed to the hybrid animal god called Ammut – "devouress of the dead" – and experienced true death – the "Second Death" – or non-existence. Thoth was also the inventor of writing and author of the "forty-two books" that were said to contain the complete knowledge required by humanity. But most important of all, Thoth was the discoverer and interpreter of the laws of *maat* – in other words the laws of the strategic *logos*. This is why I have dedicated *Dead God Rising* to him.

The role of the Egyptian gods

The Egyptian word for "god" was "ntr", usually pronounced "netjer" and written hieroglyphically as, alternatively: a staff bound with cloth; a hawk on a carrying pole; and a squatting regal figure wearing a braided divine beard. The hieroglyph showing a cloth-covered staff is the oldest and most common of the three alternatives, and is said to mean "he is buried" – a state shared by both the "justified dead" and the gods, in contrast to the unjustified, who were devoured by Ammut.

While there was an attempt in the nineteenth century AD to show that Egyptian religion developed from an "original monotheism", and in the twentieth century to demonstrate conversely that a later monotheism developed from an early polytheism, it is clear from the evidence that it was always profoundly polytheistic.[44] Creation, which was initiated by the selfcreating god, involved a process of diversification of the one into the many. What is particularly interesting today about the Egyptian concept of "the one and the many" is that it is probably the earliest theory of complexity.

In the Egyptian story of creation, the selfcreating creator separated the sky from the Earth, which provided the necessary space for both the "breath of life" and the generation of diversity in the divine and mundane spheres. The gods created in this way represented the various dynamic forces of life as perceived by the ancient Egyptians. Erik Hornung writes that: "For the Egyptians the gods are powers that explain the world"; that the gods "are formulas rather than forms"; and that "the Egyptians were always aware of this formula-like character, as is shown especially by syncretistic combinations of gods, in which names and forms are not the decisive factor, but what they stand for, what they bear witness to".[45] Essentially, the gods were responsible for sustaining the Egyptian life-system. Hornung goes on to explain:

> every god who is worshipped as a creator also sustains life – if he did not take lasting responsibility, his work of creation would be meaningless. This it is said of Ptah [creator god and patron of craftsmen] that he 'created everything that exists… (and) keeps everyone alive with his (craftsman's) fingers'.[46]

The attributes of the gods, therefore, are of both a general and a specific nature. What all the gods have in common are the attributes of "life" and "power", which are represented symbolically by the objects they hold: the ankh symbolizing life, and the flail or crook symbolizing power over the material conditions of life. Interestingly, these general attributes correspond closely to the objectives of the strategic *logos* – survival and material prosperity. Hence, the gods are the guardians of the Egyptian life-system.

In addition to these general attributes, each god is associated with one or more of the component forces of the dynamic Egyptian *logos*. The goddess Maat, daughter of the sun god, is responsible for cosmic order; Re is responsible for the daily cycle of life; Nun, god of the primeval waters, is responsible for the creative ferment (my strategic desire) that gives rise to the eternal recurrence of the gods; the selfcreating creators are responsible both for the emergence and sustenance of the Egyptian life-system (my strategic *logos*); Thoth, god of the moon and wisdom, is responsible for the development of human knowledge and for the discovery, recording, and interpretation of the laws of *maat* (equivalent to my laws of history and life); and so on, down to ever more detailed and mundane levels of human life. Yet, while the Egyptian conception of the gods was "formula-like", the deities were not just abstract concepts, as can be seen from their dedicated cult followings.

It is significant that all the major gods represented forces that were dynamic, or things that were the outcome of dynamic forces. There are no deities for static conceptions (such as mountains, lakes or rivers – only for the dynamic cycle of inundation), elements (fire, earth, air or water), stars (with the sole exception of Sirius), or human emotions (love, fear, terror, etc). Hence, the religion of the ancient Egyptians focused exclusively on the key aspects of their *dynamic* life-system.

How did the Egyptians view their gods? The central and surprising characteristic of the Egyptian gods was their ephemeral nature. Hornung tells us:

> Among the characteristics common to all gods there stands out a group that renders the deities disconcertingly transitory and subject to the march of time. Egyptian gods have a beginning and an end in time. They are born or created, they change with time, they grow old and die, and one day will exist no more.[47]

In other words, the gods reflected the Egyptian dynamic life-system, which came into being in its simplest form about 7,000 BC, waxed and waned over the millennia and was finally swept away by Rome in 30 BC. The guardians of the Egyptian *logos*, therefore, possess the same existential characteristics as the *logos* itself.

When talking of death, the ancient Egyptians invested it with a special meaning. Hornung explains:

> Many passages in texts and, from the New Kingdom on, pictures show that from a very early period the Egyptians saw rejuvenation and regeneration as the true meaning of death. 'You sleep that you may wake; you die that you may live', as the Pyramid Texts formulate the hope with archaic brevity.[48]

Only those who fail to pass the test of *maat* experience the final "Second Death". Like men, gods also die and are reborn – "dead god rising". So too the strategic *logos* goes through a process of eternal recurrence – of birth, death, and rebirth.

What, we need to ask, is the nature of this regeneration? Once again Hornung explains with his usual insight:

> Regeneration is impossible in the ordered and defined world. It can happen only if what is old and worn becomes immersed in the boundless regions that surround creation – in the healing and dissolving powers of the primeval ocean Nun. The sun god in his bark is raised from Nun every morning ... Those who sleep are rejuvenated in Nun, and in a Ramessid hymn the deceased cry out to the sun god that they too are rejuvenated through entry into Nun ...[49]

Rebirth, in other words, occurs by returning to the very conditions that gave rise to creation in the beginning.

Yet, despite this cyclical renewal – the "eternal" recurrence – the gods will finally meet their end. This will become a sort of "twilight of the gods", when the great diversity, or complexity, of the "world" will be reduced once more to the oneness of Nun. Of course, the Egyptians, who equated Egypt with the "world", were really talking about the end of Egyptian civilization, not the end of the cosmos. As in all advanced religions, the *logos* was projected onto the cosmos.

There are passages in various texts that hint at the final death of the gods. One of these is found in the Book of the Dead, in the papyrus of Ani, a royal scribe of the Nineteenth Dynasty (c. 1250 BC) in the New Kingdom. In response to Ani's question, in chapter 80, "What will be the direction of my life?" the sun gold Atum, creator of the world, replies:

> You shall be for millions on millions of years, a lifetime of millions of years. I will dispatch the Elders and destroy all that I have made; the earth shall return to the Primordial Water, to the surging flood, as in its original state.[50]

With this final act of Atum, the "many" will be absorbed back into the "one" – modern complexity will disappear into primeval oneness. This, as suggested earlier, has obvious parallels with the modern concept in thermodynamics of heat death and disorder as the result of entropy running its course.

There are strong parallels also between this Egyptian myth of creation and de-creation and my theory of the selfcreating *logos*. Like Egyptian *maat*, the strategic *logos* is also ephemeral, and it is subject to a cyclical process of expansion, exhaustion, and rejuvenation. The *logosian* guardians "die" with the old *logos* and are reborn (usually transformed in the process) with the emergence of the new *logos*. This process of rebirth is the outcome of the emergence of a new or rejuvenated dynamic strategy, driven by the primeval force of strategic desire. This "eternal" recurrence is the mechanism of "dead god rising". But there will come a time for any society, when rebirth is no longer possible owing to an inability to renew its dynamic strategies, and the strategic *logos* and its guardians will cease to exist. This happened to Egypt when it became a colony of Rome – became part of the Roman conquest *logos*. Hence the eternal recurrence of the gods – or strategic guardians – can continue only for as long as the *logos* of any society continues to exist.

Another important characteristic of the Egyptian gods is their spatial as well as temporal limits. Like all neolithic gods, the powers of the Egyptian deities were limited to their own society and country. The Egyptian gods, in other words, had national rather than universal significance. There were even times when the gods withdrew from the Nile Valley – times of invasion, civil unrest, decline of material prosperity, and monarchical heresy. These were times when the Egyptian dynamic strategy of commerce was badly disrupted and, as a result, the *logos* malfunctioned. This spatial limitation of the Egyptian gods is the reason any discussion about the "cosmos" is really a discussion about the Egyptian *logos*.

The characteristics of the Egyptian gods that has created the most confusion among scholars is what Erik Hornung has called "the one and the many", or what others such as Schelling and Müller, have called "henotheism". This is the belief that there are many gods but that any one of these can be worshipped as the supreme being at any point in time. Hornung attempts to explain this issue in terms of what he calls the Egyptian "problem of logic", whereby the many are not excluded by the one as normal logic would dictate. We are assured that "the one and the many" would not have been possible in ancient Greek thought. This "problem of logic", Hornung believes, is the "key" to understanding Egyptian society.

Hornung's hypothesis, however, encounters difficulties when forced to confront a case when the "one" does exclude the "many" – the case of Akhenaten, who worshipped Aten (the sun disk) to the exclusion of all other gods. He views this as the result of a temporary "new logic" in Egypt. While this episode was, as noted earlier, a brief interlude (1344–1328 BC) in traditional religious practice, it also suggests that there could have been no "problem of logic". If ideas evolved from some internal logic as most scholars would claim, why didn't the more sophisticated "new" logic permanently displace the traditional logic? A more persuasive explanation is that there was no new, nor, indeed, traditional logic in Egypt – logic is logic in all societies – and that ideas (as shown by the dynamic-strategy theory) are driven in the longer term by strategic demand. An important maxim of my theory is that, "desires drive, ideas merely facilitate".

Incompatible ideas and ideologies can be imposed on strategic reality in the short term, but, as they endanger the *logos*, they will be eliminated in the longer term. The real explanation, therefore, is that the Egyptians were faithful to the reality and demands of their strategic *logos*. Their "many" gods, as we have seen, personified separately perceived forces underlying the *logos*, which they believed could be addressed "one" at a time without undermining the "many" of the entire *logosian* system. Akhenaten was a metaphysicist and, hence, an antistrategist, who lost sight of the realities of the commerce *logos* in a megalomaniacal love of self. What the Greeks called hubris. He placed ideas above (strategic) desires, thereby creating, or exacerbating, internal and external problems that seriously endangered the Egyptian *logos*. That is why his "reforms" were quickly reversed following his death, not because of the inflexibility of a supposed "traditional" Egyptian logic. What was different about Egyptian civilization was not its logic, but the clarity of its perception of the reality of its *logos* and, hence, the importance it placed on strategic (materialist) rather than deductive (metaphysical) thinking.[51]

Eternal recurrence

The Egyptians understood, just as modern physicists understand, that *maat*, or order, is the outcome of a dynamic process. Through systematic observation they realized that the "cosmos" was a product of the eternal recurrence. Order is not a result of stasis. As Gunter Burkard tells us in his account of Egypt:

> The cosmos was not static but engaged in a dynamic, or rather, cyclic stream of events. It was not a world created only once but constituted a process of perpetual repetition, comprehensible most sensibly in the daily solar cycle ... Nature's cycle manifested itself in the daily solar cycle, the lunar phases, the seasonal cycle and, last but not least, in the phenomenon of the annual Nile floods.[52]

Yet, my understanding of Egyptian thought leads me to believe that "nature's cycle" was a metaphor for something less obvious and more mysterious – something they were unable to penetrate through rational discourse. That something was the strategic *logos*, which could be sensed rather than understood, and hinted at through metaphor rather than rationalised.

The Egyptian symbol of the eternal recurrence was the *shen*-sign, which was held by gods such as Isis, the "mother" of the god-kings of Egypt. In the Book of the Dead – or, as it was known to the Egyptians, the Book of Going Forth by Day – plate 33, Isis is shown kneeling before a *shen*-sign, which is represented as a doughnut-shaped object with a flat base. "*Shen*" is derived from a word meaning "to encircle, to go around", and it was widely used to describe the "eternal" cycle of the sun. It is an elongated *shen*-sign (or cartouche) that encircles – in order to protect – royal names.[53] The implication appears to be that kings play a central role in sustaining the dynamics – the eternal recurrence – of the Egyptian life-system. They are at the center of the *logos* seen as a mandala.

We need to further explore the nature of the main metaphor used by the Egyptians to comprehend and represent their hidden dynamic life-system. Clearly the solar cycle was central to this matter. The progress of the sun across the sky was characterized as a journey undertaken by the sun god Re, together with his retinue of subordinate gods and dead kings, in his divine barque. During the day they traveled in splendor across the clear-blue sky, but during the night they passed through the darkly dangerous underworld beneath the Earth (which was envisaged as a spherical disk). Yet at the same time, the watery underworld, which was part of the primeval *nun*, was regarded as a place of rebirth and regeneration. As they passed through the underworld, the gods temporarily revived the sleeping dead while combating the forces of chaos led by Apophis in the form of the giant snake. The strongest of the gods Seth, the brother and murderer of Osiris (king of the dead), took prime responsibility for preventing Re being engulfed by chaos. Dead kings and some others of the Egyptian elite were expected to join Re's barque to assist in this nightly struggle between order and chaos. And living kings and their priests needed to conduct rituals to assist the daily campaign to maintain cosmic order.

The above mythological schema was as close as the Egyptian priestly philosophers could come to understanding their strategic *logos*. Nonetheless, it is fascinating that they envisaged their life-system as a dynamic circular process – as is my independent diagrammatical representation of the strategic *logos* in Figure 12.1[54] – that was in constant danger of succumbing to the forces of chaos. And they had good reason to fear for the survival of their life-system, as the Nile Valley was dotted with the massive runs of earlier dynasties that had been highly successful for a time but ultimately collapsed.

Another metaphor for the eternal recurrence responsible for *maat*, was the flood cycle of the Nile. As the Nile was thought to have its source in the life-giving primeval waters of the *nun* that surround the world, it was seen as a powerful metaphor for eternal rebirth. The Egyptian year began with the onset of the great inundation, which was thought to arise from the return of the Distant Goddess from Nubia. Each year this goddess, who inspired fear and trepidation, had to be persuaded to return to Egypt and to take on a less destructive form as she approached their southern border. Shrines were built along the river's edge to pacify and humor the goddess as she passed by. Hence, the month before the flood was due to arrive was always a tense time, as the Egyptians waited to see whether their efforts in persuasion with this unpredictable goddess would be successful. Interestingly, while there was a goddess of the great inundation, there was no deity for the Nile itself. It was the cyclical dynamic rather than the thing-in-itself that the ancients wished to sustain.

The great cosmic cycle

The "eternal" recurrence of the solar cycle and the flood cycle were seen by the Egyptians as taking place within a great cosmic cycle. The great cosmic cycle was the mechanism by which order first emerged from primeval chaos, reached a high degree of complexity over eons of time, and then, finally, was plunged back into primeval chaos from which there appears to be no return. Clearly the Egyptians believed that their life-system and the gods who acted as its guardians were not immortal.

This idea, of the emergence from and ultimate return to the primeval waters of chaos, is usually interpreted as an example of linear time. While it is true that the priests compiled chronologies of their kings – the king lists – these chronologies should be seen as measurements on the circumference of a great circle, just like mileposts tracing out the measurement of space on the circumference of the Earth. Just as distances on the circular surface of the Earth appear linear, so time on the great cosmic cycle also appears to trace out a straight line. But by traversing these great circles of space and time, the persistent traveler eventually will end up where he started.

The mythical story of Egypt – and, hence, the world – is usually divided into seven phases of a great cosmic cycle:

- chaos (before creation)
- emergence of the selfcreating creator
- reign of the sun god
- direct rule by other deities
- rule by semi-divine kings (human history)
- return to chaos.

We will briefly outline this story.

The chaos before creation – the first phase of the cosmic cycle – was a dark watery world of infinite dimension. As we have seen, the Egyptians called these primal waters *nun*, which was personified by the demiurge and fecundity god Nun, "a kind of instinctive movement toward consciousness".[55] It was a state of unending "oneness"; a time "before two things had developed", such as the opposites of light and darkness, earth and sky, male and female, life and death. It was a time – viewed through a modern lens – before the development of complexity. But it possessed the potential for the emergence of diversity.

The selfcreating creator was the sun god, who emerged from the *nun* during the second phase of the cosmic cycle. He was regarded as the "unique one in the *nun*", the "self-created god" who "came into being alone". In different periods and different theological centers in Egypt, different gods were identified as the "unique" selfcreating deity who emerged from the waters of chaos. These gods included Atum ("the undifferentiated one", who was head of the Ennead), Re ("sustainer of the world"), Re-Atum, Shu (god of the space and light between earth and sky), Ptah (patron of craftsmen), Khnum (the ram-headed god controlling the inundation), Neith (birth goddess and protector of love, regenerator of life, renewer of the cosmos), and Isis (mother of god-kings, goddess of a happy afterlife, magician goddess). The selfcreating creator – however identified – crated a further eight gods, called "the Eight", or the Ogdoad of Hermopolis. This was done by "speaking with the *nun*", according to the Coffin Texts (spell 76), or, in the case of Atum, by self-impregnation with the god's own semen. The idea of a selfcreating creator was a way of overcoming the logical problem in creation of infinite regress – who created the creator? – which still bedevils cosmologists today.

The creation of the world and its inhabitants – which was the third phase of the cosmic cycle – began with the emergence of the "Primeval Mound" from the "great swamp", or *nun*. It was known as the "First Time", and may have been inspired by the islands that appeared in the floodplain of the Nile as the floodwaters (which were said to arise in the surrounding *nun*) receded. The essential stages in the creation of the world were: the separation of earth (Nut) and sky (Geb), which provided the necessary space for creation; the establishment of *maat*, which enabled order to emerge from chaos – enabled complexity to emerge from the undifferentiated "oneness"; and the division of beings into male and female, which enabled life to propagate and occupy the Earth.

The resulting "cosmos" consisted of a fairly familiar tri-level structure, with the divine realm in the upper sky, the Earth with Egypt at its center, and the underworld (Duat), or realm of Osiris and the "justified" dead. This simple structure, which was inherited from earlier paleolithic societies, was circumnavigated by the daily journey of the sun god Re and his retinue. With his structure and dynamic system in place, the selfcreating god created other deities responsible for its maintenance, together with the survival and prosperity of humanity. The selfcreating creator, who constructed the cosmos by drawing upon his own resources, was called "the One who made himself into millions". Creation, in other words, was a process of differentiation by which the original creative force was gradually divided into the many parts responsible for the diverse elements of the cosmos.

In this vision of reality, the selfcreating creator is responsible not only for constructing Egypt's dynamic life-system, but also for sustaining it with the assistance of the lesser deities together with that of the king and his priestly advisors and agents. This is a simple yet brilliant mythological explanation of the emergence of the selfcreating strategic *logos*. The Egyptians could accept the concept of a selfcreating and sustaining god but not that of a selfcreating and *self*-sustaining dynamic life-system. To their way of thinking, a life-system could only exist and work effectively if it was created by a divine being with supernatural powers. Why? Because Egyptian thinkers were unable to *see* their hidden life-system or understand how it could possibly work and not break down. They could just not imagine a dynamic system that was the outcome of the actions and reactions (in response to strategic demand) of ordinary people. Even their strategic leaders had to be semi-divine – to be god-kings – so as to assist in the great task of sustaining the hidden system that ensured their survival and prosperity. In the final analysis, the Egyptians were unable to imagine a selfcreating strategic *logos*. Despite the impressive mythmaking abilities of Egyptian priestly philosophers – probably unparalleled in the history of ancient civilization – they were unable to construct a demand-side general dynamic theory to explain their society. And only a demand-side theory can explain the selfcreating nature of the strategic *logos*. Still, the Egyptian thinkers are not alone in this, as even today's leading scientists and thinkers have progressed no further in this respect; as we shall see in Part II.

The fourth phase of the Egyptian cosmic cycle comprised the direct rule by the creator sun god, usually identified as Re. This sun god was known as Khepri in the morning, Re at his most powerful at noon, and Atum in the evening – but "none of these was his true name".[56] During Re's rule on Earth, which was "for a long period", no sharp distinction was made between the gods and men (Egyptians). It was not a particularly harmonious era, as the goddess Isis – the sibling wife of Osiris – schemed to make her unborn son heir to the aging Re. Finally, when even men rebelled against his rule, Re sent his Eye – a reconciled Isis – to destroy the evil rebels, while he withdrew from the Earth to live in the sky. But to keep faith with his people, the sun god sent Maat, his beloved daughter, to live among humanity. While she remained, Egypt prospered but, whenever she temporarily withdrew, chaos – disorder and strife – would revisit the land of the Nile.

Following the withdrawal of Re, the Earth (Egypt) was ruled by a series of lesser gods. This was the fifth phase of the cosmic cycle. The first to rule in Re's place was Osiris, son of Geb, who shared this task with his sister/wife Isis. Seth, their jealous brother, murdered Osiris and scattered his mutilated body throughout the land. Undeterred, Isis collected and reassembled Osiris' body parts and through her use of magic enabled him to father her child, Horus. On reaching adulthood, Horus struggled against Seth for supremacy on Earth – a struggle that was so violent it "disturbed the whole cosmos". Eventually, the dispute between them was decided by a Divine Tribunal headed by Geb, under the authority of Re.

There are many versions of this myth. Some have Horus being granted lower Egypt and Seth upper Egypt; some tell of Horus being granted all Egypt and Seth being banished; some have Seth becoming part of Re's retinue to provide, as the strongest of the gods, defense against the serpent of chaos. Most versions have Horus ruling Egypt for a time with the assistance of Maat – a time during which order and prosperity triumphed over chaos; and all versions agree that Horus became the model for each subsequent earthly king. Horus is also said to have helped his father Osiris to rise again to become ruler of the underworld populated by the "justified" dead. Osiris, the god who died and rose again – dead god rising – "seems to embody the vulnerability of the Egyptian state in dangerous transition periods".[57] Finally, other gods, such as Thoth and Maat, are also said to have ruled after Horus gave up the earthly throne to join his father in the underworld.

Eventually, all the gods withdrew to either the cosmic or underworld realms, leaving the rule of Egypt in the hands of semi-divine kings, as only beings with at least some supernatural powers could hope to understand and sustain the Egyptian life-system. This sixth phase in the cosmic cycle is the era of human history. Our interest in this myth is that it provides the link between the *logos* and the cosmos in Egyptian thinking. In the beginning the gods ruled Egypt (*logos*), but later retreated to the heavens (cosmos), leaving responsibility for the *logos* to the "sons" of Osiris – the god-kings who were closely identified with Horus. Egyptian kings were the intermediaries between men and gods, a role performed through temple ritual, oracles, and dreams. The king's priest, like the shamans of old, even possessed the power to pass between the worlds of the living and the dead, usually via false doors in tombs and temples.

The king was responsible for upholding *maat*, or order, in Egypt (the *logos*) and after life for helping the gods to maintain it in the underworld and the heavens (the cosmos). Failure by the king to uphold the laws of *maat* would plunge Egypt into extended periods of chaos – periods that would persist until a new hero-king, as the new champion of *maat*, emerged with the assistance and direction of the gods. As guardians of the *logos*, the gods could always be called upon to assist in restoring and maintaining dynamic order. This could be achieved through proper temple ritual together with "ethical" – that is, "strategic" – behavior on the part of the king, priests, justices and other Egyptian elite. And when it was achieved the gods, together with order and prosperity, returned to the land of the Nile.

Here we have a mythological account of the rise and fall of Egyptian dynasties and kingdoms in terms of the effectiveness of semi-divine kings in upholding the laws of *maat* with the assistance of strategic guardian or gods. It was this constant struggle between the forces of order and chaos that Egyptian thinkers believed was responsible for the changing patterns of history and of prospects for the future. While in reality the fluctuating fortunes of Egypt – indeed, of all human societies – was and is the outcome of the systematic exploitation and exhaustion of dynamic strategies, one can only be impressed by the basic insights the Egyptians were able to gain regarding their *logos* through their mythological imagination.

The cyclical pattern of history would, according to Egyptian thinkers, eventually come to an end. One day the profitable cooperation between kings and gods would breakdown, and the world would descend into the eternal primeval chaos from which it had emerged so long ago. This inevitable catastrophe would result from either irreconcilable disagreements between the gods, or senseless and uncontrollable rebellion by humanity. It would usher in the seventh and final stage in the cosmic cycle. Finally, in the face of this disorder, a weary creator god would reabsorb the diversity of life forms that he had originally created. Complexity would collapse into an infinite and eternal "oneness". The great cosmic cycle would be complete. Of course this story is not really about the cosmos, or even about the Earth; it is a story about the Egyptian strategic *logos*.

How the story changed over time

So far we have considered the Egyptian conception of the cosmos as if it had remained unchanged across some three millennia and throughout the entire land. While that was a convenient conceit, it is not realistic. The story already told was the one that had emerged by the time the New Kingdom was at its zenith around the fourteenth century BC, and the one told most often at the center of this dazzling commercial civilization. Some sense of the way this story developed is essential to an understanding of how the human conception of the universal life-system and its supernatural guardians has changed over time in response to an increasingly sophisticated strategic *logos* and to the growing scope faced by the priestly philosophers to exercise their metaphysical musings.

While both the strategic story (or ideology) and the degree of societal centralization grew during each great wave of commercial prosperity, both unraveled again during each period of strategic exhaustion (or Intermediate Periods). In the main, this cyclical dynamic was a response to a changing strategic demand as the Egyptian *logos* waxed and waned. From the end of the New Kingdom, any real recovery was prevented by invading armies from both north and south, which for long periods imposed their own *logoi* on Egypt. From this time the story about the guardians of the Egyptian *logos* becomes compromised and garbled, eventually to fall into silence.

It is important to realize that the relationships between deities were never fixed. In response to both strategic demand and priestly artistic license, these relationships continued to change and develop down through the millennia. While a consensus emerged in the major centers at any particular time, there was never any centralized attempt to produce a standardized version of these myths. Egyptian ideology was a wonderfully flexible strategic instrument. Essentially, the story we now possess was pieced together by scholars from a variety of visual and written sources.

By the early dynastic era (Dynasties 0–2), around 3200 to 2650 BC, a number of the central features of the above story were firmly established. The idea of an eternal struggle between order and chaos was already well developed. It took the form of the well-known battle between Horus and his murderous uncle Seth. Even at this early stage, a complex pantheon of deities had been elaborated to explain and sustain the Egyptian life-system. These had emerged from the religion of their ancestors in paleolithic times. In the pre-dynastic era, the gods assumed the forms of animals and sacred objects; but between 3000 and 2800 BC the gods were transformed into human shape; and by the end of the Second Dynasty (about 2650 BC) some of these human gods had developed animal heads – a uniquely Egyptian invention – while any given deity could assume many different forms to reflect their different functions or regions of origin.

At the beginning of the dynastic era, the king had already been identified with Horus, son of Osiris, and was regarded as the intermediary between this life and the next. The king was the political, military and religious authority – a complete strategic leader – who was responsible not only for the stability and prosperity of Egyptian society but also for the viability of their life-system. Initially religious observance was a local matter, but by the end of this early era (mid third millennium BC) a highly centralized system had emerged. Rather than attending to the deities in their local shrines, the king arranged for the deities to be brought together and celebrated in his capital.

During the Old Kingdom (Dynasties 3–6), about 2650 to 2150 BC, a number of important changes occurred in both the story about the creation of the Egyptian life-system and of its dynamic conception. This era – in the rule of King Djoser, 2630–2610 BC – provides the oldest extant evidence of the Ennead of Heliopolis, which was a group of nine deities, led by the selfcreating creator, who were central to the creation myths. By this time some 200 deities are mentioned in the Pyramid Texts, which focused only on the leading deities. The central stories in this source include the journey of Re and his retinue through the sky in his barque; the murder of Osiris by Seth; the conflict between Horus and Seth; and the resurrection of Osiris to become king of the underworld. Prior to the Fifth Dynasty (2465–2323 BC), Osiris had been a shadowy figure. The Pyramid Texts, which probably were copies of sacred papyrus and leather scrolls kept in temple archives, are only found in the tombs of kings until the breakdown of royal authority towards the end of the Old Kingdom owing to the exhaustion of the commerce strategy.

The second feature of interest in the Old Kingdom is the function of the great pyramids, which were an expensive innovation of this era. They are thought to be models of the cosmos, as well as "resurrection machines" for the kings.[58] In other words, the pyramids were mythological models of the Egyptian life-system – or strategic *logos* – as well as devices for enabling the king to make contact with the gods – or strategic guardians – in order to help sustain their society in the face of the forces of chaos. As explained earlier, this is why the Egyptians were willing to devote so much of their national income to pyramid construction. This was as much a decision of the ordinary citizen as of the elite, because pyramid construction was not a coercive activity. The whole of Egyptian society was determined to sustain their life-system.

The Middle Kingdom (Dynasties 11–13), about 2080 to 1641 BC, also made significant contributions to stories about, and mythological modeling of, the Egyptian idea of cosmos. This is know largely from the Coffin Texts, which consist of approximately 1,185 different spells. Many of these spells derive from the earlier Pyramid Texts, but they also include a number of new developments. First, the role of Osiris, king of the underworld, is expanded to provide protection not only for dead kings but also for all the elite dead. The Coffin Texts – painted on coffins, other funerary equipment, and tomb walls – provide spells and maps to enable the elite dead to negotiate the circuitous and dangerous ways of the underworld. Here we see the beginnings of the transformation of Egyptian cults from their original strategic purpose to provide for personal salvation, at least for those who could afford to pay for lavish funeral arrangements. Second, the royal mortuary complexes, as well as the temples of the Middle Kingdom, underwent further developments as models of the cosmos.

The New Kingdom (Dynasties 18–20), about 1539 to 1069 BC, witnessed a number of dramatic changes in the story about the guardians of the Egyptian life-system. As this era was the outcome of the rise of Thebes to national dominance, it is not surprising that Amun (or Amen), the patron god of that city, rose to national prominence, and became, after unification with the sun god, Amun-Re, the "King of the Gods". At the same time, the temple of Amun in Karnak became the greatest and most wealthy religious complex in Egypt. As Joyce Tyldesley tells us:

> The kings of the 18th Dynasty openly acknowledged a great debt to the god Amen, for they well understood that it was Amen who had enabled the mighty Theban warrior Ahmose to unite Egypt after the civil unrest and foreign rule of the Second Intermediate Period. Amen's protection of Ahmose soon proved to be a shrewd political move, and the devotion of successive 18th Dynasty kings allowed him to evolve from a relatively insignificant local god worshipped in and around Thebes into the patron god of the Egyptian empire ... recognised both as king of the gods and father of the king.[59]

Yet even more dramatic, as discussed earlier, was the suppression of the cult of Amun and the elevation of Aten as the one and only god of Egypt by Akhenaten. But this elevation of Aten was not deserved as Amun's had been. Aten had not led Egypt into an era of greater glory and prosperity. Indeed, he presided over a period of strategic decline, foreign threats, and internal unrest. Aten was a false god, just as Akhenaten was a false leader – an antistrategist. The elevation of Aten was not a move to monotheism, but rather a symbol of Akhenaten's decline into narcissism.[60] Akhenaten's interest in Aten was stimulated by his father Amenhotep III, who's passion for the past led to a fascination with Old Kingdom solar theology and particularly the "relatively obscure god, the Aten".[61] Amenhotep III used the cult of Aten to develop the cult of the king, stressing his own personal divinity, at a time when a burgeoning middle class was demanding access to the gods for personal salvation. It was an attempt to reverse the growing democratization of the eternal life, which was turning Egypt's strategic ideology into a personalized religion. Akhenaten took his father's innovation a large step forward by declaring that Aten was the only god, and that Aten and Akhenaten were one. Not only did Akhenaten, his wife Nefertiti, and their daughters replace the usual gods such as Horus, Osiris and Isis in Egyptian iconography but he had the royal family depicted with interesting elongated features as if to set them up as a race apart – a race of gods. These religious reforms were so unpopular that under Akhenaten they had to be implemented by a new class of bureaucrats supported by the military; and they were immediately abolished after Akhenaten's death.

Owing to the wealth generated by the highly successful commerce strategy, a great deal of attention was given to temple building and theological training during the New Kingdom. Stone replaced mud brick in the construction and rebuilding of temples throughout the empire, and these new temples became fully elaborated models of the Egyptian cosmos. The new temple complexes had undulating walls representing the world's surrounding primeval waters (the *nun*); sacred lakes for enacting the emergence of the selfcreating creator from the nun; representations of order and chaos – with the king as the upholder of *maat* – painted/inscribed on the temple walls; a subterranean crypt representing the underworld of Osiris; pylon gateways representing the mountains of the eastern horizon between which the sun god rose each morning; a small hill representing the primeval mound, on which the innermost sanctuary was built; lotus-shaped columns representing plants rising from the primeval swamp; and decorated ceilings representing the sky and solar deities. These temples were working models of the cosmos in which the king – as intermediary between the gods and men, son of both Re and Osiris, and champion of *maat* – officiated in order to sustain the Egyptian life-system. While the Egyptians had no rational model of the strategic *logos*, they did possess a well-developed and insightful mythological model that was expressed in both pictures and stone.

The Book of the Dead – or, as it was known to the ancients, Spells for Going Forth by Day – is a key source of information about Egyptian priestly (or metaphysical) philosophy in the New Kingdom. It was one of a number of "books" written to guide the newly dead through the dangerous maze of the afterlife. It first emerged in the Seventeenth Dynasty (1641–1539 BC) just before the beginning of the New Kingdom and was used for a millennium thereafter. It consists of 190 spells, which were based on earlier funerary material, particularly the Coffin Texts. There are many incomplete versions, and copies of varying quality have been unearthed all over Egypt. One of the great masterpieces of the genre is the copy described as "The Papyrus of Ani (Royal Scribe of the Divine Offerings)", held by the Department of Egyptian Antiquities in the British Museum.[62]

Thebes was the main center for the production of the Book of the Dead. While many deities are mentioned, the main ones are Re and Osiris. The "justified" dead could join either Osiris in his underworld court, or Re and his retinue in the sun barque. A new religious emphasis in this document was the "judgement of souls", supervised by Thoth in the presence of Osiris and Isis. As we have seen, the judgment of souls concerned how well the dead had served *maat*. There were forty-two possible sins against *maat*, the majority of which were in relation to the deities (guardians of the *logos*), temples (models of the *logos*), and ritual purity (service to the *logos*). In other words, these "sins" were of a strategic rather than a moral nature, in a religion that was concerned to explain and sustain the Egyptian life-system. The concern above all others was whether a citizen of Egypt was a strategist or an antistrategist. Eternal life was the reward for one, and total extinction for the other. But eternal life required participation in the never-ending struggle against chaos.

CONCLUSIONS

In this chapter we have seen how the guardians of the paleolithic strategic *logos* were transformed into the gods of the neolithic cosmos. This change in world view and religious/strategic ritual was a response to changes in the selfcreating *logos* that was communicated to neolithic society via strategic demand, and it was a response made more sophisticated by their growing material success. Unable to develop a rational model to explain and sustain their life-system, neolithic priestly philosophers developed highly imaginative, often insightful, mythological models.

In our major case study, Egyptian intellectuals developed a rich and profound metaphor for the mystery of mysteries, or life-system, that enabled them to satisfy their deeply entrenched desire to survive and prosper. Yet, as layer upon layer of richly elaborated image and metaphor were laid down, mankind was taken further and further from a realist conception of their strategic *logos*. The guardians became gods and, as we shall see in the next chapter, the gods became God. In this transformation process, religion was ultimately divorced completely from the material realties of life. Because of this, one neolithic society – ancient Greece – began to turn their serious intellectual attention from myth to science.

Chapter 4
Triumph of the One God
I: Zoroastrianism and Judaism

The transformation of paleolithic strategic guardians into neolithic gods was a response to the need for a more sophisticated explanation of the strategic *logos* together with a new capacity to finance a class of professional priestly philosophers. In contrast, the triumphant emergence of the One God from this divine pantheon was an outcome of the decision of priestly philosophers to detach the mythology from the *logos*. In this way, the *strategic* mythology that had been developed to explain and sustain the *logos* was transformed into a *metaphysical* mythology, or religion, that was employed to sustain not a strategic (materialist) society but a religious (spiritual) community. Accordingly, the polytheism previously employed to account for the various dynamic forces of the life-system was transformed into a monotheism that could provide a more satisfactory philosophical account of the creation of the cosmos. This transformation was not, however, a one-way process. Monotheism was later adopted as a strategic ideology in Europe and the Middle East.

There are two ways in which this transformation from strategic ideology to religion – from polytheism to monotheism – can be achieved. First, the priestly philosopher can, for purely personal reasons, employ elements of his society's strategic ideology as the basis for a new metaphysical system presided over by a single selfcreating creator responsible for the working of the entire cosmos. It is not meant to explain the material strategic *logos*. This was the approach taken by the Persian priestly philosopher Zarathustra in the sixth century BC. Zarathustra elevated Ahura Mazda – "wise lord" – to the role of the One God responsible for the creation of the spiritual cosmos. Of course, the mere invention of a new metaphysical system is not sufficient to establish a new religion. That requires at least one society to adopt the new system of spiritual belief. In Persia, Ahura Mazda found some loyal supporters from Zarathustra's time until the religion associated with this god was finally adopted, albeit in altered form, by the Achaemenid Dynasty (559–330 BC) as their strategic ideology. Ideas are never widely adopted unless there is a strategic demand for them.

The second way in which a strategic ideology can be transformed into a monotheistic religion is through persistent strategic failure under overwhelmingly competitive conditions. This persistent strategic failure leads both to individual psychological problems and to a form of societal neurosis, which in my book *The Selfcreating Mind* (2006) I have called **strategic frustration**.[1] It is this strategic frustration that leads to a transformation of a *strategic* ideology into a *metaphysical* mythology or religion. This was the case with the Israelite kingdom of Judah in the seventh century BC. At that time Judah was trapped in the borderlands of the world's superpowers of Egypt and Mesopotamia. The only way an ambitious Judahite elite could convince themselves that it was possible to achieve their expansionist objectives in the Levant was by seeing themselves as the "chosen people" of the One God – the one and only *universal* God, who was greater than the false gods of the surrounding superpowers. Only with the supernatural support of such a strategic guardian could they achieve their objectives against impossible worldly odds. Needless to say, Judahite expansionist plans were promptly terminated by the superpowers before they really got underway. Even the universal Creator-God YHWH was unable to defeat the worldly superpowers of the day. But this strategic failure marked the beginning of the process of transformation of Judahite strategic ideology into a monotheistic religion, which was completed by Judahite priestly philosophers during and after the Exile in Babylon (586–538 BC).

It is highly unlikely, however, that Judaism would have become a world religion had not a heretical offshoot called Christianity – also fashioned during a period of Jewish strategic failure – been adopted by the Roman state following the collapse of their conquest strategy and the humiliation of the old Roman gods of war. As Christianity possessed a more flexible metaphysical structure than Judaism, it could be easily adopted by the aspiring strategic societies that emerged from the old western Roman empire in Europe. Similarly, Islam, a metaphysical system strongly influenced by Judaism and Christianity, proved to be a very effective strategic ideology for the newly emerging conquest societies of Arabia in the seventh century AD.

Without the rise and remarkable strategic success of the Arabs, Islam would have remained a minor metaphysical system in Arabia, and, conversely, Zoroastrianism would have retained its dominance in the Middle East. Indeed, had the Persian empire defeated the Macedonians in the fourth century BC, or had the Parthians defeated the Romans around the time of Christ, or had the Sasanians defeated the Arabs in the seventh century AD, Zoroastrianism might well have triumphed over Christianity, Judaism, and Islam. Instead of YHWH, Christ, and Allah, the dominant world deity could have been Ahura Mazda! The global fortunes of the gods depend upon the unpredictable strategic fortunes of men.

There has been a considerable interaction between the four great monotheistic metaphysical systems, largely because they all emerged in the Fertile Crescent. Judaism was influenced by Zoroastrianism during and after the Exile in Mesopotamia, just at the time Judaism was making its final transition from strategic ideology to religion. Christianity, of course, began as a heretical sect of Judaism in northern Palestine. And Islam owed much to both Judaism and Christianity, not only in its formative stages in Mecca but also when it redefined itself as the conquering strategic ideology in Judeo-Christian lands. These matters are discussed in both this and the next chapter.

ZOROASTRIANISM: A METAPHYSICAL IDEOLOGY

Zoroastrianism had its origins in the vision Zoroaster (Greek), or Zarathustra (Iranian), received from the Persian god Ahura Mazda, who directed the prophet to receive and preach the truth. Zarathustra is said to have been born, probably in the early seventh century BC, into a family of knights – the Spitama – living in a town called Rhagae – now Rayy, a suburb of Tehran.[2] From time to time this pastoral community was raided by nomads from the surrounding hills. Zarathustra was concerned about the destabilizing influence of the raiding nomads, who he regarded as forces of chaos disrupting ordered communities. From this chaotic situation he attempted to draw a set of general philosophical principles that could be employed to create a better world. Zarathustra called the ordered society, which was engaged in the strategic pursuit, the followers of Truth, and the nomads, who attempted to disrupt this order for selfish reasons, the followers of the Lie.

In Zarathustra's mind, therefore, order was associated with Truth, and chaos with the Lie. Clearly this is a similar attitude to the Egyptian view of *maat* (order/truth) and *isfet* (chaos/untruth). But, instead of attempting to explain the strategic *logos* through observation and mythological generalization as the Egyptians had done, Zarathustra resorted to visions and metaphysical thinking. In the process he abandoned the pantheon of Iranian strategic guardians and elevated one of them, Ahura Mazda, to the exalted position of the One God of the cosmos, who at the end of time would triumph over the Lie/evil/chaos. As one scholar has said: Zarathustra "began his task of ousting national Mazdaism with an ascetic monotheism of his own formulation".[3] This was the beginning of revealed religion of the type – a concern with spiritual rather than strategic values and outcomes – we are familiar with today. It reflected a preference for cosmos over *logos* – for the next life over this one. To Zarathustra, this world was merely a stage on which the great metaphysical battle between Truth and the Lie could take place.

Who is Ahura Mazda? He is the creator of heaven and Earth, the source of light and darkness, the sovereign law-giver, the creator of moral order, and the judge of all creation. The ceremonial symbol of the Truth and light of Ahura Mazda was the eternal flame, which was tended by Zoroastrian priests – a ritual with much earlier origins in oil-rich Iran. Ahura Mazda created seven Amesha Spentas (beneficial and powerful immortals) to assist him in his great spiritual task. The Amesha Spentas were once Indo-European gods – "gods without being God, they are created without being creatures".[4] For Zarathustra they are the spirits of bounty, justice, truth, righteous thinking, devotion, desirable dominion, wholeness and immortality. These spirits, and the values they represent, were to be sought after by the followers of Ahura Mazda. In other words, this cult is concerned with abstract moral and spiritual values, not with strategic and materialist values as in ancient Egypt.

While Ahura Mazda is the supreme God of Truth, he is opposed by an evil representative of the Lie (Druj) known as Ahriman. Life for Zarathustra, therefore, is a struggle between two opposite forces of Truth and the Lie – of order and chaos. While this suggests a cosmic dualism in Zoroastrianism, Zarathustra asserts the monotheistic nature of his religious philosophy by claiming that Ahura Mazda, with the assistance of the Amesha Spentas, will ultimately triumph over Ahriman and his evil followers, leaving the Wise Lord in complete command of his creation. Even the time on Earth that Ahriman has to challenge the Truth is determined by Ahura Mazda.

But having introduced the concept of dualism, it is not at all surprising that after Zarathustra's death this aspect of his religious philosophy was found to be a useful explanation of the strategic (materialist) struggle between order and chaos. This opened the way for Zoroastrianism to be transformed into a strategic ideology. The apparent success of this strategic ideology is reflected in the geographical expansion of the Achaemenid Dynasty (the Persian Empire) in the 5th century BC (see Figure 4.1). In the Achaemenid Dynasty (559–330 BC), dualism was officially embraced as the mainstream of Zoroastrianism. In this form it became the state religion and strategic ideology of three successive Iranian empires: the Achaemenid, the Parthian (247 BC to AD 224), and the Sasanian (AD 224–651).[5] Hence for a millennium, Zoroastrianism was the official religion and strategic ideology of the Middle East. But it was a religion of which Zarathustra would not have approved, as it embraced a dualistic form of Zoroastrianism together with the worship of the old Iranian gods that Zarathustra had banished.

Figure 4.1 **The Persian Empire, 480 BC**

Zoroastrian teachings are found in the holy book *Avesta* and in the Pahlavi (middle Iranian) literature consisting of commentaries on the Master's ideas. Initially, the *Avesta* – of which only seventeen hymns know as Gathas are thought to have been composed by Zarathustra – was memorized and transmitted in oral form by generations of priests (Magi). The reason is that writing was considered unsuitable for sacred utterances. It is thought that this work was not written down until Parthian times.

Owing to its eventual demise, our interest in Zoroastrianism is in the influence it had on the other great monotheistic religions of the world – Judaism, Christianity, and Islam. The mechanism of this influence was the conquest of Judah by the Babylonians in the early sixth century BC and the deportation of many leading Jews to Babylon. Here they came in contact with the invading Achaemenid empire of Persia, led by Cyrus the Great, half a century later (539 BC). While the Jews were allowed by the Iranians to return to Palestine, many remained and, in particular, the influential Biblical figure Daniel is said to have served as a high official in the Achaemenid court. This court had already adopted Zoroastrianism as its official religion.

What was the nature of the impact of Zoroastrian ideas on Judaism? The most important was the shift in the focus of strategic ideology from the materialist world of everyday reality to the ethereal world to come. This was a revolution in "religious" thought. It was a shift of ideas and attitudes that was to take religion down the path of strategic irrelevance and, in the far distant future, to oblivion. It opened the way for science to become the ultimate strategic ideology. Zoroastrianism fell on fertile ground because the Judahites in Exile were searching for a new mythology to sustain their remnant community following the failure of their strategic ideology.

All other societies in the Fertile Crescent had little to offer the Judahites in this respect, because their preoccupation was with this world rather than the next. As showed in the previous chapter, Mesopotamian societies viewed the afterlife as a hellish shadow world, which was not something to look forward to. And while the Egyptians sometimes referred to the afterlife as the Field of Reeds, the objective of the "justified" dead was to assist the gods to sustain the worldly *logos* largely for the benefit of the living. In contrast, Zarathustra saw this life as a battleground hosting the great struggle between the forces of good and evil, Truth and the Lie, light and darkness; and the next life as a new and triumphal phase of existence. Zoroastrians after Zarathustra tended to emphasize "the cyclic structure of the history of 'salvation'".[6] Essentially, the strategic desire for survival and prosperity in this world would be replaced by the metaphysical desire for truth and goodness in the next. Indeed, the whole aim of creation was the destruction and elimination of evil. Yet for Zoroastrians, it was not a matter of the material world being evil *per se* (as it is in Manichaeism) rather that the spiritual pursuit is ultimately more important than the strategic pursuit. This is the core of Zoroastrianism, and it is this core that was adopted by the world religions of Judaism, Christianity, and Islam.

Monotheism was another important influence that Zoroastrianism had on these later religions. In Zoroastrianism this influence was the outcome of the revolutionary shift of emphasis from the existential material world to the metaphysical spiritual world. For priestly philosophers seduced by their own intellectual freedom, the idea of one universal God pitted against a short-term adversary (Ahriman) was a more effective way of focusing upon the mythical struggle between good and evil, light and darkness, life and death, Truth and the Lie. As the sphere of interest for these metaphysicians had shifted from the material world to the spiritual world, there was no need for a pantheon of gods representing the various aspects of a complex and dynamic life-system. Indeed, such complexity would merely obscure the simple – even simplistic – story about the struggle between good and evil and the transformation of the ephemeral material world into an eternal spiritual world. As the vision of ultimate reality had changed from a complex to a simplistic one, a similar change needed to take place amongst the deities. Monotheism was an idea that supported Zarathustra's spiritualism.

This is not to say there was no tension between monotheism and Zarathustra's vision of the eventual triumph of the metaphysical ideas of Truth and light. Because this triumph would only occur in the future, this world was to be the battleground for the struggle between these forces. For the duration of this world, therefore, the God of Truth had to endure the presence of a great and powerful adversary. The existence of two great personified forces in this world suggest that there exists a fundamental dualism not only in Zoroastrianism but also in those religions (Judaism, Christianity, and Islam) that adopted the idea of a struggle between spiritual opposites. Strictly speaking monotheism will only exist once the God of Truth disposes of his opposite number, and this material world is replaced by a future spiritual world.

The problem for Zoroastrianism – and hence for Judaism, Christianity, and Islam – is that this material world, in which evil persists, appears to be in no hurry to pass away. As God and the Adversary (Ahriman, Satan, the Devil) are thought by many religious followers to be active forces in the world, there is, as history shows, always a temptation for religious organizations to formally recognize this duality in their ritual. In Zoroastrianism after the death of Zarathustra, as we have seen, this dualism was officially recognized in Iran. Hence the practice of Zoroastrianism as a state religion cannot strictly be said to constitute monotheism. And, as shown in the next chapter, the history of Christianity displays a number of attempts to develop the theological implications of the potential for dualism inherited from Zoroastrianism.

Other influential Zoroastrian ideas included personal salvation, divine judgment, resurrection, and a spiritual afterlife. Zarathustra emphasized that every individual would be judged, both at their death and on the day when the Lie is finally defeated; and that every individual could achieve personal salvation by devotion to Ahura Mazda. On the day of judgment the dead will be resurrected, and the followers of Ahura Mazda will join him in heaven while the disciples of Ahriman will end up in hell. At the day of judgment, the material world will pass away and be replaced by an ideal spiritual world characterized by truth, light, and goodness.

What a contrast this is with Egyptian ideas about the purpose of this world, of death, and of the afterlife. As we have seen, the Egyptians did believe in personal judgment and resurrection, but only of kings and possibly the aristocratic elite. And judgment was based not on a spiritual but a strategic code – whether the individual had upheld the materialist laws of *maat* and supported the strategic *logos*. The idea underlying resurrection was that the "justified" dead, who had shown they could uphold the *logos* in life, would be able to assist the gods in sustaining the Egyptian life-system. The Egyptians did not desire a transformation of the material world into a spiritual world, they wanted to see the material world continue for as long as possible. At the end of time their complex material world would not be transformed, but be reabsorbed into primeval oneness. This contrast in ideas reflects the transformation of the world's early *strategic* ideology into *metaphysical* mythology.

JUDAISM AND THE REINVENTION OF RELIGION

In this book a distinction is made between strategic ideology on the one hand and religion on the other. Strategic ideology is, as we have seen, a body of ideas and rituals that are employed both to understand and to sustain the life-system or strategic *logos*. The relationship between a strategic *logos* and its ideology is symbiotic: they both develop together, and when the *logos* dies, the ideology is no longer relevant to life. The complex Egyptian strategic ideology, for example, ceased to have any relevance when its ancient life-system collapsed, and it was totally forgotten for thousands of years until the ancient hieroglyphic script was finally deciphered in the early nineteenth century by Thomas Young and Jean-Francois Champollion.[7]

Religion was born when the priestly philosophers found a way of divorcing the ideology from the *logos* and perpetuating its disembodied existence. Zarathustra, as discussed above, showed the way. Religion was reinvented, however, by Jewish priestly philosophers from the seventh to the sixth century BC by elevating a tribal god YHWH to universal/transcendental status, by transferring the spiritual covenant with YHWH from the Judahite *logos* to the "people of Israel", and grounding this covenant in a set of laws about family life rather than the laws of the Judahite life-system. In this way, the covenant with YHWH depended not on the survival of the Judahite *logos* but merely on the survival of the Jewish family. As the probability of survival of the family is far greater than that of the *logos* in any region of the world, religion can be more enduring than strategic ideology. While strategic ideology is practical, specific, and ephemeral, religion is mystical, general, and "eternal".

What were the circumstances that forced Israelite priestly philosophers to divorce the strategic ideology from the *logos* of the small and highly ephemeral kingdom of Judah? They included the totally unrealistic ambition of king Josiah in the seventh century BC to create a Pan-Israelite state, followed almost immediately by strategic failure in the face of Egyptian opposition and national obliteration by Babylon. With the removal of Judahite kings, the people of Israel creased to be a strategic society and became a religious community under the leadership of priestly philosophers, who exerted their authority through the exercise of metaphysical laws rather than strategic laws. Hence, the reinvention of religion in Palestine was due to the attempt made by priestly philosophers to assume control of a small community that was suffering from terminal strategic failure. To understand this transformation we need to review the history of the Israelites and their mythology.

The rise and fall of Israelite societies

Before discussing the mythology of the people of Israel, we need to determine exactly who they are and how their fortunes have fluctuated over time. The location of the Israelites in the highlands of Palestine provided considerable strategic opportunities, owing to the region's role in the wealthy trading network between Africa, the Mediterranean and Mesopotamia. But these rich opportunities were associated with considerable risk, because the superpowers in Egypt and Mesopotamia were determined to exert control over highly profitable commerce activities in these borderlands.

Owing to the more meager resource base of the Levant in comparison with both Egypt and Mesopotamia, the Canaanite city-states were able to flourish only when the superpowers were distracted by internal or external difficulties. The Canaanite window of strategic opportunity was always very limited. Once the superpowers had recovered from their temporary distractions they always reasserted their control over the Levant and crushed any Canaanite city-state that had become too successful and too independent. Canaanite societies just did not have the resource base, and hence the population size, to succeed against the superpowers. While this did not prevent Canaanite societies from dreaming about and planning for strategic glory, their dreams and plans were always rudely shattered. In contrast, modern Israel survives and prospers, because, in the technological era, science and technology (as well as friendly superpowers in the West) are more important than a rich resource base.

Israelite origins – early settlement waves, 3500–1200 BC

Until the comprehensive archaeological surveys undertaken by Israeli teams in the central highlands of Palestine following the 1967 war, the Bible's account of Israelite origins was widely accepted by historians. The Biblical story about the origins of the people of Israel is an account of the patriarchs Abraham, Isaac, and Jacob around 2000 BC; the period of captivity in Egypt under Ramesses II in the thirteenth century BC and the Exodus led by Moses; the subsequent conquest by Joshua of the Land of Canaan and the settlement there by the twelve tribes of Israel; the establishment of a united kingdom under David (1005–970 BC); the empire of Solomon (970–931 BC); the dual kingdoms of Israel and Judah (931–724 BC); the destruction of Israel by the Assyrians (721 BC) and the subsequent rise of Judah; the ambitions of King Josiah (639–609 BC) for a pan-Israelite empire, which were crushed in battle by Egypt's pharaoh Neko II; the destruction of Judah by the Babylonians (587 BC); the Exile in Babylon (587–539 BC) and the Return to Jerusalem (from 538 BC) to establish a religious community. This Biblical history is interpreted by the priestly philosophers as the outcome of the covenant between YHWH and the Israelites and the periodic failure of the people to respect that covenant. The repeated rise and fall of Israelite society, therefore, was explained in spiritual rather than material terms.

The archaeological evidence tells a very different story. Permanent Israelite settlements first appeared in the central highlands of Palestine around 1200 BC. This was a dramatic occurrence, which showed no signs of violent invasion (by Joshua) as claimed in the Bible. And it occurred far from the Canaanite city-states that the Israelites were supposed to have conquered. As we shall see later, these Canaanite cities were already in the process of collapse due to very different causes. Archaeologists have discovered about 250 small self-sufficient hill-top settlements, which were based on grain-growing and herding activities. These settlements were very similar, and they appear typically to have consisted of about fifty adults and fifty children each. They were not fortified – indeed, no weapons have been found – and none possessed any public buildings. These first Israelites appear to have worshipped Canaanite gods, as suggested by the discovery of a bronze bull figurine depicting either Baal or Il. The villages of this time were set out in a continuous oval shape, which appears to trace out the earlier Bedouin tent encampments. This evidence suggests that the first Israelites were pastoral nomads. Only later did the highland settlers adopt the more usual village design.[8]

The beginning of *permanent* settlement around 1200 BC in the Palestinian highlands was not a unique event. Modern Israeli archaeological surveys show that it was in fact the third and final wave of settlement emanating from the eastern desert fringe. The earlier two settlement waves were, however, only temporary. All three waves of settlement rolled in from the eastern desert fringe, gradually spreading *westward* through the central highlands. As can be seen from Table 4.1, these three settlement waves spanned a period of some 2,500 years. The first "temporary" wave between 3500 and 2200 BC led to the establishment of about 100 small settlements; the second, and much shorter wave between 2000 and 1550 BC, established about 220 villages, of which a small number (25) were still being occupied when the third wave occurred. This third, and permanent, settlement wave led initially (1150–900 BC) to the establishment of 250 settlements, with a population of about 45,000; but, by the time of the Babylonian destruction of Jerusalem, had grown to 500 villages, with a population of 160,000.

Table 4.1 **Israelite settlement waves, 3500–1200 BC**

	Period (BC)	Number of sites	Population	Duration (years)
First wave				
surge	3500–2200	100	NA	1,300
retreat	2200–2000	–		
Second wave				
surge	2000–1550	220	NA	450
retreat	1550–1150	25		
Third wave				
surge	1150–900	250	45,000	Permanent
consolidation	900–586	500	160,000	

Source: based on data in Finkelstein and Silberman (2002: 114–15).

The settlement patterns in each of those waves were similar, except that the south – later the kingdom of Judah – comprised a more hilly and rocky landscape with a smaller population and less wealth than the north – later the kingdom of Israel. These settlement waves also displayed, throughout the highlands, a similar material culture in terms of village design, architecture, and pottery. The usual argument is that this was due to "similar environmental and economic conditions".[9] One could add, more specifically, that it was due to the similar dynamic strategies these peoples pursued, and to their similar strategic *logoi*.

Was there anything unusual or special about these people called "Israelites", who finally established themselves in the Palestinian highlands? The archaeological answer is: no. Right from the very beginning the Israelites were indistinguishable from the Canaanites. They were Canaanites rather than the conquerors of Canaanites, and they were an integral part of the ecosociopolitical system of the Land of Canaan. They were local people on the borderlands between the nomadic herders and the settled agriculturalists who lived in towns and cities. The Israelites grazed their herds both on the eastern desert margins and in the highlands, where they later also turned to agriculture.

Israel Finkelstein and Neil Silberman argue that these herders were drawn into more permanent highland settlement by the periodic collapse of the Canaanite city-states on the western and northern lowlands that had formerly provided agricultural goods in exchange for animal products. During periods when the city-states were unable to provide grain, the nomadic herders formed their own agricultural settlements in the highlands and became self-sufficient; and when the city-states recovered, the proto-Israelites found it more economical to resume their nomadic herding existence. This generated the wave-like pattern of settlement outlined here. They conclude ironically:

> The process that we describe here is, in fact, the opposite of what we have in the Bible: the emergence of early Israel was an *outcome* of the collapse of Canaanite culture, *not its cause*. And most of the Israelites did not come from outside Canaan – they emerged from within it. There was no mass Exodus from Egypt. There was no violent conquest of Canaan. Most of the people who formed early Israel were local people – the same people who we see in the highlands throughout the Bronze and Iron Ages [3500–586 BC]. The early Israelites were – irony of ironies – themselves originally Canaanites![10]

Hence, the early Israelites were from the same stock as the surrounding peoples of Ammon, Moab and Edom, who were so despised by the writers of the Bible. Archaeological surveys in Jordan show that these peoples had the same type of villages, similar houses and pottery, and similar forms of economic activity. Even their gods were the same. The only difference in the archaeological record is that while there is an abundance of pig bones among the settlements of the Philistines, Ammonites, and Moabites, none have been found in the settlements of the Israelites. So, at least 3,000 years ago the Israelites began to define themselves as a people simply in terms of distinctive culinary practices and dietary customs. Distinctions based on religion – such as monotheism – and clan mythology – Exodus and conquest – came later, some 500 years later.[11]

While the material and religious culture of the Bronze Age (3500–1150 BC) settlements throughout the highlands was much the same, they always formed two distinctive regional societies that eventually became the separate kingdoms of Israel (931–724 BC) and Judah (931–586 BC). In the north, the Bronze Age settlements – which were all heavily dependent upon settled agriculture – ranged from large, medium, to small sites; whereas in the south, the settlements – which depended exclusively on migratory herding – were exclusively small sites. Both regions were "dominated by a single center that was apparently the focus of regional political and economic centralization – and perhaps of religious practices as well".[12] The regional center in the north was Tirzah (Tell el-Farah) – which became the first capital of the kingdom of Israel a millennium later – and in the south it was Ai (Khirbet el Tell) – see Figure 4.2. Both centers were fortified and possessed monumental temples. In the middle Bronze Age (2000–1550) – the second wave of highland settlement – the same regional distinctiveness reappeared. But this time the main center in the north was Shechem, and in the south it was Jerusalem. Once again both centers were heavily fortified and had large temples.

Figure 4.2 **Palestine–Syria, from 1000 BC**

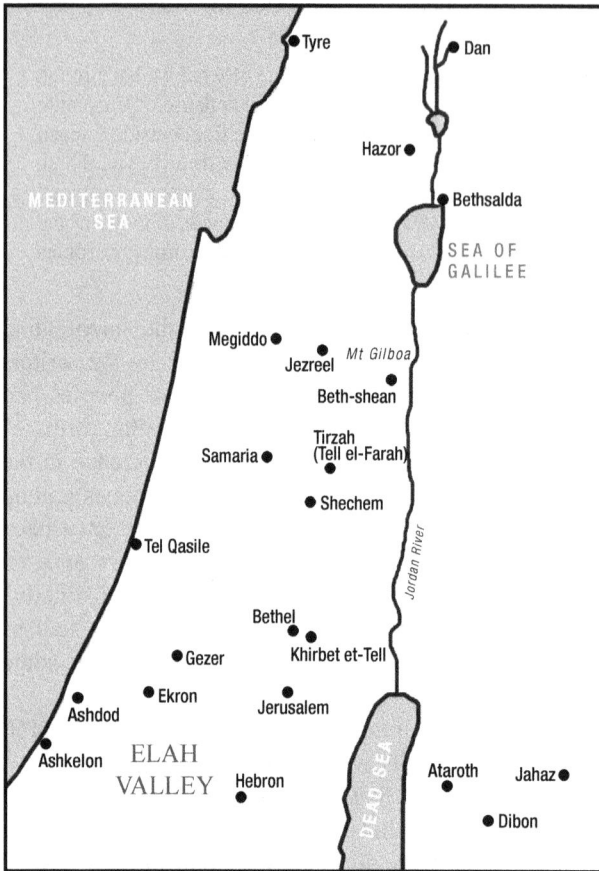

The age of David and Solomon, 1005–931 BC

Western civilization has long been dazzled by Biblical stories of heroism and grandeur concerning the united kingdom and empire of David and Solomon. European emperors such as Charlemagne (AD 742–814) even modeled their courts on Biblical descriptions of the imperial court of Solomon. Indeed, the Biblical claim about a unified kingdom that is said to have first emerged under King Saul (1025–1005 BC) was widely held to be historical fact by scholars until the 1980s and by the wider public until today. Yet, once again the archaeological evidence – compiled from intensive surveys of the hill country in the 1980s, and related by Finkelstein and Silberman – tells a very different story; a story about two distinct highland societies that continued separately from the Bronze Age into the Iron Age. The united kingdom of David and Solomon as described in the Hebrew Bible is a complete fiction.

There is just no archaeological evidence to support the Biblical claim that the northern and southern highland societies were ever united, and certainly not under the lesser developed south from which the House of David came. In fact, while the northern kingdom of Israel was booming in the tenth and ninth centuries BC – the time of Solomon and after – its southern neighbor, the kingdom of Judah, remained in the economic doldrums. And it remained small and poor.

The key to Israel's economic success was the development of olive oil as a commercial product that was exported to both Egypt and Mesopotamia. This trade was developed on a large scale by Israel in the ninth century BC and by Judah only in the seventh century BC – and only then because Israel had been destroyed by the Assyrian empire and the Israelites deported to Mesopotamia. This difference in regional wealth was, naturally enough, reflected in the different degrees of sophistication of the administrative centers in Israel and Judah. Early ninth-century administrative centers in Israel – such as Megiddo, Jezreel, and Samaria (see Figure 4.2) – were heavily fortified and possessed elaborate palaces and temples; whereas in Judah, buildings of this type did not appear until the seventh century – and, even then, they were smaller in size, of poorer quality, and reflected less cosmopolitan influences. Finkelstein and Silberman conclude:

> In sum, it is safe to say that the northern kingdom of Israel emerged as a fully developed state no later than the beginning of the ninth century BCE – at a time when the society and economy of Judah had changed but little from its highland origins.[13]

How, therefore, would it have been possible for the relatively poor and sparsely populated region of Judah, which was two centuries behind its larger, more wealthy neighbor Israel, to dominate its northern neighbor? Clearly this was no more than a Judahite daydream – a daydream that was written into the Hebrew Bible in the seventh century BC by the temporary survivor of the Palestinian clash with the superpower Assyria.

The rise and fall of Israel, 931–724 BC

The kingdom of Israel bloomed brightly, if briefly, on occasions during the ninth and eight centuries BC. The most impressive of these periods of strategic expansion was led by the Omride Dynasty between 884 and 842 BC, and again during the first half of the following century, particularly under King Jeroboam II from 788 to 747 BC. These two periods of affluence were separated by military intervention by the local Syrian state centered on Damascus, and it was finally ended by the Assyrian empire in 724 BC. While Israel's glory was brief, it showed what could be achieved even in the shadow of the superpowers. But this was a problem in itself, as it built up expectations that were totally unrealistic, leading ultimately to the debilitating social neurosis of **strategic frustration**.

The Omride Dynasty during the first half of the ninth century BC consisted of four successive kings: Omri, Ahab (and his infamous wife Jezebel), Ahaziah, and Joram. Not surprisingly, the founder of this dynasty, Omri, was an Israelite general, who was able to exploit the resources of the northern kingdom to finance his expansionist aims. This would have been impossible for the House of David to achieve a century earlier with the much poorer resources of Judah at its disposal. Hence, it was the House of Omri not the House of David that created the first "fully developed" national state in the Palestinian highlands, and even this included only Israel, not the united kingdom of Israel and Judah.

The Omri state comprised a complex bureaucracy, the use of written records, a sizeable standing army, large-scale and high-quality public buildings in a number of urban centers – Samaria, Megiddo, Gezer, Hazor, Dan and Jezreel – complex urban water-supply systems, a state-organized trade system, and a multiethnic and multicultural citizenry. At its height, the kingdom of Israel had a population of about 350,000 people, which, while it could not compare with the population of the superpowers (Egypt's population was 3.5 million at the same time[14]), made it the most densely populated state in the Levant.[15] The Omride Dynasty in Israel matched the former impressive culture – if on a modest world scale – of the old Canaanite city-states. In fact, this culture – in all its social and religious dimensions – was more Canaanite in nature than it was Israelite. As Finkelstein and Silberman conclude:

> the great Omride citadels resembled the capitals of the great Canaanite city-states of the late Bronze Age, which ruled over a patchwork of peoples and lands … That is why it is difficult to insist, from a strictly archaeological perspective, that the kingdom of Israel as a whole was ever particularly Israelite in either the ethnic, cultural, or religious connotations of that name as we understand it from the perspective of the later biblical writers. The Israeliteness of the northern kingdom was in many ways a late monarchic Judahite idea.[16]

The initial dynamic strategy of the Omrides was conquest. With this strategy they were able to expand their territory from the central hill country between Bethel in the south and Samaria and Tirzah in the north, into the rich Jezreel Valley – which included the cities of Megiddo, Jezreel and Beth-shean – and further north into the highlands of lower and upper Galilee – including the cities of Hazor and Dan. This new territory (see Figure 4.2) included rich agricultural lands, which added to the wealth of the Omri regime. Agricultural products from these lowlands, together with olive oil and wine from the highlands, provided the basis for an active participation in the Mediterranean–African– Mesopotamian trading system, which was undergoing a major revival at this time. With the acquisition of new territory, particularly of the Jezreel Valley, Israel now controlled some of the most important overland routes between the Mediterranean and Mesopotamia. Hence, following its successful conquest strategy – which was limited by the interests of the superpowers – Israel turned to the dynamic strategy of commerce to further increase its material prosperity.

This prosperity enabled Israel in 853 BC to successfully lead – under King Ahab – a coalition of neighboring countries to block (but not destroy) the advance of a mighty Assyrian army under the leadership of Shalmaneser III (858–824 BC) at Qarqar on the Orontes River in Western Syria. In this battle, Israel, according to an Assyrian account, provided 2,000 chariots and 10,000 infantry, making it the largest contingent of the coalition force. This was the first and only time a Levantine force was able to halt the advance of a superpower in full flood. An achievement that seemed to offer a new dawn for the Canaanites.

But it was a false dawn. The House of Omri fell in 842 BC and the Syrian kingdom of Damascus successfully invaded and occupied the fertile north – the rich heartland – of the new Israel between 835 and 800 BC. In fact, the Syrians attacked and destroyed the northern Israelite cities of Dan, Hazor, Bethsaida, Megiddo and Jezreel. Clearly this was a major setback for the strategic ambitions of Israel. Syrian dominance in the north only ended when the Assyrians returned in 800 BC to crush Levantine independence. What the Syrians had failed to learn from recent history was that the only possibility of success against the superpowers was through Palestinian–Syrian cooperation.

Following a period of internal strife and disrupted succession in Israel, the father and son team of Joash (800–784 BC) and Jeroboam II (788–747 BC) took charge of the country's dynamic strategy. This involved making it clear to the Assyrians that they had no imperial ambitions – for which they were permitted to reclaim some of the territories lost to Damascus – and exploiting the commercial opportunities of the Levant. This was a strategy based on the growing and processing of olives and grapes, and the export of oil and wine to Assyria and Egypt, both of which had no comparative advantage in producing these highly desirable and necessary commodities. There is also some evidence that Israel bred horses for export to their militaristic overlords.[17] As a result of this strategy, Israel experienced a recovery of prosperity and population, which at its peak may even have exceeded levels achieved in the Omride Dynasty. At a time when Judah's population was merely 100,000, Israel's was about 350,000. Israel also undertook impressive building projects in the main urban centers, which until recently were wrongly ascribed to Solomon, who in fact (archaeological rather than Biblical) *never* ruled over these northern territories.

But the prosperity was not to last, because the Assyrians under Tiglath-pileser III (744–727 BC) decided they wanted an even greater share of the lucrative Levantine trade. This could be achieved, they believed, by dispensing with vassal states and their petty rulers and establishing Assyrian provinces ruled directly by Assyrian-appointed governors.[18] When the Assyrian army began moving westward in 738 BC, Israel sensibly attempted to form a coalition – which was to include Damascus, some Philistine cities, and Egypt – as it had done successfully a century before. But Egypt was in the process of fragmentation and was being pressured by Piy of Nubia, who eventually established the Twenty-fifth Dynasty. And Israel itself was suffering from considerable civil strife and internal conflict over the royal succession at this time. Not surprisingly in these circumstances, the coalition failed to eventuate and Tiglath-pileser had no difficulty in conquering most of Israel's territory, destroying its main cities – with the exception of Megiddo, which was to become the capital of the new Assyrian province – and deporting a significant part of its population to other regions in the empire. Assyrian records suggest that some 13,500 Israelites were deported in a resettlement of conquered people that probably amounted to around 220,000 at the time.[19] Only the city of Samaria was spared, in return for the payment of tribute.

With the death of Tiglath-pileser in 727 BC, Hoshea (732–724 BC), the last king of Israel (by now the tiny city-state of Samaria) decided to gamble on gaining Egyptian support before the new king called Shalmaneser V (727–722 BC) had time to take charge. Once again Egypt failed to come to Israel's assistance and, after a long siege, Samaria was destroyed in 722 BC either by Shalmaneser V or by Sargon II (722–705 BC) who overthrew the former ruler in a civil war around that time. Once again, part of the Israelite population was resettled in other regions of the Assyrian empire, and other peoples were settled in their place. Only the rural population was left undisturbed, because they were the foundation of the prosperity that the Assyrians wanted to exploit. Possibly a total of 40,000 Israelites were deported by the Assyrians in the late eighth century BC – about 20 percent of the population west of the Jordan River.[20] This second deportation marked the end of the kingdom of Israel. The window of strategic opportunity for the northern kingdom had been firmly and finally closed.

The rise and fall of Judah, 931–587 BC

The southern highland kingdom of Judah – as already suggested – was the relatively small and poor cousin of Israel. Until the eighth century BC, the population of the Judahite highlands was only about 10 percent of that of the Israelite highlands. Earlier, in the fourteenth century BC, the kingdom of Jerusalem consisted of merely eight small settlements housing a total of 1,500 people, with about the same number living as nomadic herders. Little had changed by the beginning of the tenth century BC, when the legendary David was no more than an outlaw chief roaming the Hebrew hills and Judean desert until he was made "king" of this small rural community of a few thousand people. His "capital" – no more than his headquarters – Jerusalem was just a small hill-top village, built on a narrow ridge, with a few public buildings including a temple in which the royal cult of YHWH, together with other Canaanite gods, were attended to. In effect, YHWH at this time was the Judahite chieftains' preferred god of raiding.

Everything was to change – and to change suddenly – when the northern kingdom of Israel was finally swept away by the Assyrians in 724 BC. This was due to the large number of refugees fleeing from Assyrian control. Almost overnight the population of Judah increased from 30,000 to 120,000. While the number of settlements increased from a handful of villages to about 300, the population of Jerusalem increased rapidly from 1,000 to 15,000, and the built-up area of the city – which included public buildings, workshops, and houses – increased in size from 10 to 150 acres. New towns also appeared in the Beersheba Valley – such as Beersheba and Arad – and major fortified centers like Lachish and Azehah in the Shephelah and Hebron regions emerged forcefully.

For the first time in history, Judah could reasonably claim to be a fully emergent state, if only a small one. For the first time it was able to boast a literate bureaucracy, written records, specialized professionals, a standing army, monumental masonry buildings, a wealthy commercial elite who had elaborate tombs cut in the rock ridges close to their cities, and a national priesthood and religion. The sudden demise of the northern kingdom of Israel had provided Judah with its first, and only, opportunity to try its luck on the world strategic stage. Pity it didn't also provide an object lesson.

The dynamic strategy pursued by Judah was similar to that fueling the rise and fall of Israel. And the Judahite elite under King Hezekiah (727–698 BC) appeared to appreciate the parallels, which is why they made a considerable effort to reform their strategic ideology and to raise YHWH from a royalty cult to universal significance. If they were to succeed where Israel had failed – if they were to be able to challenge the superpowers and win – they needed to give their complete allegiance to the mightiest strategic guardian in the Universe, namely the one and only God YHWH. Although it was not their intention at the time, this was the first step in the Judahite reinvention of religion.

While they worked on their strategic ideology, they also cooperated closely with the Assyrian empire. This meant actively participating in the Arabian–Assyrian trading system. To this end they grew and processed olives and grapes in order to export oil and wine to Assyria and Egypt, just as Israel had done. In order to increase royal revenues through taxation, the commerce strategy was pursued under state direction. As with Israel before them, Judah grew wealthy though commerce. And it grew ambitious.

After reforming Judah's strategic ideology, Hezekiah apparently felt sufficiently confident to begin making preparations for war against Assyria. This is reflected in the archaeological evidence showing increased fortification of the main cities of Jerusalem and Lachish, the internalization of city water supplies, and increased capacity for food storage in case of prolonged siege. It is also shown in the attempt to form a coalition against Assyria that included Egypt. Hezekiah made his fateful bid for independence immediately following the death of Sargon II in 705 BC. While the change of Assyrian leadership gave Judah time to complete their war preparations and to secure Egyptian support, it did not prevent retaliation. In 701 BC Sennacherib, the new Assyrian king, brought a great army to Palestine, where it defeated a combined Egyptian–Nubian army at Elteka on the lowlands and, after a successful campaign in Negeb, turned on rebellious Judah.

The Assyrian army rampaged throughout the Judahite countryside, destroying many settlements as well as the major cities of Azekah and Lachish. While Jerusalem was spared, the economy of Judah was in ruins, particularly in the grain-growing Shephelah, which never recovered. Once again Palestinian strategic ambitions were dashed upon the reality of superpower strength. Only the priestly philosophers in the Temple of Jerusalem could pretend in their Biblical writings that the survival of Jerusalem was a triumph for YHWH. In the countryside, which had borne the brunt of Assyrian power, the people, who clearly had lost all confidence in Hezekiah's strategic guardian YHWH, turned once more to the old Canaanite gods for assistance.

Following the death of Hezekiah in 698 BC, the incoming Judahite king Manasseh (698–642 BC) wisely chose to cooperate with Assyria, to pay hefty tribute, and to bury strategic independence in the lucrative Levantine trade. Assyria, meanwhile, was content to allow Judah to recover as a buffer against its great rival Egypt. Once more Judah focused on growing and processing olives and grapes and exporting oil and wine to Egypt and Mesopotamia. Once more they exploited their key location on the main camel caravan routes through Beersheba Valley, the south coastal plain to Gaza, and the highlands of Edom. And in order to compensate for loss of territory in the west – which had been given to the Philistines by Sennacherib – Manasseh expanded his territories into the south and east thereby increasing Judah's agricultural and pastoral production, as well as exercising some control over the Arabian trade system, which was secured by constructing two forts in the desert under Assyrian supervision.

Perversely, the priestly philosophers who were responsible for compiling and writing the Hebrew Bible, viewed the strategic failure of Hezekiah as righteous, and the strategic success of Manasseh as wicked. As will be revealed, the Bible is a battleground between the antistrategic theorists and the practical strategists – a battleground where only the antistrategists who write the history of Judah can triumph.

The ever-changing power struggle – a struggle for control of the commerce strategy of the civilized world – between Egypt and Mesopotamia continually transformed the prospects for small states in Palestine. During the first half of the seventh century, Assyria had Egypt on the defensive, not only in Palestine but in the land of the Pharaohs itself.[21] While an invading Assyrian army was defeated on Egyptian soil in 674 BC, a second invasionary force headed by King Esarhaddon won a great battle at Memphis in 671 BC. This was the first successful invasion of the Nile by a foreign power, but it was not to be the last. Assyrian occupation, which by 664 had reached as far as the strategic center of Thebes (from where images of the Egyptian strategic guardians were taken back to Nineveh) was brought to an end in 656 BC by Psamtek I (664–610 BC), founder of the Twenty-sixth Dynasty. Thereafter, Egypt extended its influence into the Levantine coastal region to gain greater control over trading routes so as to secure its temporarily revived commerce strategy. Their task was made easier by Assyria's preoccupation with the rebellious Chaldaeans in Babylon, who captured the Assyrian capital Nineveh in 612 BC and secured the entire empire by 609 BC. Curiously, Egypt came to Assyria's aid from 616 BC until the fall of Assyria, and then continued alone against the Babylonians as far as Carchemish and Kimuhu on the upper Euphrates.[22]

With the Egyptians preoccupied with easily won coastal wealth in the Levant, the Assyrians in retreat, and a political vacuum persisting in the territories of the former state of Israel, the Judahite elite under the leadership of King Josiah (639–609 BC) were once more seduced by the idea of imperial glory. The fact that both the old kingdom of Israel and the earlier Judahite monarchy of Hezekiah had been similarly tempted and failed with disastrous consequences, demonstrates just how strong is the driving force of strategic desire in the breast of man. Even with the tempting strategic opportunities being presented during Josiah's reign, the probability of imperial success by a small power on the doorsteps of both Egypt and Mesopotamia was effectively zero.

No doubt the Judahite elite had some sense of these impossible odds. It was all a question – as far as they were concerned – of whether Judah's strategic guardian YHWH could be relied on to transform this unfavorable strategic situation so as to give them victory. While YHWH had deserted Judah in Hezekiah's time, perhaps that was because even this righteous king had failed to approach God in the correct manner. Surely the priestly philosophers in the Temple of Jerusalem could work out what had gone wrong in the past and find the correct way to approach and please YHWH in order to gain his full support. It was probably questions like these in this life-and-death situation that led to a revolution in strategic ideology during Josiah's reign.

This strategic interpretation of the development of Judaism is entirely new. Even the persuasive work of Finkelstein and Silberman emphasizes not the need to form a new strategic ideology that will maximize the probability of securing the full support of their strategic guardian YHWH, but of the need for an effective "propaganda" that will cause the nation to focus all their efforts on this great task. They consistently argue that the "great reformation" in religion was required for "propaganda" purposes "to gird the nation" for the conflict to come. They continue:

> Such an ambitious plan [to establish a Pan-Israelite state] would require active and powerful propaganda ... This is presumably the reason why the authors and editors of the Deuteronomistic History and parts of the Pentateuch gathered and reworked the most precious traditions of the people of Israel: to gird the nation for the great national struggle that lay ahead.[23]

But, of course, no matter how highly motivated the people of Judah might be – and remember that there would have been no more than 75,000 of them compared with over 4 million Egyptians[24] – there was no way they could defeat the armies of a determined superpower. Victory would only be theirs if they could obtain the supernatural assistance of the one and only God – a God who could visit terrible afflictions upon the Egyptians, part the Red Sea to allow safe passage for the Israelites, and bring the walls of Jericho tumbling down with the blast of Israelite horns. This supernatural assistance was the reason that men had always turned to strategic guardians. It was *not* primarily a matter of propaganda.

What was the "great reformation" of Judahite strategic ideology? Essentially it was the renewal of the Mosaic covenant with YHWH through strict adherence to God's laws and to the worship of YHWH as the only universal God, and only in the Temple of Jerusalem. The basis of this "the most intense puritan reform in the history of Judah"[25] was the "Book of Law" or "Book of the Covenant", which, it is claimed in the Second Book of Kings (22: 8–13), was discovered by the high priest Hilkiah in 622 BC during renovations of the Temple of Jerusalem ordered by King Josiah. This Book of Law, which has been identified as an earlier draft of Deuteronomy, was supposed to be an old lost text that "suddenly and shockingly revealed that the traditional practice of the cult of YHWH in Judah had been wrong".[26] This then was the rationalization by Josiah's advisors as to why even the righteous Hezekiah had failed in his expansionist aims a century before. All Josiah had to do now was to enforce the "correct" requirements of the Book of Law and YHWH would do the rest. To convince themselves this was true and that they would succeed where their forefathers had failed, the Judahite elite shaped the Hebrew Bible so that Josiah of the House of David could be favorably compared with Moses the great liberator and leader of the first Passover; with Joshua and David the great Hebrew conquerors; and with Solomon the great empire builder and patron of the Temple in Jerusalem. The Bible, which was a masterpiece of strategic ideology, was the second step made by the Judahites toward the reinvention of religion.

But once again YHWH failed the people of Israel. Once again he proved to be a poor choice of strategic guardian for Judah. Obviously, the new Egyptian pharaoh Neko II (610–595 BC) was less than impressed with Josiah's ambitions in the northern highlands of Palestine. And it was always going to be Neko's will that would prevail in this sphere of superpower influence. The Bible contains two versions of what happened next. In the Second Book of Kings (23: 29) we are told merely that "Pharaoh Neco slew him [Josiah] at Megiddo when he saw him"; whereas in the Second Book of Chronicles (35: 20–24) we learn that Josiah "did not listen to the words of Neco from the mouth of God, but joined battle on the plain of Megiddo. And the archers shot King Josiah ... and he died". The Bible claims that Neko was on his way to assist the king of Assyria and had encountered Josiah campaigning in the north. Others have argued that the real reason for Neko's presence in Palestine, while Assyria was in its death throes, was to obtain renewed oaths of loyalty from his vassals, which would have lapsed on his father's death the year before. On this interpretation Josiah, whose army was hardly large enough to risk open confrontation with the pharaoh's forces, would have been summoned to Megiddo to swear a new oath of loyalty to Neko. Clearly the audience did not go well – perhaps Josiah's expansionist aims had become pubic knowledge – as Neko had the ambitious king of Judah unceremoniously put to death.[27]

Whatever the circumstances of the death of the messianic king of the House of David, this single event effectively brought the unrealistic dreams of a Pan-Israelite state to a sudden and crushing end. Over the following twenty-three years Judah was ruled in quick succession by four kings – three of which were Josiah's sons – before the new Babylonian masters (Nebuchadnezzar) of Mesopotamia defeated the Egyptian overlords of the Levant and proceeded to crush those vassal states showing any signs of independence. Judah, which turned to Egypt for help rather than ingratiate itself with Nebuchadnezzar, was in 597 BC completely devastated, Jerusalem was captured and looted, and the Judahite king (Jehoiachin), its aristocracy, and priesthood were deported to Babylon. The exiled Jehoiachin was replaced by his uncle Zedekiah (596–586 BC) in what was left of Judah. But even in the face of this evidence of the brutality of the superpower, the remaining Judahite elite plotted with other Levantine kings to throw off the shackles of captivity. Unsurprisingly, Nebuchadnezzar returned in 587 BC with a great army intent on destroying all the Judahite settlements and cities, including Lachish, Azekah and Jerusalem. The last city standing was Jerusalem, which was eventually sacked and the Temple – "the only legitimate place for the worship of YHWH"[28] – was completely destroyed. This, finally, was the end of Judah and all its strategic dreams.

There is nothing unusual about this tragic story of constantly frustrated strategic ambition for a small society operating within the sphere of interest of the world's superpowers. The ancient history of the Levant has many similar stories to tell – just as do other regions of the globe in other historical eras. Perhaps it is a story better documented than most. But that is not why this small society has commanded so much of our attention in this book. The Israelites command our attention because the impossible circumstances in which they were required to exercise their natural strategic desires and ambitions was the forcing ground for the reinvention of religion – the reinvention of religion that would be felt throughout western civilization. From this time in the West, we can observe how the ideology was divorced from the strategic ambition, and how it was transformed into a metaphysical mythology or religion.

Exile, return, and the rule of priests

While the Bible treats the Exile as a major event – hardly surprising as the Hebrew scriptures were largely written and edited by those involved – it included only a minority of the Judahite population. Of a total of 75,000 people, about 20,000, or just over a quarter, were forcibly resettled in Babylon. The remaining 55,000 Judahites – who included villagers, artisans, priest, scribes and prophets (such as Jeremiah, Haggai and Zechariah) – were ruled over by a local governor called Gedaliah. Rather recklessly, a refugee military officer known as Ishmael, son of Nethaniah "of the royal family", who was under the influence of the king of Ammon, assassinated the governor. Fearing retribution from their overlords, many Judahites (including Jeremiah) fled into Egypt, leaving the highlands of southern Palestine underpopulated.

Little is known about the period of Exile, except that the Judahite community in Babylon retained their sense of identity. The old aristocracy and priesthood would have played an important role in keeping the community together and maintaining the old traditions. In fact the priestly philosophers appear to have used the Exile as a lever to finally separate Judahite strategic ideology from their frustrated strategic ambitions. It was for this purpose that the Bible was revised at this time. The priestly philosophers attempted to formulate a metaphysical mythology that would meet the psychological needs of a **nonstrategic** community, which from this time onwards could be called a "religious" community. In the process, the earlier covenant with YHWH was transferred from the monarchy (source of strategic leadership) to the "people of Israel" and their priests (the religious community). This was the third and final step in the Israelite reinvention of religion.

The Exile was far shorter than even the most optimistic Judahite could have anticipated. The surging Persian state overwhelmed the Babylonian empire in 539 BC, and the Judahites were allowed to return to Palestine. While some families decided to stay in Mesopotamia, maintaining their Judahite culture until forced to leave some 2,500 years later, others returned to the old country in a series of migratory waves. Returnees included the core of the priesthood determined to rebuild the Temple in Jerusalem and to develop a religious (or nonstrategic) community to replace the old strategic society that had failed so convincingly. The Temple was finally rebuilt by 516 BC.

In the meantime, the Persian empire had firmly established itself not only in the Levant but also in Egypt, which was entering its final struggle for existence. In 525 BC, a Persian army confronted and defeated the Egyptians near Pelusium in the eastern delta and then proceeded to occupy Memphis, remove the Twenty-sixth Dynasty, and establish a Persian dynasty (the Twenty-seventh from 525 to 404 BC) that would rule the land of the Nile as a province of the Persian empire.

Under the expansive Persian empire, the much reduced territory of Judah was renamed Yehud (in Aramaic, the Syrian language used as a lingua franca in the Levant from the sixth century[29]), and the former Judahites were known as Yehudi, or Jews. In the fifth and fourth centuries, following the rebuilding of the Temple, Yehud was a very small Persian province, with a radius of only

12 to 15 miles centered on Jerusalem. The southern part of the old kingdom of Judah was called Idumaea with Lachish as its main center; and, as ever, the old northern kingdom of Israel, now called Samaria, was much larger. Yehud had a population of only 30,000 people, who were dominated by the Jerusalem priesthood. With the ending of the royal line of David, the priesthood assumed leadership of the people of Israel. Yehud, therefore, was a religious community rather than a strategic society likes its Palestinian neighbors; and the center of the community was the Temple in Jerusalem. Back in the Promised Land the priestly philosophers were able to consolidate their newly invented religion of Judaism and to finalize the reshaping of the Bible from a strategic to a religious document.

Israelite strategic ideology

It is necessary to draw a distinction between the strategic ideology of Israelite society on the one hand, and the metaphysical or religious mythology of the Jewish religious community on the other. Strategic ideology was an important instrument of Israelite society for as long as the people of Israel pursued strategic (materialist) opportunities. This was the case between the emergence of permanent Israelite settlements in the central highlands of Palestine around 1200 BC and the final destruction of Judah by the Babylonians some six centuries later in 587 BC. Thereafter, strategic ideology was replaced by religious mythology. During the strategic-ideology era, there were two main phases of development. The first and longest phase, from 1200 to 720 BC, was dominated by Canaanite polytheism; and the second, and surprisingly short, phase from 720 to 587 BC was dominated by Judahite monotheism – not the picture painted in the Bible. It was as late as this second phase that the early versions of the Hebrew Bible – originally a strategic document – were written. Only with the reshaping that arose from strategic failure was the Bible turned into a religious work. But before examining Israelite religion, a brief survey of Canaanite strategic ideology and Hebrew acceptance of it, will be helpful.

Canaanite strategic ideology, 1450–720 BC

What is know about Canaanite ideology comes largely from clay tablets discovered in the ruins of the ancient Syrian city-state of Ugarit at Ras Shamra (on the Mediterranean coast adjacent to Cyprus), and from the Hebrew bible. While the first of these sources provides a positive view of the strategic guardians of Canaan, the latter provides only a hostile account.

Ugarit has ancient origins, but its golden age of prosperity and cultural flowering occurred between 1450 and 1200 BC. This was a great age of commerce, in which Egyptian culture – the Eighteenth and Nineteenth Dynasties of the New Kingdom – reached its highest point, and the city-states of Canaan flourished. But it was an age that came to an end in the early decades of the twelfth century BC, with the collapse of the Hittite empire, the incursions of the

Sea Peoples from the Greek world, and the exhaustion of the Egyptian commerce strategy that forced a gradual withdrawal of their presence from the Levant. In the turbulence of this period, many Canaanite city-states, including Ugarit, collapsed, never to rise again. As we have seen, it was this series of events that led to the third and final wave of Israelite settlement of the central highlands of Palestine. These Israelites thereby inherited the strategic and cultural traditions, albeit in less sophisticated forms, of the city-states of Canaan.

Ugarit developed a cuneiform writing system that was widely used in the commercial world of the Levant from the fifteenth to the thirteenth century. This written script was the only cuneiform system to employ an alphabet (rather than a word book) – developed in either Egypt or Canaan around 1900 BC[30] – which consisted of thirty letters and was written from left to right. It is claimed that the Ugarit tablets, discovered in the Temple of Baal, were "written in an Occidental Semitic language related to Phoenician and to the 'language of Canaan' adopted by the Israelites".[31] And it has been suggested that the patriarchal stories in the Hebrew Bible were "not merely transmitted orally but were based on written documents of Canaanite origin".[32]

In the Canaanite world around the time the Israelites were finally settling permanently on the central highlands of Palestine, the "supreme god" of their pantheon of strategic guardians was El. El's title was "bull" in recognition of his great powers as father of the gods and of this people; and as the "creator of created things". We are told that El, although somewhat aloof, was "a majestic guarantor of cosmic order, supervising from above *the play of forces that were embodied by other gods*, nearer to men and adored, perhaps, with greater fervour".[33] El's wife Asherah, the "mother goddess" and "creatress of the gods", was the focus of Canaanite fertility rites. She was the goddess worshipped at hill shrines by the Israelites, and condemned by the priestly philosophers who worked in the Temple of Jerusalem and wrote the Hebrew Bible. Hence, El and Asherah appear to have been two halves – together representing wholeness, order and harmony – of the cosmic principle responsible for the creation and the supervision of the forces controlling the effective operation of the Canaanite life-system – the Canaanite strategic *logos* of commerce.

The main life forces personified by Canaanite gods were those of agricultural fertility, power over the seas and rivers (on which commerce was conducted), order over chaos, and of war. The gods in charge of these forces were Baal and his twin sister/wife Anat, Yamm, and Mot, together with a number of lesser gods including: Pidray and Arsay, daughters of Baal; Ashertu, Ashratum, Athirat, and Kadesh, the fertility goddesses; Resheph, the Syrian god of war and plague; Sasuratum, the midwife goddess; and Dagan (supreme god of the Philistines) the grain and fertility god, who was the father of Baal.[34] Baal, a storm god, symbolized by a golden calf, was responsible for agricultural fertility and abundant harvests. In a drought the people prayed to Baal for relief. Even more importantly, Baal was a god constantly and actively engaged with the forces of chaos. His partner in this struggle was his sister/wife Anat, who combined both highly aggressive war-like and fertility characteristics. She assisted Baal in his battles against Yamm the god of sea and river; the god Tannin; the seven-headed serpent Loran (or Leviathan); and Mot, god of the underworld.

Baal and Anat together provided the principle of order and material prosperity in the Canaanite life-system. They were responsible for ensuring the agricultural surplus required for both survival and participation in the dynamic strategy of commerce. They also provided protection for this dynamic strategy against predatory forces on land and sea. These materialist themes were explored in Canaanite strategic ideology through the stories of Baal/Anat's struggles with both Yamm and Mot.

Yamm, the god of seas and rivers, was a potentially destructive force for a society pursuing the dynamic strategy of commerce, owing to the storms and floods that regularly disrupted agriculture and the distribution of agricultural products to local and overseas markets. In the stories about this version of the wider struggle between the forces of order and chaos, Baal and Yamm are in regular conflict, possibly over tribute demanded by the destructive force. Yamm demands the surrender of Baal, which in turn leads to war between them and their allies. With the assistance of his sister/wife Anat, Baal is finally able to overwhelm and kill Yamm, thereby taming the destructive power of the seas and flooding rivers. Here are parallels with the Babylonian order/chaos myth about the struggle between the god Marduk and Tiamet the destructive force of the ocean. Baal and Anat similarly contain and destroy other dark powers of chaos, including the dragon Tannin and the serpent Loran/Leviathan.

The myth of "dead god rising" emerges from the struggle between Baal and Mot, the god of natural adversity and death. Mot was said to have lived in the underworld – a pit within the Earth – and was responsible for the annual cycle of drought and heat that has always afflicted this Mediterranean land. We are told that Mot "has scorched the olive, the produce of the earth and the fruit of the trees".[35] This destructive god was a danger to the production and processing of olives and grapes, which was an essential basis for the profitable export of oil and wine to both Mesopotamia and Egypt. In the Ugarit myth, Mot wrestles with the rain god Baal and attempts to swallow him, a battle that ultimately leads to the national god's death. Anat, however, comes to her brother's rescue by entering the underworld and, like Isis in Egyptian mythology, bringing Baal back to life. Anat then kills Mot and grinds his body into blood and bone meal to fertilize the land of Canaan. It is thought that this myth was the basis for an annual ritual held at the beginning of the Canaanite New Year in autumn, to encourage the start of the rainy season in Mediterranean lands.

There can be little doubt that the gods El, Asherah, Baal, Anat, and others were regarded by the Canaanites as guardians of their dynamic strategy of commerce. They helped to guarantee order in a universe of chaos. They helped, in other words, to sustain the strategic *logos* in the Levant – a most unstable and unpredictable part of the Old World. And the Canaanite model of the *logos* was the Temple of Baal in Ugarit, which was meant to represent the celestial abode of their god.

In addition to these major gods common to all Canaanite societies, there were local deities who were recognized by particular clans. One of these local tribal gods was YHWH, who appears to have been the subject of a "royal" cult among the Israelites who occupied the central highlands of Palestine – a backwater in the land of Canaan – from the early twelfth century BC. In Psalms (2: 6–7; 89: 26–27) YHWH is regarded as father of the king of Israel. In earlier times he was probably central to the cult of war-like tribal chiefs and their families. He began his career, therefore, as a warrior god in the marginal desert lands east of the central highlands.[36] This royal god was also called YHWH Sabaoth, or the "God of Armies", and his role in Israelite society was similar to the Syrian god of war, Resheph – a guardian of nomadic raiding parties.

As YHWH was a god of tribal raiding parties, it was natural that the Israelites should turn to other Canaanite gods – as they lived on the margins of Canaanite society – for assurance concerning fertility, order and harmony, as well as control over the elements of rain, drought, floods, and destructive winds. Throughout most of their history, the Israelites accepted El as head of the Council of Gods, which included Baal, Asherah, Anat, deities of the sun (Shapash), moon, and morning star (Astarte), as well as YHWH. For example, in Psalm 82 we are told:

> God (YHWH) has taken his place in the divine council; in the midst of the gods he holds judgement.[37]

Only at a later time in Israelite history does YHWH claim leadership of the divine council to become "king of the gods"; only later still does he expel all other Canaanite gods; and only during the Exile does YHWH become, for the Judahite priestly philosophers at least, the only universal God. In Isaiah (2: 3–4) we are told:

> For out of Zion shall go forth the law, and the word of the Lord from Jerusalem. He shall judge between the nations, and shall decide for many peoples.

But even then, after YHWH had failed to ensure the success of the kingdom of Judah, the other Canaanite gods were worshipped by the Israelites, even in the Temple of Jerusalem.

In the course of the Hebrew Bible, therefore, YHWH is transformed from the cruel and robust tribal god of the Exodus from Egypt and conquest of Canaan, to the universal God of transcendence and compassion following the Return from Exile. At this endpoint in divine evolution, YHWH had ceased to be a strategic guardian and had become the spiritual lord of a chosen people who would take his message to the world. This transformation took place at the hands of the priestly philosophers of King Josiah and the Exile and Return, who edited and wrote the document we know as the Bible. The triumph of the One

God, therefore, was a relatively sudden event that occurred between the seventh and fifth centuries in Jewish history.

Judahite strategic ideology, 720–587 BC

With the emergence of Judah as a modest Canaanite power following the collapse of Israel in 724 BC, its royal and aristocratic elite needed to develop a new strategic ideology. They required an ideology that would reinforce and sustain a new conquest strategy; an ideology that would enable Judah to succeed where the kingdom of Israel had failed.

The kingdom of Israel had embraced the old Canaanite pantheon of strategic guardians. Their favorite deities were Baal and Asherah, which, if the Bible (I Kings, 18: 19) is correct, had 450 and 400 prophets respectively in the time of Ahab and Jezebel (873–852 BC). YHWH also had his priests in Israel, but, the Bible tells us, they were persecuted by the Phoenician princess and Israelite Queen, Jezebel. Typically, the strategic failure of Israel was seen by the priestly philosophers of YHWH as the outcome not of any unequal contest with the superpowers but of the worship of the wrong strategic guardian. Through the Bible they try to tell us that the kings of Israel failed because they incurred the wrath of YHWH for failing to follow *only* him.

As the Judahite aristocracy, particularly under Hezekia (727–698 BC) and Josiah (639–609 BC), turned their minds to conquest and empire, they were determined not to repeat the mistakes of Israel. Extreme strategic conditions – a small society struggling for survival and glory in the borderlands between two superpowers – required an extremely effective strategic ideology. They would not only reject the various fertility gods (Baal and Asherah) and embrace the local royal god of war, but they would elevate YHWH to be the one and only God – the ultimate guardian of Judah's strategic *logos*. The Judahite elite would insist on a monotheistic strategic ideology. Surely in this way their conquest strategy would succeed where Israel's had failed. This was not just a way of uniting the people of Judah behind the elite's conquest aims as Finkelstein and Silberman have suggested, but rather it was to maximize the supernatural support they desperately needed from their strategic guardian. This conclusion is supported by the new scientific evaluation of the history, nature and purpose of the Hebrew Bible.[38]

The Hebrew Bible

The Bible consists of thirty-nine "books", which in the Hebrew text are divided into three main sections: the Torah, the Prophets (former and latter), and the Writings (Poetry, Scrolls, Prophecy and History). For the purposes of exposition, these books can be more conveniently regrouped into:

The Pentateuch (or Torah): Genesis, Exodus, Leviticus, Numbers, Deuteronomy

Hebrew History: Joshua, Judges, Ruth, 1 & 2 Samuel, 1 & 2 Kings, 1 & 2 Chronicles, Ezra, Nehemiah, Esther

Poetry: Job, Psalms, Proverbs, Ecclesiastes, Song of Solomon

Prophecy:
- *major prophets*: Isaiah, Jeremiah, Lamentations, Ezekiel, Daniel
- *minor prophets*: Hosea, Joel, Amos, Obadiah, Jonah, Micah, Nahum, Habakkuk, Zephaniah, Haggai, Zechariah, M alachi.

Modern linguists and historians are convinced that the Bible as we know it was written by a large number of authors over about five centuries. The Pentateuch or Torah appears to have been written in the seventh century BC using earlier texts from the kingdom of Israel – the "E text" written between the tenth and eight centuries BC – and from the kingdom of Judah – the "J text" written in the tenth century BC soon after the reign of Solomon. The "E text" refers to God as Elohim or El in classical Canaanite fashion, while the "J text" calls God YHWH in the Judahite puritan way.

Deuteronomy is a very distinctive document and is thought to have been written for the first time in the seventh century BC, just before it was "discovered" during Temple renovations about 622 BC as the "Book of Law". To complicate the picture further, it is thought that a large number of passages discussing matters of ritual concerning laws of sacrifice, purity, and cult have been inserted into the Pentateuch by "P" – the "Priestly source". And, finally, all this work has been edited, probably a number of times, by redactors – the "R source" – between the seventh and second centuries BC.[39] The text of the Bible also reflects the contributions of many writers and editors in its many repetitions and conflicting versions of the same stories.

During this writing, rewriting, editing, and re-editing process over a period of 500 years, Hebrew strategic ideology was shaped, reshaped and finally transformed into metaphysical mythology or religion. The strategic ideology was reshaped as the strategic requirements (or strategic demand) of Israelite society changed; and, finally, it was transformed into a religious text (especially 1 & 2 Chronicles and later books) when the Jewish religious community rose from the ashes of the Judahite strategic society. While the Hebrew Bible is *myth*, it is written as if it is both the *history* of the "Chosen People" of Israel and the *revealed revelation* of the One God.

The changes in dynamic strategy that drove changes in strategic ideology can be seen reflected in the Pentateuch and the so-called Deuteronomic History (Joshua, Judges, 1 & 2 Samuel, 1 & 2 Kings). The first four books of the Pentateuch reflect the early phase of Israelite dynamic strategy, with its focus on self-sufficient agriculture and herding and family multiplication. These books provide evidence of a pluralistic society that accepted gods other than YHWH to support their materialist activities. Deuteronomy, however, displays a major change of emphasis – rejection of all gods except the royal warrior cult of YHWH, who is seen as completely transcendent, together with the complete prohibition of YHWH's worship at any place other than the Temple of Jerusalem – that was a response to the shift of dynamic strategy from family multiplication to territorial conquest. The Deuteronomic History also expresses this new strategic ideology, which takes the form of a fictional "history" of the people of Israel from the so-called conquest of the "Promised Land" to the Babylonian Exile. It comprises a series of stories cast in terms of the successes and failures of the Israelites as outcomes of their fluctuating faithfulness to the covenant with YHWH.

It is interesting to ask: as a strategic ideology, how does it compare with the Egyptian case? Both ideologies provide an explanation for the fluctuating materialist fortunes of their societies. The Egyptians believed their society rose and fell according to whether their gods favored them with their presence on Earth or whether they deserted them. The Egyptian – and particularly the Mesopotamians – regarded their gods as being unpredictable in this matter. Otherwise how could one explain how quickly success turned into failure? In contrast, the Israelites – at least from the seventh century onwards – felt that the people of Israel were to blame for any disaster that befell them. It was because they had not worshipped YHWH above all other gods; because they had lost faith and broken the covenant with God.

Yet, the most stark contrast between Egyptian and Israelite strategic ideology is that while the former offered a mythic explanation of the dynamics of their life-system, the latter does not. We do not get any real insight into Israelite thinking about their strategic *logos* from their mythology. Perhaps this is because of the far more limited time available to Israelite society to contemplate those matters before they were crushed by one or other of the world's superpowers. On the other hand, while the Egyptians never bothered to codify their mythology, the Israelite did so quite brilliantly, perhaps because of the extreme circumstances under which they had to operate on the borderlands between superpowers.

The mythic nature of the Bible

The core of the Hebrew Bible is contained within the Pentateuch and the Deuteronomic History, while 1 & 2 Chronicles is a post-Exile attempt to rewrite the Deuteronomic History from a religious rather than the earlier strategic perspective. The history of the Return from Babylonian Exile together with the building of the second Temple is contained in Ezra and Nehemiah. This account includes a series of stories about the seven-day creation of the world; the early "history" of the human race following the fall of Adam and Eve; the great flood; the origin of the nations (Egypt and Mesopotamia); the life of Abraham called by God to leave Ur in Mesopotamia and travel to the Land of Canaan; the lives of the patriarchs Isaac and Jacob; the migration of Jacob's sons to Egypt, where their rapidly growing numbers are forced into slavery; the Exodus under Moses; the wandering of the people of Israel in the desert and the covenant between God and Moses at Sinai; the priestly laws; Joshua's conquest of the Land of Canaan; the twelve tribes and their rule by "Judges" – essentially a theocracy; the emergence of the monarchy of a united kingdom under Saul, David and Solomon; the separate kingdoms of Israel and Judah; the Assyrian destruction of sinful Israel; the rise and fall of Judah and the destruction of the Temple; the Exile in Babylon; the Return and the Second Temple. What a wonderful story. Yet none of it is history, only mythology. As Finkelstein and Silberman (2002) show, the archaeological evidence and historical record demonstrate the mythical nature of these Biblical stories, which until quite recently were general regarded by scholars as history. A brief review of that evidence is made here.

Patriarchal origins?

Stories about the patriarchs – fathers of the Chosen People – begin with Abraham (initially called Abram) being called by God to leave Ur on the Euphrates in lower Mesopotamia and to migrate to the Land of Canaan. According to the Bible, this took place around 2100 BC. Once in Canaan, Abraham moved with his flocks and family between Shechem in the north, Bethel (near Jerusalem) in the central highlands, and Hebron in the south – essentially the high country of Israel and Judah. Isaac and Jacob are said to be Abraham's son and grandson.

There are many factual difficulties with these stories. First, as shown earlier, the archaeological evidence demonstrates conclusively that these central highlands were permanently settled not around 2100 BC but about 1200 BC, and they were settled not by outsiders (Mesopotamians) but by insiders (Canaanites). Second, the historical details about other societies – Assyrians, Babylonians, Arameans, Ammonites, Moabites and Edomites – relate to these regions in the period from the ninth to the seventh centuries BC rather than the twenty-second century BC. Third, the stories about Abraham take place mainly in the southern part of the hill country around Hebron in southern Judah; those associated with Isaac occur on the southern desert fringe of Judah, particularly around Beersheba; while those concerning Jacob are located mainly in the northern hill country and the Transjordan region of Israel. In other words, the writers of the Bible appear to develop a single family saga from entirely separate patriarchal stories set in different parts of Palestine. Modern scholarship concludes that this synthesis was written in Jerusalem in the seventh century BC as "a literary attempt to redefine the unity of the people of Israel – rather than as an accurate record of the lives of historical characters living more than a millennium before".[40] The purpose?: it was "a powerful expression of seventh century Judahite dreams" – dreams of uniting the kingdoms of Judah and Israel *for the first time*.

Was there an Exodus?

The Bible claims that the people of Israel, with the help of God who inflicted a series of nasty plagues on their hosts, broke out of their bondage in Egypt to spend the next forty years wandering aimlessly in the wilderness of Sinai. Scholars attempting to match this well-known story with historical events have suggested that it might have coincided with the Hyksos (western semites or Canaanites) migrations and settlements in the Nile's eastern delta around 1800 BC. These people were initially very successful, forming the Fifteenth Dynasty (1636–1528 BC) during the chaos of the Second Intermediate Period, but were driven back into Canaan by Ahmose, the founder of the New Kingdom, around 1518 BC. Some have even suggested it could have been the Hyksos who founded the city of Jerusalem and built the Temple.

But in fact, as opposed to fiction, the Temple was constructed about a century later. Second, while the Biblical story of the Captivity in Egypt mentions Ramesses, the first king bearing that name came to the throne as late as 1295 BC – in the middle of the New Kingdom era rather than three centuries earlier. Third, the Merenptah stele, which provides the very first mention in history of the name "Israel" or "Israelites", was not erected until some time during the reign of the Merenptah, son of Ramesses II, from 1213 to 1203 BC. But, this first mention of Israel in the historical record fits closely with the archaeological evidence of the first permanent settlement of Israelites in the central highlands of Palestine around 1200 BC. So, if the Exodus happened at all, it had to be in the late thirteenth century rather than the late sixteenth century BC as the Bible claims.

Is there any evidence for the exodus of a large number of people from Egypt in the late thirteenth (or any other) century? In the thirteenth century, as Finkelstein and Silberman[41] point out, Egypt was the world's greatest economic and political power, and they tightly controlled Canaan and the approaches to this vital commerce corridor. Indeed, the coastal strip between Egypt and Canaan, know as "the Ways of Horus" (or King's Highway), was guarded by a series of provisional forts, which would have been impassable for a large number of slave families. Even had they made the suicidal decision to take the alternative route through the Sinai desert, there would still be considerable evidence of a large group of people wandering there for forty years. The archaeological record, however, shows no such evidence.

Finkelstein and Silberman conclude that all the historical, geographic and ethnic details of the Biblical Exodus story reflect conditions not even in the thirteenth century but rather in the seventh century BC. While there may have been memories of earlier *small* migrations to and from Egypt, "during the time of the kingdom of Israel and Judah, the Exodus story would have endured and been elaborated as a national saga – a call to national unity in the face of continual threats from great empires". King Josiah called upon his scribes – who were in the process of editing and writing the Bible – to invent the Exodus story as a rallying call and a promise that God would lead the way in Judah's attempt to expand northwards now that the Assyrians were in retreat. We are told that "the confrontation between Moses and pharaoh mirrored the momentous confrontation between the young King Josiah and the newly crowned Pharaoh Necho".[42]

As stated earlier, where I differ from Finkelstein and Silberman is in emphasizing that this mythmaking was not just nationalistic propaganda, but rather it was primarily about ensuring a proper relationship between Judah and its strategic guardian YHWH. Even a completely united and motivated Judah could never hope to defy the might of a resurgent Egypt under the Twenty-sixth Dynasty. The only way they could succeed was with supernatural supervision and protection. Which is why the Judahite priestly philosophers invested so much intellectual effort in this remarkable exercise in strategic mythmaking.

Who conquered Canaan?

The Bible tells how Joshua, the successor to Moses, destroys the city-states of Canaan, one by one between 1230 and 1220 BC. He begins with Jericho, where, quite miraculously, "the wall fell down flat" (Joshua 6: 20); then he captured Ai; followed by the defeat of the coalition of Jerusalem, Hebron, Lachish, Jarmuth and Eglon. After destroying all the cities in what would become the kingdom of Judah, Joshua turns his divinely led force against the northern city-states in what was to become the kingdom of Israel.

While it is an exciting story, none of it can be verified by historical evidence. First, as Finkelstein and Silberman say: "How could an army in rags, traveling with women, children, and the aged, emerging after decades from the desert, possibly mount an effective invasion?"[43] Second, as the Amarna tablets (records of the court of Akhenaten established in the new city of Akhetaten) show, in the late fourteenth century BC Canaan was little more than an Egyptian province, which was effectively controlled by Egyptian administrators living in the provincial city Gaza and enforcing garrisons at key locations throughout Palestine.[44] The same would have been true of the reigns of Ramesses II and his son Merenptah during the thirteenth century when Joshua was supposed to have conquered Canaan without any opposition from Egypt.

Third, the archaeological evidence shows that the cities in Palestine at this time were not fortified. So there were no walls around Jericho to "fall down flat". Egypt provided all the security that was needed, and it didn't want the local cities to be able to defend themselves against the pharaoh. Fourth, the main cities – Jericho, Ai, and Gibeon – which the Bible claims were conquered by Joshua were, according to the archaeological evidence, not even occupied in the late thirteenth century. Fifth, while there is archaeological evidence of the violent destruction of some Canaanite cities – including Bethel, Lachish, Hazor – this occurred in the twelfth century (not the thirteenth) at the hands of the Sea Peoples, who were on the move owing to the collapse of the Hittite empire.[45] And it was the result not of a single military campaign but of many attacks taking place during the course of an entire century.

Once again we are told by Finkelstein and Silberman that the stories about

Joshua were a synthesis of local clan memories about ancient skirmishes written to serve a Pan-Israelite purpose.[46] Josiah saw himself as the new Joshua, and he identified, in the Bible that his priestly philosophers were writing, the northern cities that he *intended* to occupy. Also the strategic ideology of the Book of Joshua corresponds to that of Josiah's reign —namely that the entire land of the Israelites is to be ruled by a divinely chosen leader, who follows precisely the laws handed down by Moses. It was, therefore, a book not about the past conquest of Canaan but about the future conquest of this promised land. It was "a classic literary expression of the yearnings and fantasies of a people at a certain time and place" – the late seventh century BC in Judah's capital Jerusalem.[47] While we are told by our modern authors that the Book of Joshua was an audacious attempt to convince, through "the power of epic", the north Palestinian population that they also were part of YHWH's chosen people, I wish to re-emphasize that more importantly it was an attempt to develop a divinely inspired plan that would be supported and facilitated by Judah's strategic guardian YHWH.

A central theme throughout their work is the idea that the stories of the Bible are so powerful that they were able to determine the actions of future generations. Concerning the Joshua stories they write:

> The book of Joshua thus brilliantly highlights the deepest and most pressing of seventh-century concerns. And as we will later see, *the power of this epic was to endure* long after King Josiah's ambitious and pious plan to recover the Land of Canaan had tragically failed.[48]

Regarding the earlier story of Moses during the Exodus, they say: "And it was in the course of his [Moses] wandering as a solitary shepherd near Horeb, 'the mountain of God', that he received *the revelation that would change the world*".[49]

Both statements insist that ideas drive actions, even at a great distance from their origins in both time and space. The dynamic-strategy theory underlying this work shows the reverse – that desires drive and ideas facilitate. What we have seen so far in strategic ideology is that it is a creative response to the strategic demand generated by an unfolding dynamic strategy – an ideology thought to be essential to the facilitation of that strategic unfolding process. Hence, if an epic strategic myth "endures" over time and through space, it is because it is rediscovered in response to the unfolding of a similar dynamic strategy. It is, therefore, completely incorrect to assert, in the absence of an underlying general dynamic theory, that a "revelation" was able to change the world. The world is changed by strategic desire operating through that dynamic entity, the strategic *logos*, and not through the import from another time and place of a "powerful" mythological idea. The only reason that a modified form of Judaism, which we call Christianity, is associated with a process that "changed the world" is that it was adopted as a strategic ideology (as well as a religion) by societies that would eventually be at the center of the technological paradigm shift that we know as the Industrial Revolution. *It was the changing world that adopted this strategic ideology of Palestinian origin, not this ideology that changed the world.*

A united kingdom under David and Solomon?

The Bible claims that the theocracy ruling over the people of Israel in the time of the "Judges" – prophets and priests – was increasingly coming under attack from adjoining societies, such as Philistia. The Israelites are said to have pressured their religious leaders to provide a monarchy that could more effectively defend their economic and religious interests. God instructed Samuel, priest at Shiloh, to appoint Saul, son of Kish from the tribe of Benjamin, as the first king of the united kingdom of Israel from 1025 BC. Saul, however, was a deeply flawed character, a fact that YHWH must have recognized from the beginning because he directed Samuel to begin preparing a shepherd boy called David from the family of Jesse in Bethlehem to succeed Saul. As is well known, David came to the attention of the nation by defeating in battle the Philistine giant Goliath. David's popularity was resented by Saul who attempted to extinguish this rising star, but only succeeded in turning him into an outlaw.

Saul's reign came to an end when he committed suicide on learning his sons had been killed in battle against the Philistines. David (1005–970 BC), who was declared king by the people of Judah in Hebron, went on to rule over the entire twelve tribes of Israel from his new capital of Jerusalem. Owing to his highly successful military actions, his sphere of influence was said to extend from the Egyptian frontier to the Euphrates – a sphere of influence that in reality no Canaanite kingdom was ever able to achieve. David's son Solomon (970–931 BC) consolidated the Israelite empire, facilitated the development of commerce, and built many great buildings, including the Temple in Jerusalem. Or so the Bible tells us.

While the Biblical story of the united kingdom ruled over by the Judahite dynasty of David and Solomon had been widely accepted until the 1980s as historical fact, some scholars (the "minimalists") in the 1990s suggested that the whole story was a myth.[50] The minimalists of the early 1990s pointed out that the great Biblical kings David and Solomon were not mentioned in even one extant text in either Egypt or Mesopotamia. It was not until 1993 that archeologists found at Tel Dan in northern Israel an inscription left by Hazael, a king of Damascus around 835 BC, that boasts of a victory over an Israelite king from the "House of David". So it would appear that King David did exist – unless the "House of David" was an early mythical dynasty – but he was not sufficiently important to leave an impression on his own times either in Palestine or in the records of the superpowers.

The archaeological evidence confirms this conclusion about the insignificance of David and Solomon in the late eleventh and early tenth centuries. David's power base is said to have been Judah, which around 1000 BC was an isolated and marginal land that was only sparsely settled and had no major urban centers. There were only about twenty small permanent settlements in a region mainly suited to nomadic grazing activities; and there were no commercial olive and grape growing industries in this region at that time. The total population was no more than 5,000 people.[51] With such a small and poor population, David would not have been able to raise a fighting force of more than 500 men, and could not have kept them in the field of battle for more than short periods in the slower periods of the agricultural calendar. Clearly, David was no more than a charismatic tribal chieftain, whose brave deeds were legendary among this small group of people.

Even David's capital, Jerusalem, was no more than a typical hill village. And there is no archaeological evidence of the wealth of empire that would have been brought back to Judah by a great conqueror; or of the grand buildings that Solomon is said to have built in Jerusalem and in the northern territories during the early tenth century BC. Buildings once credited to Solomon are now dated to the period of the later northern kingdom of Israel in the ninth century BC – the time of the Omride Dynasty. In fact there is no archaeological evidence that a united kingdom of Israel ever existed. Nor could there be, because Judah did not reach the degree of economic prosperity and cultural sophistication required as a base for expansionist policies until the seventh century BC.

Accordingly, Finkelstein and Silberman conclude that the Biblical stories about David and Solomon were part of "a mythical golden age" conjured up by King Josiah, who saw himself as "a new David ... intent on restoring the glory of his distant ancestors". They go on to say:

> These were theological hopes, not accurate historical portraits. They were a central element in a powerful seventh century vision of national renaissance that sought to bring scattered, war-weary people together, to prove to them that they had experienced a stirring history under the direct intervention of God. The glorious epic of the united monarchy was – like the stories of the patriarchs and the sages of the Exodus and conquest – a brilliant composition that wove together ancient heroic tales and legends into a coherent and persuasive prophesy for the people of Israel in the seventh century BCE.[52]

Once again it was a myth about the future and not a history about the past.

Once again I depart from our author's fascinating account by stressing that it was not just positive propaganda, but more importantly an appeal for supernatural assistance. The Biblical stories about David and Solomon were part of a brilliant attempt by Josiah and his priestly philosophers to both define a role for their strategic guardian YHWH and to enlist his support for a coming conflict that they could not possibly win without supernatural protection. In demythologizing the Hebrew Bible, Finkelstein and Silberman overlook the role of the supernatural strategic guardian in sustaining the Israelite *logos*.

Was the northern kingdom of Israel so sinful?

The "histories" of the two kingdoms of Israel and Judah are presented in 1 & 2 Kings, written from the point of view of the Judahites. In general, these histories are highly critical of Israel's material and territorial successes, particularly under the Omride Dynasty in the ninth century BC – the most impressive period of Israelite civilization in ancient history. They are also highly critical and disdainful about the strategic guardians that the Omrides called on for support in their worldly endeavors. In fact the Judahite priestly philosophers attempted to show that the collapse of the kingdom of Israel was due to their sinful materialist ways. As Finkelstein and Silberman conclude:

> The writer of the book of Kings ... wanted to deligitimize the Omrides and to show that the entire history of the northern kingdom had been one of sin that led to misery and inevitable destruction. The more Israel prospered in the past, the more scornful and negative he became about its kings ... Omri and his successors earned the hatred of the Bible precisely *because* they were so strong, precisely because they succeeded in transforming the northern kingdom into an important regional power that completely overshadowed the poor, marginal, rural-pastoral kingdom of Judah to the south.[53]

It was because of the combination of material success with the worship of strategic guardians from the entire Canaanite pantheon – rather than the exclusive worship of YHWH – that, according to the writer of Kings, Israel was utterly destroyed. And it was because Judah had followed the one true strategic guardian, YHWH, that it had survived and was now positioning itself to conquer the northern territories. The prophets Hosea and Amos also "expose" and condemn the "godless" (YHWH-less) materialism – or dynamic strategy – of the northern kingdom. Hosea (12: 1), for example, writes: "they make a bargain with Assyria, and oil is carried to Egypt", thereby condemning Israel's dynamic strategy. Needless to say King Josiah intended to pursue the very same materialist strategy, albeit with the assistance of YHWH alone.

Certainly the Judahite priestly philosophers were resentful of Israel's past successes as Finkelstein and Silberman claim. My long running "strategic pursuit" project has shown that the priestly philosophers in any society usually are falsifiers of reality, antistrategic in their sentiments, and resentful of both the strategists *and* the realist thinkers. Nevertheless, the real reason they contrasted the performance of the two kingdoms is that they wanted to explain why Judah would succeed where Israel had failed. Their conclusion was that Israel had failed because it embraced the usual Canaanite pantheon of strategic guardians, whereas Judah would succeed in similar economic and political circumstances because it had reformed its strategic ideology under King Josiah and intended to follow only YHWH, and to worship him only in the Temple of Jerusalem as he had directed.

Truth was a victim of the seventh-century Judahite priestly philosophers as they shaped their society's new strategic ideology. First, while they praised

Israel's leaders inversely according to their strategic success, they did so in order to develop an ideology that would ensure Judah's strategic success. This is clearly hypocritical. Second, it is not true that the Judahites were any more faithful to YHWH in the ninth and eighth centuries than the Israelites. The people of Judah followed the most popular gods in the Canaanite pantheon to ensure fertility and commercial prosperity. Archaeological evidence for the period includes clay figurines of various gods, incense altars, libation vessels, and offering stands throughout Judah.[54] There is even evidence that gods other than YHWH were worshipped in the Temple of Jerusalem. And the Bible itself (I Kings 14: 22–24) mentions pagan altars on "high places" and "under every green tree", together with cult practices, and even human sacrifice. The point is that pagan worship was widespread in the countryside of Judah and not limited to particular times and places as suggested in the Bible. In contrast, the cult of YHWH was largely, but not exclusively, restricted to the aristocracy in Jerusalem. "Sinfulness" – both materialism and pagan worship – was definitely not restricted to the northern kingdom of Israel.

Judahite religion

The transformation of Judahite strategic ideology into Jewish religion, or Judaism, occurred, I have suggested, during the period of the Return and the building of the Second Temple — from 516 to 437 BC. During this era the priestly philosophers of the Exile and Return – including Ezra from 458 BC and Nehemia from 445 BC – wrote and edited the Hebrew Bible in its final form. Their purpose was to turn a strategic ideology – that had failed to sustain an independent Judah – into a metaphysical mythology or religion – that would sustain the religious community of Yehud, a very small province of Persia. This was a community led by priestly philosophers from the Temple of Jerusalem. These religious leaders were committed not to strategic success, as their neighbors were, but to metaphysical success. The success of ideas rather than desires. And they could do so only because they had the protection of their Persian overlords.

These priestly philosophers had backed King Josiah in the late seventh century, largely because he supported their mythological reforms, but their commitment was always less to the king (as strategic leader) than to the king's covenant with YHWH (the personification of their metaphysical ideas). After the Babylonian conquest, and the strategic failure of Judah, the priestly philosophers shifted all their support from king to God – from strategic success in this world to spiritual success in the next. They did this by rewriting the Deuteronomic History so as to shift the covenant with YHWH from the extinct Davidic kings to the stateless "people of Israel" – or "chosen people" – and by inserting retrospective prophesies into this text. Hence, there were two version of the Deuteronomic History – before and after the Exile – one strategic and the other religious. Only the religious version was retained. This rewriting also extends to the Pentateuch where the Exodus story was made to reflect the Return from Babylon. While the world's superpowers could destroy Judah's strategic ambition, they could not eliminate its religious hopes.

In this way, the Jewish priestly philosophers were able, for the first time in history, to detach the mythology from the dynamic strategy of society. This is why the mythology, which we call religion, was able to survive even though the strategic *logos* of the Judahites no longer existed. A strategy-less mythology is also more transferable and amenable to metaphysical changes – as in the cases of Christianity and Islam – and to worldwide distribution. This is the explanation that eludes Finkelstein and Silberman when they, otherwise correctly, observe:

> While most other nations of the ancient Near East would have been content to accept the verdict of history, shrug their collective shoulders, and transfer their reverence to the god of the victor [Ahura Mazda], the later editors of the Deuteronomic History went back to the drawing board.[54]

But these authors underestimate the role of strategic frustration. It was the emergence of a strategy-less mythology, or religion, that also enabled Judaism to survive in the religious community when the Second Temple was destroyed.

The core of the religion of Judaism was "the Law" of the Torah (or Pentateuch), which first appeared in 622 BC as the scroll "discovered" during Temple renovations. This scroll, as discussed earlier, was an early draft of Deuteronomy, and was introduced to the public by Josiah through this fictional device. During the Second Temple period, 450 BC – 70 AD there were three main approaches to Judaism: the "priestly viewpoint", emphasizing "sanctification" – or maintenance of proper *order* as established at creation – in the Temple, with a focus on doctrine, law, and "a way of life"; the "sage viewpoint", emphasizing the sacred laws and rules needed to regulate the life of the community rather than the priests; and the prophet's viewpoint concerning the resolution of Judahite strategic failure by emphasizing restitution at the end of time. The Pharisees adopted the "sage viewpoint" by insisting that Jews live in their family homes like priests in the Temple. This required the practice of ritual purity domestically, with the home becoming the Temple, and the family table the altar. In this way the responsibility for "sanctification" – maintaining God's order embodied in creation – would be transferred from the Temple to the family.

As chance would have it, the Pharisaic approach was the key to the survival of Judaism when the Temple was destroyed by the Romans in AD 70 and Jerusalem was closed to the Jews. From this time, Rabbinic Judaism, based on the "Pharisaic method" stressed the importance of keeping the Law and the need for every Jew to do what only priests had formerly done. An early statement of Rabbinic Judaism – the Mishnah – appeared around 200 AD and stressed "sanctification ... understood as the correct arrangement of all things, each in its proper category, and each called by its rightful name, just as at creation".[56] In other words, the observance of the Law contained in the Torah –

the outcome of the covenant between God and the chosen people of Israel – was meant to sustain the ordered world that God had created out of primeval chaos. In the words of Jacob Neusner, Distinguished Research Professor of Religious Studies, University of South Florida:

> Standing in contrast with the world to which it speaks, the Mishnah's message is one of small achievements and modest hope intended to defy a world of large disorders and immodest demands. It offers this message to an Israelite world that could not shape affairs in any important ways and speaks to people who by no means willed the way things were. The Mishnah lays down a practical judgement on and in favor of a people who must go forth with the imagination and will to reshape their reality, regain a system, and establish an order upon which trustworthy existence is to be built.[57]

The Jews, like people in all other communities, were driven to generate order out of chaos so as to survive and prosper. But, increasingly after the destruction of Judah and particularly after the destruction of the Second Temple, they attempted to do so by creating a *static* metaphysical system to replace the failed *dynamic* strategic system. They had finally accepted that they could not create and sustain a viable strategic society on the borderlands of the superpowers, and opted instead for the fashioning of a religious community based on the extended family. It was this micro approach to survival and prosperity that enabled Judaism to survive in the face of concerted state opposition after the Roman emperor Constantine I adopted Christianity as his strategic ideology in AD 312, and subsequently established it as the strategic ideology and official religion of the Mediterranean world.

It should be realized that Mishnah Judaism was an antistrategic system, as it was based on a set of metaphysical laws (rather than strategic laws) that, if implemented as a sociopolitical system, would have undermined the material success of society. Using slightly different language, Jacob Neusner writes:

> Since the Pentateuchal face of Judaism began as a paradigm, not a set of actual events, the conclusions generated by the paradigm, derived not from reflection on things that happened but from the logic of the paradigm ... This self-generating, self-renewing paradigm formed the self-fulfilling prophecy that all Judaisms have offered as the generative tension [resentment in the myth of exile] and critical symbolic structure of their systems.[58]

This "paradigm" or, in my own language, metaphysical mythology, was the product of Israelite priestly philosophers who deliberately distorted their history and created a mythological structure that obeyed its own metaphysical laws rather than the strategic laws under which the rest of the world operated.

When subsequent Israelite kingdoms were formed in the ancient world – the Hasmonean kingdom from 142–63 BC, the kingdom of Herod the Great from 40–4 BC – they were run on strategic rather than metaphysical lines, with a clear distinction being maintained between political and religious leadership. In the modern world the Zionists established the state of Israel in

1948 as a democratic republic, not a Jewish theocracy. A theocracy based on the laws of the Torah would have quickly failed. The reason the modern state of Israel has been able to succeed where its ancient counterpart failed is that a technological paradigm shift has occurred, which has not only transformed the foundations of the strategic pursuit but also caused a relocation of the world's geopolitical center. With the technological paradigm shift known as the Industrial Revolution – which occurred in Western Europe, not in the Fertile Crescent – global economic and political power, which became dependent upon technological change, shifted from East to West. Palestine was no longer in the borderlands between the global superpowers, but rather in a Third-World backwater. Also in the modern era economic and political power depends not on the natural agricultural advantage possessed by ancient riverine powers – a natural advantage not possessed by the Canaanites – but on the skilful employment of the technological strategy. When the Zionists established a modern state in Palestine, they did so with the technology and the political support of the Western superpowers.

In the end, Israel was able to take its place among the strategic nations of the world not through observance of the Law of the Torah, or the coming of the Messiah in whom many generations of Jews had placed their faith, but through the fortuitous outcome of global strategic dynamics. Yet it was the Law that sustained the cultural identity of the Jews, which, in turn, enabled them after 2,500 years to create the strategic society that King Josiah of Judah had dreamed about. If, in the end, the Jews were the unintended beneficiaries of the strategic guardians of the West — the Christian gods — these guardians had their origins in Josiah's strategic dreams.

Chapter 5
Triumph of the One God
II: Christianity and Islam

The idea that metaphysical mythology or religion – the triumph of the One God – is forged in the furnace of superpower oppression, is the theme in both Chapter 4 and Chapter 5. And the mechanism by which this transformation takes place is **strategic frustration** – a form of individual and community neurosis generated by a persistent failure to achieve or sustain strategic success. Chapter 4 is concerned with the first phase of this process – the response of elite priestly philosophers from the Temple of Jerusalem in the fundamentalist south – that failed to effectively resolve strategic frustration on the part of the Israelites. And Chapter 5 deals with its second phase – the response of the charismatic peasant sage in the multicultural north – which inadvertently provided the materialist ideology for ultimate **strategic success** in the West.

The first part of the chapter provides an outline of the fluctuating fortunes of Palestine from the return from the Exile (538 BC) until the Roman–Jewish war (AD 66–73), in order to show how this exacerbated the existing problem of strategic frustration. In the first century AD there were a number of local responses to this psychic-societal problem, including: "messianic claimants", such as the Maccabees, organizing military uprisings; apocalyptic prophets appealing to YHWH to reenact the old Moses/Joshua model of crossing the Jordan into the Promised Land and conquering the hostile cities of Canaan; eccentrics joining groups of cynics and rejecting all material values; and charismatic sages building new communities based on the radical idea of the emergence of the Kingdom of God in the here and now. Jesus of Nazareth — the focus of the first part of the chapter — was a charismatic sage who chose the latter approach at a time of Roman domination. We also see how, in the following two centuries, the Jesus movement was transformed into a nonstrategic religious community that initially suffered state persecution, but later was surprisingly supported by Emperor Constantine, who adopted Christianity as the strategic ideology of an empire in long-term decline. And we examine the rise and fall of this strategic ideology in the Western world from the collapse of Rome to the rise of the West. In the second part of the chapter the rise and fall of Islam as a strategic ideology, as well as a religion, is also examined.

THE RISE AND FALL OF CHRISTIANITY

The argument in the first part of the chapter is that the origins and development of Christianity were outcomes of a series of responses to the changing nature of the strategic pursuit in the Western world. For this purpose it is necessary to briefly trace out the fluctuating strategic fortunes of Palestine and the West, including Rome and Western Europe. These fluctuating strategic fortunes provided the forcing ground for the emergence and development of Christianity, initially as religion but, later, also as strategic ideology. Our focus here is on the superpowers in Palestine from the Exile to the Roman–Jewish war, the last days of the Roman empire, and the rise of Western Europe from the fifth to the twenty-first centuries.

The forcing grounds for Christianity

Palestine and the superpowers, sixth century BC to first century AD
The emergence of Christianity, initially as a disaffected offshoot of Judaism, was the outcome of the very forces that had led to the Jewish reinvention of religion – the outcome of strategic frustration resulting from superpowers oppression of the Palestinians. From the sixth century BC to the first century AD, Palestine suffered the age-old frustration of long periods of superpower domination punctuated by short periods of self-rule. Consequently, Palestinian societies were not able to generate their own pattern of strategic development as did Egypt, Mesopotamia, Greece, or Rome. Throughout the era of colonial domination, Palestinians never lost their intense desire for political independence, which was needed to pursue their own dynamic strategies of conquest and commerce. But their successes were tantalizingly brief and generated considerable strategic frustration. From this pressure of continuous strategic frustration arose both individual and societal neurosis – a psychological condition examined in detail in my recent book *The Selfcreating Mind* (2006) – and led to a search for nonstrategic alternatives. This was a search for a way out of this eternal cycle of strategic promise followed quickly by crushing strategic failure.

After returning from Exile in Babylon from 538 BC, the Judahites became colonials in the mighty Persian empire. Their consolation, as we have seen, was that they were encouraged to take their former cultic treasures with them to rebuild in Jerusalem the Temple dedicated to YHWH. They may not have been able to reconstruct their former independent kingdom – their strategic *logos* – but they were able to form a religious community as their priestly philosophers had successfully divorced their mythology from their former strategic ambitions. This was a state of affairs that might have continued indefinitely had not Alexander the Great destroyed the Persian empire in 333 BC. For a generation, Palestine came under direct Macedonian rule and then, from 301 BC, it was controlled by Ptolemaic Egypt, which was ruled by a Greek aristocracy. For almost two centuries, Palestine was absorbed into an international Hellenic culture resulting in the construction of many Greek-style cities; the adoption of the Greek language, customs and gods; and the influx of Greek migrants.

Yet, it was not long before Palestine reverted to being the battleground between the Egyptian and Mesopotamian superpowers, despite the Macedonian origins of their rulers – the Ptolomies in the south and the Seleucids in the north-east. Gradually the Seleucids forced their way from Mesopotamia into Syria, Turkey and, by 200 BC, all of Palestine. While the Seleucids maintained the Hellenic culture of Palestine, they became increasingly oppressive – raising taxes and plundering indigenous temples, including that in Jerusalem – as they came under increasing military pressure from Rome in the west, Parthia in the east, and Egypt in the south. Not surprisingly, this predatory behavior generated growing unrest among the indigenous Palestinians.

The final straw was an attempt by Antiochus IV, Epiphanes of Seleucia to reverse his empire's military defeats by unifying all cultures in the worship of a single strategic guardian, Olympian Zeus, father of all the gods who was thought to determine the outcome of battles. To this end, the Temple of Jerusalem was forcibly converted into a Hellenistic cult center, complete with Greek-style altar, devoted to the worship of Zeus. The demoted Jewish god YHWH – the former military god of the House of David – was merely identified with the Greek god Zeus.

This intolerable situation incited the revolt of the Hasmons, a priestly family, in 167 BC. Following a guerilla war, Judas Maccabees – son of the rebellious priest Mattathias – retook Jerusalem, cleansed the Temple, and rededicated it to YHWH. The internationally besieged and weakened Seleucids were finally driven out of Judah in 141 BC and, for the first time since 586 BC, an independent Judahite kingdom was established under the Hasmonaen dynasty. Needless to say, the Maccabees were extremely fortunate that their rebellion occurred at a time when the Seleucid empire was on the brink of disintegration.

Through conquest, the small Hasmonean kingdom continued to expand steadily until, just prior to the reign of Alexander Jannaeus (103–76 BC), it included all the lands of Palestine. This was the first time in history – as opposed to Biblical mythology – that the Judahites had ruled over all of Palestine. But, as usual, Jewish independence on any scale was not to last long. In 63 BC, just 78 ears after Judah had secured its independence, the Romans under Pompey reduced Palestine to its former colonial status.

Pompey reduced the Hasmonean kingdom to the territories of Judaea, Galilee, and part of Idumaea (south of Judaea), while the Hasmonean prince, Hyrcanus II (63–40 BC) was made Ethnarch and high priest (but not king). The real power in Palestine was invested in Antipater, who was of Idumaean origin (recent converts to Judaism). As a reward for supporting Julius Caesar when Pompey was assassinated by Ptolemy in Egypt, Antipater was made procurator of Judaea, and he in turn appointed his sons Phasael and Herod as governors of Jerusalem and Galilee respectively. While the Jews lost their recently acquired strategic power, they were at least granted religious freedom.

Civil war in the Roman world followed the assassination of Caesar in

44 BC, but with the victory of Antony and Octavian, Herod was proclaimed king of Judaea in 40 BC – owing to the death of Antipater from poison three years earlier – by the Roman senate. Even before beginning his rule, Herod the Great (40–4 BC) had to dispose of his nephew Antigonus, who had gained the support of a Parthian army. Then, after a struggle for control of the Roman empire between Octavian and Antony, which was finally settled by the Battle of Actium in 31 BC, Octavian, now Augustus, confirmed Herod's kingship over most of Palestine.

Herod was an able yet ruthless king, who retained power by enthusiastically supporting the Roman leadership. He was also an energetic builder of grand public buildings throughout Palestine, an activity that imposed a heavy fiscal burden on his subjects. While Herod lavishly rebuilt the Temple of Jerusalem, he also built grand pagan temples in other Judaean cities. With Herod's death in 4 BC, considerable social unrest emerged, which led Rome to depose his successor and reduce Judaea to a mere province of Rome, governed by a Roman prefect installed in the Herodian part of Caesarea. So, the strategic hopes of the Jews, which were briefly raised by the death of Herod – a Roman puppet – and recent memories of Hasmonean rule, were crushed once again by Roman power. Once again the residents of Palestine suffered an extreme degree of strategic frustration. This tense and difficult sociopolitical climate was a fertile breeding ground for charismatic leaders, who attempted to lead the people out of strategic frustration. Jesus of Nazareth, as we shall see, was one of those sages. But before exploring this theme we need to outline the changing nature of the Roman world and the western kingdoms that replaced it.

The last days of the Roman empire

It was the impending fall of the Roman empire that provided Christianity with the possibility of transforming itself from the religion of the strategically dispossessed to the strategic ideology of the Western world. The dynamic pathway of Rome's unfolding conquest strategy is charted in Figure 5.1, where we see the expanding territory of Rome from 260 BC to AD 476 as the army – the major strategic instrument of both the republic and the empire – fought its way throughout the Italian peninsula, around the Mediterranean, and into Asia minor, the Middle East, and Europe. All in an effort to increase their wealth and prosperity (Snooks 1997: ch. 6).

Roman territorial expansion was achieved via four great steps in time: the early second century BC; the late second century BC; the second half of the first century BC; and the first century AD. Each major phase of conquest was followed by a period of consolidation during which the gains made were digested and the institutional structure of society was extended to provide a basis for the next major conquest initiative. Throughout this long period of expansion through conquest, the Roman gods of war smiled on the people of Rome, who repaid their strategic guardians by investing heavily in temples and the associated priesthood. These Roman gods – discussed in my *The Ephemeral Civilization* (1997) – owed much to those in the Greek world.[1] Interestingly these Graeco-Roman gods had little more than literary influences on the subsequent rise of the West and the future of humanity. For this reason they are not discussed in this book.

Figure 5.1 **Roman territorial expansion, 300 BC – AD 1200**

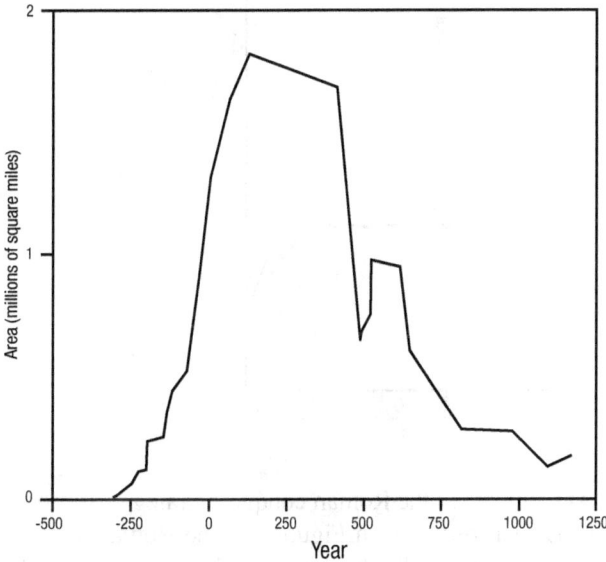

Source: Snooks 1997:138

In absolute terms, these territorial steps got bigger as the Roman conquest strategy unfolded; yet in relative terms they actually became smaller. This can be seen in Figure 5.2, which shows the *rate* of change of empire territory over the period of the rise of Rome to the collapse of the western half of the empire. We see that the rates of expansion rose progressively from 510 BC to 190 BC, but that they declined gradually thereafter, until ultimate collapse in the early fifth century BC. This shows, as I have argued in *The Ephemeral Civilization*, that the years around 190 BC witnessed the exhaustion of Rome's conquest strategy and the replacement of *increasing* with *decreasing* strategic returns.

Nonetheless, for over seven centuries, between 340 BC and AD 420, Rome's rate of expansion due to conquest was about 2% p.a.; which compares more than favorably with the long-run rate of expansion of the modern world measured by real GDP. For example, real GDP for England over the six centuries to AD 1700 was 0.5% p.a.; and for the world economy over the five centuries to the end of the twentieth century it was 1.0% p.a.[2] And there were shorter periods when the rate of Roman expansion was much greater than rates that the modern world has been able to achieve (except in catch-up mode like modern China). Can there be any doubt that Rome's strategic guardians had more than repaid the people's faith in them. The Roman gods were able to sustain the viability of the strategic *logos* of Rome for many centuries.

Figure 5.2 **Economic fluctuations in the Roman empire, 300 BC – AD 470**

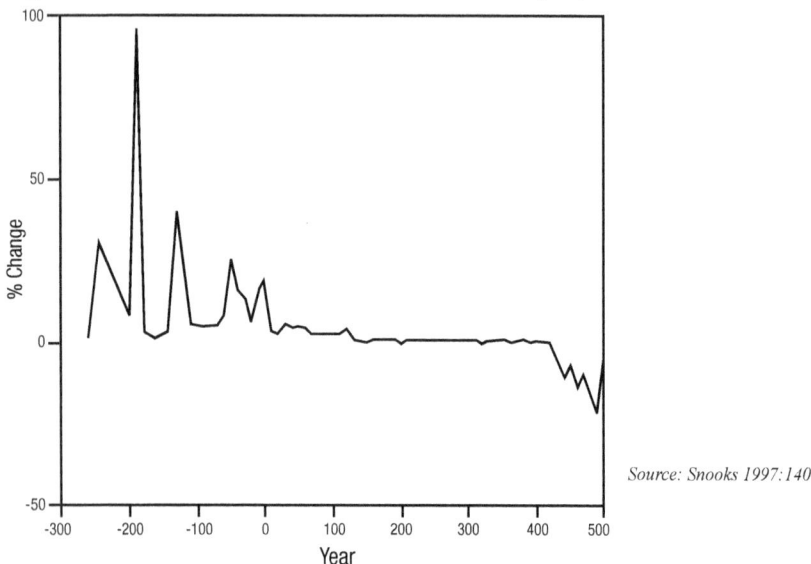

Source: Snooks 1997:140

Until, that is, about AD 190, when the Roman conquest strategy had finally exhausted itself. As can be seen reflected in Figure 5.2, the Roman strategic *logos*, which began with great energy, finally found itself spent by the close of the second century AD. If this graph were the record of a human heartbeat, the attending physician would have concluded that by AD 190 the patient was on the point of expiring. We can say the same about the Roman strategic *logos*, which from that time was plugged into an artificial life-support system. Clearly the old strategic guardians of conquest had abandoned Rome. In these circumstances it is not surprising that the state and individual citizens began searching for a new strategic guardian. As we shall see, they found one in the new god of the Christians. But, as is clear from Figure 5.2, this was no more than a artificial life-support system that was unable to revive the strategic *logos* of Rome, which finally expired in the fifth century AD.

Western Europe, 500–2001

In the millennium-and-a-half following the collapse of Rome, Western Europe was transformed from a backwater into the powerhouse of the global economy. Only a brief outline of this remarkable transformation, together with the dynamic mechanism by which it was achieved, can be provided here. Nevertheless this is essential if we are to understand the rise and fall of Christianity.

A rough outline of the development of Western Europe is provided by population estimates presented in Figure 5.3. Population grew from the time of the birth of Jesus of Nazareth until the exhaustion of Rome's conquest strategy in the late second century. As the Roman empire turned in on itself, the population of Western Europe fell steadily, reaching its lowest point in the sixth century. Thereafter, with the expansion, through conquest, of the Frankish kingdom — and, under Charlemagne (742–814), of the Frankish empire — population began to expand once more. From about 1000, the rate of population expansion began to accelerate, owing to the growing territories and wealth of the conquest kingdoms of Western Europe, including France, Germany (plus northern Italy), England, Denmark, and Sweden.[3]

Figure 5.3 **Western European population levels, 0–2003 AD ('000)**

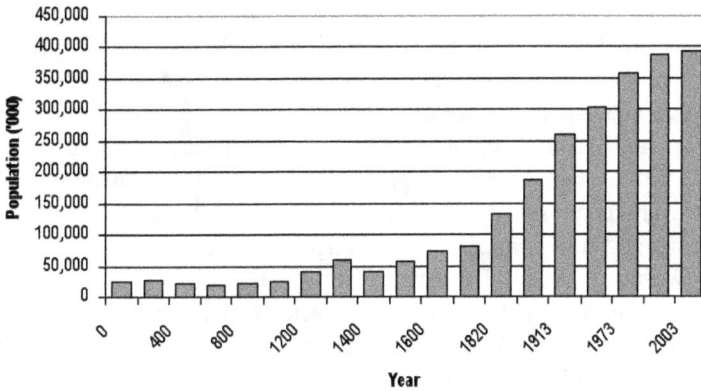

Source: Drawn from data in Maddison (2003:42–45).

A population peak was reached around 1300 followed by a significant decline during the thirteenth and fourteenth centuries, owing to the devastating impact of plague, which wiped out a third to a half of the population of the worst affected regions. The exhaustion of the old conquest strategy – after prevailing for about three centuries – in the most advanced parts of Europe, also played a role in economic stagnation and decline. Population growth resumed after 1500, owing to the prosperity generated by the new commerce strategies of England, the Low Countries, and parts of Germany. And it increased after 1700 as the commerce strategy became more widely adopted, and as Britain pioneered the Industrial Revolution from the 1780s.

Needless to say, the geographical distribution of the West European population changed considerably over the two millennia following the birth of Jesus.[4] At the beginning of this period, the region with the largest population was, of course, Italy with about 28% of the total, followed by France with 20%, Germany 12%, and Britain merely 3%. By 2001, the largest country was Germany (21.0%) followed by Britain (15.2%), France (15.2%) and Italy (14.8%) which had halved over the two millennia. In 1600, at the end of the conquest phase (in the most advanced societies at least), France had the largest population (25%), followed by Germany (22%), Italy (18%) and Britain (8%). And in 1913, following the unfolding of the commerce and industrial-technological strategies, the order changed to Germany (24.9%), Britain (17.5%), France (15.9%) and Italy (14.3%). Clearly, while the strategic guardians of conquest favored France and Germany, the gods of commerce and technology favored Britain and Germany.

The dynamic-strategy theory tells us that the functional character of a society's institutions and organizations – including religion – are determined and driven by the type of dynamic strategy pursued. The causal mechanism operates through strategic demand, which changes as the dynamic strategy unfolds. For Western Europe during the past two millennia, the overall **strategic sequence** has been conquest → commerce → industrial technological change. This underlying mechanism, which is driven by **strategic desire**, involves the adoption, exploitation, exhaustion and replacement of dynamic strategies. It also takes place against, and interacts with, a background of *paradigmatic* exploitation, exhaustion and replacement – as seen in the unfolding of the Neolithic/agricultural technological paradigm and its replacement by the modern/industrial technological paradigm –discussed in Chapter 11. Needless to say, the timing and significance of this strategic sequence varied from region to region in Western Europe. To illustrate how it operated, I will focus on England, which was the most effective exponent of this strategic sequence, increasing its share of total Western European population from 3% to 17.5% over the period AD 1 to 1913.

The material outcomes England was able to achieve by exploiting the strategic sequence of conquest → commerce → technological change for the period 1000 to 2000 are shown graphically in Figure 5.4. This English strategic sequence generated the fairly typical great waves of economic change of about 300 years in duration: 1000 to 1300; 1480 to 1750; and 1760s to beyond 2000. Each of these great waves was generated by a very different dynamic strategy – the first by conquest, the second by commerce, and the third by technological change. Each of these surging waves is separated from the others by periods of downturn and stagnation, during which England desperately searched for a replacement dynamic strategy. A detailed analysis of this strategic sequence and its transforming sociopolitical impact on England can be found in my book *The Ephemeral Civilization* (1997).[5]

Of interest here are the implications of the strategic sequence of conquest → commerce → technological change for the institutional and organizational structure – particularly of a religious nature – of Western Europe. Each dynamic strategy generated a demand for very specific organizations (social networks) and institutions (social rules). In general terms, as far as organizations are concerned, a conquest society requires both a military system (armed forces, engineering, logistics) and an imperial organization; while a commerce society needs a commercial system (trading networks; finance, insurance, and shipping organizations), a state navy, and a foreign service; and a technological society requires a research establishment (universities, scientific bodies, research funding), an industrial system (factory organizations, multinational corporations), a commercial system, and a state bureaucracy. And as far as institutions are concerned, a conquest society requires a highly centralized political system (monarchy, dictatorship, or oligarchy), a centralized economic system (feudal, totalitarian), a hierarchical legal system, state-controlled systems of factor and commodity exchange, elite property rights, and elite codes of conduct. A commerce society needs a political system controlled by the merchant elite, with a state-controlled market system, middle-class-dominated legal system, regulated commodity and factor markets, and property rights biased towards the growing middle classes. And a technological society demands democratic political institutions, a free market system, free commodity and factor markets, a universal legal system, and universal property rights.

Figure 5.4 **The strategic sequence of conquest → commerce → technological change, England 1000–2000**

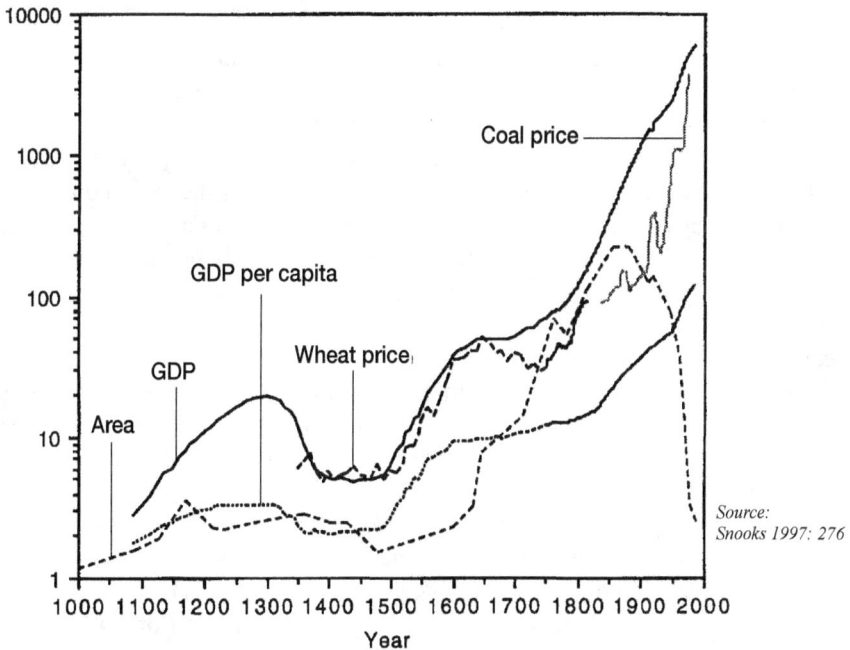

Source:
Snooks 1997: 276

The only reason that most intellectuals have been able to convince themselves that democracy is a key component of the "evolution" of complex systems is that over the past millennium in Western Europe the strategic sequence has been precisely conquest → commerce → technological change. As it turns out, this very particular sequence is unique in history. It only occurred because the exhaustion of England's commerce strategy in the mid-eighteenth century coincided with the exhaustion of the neolithic (agricultural) technological paradigm. In *all* other periods of history, where the sequence began with conquest → commerce, it ended by reverting back to conquest. Hence, the typical sequence was conquest → commerce → conquest. This had a predictable impact on institutional and organizational change. As conquest was replaced with commerce, there was a shift to more democratic institutions; but as commerce was replaced with conquest (as the neolithic paradigm was far from exhausted) there was a shift back to authoritarian institutions. Social institutions, therefore, do *not* evolve according to some sort of Darwinian mechanism as most scholars (such as Doug North) believe. This is also the case with religious ideology, institutions, and organizations.

What then are the implications of this dynamic mechanism for religion in general and Christianity in particular? In a conquest society the chief deities will be authoritarian and war-like. The strategic leaders will appeal to the Old Testament god YHWH rather than to the sage and teacher Jesus of Nazareth. Like the political system, the church will be ruled by the wealthy elite (who are all male), its key rituals will be kept a secret from ordinary citizens, and its ceremonies may even be imposed upon the population in an unknown language (such as Latin or Coptic). In a commerce society the deities will be more benign, even benevolent, yet still majestic. The European model is that of the risen Christ. The church is more likely to be open to the participation of a wider proportion of the population, its rituals will be widely accessible to the middle classes, and services will be conducted in the vernacular by a minister (always male) who is closer to his community than priests of the past. Finally, in an industrial-technological society, the deity will be more avuncular, with the model being that of Jesus as sage and teacher. The nature of church participation no longer depends upon socioeconomic status, and services are reduced to forms of pleasurable and uplifting entertainment where the doctrinal content is reduced to a bare minimum. Increasingly in this system, the ministers and priests (except in the Roman Catholic Church) have become women. It should be noted, however, that this change in religious ideas and practices is not evolutionary in nature, because a reversal of dynamic strategy from commerce to conquest would cause a return to more hierarchical, elitist, and male-dominated institutions; and to gods that are more authoritarian and war-like.

Only by understanding this underlying dynamic mechanism of the strategic *logos* can we make any sense of the emergence, rise, and fall of Christianity. The *logos* is the hidden key to it all.

The origins of Christianity

The origins of Christianity are to be found in the same type of conditions that generated Judaism – a determination of the superpowers of the ancient world to control the crossroad of commerce know as the Levant. For four millennia the superpowers – including the Egyptians, Sumerians, Babylonians, Hittites,

Assyrians, Persians, Greeks, and Romans – struggled against each other and the local societies for control of the lands at the eastern end of the Mediterranean. We have seen how there were rare and very brief intervals between this constant power play, when ambitious locals managed to control the Levant themselves, but that they were always savagely swept aside. For local populations these four millennia constituted an unending era of massive strategic failure, which generated **strategic frustration** – individual and societal neurosis. The rare and brief periods of strategic success only exacerbated this condition.

After four millennia of strategic failure and strategic frustration, the indigenous people of Palestine were receptive in the extreme to charismatic sages, teachers, healers, messiahs, apocalyptic prophets, even bandit leaders, who could offer a solution to the destructive effects arising from this problem. Strategic frustration induced deep depression in many people, who also experienced a loss of psychic energy, purpose, and direction in life – some to the point where they seemed to be possessed by "evil spirits". In these circumstances the Temple culture of the Sadducees and the purity laws of the Pharisees offered little relief. Judaism was the religion of the educated elite who achieved accommodation with the imperialists. But it provided little consolation for the majority of the Palestinians in the face of strategic frustration. It merely offered restitution at the end of time, which seemed no closer under the Romans than it had under the Egyptians, Assyrians, Babylonians or Persians. What the people of Palestine badly wanted was psychic relief in the here and now, not in a distant and uncertain future. As we shall see, many appeared to find this relief from strategic frustration initially in the Jesus movement and, later in Christianity.

The early Jesus movement

What was it about Jesus of Nazareth and his teachings that ordinary Palestinian people found so helpful in these difficult times? The answer to this question has only become clear since the 1980s with the discovery of the "lost gospel" – called the Q text – of the early Jesus movement. This gospel consists of about 250 sayings attributed to Jesus. While most of these sayings were composed by his followers during the first generation or so after their teacher's death, about 10 percent are thought to be the actual sayings of Jesus. The Q gospel, therefore, is considered representative of the teachings of Jesus in Galilee.

Where was the lost gospel found? It was found embedded in the most visible, but overlooked, of places – the well-known gospels according to Matthew and Luke in the Christian New Testament. The history of its discovery is a fascinating story, well-told by Burton Mack in his book *The Lost Gospel: the Book of Q and Christian Origins* (1994).

It has long been hypothesized – since the 1830s in fact – that Mark's history was the first narrative gospel to be written (in the 70s of the first century AD), and that both Matthew (in the 80s) and Luke (early second century) independently wrote their more inclusive gospels using both Mark and very similar copies of sayings attributed to Jesus. Hence, by comparing the gospels of Matthew and Luke, it was possible to isolate a body of Jesus sayings that amounted to at least 225 verses. This is the text of the early Jesus movement now known as Q, an abbreviation of the German word "Quelle", meaning "source". This hypothesis was successfully tested by a number of critical scholars in the nineteenth and twentieth centuries, and by the 1920s had "largely been accepted by scholars in the liberal tradition".[6] Surprisingly, it took another fifty years before scholars turned to Q as the earliest and best evidence of the early Jesus movement, which predates "Christianity".

Why did it take so long for Q to be recognized for what it really is? Largely because this material was regarded as a collection of isolated sayings, rather than a "book of instructions with its own history, much less a charter for a Jesus movement that did not have a narrative gospel".[7] Also, access to these sayings as a systematic body of thought required comparing and contrasting two narrative gospels that employed these aphorisms – brief statements of principle – in a different order and in different contexts. Between the 1920s and 1970s, however, these aphorisms were subjected to both micro and macro textual criticism, which, during the last quarter of the twentieth century, finally led to their study as a cultural – not just a religious – phenomenon. By the 1990s, therefore, Biblical scholars had placed their studies within the wider human sciences, which viewed Christianity as a major force in Western civilization. Also by the end of the twentieth century, Q, together with other early Christian documents (such as the Gospel of Thomas), was seen as an important source for cultural studies. This provided a greater urgency for the reconstruction of Q as a text of the early Jesus movement.

In 1988 John Kloppenborg published a "parallel" text (from Matthew and Luke), and in 1993 Burton Mack published a "unified" text. The Mack text has also been divided into three parts, reflecting the main stages in the development of the Jesus movement, from the 20s to the 70s of the first century AD: Q^1 includes the "wisdom sayings" of Jesus (6/5 BC – AD 30/33) and those attributed to Jesus by his earliest followers; Q^2 includes the announcement of divine judgment; and Q^3 includes material about the "son of God" added during and immediately after the Roman Jewish war (AD 66–73).

The other document that provides information about the earliest phases of the Jesus movement is the Gospel of Thomas. Rather than being discovered in the most published book in the world, the Gospel of Thomas was excavated in upper Egypt near the modern city of Nag Hammadi in December 1945.[8] It was part of a collection of manuscripts written in Coptic and known now as the Nag Hammadi library. The Gospel of Thomas claims to be the sayings of Jesus that were recorded by Judas Thomas the Twin. The text is very similar to Q, and approximately 35 percent of the Thomas sayings can be found there. This suggests that documents containing sayings attributed to Jesus were widespread between the death of Jesus (AD 30–33) and the appearance of the narrative gospels that displaced them in the last quarter of the first century AD.

The fact that the Thomas gospel does not include the apocalyptic material in Q^2 – apart from a reference to the apocalyptic prophet John the Baptist – leads some to conclude that the "Thomas people" disagreed with the "Q people" and their idea of an apocalyptic Jesus associated with future divine judgment, and hence decided to disassociate themselves from the mainstream Q movement.[9] The Thomas people, therefore, continued to think of Jesus as he had been during his ministry – a sage-teacher rather than an apocalyptic prophet. This suggests that the Thomas people, and their handbook of instructions, were associated with the earliest phases (Q^1) of the Jesus movement.

To discover why ordinary Palestinians found the teachings of Jesus to be a solution to the problem of strategic frustration, we need to examine the nature of the sayings in both Q and the Gospel of Thomas. Burton Mack's division of Q into three layers is useful for this purpose. The first layer, or Q^1, consists of seven clusters or 21 blocks of sayings concerning: Jesus' teaching (7 blocks); instructions for the Jesus movement (2 blocks); confidence in the Father's care (2); on anxiety and speaking out (2); on personal goods (3); parables of the kingdom (1); and the true followers of Jesus (4).

These sayings are all aphorisms (or short pithy statements) taking the form of either maxims (general truths) or imperatives (instructions or commands). The maxims – such as, "life is more than food" – constitute a critique of the existing, or **strategic,** society but are not directives about changing it. In other words, the critique is **nonstrategic** rather than **antistrategic.** Burton Mack summarizes this critique as follows:

> Overall, the message of these sayings is that customary pretensions are hollow. Claim to superior status based on such things as wealth, learning, possessions, secrets, rank, and power is exposed as questionable if not ridiculous. The perspective is that of the underdog, and the vision is that of those who can see through the emptiness ... There is no sign of hostility toward those caught in the usual binds, and there is no suggestion of a program to change the system that supports questionable values ... [but] implicit in the critique is the assumption that there must be a better way to live.
>
> The better way is not spelled out in these aphorisms. One has only the sense that simplicity is better than pretension, that realistic assessment is a better guide than status, and that life would be more rewarding if lived another way. In general it is clear that sympathies lie with the poor, the least, the humble, the servant, and those consigned to positions without privilege, more than with their social opposites.[10]

These early maxims imputed to Jesus, constitute a critique of strategic society, its successes, and its failures in early to mid-first century Palestine, together with the suggestion that a nonstrategic alternative (i.e. opting out of the mainstream strategic society) would be better. While it supports those who have not fared well in strategic (materialist) society, it does not attack those who have prospered. These maxims, in other words, are not antistrategic.

But what of the "imperatives" in Q[1] and the Gospel of Thomas? These imperatives – which take the form "love your enemies", "judge not and be not judged" – are suggestions about how to live a better life in the Roman province of the time. The message is: live a simple, unencumbered life; be cautious but courageous; give when asked and ask when in need; respond without aggression to the aggression of others; and don't be consumed by anxiety or ill-feeling.

What was the philosophical basis for this critique of Roman strategic society and suggestions of how to live within it? Some scholars have claimed that Jesus was influenced by the Greek school of Cynics, who were critics of conventional values for a thousand years between the fifth century BC and the sixth century AD.[11] To support this hypothesis they point to the Cynic-like sayings of Jesus, and to the fact that Jesus and his followers in Galilee were in close proximity to Hellenized cities that were widely known to be inhabited by some famous Cynics. Mack, for example, tells us:

> The crisp sayings of Jesus in Q[1] show that his followers thought of him as a Cynic-like sage. Cynics were known for begging, voluntary poverty, renunciation of needs, severance of family ties, fearless and carefree attitudes, and troublesome public behavior. Standard themes in Cynic discourse included a critique of riches, pretension, and hypocrisy, just as in Q[1]. The Cynic style of speech was distinctly aphoristic, as is that in Q[1]. And Cynics were schooled in such topics as handling reproach, nonretaliation, and authenticity in following their vocation, matters at the forefront of Jesus' instruction in Q[1].[12]

No doubt Jesus and his early followers were familiar with the Cynics in the larger Palestinian cities, and no doubt there are some points of similarity between these two groups, but there are also some important differences. What the Jesus movement and the Cynics have in common is their critique of strategic society, which they both regarded as oppressive and morally bankrupt. They both detail the characteristics of strategic society that they regard as unattractive and demeaning. And by rejecting or inverting these features they both attempt to outline a more ethical and meaningful lifestyle. There is nothing uniquely Cynic-al about this procedure, which has been pursued widely through time and history by dissident thinkers. It can be seen, for example, in Buddhism in the Orient, in the Puritan settlements in North America, in various utopian colonies (by Germans and Australians) in South America, in the counter-culture movement in the Western world in the 1960s, and various environmental groups in the West ever since.

There are two major characteristics of the early Jesus movement that distinguish it from the Cynics – their motivation and their ultimate objective. The sage and teacher, Jesus of Nazareth, attracted a mass following that the Cynics were never able to achieve, because he was able to offer a healing solution to the psychic angst and mental disorders created by the intense strategic frustration of millennia of crushing colonial oppression. This geopolitical experience also generated a driving force in the Jesus movement that was lacking in the Cynics' philosophy.

Jesus, a Galilean Jew, was motivated by the need to resolve the problem of endemic strategic failure. He attempted to do this by showing the people of Palestine – both Jew and Gentile – how, in the midst of colonial oppression and strategic deprivation, they could construct an alternative *nonstrategic* community. In contrast, the Cynics, being part of the ruling Hellenistic culture, were motivated not by strategic failure but by disgust at the excesses of strategic success. Their objective was not to establish an alternative nonstrategic community but to act as an *antistrategic* constraint on the excesses of their materialistic culture. Hence, we must reject Mack's conclusion that "the Jesus movement began as a home-grown variety of Cynicism".[13]

Interestingly, as John Crossan points out, one of the set of Jesus' imperatives on dress and remuneration shows that he was aware of the Cynics and wanted to distinguish himself and his followers from them. Here I quote from the "unified" Book of Q edited by Mack.

> Go. Look, I send you out as lambs among wolves.
> Do not carry money, or bag, or sandals, or staff;
> and do not greet anyone on the road …
> And stay in the same house, eating and drinking
> whatever they provide, for the worker deserves his wages.
> Do not go from house to house.[14]

Here the followers of Jesus are being instructed to give their teaching and healing services in exchange for whatever hospitality a household could provide. They should, Jesus implied, lead a community-dependent lifestyle. Cynics on the other hand were fiercely independent and self-sufficient, as symbolized by their widely recognized uniform of coarse cloak, bag (or wallet), and staff. Crossan quotes the following from *Pseudo-Diogenes*, a collection of letters fictionally attributed to Diogenes, the founder of Cynicism:

> [To Hicetas] do not be upset, Father, that I am called a dog and put on a double, coarse cloak, carry a wallet [or bag] over my shoulders, and have a staff in my hand … living as I do, not in conformity with popular opinions but according to nature, free under Zeus.[15]

Similar references to bag and staff appear regularly in Cynical literature.

Hence, it seems quite clear that Jesus' instruction – *not* to carry money, bag, sandels, or staff – is to contrast his objectives with those of the Cynics. Indeed, Crossan concludes:

> The Jesus missionaries, in contrast, are told precisely to carry *no* knapsack [nor bag] and hold *no* staff in their hands. Why this striking difference? Since a reciprocity of healing and eating is at the heart of the Jesus movement, the idea of no-staff and no-knapsack is symbolically correct for the Jesus missionaries. They are … on a house mission to rebuild peasant society from the grass roots upward.

> Since commensality [communal equality] is not just a technique for support but a demonstration of message, they could not and should not dress to declare itinerant self-sufficiency but rather communal dependence. Itinerancy *and* dependency: heal, stay, move on.[16]

The point is that while the Cynics were interested in social criticism for its own sake, the Jesus people were interested in forging an alternative and *nonstrategic* community.

What was this alternative and nonstrategic community that Jesus of Nazareth offered and which the indigenous Palestinians found so attractive? Jesus called it the "kingdom of God", not in some teleological future but in the here and now. What did he mean by the kingdom of God in the here and now? This is a question that can only be answered by reference to Q[1] and the Gospel of Thomas. The account give by John Crossan is both brilliant and persuasive. It is particularly persuasive because it is what the dynamic-strategy theory that underlies this book leads one to expect to find. Crossan's interpretation even survives his attempt to force it into the supply-side theoretical straightjacket of "cross-cultural anthropology" – using the body as a model of society – and his incorrect analysis of the Galilean economic system and, hence, of Jesus' socioeconomic position.

Crossan's argument is that Jesus' version of the kingdom of God in the here and now was an ethical lifestyle based on a "radical egalitarianism". Jesus set about trying to achieve this *not* by attacking the political authorities as many Jewish messiahs did before and after the time of Jesus, and *not* by calling down God's judgment on these authorities as the apocalyptic prophets (like John the Baptist) were prone to do, but by changing the power relationships at the grassroots level through personal example. Crossan insists "Jesus was not just a teacher or a preacher in purely intellectual terms ... He not only discussed the Kingdom of God; he enacted it, and said others could do so as well".[17]

What then was the "radical egalitarianism" that characterized Jesus' view of the kingdom of God? Crossan tells us:

> for Jesus, the Kingdom of God is a community of radical or unbrokered equality in which individuals are in direct contact with one another and with God, unmediated by any established brokers or fixed locations.[18]

What did this involve? It meant going out to the indigenous people of Galilee and visiting them in their own homes; telling them about a new ethical (or nonstrategic) way of life – the kingdom of God in the here and now; "healing" their anxieties, frustrations, distress, and neurotic disorders; and sharing whatever food and shelter their hosts felt able to offer. The "healed" were then encouraged to become "healers". In this way, Jesus attempted to overcome the intense strategic frustration being experienced by his fellow Galileans. The idea was not to overthrow the existing strategic society through political or religious (apocalyptic) means but by quietly and steadily developing a nonstrategic community of equals liberated from strategic power relationships but still located in Roman conquest society from which they could not hope to escape.

The radical nature of this new community was demonstrated by Jesus in his attitude to meeting, healing, and eating with other Galileans. First, he conducted his ministry not by establishing a preaching practice in a fixed place and insisting that people come to him and pay for his teaching/healing services, but by going out to the people in their own homes and accepting their hospitality. This shifted power from the preacher to the people. Second, everyone was welcome at Jesus' table, irrespective of gender, ethnicity, or social rank. And at such meetings it was Jesus who broke and distributed the bread, fish, etc – a role played by servants in a rich household and by women in a poor household. For Jesus, the radically egalitarian rules of meeting and eating at the communal table provided the micro model for "rules of association and socialization" at the societal level.[19]

Third, Jesus implicitly attacked social attitudes of the day together with Pharisean laws of purity by his association with the sick and diseased. Crossan sensibly draws a distinction between "disease", a physical condition, and "illness", the "personal and social stigma of uncleanness, isolation, and rejection" arising from Pharisean purity laws. He then argues convincingly about a particular case that "Jesus, who did not and could not cure that disease [psoriasis] or any other one, healed the poor man's illness by refusing to accept the disease's ritual uncleanness and social ostracization".[20]

Crossan widens this argument about disease/illness to including the healing of "demonic possession". He asks: "could there be a connection between colonial possession and forms of mental illness easily interpreted as demonic possession?" Jesus, by inviting "possessed" people into his new community – the kingdom of God in the here and now – was able to cast out the "unclean spirits" of possession caused by colonial oppression. To support his case, Crossan draws attention to the story about the Gerasene demoniac in the Gospel of Mark (5: 1–17). In this story the unclean spirit calls itself "Legion, for we are many" – a clear reference to Roman power – and begs Jesus not to send them out of the country but to let them inhabit a nearby herd of swine (an unclean animal to the Jews) that then rushed down a steep bank into the sea (what every Palestinian wanted to see happen to the Romans). The former demoniac was left "in his right mind", owing to this symbolic release from colonial oppression.

Crossan's argument about colonialization and mental disorders intersects with the more general proposition in this book about superpower involvement in Palestine generating an intense form of strategic frustration in individuals and societies. This condition, which was discussed in my earlier book *The Selfcreating Mind* (2006), was capable of inducing in susceptible people, not only deep depression and malaise, but also psychosis that could be popularly interpreted as "demoniac possession". By bringing these people into a caring nonstrategic community, the impact of strategic frustration would be suddenly and massively reduced, thereby helping to heal the "possessed" individual. My argument is more general than Crossan's, owing to the fact that I am using it as part of a general dynamic theory of complex living systems to explain the transformation of a strategic ideology — required to sustain the strategic *logos* — into a religion — required to give individuals access to divine assistance in their daily lives.

In Jesus' kingdom of God – a nonstrategic community – all forms of strategic frustration were supposed to wither away. All mental problems – depression and psychosis – were supposed to be resolved. Galileans, despite being subjected to Roman power, would be able to live in peace and harmony with themselves, each other, and their God. The pressure to survive and prosper would be eased, and strategic desire would be redirected into socially creative activities, such as healing, teaching, and welfare. This was supposed to be a wonderfully liberating and creative solution to Palestinian strategic problems.

While it was a brilliant idea generated by an amazing man, it lead to a number of unforeseen problems that arose inevitably from being a nonstrategic solution to superpower oppression. First, a nonstrategic community could only survive in the longer term in a completely nonstrategic world. And the only nonstrategic world is the invention of priestly philosophers – heaven. In this life's strategic world, *nonstrategic* communities are inevitably seen as being *antistrategic*, even if that is not their objective. They are seen as undermining the objectives and values – of survival and prosperity – of the host strategic society. Consequently, the host strategic society will take decisive action to eliminate any antistrategic threat. It is not surprising, therefore, that as the Jesus movement grew in popularity and influence, its leader was unceremoniously eliminated and its members were persecuted.

The second unforeseen problem was the impossibility of either eliminating or effectively redirecting strategic desire. Consequently, after the unattended crucifixion of Jesus, the survivors jostled for power and authority within the movement and to shape and control is mythology. The purpose of the New Testament, as we shall see, was to establish the power and authority of the fictional apostolic succession from Jesus to the apostles to the bishops of the new church. This had not been desired nor anticipated by Jesus and his earliest followers, despite what the narrative gospels of Mark, Matthew, Luke, and John might say. Because of this outburst of strategic desire, the early Jesus movement was transformed in just a few generations into an organization – the Christian Church – based on a hierarchical, male-dominated power structure. In doing so, it not only mimicked the organizational structure of the strategic world, but made it possible for later societies to adopt Christianity not only as a spiritual discipline but also as a strategic ideology. This indicates how quickly and how far Christianity traveled after the death of Jesus, in an effort to survive and prosper.

From sage to apocalyptic prophet

The promise of initiation into the kingdom of God was not easily fulfilled for ordinary Palestinians. As soon as the Jesus movement was seen by the Roman and Jewish authorities as a public challenge to their respective status, action was taken against its members. Clearly the biggest setback was the arrest and crucifixion of their leader and teacher, Jesus of Nazareth. Apart from the crucifixion itself, which is mentioned in the histories of Josephus, there is no independent evidence as to how it occurred. Some, like Crossan, accept the testimony of the narrative gospels that it occurred in Jerusalem at the time of the Passover, following Jesus' disruption of Temple activities. Others, like Mack, are disinclined to believe any aspect of the crucifixion story. What both liberal scholars do agree on is that Jesus' body was never recovered, as in all probability it was taken by wild animals. This was the fate of virtually all crucified Palestinians, as only one crucified skeleton has ever been discovered in or around Jerusalem. They also agree that the followers of Jesus never encountered the risen Christ. The idea of the resurrection was, as we shall see, the invention of Paul, the self-proclaimed apostle.

With their leader crucified, the Jesus movement encountered increasing opposition as they extended their teaching and healing mission from rural villages to the cities of Galilee and beyond. In particular they appear to have run into opposition from the Pharisees, who attacked them for abandoning the purity laws of Judaism in their healing and eating practices. The strategic frustration they had tried to escape by establishing their nonstrategic community was coming back to haunt them. Their response to these new circumstances was to change the message and character of their dead leader by adding a group of new sayings to the "instruction handbook" of their movement. This new block of sayings is known as Q^2 and it introduces an entirely new and apocalyptic element. As Mack argues:

> The apocalyptic imagination served only one purpose for the people of Q, and that was to guarantee the threat of judgement that they wanted to bring down upon people who had *frustrated* their mission ... It is obvious that the people of Q were distressed and incensed, and that they targeted certain people such as the Pharisees for their fire ... The beauty of apocalyptic projection was that it could turn a contemporary critique or a charge into a threat with a tinge of ultimacy: 'You will surely get your just deserts'.[21]

And they surely did. A short time later (AD 70) the Temple in Jerusalem was totally destroyed by the Romans. This reaction by the Jesus movement was similar to that of the Jews returning from the Exile in the mid-fifth century BC. It will be recalled that the Judahites responded to strategic frustration in the face of superpower supremacy – in that case Persia – by retreating into spiritual mysticism and by threatening retribution on their enemies by the final judgment at the end of time. And it has a modern equivalent in the scientism of the environmental movement, which, being persistently overlooked by policymakers in the past, have responded with a similar threat of retribution: "Listen to us now, or the world will collapse tomorrow!". The apocalypse is the chosen weapon of the strategically powerless of this world.

This apocalyptic element in the Gospel of Q was introduced through the figure of John the Baptist – an apocalyptic prophet – who, the later narrative gospels tell us, saw himself as paving the way for someone greater than himself – for the "son of man". Also, apocalyptic judgment was introduced into some of the sayings of Jesus. It was John who is supposed to have baptized Jesus. Once again our two liberal biblical scholars, Crossan and Mack, part company. Mack considers John a fictional construct of the Q people during the 60s, rather than a real person in the 20s of the first century AD. Crossan (who is more willing to believe the secular stories of the narrative gospels where two or more independent sources agree), on the other hand, argues that Johns' ministry involved leading small groups of people, who had made the journey from Palestine into the eastern desert, through the Jordan River and, via a baptismal ritual, back into the "Promised Land". By symbolically recreating the Biblical story of the conquest of the Land of Canaan following the Exodus from Captivity in Egypt, John was attempting to induce YHWH to invoke the final judgment promised in the Hebrew Bible. Crossan further claims that Jesus, who he sees as being initially a follower of John, decided, after the Baptist's death at the hands of Herod Antipas, that a new non-apocalyptic way was required. This is when Jesus might have begun his own highly popular form of nonstrategic societal formation, which involved invoking the kingdom of God in the here and now rather than at the end of time. According to the ancient Jewish historian Josephus there were many "false prophets" at this time, who encouraged such apocalyptic reenactments, usually followed by brutal retaliation from Roman authorities. So, even if John never existed, Jesus could have decided that there had to be a better way.

By introducing apocalyptic judgment into the sayings of Jesus, the people of Q transformed their dead leader from a sage-teacher into an apocalyptic prophet called the "son of man". Further, they placed the son of man securely within the epic tradition of Israel as an agent of divine wisdom. In this way they created a powerful myth of origin for their movement, which displaced Judaism as the force determining the course and conclusion of world history. And they relocated the kingdom of God from the here and now to the end of time. Surely, had Jesus been afforded the dignity of a grave, he would have been turning in it!

From apocalyptic prophet to Son of God

But the people of Q had not completed their mythmaking. Quite unexpectedly, and not at all fortuitously, war broke out between Rome and its vassal Jewish territories, and raged between AD 66–73. In the process, Jerusalem was sacked and the Temple destroyed for all time. While the retribution that the Q people had promised their Jewish persecutors had miraculously come to pass, it also threatened their own survival. The Q people responded to this strategic threat by transforming Jesus from "son of man" to "son of God" in the Q^3 sayings. Yet even this new myth about the son of God did not yet include the idea of divinely inspired martyrdom and resurrection. That idea was contributed by later, non-Q, groups.

In discussing the emergence of the idea of the son of God, Mack writes:

> Jesus was no longer imagined as a sage whose knowledge was divine. He was imagined as an otherworldly being, heir of the father's kingdom (QS 24) in battle with the accuser for the authority to rule over the kingdoms of the earth, whose hour for full disclosure would come in the future (QS 49), at which time he would turn the father's kingdom over to his followers so they could rule over the twelve tribes of Israel (QS 62).[22]

He argues that Q^3 provides a "unified mythology" created by "merging all of the earlier mythological concepts [sage, apocalyptic prophet, child of wisdom] in the single figure of the son of God". This transformation involved "a radical shift, and the mythic frame now gives the sayings of Jesus an ethereal cast". What caused this radical shift? Mack suggests that "one has the sense that the people of Q lost their public bearings during the war and turned within to cultivate an esoteric confidence".

This argument by Mack supports my strategic-frustration hypothesis: the Roman–Jewish war was a savage blow to the community's growing feeling of success in reversing the burden of colonial oppression and strategic failure. Each advance in spirituality in Palestine was driven by a deepening of the age-old affliction of strategic frustration.

From Son of God to risen Christ

The early Jesus movement – as reflected in the Gospel of Q – had gone a long way in reworking the mythology of their founder, but they held out against the Pauline idea of the risen Christ well into the 70s of the first century AD. They stubbornly resisted the Christ cult that was central to Paul's mission to the gentiles in northern Syria, Asia and, finally, Rome between the 40s and early 60s. The Q people were interested primarily in societal formation, but, in the face of resistance from Palestinian authorities, also looked to the end of time when Jesus would proclaim God's final judgment. In contrast, Paul, who had never met Jesus and had difficult relations with the early Jesus movement (as their chief Jewish prosecutor!), believed in a *spiritual* kingdom of God that could be entered through personal redemption, owing not to the law but to the grace of God.

Essentially, Paul's views constituted a theology of personal redemption, or salvation, through a mystical "union with Christ". It was a union made possible by the Holy Spirit operating through the sacraments of baptism and holy communion. In this way the convert shares in Christ's death and resurrection in order to participate here and now in a *spiritual* kingdom and after death in the *eternal* kingdom of God. Paul had no interest in forming a nonstrategic community on Earth as had Jesus and his early movement. Paul's interests were not of this world but of the next. Hence, his Christ cult must be regarded as a perversion of the teachings of Jesus of Nazareth.

If the teachings of Jesus were not the source of Paul's theology, what was? This is a highly controversial matter in theological circles. Two main sources of Pauline theology have been suggested over the past century or so. They are Jewish apocalypticism as reflected in the Dead Sea scrolls, and Hellenistic thought as reflected in Greek mystery religions and Gnosticism. The mystery religions, which focus on the dying-rising god, are of interest, particularly as the concept of "dead god rising" is an important focus of Egyptian and Mesopotamian mythology. No educated Palestinian would have been unaware of this mythology. Similarly, Gnosticism stressed a metaphysical dualism – of body and spirit – that could be resolved though the divine grace and power of *gnosis*, or a special knowledge of God. These ideas would provide a solution for a Jewish apocalyptic theologian like Paul, who possessed a frustrated desire for an immediate proclamation of the end of time and God's final judgment. Even in the face of a receding Day of Judgment, the Christian convert could immediately enter into the *spiritual* kingdom of God. This was the very antithesis of a strategic ideology, as well as being a perversion of the message of Jesus of Nazareth.

The authors of the narrative gospels – Mark, Matthew, Luke and John – had to decide what to make of the two main traditions of "Christianity" that had flourished during the generation or so after the death of Jesus. There was the Book of Q, containing the sayings attributed to the sage-teacher Jesus, and the letters of Paul telling of a mystical union with the crucified and resurrected Christ – the dead god rising. As we know, the New Testament gospel writers used both sources – together with other writings, such as the Jesus "pronouncement" and miracle stories – in a way that advanced the objectives of the church groups with which they were affiliated. The resulting gospels were less austere and more worldly (more strategic) than Paul's theology, but more metaphysical and apocalyptic than the teachings of Jesus of Nazareth. Christianity, therefore, was as much a product of the ideas of Paul as it was of Jesus.

As has been remarked upon many times, the four gospels are very different in their approach. Mark, who invented the narrative gospel form, wrote his account around AD 75–80. His central focus was the crucifixion and resurrection of Jesus, which he regarded as divinely ordained. This is hardly surprising as he was Paul's companion and assistant on his missionary work. Yet, at the same time, Mark lays the blame for the rejection of Jesus' message and the crucifixion of the Lord on Jewish leaders. It was this failure of the Jewish leaders to respond to God's intention that led to the sacking of Jerusalem and the final destruction of the Temple.[23] Clearly there is a logical tension in this argument. To make his story work, Mark had to indulge in considerable mythmaking about Jesus' relationship with John the Baptist, his focus on twelve apostles, the journey to Jerusalem, the last supper, the denial by Peter, the betrayal by Judas Iscariot (now reprieved in the eyes of some by the recent discovery of the Gospel of Judas[24]), the role of Pilate, the crucifixion, the burial by Joseph of Arimathea, and the appearances of the risen Christ to the women and, later, the disciples.

Matthew, who wrote his gospel around AD 85–90, focuses on Jesus' teachings rather than on his apocalyptic role. Essentially, he employs Mark's narrative, with various embellishments of his own (such as the birth story), as a vehicle for presenting many of the saying of Jesus. Owing to this it is thought that Matthew may have been a member of the Q people. He also presents Jesus as heir to Jewish hopes, which he links to the prophesy of Malachi about the future Messiah. It was for this reason that the Christian church placed the Book of Malachi at the end of the Old Testament (not the position it has in the Hebrew Bible) and immediately before the gospels in the New Testament.

Luke's gospel – written early second century – had a more pragmatic objective. He wanted to tell a story about the development of Christianity from the time of Jesus to the founding of the apostolic churches, in order to show that the Church of his time was true to Jesus and its early followers, that God's people are both good and good for society, that Jesus was part of a long line of God's agents sent to declare his purpose to the world, and that this purpose was as relevant to the gentiles as to the Jews. In the process, Luke, an educated Greek gentile, toned down the more extreme aspects of early Christian mythology – including Jesus as Messiah, the vindicated martyr, wisdom's child, son of God, son of man, apocalyptic prophet – that characterized the later editions of the Book of Q and the Gospel of Mark. And he attempted to place the story within the framework of world history.[25]

Luke viewed Jesus as a great teacher and prophet, who brought God's word to the gentiles. In a sense, Luke was positioning the Church of the early second century to become a strategic institution in the Western world. It is not surprising, therefore, that the Church, which clearly wanted to survive and prosper, regarded Luke's two-volume history – his gospel and his "acts of the Apostles" – as a central document to be preserved in their New Testament. The Church was also attracted to Luke's writings because they contained an account of the "apostolic mythology".[26]

The early Christian churches generated a large volume of written work, of which only a small, and not particularly representative, sample was preserved in the New Testament. It has been argued, quite convincingly, that the main criterion for selection was whether or not they could "demonstrate" the line of authority – entirely fictional – from Jesus to the Apostles (who have no role in the early Jesus movement) to the bishops of the second-century church. Fictional letters of Paul (1 & 2 Timothy and Titus) and Peter were included because they are "instructions" from the "Apostles" to church communities about the essential role of bishops. This is, of course, a direct contradiction of Jesus' radical egalitarianism, but an essential requirement for a Church that was intent on survival and prosperity, just like any other strategic "society". Just like a strategic society, the Church adopted a dynamic strategy – of increasing membership and resources (a variant of family multiplication) – that generated a growing demand (just like strategic demand) for organizational and institutional change, and for a changing mythology (like a strategic ideology) about its origins, history and theology. In the process Jesus was transformed from a sage-teacher into a divine figure of redemption, and his radical egalitarianism was transformed into a hierarchical power structure that mimicked that of the strategic world.

The nonstrategic Jesus movement, therefore, was transformed into a strategic "society" – albeit embedded in the wider strategic civilization of the Roman world – positioning itself to compete with the superpowers that were responsible for its birth. How was this to be done? Through infiltrating those superpowers by posing as their strategic ideologies. If you can't defeat them, then join them in a mutually advantageous strategic pursuit.

Christianity in the Roman empire

The early years

Following the first-century missionary work of Paul, Peter, and others among the Greek-speaking communities of Asia Minor, Christianity spread gradually throughout the eastern part of the Roman empire. This expansion was aided by the common language and culture of the Mediterranean world at a time of *Pax Romana*. Gradual expansion in the second century turned into exponential expansion in the third, owing to the exhaustion of Rome's conquest strategy (around AD 190) and the glaring impotence of the empire's old gods of war. Roman citizens were actively seeking new guardians, and by the middle of the third century, Christianity had permeated all classes of Roman society.[27] This was a staggering achievement that would have astounded the early members of the Jesus movement just nine generations earlier.

It is hardly surprising that in the second century the bishop in Rome – metropolis of the empire – asserted his dominance over the Church, despite the fact that it continued to be Greek-speaking until the mid-third century. It was at this time (late second century) that the Church formulated the New Testament canon, emphasizing apostolic succession; established an administrative network based on urban-centered bishoprics; raised funds to finance church activities (clergy, poor relief, manumission, even loans to Christian merchants); and attempted to rationally sort out its convoluted theology arising from its messy ad hoc origins.

Doctrinal issues took centuries to resolve, and even then they appeared absurd to nonbelievers. The main difficulties arose over the nature and status of Jesus in relation to YHWH and the Holy Spirit. Early theologians involved in this protracted debate included Justin (100–165), Hippolytus (170–235), Tertullian of Carthage (160–220), Tatian of Mesopotamia (second century), Clement of Alexandra (150–215), and Origin (185–254). From this debate emerged the logically difficult concepts of the Trinity of Father, Son and Holy Spirit, and of Christ, who simultaneously possessed a divine and human nature. While these unusual ideas subsequently became articles of faith for Christian believers, they have always appeared absurd to rationalist thinkers. Still, that is true of all religious ideas, Christian or non-Christian.

This orthodox doctrine was also challenged from within Christian ranks. Indeed one is left wondering what Jesus of Nazareth, the pragmatic sage and teacher, would have made of all this complex theology. In the second century the chief dissident was Marcion of Pontus (100–165), who went to Rome in about 140, where he came under the influence of Cerdo the Gnostic. Marcion was a dualist, who taught that there were two cosmic gods – an angry, war-like creator god who was responsible for the material world and who ruthlessly imposed his idea of justice; and, in contrast, a loving god, who, out of sheer goodness, sacrificed his son Jesus Christ in order to save humans from the material world and to gather them to himself. According to Marcion, the loving god was the "unknown" god or the "stranger". In effect, Marcion was challenging – denying, really – the Judahite transformation of the old strategic guardian of conquest into a universal and transcendent God. Surely he was correct to challenge this shift from strategic ideology to religion. If there is a universal God – and there is no evidence one way or another – he must be unknown, because he can hardly be the transformed strategic guardian of the seventh-century BC Judahites and/or of first century AD Galileans.

Marcion, who was declared a heretic in 144, was a catalyst in the Church's formulation of its New Testament canon, which stood in opposition to Marcion's edition of collected gospels, and of its concept of the Trinity, which denied Marcion's duality. Marcionite dualism was never really extinguished and was to reemerge as the Cathar heresy in medieval Europe in the eleventh to fifteenth centuries. Clearly there are parallels between the dualistic beliefs of both Marcion of Pontus and Zoroaster of Persia.

Strategic exhaustion and religious persecution

During the century or so following the final exhaustion (AD 190) of Rome's conquest strategy, the Roman elite and people became increasingly concerned about the future. With the end of conquest, income from beyond the frontiers ceased to flow into Rome, with the result that real income and wealth declined, taxes increased, excessive (nonstrategic) inflation emerged, capital works were curtailed, poverty increased, and government became more arbitrary. In a growing atmosphere of uncertainty and apprehension, there was a great need and desire for scapegoats. Christians who refused to offer sacrifices to the old gods were obvious candidates. They were regarded as "atheists". As Jacob Balling tells us:

> In the light of the 'political theory' of Rome, the Christians must necessarily appear as atheists in the full sense of that word: rebels against the gods and their order, against peace, security, and prosperity.[28]

These Christian "atheists" had to be called to account so as to prevent the further deterioration of Roman order, peace, security, and prosperity.

Throughout the second and early third centuries, the persecution of Christians was haphazard, erupting from occasional mob violence directed at these new religious fanatics and "terrorists". Christians appeared to be antistrategists (or terrorists) because they refused to support the strategic guardians of Rome. The Church's prospects deteriorated during the middle of the third century owing to "threats to the survival of the empire and resentment at the Christian attitude to the celebrations of Rome's millennium in 248".[29] In 250 the emperor Decius began his brief reign by ordering a general celebration of sacrifices to the gods. Those who refused to support Rome at its time of need – as the Germanic tribes were pressing on the northern border – in this way were to be executed or sent to the mines. This was the beginning of systematic and severe persecution of Christians, who, of course, felt unable, or at least reluctant, to sacrifice to pagan gods. It was, however, a persecution cut short by the death of Decius – the first Roman emperor to be killed by the barbarians – in battle against the Goths in the Balkans.

Clearly a new strategic guardian was required to lead Rome out of a growing strategic crisis. This frightening situation prompted the emperor Aurelian (270–275) to introduce the worship of the sun as the supreme god and the emperor as the earthly image of his life-giving power. This new religion appears to be an echo of the equally ephemeral worship in Egypt of the sun god Aten by King Akhenaten. Interestingly, the feast day of Rome's new solar guardian of conquest was 25th December, later adopted as the day on which the birth of Christ was celebrated. The new sun god of Rome was brilliantly successful at first. Emperor Aurelian, known as the "Restorer of the World", was able to revive army discipline and domestic order, and to crush the breakaway Gallic and Palmyrene kingdoms. Both the "restoration" and the new strategic guardian, however, were ephemeral. Just like all other attempts to revive the Roman empire, which was by now dead at heart.

Christian persecution was renewed by emporers Diocletian (284–305) and Galerius (305–311), who ruled Rome at a time when the barbarians threatened to break through on every part of the frontier from Britain to Egypt. In these perilous times, official attempts to prevent Christian "atheists" penetrating the civil service and army led to very severe persecutions, described as "downright terror", for a decade after 303. The most savage actions were taken by Galerius, who, nevertheless, on his deathbed issued an order that the persecutions would be ended "on the condition that the Christians prayed for the state in return for their freedom of worship".[30] This was a landmark decision for the Christian Church, as it was the first time that their God had been called upon to act as a strategic guardian for the failing Roman empire. It was clear evidence that by the early fourth century even the Roman leaders despaired of receiving any assistance from the city's old gods. In effect, the old strategic guardians were well and truly dead.

The persecutions, although savage, failed to eradicate the atheist Christians. This is usually explained in terms of: the rallying effect of martyrdom ("the martyrs' blood is the seed of the Church"); Rome was not a very efficient police state, owing to its decentralized character; and that Christians were, in the main, good citizens prepared to pray to their God to support the emperor and empire so as to maintain an ordered society.[31] While there is some truth in this type of explanation, it overlooks the real reason. The persecutions were the result of the exhaustion of Rome's conquest strategy, which left the empire stranded in highly vulnerable circumstances, and requiring public scapegoats. Once it was realized that the old conquest gods were no longer of any use as strategic guardians, Roman citizens turned in increasing numbers to the new Christian God, who at least promised order and security in the next life, and might even be prevailed upon as the one and only God to reinvigorate the failing empire. As is well known, Romans also turned to other mystery religions, such as the cults of Bacchus (Greece), Isis and Osiris (Egypt), Attis (Asia Minor), Mithras (Persia) and the sun god – all of which held out similar hopes. The explanation for the failure of official attempts to eliminate these new religions, therefore, is strategic in nature.

Needless to say, not all Christians were model citizens. As with Islam today, there were fanatical Christian believers in the Roman world who actively sought martyrdom, and who could justifiably be regarded as "terrorists", or antistrategists. At the mild end of this spectrum were Christians who smashed pagan images and displayed disrespect towards Roman authorities, while at the militant end were radical North-African Christians who were determined to die as martyrs.[32] In contrast to these willing martyrs were the wealthy Christians, who "compromised" their faith during the persecutions, for fear they would have their property, and even lives, confiscated by the state. Clearly, this was the more usual reaction. Indeed, owing to the scale on which it occurred, it raised the difficult problem for the later Church of "restoring" apostates who had, under extreme pressure, returned to pagan rites. Canon law in the Church had its origins in the apostate issue.[33]

Christianity as strategic ideology

The transition of Christians from "atheists" and "terrorists" to model citizens must have been as surprising as it was swift. Within two years of the ending of the most sever persecutions under Galerius, Christianity was declared (in 313) the official religion of the western half of the Roman empire, and was tolerated in the eastern half despite being still officially pagan. How had this dramatic transformation occurred? The well-known answer is that the brilliant general Constantine had, under the banner of Christ, fought his way out of York in 306 to become ruler of the western half of the empire by 312, whereupon he persuaded the pagan ruler of the eastern half to grant tolerance to law-abiding Christian citizens. Constantine attributed his military success to Christ, who he believed had acted as his strategic guardian against the failing old guardians of Rome.

Constantine was the son of Constantius, who was appointed in 293 as one of the two "Caesars" (the other was Galerius) under the two "Augusti", Diocletian and Maximian. This unusual form of leadership structure was a bold and successful attempt by Diocletian to throw back the barbarians invading on a wide front. Ceasar Constantius was responsible for retaking the Rhine and Britain from the invading Germanic tribes, while Galerius took charge of the Persian war. In 305 both Diocletian and Maximian abdicated in favor of Galerius and Constantius, who in turn appointed two new Ceasars.[34] On Constantius' death in 306, his son Constantine was proclaimed Augusti by his troops, and Maximian's son Maxentius seized power in Italy. In 312 Constantine, who had adopted the Christian God as his strategic guardian, defeated Maxentius — who vainly sought protection from the old gods — at the battle of Milvian Bridge just outside Rome. Constantine, who believed his victory was the outcome of divine assistance, now found himself to be emperor of the western empire. With his victory over Licinuis in 324, he became sole emperor of the entire empire and declared Christianity its official religion.

Constantine made Christianity the strategic ideology of the Roman empire and encouraged its acceptance by the people as its religion. Owing to the exhaustion of conquest as a dynamic strategy and its replacement with commerce, Christianity became the strategic ideology of the dynamic strategy of commerce. To take full advantage of the new commerce strategy, Constantine established, in 330, the new capital of Constantinople at the very center of trade between the resource-rich north and the ancient commerce network linking the Aegean, Egypt, the Levant, Mesopotamia, and India. Rome was too far west – too far up a dead strategic alley – to play this important new role. To symbolically demonstrate the empire's new direction, Constantinople was dedicated to the new strategic guardian – the Christian God – by Constantine's new priestly philosophers. Constantine also conferred great material benefits on the Christian Church – as befitted its new role, as the link with the empire's new strategic guardian – by granting tax concessions and building great basilicas in Constantinople, Rome, Jerusalem, and Bethlehem. At the same time, the pagan temples and their priests lost their old endowments, as they were no longer relevant to the new strategic *logos* of commerce. In this way, Constantine made a mighty effort, in his words, to "renew the body of the world".[35]

As it turned out, the new strategic *logos* of commerce only made it possible to "renew" part of the "body of the world".[36] The new commerce *logos* centered on the Greek world could not breathe life into the old conquest *logos* of the Latin world. The old *logos* and its strategic guardians departed this world together. In the early fifth century, the conquest city of Rome and its western empire was finally abandoned, whereas the mercantile city of Constantinople and its eastern empire lived on until it was taken over in 1204 (the prime objective of the Fourth Crusade) by Western Europe, the inheritors of the Latin world.

The commerce *logos*, in contrast to the conquest *logos*, does not require such a large amount of territory to generate a given level of income and wealth. It was possible for the elite in Constantinople, therefore, to become fabulously wealthy – even more wealthy than the elite in Rome – by occupying less than half the territory of the old conquest empire. While the conquest *logos* is land (i.e. resources) intensive, the commerce *logos* is transactions intensive.

The adoption of Christianity as the strategic ideology of the Roman empire – as well as the religion of its citizens – created tensions within the Church that were to last for the next 1,500 years, until the Industrial Revolution opened the way for science to replace religion in this respect. As one Church historian has said:

> the [early] Christians were predominantly, if not entirely, world-renouncing. They were dissenters from and critics of the worldly values of power, pleasure, and opulence, and therefore in the long term the creators of the modern secularizing notion that such pursuits are irrelevant to religion and vice versa. Yet from Justin [100–165] onwards, they were seeing the destinies of the empire mysteriously bound up with God's purposes being worked out through his church.[37]

It is shown above that Christianity had its origins in the Jesus movement, which was an attempt, born of strategic frustration in the face of Roman oppression, to forge a nonstrategic community based on a radical egalitarianism. Three centuries later, the Church which emerged from that nonstrategic community found itself supporting and, through the Christian God, sustaining that very same materialist/ strategic empire. Under Constantine, the Church was required to serve both God *and* the Roman *logos,* the purpose of which was to generate wealth and income. This was hardly compatible with the well-known sayings of Jesus:

> Ye cannot serve God and mammon (Matthew 6: 24)

> For what shall it profit a man, if he shall gain the whole world, and lose his own soul? (Mark 8: 36)

> Lay not up for yourselves treasures upon earth, where moth and rust doth corrupt, and where thieves break through and steal (Matthew 6: 19)

While the majority of Roman's Christian citizens experienced no intellectual/ moral qualms – because they were "Christians" for strategic not spiritual reasons – this inconsistency was a source of much soul-searching for a small proportion of religious devotees. But the tension was real enough and could have been responsible for the development of monastic orders, which attempted to maintain the early religious traditions of the Church in the face of strategic pressure and of the materialist desires of the majority of citizens.

The Byzantine Church

The Byzantine Church from 330 included the Greek (Constantinople), Coptic (Alexandria), Syrian (Antioch), and Armenian (Jerusalem) branches. Which was the case until the early seventh century when the Persians (Zoroastrianism) and then the Arabs (Islam) captured Syria, Palestine and Egypt, leaving the Byzantine empire in control only of the Greek Church. There was no change in this situation until the Fourth Crusade (1204), when Western Europe imposed the Roman Church on Constantinople; and in 1453 when the Islamic Ottoman Sultanate finally sacked the great city, which had been in Christian hands for a millennium. Finally, even the commerce *logos* of the old Roman empire was swept away, and its Byzantine strategic guardian sought sanctuary in the Principality of Moscow and the Kingdom of Georgia.

Throughout the history of the Byzantine empire, the Church played both a strategic (materialist) and nonstrategic (religious) role. Its strategic role was indistinguishable from that played by the strategic ideologies of all ancient societies, such as those of Egypt or Mesopotamia examined in Chapter 4. In this respect, one historian tells us:

> Our modern distinction between church and state would have been meaningless to the Byzantines. They did not envisage church and state as two contrasting entities, subsisting in cooperation or conflict, but they thought of society as a single integrated whole. The emperor had religious as well as civil responsibilities.[38]

But our historian is unable to tell us why this was so. The modern distinction between church and state with which we are familiar in the West, is a recent and novel idea, which emerged as recently as the nineteenth century when Christianity as a strategic ideology was replaced by that of scientism. And the reason for this substitution of ideologies was the occurrence of the industrial technological paradigm shift or Industrial Revolution. The entire ancient, medieval, and premodern world would have found the modern distinction between "church" and state puzzling in the extreme.

The Byzantine emperors, from 330 to 1453, conformed to the age-old role of kings as strategic leaders and intermediaries between God – or the strategic guardian – and the people he represented. The emperor was charged with securing divine support for his society's strategic pursuit, together with the maintenance of societal order. In other words, the Byzantine emperor was *custodian* of the strategic *logos*, just as God was *guardian* of the entire cosmos. Church historians have expressed this relationship as follows:

> The emperor is to be seen as the living icon of Christ, God's viceregent on earth. The terrestrial rule of the emperor reproduces God's rule in heaven ... Just as God regulates the cosmic order, so the emperor regulates the social order.[39]

This was the view of Eusebius of Caesarea (264–340), historian of the early Church in the 330s, and it was the view of all emperors of the Byzantine empire until 1453. And, as shown in Chapter 4, it was the view of all priestly philosophers throughout the ancient world.

This essentially pagan role of the Church generated considerable tensions for those who looked back to the non-materialist origins of the Jesus movement.

Just as it had for the Church in Rome at an earlier time. It is no coincidence that eastern monastic communities emerged soon after Christianity had been formally adopted as the empire's strategic ideology. According to historians of the Byzantine Church:

> They [monastic communities] acted as a counterbalance to an *established* [or state] Christianity, reminding the church at large that God's kingdom is not to be identified with an earthly realm. In this way they filled an eschatological role, serving ... as the prophets of the second coming of Christ.[40]

In effect, monastic life recreated the nonstrategic community of the Jesus movement at a time when the Church became closely identified with the empire's materialist strategic pursuit. Certainly the monks and nuns who worked as laypeople, helpers, and craftsmen, were more in touch with the origins and principles of the early Jesus movement than the priestly philosophers and bishops. Monasteries took seriously their mission of helping the poor and oppressed – just as the Jesus movement distributed food and healed the sick – through the establishment of hospitality, orphanages, and hostels for the disadvantaged. This is not to deny that, from time to time, some of these institutions were subverted by materialism.

The chief task of the monasteries, however, was to pray for the souls of those closely involved in society's strategic pursuit — those who paid for their upkeep. We are told:

> This, then, was what the Byzantine expected from the monasteries: not, on the whole, learning, evangelism, or organized charity, but holiness. He expected to find there men and women who would pray for his sins, and who could offer him at moments of crisis a healing word of counsel ... Such is the true contribution that, in Byzantine eyes, the monasteries made to society: prayer, holiness, spiritual guidance.[41]

The role of the monasteries, then, was to maintain the religious role of Christianity in the face of its highly materialist strategic role; to prevent Christianity totally abandoning the religious for the strategic function; to maintain a link with the early Jesus movement and its nonstrategic character; to do, in other words, what the state church had abandoned. The state church in contrast, was concerned through its public rituals and ceremonies to gain access to the divine strategic guardian and persuade him to sustain their strategic *logos* and to advance their strategic pursuit. Perhaps in this dual capacity the church might be able to serve both God and mammon after all.

Christianity in Europe

From empire to warring kingdoms, 500–1000

In contrast to the Roman empire, which regarded the Mediterranean as its own great "lake", the replacement Germanic kingdoms of Western Europe turned away from the sea to focus their expansionist aims on inland territories. To assist them in this strategic task, European kings adopted Christianity as their strategic ideology and the Christian God as their strategic guardian. In the early middle ages, whole communities adopted Christianity because of its perceived superiority as a strategic ideology. One church historian tells us that

> conversion to Christianity generally took the form of a collective act: common acceptance of the new *sidr* (as the Norsemen called it), the new way of life that was believed to safeguard human society more effectively than the old one.[42]

Christian missionaries also played on the alleged power of the Christian God to provide his people with greater prosperity than they had under pagan gods. In 723–24, according to Henry Mayr-Harting, Bishop Daniel of Winchester wrote a letter advising Boniface (680–754) in his mission to the Germans as follows: "ask them what sort of gods have allowed the Christians to have all the lands rich in wine and oil and other goods, and have left the heathens only with the frozen north". Mayr-Harting comments that: "this letter sets a tone for such missionary work in the early Middle Ages".[43] Even among gods, nothing succeeds like material success.

Each Germanic kingdom developed its own church and its own form of Christianity, over which the king exercised considerable control. Historians of Christianity tell us that:

> The new rulers – Germanic warlords – considered themselves the natural governors of 'their' churches and tolerated no papal interference. In this situation the groundwork was laid for the form of intermingling between political and ecclesiastical power that was to become so marked a characteristic of European history.[44]

This political – in fact, strategic – control of the Church in each European kingdom can be seen at both the "national" and local levels. The king exercised control over the leaders of the "national" church, while the king's knights built parish churches on their own estates, thereby manipulating the lesser clergy and religious ritual (or strategic ideology). While many leading clerics were from the same families as the king's barons, the rest were treated as tenants by the manorial lords. Prior to the papal reforms of Pope Gregory VII (1073–85), the Roman see had little influence on the European churches, which were employed as strategic instruments by national leaders.

What Church historians do not explain is that by developing their *own* Churches and their *own* forms of Christianity to sustain their *own* conquest strategies and *logoi*, these early European kingdoms were creating their *own* strategic guardians – their *own* gods. Just as each competing kingdom's conquest strategy was designed to maximize their *own* probability of survival and prosperity, so each kingdom's god was expected to provide them, and them alone, with military victory. In other words, the conquest strategies and, hence, *logoi* of Western Europe gave rise not to one Christian God worshipped in common by all kingdoms, but to a large number of parochial gods. Each god favored its own *logos* over all others, even though each god was described as "Christian". The fragmentation of the western half of the Roman empire, therefore, gave rise to a situation similar to the multiplicity of city gods in Sumerian civilization, whereby each city-state was supported by its own parochial god despite the common background mythology. Christianity provided a common mythology with which the national European gods were identified.

What influence did "Christianity" have upon the sociopolitical development of Europe in the five centuries after the fall of Rome? One Church historian has suggested that

> During the eighth and ninth centuries the Christian Church effected nothing short of a revolution in the forms of Western politics. Put briefly, there developed an idea of the pervasive religious and moral responsibility of the ruler. Christianity enormously expanded the perspectives in which rulers could think of themselves, and these perspectives in turn became an engine of expanded royal government.[45]

It is claimed that Charlemagne, king of the Franks and Holy Roman Emperor (crowned in Rome) from 800, embraced "a new Christian ideal of the ruler as a generous builder of churches and a devout man of prayer".[46] Charlemagne is supposed to have employed the Judahite King David as his model – rather than Christ! – and to have compared himself with King Josiah of Judah. Other European kings, such as Charles the Bold (Charlemagne's grandson) and Alfred of England, apparently made comparisons of their kingship with that of Solomon.

This interpretation by Church historians requires a response. First, the idea of "persuasive religious and moral responsibilities of the ruler" was neither novel nor the outcome of Christian – even religious – thinking. As demonstrated throughout this book, strategic leaders have always seen their responsibilities as being both secular and "religious". As well as assuming the leading role in the strategic pursuit, the ruler has always seen himself as the intermediary between the people and the strategic guardian(s) or god(s) – often in the role (as in Egypt) of chief priest. The changing nature of this secular/religious role over time is a function not of any particular religion such as Christianity but of the unfolding dynamic strategy of the strategic *logos*.

Second, the building of churches/temples was hardly "a new Christian ideal". Rulers, as intermediaries between the gods and the people, have always built temples on a lavish scale. The more successful the dynamic strategy, the more lavish the scale. Of course, Charlemagne's church-building campaign hardly compares with that of ancient Egyptian kings. Third, it is curious that the use of David, Solomon, and Josiah as role models could be regarded as a unique Christian contribution, when these kings were not Christian but Jewish! The reason they were chosen as role models was due to the fact that these Judahite kings were strategic conquest leaders, whereas Jesus was a nonstrategic sage and teacher. Only later Holy Roman Emperors, who had ceased pursuing a conquest strategy, turned from the Old to the New Testament when looking for role models. Otto III (980–1002), for example, associated himself with "Christ seated in majesty". Fourth, it is ironical that Frankish, and other European, kings should regard these Judahite kings as role models. As shown in Chapter 4, David and Solomon were little more than minor Palestinian tribal chiefs, and Josiah was a strategic failure. European kings aspired to greater strategic success than these examples provided.

My point here is that the sociopolitical developments of Western Europe were the outcome not of Christianity but of the unfolding conquest strategies of successful kings and kingdoms. While Christianity provided a set of ideological concepts and institutions that could be used, in part, in response to the unfolding conquest strategy, it was strategic demand driving this process. And it was Christianity as a materialist strategic ideology (fashioned by the declining Roman empire), rather than as a spiritual mythology, that played this role. Even without Christianity, a similar sociopolitical system (in the basic functional sense) would have emerged in Western Europe, as all conquest societies possess common functional characteristics. Zoroastrianism or Islam would have done just as well. This has been demonstrated in my book *The Ephemeral Civilization*.[47] Of course, by carrying established ideas and institutions from the old Roman empire – ideas and institutions reshaped by *local* strategic demand and supply conditions – and mixing them with existing Germanic ideas and institutions, Christianity helped reduce the costs of building these new sociopolitical systems. It is useful to recall here that desires drive and ideas facilitate.

The European council of conquest gods, 1000–1500 – a heavenly drama!

During the few centuries prior to AD 1000, the European vision of the heavenly realm resembled a battleground on which a variety of different Christian, Islamic, and pagan gods struggled for supremacy. While the pagan gods had been eliminated by AD 1000, the European cosmos was populated by a dozen competing Christian gods and a smaller number of Islamic deities. All battling with each other on behalf of their own human supporters. Over the next five centuries, the gods of the Germans, Castilians and, for a while, the English, appeared to gain the upper hand over the gods of the Italians, the Islamic societies in Spain, the French, and the Celtic societies in Britain.

One of the gods – the old imperial god of Rome – had a different agenda from the rest. Instead of struggling against his fellow Christian gods – who were younger and more energetic – the old god of Rome attempted to form a Heavenly Council on which all the Christian gods of Western Europe would be represented, and over which he would preside. The old Roman god had some success in this venture. He even gained the grudging acceptance of his brother gods to allow his representative on Earth, the Pope, to interfere in the appointment of their bishops in their chosen societies. In this way the Roman god came to preside over the war games played out by the other gods and their earthly vassals.

The old god's leadership abilities were most consciously displayed by being able to persuade his brother gods to divert part of their energies from warring with each other to attacking the real enemy, the gods of the Islamic world, who now resided in his country of origin – Palestine. These new wars in the heartland of his youth were to be called the Crusades. These Crusades against the upstart Muslim gods were, in the beginning, quite successful. And for a time the old god of Rome was able to revisit the land of his youth and even to oust his younger sibling from Byzantium under the guise of further attacks (the Fourth Crusade) on the gods of Islam. But the good times were not to last. The Islamic gods staged a recovery, taking back Palestine and even overwhelming Byzantium; and the younger Christian gods of Europe resumed their internecine wars on their own terms, thereby breaking up the European Council of the Gods. Only in Spain were the Islamic gods routed, and this by the Castilian god without the assistance of Rome. Yet worse was to come. New non-conformist gods were to emerge, struggle with the older Catholic gods, and eject these older gods from the more progressive parts of Western Europe.

Medieval Christianity specified clear-cut roles for Church, king, monasteries, priestly philosophers, and ordinary people. These roles will be familiar to readers of the earlier chapters of this book. As these roles are common to all successful strategic societies, they can be seen as responses to a dynamic strategic *logos* rather than to Christianity as a set of independent ideas and institutions. Within each of the kingdoms of Europe, the Church was seen as reflecting the order of the cosmos created by their own national god. And they saw it as their mission to transfer this order to society in general. This was their strategic role. Accordingly, the medieval Church focused on strategic issues rather than personal piety, which was left to the monastic orders to deal with. In particular, the Church reinforced the strategic structure of society by developing a set of ethics – rules of conduct – and attitudes relevant to every rank in society, including the military (the ceremony of knighthood admission, with its fidelity to one's lord), the merchants (usury laws), the guilds (contributions to the Church), and urban elites (provision of hospitals, schools and leper houses). The churches also used the confessional as an instrument of social control, "which helped to ensure that the laity performed the duties appropriate to their station".[48] But these rules of conduct – these strategic instruments – were those required by the strategic *logoi* of Western Europe to sustain their dynamic pathways, not those of an independent institution pursuing a nonstrategic purpose.

The king in European Christendom adopted the role played by rulers in all other strategic societies. One historian of Christianity claims that: "when Christianity arrived in Europe, it carried with it a tradition for regarding the secular ruler as appointed by God and endowed by him with a special task"; a role that was reinforced by "the Germanic tradition of regarding the king as mediator between the people and the gods: his was a special relationship with the powers on which the peace and well-being of human society depended".[49] This role of divine mediation provided the king with power to exercise control over the people, but only within limits. We are told that both traditions gave the people the right to criticize bad strategic leadership and to remove bad strategic rulers. This is "found in the Germanic 'right of resistance': an idea and a practice according to which the relationship between the king and people was of reciprocal obligations, which could not be broken by the ruler without the people taking countermeasures"; and it is found in Roman Christianity in "a tradition of viewing all earthly rulership in a critical light".[50] What we are *not* told, is that these attitudes and institutional arrangements were an outcome of the type of dynamic strategy pursued and the stage reached in the dynamic unfolding process. They are *not* the result of some inherent characteristic of Christian or Germanic ideology. They can be found in all societies. Christian and Germanic ideology merely provided the superficial characteristics of these fundamentally strategic institutions.

The models of European kingship are said to go back to the Bible. In the Germano–Roman empire:

> The royal cloak ... is made to resemble that of the high priest of Israel. One of the plates of the crown imitates the high priest's breastplate, beset with twelve precious stones symbolizing the twelve tribes of Israel; and another plate, also with twelve stones, points at the twelve apostles, the leaders of the new people of God. In its entirety the crown, by its form, its colors, and its numerous entities of stones and pearls, refers symbolically to the heavenly Jerusalem as described in the book of Revelation as the goal of the Church's pilgrimage through history.[51]

In European Christendom, "the king simultaneously appears as God's representative to the people and the people's to God. In other words, he is some sort of priest in his capacity as king, exactly as the priest is some sort of king in his capacity as priest".[52] While this role certainly provides the king with power over the people, which he might employ to achieve selfish personal ends, this is secondary to the desire of both king and people to exercise some control over the mysterious life-system that is responsible for their mutual survival and prosperity. Further, as will be clear from our study of other societies in this book, despite the fact that the strategic ideology of medieval European societies was woven from ideas, symbols and myths from the Bible, the fundamental role of their kings was the same as that of the rulers of all other successful strategic societies. It is a role determined by the needs of the strategic *logos*.

The role of the Pope in European Christendom changed dramatically in the five centuries following AD 1000. Until 1046, the popes were recruited from Roman aristocracy and their interests were largely limited to the see of Rome. Thereafter, with the election of a series of German popes by the German emperor – who ruled the northern half of Italy as well as Germany – the Roman see took a greater interest in Church administration in the various West European kingdoms. Many of these German popes had monastic backgrounds and they attempted to reform the priesthood of Europe in the light of monastic norms, which, as suggested above, tended to be nonstrategic. What started as an attempt to renew the apostolic spirit of the Church, soon became a radical attack on the strategic role that had been adopted by the various national churches over the previous few centuries.

The most notable of these reforming popes was Gregory VII (1073–85), who was particularly concerned about the secularization – or strategic nature – of the national churches and attempted to break the power of national secular rulers over them. Gregory asserted, in effect, that the God of Rome was the universal God and that he alone, operating through the successors of Saint Peter, must determine the election of bishops. And these bishops and their churches must serve the universal God, not the national gods of the warring European kingdoms. Clearly Pope Gregory failed to understand either the strategic role that the national churches were playing, or the fact that this role was the sole reason for the success of the Church in Western Europe.

Not surprisingly, the German emperor and the other European kings saw this papal interference as a threat to their strategic interests. Papal interference, one Church historian tells us:

> made it impossible for the German king to remain passive when confronted with the Roman claims. The coherence and stability of the realm depended on the king's control of the episcopal sees; therefore, the Roman attack resulted in a long and bitter controversy, ending only with the pope's death in exile.[53]

What was at stake here, however, was more than just the "coherence and stability of the realm". The German emperor believed that the very future of German strategic opportunities depended on their strategic ideology remaining in German hands. Other European kings felt the same. During the course of this struggle for Church control, Gregory VII excommunicated the emperor Henry IV (1084–1106), absolved his vassals from their oaths of fealty, claimed the right to elect a successor, and even attempted to establish a papal military force – the *Militia Sancti Petri* – to back up his insistence on "ecclesiastical liberty". In this turn, Henry appointed an "antipope" (Clement III, d. 1191), took possession of Rome in 1084, and forced Gregory into exile.

The reforming efforts of the popes during the eleventh and twelfth centuries, however, gradually provided Roman control over the religious – as opposed to the strategic – activities of the national churches. In particular, the papacy developed a system of appeals to Rome, with "judges delegate" hearing cases in their own kingdom with papal authority. In effect the Roman god had become head of a "Council of National European gods". But, at the same time, Rome was struggling for its own freedom of action from the German empire, which challenged papal authority by "electing" a series of imperial antipopes. Rome, however, achieved considerable success against the German empire under Pope Innocent III (1198–1216), who claimed to be the "vicar of Christ on earth". During the reign of Innocent, the papacy exercised authority over the empire; achieved a degree of political intervention in other kingdoms of Western Europe; founded the Papal states; played a role in the election of the Holy Roman Emperor; became spiritual "overlord" of a number of kingdoms (including England in 1214); initiated, but lost control of, the Fourth Crusade that invaded and partitioned the Byzantine empire; urged reform on the Western churches; encouraged the development of new religious orders, including those founded by Dominic and Frances; and attempted to pursue the Pope's concerns through the Fourth Lateran Council of 1215, which was attended by over 400 bishops and 800 abbots, as well as other clergy.

This reforming religious spirit, however, was soon transformed into a desire by Roman popes for political control in Europe. The first half of the thirteenth century was a golden age of papal power, when the papacy achieved a great victory over the German empire. After two centuries of struggle between emperors and popes, the Hohenstaufen family was finally brought to its knees, the power of the emperor was virtually restricted to Germany, and the pope and his Italian allies gained control of the Italian peninsula. But the triumph was brief, as the German threat was replaced by a French one. It was impossible to keep the strategists at bay. Pope Boniface VIII (1294–1303), who was soon embroiled in conflict with Philip IV (1268–1314) of France, issued the bull of *Unam Sanctum* in 1302 in which he asserted the supremacy of the Roman Church over all temporal powers, but particularly over the kings of France and England. Following his excommunication by the pope, the French king arrested Boniface, who died the following year, and in 1309 established a new papacy at Avignon in southern France. Not until 1377 did the popes return to Rome. The national gods of Europe had effectively deposed the would-be universal God of Rome.

Also, from the early fourteen century the religious institution of the papacy in Rome became, what the Church historians have termed, "corrupt". Essentially, Rome became a small strategic state in competition with other strategic states, and employed its religious institutions and personnel as strategic instruments. In effect, the Roman god engaged in an unequal war – owing to his limited resource base – with the national gods of Western Europe over which he had formerly attempted to preside. Thereafter, Rome had little influence over the national churches of Europe.

Monasteries, during the first half of the second millennium, continued to play a balancing role in the Church. While the mainstream clergy carried out a strategic role, members of monastic and mendicant orders kept alive the values of the early Jesus movement as they understood it. The Benedictine rule by which the daily life of the monastery was to be conducted, aimed to achieve a balance between three main activities: "the work of God" (or liturgical prayer in common); "the work of the hands" (or productive manual work); and "the divine reading" (or individual study of the Bible, works of the "Fathers", and devotional texts). This radical alternative to the mainstream strategic lifestyle, involved a Jesus-like renunciation of property, family and personal autonomy. Needless to say, this material renunciation was expressed by the ordinary monks and nuns, not by the abbots, who, like the bishops, were great landowners and, therefore, an integral part of aristocratic society. There were many inconsistencies and tensions in the medieval Church.

Essentially the monasteries were engaged in a striving for spirituality in a materialist world. This was meant to reduce the tension created by transforming a nonstrategic philosophy into a strategic ideology, and it helped to ease the consciences of the classes devoted entirely to the strategic pursuit. But the main reason the strategists invested a significant proportion of GDP in the monasteries (through land grants, gifts, taxation concessions etc) was because the monks and nuns prayed not only for the souls of their benefactors but also for the success of the strategic pursuit; because monasteries were pioneer land-developing organizations; and because they provided educational, health, and welfare services for the population, thereby minimizing the probability of popular rebellion. Despite their best intentions to the contrary, therefore, the monasteries also played an important strategic role.

The priestly philosophers played their (by now) accustomed role of developing the theology of Christianity and adapting it to each of the strategic requirements of the kingdoms of Western Europe. But, in contrast to the mythmaking of a society like Egypt, Christian mythmakers began not with the reality of their life-system, but with a number of fantastical claims about their religious founder. Much intellectual work was required to rationalize the internal contradictions and lack of rational coherence in Christian dogma. Accordingly, these Christian priestly philosophers constructed a strategic ideology that, unlike Egypt's, had nothing to say about the workings of the European strategic *logos*. While it is claimed by some Christian historians that "Christianity as a theoretical and doctrinal quantity claimed to provide a full explanation of world order, past history, contemporary and future existence"[54], the truth is that its views on all these issues was, and is, highly superficial and, from a strictly rational point of view, totally absurd. These Christian priestly philosophers also developed a tradition of metaphysical musing that has dominated the philosophical disciplines of European universities, which they established, down to the present day.

It was noted above that in the early Church the bishops were also theologians. By contrast, in medieval Europe, there was a greater degree of specialization, with bishops focusing on administration and politics, and the professional teachers and thinkers devoting themselves to theology. Initially theology was developed in the monasteries, as a result not of professional scholarship but of daily devotional studies of the Bible and writings of the Church Fathers. From the eleventh century, economic expansion and urbanization led to the establishment of cathedral schools, which, in major centers like Paris, Oxford, and Cambridge, developed into universities studying Greek writers as well as early churchmen. While Gregorian reforms in the late eleventh century (which required men trained in Church history, law, and theology) together with contact with the Islamic world, stimulated this process of European learning, of more fundamental importance was the changing nature of strategic demand for formal knowledge as the conquest strategy unfolded and European society became more complex. Like the Church, the monasteries, and the monarchy, the priestly philosophers were essential instruments in developing the European strategic *logos*.

The rise of the gods of commerce, 1500–1700

While the national gods of war struggled against each other, they failed to notice the emergence of the new gods of commerce. And when they did notice them, the conquest gods failed to take these upstarts seriously. There was no way, they scoffed, that gods with mercantile interests could compete with those expert in the ways of war. But the powers of the old European gods of war were declining as the conquest strategies of their adopted nations approached exhaustion. Indeed, as some of the old gods had become so senile they were rejected in favor of the new gods of commerce. And as the commerce strategies of these rejuvenated nations were effectively exploited, their prosperity increased and the powers and reputations of their new gods rivaled and, eventually, surpassed those of the few remaining European gods of war. In an effort to understand these remarkable changes in the heavenly and earthly spheres, the people of Europe either praised or blamed a few prominent priestly philosophers for encouraging the emergence of these new gods. No one seemed to understand that desires drive and ideas merely facilitate.

Church historians view the mid-sixteenth century as a major turning point in the development of Christianity. This period saw the emergence of the protestant Church in Western Europe – known as the Reformation – a growing control exercised by the state over their national Churches, and an increasing "secularization" of the state. The essence of protestantism involved a greater emphasis on the relationship between the individual and a loving God, rather than between the Church as representative of all individuals and the sterner, more judgmental God of catholicism. In the protestant churches, the individual was encouraged to read the Bible for himself and to actively participate in the service. To enable this development, both Bible and service were rendered in the vernacular rather than Latin. And the individual was encouraged to support a national church against Rome, together with the mercantile protestant coalition against the catholic conquest states.

Most histories of this religious transformation focus on the role of prominent churchmen, such as Martin Luther (1483–1546) in Germany and John Calvin (1509–1564) in Switzerland. These histories differ as to the relative importance of these (and other) priestly philosophers and the more impersonal "forces of history". One historian poses the following question:

> Did one man, Martin Luther, begin the reformation which otherwise would never have happened, by inventing a new theology ...? Thomas Carlyle ... thought so, pronouncing that if Luther had not stood his ground at the Diet of Worms, when called upon by the Holy Roman emperor to recant, there would have been no French Revolution, no America, no modern freedom.[55]

This historian clearly believes that Carlyle has exaggerated the role of Luther. He suggests that while Luther, Calvin, and other priestly philosophers played an important role in the emergence of protestantism, other forces were also involved, particularly those "at a high political level" in church and state. His difficulty, like many other historians, lies in deciding where the balance should be between the personal and impersonal, the elite and the popular. Indeed, he claims that no one can sort out the causal factors involved in this complex process: while we "have been asked that question in one form or another for generations ... no one supposes that some candidate somewhere is about to discover the right answer, so laying to rest all further discussion".[56] Nor is it possible, our church historian believes, to answer the related question of whether the Reformation could have been evolutionary rather than revolutionary:

> Historians will only have to argue, from their different ideological premises, whether the revolution of the Reformation could or could not have been avoided, by encouraging a liberal process of more gradual institutional and constitutional change.[57]

This difficulty our historian has in explaining the Reformation emerges in other histories of Christianity. Jacob Balling, for example, claims:

> the picture of Christian Europe cannot be drawn in the same way after the middle of the sixteenth century as before. That is due to a strengthening and deepening of the old forces for change: nationalization, individualization, rationalization. But above all it is due to a religious and ecclesiastical reorientation with its point of departure in the experiences of one European, the Saxon friar and academic Martin Luther.
>
> Those two things are in some ways interdependent, both because the Lutheran reform movement acquired its mass effect from the old forces for change and because Luther himself was to some extent one of their exponents. But if ever there has been a case in European religious history where a course of events has been decisively determined by one man's highly personal experience, reflection, choices and action, then the Protestant Reformation can confidently be claimed as it.[58]

While Carlyle clearly understood nothing about causation in history, scholars since his time may be less comfortable with the "great man" view of the past but they are still unable to explain major social changes such as the Reformation. Vague references to "historical forces" such as "nationalization, individualization, rationalization", or forces "from above or below", do not provide the answers we are looking for. These "forces", like the Reformation itself, are outcomes of a more fundamental societal transformation that these histories have been unable to even detect let alone explain. For that purpose we need to employ a general dynamic theory of human society.

The Reformation emerged in those European societies – England, Germany and the low countries – that had exhausted their conquest strategies and had successfully adopted commerce as a replacement strategy by the late fifteenth century. The dynamic strategy of commerce in each of these nations saw the emergence of a new middle class, as a larger proportion of the population was drawn into the new engine of prosperity. This increasingly prosperous middle class generated a growing demand for greater political control over the sources of their new wealth, improved education to facilitate this, and greater access to the strategic guardian who guaranteed their continued commercial success. As the commerce strategy unfolded, individualism and secularization grew in extent and intensity. For those readers interested in detailed case studies, they can follow the fortunes of England in my book *The Ephemeral Civilization* (1997).[59] These strategic changes led to a widespread demand among the middle classes for the reform of the old, corrupt, authoritarian, and, most important of all, *irrelevant* organization of the Catholic Church in commerce societies. Hence, it was this new strategic demand generated by the unfolding commerce strategy that stimulated priestly philosophers like Luther and Calvin to develop a new theology – a new strategic ideology. Had this strategic demand for a new ideology not existed, any theological ideas that Luther and Calvin may have created would not have taken hold. Once again, desires drive, ideas merely facilitate.

Italy, at face value, seems to be an exception. It adopted the dynamic strategy of commerce earlier than north-west Europe, but it retained catholicism as its strategic ideology, even after protestantism had emerged elsewhere. I will argue that it is the exception that proves the rule. The fundamental difference between these two regions is that Italy adopted the commerce strategy many centuries before the latter. Indeed some societies like Venice knew no other dynamic strategy. The reason is that Italy had long been – since the seventh century – on the major trade route between Constantinople and northern Europe and, hence, it was in an ideal position to extract economic rents from societies wanting to participate in this trade. At a time when the warrior aristocracies of northern Europe dominated their national catholic churches, the commerce elite of the Italian city-states (ultimately including Venice, Pisa, Rome, Florence, and Genoa) had become princes, even popes, of their Catholic Church. In doing so they were able to shape Italian catholicism to reflect their strategic interests. Unlike northern Europe, the wealthy Italian commerce families did not have to wrest control of the church from a warrior aristocracy. There was no need for a reformation in Italy, precisely because the existing church provided an effective strategic ideology.

The old catholic strategic ideology held on in those societies – Spain and France – that continued to pursue the conquest strategy. But, some readers might ask, why didn't Spain and France adopt protestantism once they too had abandoned the dynamic strategy of conquest? The answer is that the strategic sequence was swamped by the paradigmatic sequence. What this means is that the industrial technological paradigm shift – the Industrial Revolution – which began in England about 1780, led to the abandonment of Christianity of all types as a strategic ideology in favor of science, *before* the strategic shift from conquest to commerce in Spain and France required a substitution of protestantism for catholicism. Reforms in catholicism, in response to the protestant challenge, slowed down the inevitable strategic effect until the swamping paradigmatic effect occurred. In a world where religion no longer played a strategic role – where it no longer mattered in a materialist way – nostalgia about the old faith played a role in the continuance of catholicism. Nostalgia, however, is never a factor in the adoption and maintenance of strategic ideology, as strategic ideology matters. Strategic ideology is driven by changes in the strategic *logos*.

The debate about protestantism and the rise of "capitalism" initiated and developed by Max Weber (1904) and Richard Tawney (1926) is usually mentioned by historians in this context.[60] The thesis, however, is fundamentally flawed. "Capitalism" was the outcome not of protestantism, but of the exhaustion of the old conquest strategy and the adoption of the new commerce strategy in north-west Europe at a time when south and central Europe were still finding the conquest strategy profitable. As we have seen, it was the subsequent change in strategic demand in the "capitalist" commerce societies for a new strategic ideology that led to the emergence of protestantism, rather than the other way around. And these "first" commerce societies were also the first to exhaust their traditional dynamic strategies and to adopt the entirely new industrial technology strategy that powered the further development of "capitalism" in the modern world. Ideology plays a facilitating not a driving role in the dynamics of human society.

THE RISE AND FALL OF ISLAM

Only the briefest outline of the rise and fall of Islam as a strategic ideology – not necessarily as a spiritual idea or experience – can be provided here. This is a reflection not of its relative importance but of my familiarity with the subject area. To keep this vast subject within the confines of a single volume, I have focused on a limited number of historical case studies associated with the rise of the modern world. But as Islam has had such an important impact on the world in the past it cannot be passed over in silence.

The dynamic strategy of Islam

Muhammad and the conquest of Arabia

For the Prophet Muhammad (570–632), Islam was not a *new* religion, if indeed it was meant to be a religion at all. His primary objective was to bring the

"One God" experienced by the Jews and Christians to the Arabs as a strategic guardian. And his reason for doing so was to unify the fragmented warring tribes of Arabia so that they might be able to achieve the "national" peace and prosperity experienced by the prevailing Byzantine (Christian) and Persian (Zoroastrian) empires. Muhammad was not interested in establishing a religious – or nonstrategic – community, along the lines of the early Jesus movement. We are told that "he had long been worried by what he perceived to be a crisis in Arab society ... Throughout Arabia one tribe fought another, in a murderous cycle of vendetta and counter-vendetta"; and in the process "some of the old tribal values had been lost ... making money at the expense of some of the tribe's poorer family groupings, or clans".[61]

The societal chaos in Arabia was the outcome of the location of these tribal societies in the borderlands between the superpowers of Egypt, Mesopotamia and the Mediterranean. As we have seen with Palestinian society, this superpower oppression led to persistent strategic failure, which in turn generated intense strategic frustration. It was this strategic frustration that led to the emergence of the new strategic ideology of Islam. But the remarkable success of this strategic ideology, as we shall see, was the outcome of fortunate timing. Islam was born into a world where the superpowers had fought each other to a standstill.

The Prophet's lifework was to create and maintain the "unity of the *ummah*" (or Muslim community) as an ordered, prosperous, and just society. This "unity" was similar in nature to the Egyptian concept of *maat*, or community order, and it involved achieving societal survival and prosperity. One religious historian has expressed it thus: "the political and social welfare of the *ummah* would have sacramental value for Muslims. If the *ummah* prospered, it was a sign that Muslims were living according to God's will"; and again: "the Quran did not put forward any philosophical arguments for monotheism; its approach was practical ... The old religion, the Quran claimed, was simply not working"[62] – not working as a strategic ideology. In other words, Muhammad's objectives were strategic (materialist) rather than merely religious (spiritual). Islam was to be a new strategic ideology for the Arabs – although not new to the prevailing world empires – with a new strategic guardian smiling on a new strategic *logos*.

The key to success for the new Islamic society of Arabia was the adoption of a viable dynamic strategy at a propitious time in the history of the Middle East. Muhammad's choice of dynamic strategy was conquest. This was an interesting choice for a prophet of God, particularly if we make the mistake of assuming that Islam was a religion rather than a strategic ideology. Muhammad could have adopted the alterative dynamic strategy of commerce. In the early seventeenth century Mecca was an important center of commerce, with some Arab merchants growing rich on trade with Syria in wool, leather, grain, olive oil, wine, and, particularly, precious metals mined in the Hijaz.[63] Clearly, Muhammad had decided that commerce, and the old gods of commerce centered on the pagan shrine in Mecca, might generate wealth for certain tribes like the Quraysh, but they could not unite the Arabs in a prosperous, peaceful, and just society. Even the Prophet's early preaching in Mecca was seen as "an attack on the shrine at Mecca and the prosperity it brought".[64]

Only through conquest, Muhammad believed, could the unity of *ummah* be achieved. This explains why conquest as a strategy is discussed at length in the Quran. There are a score or more topic references in the Quran to warfare, battle, and the distribution of plunder – even a six-page *sura* (chapter) entitled "Battle gains" (*sura* 8). In the Quran the ultimate justification of conquest is strategic: "To anyone who fights in God's way, whether killed or victorious, We shall give a great reward"[65] – meaning material or spiritual reward. The Quran even instructs on the art of war and the role of the strategic guardian: "Believers, when you meet a force in battle, stand firm and keep God firmly in mind, so that you may prosper".[66] In other places, the Quran attempts to justify conquest as a just war, as it is necessary in order to maintain and extend unity of the *ummah*.

This new approach for Arabia – unity and prosperity through conquest – was first revealed to the Prophet in 610, but initial progress in developing the new Islamic society was slow, as resistance in Mecca to these new ideas was considerable. How could the Arabs – a fractious people living in the borderlands between the superpowers – possibly succeed through the pursuit of conquest when so many had tried before and failed? Muhammad must be mad! And it was not until 622 when he was forced to leave Mecca for Medina – known as the *hijrah* – where he became the leader of a collection of some of the poorer tribal groups that were united not by blood but by the new Islamic strategic ideology, that his radical approach began to bear fruit.

Muhammad's new multi-tribal community – considered "an astonishing innovation in Arabian society" – were quick to accept the conquest strategy in order to survive and prosper. This strategy was euphemistically called the *ghazu* or "raid". No doubt these raids on prosperous Meccan caravans were calculated to provoke a response from the dominant tribe of Quraysh. And when the response came, the Prophet's well-drilled army was ready. After a number of battles in the second half of the 620s, Muhammad eventually marched on Mecca, which capitulated without a fight in 630. This major victory demonstrated the power of the new strategic guardian Allah, together with the viability of the new Islamic strategic *logos* or *ummah*. Not surprisingly, the scattered Arab tribes were mightily impressed and keen to join the new *ummah*, in order to participate in the new prosperity rather than to adopt a new religious faith. By the death of the Prophet in 632, all the Arab tribes had been incorporated into the *ummah* – the new strategic *logos* of Arabia.

The early Islamic empire and strategy

To sustain the dynamics of the *ummah* it was obvious to the "companions" of the dead Prophet that their conquest strategy must be pursued beyond Arabian borders. One scholar tells us that after Muhammad's death "the leaders of the new state were fully aware that it had to expand or collapse. For them there was only one possible course of action: conquest".[67] But it was a conclusion that Muhammad had already reached before he died. We are told that he had plans to conquer Syria, and had already sent a "carefully planned expedition against Tabuk in the northern Hijaz, which may have been a trial run for attacks on Syria ... There can be no doubt that when the early Muslim high command embarked on a conquest of Syria they were pursuing a policy already begun by their Prophet".[68] Muhammad, therefore, was a prophet of the new strategic guardian of conquest — of Allah — and the early *ummah* was a conquest *logos*.

The companions of the Prophet – the *Rashidun* – included Abu Bakr, Umar ibn al-Khattab, Uthman ibn Affan, and Ali ibn Abi Talib, the four "rightly guided" caliphs who ruled the *ummah* from 632 to 661. The Rashidun's decision to pursue the conquest strategy beyond the boundaries of Arabia, was akin to the Roman decision to pursue conquest beyond the Italian peninsula some 900 years earlier. All conquest societies are driven by the same motivation – to maximize the probability of survival and prosperity – irrespective of their strategic ideology, whether pagan, Christian, or Islamic. As Karen Armstrong has confirmed:

> There was nothing religious about these campaigns ... The objective of Umar and his warriors was entirely pragmatic: they wanted plunder and a common activity that would preserve the unity of the *ummah*.[69]

The close relationship between Islamic strategic ideology and the conquest strategy is reflected by the key public buildings in Arab cities that sprang up in the conquered territories. We are told that "the mosque and the palace [military headquarters] ... shared a common wall". This became the "classic central architectural layout of the Islamic city ... a layout that had no direct parallel in pre-Islamic architecture and which was to persist for centuries to come".[70]

The Islamic conquest strategy was pursued with remarkable success in the seventh and eight centuries by the Rashidun (632–661) and by the Umayyads (661–750) who, under Muawiyyad (661–680), seized power by overthrowing Ali ibn Abi Talib the cousin and son-in-law of the Prophet. This success was aided by the military exhaustion of the Byzantine and Persian empires, which had been engaging in debilitating warfare for some time. But it was also aided by the determination and fighting qualities of the Arab tribes united by a new strategic ideology. We are told by an expert, Hugh Kennedy, on the Arab conquests that:

> The early Muslims had no secret weapons, no mastery of new military technology with which to overpower their enemies. Their advantages were simply those of mobility, good leadership and, perhaps most important of all, motivation and high morale.[71]

And, as just suggested, extremely good luck in the timing of their breakout from Arabia.

Under the Rashidun, the Islamic armies successfully invaded Syria, Iraq, Egypt, Libya, Iran, Afghanistan, India, Cyprus, and Armenia; and under the Umayyads the empire was extended into north-west Africa, Spain, and the Khazar homeland.[72] In this way, Islam replaced Christianity and Zoroastrianism as the strategic ideology of much of the civilized world.

By the late seventh century, the Arab empire increasingly resembled all other empires, despite its Islamic ideology. It was ruled by an absolute monarchy; it settled the empire with people from the homeland (outlawed under early caliphs); it permitted conquered peoples to convert to Islam; and it imposed Arabic as the lingua franca of the empire. And the strategic *logos* of the new empire was determined not by any metaphysical principles of Islam that might be contained in the Quran, but rather by the requirements of the dynamic strategy of conquest, communicated via strategic demand. In part this is recognized by the standard historical treatments of the new Islamic societies. Ira Lapidus, for example, writes:

> Islam was never the sole organizing principle of pre-modern Islamic societies. Each inherited and maintained cultural identities, social organizations, political institutions, and economies defined in non-Islamic terms. ...The economies of Muslim peoples were almost never organized in Muslim terms except for certain modifying ethical concepts such as opposition to usury and demand for fairness, justice, and charity.[73]

Of course, there was nothing unique to Islam about these ethical considerations (including opposition to usury), which were used and abused in Christian and Islamic societies alike.

While the Arab empire increased via two waves of conquest between 634 and 650 and 696 and 737, the realization that there were limits to empire must have dawned on the Islamic leaders with the dismal failure of the attempted seaborne invasion of Constantinople in 717–18 under Umar II (717–720). As can now be determined, the Arab conquest strategy had exhausted itself by the late 730s. With this exhaustion, the huge additional returns to conquest in the form of land, slaves, mines, booty, and incomes from new tenants came to an abrupt halt. But this did not mean that the empire was about to enter a phase of slow decline and collapse as had happened to Rome three centuries earlier. Why? Because the Arab empire spanned the great trade routes between wealthy societies in China, India, the Black Sea region, Mesopotamia, the Levant, Egypt, Africa, the Aegean, and a rejuvenating Western Europe. The rich material returns to conquest were effectively replaced by the equally impressive returns to commerce as the Umayyads and their successors exerted control over much of the civilized world's commerce.

Yet, although the Islamic empire in some form was guaranteed by the dynamic strategy of commerce from the 730s, this did not prevent the rise and fall of political and ethnic dynasties – as had occurred in ancient Egypt. Indeed, the Umayyads were swept from power in 750 by the rebellious Abbasids, who initially pretended to support the disaffected Shii (who could not forgive the Umayyads for deposing Ali ibn Abi Talib, the Prophet's closest male relative) in order to seize power for themselves. Only Spain survived as an Umayyad Emirate. The ruthless Iraq-based Abbasids (750–935) merely stepped into the shoes of the Syria-based Umayyads to reap the benefits of the fabulously profitable commerce strategy. It was a period of political rule, know as the "high caliphate period", during which the caliph, located in Baghdad, was styled the "Shadow of God on earth" – the earthly representative of the Islamic strategic guardian. The caliph was the symbolic link between humanity and God, while the affairs of the *ummah* were left in the hands of a vizier.

The peak of the caliphate period was reached during the reign of Harun al-Rashid (786–809), who was a great patron of the arts. At this time there was a cultural renaissance, during which ancient Greek texts were translated into Arabic, and important scientific discoveries were made. There was a vast gulf between the imperial caliphate, which looked to Persia rather than Arabia for cultural influences, and the simple *ummah* of the Quran. To accommodate these two different parts of society, a dualistic legal system was developed. While shariah law was followed by the *ulama* (learned men, or priestly philosophers) and the ordinary people, the court and mercantile elite adopted the autocratic legal system of former Mesopotamian empires. This reflected the intense tension in Islamic society between the dynamic strategists who were focused on strategic issues of survival and prosperity, and the priestly philosophers concerned with developing Islamic strategic ideology into a spiritual mythology. It is a tension that has always existed in Islamic society – a tension that today increases the cost of modernization.

The later Islamic empire and strategy

Once the dynamics of the Arab empire – fed sequentially by both the conquest and commerce strategies – had ground to halt in the early ninth century, the ever-present regional centrifugal forces of fragmentation were able to overwhelm the centripetal force of strategic leadership. In other words, once the commerce strategy had been exhausted, the benefits of empire no longer exceeded the costs of maintaining it. Consequently, there was considerable material incentive for regional strongmen to break away from the Abbasid caliphate. By the 820s the old empire had fragmented into five separate caliphates or emirates; and into eight separate states by the 880s. Throughout the ninth century, the Abbasid caliphate retreated to its Mesopotamian heartland, then, in the early tenth century, it staged a temporary revival by retaking western Arabia and Egypt. But this was a false dawn. The Abbasid dynasty was extinguished in 935 by a pro-Shiite Persian dynasty, the Buwayhids. Finally, the Shiites had their revenge over the traitorous Abbasids.

Quite predictably, the fragmentation of the old Arab empire opened the way for opportunistic outsiders to make their bid for power in this immensely rich part of the civilized world. Various Turkish societies had for centuries been operating vigorously on the northeastern borders of the Arab empire, and Turkish soldiers had been in its employ. Some of the Ghaznavids had even been converted to Islam. From about 1037, a clan of the Ghuzz, who had been employed as mercenaries by the Ghaznavids, rebelled against their masters and defeated the neighboring Buwayhids in Mesopotamia in 1055 to form the Seljuk Sultanate. Flushed with success, the Turkish Seljuks continued their offensive, defeating the Byzantine army at Manzikert in 1071 and occupying Anatolia as far west as the Bosphorus; and they also attacked and pushed the Fatimid Caliphate out of both the Levant and western Arabia. But, from the early twelfth century, the Islamic Seljuk dynasty began to fragment, opening the way for the Byzantines and the Western European Crusaders to go on the offensive in the west, and for the Mongols to close in from the east.[74]

The Crusades were a series of events with more significance for Christendom than for Islamdom. Together with the Castilian offensive in Spain, they heralded the growing confidence, power and common identity of the West. The proximate cause of the Crusades was the Seljuk's conquest of Fatimid Syria in 1070, because during this campaign they came into conflict with the Byzantines in Anatolia, pushing them back to the Bosphorus over the following two decades. In 1091 the Byzantine emperor requested help from the French Pope, Urban II (1042–99), who responded by summoning the First Crusade in 1095. But right at the beginning, the Pope lost control of the Crusade to the materialist warriors from northwestern Europe, who were determined to make their fortunes. The First Crusade, therefore, was conducted for strategic, not religious reasons. Men do not fight wars for ideas.

In July 1099 the Crusaders laid siege to Jerusalem and established four separate states in Palestine, Lebanon, and Anatolia. Owing to their fragmentation and infighting, the Seljuks were powerless to prevent this invasion of territory they had held for four centuries. But a century later, in 1187, the Kurdish general Salah ed-din Yussuf ibn Ayub (or Saladin, 1137–1193) retook Jerusalem, and the Third Crusade (1189–92) failed to recover it. And of course the Fourth Crusade (1204) was hijacked by the Venetians in order to take Constantinople and break up the Byzantine empire – something that even Islamic forces had been unable to achieve. Despite their failure, the Crusaders retained a small presence on the Levantine coast for a further century. While this insignificant presence was tolerated by the Ayyubids, who held Egypt and Palestine for the first three-quarters of the thirteenth century, it was finally swept away by the succeeding Mamluke dynasty formed by the former Turkish palace guards.

The Mongols also took advantage of the fragmenting empires of the Seljuks and Byzantines.[75] Genghis Khan, "Lord of the Earth", whose real name was Temujin (1162/67–1227), initiated the greatest disturbance in the Middle East since the Arab invasions of the seventh century. When he died Temujin's empire extended from Persia to Korea. Within a decade, Temujin's successor began exploiting weaknesses in the Middle East and Eastern Europe that had been exposed by earlier raids. By the early 1260s, the Mongol Khanate of the Golden Horde had been established in Eastern Europe (with campaigns that had punched into Poland and Hungary as far as the borders of the German empire, and deep into northern Russia); the Khanate of Persia had been formed in the Middle East (with the Seljuks in Anatolia forced into vasseldom); the Khanates of the White Horde and of Chaghatay dominated central Asia; and the empire of the Great Khans ruled China. These Mongol empires lasted until the mid to late fourteenth century in the Middle East, Mongolia, and China; and to 1502 in Eastern Europe.

While the Mongols developed a highly efficient military machine, they did not possess a sophisticated societal system. Accordingly, they adopted the institutions and organizations of the more culturally advanced states they conquered. By the end of the early fourteenth century, all Mongol states had adopted Islam mythology as their strategic ideology and Islamic principles for their legal system.

The declining power of the Mongol empire in the Middle East allowed the Turkish emirates of Anatolia (successors of the Seljuks) to reassert themselves in the mid-fourteenth century. The most vigorous of these was the Ottoman Sultanate on the Bosphorus, which, by 1400, had taken over the former territory of the Byzantine empire on both sides of the Bosphorus. Hence, the Ottoman empire became the flag carrier for the Islamic strategic ideology. Only the city of Constantinople resisted invasion. At least until 1453, when the occupying Ottomans changed its name forever from Constantinople to Istanbul. Finally, the old Christian God had been displaced by the younger Islamic God.

During the second half of the fifteenth century, the Ottomans pushed into Hungary and took over the Crimea, almost encircling the Black Sea and making it a private Islamic lake (actually not achieved until the conquest of Georgia a century later). But during the sixteenth century the Ottomans – particularly under Selim I (1512–20) and Suleiman the Magnificent (1520–66) – included Syria, Palestine, Egypt, Algeria, the rest of North Africa (Tunis, Tripoli, Barqa), Iraq, Arabia, Hungary, and Moldavia in their empire. By the end of Suleiman's reign, even the Mediterranean could be regarded as largely a private Ottoman lake. Only the earlier Romans had a better claim to private ownership of this vast body of water.

But by the late seventeenth century the Ottomans had finally exhausted their conquest strategy and their alternative commerce strategy was being slowly strangled by Western Europe. In the late fifteenth century the Spanish, Portuguese, and British explored sea routes to north and central America, and around Africa to India rather than conduct commerce through the Ottoman-controlled Levant. And during the sixteenth century these European countries began settling the Americas and establishing trading centers along the west and east coasts of Africa, and throughout India and Southeast Asia. By the mid-seventeenth century, Spain and Venice dominated trade in the western and central Mediterranean and even as far as the Black Sea and the Levant; both Spain and Portugal commanded trade with the Americas; and Britain, Holland, Portugal and France monopolized the sea trade between Western Europe, Africa, India, Southeast Asia, and China.[76]

By the mid-seventeenth century, therefore, the Ottoman empire had lost its monopoly of east-west trade, and was quickly becoming cut-off from the wellsprings of growth and prosperity that had fueled the superpowers of the Middle East for millennia. The geopolitical center of the world was shifting from East to West. Hence, it is hardly surprising that this once mighty empire began to stagnate in the seventeenth century and to decline in the eighteenth. With the result that, by 1800, Muslims, not only in the Ottoman empire but throughout Asia as well, began to realize that Islamdom had finally been overtaken by the West. This reality was put beyond any doubt by the technological paradigm shift in Western Europe known as the Industrial Revolution, which occurred in the first half of the nineteenth century. The Christian strategic guardian was now in the ascendancy.

The metaphysics of Islam

A major thread running throughout the fabric of Islamic history is the tension between material progress and the ethnical system outlined in the Quran. It is a tension between the strategic and metaphysical conceptions of the world; between the materialist and spiritual quests; and between the dynamic strategist and the priestly philosopher. This tension existed at the very beginning when Muhammad developed a mystical dimension to his Islamic strategic ideology, and when Islamic societies subsequently experienced strategic crisis and, hence, strategic frustration, this tension led to the emergence of fundamental religious reform.

Muhammad, as shown above, established a simple egalitarian social system, the rules for which are enshrined in the Quran. This system was based on his interpretation of old Arabian tribal values and social relationships. He had no way of knowing that this Quranic social system would soon become obsolete as Arab armies unexpectedly overwhelmed Mesopotamia, Persia, Egypt, North Africa and Spain. While retaining an Islamic strategic ideology, the new Arab empire needed to develop a new sociopolitical structure if it was to survive. By the time of the Umayyad dynasty, the leadership, legal, and other sociopolitical structures had more in common with other great conquest empires than with the simple Quranic social system. Yet, because the Quran was well drilled and, later, written down, it became the benchmark against which more sophisticated sociopolitical systems were measured. In the eyes of the priestly philosophers, the Quranic system became the ethical standard.

This tension between the strategic and Quranic views of the world began with Muhammad's confusion about the difference between a strategic ideology and a religion. Despite the fact that Muhammad himself adopted the conquest strategy to generate both social unity and prosperity, the Quran speaks out against unjust wars – all wars except those in defense of the *ummah*. The modest success of the conquest strategy in the Prophet's life time may not have provided an insurmountable ethical problem for the Quran reciters (or priestly philosophers), but the unexpected and remarkable success of Muhammad's companions, particularly Umar and Uthman, certainly did so.

While the strategic leaders of the Arab empire developed radically new (to Arab eyes) sociopolitical structures in response to a rapidly changing strategic demand of the new Islamic *logos*, the typically conservative *ulama* compared these institutions critically with the old Quran ideal. The priestly philosophers were particularly concerned about the emergence of new absolute forms of leadership, the displacement of egalitarian Sharah law by a new autocratic and imperial law, and the growing focus on material success. Their opposition to these strategic changes led to the development of a new spiritual form of Islam that expressed an antistrategic ethic foreign to the intentions of Muhammad and the Quran. In this way, the strategic ideology of the Prophet was, for the first time, transformed into a metaphysical mythology. A leading exemplar of this new religious approach to Islam was Hasan al-Basri (d. 728). We are told that

> Hasan initiated a religious reform in Basrah, teaching his followers to meditate deeply on the Quran, and that refection, self-examination and a total surrender to God's will were the source of true happiness, since they resolved the tension between human desires and what God desired for men and women.[77]

The priestly philosophers of the early eighteenth century had created a new religion and a nonstrategic community within Islamic strategic society.

It was a religion renewed each time materialist Islamic societies experienced strategic crisis. And this religious renewal always involved a return to the fundamentalism of the Quran – or at least those parts that suited the priestly philosophers. For example, with the decline of the Caliphate – the fragmentation of Islamdom – in the tenth and eleventh centuries, there was an attempt by the *ulama* to extend their influence in the Islamic world. They did this by establishing Islamic colleges, or *madrasahs*, to increase their numbers and to take over the bureaucracies and legal systems of the various emirates. In this way the priestly philosophers gained a degree of independence from the military leaders, or *amirs*, and the influence of religious ideas and institutions in Islamic society increased significantly. Further, this religious influence became increasingly mystical in nature. Abu Ali ibn-Sina, or Avicenna (980–1037), for example, thought that prophets were the ideal philosophers and emphasized the role of mystical experience.

An important, but generally neglected, exception to this mystical approach to both philosophy and the understanding of strategic crisis, was the approach taken by Abd al-Rahman ibn Khaldun (1332–1406).[78] Rather than asserting that Allah was the cause of the rise and fall of human society, ibn Khaldun sought an explanation in history. This was a radical intellectual innovation, because all other *ulama* regarded history as an inferior discipline, owing to its preoccupations with ephemeral events and institutions rather than the eternal truths of metaphysics. What ibn Khaldun's detractors did not understand – what the priestly philosophers in all societies and in all ages fail to understand – was that "eternal" truths can only be found underlying the ephemeral patterns of civilization.

Our interest here in ibn Khaldun is that he developed a theory of history in which survival and prosperity is the outcome of a strong sense of group solidarity (*asibiyyah*). He also developed a theory of cycles based on human psychology, whereby the vitality of the ruling class that creates prosperity is undermined by their very wealth, leading to complacency and a loss of vigor. While an outstanding intellectual achievement for its time and setting, ibn Khaldun's hypothesis is a supply-side construct that may provide a partial explanation of the disintegration of leadership in some dynasties but is unable to explain the recurrent rise and fall of their societies. Only a demand-side theory can do so. Even so, ibn Khaldun's work is on an entirely different plane to that of all other Islamic priestly philosophers.

The Mongol invasions of the thirteenth century also led to religious revival in the Arab world. As usual, strategic crisis followed by strategic frustration, turned Arab minds to the spiritual alternative to strategic success. As Karen Armstrong has written:

> The Mongol invasions had led to a mystical movement, which helped people come to terms with the catastrophe they had experienced at the deeper levels of psyche ...[79]

And again:

> Throughout Islamic history, at times of great political crisis – especially during a period of foreign encroachment – a reformer (*mujdadid*) would often renew the faith so that it could meet the new conditions. These reforms usually followed a similar pattern. They were conservative, since they attempted to go back to basics rather than create an entirely new solution.[80]

One such reformer was Ahmad ibn Taymiyyah (1263–1328) of Damascus, who reformed shariah law by purging post-Rashidun accretions and applying Quranic notions to the current situation. He also attempted to counter the influence of Sufism, the mystical tradition of Islam.

Finally, strategic crisis experienced by the Ottoman empire in the late eighteenth century also resulted in the usual religious reform, involving a fundamentalist return to the Quran and the *sunnah* (or habits and religious practice of the Prophet). If strategic crisis could generate a revival of religious fundamentalism in the past, it is not difficult to understand the psychic force of strategic frustration among Islamic peoples today, when the global dominance of the West – the former Crusaders – has been overwhelming for more than two centuries and must appear endless. It is hardly surprising, therefore, that Islamic fundamentalism today is more fanatical than religious. Islamic terrorism is an outcome of the age-old problem of strategic frustration.

A TENUOUS TRIUMPH?

By the mid-eighteenth century, the triumph of the One God appeared complete. In Christian form he dominated Europe, northern Asia, significant parts of China and Southeast Asia, much of the Americas, and a growing part of Oceania; while in Islamic form he presided over the Middle East, the eastern Mediterranean, northern Africa, Egypt, central Asia, India, and parts of Southeast Asia. Only in Jewish and Zoroastrian forms did he appeal to boutique markets. The One God, therefore, was the strategic guardian of most of the pre-modern world, as well as the spiritual guide for its vast populations. Only parts of China, Indo-China, Japan and south-west Africa seemed able to resist his charms.

What a contrast this provided to the world just two millennia earlier, when the heavens were crowded with tens, possibly hundreds, of thousands of gods.[81] Surely it would not be much longer before the One God emptied the heavens of the last of his competitors and became the sole guardian of a global strategic *logos*. Surely. But then something totally unexpected happened. Just as he had total victory in his grasp, the One God ... died!

Chapter 6
Death of the Old God

Life is profoundly ironical. The glory and triumphs of mankind are, as history shows, closely followed by its humiliations and failures. So it was with the One God. After emerging triumphant and providing unquestioned strategic guidance for the late Roman empire and the kingdoms of Europe for one-and-a-half millennia, the Old God was abruptly cast aside and pronounced dead. No longer would he be looked to by Western civilization – or by the later followers of the West – to sustain its strategic *logos*.

Instead, during the nineteenth century, the European God was displaced as strategic guardian by that upstart deity of science. Only in strategically backward Islamic societies would the Old God continue to be regarded with a respectful nostalgia, despite his strategic impotence. But even this misplaced devotion will evaporate once the Islamic world fully embraces the modern world – as it inevitably will. Divine fate clearly is inextricably entwined with the fate of mankind.

"GOD IS DEAD"

In 1882 Friedrich Nietzsche famously announced the death of God in his book entitled, with unintentional irony, *The Gay Science*.[1] And in the following year he explained what he meant, in his most famous book, *Thus Spoke Zarathustra*.[2] Here we are told the story about Zarathustra leaving his home in the mountains to bring mankind a unique gift. On this journey Zarathustra meets a saintly old hermit who loves not mankind, as Zarathustra does, but only God. After an exchange of views, Zarathustra resumes his journey to mankind and says to himself: "Could it be possible! This old saint in his woods has not heard the news that *God is dead!*". For Zarathustra, the only meaning left in life after the death of God is the idea of the "overman", which is the gift he is bringing to mankind. Zarathustra says to himself:

> The overman is the meaning of the earth. Let your will say: the overman *shall be* the meaning of the earth! I beseech you, my brothers, *remain faithful to the earth* and do not believe those who speak to you of extraterrestrial hopes! They are mixers of poisons whether they know it or not.
> They are despisers of life, dying off and self-poisoned, of whom the earth is weary: so let them fade away!
> Once the sacrilege against God was the greatest sacrilege, but God died, and then all these desecrators died. Now to desecrate the earth is the most terrible thing, and to esteem the bowels of the unfathomable higher than the meaning of the earth!

The "overman" was Nietzsche's term for a process by which mankind could achieve power over itself and the Earth, and, thereby, do for itself what only

God had formerly been able to do. Mankind's new power would enable it to sustain society through knowledge of self and nature, rather than through a mystical approach to the Old God, now dead. Both the old approach and the nature of mankind had to be overcome in order to turn away from "the bowels of the unfathomable" and to embrace self-determination with joy and hope. Nietzsche believed that human knowledge would replace the Old God in determining our future. Zarathustra says: "Behold, I teach you the overman" – the new strategic guardian of knowledge. As the Old God is dead we have to become our own gods.

THE REAL MEANING OF "SECULARIZATION"

In the early 1880s Nietzsche gave imaginative expression to an earth-changing transformation that had been underway for the past century – the technological paradigm shift, known as the Industrial Revolution. This transformation, which is analyzed in Chapter 10, was the first technological paradigm shift in eleven thousand years, and it had a dramatic transforming impact on human society, the natural world, and the realm of the gods

By the late nineteenth century in the most strategically advanced parts of Western Europe, and its offshoots in the New World, the technological strategy had replaced the exhausted commerce strategy; and the modern (or industrial) paradigm had replaced the neolithic (or agricultural) paradigm. These changes were seismic in their impacts on the strategic *logos* of the modern world, and on its guardians. For the first time, the modern strategic *logos* became dependent upon the development of both science and technology for its survival. And science gradually, but inevitably, replaced religion as the strategic ideology of the world's most complex and progressive societies.

Under the new technological paradigm, the Old God was displaced by the deity of science as the guardian of the modern strategic *logos*. As far as the West was concerned, therefore, the Old Strategic God was well and truly dead. And it was Nietzsche who broadcast the mind-shattering news. Only the memory of this, once, triumphant and dominant God lived on as a personal deity in the minds of some pious individuals.

Over some two millennia, Christianity had come full circle. It began with the Jesus movement, taking the form of a nonstrategic community based on a radical egalitarianism. Over the following three centuries the Church abandoned its initial egalitarianism, developed a hierarchical organizational structure, and adopted a mythical history and a mystical theology. In the early to mid-fourth century, this mystical religion was adopted as a strategic ideology by the declining Roman empire, which had been abandoned by its old pagan gods of conquest. In the process, Christianity became a strategic instrument of empire and its God became a strategic guardian – a role identical to that played by the strategic ideologies of all aspiring societies. With the final collapse of Rome and its western empire, the strategic ideology of Christianity was adopted by the conquest societies of Western Europe. The religious, as opposed to the strategic, character of European Christianity was maintained by the Church's monastic orders.

While Christianity proved to be an "effective" European strategic ideology for both the conquest and commerce strategies – presiding over the rise of the West until the late eighteenth century – it was not able to extend this role to the technological strategy. For its sustenance, the new technological *logos* of the West required a rational scientific ideology, not a mystical metaphysical ideology. With the abandonment of religion as a strategic ideology, the Christian Church was transformed back into a nonstrategic, largely egalitarian, community. By the twentieth century the circle was complete. Perhaps this is the real, if unintentional, meaning of the "Second Coming" of Jesus.

This reality is very different from the usual historian's explanation of the rise of modernity – of the emergence of industry, technology, science and "secularization". It is worth quoting one historian of Christianity on this topic at some length. Jacob Balling claims that:

> The modern European industrial economy has many other roots than Christian ones. But it could hardly have come into being without the Christian tradition of renouncing the impulses of the 'flesh' by an ascetic discipline and a rational planning of life with a defined purpose, carried through on the basis of time schemes and universally valid sets of rules. In other words, it is unthinkable without monasticism. It is not thinkable, either, without Christian insistence on a critique of tradition based on a concept of past and future perfection. And it would not exist at all without the natural sciences, which can only be understood in the light of the Jewish and Christian assertion about God, in relation to whom everything else, all individual phenomena, is both 'accidental' and 'regular' – governed by laws.[3]

This is an amazing series of assertions unaccompanied by any supporting evidence. Yet it is widely accepted in scholarly circles. It is part of the flawed supply-side approach, typical of religious historians (and all other scholars), resulting in the totally false claim that Europe's industrial transformation required preconditions that only Christianity could supply. The Industrial Revolution, we are told, was an outcome of "ascetic discipline", "rational planning", "time schemes" and "universally valid sets of rules" that could be provided only by monasticism! What is wrong with this? First, in a society undergoing strategic and paradigmatic transformation, facilitating instruments like discipline, planning, and rules emerge not from a pre-existing philosophy, but directly in response to strategic demand. The theory and the evidence for this is provided in my *The Ephemeral Civilization* (1997). Facilitating institutions and organizations are not conveniently extruded from supply-side structures like religion, but rather arise in response to the requirements of an unfolding dynamic strategy. Otherwise, totally unexpected developments that have no preconditions could never occur. And there were no preconditions for the seismic technological paradigm change of the late eighteenth to early nineteenth century.[4]

Second, monasticism was not a forcing ground for the requirements of the Industrial Revolution, but a way of maintaining the early nonstrategic, or religious, function of Christianity in the face of the strategic (materialist) role adopted by the medieval Church. Third, natural science in Europe emerged in response to the strategic demand generated by both a mature commerce strategy and the closely following technological strategy; and not as the supply-side outcome of Judaeo-Christian traditions. In fact, the Christian Church acted as a brake on this intellectual response by persecuting major scientists such as Giordano Bruno (1548–1600) and Galileo Galilei (1564–1642); intimidating many others, such as René Descartes (1596–1650) and Charles Darwin (1809–1882); and banning the books of thousands of intellectuals (the infamous *Index Librorum Prohibitorium*, operative from 1559 to 1966, and administered by the Roman Inquisition), including those by Bentham, Bergson, Comte, Defoe, Diderot, Flaubert, Gibbon, Hobbes, Hume, Kant, Kepler, Locke, Mill, Montaigne, Montesquieu, Pascal, Rousseau, Sand, Spinoza, Stendhal, Voltaire, and Zola.[5]

Fourth, the *idea* of spiritual progress is irrelevant to the *fact* of material progress, which is the outcome of a blind striving to survive and prosper.[6] As always, desires drive and ideas, which respond to strategic demand, merely facilitate. Finally, my dynamic-strategy theory suggests that even had Christianity died on the cross with its luckless founder, Europe would still have given rise to the Industrial Revolution within a similar time frame. The truth is that Christianity was shaped by the European strategic *logos*, not the reverse. Zoroastrianism – had the Parthians rather than the Romans dominated the Mediterranean – would have provided an equally effective strategic ideology for pre-modern Europe. A strategic ideology merely provides a society with the confidence to act as if their strategic *logos* is going to survive and prosper.

Similar claims are made about the role of Christianity in the growing "secularization" that characterizes the modern world. Somewhat paradoxically, it is claimed that Christianity was responsible for its own strategic demise. If God is dead, then it was the European Christians who killed him! In this context, Balling asserts:

> Perhaps the most important contribution of Christianity to the birth of the modern world is secularization itself ... one could say that secularization came about *both* because Christianity talked about man as a free creature whose shape was assumed by God himself, *and* because the church did not dare take its own statements about that free creature seriously ... More directly important was the steadily growing differentiation and professionalization of European life, which ... often enough happened on distinctly Christian premises ... Another highly important factor is the general tendency toward rationalization, which ... had one of its points of origin in the claim made by Christian religion itself: it was entrusted with a rationally accessible explanation of the world and history as well as a set of rationally coherent rules of conduct.[7]

Clearly, "secularization" is a name employed by historians for the process by which science replaced religion as the strategic ideology of the modern world, even though its real nature is not fully understood. But Balling seems to miss the point that Christianity was neither responsible for this process nor a willing participant in it. Secularization was the outcome of the industrial technological paradigm shift, which generated a world that had no further use for religion as a strategic ideology. A belief in the "power of science" – what might be called "scientism" – replaced the Christian God as the strategic guardian of the modern *logos*. Similarly, the growing professionalism and rationalization of modern society were necessary responses to changing strategic demand as the industrial technology strategy unfolded in the nineteenth and twentieth centuries. An interesting proof of my view that desires drive and ideas merely facilitate is the fact that the ideas of intellectuals can be completely false and inappropriate, like those of the historians discussed here, and yet they have no adverse long-term impact on the strategic pursuit.

THE GREAT DEBATE BETWEEN SCIENCE AND RELIGION

Science on the offensive

Prior the early nineteenth century, most, if not all, educated people in Western society accepted the Biblical account of the origin and workings of the cosmos, nature and human society. Indeed, Isaac Newton's (1642–1727) theories of the physical world – his "celestial mechanics" – were viewed by its author, as well as many other eighteenth-century scientists, as confirmation of the existence of God the creator. This idea was popularized by William Paley (1743–1805) in his book *Natural Theology* (1802) as the work of the divine "watchmaker". The Earth, considered to be no more than 6,000 years old, was thought to display the marks of God's creative hand. All human, animal and plant forms were believed to be exactly as God had created them. God's hand was also seen behind the rise and fall of societies and civilizations, and particularly behind the rise of the West.

But, with the demise of the strategic gods of Western Europe and the rise of the deity of science, new explanations of nature, society and, later, the cosmos began to emerge after the 1830s. This led to a great debate between the older generation of dilettantish parson-scientists and a younger generation of professionally trained secular scientists. It was a debate that also spilled over into the social sciences as scholars developed secular theories about the dynamics of human society. In England, the new class of natural scientists included the geologist Charles Lyell and the naturalists Charles Darwin, Alfred Wallace, and Thomas Huxley.

In this *Principles of Geology* (three volumes published between 1830 and 1833), Charles Lyell (1797–1875) exploded the arguments of the static creationists, together with those who also believed that the Earth's present geological features had either been shaped that way by a divine creator or were the outcome of catastrophic God-caused events, by demonstrating that the Earth was subject to forces of continuous gradual change. He persuasively argued that although the physical forces on the planet operated via small steps, the accumulation of those small steps over long periods of time brought about remarkable changes in the environment. Mountains and deep ravines, therefore, were the outcome of slow-acting forces operating on the crust of the Earth, while other, equally slow-acting forces, such as erosion by wind, water and ice, were responsible for wearing away these mountains and filling in the ravines.[8]

The young Charles Darwin was attracted by Lyell's argument about the gradual transformation of the Earth by small steps over long periods of time. He read Lyell's first volume prior to his embarking on the *Beagle* (1831–1836) and the second volume during the voyage itself. Darwin realized that the evidence he was gathering on this world trip supported the great man's argument. At first hand Darwin witnessed the impact of those forces constantly changing the face of the Earth – earthquakes and volcanoes – which could devastate human settlement (such as the collapse of the cathedral of Concepción[9]) but changed the physical environment only marginally. But, as he was able to confirm, the accumulation of those marginal changes over vast periods of time was sufficient to transform the physical environment. Darwin noted fossilized trees, formerly at sea level, in the Andes at 7,000 feet; seashells on St Helene at 2,000 feet; and coral atolls that, he theorized, had been built up gradually as former mountains sank slowly into the seas.[10]

Darwin wondered whether animal and plant life might also have been transformed slowly over vast periods of time by the accumulation of very small changes. He was encouraged in these speculations by his knowledge of selective animal breeding programs. Could there be a natural equivalent of this barnyard process of breeder selection? Curiously, Lyell, who had revolutionized thinking about the physical world, was a conservative when it came to the question of the possible transformation of life. In the second volume of *Principles*, Lyell argued that each species of animal and plant life was entirely dependent on its geographical "centre of creation", and that any change in the physical conditions of life would exterminate rather than transform it — a bit like the climate-change scientists today.

But the evidence Darwin was collecting on his long *Beagle* voyage caused him to question and then to reject Lyell's views on life. Darwin's observation of primitive life forms on coral atolls suggested that both plant and animal life had a common origin, and that new varieties emerged from parent species. This particularly appeared to be the case for bird and reptile life on the Galapagos Islands. Life, rather than being fixed as Lyell claimed, appeared to Darwin to possess the ability to adapt to changing environmental conditions. At the same time, the fossil evidence he was amassing suggested that the traditional catastrophe (such as the Biblical flood) argument could not explain the widespread incidence of extinct animals. Slowly it dawned on Darwin that, over vast periods of time, new species replaced earlier ones in a gradual and continuous way. And finally, his observations in the jungles of South America convinced him that life involved an intense struggle for existence in which there were few winners and many losers.

Clearly this evidence about the dynamics of geology and life challenged the Biblical account of creation. Both the Earth and life as we know it had taken vast periods of time to emerge and, in the case of plants and animals, involved a long slow process of biological change that Darwin called "transmutation". If this was the case with animals, Darwin reasoned, it must also be true for human beings.[11] What did this imply, then, for the Biblical assertions that man was created in the image of God and that man and the world was created only some six thousand years ago (as calculated by Archbishop James Ussher [1581–1656] and other conservative biblical scholars)?

Darwin, a pillar of the Victorian social establishment, shuddered to think. Even before he had developed the natural selection hypothesis to explain transmutation, Darwin was deeply concerned about the impact that his discoveries and insights would have upon Victorian society. He was not the man to publicly declare that God was dead! This is why there was a seventeen-year delay between Darwin's first thirty-five page handwritten sketch of the process of transmutation via natural selection (May 1842) and the publication of the final expanded account as *Origin of Species* (1859). Indeed, it is possible that Darwin's ideas might have died with him in 1882 had not Alfred Wallace (1823–1913) arrived at the same hypothesis in the mid-1850s and sent a copy of his ideas to Darwin. Somewhat appropriately, this competitive threat to the survival of his priority to the idea of natural selection was the spur Darwin needed to finally publish *Origin*. Nonetheless, he suffered greatly, both mentally and physically, from challenging the metaphysical mythology of his era.

A younger generation of naturalists, which was not so closely associated with the old ruling elite of Britain, was far less inhibited about taking on the religious establishment. There was more at stake here than ideas, as central to life as they were. The real battle was about the social and economic status of the new professional scientists on the one hand and of the establishment parson-scientists (the priestly philosophers) on the other.[12] And in more fundamental terms it was a struggle between the old strategic ideology of religion and the new strategic ideology of science. Indeed, there was one famous young naturalist, Thomas Huxley (1825–1895), who delighted in baiting the priestly philosophers of his time. Huxley, who coined the term "agnostic", insisted that "Theology and Parsondom" were "irreconcilable enemies of Science".[13] While Huxley initially resisted Herbert Spencer's earlier metaphysical evolutionary arguments, he responded positively to Darwin's more practical theory of natural selection. In fact he was so pugnatiously supportive of Darwin's views that he will forever be known as "Darwin's bulldog". Huxley played an important role in the secularization of Victorian Britain by attacking the old religious institutions now they served no strategic role. God was dead, but many of his old followers just pushed on regardless. The agnostics and atheists played an important role in dismantling an institutional frameworkthat had been rendered obsolete by economic revolution.

From the mid-nineteenth century, social scientists joined in the attack on obsolete religious institutions. Some of the most important of these were Auguste Comte (1798–1857), Ludwig Feuerbach (1804–1872), John Stuart Mill (1806–1873), Karl Marx (1818–1883), Henry Buckle (1821–1862) and Herbert Spencer (1820–1903). These and associated thinkers viewed human society as operating according to historical laws totally independent of any divine force.[14] In their different ways they attempted to understand the nature of these historical laws and how they shaped the observable patterns of historical experience. Religion, they argued, was associated with a more primitive phase of history, and that its perpetuation in the modern world merely restricted the liberty and achievements of mankind. While some of these thinkers (particularly Marx and Spencer) may have merely replaced divine laws with an alternative set of metaphysical laws, they played an important role in dismantling the ideas and institutions of an outmoded strategic ideology. A few brief examples will suffice.

In *The Positive Philosophy*, published in the early 1850s before the *Origin of Species*, Auguste Comte advocated a form of "social physics", or sociology, which he viewed as being the final stage in the development of scientific thought. Its nature will, Comte argued, depend upon the accumulated methods and results of the other sciences. The simple sciences – astronomy, physics and chemistry – emerge first, and the more complex sciences – biology and sociology – appear last. The most complex sciences, Comte argued, require a more complex methodology, which is historical induction rather than logical deduction. And the emergence of scientific thought from primitive mythological and religious thought is the outcome of an evolutionary process. This evolutionary process is determined by Comte's famous "law of three stages", by which the human mind passes through the three stages of: the "theological"; the "metaphysical"; and the "scientific". Comte asserts:

> From the study of the development of human intelligence, in all directions, and through all times, the discovery arises of a great fundamental law, to which it is necessarily subject, and which has a solid foundation of proof, both in the facts of our organization and in our historical experience. The law is this: – that each of our leading conceptions – each branch of our knowledge – passes successively through three different theoretical conditions: the Theological, or fictitious; the Metaphysical, or abstract; and the Scientific, or positive.[15]

While Comte predicted the displacement of religious thinking by scientific thinking, he employed a uni-directional supply-side model that doesn't have universal relevance.

Although J.S. Mill was strongly influenced by Comte's positivism in his youth, he was unable to escape the pull of the master's second phase of "metaphysical, or abstract" thinking — he was unable to make the transition to the final Comtian stage of "scientific, or positive" knowledge. Mill tried, with the publication of his *A System of Logic* (1843), to develop an empirical theory of dynamics, but reverted to older and easier ways of thought after failing to do so.[16] It was Henry Buckle who came closer than any other nineteenth-century thinker to respond to the positivist challenge. With the publication of *History of Civilization in England* in three volumes between 1857 and 1861, Buckle became an overnight sensation, being fêted by London's intellectuals dedicated to liberty and the destruction of liberty's enemies – namely the old aristocracy and the Church. This was a time when serious writers and thinkers could become widely read in their own day, in contrast to today when this only happens to trivial and imitative popularists.

Buckle was a man of his times. As the technological strategy unfolded, a greater proportion of the population had the opportunity to exercise political influence. This led to a struggle between the old strategists – the aristocrats and clerics – and the new strategists – the industrialists and intellectuals – for economic and political influence. Some intellectuals – such as Hegel, Mill, Marx and Buckle – rationalized this materialist struggle as a quest for liberty. In particular, Buckle focused upon the emergence of liberty, which he interpreted as the struggle for the "spirit of inquiry" against the "spirit of protection". It was a deadly struggle between the skepticism of great men of ideas (including himself!) and the oppressive tradition of interference and control exercise by state and church.

Buckle explains this struggle:

> To scepticism we owe that spirit of inquiry, which, during the last two centuries, has gradually encroached on every possible subject; has reformed every department of practical and speculative knowledge; has weakened the authority of the privileged classes, and thus placed liberty on a surer foundation; has chastised the despotism of princes; has restrained the arrogance of the nobles; and has even diminished the prejudices of the clergy.[17]

To explain the rise of the "spirit of inquiry", Buckle developed a theory about the progress of human society from historical observation – using the Comtean inductive method – that had no role for God and his clerical agents. He argues that the progress of civilization depends on the interaction between the laws of nature and the laws of the human mind. In societies like England and Western Europe, where the laws of the mind dominate those of nature, civilization emerges first and progresses most rapidly. Progress is the outcome of the struggle between intellectual forces and repressive forces that dominate pre-modern society – namely religious intolerance and mankind's warlike spirit. The failure to overcome the repressive forces leads to crisis and collapse.[18] In Buckle's account, ideas drive and desires frustrate – the reverse of reality – but at least he assisted in overcoming the residual influence of an outdated ideology being employed by the old strategists to protect their declining material interests.

Ludwig Feuerbach's most important work was *The Essence of Christianity*, published in 1841. He argued that the essential difference between mankind and the rest of the animal world is that animals are driven by instinct alone, whereas humans possess the power of reflection and are influenced by the essential properties of intelligence, love, sympathy, and benevolence. Mankind, however, falls short of perfection – of its species-essence – owing to the mistaken notion that only God is perfect. God rather than our own humanity has become the focus of our love and concern. But as God is an illusion, we have not only misdirected our efforts but also entirely wasted them. Hence, mankind needs to abolish the illusions of God and religion and to redirect its concern to humanity.

Karl Marx, who was considerably influenced by Feuerbach, believed mankind could achieve perfection in this life without God or religion. He argued that history is driven and shaped not by any deity but by its own "dialectical" laws. In this Marx was influenced also by G.W.F. Hegel (1770–1831), who had earlier elaborated his famous "dialectic triad" of thesis, antithesis and synthesis (which in turn was inspired by Heraclitus' – around 500 BC – "principle of opposites"[19]). Marx, however, was quick to emphasize a fundamental difference between Hegel and himself. While Hegel believed history was driven by ideas, Marx was adamant that it was driven by material forces – hence his "dialectical materialism". While Marx liked to claim that his theory – unlike that of other socialists – was scientific, in reality it was a metaphysical system driven by the forces of destiny – a dubious substitute for divine forces.[20] Hence, Marx's theory had more in common with Hegel and with the theological theorists than its author cared to admit.

According to Marx, his dialectical materialism was responsible for the inevitable passage of European history through the stages of tribalism, feudalism, capitalism and, finally, communism. In the future state of communism all the contradictions underlying the operation of dialectical materialism would be eliminated and the spirit of mankind would be set free. In this final state, man will no longer be oppressed by a class of exploiters and will have no need for the illusion of God and religion. Communism would eliminate dynamic forces and become a society suspended in a state of perfect equilibrium and order. History would come to an end.

Herbert Spencer was the first to advance a theory of evolution that encompassed the physical world, organic life, and human society. It is wrong, therefore, to categorize him – as many have done – as a social Darwinist. It is quite clear from the historical record that Darwin had only a minor influence on Spencer's ideas after they had been more or less fully developed. Spencer had developed and published a general theory of evolution to explain the "progress" of both the organic and inorganic worlds as early as 1852, some seven years before the publication of Darwin's *Origin of Species* (1859). Darwin even responded to the publication of Spencer's book by sending him a letter of warm approval.[21] Also, Darwin, Wallace and Huxley rated Spencer's contribution to the idea that the cosmos, Earth, and life on Earth embodied a great "law of progress", which could explain their transformation from simple to complex forms without invoking divine intervention, as greater than theirs.[22]

The great natural and social scientists of the Victorian age, therefore, played an important role in stripping the old religious institutions of any vestige of strategic status – of purging Western society of Christian strategic ideology – now that the old God was dead. While this only occurred *after* the industrial technological paradigm shift had made the old strategic God obsolete – their role being that of strategic instruments responding to massive changes in strategic demand – they provided the rationalization as to why God should no longer be regarded as a strategic guardian: why nature and society possessed dynamic principles of their own. Their theoretical arguments successfully accomplished this important task, and helped to shift the focus of public perception from religion to technology and science as the key to ensuring survival and prosperity. One would have been more impressed, of course, had any of these thinkers made their arguments before the technological paradigm shift had actually occurred; had they anticipated it rather than merely responded a generation or two after this momentous event. It is an interesting irony that the majority of these Victorian theories – in contrast to the facts they purported to explain – have been shown to be wrong. Not wrong about the irrelevance of God to the dynamics of life and modern society, but wrong about how this might be explained.[23] The Victorians seemed incapable of developing a general dynamic theory of human society and life.

The retreat of religion

As Christian apologists initially responded to the secular scientists with considerable vigor, Victorian society was well aware of an ongoing war of words between religion and science. Books with titles like *The Warfare of Science with Theology in Christendom* (1896) by A.D. White, and *History of the Conflict between Religion and Science* (1874) by J.W. Draper, were avidly read by a growing literate class in modern society. But in a world growing secular, the religious apologists gradually lost ground. Eventually it was realized there was little to be gained by engaging with atheists in public debate, because astute and intellectually flexible people can always change their views about the way the world works while retaining belief in the central dogma of Christianity. But to do so required an acquiescence in the retreat of religion from the strategic world of national and global affairs to the personal world of "spiritual" values.

The Christian Church responded to the changed strategic nature of the modern world in a number of predictable ways: the embattled Roman Catholic Church declared war on liberal change; some protestant churches attempted to return to the nonstrategic origins of the Jesus movement; and most protestant churches explored the possibility of ecumenical union. As one historian of Christianity has written:

> To a large extent the churches went in other directions from the 'spirit of the times', and their powerlessness before some of the burning problems of the age was painfully evident in the eyes of friend and foe. Nevertheless, the idea and reality of such a church refused to die, and did not die.[24]

The Christian Church did not die globally because it found new converts in strategically underdeveloped societies that had yet to adopt the new science-based technological strategy. In these societies, metaphysical mythology still had a strategic role to play. But in strategically advanced societies, church membership declined significantly because survival and prosperity no longer required divine assistance. Those who stayed with the Christian churches did so because they continued to find personal solace in religion – in an escape from the harshness of reality.

The response of the Roman Catholic Church to Christianity's loss of strategic influence in the West was to develop a fortress mentality, to develop greater institutional centralization and authority, to eliminate liberal movements in its ranks, and to stage theatrical religious events (such as the absurd spectacle of investigating and testifying to "miracles" in order to establish sainthood – even as late as 2010!). During the nineteenth century there was a growing centralization in the Roman church, which culminated in the unprecedented decree concerning papal infallibility on matters of faith and morals by the First Vatican Council in 1869–70. This decree can never be modified or abolished. Centralized control exercised by the Vatican over the entire Catholic Church was achieved by the establishment of the Roman Curia (or papal court), by a rejuvenated Jesuit order, and by modern forms of communication that acted to reduce the authority and influence of dissenting bishops and theologians. In this way, the Vatican has attempted to resist modernity and to control the lives and faith of Catholics throughout the world. It provides a modern echo of the myth of King Canute trying to stop the incoming tide.

The success of a fortress mentality will always be limited. Institutions must change in response to the requirements of society or be swept away. Needless to say, many in the Roman church realized this iron law and initiated a reform movement that was recognized by the liberal Pope John XXIII (1958–1963) and the delegates at the Second Vatican Council, 1962–1965. This Council attempted to modify the highly centralized and authoritarian structure of the Roman church by establishing a consultative synod of bishops; by recognizing, finally, that in a technological world the role of the church would be more "religious" and less "juridical" (or, in my terms, "strategic"); and by catering to the needs of a liberal and democratic society through the introduction of vernacular languages into the liturgy.

Since the Second Vatican Council, the Roman church has resisted further liberalization. The fortress walls have been reinforced once more. And as a result, the Roman church in the West is rapidly losing the ability to hold, let alone attract, parishioners and, particularly, potential recruits for the old religious orders that are just fading away. The only way congregations have avoided disappearing completely is by being able to tap into the flow of migrants from strategically backward countries. But this is only a short-term expedient. Further, the Roman church's moral authority has suffered a major blow from the ill-advised attempt – all part of its fortress mentality – to shield sexual predators in their midst.

Some of the protestant churches responded to the abandonment of Christianity as state strategic ideology by going back to the nonstrategic origins of the early Jesus movement. The Jesus movement – discussed in Chapter 5 – emerged in response to the strategic frustration experienced by indigenous communities in Palestine under Roman occupation. These followers of the Galilean sage embraced a radical egalitarianism and undertook a teaching and healing (of the psyche) mission among the poor, oppressed, and anxious Palestinians. Churches such as the Methodists and Salvation Army also embraced a learning and teaching ministry among the casualties of the Industrial Revolution in Britain. While much beneficial social work was achieved by these religious organizations, they did not flourish in the same way as the early Jesus movement. Why? Because the problems of poverty and oppression in early nineteenth-century Britain, while severe, were only temporary in this technological society generating rapid material improvement, and because other better-funded organizations were established by an increasingly democratic state to cater for these economic and social needs. Unlike Palestine at the time of Jesus of Nazareth, Britain (and ultimately Western Europe), experienced strategic success, not strategic failure and frustration.

Stripped of strategic purpose, the protestant churches have become increasingly interested in the possibility of union – of developing a single Church under a single God. This was only possible because of the "destrategization" of the Church in Western countries. When Christianity provided a strategic ideology, each Western nation had its own strategic guardian, just as all societies had before them. In this very real sense, there was no universal God, but a pantheon of strategic gods in Christendom. Each Western nation looked to its own strategic god – which was differentiated in cultural, linguistic and liturgical terms – to enable them to defeat their "Christian" neighbors in war and commerce.

In these strategic circumstances, the ecumenical ideal of Christian unity under a universal God was entirely out of the question. The first "ecumenical conference" was not convened until 1874. It was organised in Bonn by Professor Johann Döllinger (1799–1890), a Roman Catholic theologian at Munich, in opposition to the 1870 Vatican Council determination on papal infallibility. Although on only a small scale – with about fifty delegates – this marked the beginning of the modern search for Christian unity and the universal

God. It also led to the excommunication of Döllinger. Two other sources of ecumenicism were the Evangelical Alliance of 1846 and the World Missionary Conference in Edinburgh in 1910, which led directly to the creation of the Faith and Order movement at Lausanne in 1927 and, finally, to the establishment of the current World Council of Churches at Amsterdam in 1948. In 1961, the World Council of Churches was joined, for the first time, by delegates from the Russian Orthodox Church and by official observers from the Roman Church.[25]

Since 1948 the World Council of Churches has held regular meetings to develop policy in relation to a wide range of religious, ethical, social and economic issues. There has also developed a greater informal interaction between the Roman and other churches, including the attendance of Pope John Paul II at Canterbury Cathedral in England in 1982 and Pope Benedict XVI in 2010. One can only wonder what Henry VIII, the strategic leader of Tudor England, would have thought of such an occurrence. Certainly he would have found it impossible to view religion in a nonstrategic way. As in most matters of human relations, international union only takes place when material considerations are no longer an issue.

CHRISTIANITY AS A WORLD AND FUTURE RELIGION

The most striking development in Christianity since the death of the strategic God, has been its transformation from a European to a world religion. Prior to the start of the Industrial Revolution around 1780, almost all Christians lived in Europe (including Russia), and in the colonial offshoots of Europe (namely North America and Australasia). By 1900 only two-thirds of all Christian lived in Europe, and only 80 percent in Europe and North America combined. And by 2000, while only a little more than a quarter lived in Europe — with about 40 percent in both Europe and North America combined — as many as one-third of all Christians could be found in Latin America, 20 percent in Africa, and the rest (as numerous as those in North America) in Asia.[26] Hence, in just two hundred years, the center of Christian demographic gravity had shifted from Europe to the rest of the world – namely to the Third World.

There are two main reasons for the adoption of the Christian God in the Third World following his abandonment as the strategic guardian of the West. First, the Third World was keen to emulate the material success of the West. As outsiders, the Third World associated this success with the power of the Christian God (or gods) in his role as strategic guardian. Missionaries regularly reported the importance of the idea of "god power" in their conversion of Third-World societies to Christianity. This adoption of the strategic ideologies of successful societies is a common theme running throughout human history. It is another example of the powerful mechanism of **strategic imitation**. Second, for Third-World societies, religion as strategic ideology was considerably more affordable than science with its massive infrastructure requirements. Conversion to Christianity, in other words, was much cheaper and quicker than transition to a technological society. Unfortunately it was also much less effective. Perhaps uneducated people in these societies thought that the adoption of Christianity would eventually led to the flourishing of science and to technological transformation, as it *appeared* to do in the West. But, as shown in this book, appearances can be very deceptive.

Between 1920 and 2000, the number of Christians in the world tripled to about 2,000 million; the number of Muslims quadrupled to about 1,200 million; the followers of Judaism experienced only a small increase (mainly recovery from the Holocaust of the 1940s) to about 50 million; while Buddhists doubled to about 400 million, and Hindus more than doubled to over 800 million.[27] By the end of the first decade of the twenty-first century Islam will probably become the most populous world religion. Yet despite these substantial gains for God, the stand-out category in growth-rate terms was "no religion", which increased ten-fold to about 1,000 million in 2000, making it the third-largest "religious" group (about 16% of the total) in the world.

This rough outline – as it is difficult to obtain accurate figures – suggests that the death of the strategic gods have also had a massive impact on the personal religion of the citizens of the Western world. While all Western countries have witnessed a decline in church membership, that decline has been most rapid in Western Europe, the old incubator of modern Christianity; and it has been least rapid in the USA, where the Judeo-Christian God has been "Americanized".

The most fascinating feature of Christianity since the death of the strategic gods is the Americanization of the Judeo-Christian God. Because the USA was established at the beginning of the industrial technological paradigm shift – at a time when Christianity was being abandoned as a strategic ideology in Western Europe – the separation between church and state was actually enshrined in the American constitution. Despite this, Americans regularly refer to "this nation under God", or to the USA as "God's country". As one historian has put it: many Americans

> assent to the notion that the United States is somehow a covenanted nation, called into being by a provident God, guided by such a God, impelled into a mission and inspired by a 'destiny' under God.[28]

This would appear to have something in common with the old Judahite idea of King Josiah that they are a "chosen people" – but without much religious content.

What do Americans mean by God? In my opinion, most Americans employ the term "God" as a rhetorical device. It is another name for "*American* progress and democracy" or "*American* destiny". Church services appear to be strong on emotional and patriotic expression, but rather weak on religious and spiritual content. This can be seen most clearly in the popular mega-church services involving tens of thousands of people and conducted in huge indoor venues. Participants have the opportunity to address themselves emotionally to the "god" of American progress and democracy by singing, shouting, and dancing together in view of massive television audiences. While this is probably emotionally fulfilling it is hardly spiritually uplifting or intellectually or morally demanding. Having recharged their emotional batteries, these people are able to plunge back into the workday world of making money and consuming goods and services on an indulgent scale. Essentially it is societal validation that greed is good — or that greed is god.

While this type of despiritualized religion may have some psychic benefits for the participants, it doesn't play the traditional role of religious strategic ideology. This god of greed is *not* the guardian of the American strategic *logos*. That role is played by the secular deity of science, which underpins the strategic success of the American economy. An essential characteristic of strategic ideologies of the past and present is their ability to attract a great deal of public and private investment. In ancient Egypt, for example, a substantial proportion of GDP was invested in temples, priestly orders and royal burials, only because it was believed that this would generate a high strategic return on this abstinence from current consumption. In the USA today – as in all Western societies – an equally substantial proportion of GDP is invested by public and private bodies in the buildings, equipment, and staff of the nation's scientific, educational, technological, and research organizations for exactly the same reason – to ensure the survival and prosperity of the strategic *logos*.

Nothing, however, is invested by the state or American strategists in the infrastructure of religion as a way of ensuring strategic success. Clearly, religious businesses do invest in religious facilities – such as large auditoria, and electronic and television equipment – but they do so in order to generate a lucrative livelihood for themselves, not to ensure the strategic success of the nation. And the public is happy to spend part of its income on the consumption of "feel good" religious entertainment. Once again, this has nothing to do with sustaining the strategic *logos* as it once did.

Undoubtedly, once the USA is surpassed in economic size and wealth by that emerging giant China – something that will be achieved this century – this "religious" form of American self-celebration and self-congratulation will begin to decline. As a second-tier strategic nation – like many European countries today – the USA may not be so eager to see itself as the world's "chosen people" or even "this nation under God". Instead they will become less self-confident and more like the Western Europeans today, who are abandoning the Christian God in their personal lives as well as in the strategic sphere – in favor of faith in science and technology.

THE FUTURE OF ISLAM

While the old God has been pronounced dead in the West, many are convinced he still lives on in the lands of Islam. They take comfort in the recent resurgence of Islamic fundamentalism in the Middle East and Southeast Asia, and are convinced that the East can modernize under the protection of Allah. This Islamic resurgence, they believe, proves that Western secularism is not a universal development but merely a reflection of the temporary godless success of Europe and North America.

Even some Western observers are beginning to doubt the universal validity of the modernism thesis about economic development and secularism. One authoritative religious historian has concluded:

> the secular presuppositions and expectations of modernization theory were swept aside by an Islamic tide that seemed to come out of nowhere and challenged much of the Muslim world, from North Africa to Southeast Asia to the West.[29]

And more specifically he writes:

> Islam reemerged as a potent global force throughout the 1970s and 1980s. Much of its impact in the 1970s went unnoticed. It was the Iranian revolution that shattered the secular bias and expectations of modernization and development theories and cast a light on the significant changes that had already been taking place in many Muslim societies throughout the 1970s.[30]

It is essential, of course, to draw a clear distinction between modernization theory on the one hand and the death of God on the other. While modernization theory is deeply flawed, the death of God is a strategic reality. Modernization "theory" predicted the emergence of secularization in Islamdom on the basis of what happened in the West *when it grew rich*. Herein lies its flaw. As shown earlier in this chapter, it is not wealth that led to the abandonment of the old God as strategic guardian of the West, but rather the transition from the neolithic technological paradigm to the industrial technological paradigm. The reason that some Islamic countries – such as Iran and Egypt – which attempted to modernize in the twentieth century, have, more recently, experienced a religious resurgence, is that they adopted only the superficial characteristics of Westernization. The critical point is that they failed to pass through a paradigmatic transformation. Instead they have relied on their easily won wealth in oil rather than the hard-won paradigmatic transformation through science. They have failed, in other words, to transform their strategic *logos* from a neolithic to a modern form. Accordingly, they have continued to look to the old strategic guardian, and to employ Islam as their strategic ideology, rather than to adopt the new strategic ideology of science and technological change.

We need to briefly review the failed attempts by Islamic countries to undergo the necessary paradigmatic transformation. In the seventeenth and eighteenth centuries it was becoming clear to the Islamic world that, for the first time, the West was beginning to present a major challenge to their continued survival and prosperity. Their response was predictable. They either attempted to reform their sociopolitical system by revisiting ideological basics and restoring the beliefs of the past when Islamic societies had been dominant – the usual response in times of crisis – or they invested in military resistance, which had been so successful in the past. But neither approach effected the desired outcome, owing to the growing technological and military superiority of Europe.

But it was the European Industrial Revolution – the industrial technological paradigm shift – of the late eighteenth and early nineteenth centuries that drew a desperate response from the Islamic world. The choice for Islamic societies appeared crystal clear – either they "modernized" or failed to survive. But what did it mean to modernize? Muslim rulers in the Ottoman empire – namely Morocco, Egypt and Iran – during the nineteenth and early twentieth centuries interpreted this concept in terms of creating a strong military and central administration in their countries through the acquisition of European technology and weapons. This political and rather superficial response involved sending students to Europe to study science, politics and languages; modernization of their systems of education, law and economics; establishing new universities with modern curricula; creating modern armies trained by European experts; and establishing printing presses and translation bureaus to make new ideas and information more accessible. At the same time these new leaders restricted sharia law to issues of personal status and family matters (marriage, divorce and inheritance); and they regulated mosques, sharia courts, religious schools and endowments, and religious orders. Needless to say, these measures were directed largely towards bolstering the wealth and power of the political elites and had little impact on the standing of the people, and none on paradigmatic transformation. The strategic *logos* cannot be transformed from above in this superficial way.

While Islamic states attempted to emulate the superficial aspects of the industrialized West, there also emerged a widespread Islamic movement calling for the "reformation" or reinterpretation of Islam to enable an effective response to Europe.[31] The objective was to create a synthesis of Islam and modern science, technology and learning. This could be achieved, it was thought, by reinterpreting and reapplying the basic principles of Islam. Major intellectual figures in this movement included Jamal al-Din al-Afghani (1838–1897) and Muhammad Abduh (1849–1905) in the Middle East, and Sayyid Ahmad Khan (1817–1898) and Muhammad Iqbal (1877–1938) in South Asia. Their belief was that religion, reason and science were compatible, because they were able to make the distinction between the eternal principles of Islam (shariah) and those regulations that arise from human responses and, hence, were subject to change. Some, like al-Afghani, even made a clear distinction in their thinking between Islam as religion and as civilization.[32] What they did not understand was that the new dynamic strategy of technological change, if successfully negotiated, would transform their strategic *logos* and, hence, undermine Islam as a strategic ideology (if not as a religion of reduced significance).

In the twentieth century, a number of nationalist movements in Algeria, Iran, Tunisia, and the Asian sub-continent emerged in response to European hegemony. This led to the creation of a large number of Islamic states following both world wars. The European powers were responsible both for drawing the artificial boundaries of these new states and for choosing their ruling dynasties. Muslim states in the mid-twentieth century ranged from secular Turkey to Islamic Saudi Arabia, with the rest taking a stance somewhere between these extremes.

Initially these new Islamic states equated "modernization" with "progressive westernization" and "secularization". But with a growing dissatisfaction among the intelligentsia – the priestly philosophers – movements such as the Muslim Brotherhood and the Islamic Society (Jamaat-i-Islami) emerged. These movements promoted the idea of a need for, and the possibility of, a self-sufficient Islamic alternative to capitalism, Marxism, and socialism, which would be based on a reunion of religion and politics – on "true Islam" and the shariah. Basically this was an admission that the Muslim states had failed in their immediate quest for technological transformation – a state in which the sociopolitical system would be determined not by metaphysical philosophy but by the *logos* through strategic demand.

With the failure of the Islamic world to transform itself technologically, despite the windfall oil wealth enjoyed by many of its constituent societies, there was a resurgence of political Islam from the 1970s. There is, however, much confusion among political commentators as to its cause. One, normally acute, observer – John Esposito – has written that

> Ironically, its most potent manifestations of the Islamic resurgence, both in the 1970s and in later decades, occurred in those societies regarded as the most "modern" or modernizing, those possessing a well-trained, Western-oriented, secular elite: Iran, Egypt, Lebanon, Tunisia, Turkey, and Algeria.[33]

Esposito is only able to find this situation ironical because of his acceptance of the flawed modernization hypothesis discussed earlier. In contrast, the dynamic-strategy theory, which shows that secularization is a function not of wealth but of paradigmatic transformation, predicts that strategic frustration will be greatest in those societies that have invested most in strategic failure. And as we have seen throughout this book, it is strategic failure and its concomitant strategic frustration that lies behind the attraction and resurgence of religion. Religion is the compensation for strategic failure. Political opportunists, as always, were quick to exploit this religious resurgence. Established leaders – like Numayri in Sudan, Qaddafi in Libya, Sadat in Egypt, and Bhutto in Pakistan – adopted Islamic disguise to secure political support; and opposition groups in countries such as Iran and Afghanistan used Islam as propaganda to assist in the overthrow of existing governments.

It remains to be determined whether Muslim countries will break the stranglehold of metaphysical ideas peddled by the priestly philosophers, will see beyond the seductive surface of "modernization", and will, finally, embrace the core process of paradigmatic transformation. The great barrier is not the metaphysical ideas as such, but rather the large number of influential *ulama*, who, in a country such as Iran, control a massive network of mosques that serve as centers for organizing the "war on modernization". These reactionary priestly philosophers, who spin their deadly webs, are also intermarried with the old commerce strategists who wish to prevent the rise of the new technological strategists. But it is a war that the conservative forces will eventually lose, although they will create much suffering in the process.

Once the new technological strategists win this war, and the Islamic states pass through paradigmatic transformation, then Allah, like Christ before him, will be abandoned as their strategic guardian. Just as in the Christian West, the Islamic East will declare the death of the old God and will embrace the new deity of science. Islam, like Christianity, will survive only as a metaphysical mythology, embraced by those who are unable or unwilling to face the future reality of former Islamic societies. In the end, it will come down to a choice between the death of God or the death of the Islamic *logos*. This is an iron law. But the death of the old God (Islam) leads to the birth of a new god (science) – dead god rising.

PART II
THE NEW STRATEGIC GODS

Chapter 7
Dead God Rising

The old God is dead, long live the new god. Certainly he will live for as long as the strategic *logos* of mankind has a need for his support and guidance. And no longer. The old metaphysical gods, who sustained human society for eleven thousand years, were finally abandoned as the industrial technological paradigm replaced the neolithic technological paradigm in the West. And their place was taken by the new deity of science, and the strategic ideology of scientism. Scientism is the belief – for it is no more than a belief – that science, by discovering the laws that govern all that happens in the Universe, can provide a true explanation of material existence. More importantly, scientism is the belief that science can anticipate future crises – such as any impending climate change – can resolve those crises, and can guarantee the survival not only of human society but also of the planet. The deity of science, it is believed, can do what no other strategic guardian has ever done. The risen god is more powerful than the dead god.

GOD-MAKER AND GOD-BREAKER

Throughout this book, references have been made to the great transforming mechanism that I have called the technological paradigm shifts. By now the reason for these references will be clear. The technological-paradigm-shift mechanism is the "god-maker/god-breaker" of human society: it is the driving force behind dead god rising. This mechanism was responsible for the birth of the gods as guardians of the strategic *logos* of early man, for the transformation of these strategic guardians into gods of the cosmos during the early phases of civilization, for the death of the old God in the nineteenth century, and for the rise of the deity of science in our own age. It will also determine the nature of the gods in the future, both on this planet and beyond.

While a general outline of the wider genetic/technological paradigm shift mechanism, operating over the past 4,000 myrs, is provided in Chapter 10, we need to focus here in greater detail on the way it has operated over the past 2 myrs and, in particular, over the past two centuries.[1] We will also consider the future. The underlying dynamic mechanism represented in Figure 7.1 – the god-maker/god-breaker – involves the exhaustion of an existing technological paradigm, the adoption of an entirely new technological paradigm through a major economic revolution (or technological paradigm shift), a conjoint transformation of the strategic *logos* of the pioneering society, and a global strategic transition affecting the *logoi* of all societies. In turn, the transformed strategic *logos* generates a changing strategic demand for a wide range of economic, institutional (social rules), organizational (social networks) and cultural inputs. Most important of all, the new *logos* causes a transformation in the nature and societal role of the strategic guardians – commonly called gods (or, in my schema, **G**uardians **O**f **D**ynamic **S**trategies).

Figure 7.1 **The god-maker/god-breaker mechanism – global technological transformations**

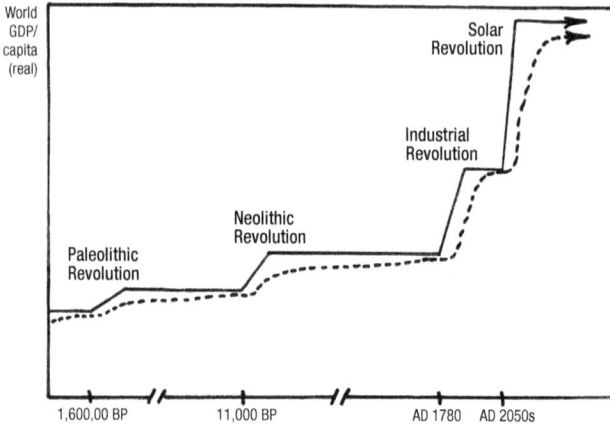

Source: Snooks 1996: 403; and Snooks 2010: ch.5
Notes: 1. Not to scale
2. Solid line represents "potential" WGDP; Dashed line represents "actual".

From Figure 7.1, we can see that the paleolithic technological paradigm shift – paleolithic shift for short – coincided with the birth of the simple strategic guardians discussed in Chapter 2; the neolithic shift, with the transformation of simple strategic guardians into complex gods of the cosmos that eventually gave rise to the One God; and the modern shift, with the death of the old God and the rise of scientism. As we shall see, this god-making mechanism also has implications – even if unknown – for the future.

Figure 7.1 requires a brief explanation. Each of the paradigm shifts that it portrays, opens the door for an extended period of material expansion through the exploitation of the new technological capacity it provides. The new and higher level of technological capacity is represented by the "potential" curve, and the exploitation of this potential is shown by the "actual" curve. When the two curves coincide, the paradigm is exhausted. In other words, at this point the entire technological capacity of the paradigm has been fully exploited.

The paleolithic shift, as we saw in Chapter 2, involved a substitution of a hunting for a scavenging technology. This caused a major change in the strategic *logos* of human society, which in turn generated a significant change in strategic demand for material, institutional, and cultural inputs for humanity's strategic pursuit. Of particular importance for this study is the new demand for assistance from strategic guardians in sustaining this more complex life-system. In this new, unknown and frightening world there was an urgent need for assistance from beings more knowledgeable and powerful than themselves. Such a being had to be greater than any human being precisely because mankind was unable to understand or directly influence the mystery of mysteries on which their survival and prosperity depended. These strategic guardians, as we have seen, were directly responsible for sustaining key aspects of the strategic *logos*, by ensuring regular patterns of rainfall; adequate numbers of wild herds, plants, and fruit; appropriate human fertility; and effective protection from predators, both animal and human. These strategic guardians were not yet cosmic beings.

The neolithic shift, as shown in Chapter 3, involved the substitution of an agricultural/herding technology for a hunting technology. Once again this technological paradigm shift was responsible for transforming the strategic *logos* of mankind. And the transformed *logos* generated a changing strategic demand for a wide range of strategic inputs, including a more complex understanding and mastery of the mystery of mysteries and its protective strategic guardian. To provide this greater understanding and mastery, a professional class of priestly philosophers emerged, financed by the surplus that could now be generated through agricultural production. And the greater the scale on which this agricultural production and associated commerce or conquest strategic pursuit occurred – the greatest examples being in the irrigated lands of Egypt and Mesopotamia – the greater the investment in the infrastructure of strategic ideology. In these agricultural societies the strategic guardians were transformed into gods that not only sustained the strategic *logos* but also took on cosmic significance. The most impressive strategic ideology was developed by the ancient Egyptians, who came closest to understanding and mastering the mystery of mysteries, owing to the great longevity of their civilization. They finally failed, because in the end metaphysics and mythology are self-referential not existential.

The transformation of strategic ideology into metaphysical mythology or religion was a product not of strategic success but of **strategic failure**. Religion emerged in those societies located in the borderlands of the superpowers of the ancient world. Owing to their oppression by the great powers of the Fertile Crescent and Mediterranean, the semitic peoples of Palestine and the Red Sea region experience extreme forms of **strategic frustration**, which led them to transform their failed strategic ideologies into religions. What could not be achieved in the material world could always be achieved in the spiritual world – self-satisfaction.

In this way, the vast numbers of strategic gods were displaced by a sole, universal God. This was the case with the exasperated Judahites in the sixth century BC, the frustrated Galileans in the early first century AD, and the marginalized Red Sea Arabs in the early seventh century AD. It was the Christian form of this One God that was, ironically, adopted as a strategic ideology by the failing Roman empire and, thereby, transmitted to the European kingdoms that emerged in the West. From the seventh century AD it was the Judeo–Christian–

Islamic God that provided the model for the strategic guardians that dominated the societies of Europe, Asia Minor, the Fertile Crescent, and North Africa for the next two millennia. It also provided the basis for the spiritual needs – as compensation for the highly inequitable distribution of material surpluses – of its people.

The technological paradigm shift that has shaped our own strategic *logos* is the Industrial Revolution (Figure 7.1). This modern shift involved the substitution of an industrial for an agricultural technology. And at the core of this technology was the use of fossil fuels and inorganic construction materials, which replaced the old technology centered on organic fuels and materials. Science played a central role in this more complex process of substitution, particularly as the industrial paradigm unfolded – as the Industrial Revolution passed from its initial pioneering mechanical phase (in Britain, 1780 to 1830) into its more sophisticated chemical and electrical phases (in Germany and the USA during the later nineteenth century).

With the rise of science, some of the mystery of the strategic *logos* seemed to dissipate. Governments and the educated public believed that science was the solution to the age-old problem of how to sustain a vital life-system and, thereby, how to maximize the probability of survival and prosperity. As belief in science rose, faith in the old strategic God fell. Accordingly, governments, businesses, and individual consumers shifted their expenditure on **strategic insurance** from the infrastructure of religion to the infrastructure of science. Since the nineteenth century, the most strategically advanced societies have invested a substantial proportion of their GDPs (7–8 percent – OECD 2003) in the fields of science, technology, and education, in the belief that this will guarantee their strategic success – success in the attempt to sustain their strategic *logos* and, thereby, maximize the probability of their survival and prosperity.

At the same time, investment by advanced societies in the infrastructure of religion has declined dramatically. Can anyone imagine a modern strategic society building the contemporary equivalent of the Great Pyramid (which absorbed 10 percent of Egypt's GDP at the height of its building program), Notre Dame Cathedral, or St Paul's Cathedral? Instead we construct great universities, scientific institutions, and research establishments. This shift in the relative importance of religion and science is also reflected in the numbers of trained professionals entering both fields; in the relative status, prestige, and remuneration of these professionals; and the relative importance of science and theology in the halls of higher learning. But, of course, neither field is as prestigious or as well remunerated as strategic activities. This has always been the core of our strategic *logos* throughout the course of human history. It is a reflection of the dynamic-strategy maxim that "desires drive, ideas facilitate".

What of the future? In *The Dynamic Society* (1996) I argue that owing to the exponential pace of technological paradigm transformation – identified and measured by the Snooks-Panov algorithm[2] – the next great shift will begin during the middle decades of the twenty-first century.³ I have called this the **solar shift** or **Solar Revolution** (Figure 7.1).⁴ It will completely transform the strategic *logos* of humanity and, therefore, will generate a very different strategic demand for cultural institutions and strategic ideology. However, at this distance we are unable to predict what form the new strategic guardian might take. Certainly our ideas about the universal life-system and the natural and social sciences that will attempt to explain, model, and predict it, will change dramatically. Perhaps that revolution in thinking will be influenced by the radical ideas about the strategic *logos* presented in this book.

THE RISE OF MODERN SCIENCE
A new explanation

Just as the dynamic strategy theory can explain the emergence of the gods and their transformation over time, so it can account for the rise of modern science. It can even explain the precocious emergence but ultimate stagnation of ancient science. Essentially, science is a strategic instrument and, like other strategic instruments, it is a response to the changing strategic demand generated by an unfolding dynamic strategy. Where there is a strategic demand, there will always be a supply response. But when that strategic demand levels off or even disappears, the supply response will eventually wither. In other words, science does not possess an internal driving mechanism – it does not have a momentum of its own. At least, not in the long run.

While all four dynamic strategies generate a dynamic demand for new techniques, only in the commerce and technological strategies is this demand sufficient to give rise to an integrated body of knowledge that could be called "science" – from the Latin *scientia*, meaning knowledge. For example, the paleolithic family-multiplication strategy generated a dynamic demand for tools (stone, wood, and bone) for hunting, and simple devices for transport (rafts and canoes); while the conquest strategy generated an unfolding demand for military equipment, siege machines, engineered infrastructure (roads, aquaducts, ports, docks and buildings), naval equipment, transport and communications. Owing to the lack of writing in paleolithic societies, simple technological ideas were passed from parent to child, with the result that no independent body of knowledge was built up. In conquest societies – particularly before the time of the Greeks (1000–150 BC) – manuals containing military technology were written, but the knowledge they contained remained practical rather than abstract or theoretical. Changing techniques were a direct response to strategic demand and existed as a working collection of inventions. Conquest societies had little need for abstract ideas about the natural world.⁵

The world of commerce was an entirely different matter. The unfolding commerce strategy generated a dynamic demand not only for new strategic techniques – such as larger and faster ships, better naval protection, efficient wharfs and docks, lighthouses, better handling and storage techniques, more effective forms of communication – but also for abstract ideas about the natural world. As merchants needed to travel large distances over dangerous seas and deserts, they required effective navigation techniques, accurate maps, sextants, chronometers, and mathematical systems. Their businesses also generated a demand for effective accounting techniques, business forecasting, together with systems of balances, weights, and measures.

To meet these demands for specific strategic instruments, commerce societies – from the Egyptians, Greeks and Phoenicians in the ancient world to the Arabs, Italians, Portuguese, Dutch and British in the pre-modern world – found it necessary to develop abstract bodies of knowledge about the natural and human spheres. These scientific fields included observational and theoretical astronomy; mathematics; accounting; cartography; the accurate measurement of time, dimension, and mass; the theory and craft of precise instruments; and the chemistry of metals, clays, glazes and dyes. Commerce societies, in contrast to conquest societies, regarded intellectual activities as an acceptable male pastime alongside the more familiar war games of gladiatorial combat, jousting, wrestling, archery, and hunting. The reason, of course, was that the outcomes of new intellectual activities fed into the viability of the commerce strategy, which in turn generated material prosperity. And, finally, the growing surpluses of commerce societies created middle classes with the leisure and private resources to engage in these intellectual activities.

In the ancient world, the normal strategic sequence for societies inhabiting an internationally competitive environment was conquest → commerce → conquest. Each of the Greek strategies in this sequence was exploited for about 300 years before they were exhausted. When the initial conquest strategy had been exhausted, it was replaced with the commerce strategy, and when the commerce strategy had been exhausted it was replaced with conquest.[6] Hence, while the Greeks developed science during the commerce phase (800–500 BC), once this strategy had been exhausted, the development of classical science was brought to an end. Science was not a requirement of their conquest strategy.[7] As the role of science declined, that of religion and the dark arts rose.[8] Only societies that were effectively shielded from intense and aggressive international competition for millennia – the chief example being Egypt – were able to focus largely on commerce and the development of their sciences in a more sustained fashion.[9]

Greek experience in the field of science can be contrasted with that of Western Europe. Take the case of Britain, which was the pioneering society in the industrial technological paradigm shift that began in the late eighteenth century. It embarked on the classical strategic sequence, for a society exposed to intense international competition, of conquest (1000–1300) followed by commerce (1480–1750). And Britain would have reverted to conquest – there are signs that in the mid-eighteenth century it was preparing to do so – except that its commerce strategy fortuitously exhausted itself at the very time that the neolithic technological paradigm was also exhausted. For the first time in history, the strategic sequence became, in the case of Britain: conquest → commerce → technological change (1780 to date). This, with individual variations, became the general experience of Western Europe. So the rise of pre-modern science in Western Europe, which was a response to their commerce strategy, continued to rise in the modern era owing to the adoption of the technological strategy. Had the industrial technological paradigm shift not occurred after 1780, the so-called "science revolution" that began in Western European commerce societies, would have been aborted. Just as it had in the ancient world when conquest replaced commerce. Science has no long-term internal dynamic; rather it is a response to changes in strategic demand.

The unfolding technological strategy of the West generated a dynamic demand for a new and more sophisticated range of technological and scientific ideas. It is interesting that the pioneering British Industrial Revolution did not at first make great demands on the scientific community, precisely because the scientific developments of the nineteenth century were a response to rather, than the cause of, this technological paradigm shift. The British Industrial Revolution was the result of practical and resourceful men attempting to find new ways to maintain their profits in the face of an exhausting commerce strategy.[10] Innovations in the textile, iron and steel, coal-mining, and transport industries were generated by men familiar with the practical aspects of their industries. One of the few partial exceptions to this generalization is the work that James Watt (1736–1819) – whose employment as a scientific-instrument maker led to an interest in improving Thomas Newcomen's (1663–1729) atmospheric steam engine – undertook in developing the modern steam engine. Even in this case, the invention of the steam engine gave more to science, in the form of the theory of thermodynamics, than science gave to steam technology. It was not until the pioneering phase of the Industrial Revolution was over (by 1830) that the transformed science profession made a significant contribution to the further unfolding of the technological strategy, particularly in the fields of alloy steels, chemistry (artificial dyes), electricity, and magnetism (the electric dynamo and motor).

From the mid-nineteenth century there was a growing interaction – a symbiosis – between science and the unfolding technological strategy. Yet is must be understood that the driving force in this relationship was the motivation underlying the strategic pursuit. If, at any time in the future, the industrial technological paradigm exhausts itself *without* being replaced by a new paradigm, the rise of science will cease, stagnate, and then fall, because there will be no further demand, and no further funds, for scientists or their ideas. As in the rest of life: desires drive and ideas merely facilitate. That is the central maxim of the strategic *logos*.

Redefining the Renaissance

Much is made of the new sixteenth-century intellectual view of the natural world known as the Renaissance (or "rebirth") as a precondition for the "scientific revolution" of the sixteenth and seventeenth centuries. The Renaissance is usually seen as a process of "emerging from the dark".[11] And it arises from the conception of the period in Western Europe between the Greco-Roman civilization and the Renaissance as the "Dark Ages" – a reference to the nature of intellectual activity in society. This is a common misconception that has arisen from a total misunderstanding of the dynamics of human society.

In strategic terms, the middle ages in Western Europe were not "dark", but as enlightened as any other age. They cast all the light that was required by their strategic *logos* to ensure the survival and prosperity of their populations in the circumstances of the time. Life is always focused on maximizing the probability of survival and prosperity, not on maximizing the development of ideas. The latter is merely a myth perpetuated by intellectuals either for self-serving ends or out of ignorance — or both. Western European culture and ideas in the middle ages were as appropriate and enlightening to their times as Renaissance culture and ideas were to the sixteenth century.

A comparison is usually made between Greek culture in the "enlightened" age of commerce (rather than their "dark" ages of conquest) and European culture during their "dark" age of conquest. One culture emphasized the science and learning required for the materialistic pursuit of commerce, while the other focused on the metaphysical mythology required by the materialistic pursuit of conquest. To argue that one culture is superior to the other requires the establishment of a set of arbitrary, nonstrategic values. This, of course, is the standard practice of the priestly philosophers – the purveyors of metaphysics. In strategic terms – the terms by which societies live or die – both cultures are equally appropriate and vindicated. To paint these societies in shades of "light" and "dark" amounts to caricature.

Even the basic notion of the Renaissance as "rebirth" is false. Culture in the sixteenth century was not a "rebirth" of classical Greek culture, it was entirely a response to the dynamic demand of a very Western European commerce strategy. Just as classical culture was a response to the Greek commerce strategy between 800 and 500 BC. The revival of classical learning was merely belated recognition by intellectuals in Western Europe that they were going through a similar process to the Greeks some 2,300 years earlier. In doing so, the West was merely looking for precedents of what they were experiencing in order to enhance their confidence in changing times. Basically, my point is that the intellectual ferment in Western Europe in the sixteenth century was strategically determined and would have taken the same fundamental course, *even if ancient Greece had never existed;* although it would have been dressed up in different clothes. While we may be stuck with the inappropriate term

"Renaissance", it needs to be redefined in strategic terms. And, of course, it was only a matter of time before the achievement of the new learning outpaced that of the Greeks, as the ancients had no hope of riding the industrial technological paradigm shift (as the neolithic paradigm was far from being exhausted. Here the West was entering entirely new territory.

Surveying the new science

The story about the rise of science usually begins with a discussion of the new cosmic theory of Nicolaus Copericus (1473–1543), Tycho Brahe (1546–1601), Johannes Kepler (1571–1630), and Galileo Galilei (1564–1642), concerning the revolution of the Earth and other planets in the solar system around the sun. This theory, beautiful in its simplicity, finally refuted the agonizingly complex Earth-centered theory of the Greek astronomer Ptolemy – or Claudius Ptolemaeus, who was writing around AD 127 to 145 in the great library of Alexandria – and the official dogma of the Roman Church.

For his part in promoting this heresy, Galileo, who is regarded as one of the first modern scientists, was threatened by the Inquisition in 1616, officially tried in 1633 for heresy, and in 1634 placed under house arrest for the remainder of his life.[12] Kepler, who was of more timid disposition, deliberately buried his "heretical" laws of elliptical planetary motion (which formed the background to Newton's discoveries) in impenetrable Latin prose. But it would take another half century before Isaac Newton (1642–1727) was able to provide a complete explanation of the Copernican cosmos, using just three simple laws of motion together with the concept of gravity. Newton also developed calculus (simultaneously with Gottfried Leibniz, 1646–1716) to analyze the interaction between bodies; studied the nature of light (which he argued consisted of a stream of particles); devised the first reflecting telescope; and employed the systematic scientific technique of observation, hypothesis, prediction, and law-making. This pioneering work in the sixteenth and seventeenth centuries, riding the great wave of commerce, directly challenged the prevailing religious mythology developed in response to the dynamic strategy of conquest. But, as we have seen, old strategic ideologies are only swept away by the emergence of new dynamic strategies, not new ideas.

With the rise of science in the seventeenth century, there came a demand for a more effective form of distribution of new scientific ideas. The old method of publishing prohibitively expensive books written in Latin was replaced by the emergence of scientific societies that organized lectures and discussion sessions and published scientific papers. Scientific societies appeared in Italy in the mid-seventeenth century, then in England (the Royal Society in 1662) and France (Académie des Sciences in 1666), which published the *Philosophical Transactions* and *Mémoires* respectively. Through these new institutions, which were responses to a changing strategic demand, the scientific method – careful observation and generalization followed by replication – as initiated by Galileo and, particularly, Newton, was institutionalized. Hence, the way forward for the systematic development of science had been laid down by the last quarter of the sixteenth century, provided only that there would be a continuing strategic demand for this new way of thinking.

Physics maintained is priority among the sciences in the eighteenth century as the commerce strategy reached and passed its peak. Increasingly, physics was becoming a mathematical discipline, with physical problems being solved not by Newtonian observation but by complex mathematical techniques. This new work was undertaken by Leonhard Euler (1707–1783) in Switzerland, together with Joseph Louis Lagrange (1736–1813) in France. Nonetheless, chemistry became part of the new scientific movement in experimental techniques. In the eighteenth century the main advances in chemistry concerned the role of gases in chemical reactions, the nature of heat and combustion, the composition of the atmosphere, the discovery of specific gases such as oxygen and nitrogen, and the classification of chemical compounds. The major chemists of that century were Joseph Black (1728–1799) in Scotland (born in Bordeaux to Scottish parents) and Antoine Laurent Lavoisier (1743–1794) in France.

Progress in the eighteenth century was also made in the understanding of electricity and magnetism, which were thought of in Newtonian terms as consisting of a stream of particles. Electrical and magnetic forces were identified and measured by Charles Augustin de Coulomb (1736–1806) using the torsion balance; and the electric battery was developed by Alessandro Volta (1745–1827) in Italy.[13] Hence, the so-called "Enlightenment" – the superiority of reason over superstition – was the outcome not of intellectual or moral improvement, but of the unfolding of the commerce strategy in Western Europe.

The future of science, however, was called into question in the mid-eighteenth century as the long wave of prosperity generated by the commerce strategy exhausted itself in the leading societies of Western Europe. This new form of enquiry, which challenged the old metaphysical mythology, teetered on the edge of collapse as countries like England explored the alternative strategy of conquest in the second half of that century. Its future was only secured once England, for purely material reasons, rejected conquest in favor of technological change. It was this, and only this, fundamental strategic choice that enabled the "scientific revolution" to continue.

In the nineteenth century, the new sciences were driven by the Industrial Revolution. Developments in our knowledge of metallurgy, chemistry, electricity, and magnetism were a direct response to the rapidly changing strategic demand generated by the new industrial *logos*. The science of metallurgy developed to supply the alloy steels required by an increasingly sophisticated market for machinery and construction materials; chemistry responded to a growing consumer demand by creating new substances such as aniline dyes; and electricity and magnetism were subjects explored to develop new sources of power, such as the electric motor by experimental physicists like

Michael Faraday (1791–1867). Even James Watt's steam engine – the invention of which in 1769 was influenced by the experiments on heat undertaken by his friend Joseph Black and by his practical knowledge of the Newcomen engine – only went into production *after* the British Industrial Revolution had got underway by the end of the eighteenth century.

The science of heat and motion, which came to be known as thermodynamics, was also a direct response to the Industrial Revolution – to the strategic demand of the new industrial *logos* – which provided physicists with practical demonstrations in the form of the steam engine, of the wasteful transformation of heat into energy. Thermodynamics began to be recognized as a science in the 1820s through the work of Sadi Carnot (1796–1832) of France, but its principles were not fully worked out until the 1860s, largely by William Thomson, or Lord Kelvin (1824–1907)— who coined the term "thermodynamics" in 1849 – in England, and Rudolf Clausius (1822–1888) in Germany. Their concept of entropy – the famous second law of thermodynamics – which implied that the Universe not only had a beginning but that it would eventually end in complete disorder or heat death, was a further challenge to the role of God in sustaining the cosmos.

While the rapid development of other sciences, such as geology and biology, may not have been a direct response to the Industrial Revolution, they only flowered because of the emergence of the industrial *logos* and its abandonment of Christianity as a strategic ideology. We have already seen that the concept of slow evolutionary development of geological and biological structures only became acceptable in a world in which the old God was already dead. The pioneering figures in both modern geology and biology – Charles Lyell and Charles Darwin – were particularly sensitive to the conservative ideas of their landowning class. Darwin as we have seen, delayed the publication of his *Origin of Species* for decades.

By the second half of the nineteenth century, the relationship between the industrial strategic *logos* and science had become a symbiotic one. Science responded to strategic demand and was financed from the growing surpluses of modern society; but at the same time science had become indispensable to the further development of the strategic *logos*. The science of thermodynamics, for example, which had been stimulated by the engines driving the Industrial Revolution, provided the knowledge necessary to design and build engines capable of generating greater and more efficient energy in the second half of the nineteenth century. This feedback mechanism was recognized by leading industrialists and their governments and resulted in public support for science. This took the form of technical schools – beginning with the Ecole Polytechnique in Paris in 1794 and leading to the mushrooming of technical schools throughout the Western world during the nineteenth and twentieth centuries —science departments in modern universities; research grants, prizes, official posts, and honors made to leading scientists; and public research institutes. It was during the second half of the nineteenth century that the professional scientist replaced the aristocratic dilettante and priestly philosopher, who, increasingly, retreated into schools of theology and philosophy.

In the Western world by 1900, an empirical and rational view of reality had displaced the metaphysical and mythical view that had existed only a century earlier. By 1900, science had totally displaced religion both as the strategic ideology and the story of life in the Western world. Some scholars were even bold enough to suggest that science had developed so far it had little more to tell us about life. No less an expert than Lord Kelvin declaimed at the British Association for the Advancement of Science in 1900 that "There is nothing new to be discovered in physics now. All that remains is more and more precise measurement".[14] This was wrong for three main reasons. First, there was still much more to be discovered about the physical world; second, that virtually *everything* remained to be discovered about the mystery of mysteries – the strategic *logos*; and third, strategic demand had not, and never will, run its course.

As far as the physical world was concerned, the critical issue of the atomic structure of objects remained to be solved; and the theoretical concept of the "ether", on which physics had come to rely, had yet to be demonstrated empirically. The game was far from over. In the decade that straddled the year 1900, work by Max Planck (1858–1947) and Albert Einstein (1879–1955) not only proved the existence of atoms and disproved the existence of the "ether" (together with all the physics that had been built upon it), but it "redefined physics as the study of relations between observers and events, rather than of events themselves".[15]

This twentieth-century redefinition of physics was the outcome of Einstein's 1905 paper on the special theory of relativity, in which he showed that the central Newtonian idea of absolute space was a fiction, because any observed event was a function of the observer's location and motion relative to that event. Einstein was able to generalize this result in his famous 1915 paper on the general theory of relativity. In addition, Max Planck's work on thermodynamics and black-body radiation led him reluctantly to challenge classical Newtonian principles and to construct the basis for quantum theory. Both the demolition of the absolute status of Newtonian physics and the firm establishment of quantum theory were achieved by Einstein in another 1905 paper on light quanta.[16]

Einstein spent the rest of his life trying unsuccessfully to develop a general theory – the so-called unified field theory – that would integrate the disciplines of relativity theory and quantum theory that he had introduced in 1905. As he grew older, like Planck before him, Einstein expressed deep concern about the direction in which the young Turks were taking quantum theory – a place where physicists could no longer speak with confidence about an independent physical reality, but only about the probability of measuring reality. Einstein's concept of reality involved the following three characteristics: reality exists independently of the ability and method of scientists to observe it; objects are located at certain points in spacetime, which he called separability; and causality is of the classical determinist kind and not a matter of probabilities or chance – as he was fond of saying: "God does not play dice".[17] In his highly successful textbook called *The Evolution of Physics* (1938), Einstein expressed his belief in "objective reality" and claimed that "without the belief that it is possible to grasp reality with our theoretical constructions, without the belief in the inner harmony of the world, there would be no science".[18] This, however, was not the belief of Niels Bohr (1885–1962) and subsequent quantum theorists. They believed that scientists could only hope to know the results of their experiments and observations, not an ultimate reality that might be beyond their perceptions.

Clearly the view of reality expressed in this book is similar to that held by Einstein. While the strategic *logos* – see Chapter 12 – is invisible and can only be detected indirectly through its impact on our lives, nonetheless it is very real. It has always existed, and we have always been able to sense its presence and experience its material outcomes. The entire history of strategic ideology and religion is a testament to that fact. The problem for humanity has been how to approach, understand, and influence this hidden reality. This is a problem far more difficult than the one faced by quantum physicists. It is this difficulty that has led mankind down through the ages to employ metaphor and mythology. But, as suggested in this book, there is a better way. We can scientifically approach the strategic *logos* – that mystery of mysteries – by observing the patterns of life and human history; by developing a general dynamic theory to explain these patterns; by deducing the laws of life and history from this general theory; and by reconstructing – on the basis of these laws and theory – the dynamic demand and supply forces of the hidden strategic *logos*. This is achieved in Chapter 12, and presented graphically in Figure 12.1. The strategic *logos* is the ultimate reality, because it is the vehicle of life — the vehicle in which we are all embodied — journeying through a hostile Universe.

But back to our story of science. The twentieth century experienced a revolution in physics, which was based on the work of Einstein and his European colleagues a century ago. This revolution, which consisted of relativity theory, quantum mechanics, and particle physics, displaced the old Newtonian physics and shattered the confidence of the old guard represented by Lord Kelvin. It led physicists to explore worlds we cannot see – hidden worlds – at both the subatomic and cosmic levels. The scientific revolution has also been extended to the fields of chemistry and biology; with chemists able to tailor molecules on demand, and biologists able to map the human (and animal) genome and to engage in genetic engineering.

Owing to the deeply entrenched and widespread misconception concerning this matter, it is worth reemphasizing that the modern "revolution" in science has only taken place because of the unfolding industrial technology strategy, which employs science as a strategic instrument. If, for some reason, the current technological strategy were prematurely derailed – perhaps due to the emergence of a strategically irrational climate-mitigation dictator at the global level – then the science revolution would come to an abrupt end.[19] Also, it is totally incorrect to call, as one historian has done, this scientific revolution "the most important event in the history of mankind".[20] Indeed, there is no "most important *event*" in the history of mankind, rather a sequence of important *transformations* – namely the technological paradigm shifts that have taken place in human history over the past two million years, and which will continue to take place in the future (see Chapter 10). Without this sequence of paradigm shifts there would have been no science "revolution", because science has no long-term momentum of its own. There is, in other words, no such thing as an independent revolution of ideas, whether scientific or non-scientific, only a symbiotic relationship between the strategic *logos* and science.

SCIENTISM – A NEW STRATEGIC IDEOLOGY

While science is a strategic instrument employed by the modern strategic *logos*, **scientism** is the strategic ideology of advanced, twenty-first century societies. Scientism, therefore, is the equivalent of state religion in the pre-industrial age. But what is scientism? In a *Scientific American* article, appropriately called "The shamans of scientism", Michael Shermer defined scientism as follows:

> Scientism is a scientific worldview that encompasses natural explanations for all phenomena, eschews supernatural and paranormal speculations, and embraces empiricism and reason as the twin pillars of *a philosophy of life* appropriate for an Age of Science.
>
> Scientism's voice can best be heard through a literary genre for both lay readers and professionals that includes the works of such scientists as Carl Sagan, E.O. Wilson, Stephen Jay Gould, Richard Dawkins and Jared Diamond. Scientism is a bridge spanning the abyss between what physicist C.P. Snow famously called the 'two cultures" of science and the arts/humanities (neither encampment being able to communicate with the other). Scientism has generated a new literati and intelligentsia passionately *concerned with the profound philosophical, ideological and theological implications of scientific discoveries.*
>
> Although the origins of the scientism genre can be traced to the writings of Galileo and Thomas Huxley in centuries past, its modern incarnation began in the early 1970s with mathematician Jacob Brownowski's *The Ascent of Man*, took off in the1980s with Sagan's *Cosmos* and hit pay dirt in the 1990s with Hawking's *A Brief History of Time*.[21]

Shermer makes the additional points that: "cosmology and evolutionary theory ask the ultimate questions that have traditionally been the province of religion and theology"; "this being the Age of Science, it is scientism's shamans who command our veneration"; and "we are also storytelling, mythmaking primates, with scientism as the foundational stratum of our story and scientists as the premier mythmakers of our time". Shermer sees himself as an exponent of scientism.

This is an interesting starting point for our exploration of scientism as a strategic ideology. We can agree that scientism provides a science-based worldview; that it has spawned a popular literature advancing a scientific philosophy; that it asks ultimate questions about the beginning and end of the Universe, which were once the sole province of religion; and that the public advocates of scientism are the shamans of the modern world. But there are also distinct points of disagreement and differences of focus.

As will be demonstrated in the chapters that follow, the worldview of scientism may be based on science, but that is not enough to make it scientific. Even Shermer makes the point that the advocates of scientism are both the "shamans" and the "premier mythmakers of our time". Mythmaking, however, is not a scientific activity that necessarily "embraces empiricism and reason as the twin pillars of a philosophy of life appropriate for an Age of Science". Secondly, it is hardly correct to assert that scientism is a bridge between science and the arts in any meaningful sense. Science in the hands of advocates like Edward Wilson has failed to embrace the arts, despite its intention to do so, precisely because of its own scientific limitations. Sociobiology has failed to colonize the social sciences because of its own difficulties in coming to an understanding of biological transition.[22] There is just no way that sociobiology can identify let alone analyze the nature and role of the strategic *logos*. The same can be said for those who make claims about social physics.[23] Despite the twentieth century's science "revolution", the truth is that scientists are no closer to understanding the universal life-system than are theologians. Advocates of scientism – in contrast to science – are the new priestly philosophers; the new metaphysicians of the modern world.

Third, we must be careful employing a term like the "Age of Science", because this age is not the creation of science. Rather it is the outcome of the industrial technological paradigm shift and the ongoing dynamic strategy of technological change, which are driven by desires not ideas. Fourth, it is not correct to say that the *modern* form of scientism can be traced back only to the 1970s. Its roots go back to the early nineteenth century when the Industrial Revolution was being pioneered. Its advocates, as discussed in Chapter 6, included Lyell, Darwin, Wallace, Nietzsche, Marx, Buckle and so many more, who attempted to substitute a scientifically based world view for the monotheistic world view.

Finally, it will be clear from his view of its origins, that Shermer's definition of scientism is far too narrow. It is not the worldview of just those who write and read the popular works of articulate scientists such as Sagan, Wilson, Gould, Dawkins, Hawking, etc; rather it is the worldview, however inadequately articulated, of all those who *believe* in the power of science in the struggle to survive and prosper – just as in the pre-modern world ordinary people *believed* in the power of religion to do the same thing. Afterall, it is "the people" who drive the strategic *logos,* not the intellectuals.

The modern article of *faith* is that science will guarantee the survival and prosperity of our life-system. Because of this *belief,* modern society has invested massively in the infrastructure of science, technology, and higher learning. This is not just a simple belief that investment in science will generate an increase in incomes and wealth. It is a belief that science is able not only to detect looming crises – such as climate change – but also to resolve them. A massive leap of faith is involved here, because mankind has demonstrated repeatedly that our intellectual models of society and nature are so simplistic that they are totally incapable of analyzing complex dynamic systems in the past and present, let alone predicting how they might work themselves out in the future. Even if we were able to make accurate predictions about the emergence of future crises, our track record of remedial intervention is so abysmally poor, that the outcome of significant interference is likely to be more catastrophic than the crisis itself. To make a life-system operate more sustainably, we need to understand the nature and processes of that system. As I have shown in this book, neither natural nor social scientists have any effective understanding of the strategic *logos* that they are determined to substantially alter. To change one or two parameters in a complex dynamic system is likely to send that system spiraling out of control. These issues are discussed in my recent book *The Coming Eclipse* (Snooks 2010).

There are a number of classical examples of instability caused by large-scale interventions. The first of these is the attempt by the USA after September Eleven to secure oil supplies in the Middle East by invading Iraq and deposing Saddam Hussein. The problem seemed simple and tractable. Certainly it was a simple matter to destroy the conventional military forces in Iraq and to eliminate the antistrategic leadership of the Hussein family and the Bathist party, but it proved to be impossible to predict and shape the longer term outcomes of interference in a complex sociopolitical system. All the USA has so far achieved is to destroy the old Iraqi strategic *logos* and fail to replace it with a more satisfactory one. The Bush administration had no conception of the complexity of what they were attempting because they, and their "expert" advisors, had no understanding of the workings of the strategic *logos*. And the Obama administration merely wanted to wash their hands of the whole debacle.

On a smaller, but still significant, scale is the misconceived policy of inflation targeting in advanced strategic societies. These societies – such as the USA, Britain, Australia – have charged their reserve (or central) banks with keeping inflation under control. The governors of these reserve banks are usually people trained in orthodox neoclassical economics, with working experience somewhere in the financial sector. The problem is that neither the discipline of neoclassical economics nor financial experts understand how the strategic *logos* operates. Indeed, they have no idea even of its existence. Nor do they understand the dynamics of complex living systems. Their discipline employs a comparative static methodology with a focus on equilibrium solutions. While they have no body of theory to explain the role of inflation in a dynamic society, they have a vague fear that it will lead to instability and away from equilibrium. Like the priestly philosophers of Egypt, modern deductive (metaphysical) economists are concerned to maintain order and stability. Their solution is to eliminate inflation – or at least reduce it to low levels – by increasing interest rates so as to slow the growth process and to deflate the economy. Hence, the economy alternates between phases of growth and inflation on the one hand and stagnation (even negative growth) and deflation on the other. As I show in *Longrun Dynamics* (1998b), *Global Transition* (1999) and *The Global Crisis Makers* (2000), *strategic* inflation plays a positive role in the dynamic process by orchestrating the strategic demand-response mechanism. While it is possible to eliminate inflation by deflationary policies, to do so successfully in the long run would also eliminate economic growth. My discovery of the growth-inflation curve demonstrates that inflation is a non-accelerating function of economic growth.[24] Hence, owing to their ignorance of the dynamic mechanism of the strategic *logos*, orthodox economists and gullible politicians run the risk of reducing the efficiency of, even derailing, the dynamic process of advanced strategic societies.

What unintended impacts will current attempts to control climate change have on the complex living systems on this planet? The simple truth is that because these systems are so complex and the existing models of natural and social sciences so simplistic, scientists cannot answer this question. But the belief in the power of science is so strong that these "experts" believe they can manipulate the dynamic systems of the planet, together with the life-systems of all its species, despite not recognizing or understanding the nature of the strategic *logos* and how it interacts with climate change. What man once did in the name of God, he now does in the name of science. Science itself has become our highest deity. To continue in this myopic way is to invite disaster – a disaster that the deity of science will not be able to deflect.

Scientism also invites a belief in the ability of science to deliver an endless stream of new ideas that will continue to drive the increase in wealth and living standards. This view is based on a fundamental misunderstanding of the role of science – and of ideas in general – in modern society. As emphasized throughout this book, desires drive and ideas merely facilitate. The occasional suggestion that a "national ideas summit" (as in Australia in early 2008) will somehow improve our strategic pursuit and/or our sociopolitical system is badly flawed (as the collapse of the Rudd government in 2010 clearly demonstrated). Strategic demand creates its own ideas, but ideas never create their own strategic demand. Ideas without a demand for their application will merely wither on the vine. Ideas summits are all about elitist feelings of self-importance. The only way that human society will continue to generate innovations is if the strategic *logos* continues to require them. Human society solves its problems strategically rather than scientifically. This is true of issues like climate change as well as material living standards. Indeed, climate change will only be resolved – to the extent that it can be resolved – if it becomes part of the strategic calculus of mankind. It will be resolved, in other words, through the operation of desires rather than ideas.

Scientism also fulfills the secondary function of strategic ideologies down through the ages – that of a personal religion. Some people have always needed something greater than themselves to believe in. Just as we need to believe in a strategic guardian that knows more than we do about the life-system that sustains our society, so individuals need to believe in something greater than themselves to give their lives meaning in an apparently meaningless Universe. In the pre-modern world, strategic guardians were transformed into personal gods; while in the modern world, in the absence of a deity of scientism acceptable to a "sophisticated" modern, many people have looked to a personified nature. This is the outcome of a romantic approach to scientism, which is similar to eighteenth-century Romantism in the West. Today the so-called "green movement" has revived the Romantic attitude to nature, by providing it with a sensible personality. Some have gone as far as to regard the Earth – rechristened Gaia – as a living organism worthy of veneration. Others have projected the same quality onto the cosmos, thereby generating a sort of cosmotheology. Just like religious fundamentalists, the radical ecologists/environmentalists, and followers of Gaia have unwittingly become antistrategists dedicated to undermining the strategic *logos*.

The ancient Egyptians called their antistrategists "criminals" while the ancient Romans called them "atheists". What will future generations call the destabilizing climate mitigationists: heros or knaves? In chapter 9 we will examine how science has been transformed into religion. But first, in Chapter 8, we consider how some scientists have attempted to make a science of religion.

Chapter 8
A Science of Religion?

In the continuing struggle between the old and new *strategic* ideologies in the West – between Christianity and scientism – some scientists have been striving to displace religion entirely. This is being attempted by providing a scientific explanation for the role of religion in general and of God in particular. One group of natural scientists consider themselves especially ordained to assert their dominance over the theologians. They are the neo-Darwinists, or sociobiologists, some of whom appear to feel particularly threatened by the priestly philosophers of Christianity.

Neo-Darwinists have revived the old nineteenth-century war against the creationists, because these latter-day supporters of Darwinian natural selection are the purveyors of what they (incorrectly) regard as the only alternative to the old idea of divine selection. As cosmologists seem less sensitive to the arguments of creationists – some are even quite sympathetic – it is difficult to understand why the neo-Darwinists are so defensive. They appear to be caught in a Victorian time warp, because they fail to realize that Christianity has already been abandoned as a strategic ideology owing to the industrial technological paradigm shift – that Christianity no longer matters in the strategic pursuit.

In this chapter we will consider the arguments of the neo-Darwinists and their camp followers concerning the origin and nature of religion and ethical values; and concerning their own attempt to develop a science of religion. The authors included in this survey are Edward Wilson, the father of sociobiology, Richard Dawkins, the contemporary popularizer of Darwin's "dangerous idea", and Dean Hamer, author of *The God Gene*. Despite the common ground held by all three writers on the role of natural selection in determining mankind's genetic inheritance, they have very different explanations of the origins and role of religion: religion as a "superorganism"; religion as an "evil virus"; and religion as the outcome of the god gene. Prominent among neo-Darwinism's campfollowers is Daniel Dennet, a philosopher who wishes to develop a "natural science" of religion.

RELIGION AS A "SUPERORGANISM"

Edward Wilson, the father of sociobiology, displays considerable respect for religion and religious-based ethics. This contrast starkly with the attitude of his more combative neo-Darwinist colleague Richard Dawkins. Nevertheless, Wilson is convinced that religious metaphysics can be transformed into a science of religion. In his somewhat conciliatory book *Consilience* (1999), Wilson writes:

> On the one side, ethics and religion are still too complex for present-day science to explain in depth. On the other, they are far more a product of autonomous evolution

> than hitherto conceded by most theologians. *Science faces in ethics and religion its most interesting and possibly humbling challenge*, while religion must somehow find the way to incorporate the discoveries of science in order to retain credibility ... *Science for its part will test relentlessly every assumption about the human condition and in time uncover the bedrock of the moral and religious sentiments.*[1]

While the natural sciences – namely sociobiology – will eventually explain religion and, presumably God, the challenge, according to Wilson, will not be an easy one. Needless to say, Wilson has completely underestimated the role of the social sciences (as in the present book) in meeting this challenge. This is because he believes that sociobiology will eventually subsume the social sciences, and that fundamental progress in this field must wait until then. He will have a very long wait.

Wilson, unlike Dawkins, is willing to concede that there are two approaches to ethics and religion – the transcendental (which can be secular as well as religious) and the empirical – that should be taken seriously. While he admits to a "leaning toward" deism – the idea of a creative force based on reason rather than revelation – he also claims to be an ethical "empiricist". By "empiricist" he means that ethical codes are, and should be, based on "hereditary predispositions in mental development" that cause "broad convergence across cultures, while reaching precise form in each culture according to historical circumstances"; and he believes that these ethical codes "play an important role in determining which cultures flourish, and which decline".[2] It is because of these "biological roots of moral behavior" that Wilson and his followers believe a science of religion will eventually be constructed. Once again we see here the flawed supply-side approach of orthodox scholarship.

Human nature and coevolution

Ethical and religious codes are, for neo-Darwinists like Wilson, the products of the Darwinian brain. It is, for them, the biologically determined brain – an outcome of processes of natural selection – that constructs human nature. And it is human nature that shapes society in general and religion in particular. In answering the rhetorical question: "What is human nature?" Wilson tells us:

> It is not genes which prescribe it [human nature], or culture, its ultimate product ... It is the epigenetic rules, the hereditary regularities of mental development that bias cultural evolution in one direction as opposed to another, thus connecting the genes to culture.[3]

In other words, human nature is merely the outcome of our genes operating at one remove in a social context. And the human brain is the link between genes and culture – a link made possible by natural selection. Wilson writes:

> Thousands of genes prescribe the brain, the sensory system, and all other physiological processes that interact with the physical and social environment to produce the holistic properties of mind and culture. Through natural selection, the environment ultimately selects which genes will do the prescribing.[4]

This is why Wilson believes that biology is the linchpin of human knowledge – of "consilience" as he likes to call it.

Wilson deepens his analysis by introducing what he calls "epigenetic rules". He tells us that "the search for human nature can be viewed as the archeology of the epigenetic rules".[5] Epigenetic rules are, according to Wilson, the genetically determined constraints that operate on the "anatomy, physiology, cognition and behavior of organisms". And, of course, they are the outcome of the neo-Darwinian version of natural selection:

> During hundreds of millennia of Paleolithic history, the genes prescribing certain epigenetic rules increased and spread at the expense of others through the species by means of natural selection. By that laborious process human nature assembled itself.[6]

As usual, no evidence is given – nor could it be given – for this assertion. It is, therefore, metaphysical in nature. There is nothing "empirical" here!

Epigenetic rules are said to operate at two distinct levels. The "primary" epigenetic rules are "the automatic processes that extend from the filtering and coding of stimuli in the sense organs all the way to perception of the stimuli by the brain. The entire sequence is influenced by previous experience only to a minor degree, if at all". And the "secondary" epigenetic rules are "regularities in the integration of large amounts of information. Drawing from selected fragments of perception, memory, and emotional coloring, secondary epigenetic rules lead the mind to predisposed decisions through the choice of certain memes and overt responses over others".[7] Wilson regards this division as subjective and suggests that there will also be intermediate levels for these genetically influenced rules.

Clearly, Wilson, together with other sociobiologists, regards variations in behavior, as well as in physical characteristics, as genetically determined to a high degree. While the degree of determination is not precisely stated, it has to be considerable, otherwise the sociobiological position would not be distinguishable from that of the existing social sciences, which Wilson claims will be taken over by his sociobiological project. In the mid-1970s, Wilson proclaimed somewhat triumphantly that:

> It may not be too much to say that sociology and the other social sciences, as well as the humanities, are the last branches of biology waiting to be included in the Modern Synthesis [i.e. neo-Darwinism]. One of the functions of sociobiology, then, is to reformulate the foundation of the social sciences in a way that draws these subjects into the Modern Synthesis.[8]

More than thirty years later the social sciences are still "waiting" to be embraced! The great sociobiological vision is no closer to being realized now than at its birth. Accordingly, Wilson's tone today is more conciliatory. Now he is offering not an unconditional takeover but a junior partnership to social scientists, who have been harder to convince — or, indeed, to rout — than he at first thought. Yet, even now, he insists that human culture will only be fully understood through a Darwinian study of the human brain and of human nature.

Wilson's belief in the central role played by genetics in human behavior and, hence, human society, is conveyed rather aptly by his provocative metaphor – the "genetic leash". Employed at least as early as the 1970s in *On Human Nature* (1978), the "genetic leash" was still part of his vocabulary at the turn of the century in *Consilience* (1998). In responding to a rhetorical question on that earlier occasion, Wilson proclaimed:

> Can the cultural evolution of higher ethical values gain a direction and momentum of its own and completely replace genetic evolution? I think not. *The genes hold culture on a leash*. The leash is very long, but inevitably values will be constrained in accordance with their effects on the human gene pool.[9]

The human "dog", therefore, is controlled by its "master" the gene. This is, of course, merely an alternative – although a far more provocative and offensive – metaphor to Richard Dawkins' "selfish gene", with talk of "lumbering robots" and "gene machines". There have always been some evolutionary geneticists, such as Steven Gould, Richard Levontin, Niles Eldredge and Steven Rose, who have found these metaphors both ridiculous and offensive, and who are highly critical of the sociobiological focus on genes rather than organisms.[10] The geneticist Steve Jones even regards the various attempts "to apply Darwinism to civilization" as "more or less infantile".[11]

Despite the more conciliatory tone in *Consilience*, Wilson continues to employ the "genetic leash" metaphor. When discussing the alleged parallel "evolution" of genes and culture throughout mankind's prehistory, Wilson asks: "How tight was the genetic leash? That is the key question, and it is possible to give only a partial answer". And that answer is:

> In general the epigenetic rules are strong enough to be visibly constraining. They have left an indelible stamp on the behaviour of people in even the most sophisticated societies.[12]

Also, when explaining that different scholars have different views on how tight the "leash" might be, Wilson writes:

> Nurturists think that culture is held on a very long genetic leash, if held at all, so that the cultures of different societies can diverge from one another indefinitely. Hereditarians believe the leash is short, causing cultures to evolve major features in common.[13]

Wilson is a hereditarian. As I show in *The Collapse of Darwinism* (2003), there are other leading geneticists who disagree strongly with Wilson's "tight leash" interpretation.[14]

Yet, having argued a case for the "genetic leash", Wilson is forced to admit there is very little hard evidence for any connection between genes and epigenetic rules! This, he insists, is not because such an oppressive relationship does not exist, but because coevolution is "an infant field of study". The argument, however, is not very convincing, particularly in the twenty-first century. Evidence that Wilson does provide – dyslexia and irrational aggressive behavior – hardly inspires confidence. Nonetheless, despite the absence of empirical support, he is prepared to assert that "variation in virtually every aspect of human behavior is heritable to some degree, and thus in some manner influenced by differences in genes among people".[15] For the sociobiologists, no matter what the nature of the evidence, human behavior is "in some manner" genetically determined. Human culture, in other words, is extruded from the Darwinian brain. On this basis, neo-Darwinism is ultimately a matter of faith – hardly a sound basis for a science of religion, but possibly a good basis for a religion of science.

This brings us to what, in *The Collapse of Darwinism,* I called "the myth of coevolution".[16] Sociobiologists allege that coevolution is a dynamic process in which genes and culture interact under the shaping influence of natural selection. As this is a rather shadowy process, Wilson should speak for himself. In a chapter of *Consilience,* entitled "From Genes to Culture", he writes:

> Culture is created by the communal mind, and each mind in turn is the product of the genetically structured human brain. Genes and culture are therefore inseverably linked. But the linkage is flexible, to a degree still mostly unmeasured. The linkage is also tortuous: genes prescribe epigenetic rules, which are the neural pathways and regularities in cognitive development by which the individual mind assembles itself. The mind grows from birth to death by absorbing parts of the existing culture available to it, with selections guided through epigenetic rules inherited by the individual brain.[17]

Not only is the human brain genetically determined at birth, according to Wilson, but its subsequent development is shaped by epigenetic rules that are "prescribed" by one's genes. And all this is the outcome of natural selection as genes attempt to maximize their survival and influence in the gene pool.

Wilson goes onto explain the cultural implications:

> The nature of the genetic leash and the role of culture can now be better understood, as follows. Certain cultural norms also survive and reproduce better than competing norms, causing culture to evolve in a track parallel to and usually much faster than genetic evolution. The quicker the pace of cultural evolution, the looser the connection between genes and culture, although the connection is never completely broken.[18]

Darwin, therefore, is never far away. As Wilson expresses it: "gene-culture coevolution is a special extension of the more general process of evolution by natural selection", which he regards as an "impersonal force". Only those genes that "confer higher survival and reproductive success on the organisms bearing them, through the prescribed traits of anatomy, physiology, and behavior, increase in the population from one generation to the next". And he concludes:

> To genetic evolution, putting the matter as concisely as possible, natural selection has added the parallel track of cultural evolution, and the two forms of evolution

are somehow linked. We are trapped, we sometimes think, for ultimate good or evil, not just by our genes but also by our culture.[19]

But, of course, for sociobiologists even our culture is shaped by our genes.

All this merely begs the question: How can Wilson's imprecise model of coevolution – genetic and cultural evolution are "somehow linked" – that lacks empirical support, possibly explain the structure and dynamics of human society? To answer this ultimate and demanding question, we need to consider what Wilson means by "culture". It is, as we shall see, a very simple concept that does little to improve our understanding of the complexity or dynamics of human civilization or religion. Belatedly and briefly Wilson tells us that, "strictly defined", culture is the "complex socially learned behavior" of humans, which, of course, is constrained by the "genetic leash". Wilson's only other comment in *Consilience* on the nature of human culture concerns what he calls the "cultural unit". He explains:

> We [Lumsden and Wilson (1981)] recommend that the unit of culture – now called meme – be the same as the node of semantic memory and its correlates in brain activity. The level of the node, whether concept (the simplest recognizable unit), proposition, or schema, determines the complexity of the idea, behavior, or artifact that it helps to sustain in the culture at large.[20]

This definition of "meme" is very different to that employed by Richard Dawkins, for whom the cultural "replicator" is largely independent of genetic constraint – as we will see shortly.

In effect, Wilson equates the idea of culture (including religion) with the way our genetically engineered brains view the world. Human ideas, behavior, institutions (including religion) and artifacts are somehow extruded from our brains to form the complexities of our sophisticated civilizations. He explains:

> The epigenetic rules of human nature bias innovation, learning, and choice. They are gravitational centers that pull the development of the mind in certain directions away from others. Arriving at the centers, artists, composers, and writers over the centuries have built archetypes, the themes most predictably expressed in original works of art.[21]

He further believes that a biological study of these archetypes will place the "flawed" psychoanalysis of Freud and Jung back on the correct – the neo-Darwinian – track. In this context, Wilson claims that "mysticism and science meet in dreams". This tilt at evolutionary psychology is analyzed and exposed in my recent book *The Selfcreating Mind* (2006).[22] In particular, I reject the bizarre concept of the Darwinian modular brain, and show that the developing brain is a response not to epigenetic rules but to strategic demand generated by the strategic *logos*.[23] The brain, in other words, is a response to demand-side rather than supply-side forces – to the *logos* rather than the gene.

Before examining how this sociobiological approach to the dynamics of human society has been employed by Wilson to explain ethical codes and religion, we need to briefly consider its status as social science. Coevolution is a rather naive supply-side hypothesis. It should not be called a model, because it does not tell us anything about the transition from genetically shaped products of the human brain to the complex and varied ecosociopolitical structures of human civilization. Exactly how does "coevolution" explain, for example, the building of the Egyptian pyramids, the rise and fall of ancient Greece, the waxing and waning of Greek democracy, the sudden and radical transformation of Arab society and the rise and fall of its world empire, the equally sudden rise of Japan following the Meiji restoration, the rise and fall of the USSR, or the recent sudden modernization of China? The simple and telling fact is that it cannot. Sociobiology will never achieve its imperial ambitions in the social sciences because it is based on the simplistic and flawed supply-side concept of natural selection. Wilson and other sociobiologists are simply unable to explain the dynamic complexities of the human world from the viewpoint of the selfish gene.

Ethical codes and religion

Wilson attempts to apply the coevolution hypothesis to the study of ethical codes and religion. "Ethical and religious beliefs", he writes, "are created from the bottom up, from people to their culture" – from genetically determined organisms to institutional structures. Ethical codes are "reached by consensus under the guidance of the innate rules of mental development", whereas religion "is the ensemble of mythic narratives that explain the origin of a people, their destiny, and why they are obliged to subscribe to particular rituals and moral codes".[24]

Wilson argues that "ethical codes have arisen by evolution through the interplay of biology and culture". He maintains this occurs in two stages. The first stage involves the emergence of *genetically determined* "moral sentiments" or moral instincts. Darwinian evolution favors cooperation, which becomes "heritable" owing, we are told, to the "fact" that "cooperative individuals generally survive longer and leave more offspring". This Darwinian process "repeated through thousands of generations inevitably gave birth to the moral sentiments" of "conscience, self-respect, remorse, empathy, shame, humility, and moral outrage". In the second stage, these moral instincts are said to "bias cultural evolution toward the conventions that express the universal moral codes of honor, patriotism, altruism, justice, compassion, mercy, and redemption". Human beings, therefore, possess an "inborn propensity to moral behavior" owing to our innate epigenetic rules of moral reasoning.[25]

Ethical codes, in other words, are genetically determined and, in effect, extruded from the human brain. This is the usual metaphysical supply-side hypothesis that runs into all sorts of real-world difficulties. Two of the most important are the inconsistent manner in which moral codes are applied in human society, and the obvious inflexibility of a set of codes that are genetically determined. As Wilson himself notes:

> The dark side to the inborn propensity to moral behavior is xenophobia ...
> People give trust to strangers with effort, and true compassion is a commodity
> in chronically short supply ... They are quick to imagine themselves victims of
> conspiracies by competing groups, and they are prone to dehumanize and murder
> their rivals during periods of severe conflict.[26]

What he doesn't tell us is that when conventional society breaks down under
great stress, its citizens — even close family members — turn violently against
each other. How is this possible in Wilson's strange world of kin-selection and
genetically determined moral codes? In contrast, it is completely explicable
in the real world of the strategic *logos*, where ethical rules are generated by
strategic demand, which, in extreme circumstances, can collapse completely,
leaving individuals free to act in whatever way that will ensure their survival –
even cannibalizing members of their own family.

Wilson's system of genetically determined moral codes also lack the
remarkable flexibility observed in the real world. How, for example, would
he explain the sudden change in moral codes that occurred in Germany in the
mid-1930s? He cannot, using his supply-side sociobiological hypothesis. In
contrast, the demand-side dynamic-strategy theory can explain it in terms of
an abrupt shift in dynamic strategy from technological change to conquest,
owing to the rise of Nazism during a time of severe economic crisis. Germany's
new conquest strategy generated a strategic demand not only for a new type
of ecosociopolitical system but also for a new set of darker ethical principles.
Each of the four possible dynamic strategies – family multiplication, commerce,
conquest and technological change – generates a characteristic need for a set
of distinctive and predictable ethical principles. This cannot be explained by a
simplistic supply-side hypothesis such as sociobiology.

Finally, in *Consilience* Wilson briefly turns his attention to religion; but only
briefly, as sociobiology is unable to explain human culture or the underlying
logos. He writes:

> Religions are analogous to superorganisms. They have a life cycle. They are born,
> they grow, they compete, they reproduce, and, in the fullness of time, most die.
> In each of these phases religions reflect the human organisms that nourish them.
> They express a primary rule of human existence, that whatever is necessary to
> sustain life is also ultimately biological.[27]

This vision of religion is typical of the sociobiological mind. Religions are
seen as biological entities operating according to Darwinian principles. This
vision is in stark contrast to the strategic interpretation presented in this book,
whereby "religions" were initially strategic ideologies considered necessary by
their adherents to sustain the viability of their strategic *logos*. These strategic
instruments rise and fall according to the demands of the *logos*, which is shaped
by both strategic and paradigmatic change. Within these broad parameters,
the detailed nature of strategic ideologies and religions are influenced by the
material and intellectual interests of the priestly philosophers and their social

environments. While the strategic approach can explain major changes in strategic ideologies and religions, the sociobiological approach is all at sea. How can Darwinian natural selection explain the transition of a particular society's strategic ideology (even if it could recognize it as such) to a religion, followed by a reversal to a strategic ideology, and a final reversal to a religion, as occurred in the case of Christianity (see Chapter 6)? Natural selection cannot explain "evolutionary" reversals, as I explain in *The Ephemeral Civilization* (1997). The dynamic-strategy theory enables us to explode the myth of religious evolution. [28]

Wilson views the origins of religion as multi-faceted. Religions arise in order to satisfy a number of aspects of the Darwinian mind: the desire for "permanent existence", arising from some sort of primitive fear; and a need to "explain the meaning of life".[29] And, as we have come to expect by now, religion arises in this context from "biases in mental development encoded in the genes" – a result of "instinctual behavior". Wilson explains: "If the religious mythos did not exist in culture, it would be quickly invented ... Such inevitability is the mark of instinctual behavior in any species". Why? Because "there is a hereditary selective advantage to membership in a powerful group united by a devout belief and purpose".[30] So, we are told without a scrap of evidence, "much if not all religious behavior could have arisen from natural selection", and that "the human mind evolved to believe in the gods".[31] This is an issue taken up by Dean Hamer below. Finally, Wilson claims that "religion arose on an ethical foundation, and it has probably always been used in one manner or another to justify moral codes".[32]

The idea of religion as a superorganism has little substance and could never be employed to explore the religious experience in the real world, as we have done in this book. Wilson's supply-side hypothesis, with religion and ethics being extruded from the Darwinian brain, is an over-engineered biological system. As such, it is an inflexible and inappropriate hypothesis about human culture in general and religion in particular.

RELIGION AS AN "EVIL VIRUS"

Richard Dawkins, unlike Edward Wilson, displays considerable hostility towards religion. No doubt many readers of his recent book *The God Delusion* (2006) consider the degree of hostility it contains as strangely irrational.[33] Surely the claim that religion is an "evil virus" is completely over the top. Many will be left wondering about the real, rather than the stated, cause of such an exaggerated response. As we shall see, Dawkins' arguments in this book are based on a totally *unscientific* evaluation of the nature and role of religion in human society.

Despite their different attitudes toward religion, both Dawkins and Wilson share a common view of life – that of neo-Darwinism – and a belief in the ability of science to ultimately explain the nature of religion and human ethical codes. Dawkins, however, wants to go a couple of steps further. He claims that science will eventually demonstrate conclusively that God doesn't exist. Dawkins insists that:

> Science can chip away at agnosticism, in a way that Huxley bent over backwards to deny for the special case of God. I am arguing that, notwithstanding the polite abstinence of Huxley, Gould and many others, the God question is not in principle and forever outside the remit of science. As with the nature of stars ... and as with the likelihood of life in orbit around them, science can make at least probabilistic inroads into the territory of agnosticism.[34]

Dawkins considers and rejects the idea of the "God hypothesis" – the hypothesis that "there exists a superhuman, supernatural intelligence who deliberately designed and created the universe and everything in it, including us".[35] In its place he substitutes the "Darwinian hypothesis", to the effect that

> any creative intelligence, of sufficient complexity to design anything, comes into existence only as the end product of an extended process of gradual evolution. Creative intelligences, being evolved, necessarily arrived late in the universe, and therefore cannot be responsible for designing it. God, in the sense defined, is a delusion; and ... a pernicious delusion.[36]

There are two interesting issues here. The first is: why would anyone claiming, as Dawkins regularly does, to be an objective scientist, bother with either the God hypothesis or its Darwinian alternative? Surely, a real scientist would marshal the evidence to answer the obvious question: why have so many individuals and societies across space and time accepted the God hypothesis. In other words, what we need to do as scientists is to explain this universal phenomenon rather than to engage in impassioned verbal warfare about it. This is what I have attempted in the present book. The second issue is that, as the dynamic-strategy theory shows, life is a selfcreating, or autogenous, process, by which organisms have been involved, through the creative process of **strategic selection**, in the shaping (or "designing") of life.[37]

On the question of scientific attitudes, it is strange that Dawkins attacks religious fundamentalism, but defends atheistic fundamentalism on the grounds that it is based on scientific Darwinism. Surely the objective scientist would regard both matters as unscientific. In attacking religious fundamentalism, Dawkins claims that:

> Fundamentalists know they are right because they have read the truth in a holy book and they know, in advance, that nothing will budge them from their belief. The truth of the holy book is an axiom, not the end product of a process of reasoning. The book is true, and if the evidence seems to contradict it, it is the evidence that must be thrown out, not the book.[38]

Ironically, as I pointed out in *The Collapse of Darwinism* (2003), Dawkins takes precisely this stance in relation to the holy book of Darwinism called *Origin of Species*. Being an astute intellectual, Dawkins appears to anticipate this criticism by writing, almost innocently, that: "By contrast, what I, as a scientist, believe (for example evolution) I believe not because of reading a holy book but because I have studied the evidence. It is really a very different matter".[39] As devil's advocates, we should ask at least two questions here: first, did Dawkins really study the evidence before he accepted the dogma of Darwin's *Origin of Species*; and second, how systematically has Dawkins studied the evidence? I suspect the answer to the first question is that, as a student, Dawkins was presented with, and accepted, Darwin's theory of natural selection *before* he actually studied any evidence, and that when he did study the evidence he did so in a Darwinian framework. As far as the second question is concerned, I know of no attempt ever made by Dawkins to systematically examine the historical evidence of species – whether plant, animal, or human – specifically in order to falsify the Darwinian hypothesis of natural selection. Instead, unlike the paleontologist critics (Gould and Eldredge[40]), Dawkins uses a deductive approach to take the ideas of Darwin and the neo-Darwinists to their logical, but absurd, extremes.[41] Dawkins extends – and unwittingly exposes – Darwinism, he does not test its scientific status. In this he is at one with the theologians he attacks — he is a **priestly philosopher**.

But, in a burst of enthusiastic overstatement, Dawkins claims:

> We [scientists] believe in evolution because the evidence supports it, and we would abandon it overnight if new evidence arose to disprove it. No real fundamentalist would ever say anything like that ... [M]y belief in evolution is not fundamentalism, and it is not faith, because I know what it would take to change my mind, and I would gladly do so if the necessary evidence were forthcoming.[42]

This is a fascinating claim. But is it true? A fundamentalist might very well claim to be willing to change his mind if evidence to the contrary were provided; but then either not make reasonable efforts to examine scholarly claims that this evidence does exist, or deny the validity of this evidence when they are no longer able to ignore it.

The evidence suggests that Dawkins has made up his mind unalterably that "natural selection is not only a parsimonious, plausible and elegant solution; it is the only workable alternative to chance that has ever been suggested".[43] This sentiment is expressed in similar words on at least five further occasions in *The God Delusion*, which leads one to suspect that, like the "Player Queen" in Hamlet's play, he "doth protest too much, methinks".[44] Indeed, had Dawkins been at all concerned to refute this very strong hypothesis – as a real scientist would – he would have regularly scoured the literature on the internet to see if any such evidence existed. Had he done so, he would have known that for the decade prior to the publication of *The God Delusion* there has been a growing neo-Darwinian challenge to natural selection as an explanation of life. That challenge is my own dynamic-strategy theory, which is a realist (i.e. empirical), demand-side, general dynamic theory of life and human society based on a systematic examination of the historical (both biological and cultural) evidence that Dawkins studiously ignores. This challenge began with *The Dynamic*

Society (1996) and consists of a total of eleven books including *The Collapse of Darwinism* (2003) and *The Selfcreating Mind* (2006), together with a number of articles in natural science journals, including *Advances in Space Research* (2005) and *Complexity* (2008). Could Dawkins really have missed this?[45] Only if he had been determined to do so, particularly after I brought it to his attention. So far he has failed to even acknowledge either this evidence or my prompting – hardly the action of a scientist determined to avoid being branded as a "fundamentalist".

The roots of morality

Not surprisingly, Dawkins, like his fellow neo-Darwinist Edward Wilson, believes that moral codes – or "moral sense" – are an outcome of our genetic inheritance. Indeed, he is convinced that the moral sense of mankind has a Darwinian origin. This leads Dawkins into a restatement of the distinction between the "selfish gene" and the "altruistic organism" first discussed in *The Selfish Gene* some three decades ago. It is worth quoting Dawkins at some length on this issue:

> The logic of Darwinism concludes that the unit in the hierarchy of life which survives and passes through the filter of natural selection will tend to be selfish ... [and] that the unit of natural selection (i.e. the unit of self-interest) is not the selfish organism, nor the selfish group or selfish species or selfish ecosystem, but the selfish *gene*. It is the gene that, in the form of information, either survives for many generations or does not. Unlike the gene (and arguably the meme), the organism, the group, and the species are not the right kind of entity to serve as a unit in this sense, because they do not make exact copies of themselves, and do not compete in a pool of such self-replicating entities ...
>
> The most obvious way in which genes ensure their own 'selfish' survival relative to other genes is by programming individual organisms to be selfish. There are indeed many circumstances in which survival of the individual organism will favour the survival of genes that ride inside it. But different circumstances favour different tactics. There are circumstances – not particularly rare – in which genes ensure their own selfish survival by influencing organisms to behave altruistically.[46]

The circumstances favoring altruism in a Darwinian world are, according to Dawkins, genetic kinship, reciprocal altruism ("you scratch my back and I'll scratch yours"), the "Darwinian benefit of acquiring a reputation for generosity and kindness"; and "the particular additional benefit of conspicuous generosity as a way of buying unfakeably authentic advertising".[47]

These circumstances favoring altruism emerged in "ancestral times", when members of our species "had the opportunity to be altruistic only towards close kin and potential reciprocators". But today, we live in big cities and interact with large numbers of people, only a very small proportion of whom are family or people with whom we have repeated interactions. Despite this we still respond to other people with varying degrees of generosity and kindness. Why? Because,

Dawkins tells us, the rules of thumb by which the human brain operates – as a result of natural selection in ancestral times —persist into the modern world. As this was not the intention of the selfish gene, Dawkins argues that it is the outcome of a "misfiring", or a "mistake", of the genetically determined rules of thumb. They are "Darwinian mistakes: blessed, precious mistakes".[48] Hence, for Dawkins, our moral sense is rooted deeply in our Darwinian past. "Moral sense", we are told, "is built into our brains, like our sexual instincts or our fear of heights".[49]

Elsewhere I have not only discussed and refuted the absurdity of the selfish-gene argument, but have shown that the underlying concept of natural selection is wrong.[50] Here I will limit my discussion to the points raised specifically by Dawkins in relation to moral principles. First, I suggest a re-reading of the long quotation from Dawkins on the selfish gene and the reason it is "the unit of natural selection" or "the unit of self-interest". We are told that only genes are able to "make exact copies of themselves" or to "compete in a pool of such self-replicating entities". This is like saying that technical ideas are units of self-interest and of technological dynamics because they, rather than the entrepreneurs who adopt them, replicate, compete and survive in the technique pool. Clearly this is absurd; just as the selfish-gene argument is absurd. Technical ideas certainly do *not* compete for survival in the technique pool by manipulating entrepreneurs. Techniques are created, applied to the processes of production, and are retired by entrepreneurs attempting to maximize their profits. In doing so, the entrepreneurs (or selfish organisms) are responding to a changing strategic demand generated by the prevailing dynamic strategy of the *logos*. The same – as I have shown in *The Collapse of Darwinism* (2003) – is true of genes and strategic organisms of all types. Genes are not "selfish", even in "the special Darwinian sense of selfishness", and they do not compete with each other. Indeed, genes are indirectly selected – through the process of **strategic selection** – by selfcreating selfish organisms in response to **logosian** strategic demand.

Second, to argue that the process of replication – whether genetic or technological – has to be the logical criteria for determining "selfishness" is both absurd and illogical. What is special about the process of replication of "ideas" from a causal perspective? The real criterion is the unit of life that responds directly to logosian strategic demand in both the human and natural worlds. And that unit of life is the selfish organism. Ideas, whether genetic or technological, are merely strategic instruments in the real world of the strategic *logos* and the selfcreating decision maker driven by strategic desire. Once again: desires drive, ideas merely facilitate. It is the *logos* that survives for many generations, not units of information or ideas, which are in a constant state of flux. The strategic *logos* is the universal life-system, which determines the nature of the strategic response by the suppliers of ideas, both genetic and technological – by, in other words, the selfish organism.

Third, the selfish-gene argument is unable to explain the historical development of life over the past 4,000 myrs. In discussing the anthropic principle – the idea that although the emergence of life is highly unlikely, the fact that we are contemplating it suggests that our experience is one of a very large number of possibilities that proved to be the exception – Dawkins admits that natural selection has difficulty explaining how life on Earth "bridged" a large number of "gaps" or discontinuities in the historical record. He is forced to admit that "sheer luck" was involved:

> it may be that the origin of life is not the only major gap in the evolutionary story that is bridged by sheer luck, anthropically justified. For example … the origin of the eukaryotic cell (our kind of cell, with a nucleus and various other complicated features such as mitochondria, which are not present in bacteria) was an even more momentous, difficult and statistically improbable step than the origin of life. The origin of consciousness might be another major gap whose bridging was of the same order of improbability …
>
> Natural selection works because it is a cumulative one-way street to improvement. It needs some luck to get started … Maybe a few later gaps in the evolutionary story also need major infusions of luck, with anthropic justification.[51]

What is the primary Dawkinsian explanation here, natural selection or "sheer luck"? Clearly, on its own, natural selection and the concept of the selfish gene are unable to explain either the origin of life (as I show in Snooks 2005) or the great genetic and technological transformations that have taken place on Earth over the past 4,000 myrs. In contrast, my dynamic-strategy theory can explain the entire history of life and society – see Chapters 10 and 11 – without recourse to "sheer luck". It should be clear which is the superior theory.

Fourth, it is not true that moral values are hard wired. As I show in *The Selfcreating Mind* they are a response to logosian strategic demand. The similarities and differences between the moral codes of different societies in space and time – even the same society over time – reflect the fact that there are only four basic types of strategic *logos*, but that there are significant differences between all four. Types of strategic *logoi* include the technological, the commercial, the conquest and the familial. Each *logos*-type generates a characteristic set of moral codes, ranging from the most humanitarian generated by the technological *logos* through those of the commercial and familial *logoi* to the least humanitarian in the conquest *logos*. The Darwinian hypothesis, however, is unable to explain either this spectrum of logosian moral values or the rapid transition in these values that takes place when one dynamic strategy (say technological change) is replaced by another (say conquest) as in the case of Germany in the 1930s.

Once again we can see how inadequate is the neo-Darwinian explanation of ethical or moral codes. It is a deeply flawed supply-side hypothesis in which moral codes are the outcome of mythical mental "rules of thumb" projected onto the mind of modern man. As these mental rules of thumb are said to have been generated by Darwinian evolution in paleolithic times, they can only be made relevant to the modern world by hypothesizing accidental "misfiring" or "Darwinian mistakes". These Darwinian mistakes join the "sheer luck" required to enable Dawkins to employ a flawed Darwinian explanation. "Darwinian mistakes" and "sheer luck" are just further flying buttresses erected to prop up the collapsing core hypothesis of natural selection.

The roots of religion

If neo-Darwinism was a real science, one would expect its practitioners to have an agreed position on the "roots of religion". Wilson, it will be recalled, views religion as analogous to a "superorganism" – a large-scale biological entity operating according to Darwinian principles. According to this interpretation religion does confer a Darwinian benefit, because there exists "a hereditary selective advantage" from belonging to a strong community held together by "devout belief and purpose". Curiously, Dawkins, a fellow neo-Darwinist, sees no such benefit. He declaims:

> Religion devours resources, sometimes on a massive sale. A medieval cathedral could consume a hundred man-centuries in its construction, yet was never used as a dwelling, or for any recognizably useful purpose ... What is it all for? What is the benefit of religion?[52]

Instead of a Darwinian benefit – by which he means "some enhancement to the survival of the individual's genes" – Dawkins sees only waste of time and resources, the perversion of the human mind, and the destruction wreaked by religious wars.

As Dawkins sees no Darwinian benefit arising from religion, he concludes that humans must be abnormally "*vulnerable* to the charms of religion and therefore open to exploitation by priests, politicians and kings".[53] But why is this so? Once again Dawkins falls back on the very weak idea of a Darwinian accident" – the "misfiring" of Darwinian modules in the brain. He suggests that "perhaps the feature we are interested in (religion in this case) doesn't have a direct survival value of its own, but is a by-product of something else that does". In other words "the propensity that was naturally selected in our ancestors was not religion *per se*; it had some other benefit, and it only incidentally manifests itself as religious behaviour".[54]

One possibility Dawkins suggests, is the genetic rule of thumb that says "believe, without question, whatever your grown-ups tell you. Obey your parents; obey the tribal elders, especially when they adopt a solemn, minatory tone". "But", he continues, "the flip side of trusting obedience is slavish gullibility. The inevitable by-product is vulnerability to infection by mind viruses".[55] And further, "the idea of psychological by-products grows naturally out of the important and developing field of evolutionary psychology", which postulates that the human brain is a collection of modules for handling specialist data-processing needs. In this context, "religion can be seen as a by-product of the misfiring of several of these modules, for example the modules for forming theories of other minds, for forming coalitions, and for discriminating in favour of in-group members and against strangers".[56] In this way, Dawkins believes, it will be possible to generalize the issue he claims to have detected in the "misfired" rule of thumb of authority that leads to human gullibility and vulnerability to religious ideas. He concludes this discussion by writing: "The general theory of religion as an accidental by-product – a misfiring of something useful – is the one I wish to advocate".[57]

But the issue cannot be left there. The question now becomes: "Vulnerable the mind may be, but why should it be infected by *this* virus rather than that? Are some viruses especially proficient at infecting vulnerable minds?"[58] This is where Dawkins' old, flawed hypothesis about "memes" (or ideas) comes in.[59] Successful memes, we are told truistically, are those "that happen to be good at getting copied". But why is the religious meme good at getting copied? Some, we learn, may have "absolute merit" – which is merely the "ability to survive in the pool" – and "some religious ideas survive because they are compatible with other memes that are already numerous in the meme pool – as part of a memeplex".[60] None of this, however, is at all convincing. He is unable to show why religion, which he regards as a useless and evil set of ideas, is so successful in infecting gullible minds. Why more successful than any other set of ideas? We are just not told.

The misfiring successful meme theory is extremely weak and very messy. As we have come to expect from neo-Darwinism, the core hypothesis of natural selection has to be surrounded by a vast number of flying buttresses to stop it collapsing before our eyes. This theme was explored in my book *The Collapse of Darwinism* (2003) in a part (II) entitled "The collapsing cathedral of Darwinism". Flying buttresses, it is argued there, are a sure sign that the core hypothesis is flawed and unable to explain what is required of it. In *The God Delusion*, a recent book, Dawkins has added another set of buttresses to those he has been constructing over the past three decades. Darwinism is a dead man standing.

As with all neo-Darwinian theories, Dawkins' explanation of religion is a supply-side construction. But a supply-side theory with a difference. While Wilson views religion as an extrusion from the Darwinian brain that provides a Darwinian benefit, Dawkins sees it as a Darwinian mistake – a malfunctioning of the brain that makes it vulnerable to a takeover by the virus of religion, which for some unspecified reason is consistently more successful than all other "memes". There are two problems here. The first is the idea that religion, which has been of great significance to every society in every phase of history, must be regarded as an aberration. It is an outcome, we are told, of the failure of natural selection rather than of its success. The very fact that Dawkins' selfish gene theory cannot recognize the beneficial role played in society by religion challenges its validity. In stark contrast, I have been able to demonstrate in this book that religion can be explained – using a general demand-side dynamic theory – as playing a positive role in man's desire to survive and prosper. It has been a response to the logosian strategic demand for a protective strategic ideology and a way of negotiating strategic frustration.

The second major problem with the Dawkins view of religion is the very silly hypothesis about memes – self-propelled ideas that flit from mind to mind, with successful memes, like successful genes, being good at replicating themselves. Once again we are in a supply-side fantasy world – a sort of Alice through the looking glass. As I have been able to demonstrate in a succession of books – including *The Dynamic Society, The Ephemeral Civilization, The Collapse of Darwinism*, and *The Selfcreating Mind* – ideas merely respond to logosian strategic demand. They have no motive force of their own. This is true of genetic, technological, and intellectual (including religious) ideas. Ideas for which there is no strategic demand just wither on the vine. As the "God delusion" will do.

An evil virus?

This is the silliest idea in a book that, at best, is not very sensible. But it is a silly idea that is consistent with the wider selfish-gene hypothesis. Dawkins spends most of *The God Delusion* vilifying religious faith and blaming it for many of the evils of this world. The reason he does so – apart from any hidden personal matters involved – is because of his flawed neo-Darwinian theory about the selfish gene/meme. It is a theory that leads him to the false conclusion that ideas are the driving force in society through their manipulation of human "meme machines". This is the central fallacy of Dawkins' book – indeed of his entire career. I have shown that, to the contrary, it is strategic desire embodied in all organisms that is the driving force in life and human society, and that ideas merely facilitate, and are shaped by, this force.

A few quotes will expose the absurdity of the type of anti-religious argument employed by Dawkins. First, he believes that religion is the source of much of the world's evil:

> Imagine ... a world with no religion. Imagine no suicide bombers, no 9/11, no 7/7, no Crusades, no witch-hunts, no Gunpowder Plot, no Indian partition, no Israeli/Palestinian wars, no Serb/Croat/Muslim massacres, no persecution of Jews as 'Christ-killers', no Northern Ireland 'troubles', no 'honour killings', no shiny-suited bouffant-haired televangelists fleecing gullible people of their money ...[61]

Only someone with very little understanding of human nature or human society could possibly claim that these matters would not have occurred in the absence of religion. They are all outcomes of the strategic pursuit (materialism) rather than religion (spirituality). The interpretation is silly, because the theory on which it is based is so obviously absurd.

Second, when discussing terrorism, Dawkins insists we blame religion and not the terrorists, who are merely faithfully following the dictates of their religion. He writes:

> Western politicians … characterize terrorists as motivated by pure 'evil'. But they are not motivated by evil. However misguided we may think them, they are motivated … by what they perceived to be righteousness, faithfully pursuing what their religion tells them. They are not psychotic; they are religion idealists, who by their own lights, are rational.[62]

He continues: "The take-home message is that we should blame religion itself, not religious *extremism* – as though that were some kind of terrible perversion of real, decent, religion".[63] To which he adds: "this story of the Italian Inquisition and its attitude to children is particularly revealing of the religious mind, and the evils that arise specifically *because* it is religious".[64] Only someone who fails to understand the origin and real role of religion could make such a foolish claim. As I show in this book, leading terrorists are not gullible, rational men and women of faith; rather they are antistrategists attempting to disrupt a strategic world in order to achieve their own selfish personal/group desires. In the process they may seduce more gullible, even idealistic, people. But these people are followers rather than instigators of terrorism. In a strategic world it is the antistrategist who is evil, not the ideology he may employ to disguise his real intent. Only gullible neo-Darwinists could possibly be fooled in this way.

Third, Dawkins has some very strange ideas about religion in the USA. For example, he quotes with approval "a concerned American colleague" as follows: "If secularists are not vigilant, Dominionists and Reconstructionists will soon be mainstream in a true American theocracy".[65] In terms of Dawkins' neo-Darwinist theory, this is a struggle between selfish religious and secular memes for dominance in the American meme pool! What is strange about this? Absolutely everything! Does Dawkins really expect roundly educated (as opposed to narrowly specialized) people to believe his neo-Darwinist myth about the battle of the memes? It is no more sophisticated than early neolithic myths about the battle of the gods. Also, Dawkins fails to understand that the USA is in no danger of becoming a "theocracy" for reasons discussed in Chapter 5 above. The American God is a personification of their strategic *logos*. Just ask where all the infrastructure investment is going: into religion or the economy? Dawkins even trumps himself in this matter. We are warned of an impending theocracy, then we are told:

> A Gallup poll in the United States of America found the following. Three-quarters of Catholics and Protestants could not name a single Old Testament prophet. More than two-thirds didn't know who preached the Sermon on the Mount. A substantial number thought that Moses was one of Jesus's twelve apostles.[66]

Does this sound like a society in the grip of the Christian meme?

Fourth, Dawkins' views on atheism are not well informed or argued. In the first place, he is beating a dead horse. Atheism was, as shown in Chapter 6 above, a useful strategic device in the nineteenth century when Western societies were attempting to divest themselves of the remains of an obsolete strategic ideology following the industrial technological paradigm shift. Dawkins, and his fellow latter-day-atheists, have turned up to the party a century too late (as with his support of an obsolete Darwinism), when his bad-tempered attack on religion merely appears grotesque. Compare his steam-hammer approach to the wit and elegance of Nietzsche's far more effective attack on religion a century earlier. In the second place, no matter how much he insists to the contrary, it is illogical to argue that atheism, rather than agnosticism, can be rationally demonstrated or defended. After all is said and done, atheism is as much a faith as is religion. And in the third place, Dawkins is unable to understand the reaction against atheism, because he doesn't understand the nature of religion. For most of human history, what we call religion was really strategic ideology. An atheist – as we saw in the case of pagan Rome when Christianity first emerged – was an antistrategist – someone who wanted to undermine the existing strategic *logos* by attacking (or not supporting) its official strategic guardians. And a blasphemer was someone who cursed the strategic guardians. It is because these "atheists" undermined the strategic *logos* and threatened society's probability of survival and prosperity that they were attacked so fiercely. It is a premodern attitude that lingered on in the statute books until the early twentieth century, and continues to color the attitudes of some Western leaders even today.

But it is time to move on. I will conclude by observing that Dawkins has failed to make the case that neo-Darwinism can provide a scientific analysis of religion. I suspect Charles Darwin would have agreed. Certainly he would have been embarrassed to know that his name was being used to call religion an "evil virus". Dawkins has merely demonstrated that his talent is as a mythmaker rather than a scientist or even a rationalist. He is in fact a propagandist for an obsolete faith – the faith of Darwinism. What he has failed to grasp, is that Darwinism died just as surely as the old God died. The old God died because of the technological paradigm shift, and Darwinism died because of the discovery of the strategic *logos*. Dawkins is feuding with phantoms. While the creationists are unable to provide any significant intellectual opposition, the only real opposition – the dynamic-strategy theory – has been carefully avoided.[67] In *The God Delusion*, Dawkins is like an aging boxer, who is attempting to get a title fight by competing with known losers.

THE "GOD GENE"

It was only a matter of time before someone in the neo-Darwinist camp claimed to have discovered a gene responsible for the longstanding interest of mankind in religion and God. That someone is the geneticist Dean Hamer, who recently published a book entitled *The God Gene. How faith is hardwired into our genes* (2004). Hamer takes a more fundamentally genetic approach to developing a science of religion. He tells us that:

> both Wilson and Dawkins have set their sights so broadly. Both ... attempt to derive single explanations for multiple phenomena, mixing purely cultural traits ... with those that may have a more biological basis ... The two traits are as dissimilar as apples and oranges. If we want to understand the evolution of genes that influence our need to believe, then we need to focus on those traits known to involve genes.[68]

Accordingly, Hamer focuses on an issue that he claims has a genetic basis – the spirituality of mankind and the source of the idea of God – which he separates from the context of religious ideas that he claims are cultural and subject to the activity of memes. In his own words: "spirituality is genetic, while religion is based on culture, traditions, beliefs, and ideas. It is, in other words, mimetic."[69]

Hamer's thesis is contained in five interlocking arguments. A mistake in any one of which will bring his entire case about the God gene crashing down. First, he begins by claiming that it is possible to measure "spirituality" by using a "self-transcendence" scale developed by Robert Cloninger, a psychiatrist at Washington University's medical school in St Louis. This measure has three components: "self-forgetfulness" (losing oneself in one's daily activities); "trans-personal identification" (a sense of unity with the rest of life); and "mysticism" (a "spiritual" connection with others and belief in mystical experiences). In developing this index, Cloninger refers to it as "spiritual acceptance versus rational materialism".[70]

Second, Hamer employers this "self-transcendence" scale in the study of twins, finding that the scores for identical twins were more alike than for fraternal twins in a ratio of 2 to 1. This, he claims, is what would be expected for a "genetically mediated trait", since identical twins are twice as similar at the DNA level as fraternal twins.

Third, Hamer attempts to identify "a specific individual gene associated with the self-transcendence scale of spirituality".[71] This is his so-called "God gene". He admits he cannot say where in the human genome the God gene is located, as one-third of all genes at the time of his analysis were not understood. For this reason, Hamer attempts to compare DNA sequences in people displaying different degrees of "spirituality" —people at different locations on the self-transcendence scale. He is bold enough to highlight a single gene – called $VMAT_2$ – that deals with all the monoamines (the biochemical mediators of emotions and values) simultaneously. Hamer claims that "there was a clear association between the $VMAT_2$ polymorphism and self-transcendence", and concludes that "while this one gene might not make one a saint, a prophet, or a seer, it was enough to tip the spiritual scales and predispose one toward spirituality."[72] His study of siblings suggested that the influence of this "God gene" was "the same for males and females, for all age groups, and for race and ethnicity".[73]

Fourth, he attempts to identify the brain mechanism involved in this biological process of spirituality. He argues that the God gene controls (by wrapping and unwrapping) the monoamine (brain chemicals), which "influence spirituality by altering consciousness". There is, he claims, an "intimate relationship between spirituality and consciousness", which "becomes most conspicuous through mystical experiences".[74] By controlling the monoamines in the brain, $VMAT^2$ is able to produce different intensities of feeling, either "a profound sense of joy, fulfillment, and peace", or more mundane feelings. What has this got to do with God? Hamer tells us that "we do not know God; we feel him" – spirituality is "a matter of emotions rather than intellect".[75]

Fifth, what precisely is Darwinian about all this? Does the "God gene" offer an evolutionary advantage, despite the scorn poured on this question by Richard Dawkins? Hamer replies in the affirmative: "one of the important roles that the God genes play in natural selection is to provide human beings with an innate sense of optimism ... the will to keep on living and procreating, despite the fact that death is ultimately inevitable".[76] He elaborates thus:

> Genes are selfish. The only thing they care about is being passed on to the next generation. Since the only way that can happen is through reproduction, the essential point to consider about the evolution of God genes, or genes that help to promulgate one's need to believe, is how they contribute to procreation ... [For example,] somebody who feels good about the future may be more likely to get up and hunt for food, build a shelter, and – above all – want to have children.[77]

He admits that this is not a complete explanation of spirituality, as he has only employed a single measure, and as genes explain only half the variation on this measure.[78]

Hamer draws a distinction between a genetically determined "spirituality" and a culturally determined religion. He explains: "While it is our genes that initially make us receptive to spirituality and faith, it is our memes that carry religion from one generation to the next and that make each religion distinct".[79] And he repeats the same absurd mantra espoused by Dawkins: "The critical feature of memes is their ability to be replicated ... memes are like genes in another way. They are selfish. They only care whether they are copied or not, not what happens to the copier".[80] Hence, while "spirituality" is beneficial to both genes and people because it is the outcome of natural selection, religion may or may not be beneficial to people even though it is beneficial to the successful memes.[81]

Hamer's "God gene" hypothesis at least possesses the virtues of clarity and falsifiability. Neither of which can be said of the "superorganism" hypothesis of Edward Wilson or the "evil virus" hypothesis of Richard Dawkins. At least Hamer's argument is scientific rather than merely metaphysical. His hypothesis about spirituality has the added virtue of being the outcome of natural selection rather than merely a "Darwinian accident" as in the case of Dawkins. But clarity and falsifiability do not make it true. We now need to test just how robust Hamer's five-argument system really is.

In the first place, the "spirituality" scale employed by Hamer is not in fact a measure of spirituality but of strategicality. The originator of the index, Robert

Cloninger, views the measure as a way of distinguishing between people who are, in his words, "rationally materialistic" and those who are significantly less so, who he calls, misleadingly, "spiritual". This is the same distinction that I make in the dynamic-strategy theory between people who are "strategists" and "nonstrategists" — those actively involved in the materialist pursuit and those not. The crucial point here is that what we now call "religion" was a strategic ideology that initially emerged to sustain the strategic *logos*. Hence, the gods, or strategic guardians, were a response to the needs of the strategists not the nonstrategists – to materialism not spirituality. Ironically, Hamer's measure of self-transcendence is really a measure of strategicality.

In the second place, the neo-Darwinian assertion, that genes enhance their survival by regulating their host's feelings of optimism by generating ideas about a divine creator, is entirely wrong. This is the familiar supply-side neo-Darwinist hypothesis about God being an idea extruded from the Darwinian brain in order to benefit the genes that constructed it. The idea of the Darwinist brain and its selfish genetic creators is, as I show in *The Collapse of Darwinism* and *The Selfcreating Mind*, a totally flawed theory with no substance. In reality, the idea of "God" arose as a response to logosian strategic demand for supernatural assistance in sustaining their life-system. The strategic guardians emerged for the benefit not of genes (or ideas) but of strategists and their life-supporting *logos*. This can be seen throughout the history of human society – as shown in part II above – but particularly today in the West, where the old strategic guardian – the Christian God – has been replaced by the deity of science. Would anyone claim that science is the outcome of a "God gene"?

In the third place, as suggested earlier, the idea of selfish memes determining the rise and fall of the great religions of the past and present is completely absurd. Neo-Darwinists provide no evidence for the hypothesis that ideas are self-propelled, that they act in a selfish way, that they compete with each other to maximize copies of themselves in a "memeplex", or that they are able to manipulate mankind into achieving their ends. And they have not attempted to systematically examine the historical development of the world's religions to show in practice how this might have been achieved. It is the usual supply-side fantasy that only neo-Darwinists – intellectual imperialists from the biological sciences – are able to believe. Practicing social scientists are left amazed at its absurdities. Ideas, as I have demonstrated in all my books, are not a driving force in human society. It is desires that drive and ideas that facilitate. We need to reject this supply-side cultural model, just as we have rejected the supply-side genetic model on which it is based (initially a tongue in cheek suggestion by Dawkins in *The Selfish Gene,* but an idea he now embraces owing to its unexpected popular appeal). Religious ideas are a response to logosian strategic demand. Hence, Hamer's "God gene" hypothesis, like the other neo-Darwinian hypotheses examined in this chapter, falls to the ground.

NEO-DARWINISM'S CAMP-FOLLOWERS

Although neo-Darwinism, or sociobiology, has been widely rejected by social scientists, there are some, mainly philosophers, who feel comfortable with the absurdities of the selfish-gene/meme hypotheses. They can be thought of as the priestly philosophers of scientism. Members of this group who have discussed religion including Pascal Boyer, Scott Atran and Daniel Dennett. David Wilson is regarded as a heretic by the neo-Darwinists for his advocacy of group selection in the religious context.[82] I will briefly focus on Dennett's views.

Daniel Dennett appears to have accepted many of the core ideas of neo-Darwinism and atheism, but he expresses them in a more moderate and subtle manner. While his objectives in a recent book entitled *Breaking the Spell* (2006) are much the same as those of Dawkins in *The God Delusion*, he is concerned to minimize the degree of offence experienced by his readers. Dennett attempts to demonstrate that religion is a "natural phenomenon" that can, and must, be subjected to scientific investigation. It is his intention to "break the spell" that religion has cast upon the minds of people to prevent their intellectual freedom. But, in contrast to Dawkins, he wants to do so by employing gentle as well as rational persuasion.

In this reasoned way, Dennett hopes to clear the ground in order to "develop the natural science of religion".[83] Why? Because, like Dawkins, he believes that religion is an evil meme, even though he is far more cautious in the way he expresses this. We are told, for example, that: "I, for one, fear that if we *don't* subject religion to such [scientific] scrutiny now, and work out together whatever revisions and reforms are called for, we will pass on a legacy of evermore toxic forms of religion to our descendants".[84] Yet although Dennett treads softly, he nevertheless carries a big stick. He is determined to employ all his powers of persuasion to eliminate the influence of religion, which he believes "will be of tremendous significance to the planet".[85]

Despite the stark contrast with Dawkins concerning the method of attack, Dennett accepts the flawed supply-side arguments of the neo-Darwinists. While he refers approvingly to Pascal Boyer and Scott Atran, Dennett's position is similar to that of Dawkins – namely, that religion, like many other human institutions, is the outcome of "Darwinian mistakes". Essentially his argument is that Darwinian brain modules, which emerged in the paleolithic era owing to the operation of natural selection in response to specific environmental conditions, interact in some unanticipated and accidental way to produce patterns of behavior that fortuitously end up by being useful to human society. In order to make neo-Darwinism "work", it is necessary to introduce large doses of chance and Darwinian mistakes. Hence, it is only through the fortuitous errors of natural selection – which cannot anticipate something like civilization for which there is no precedent in the formative paleolithic era – that neo-Darwinists can "explain" human society in general and religion in particular.

What is Dennett's particular "take" on the idea of religion as a Darwinian mistake? He views religion as an "overreaction" to environmental stimuli – an "overactive disposition to look for agents"; and "overshooting of the intentional stance in the lives of our ancestors. The practice of overattributing intentions to moving things in the environment is called *animism*, literally giving a soul … to the mover"; and "a hyperactive habit of finding agency wherever anything puzzles or frightens us".[86] Why mankind should be hard-wired to "overreact", we are not told. It is just another supply-side attempt to explain what in reality is a response to logosian strategic demand.

Because of the supposed modular cross-wiring in the Darwinian brain, Dennett believes that "folk" religion emerges without design in the minds of people. He explains:

> Extrapolating back to human prehistory with the aid of biological thinking, we can *surmise* how folk religions emerged without conscious and deliberate design, just as languages emerged by interdependent processes of biological and cultural evolution.[87]

Here is a link to the coevolution argument of Edward Wilson discussed above. This is the usual supply-side argument, whereby human institutions like religion are extruded unaided by human intention from the Darwinian brain. Of course, none of this elaborate biological launching equipment is required, because religious (and all other) institutions are the creative response of a general strategic mind (rather than a specialist Darwinian modular mind) to changes in the strategic *logos* communicated via strategic demand. Social scientists and humanists like Dennett have been hoodwinked by the priestly philosophers of neo-Darwinism.

CONCLUSIONS

In this chapter three different versions of the neo-Darwinist "explanation" of religion and God have been reviewed. What they have in common is that they are all flawed supply-side hypotheses, which attempt to explain religion, ethics, and/or spirituality as extrusions from the human brain. They are all based on the absurd but logical contention of Darwinian natural selection known as the selfish-gene/meme hypothesis. This approach lends itself to a rather extreme "overreaction" to the nature and role of religion — an overreaction that in the hands of Richard Dawkins leads to the grotesque.

Such hypotheses lack the reality and flexibility required by social scientists to explain a central human institution like religion that has been so widespread throughout time and space. It is not difficult to conclude that the neo-Darwinists have failed in their quest to construct a science of religion.

Chapter 9
A Religion of Science

With the great transformation of human civilization known as the Industrial Revolution, the new strategic ideology of science replaced the ancient one of monotheistic religion. This, however, was not the end of the intellectual process of mythmaking. Like all strategic ideologies, science has been used to create a new religion.

As shown in this book, materialist strategic ideologies have always been targeted by the priestly philosophers in order to transform them into metaphysical mythologies generally known as religions. This occurs because priestly philosophers become frustrated with a society led by material interests. It is a frustration with both the materialistic objectives of society and the way science has been neglected by strategic policymakers. It is a frustration that has led to a new round of mythmaking. Over the past generation, a variety of metaphysicians have emerged to make a religion out of science. These intellectuals make strong claims for their credentials as scientists or as rational thinkers able to publish in serious scholarly journals. While there is a serious scholarly side to their lives, they are also dedicated to spiritualizing the materialist quest of mainstream science.

WHY A RELIGION OF SCIENCE?

The new religion of science has arisen from the failure of the natural sciences – of physics and biology – to recognize, let alone understand, the strategic *logos*. Had the metaphysically inclined among the physics community understood how the strategic *logos* worked, it would not have been necessary to fill the gaps in their knowledge with scientific mythmaking – with the search for some sort of absolute meaning underlying the cosmos that could account for what they regard as unfathomable mysteries. One well-known physicist caught in this web is Paul Davies.

There are a number of issues in life that Paul Davies – in a book titled *The Mind of God* (1993) – believes can only be explained if we recognize some sort of supernatural purpose. These issues include the "mysterious" ability of the human mind – which, Davies tells us, evolved through natural selection on the African savannah – to understand the laws of physics; and the role of mathematics as "the language of nature". Davies sees these matters as being highly mysterious and only capable of resolution if we recognize that the cosmos embodies an ultimate purpose.

The first issue concerns the "amazing" ability of the primitive human mind to unlock the secrets of the Universe. On this matter Davies writes:

The success of the scientific enterprise can often blind us to the astonishing fact that science works ... it is both incredibly fortunate and incredibly mysterious that we are able to fathom the workings of nature by use of the scientific method ... we find a situation in which the difficulty of the cosmic code seems almost to be attuned to human capabilities ... The mystery in all this is that human intellectual powers are *presumably* determined by biological evolution, and have absolutely no connection with doing science. Our brains have evolved in response to environmental pressures, such as the ability to hunt, avoid predators, dodge falling objects, etc. What has this got to do with discovering the laws of electromagnetism or the structure of the atom?[1]

He goes on to ask, what to him is, the key question in life:

Why should human beings have the ability to discover and understand the principles on which the universe runs? ...Is the spectacular progress of our science just an incidental quirk of history, or does it point to a deep and meaningful resonance between the human mind and the underlying organisation of the natural world?[2]

Dawkins and Wilson, as we have seen, opt for the first of these possibilities, which they call "Darwinian mistakes", whereas Davies believes "we have been written into the laws of nature in a deep and ... meaningful way".[3]

On the issue of mathematics as "the language of nature", Davies writes at some length. He tells us, with his usual sense of awe, that:

To the scientist, mathematics is the guarantor of precision and objectivity. It is also, astonishingly, the language of nature itself ...Because of its indispensable role in science, many scientists – especially physicists – invest the ultimate reality of the physical world in mathematics. A colleague of mine once remarked that in his opinion the world was *nothing but* bits and pieces of mathematics. To the ordinary person ... this must seem astounding. Yet the contention that mathematics is a key that enables the initiate to unlock cosmic secrets is as old as the subject itself.[4]

What, Davies asks, is the true nature of the relationship between mathematics and physical reality? He notes that "there is evidently a crucial *concordance* between, on the one hand, the laws of physics and, on the other, the computability of the mathematical functions that describes *those same laws*"; and he asks, rhetorically, "does it point to some deeper resonance between mathematics and reality?"[5] Could mathematics be somehow embedded in nature? And what would that imply about the possibility of ultimate meaning?

Given this apparent "deeper resonance" between mathematics and reality, the ability of the human mind to comprehend mathematics is, for Davies, a great "mystery". As he accepts the Darwinian hypothesis of natural selection, Davies puzzles over the role that mathematics plays in human society, and he concludes: "it is very hard to see how abstract mathematics has any survival value. Similar comments apply to musical ability."[6] Sound familiar? It will be recalled that Edward Wilson makes the same point (although somewhat later) in a more poetic way when he draws our attention to "the great mystery of human evolution: how to account for Calculus and Mozart".[7]

While Wilson draws a broad line between his science and his faith, Davies is tempted to resolve these "mysteries" about mankind's ability to employ mathematics in exploring the laws of the cosmos by an appeal to supernatural influence and design. He concludes *The Mind of God* as follows:

> What is Man that we might be party to such privilege? I cannot *believe* that our existence in this universe is a mere quirk of fate, an accident of history, an incidental blip in the great cosmic drama. Our involvement is too intimate. The physical species *Homo* may count for nothing, but the existence of mind in some organism on some planet in the universe is surely a fact of fundamental significance. Through conscious beings the universe has generated self-awareness. This can be no trivial detail, no minor byproduct of mindless, purposeless forces. We are truly meant to be here.[8]

This type of conclusion – this leap of faith – by practicing scientists, is the beginning of the religion of science.

None of this agonizing over the "mind of God" would have been necessary had Davies – and like-minded colleagues – been aware of the selfcreating strategic *logos*. The rebuttal of the type of thesis forwarded by Davies can be briefly stated. First, the neo-Darwinists are trapped by the Darwinian modular theory of the brain, which I exposed in *The Selfcreating Mind* as being historically inaccurate as well as completely unworkable. Rather than being an inflexible instrument consisting of a collection of independent modules each of which has evolved for an environmentally specific purpose (like a Swiss army knife — a favorite metaphor of evolutionary psychology), the mind of man is a highly integrated general organ that emerged through **strategic selection** in response to logosian strategic demand. The human brain developed in order to recognize patterns, to generalize about those patterns, and to predict future outcomes – in order, that is, to think strategically. As this strategic instrument is able to handle all dynamic strategies – technological change, commerce, and conquest, as well as family multiplication (hunting/gathering) – it is also able to pursue science, which is based on a similar methodology. Science is just a natural extension of strategic thinking – of recognizing patterns and generalizing about them. Hence it is not at all remarkable that we can engage in both the strategic pursuit and science. Indeed, science is part of the strategic pursuit and was developed in response to logosian strategic demand. Davies could not be more wrong than when he says that "human intellectual powers are presumably determined by biological evolution, and have absolutely no connection with doing science".

Second, there is nothing "mysterious" about the relationship between mathematics and reality, or about mankind's use of the former to explore the latter. Mathematics, which is just a form of deductive thinking, is an instrument to increase the power and precision of strategic thinking. Calculus was a very late development – independently invented by Newton and Leibniz around the end of the seventeenth century – whereas strategic thinking has existed for 2 to 3 myrs. As mathematics (and deductive thinking) is a product of man's pattern-recognizing and generalizing mind, it is not the language *of* nature but a langue *about* nature. Mathematics gives the appearance of being closely related to the physical world because it was designed by the strategic mind for this purpose. Interestingly, while mathematics can model the relatively simple physical world, it is unable to model the complex world of the strategic *logos*. Indeed, the use of mathematics and deductive thinking has actually limited science's understanding of societal dynamics. This is why social physics and complexity theory have failed to take the social sciences by storm.[9] Clearly the "mind of God" has its limitations.

Yet this mystical approach to life and the Universe has led to a number of metaphysical mythologies that claim to be based on science. Rather than superficially outlining the work of many of the priestly philosophers, I have selected two of their number – James Lovelock and James Gardner – for a more in-depth examination. Lovelock, as is well known, is the inventor of the Gaia hypothesis about the "living" Earth, and Gardner is the author of the Biocosm hypothesis about the "living" cosmos. The recent Biocosm viewpoint is an outcome of taking the earlier Gaia thesis to its ultimate extreme. Both have their sources in the failure of the natural sciences to detect the strategic *logos*, and both are examples of how the strategic ideology of science is being transformed into religion by strategically frustrated priestly philosophers.

GAIA – GODDESS OF THE "LIVING" EARTH

The Gaia hypothesis is long on history — its own that is — but short on theory. It had its origins, we are told by its author James Lovelock, in the work he did for NASA on their Mars project back in the1960s. The first "preliminary ideas" were "expressed" by Lovelock in the late sixties and early seventies; published as journal articles jointly with the biologist Lynn Margulis in 1973; and developed further in books by Lovelock in 1979, 1988, 1991 and 2006.[10] Yet, despite this long period of incubation and development, Gaia "theory" – as Lovelock now calls his former "hypothesis" – is vague, unconvincing, and has more in common with theology than science.

What is Gaia? We need to distinguish here between the physical and metaphorical dimensions of this concept. Lovelock tells us that:

> Gaia is a thin spherical shell of matter that surrounds the incandescent interior; it begins where the crustal rocks meet the magma of the Earth's hot interior, about 100 miles below the surface, and proceeds another 100 miles outwards through the ocean and air to the even hotter thermosphere at the edge of space. It includes the biosphere and is a dynamical physiological system that has kept our planet fit for life for over three billion years.[11]

Despite the fact that Gaia includes inanimate (rocks, ocean, atmosphere) as well as animate (a multitude of biological life forms) components, Lovelock regards this entire "system" as the "living Earth". Indeed, the reason for calling this "system" Gaia – a suggestion made by his novelist friend and neighbor, the late William Golding (1911–1993) – after the Greek goddess of the Earth, was to metaphorically reinforce the idea that the biosphere is a living entity.

What is the Gaia hypothesis?

In the late 1980s Lovelock outlined the Gaia hypothesis as follows:

> Through Gaia theory, I see the Earth and the life it bears as a system, a system that has the capacity to regulate the temperature and composition of the Earth's surface and to keep it comfortable for living organisms. The self-regulation of the system is an active process driven by the free energy available from sunlight.[12]

While the Gaian system is "empowered" by living things, it operates under physical constraints that affect both organisms and the physical/chemical environment. Hence, Gaia is a dynamic physiological system that possesses the "unconscious goal" of sustaining life by regulating the climate and chemistry of the planet; that adapts to dominant life forms and "regulates itself on life's behalf"; and that has "goals [that] are not set points but [are] adjustable for whatever is the current environment and adaptable to whatever forms of life it carries".[13]

As a general *description* this is fine, but just how does Gaia work? In the face of this question Lovelock, despite having spent almost half a century attempting to develop this concept, runs into difficulties. After all this time, Lovelock is forced to admit: "I find explaining Gaia is like teaching someone how to swim or to ride a bicycle: *there is much that cannot be put into words*".[14] He goes on to suggest that those wanting to know more should "try to *sense* Gaia".[15] Indeed, after attempting to give a "sense" of Gaia by employing a simple thermostatically controlled mechanical system, Lovelock concludes:

> The ideas I have just presented are part of the basis of Gaia theory, but a full explanation would require an account of how self-regulation works. In some ways this is not just difficult, it is impossible: emergent phenomena like life, consciousness and Gaia resist explanation in the traditional cause-and-effect sequential language of science. Emergence has similarities with the quantum phenomena of 'entanglement', and we may never be fully able to explain them. What we can do is to express them in the language of mathematics and use them in the cornucopia of our inventions. Engineers are well able to design complex self-regulating systems, such as automatic pilots for ships, aircraft and spacecraft … But I doubt if any of them have a conscious mental image of their inventions; they develop and understand them intuitively.[16]

And again we are told that: "Life, the universe, consciousness … are inexplicable in words".[17] He even goes as far as to say: "A theory in science is no more than what seems to its author a plausible way of dressing up the facts and presenting them to an audience".[18] And he seems to find vindication in the arcane fact that the word "theory" in ancient Greek has the same root as "theatre" – both are there to put on a show! This is why Lovelock feels able to call Gaia – his rather theatrical construct – a theory.

How then are we to understand the Gaia hypothesis if words are of little or no help? Lovelock suggests two ways – metaphor and analogy. Of metaphor – "the living Earth" – Lovelock writes:

> Metaphor is important because to deal with, understand, and even ameliorate the fix we are now in over global change requires us to know the *true nature* of the Earth and *imagine* it as the largest living thing in the solar system, not something inanimate like that disreputable contraption 'spaceship Earth'. Until this change of *heart* and mind happens we will not *instinctively sense* that we live on a live planet that can respond to the changes we make, either by cancelling the changes or by cancelling us.[19]

So we are to *imagine* that the Earth is alive – a "superorganism" – that can either be our friend or our enemy. And if it is to be our enemy, it is highly likely – as Lovelock informs us in a book entitled *The Revenge of Gaia* (2006) – that this "superorganism" will retaliate against our troublesome species. Gaia, then, is a "superorganism" – "the largest manifestation of life"[20] – beyond the scale imagined by Edward Wilson (in the case of religion), but nowhere near the scale imagined by James Gardner for his Biocosm.

Metaphor has its place in scientific exposition, but one is left with the impression that Lovelock moves a little too slickly between metaphor and explanation when treating Gaia as "the living Earth" and as "superorganism". Metaphor is a useful literary device to illustrate or reinforce a truth conveyed in more formal intellectual terms, particularly for a more general audience. What it should *not* be employed for in scientific discourse is as a *substitute* for more formal analysis, or theory, or models. Needless to say, in the absence of any formal theory – as with Lovelock's Gaia *hypothesis* – it is inevitable that a strong metaphor will be employed as if it were a scientific theory. Despite his claims to the contrary, Lovelock treats Gaia as a living, goal-directed superorganism that can operate proactively, even taking its "revenge" on mankind.

Lovelock also employs the dangerous method of analogy. Why dangerous? Because there is no guarantee that the object or process used in the analogy will have any real similarity with the object or process we wish to understand. This method is particularly fraught where there is no easy way of testing the reality of the analogy. There is a notorious example of how analogy has led scientists astray for centuries. It is Charles Darwin's barnyard analogy – artificial selection – discussed in detail in my book *The Collapse of Darwinism* (2003). While a more appropriate method is the process of strategic thinking – of pattern recognition and generalization – it requires a higher level of imagination and intellectual skill.

Because Lovelock has been unable to develop a general dynamic theory of Gaia using observation and generalization, he takes a shortcut and postulates that Gaia operates like a self-regulating "climate control system" – a closed system with feedback loops.[21] He tells us that: "To me it was obvious that the Earth was alive in the sense that it was a self-organising and self-regulating system", but the scientific community "not seeing a mechanism for planetary control ... denied its existence as a phenomenon and branded the Gaia hypothesis as teleological".[22] In particular, these scientific critics believe that life forms do not possess the capacities for inter-species communication, foresight, and planning that would be required for the biosphere to operate as a integrated system.

To meet this scientific challenge, Lovelock decided in the early 1980s to develop a computer model known as Daisyworld to "illustrate" what he "sensed" about the working of Gaia. In Daisyworld, two groups of differently colored daisies – one light and the other dark – react differently to the steadily increasing luminosity of the sun and, in turn, have a differential impact on the total absorption or reflection of the sun's heat. By changing the proportion of light and dark daisies, and of surface area colonized by daisies of all types, the temperature of the virtual planet is "automatically" regulated. Lovelock writes:

> The simple model Daisyworld illustrated how Gaia might work ... On this world, the competition for territory between two species of daisies, one dark and one light in color, led to the accurate regulation of planetary temperature close to that comfortable for plants and daisies. No foresight, planning, or purpose was invoked.[23]

He goes on to triumphantly claim that:

> Very few assumptions are made in this model. It is not necessary to invoke foresight or planning by the daisies. It is merely assumed that the growth of daisies can affect planetary temperature, and vice versa.[24]

Despite Lovelock's claims, Daisyworld was intentionally and carefully constructed to operate as a closed-loop engineering system. Hence, the "agents" in his system do not require foresight and planning, because the necessary "self-regulation" was built into the system by Lovelock. In other words, Daisyworld was constructed to operate according to a predetermined set of rules. Lovelock even comes close to admitting this truth when he writes:

> Daisyworld differs profoundly from previous attempts to model the species or the Earth. It is a model more like those of control theory, or cybernetics ... Such models are concerned with self-regulating systems; engineers and physiologists use them to design automatic pilots for aircraft or to understand the regulation of breathing in animals, and they know that the parts of the system must be closely coupled if it is to work. In their parlance, Daisyworld is a closed-loop model ... Daisyworld is not identical in form to an engineered device; a key difference is the absence in Daisyworld, and perhaps in Gaia also, of 'set points' ... Daisyworld does not have any clearly established goal like a set point [for temperature]; it just settles down, like a cat, to a comfortable position and resists attempts to dislodge it.[25]

The last assertion, of course, is nonsense. Only a real living system could "settle down like a cat". Daisyworld is definitely not a real living system. It is a simple, virtual system that is clearly based on an "engineered device" – an engineering "invention" as he suggests elsewhere. No set points for temperature are required, owing to the way the model, with its inbuilt rules of operation, is constructed. A simple computer model can only do what it is designed – either explicitly or implicitly – to do. Lovelock is self-deluded if he really believes otherwise.

In the absence of a realist general dynamic theory of Gaia, Lovelock merely *assumes* that the biosphere operates like a self-regulating engineering device. There are a number of difficulties arising from this procedure. First, this analogical method would only be appropriate if it could be shown that Gaia and Daisyworld had a large number of key processes in common. Lovelock has been unable to make this link, largely because he is unable to explain in words or mathematical terms how Gaia works in reality. Second, Lovelock's analogy breaks down in a similar way to Darwin's barnyard analogy. The fact that artificial selection depends on a human selector, suggests by analogy, that natural selection requires a divine selector. Alfred Wallace, the co-inventor of natural selection, was sensitive to this implication and, as a result, preferred Herbert Spencer's alternative term of "survival of the fittest". In a similar respect, Daisyworld is only self-regulating because it was constructed to operate that way by its computer operator; which implies that Gaia requires a divine operator to be "self" regulating. These implications should be greatly embarrassing for both Darwin and Lovelock. The only way to overcome this difficulty is by abandoning the analogical method for the historical (or inductive) method in order to develop a realist general dynamic theory of biotransition (in Darwin's case) and of life on Earth (in Lovelock's case). Such a general theory relevant to both cases is supplied by my dynamic-strategy theory. Third, the mechanical/engineering nature of Daisyworld is hardly compatible with the idea of Gaia as a "superorganism" – a living Earth. What is Lovelocks' real metaphor: the Earth goddess or the engineer's machine?

As Lovelock has been unable to develop a sound theoretical structure for Gaia, what are we to make of his predictions about the future condition of the Earth? Owing to these circumstances, it will hardly come as a surprise that Lovelock's predictions have changed dramatically over the past twenty years, even though there has been no change in his description of the Gaia concept. It follows, of course: no theory, no consistent predictions. In his book *Ages of Gaia*, first published in the late 1980s, Lovelock predicted the coming of a new ice age – yes, an *ice age*! He wrote:

> Left to herself, Gaia will relax again into another long ice age. We forget that the temperate Northern Hemisphere, the home of the rich First World, now enjoys a brief summer between long, long periods of winter that last for a hundred thousand years ... The natural state here in Devon [his home at the time] has been, for most of the past million years, a permanent arctic winter ... So why should I fret over the destruction [by agribusinesses] of a countryside that is, at most, only a few thousand years old and soon to vanish again?[26]

Admittedly Lovelock was aware of the growing accumulation of carbon dioxide in the atmosphere, which he believed would lead to some global warming –

a "warm spell" – but this would be swept aside when the "*permanent* arctic winter" inevitably reasserted itself and a new ice age would bear down on us again. He refers to this short warm spell as "the carbon dioxide fever" – a brief illness that Gaia had caught from its currently dominant life form, humanity. Lovelock writes:

> I can only guess the details of the *warm spell* due. Will Boston, London, Venice, and the Netherlands vanish beneath the sea? Will the Sahara extend to cross the equator? The answers to those questions are likely to come from direct experience. There are no experts able to forecast the future global climate.[27]

In the late 1980s – just twenty years ago – Lovelock believed it would be unwise for humanity to continue to contribute to the build-up of carbon dioxide, because "from control theory and from physiology, we know that the perturbation of a system that is close to instability can lead to oscillations, chaotic change, or failure".[28] By curbing carbon dioxide growth, Gaia would be free to return to its more normal icy climate, which, he claimed, is more life affirming. But, of course, less beneficial to humanity. Humanity, however, has never been his real concern, as Gaia comes first, man second.

By the time he published *Revenge of Gaia* in 2006, Lovelock had abandoned his new-ice-age prediction, and replaced it with a story about the steadily increasing luminosity of the sun, which will eventually burn up the Earth. He tells us:

> only for a brief period in the Earth's history was the sun's warmth ideal for life, and that was about two billion years ago. Before this it was too cold for comfort and afterwards it has progressively grown too hot. In the very long term, solar warming is a far greater problem for life than our present-day battle with man-made global heating.
>
> In about one billion years, and long before the sun's life ends, the heat received by the Earth will be more than two kilowatts per square metre, which is more than the Gaia we know can stand; she will die from overheating.[29]

The intellectual problem faced by Lovelock was how to make compatible the new argument about increasing luminosity with the well-known evidence of past ages. He found a solution in the engineering models on which Daisyworld is based. It is, however, a solution only for those with faith in Gaia. He writes:

> Gaia regulates its temperature at what is near optimal for whatever life happens to be inhabiting it. But like many *regulating systems with a goal*, it tends to overshoot and stray to the opposite side of its forcing. If the sun's heat is too little the Earth tends to be warmer than ideal; if too much heat comes from the sun, as now, it regulates on the cold side of ideal. This is why the usual state of the Earth at present is an ice age. The present crop of glaciations the geologists call the Pleistocene is, I think, a last desperate effort by the Earth system to meet the needs of its present life forms ... [But] in less than 100 million years the sun's heat will be too much for the Earth to regulate at its current state, and it will be forced to move to a new hot state inhabited by a different biosphere. The brief interglacials, like now, are, I think, examples of temporary failures of ice-age regulation.[30]

This appears to be stretching the engineering analogy somewhat. A thermostatically controlled system may overshoot a set temperature target in the very short run, but it soon gets to approximately the desired temperature. The very-long ice ages experienced on Earth hardly qualify as short-run overshooting. It is more than a little difficult to believe that the outcome of growing luminosity over the past 4,000 myrs is a "permanent arctic winter" or that "the usual state of the Earth at present is an ice age". It is also a long shot to interpret the interglacials as "examples of temporary failures". But, in the absence of a general dynamic theory of the "living Earth", Lovelock is forced back on simplistic engineering explanations.

Despite these disabling methodological limitations, Lovelock is willing to make some very strong predictions for the twenty-first century. He identifies three thresholds of no return for the current state of Gaia – thresholds he is convinced will be reached early this century. They are as follows: the Greenland glacier will melt irreversibly if the global temperature increases by more than 2.7°C; the tropical rainforests will disappear if the global temperature increases by more than 4°C; and the ancient algae life form will fail if carbon dioxide levels reach 500 parts per million (ppm). Lovelock sees the tropical rainforests as not only absorbing carbon dioxide but also providing a reflective cloud cover; the algae also absorbs carbon dioxide; and the ice cap reflects the heat of the sun. The overall effect of the destruction of these "heat shields" will be to increase global "heating" (not "warming", Lovelock insists).

While he believes that technology may help to combat global heating – through a combination of terrestrial or space-mounted sunshades, aerosol particles released into the atmosphere to reflect some of the incoming sunlight, injecting sequestered carbon dioxide into the ground – he is pessimistic about the outcome. In fact, he believes we have finally passed the point of no return and that, while a much-reduced population of about 500 million (less than ten percent of the existing population) might survive in the Arctic regions, human civilization as we know it is irretrievably doomed.

Why has this come about? Because, Lovelock claims, humans lack any "instinct" about the dangers facing Gaia. He tells us "understanding is still in the conscious mind alone and not yet the visceral reaction of fear. We lack an intuitive sense, an instinct, that tells us when Gaia is in danger". Indeed, "because of the circumscribed nature of its origins, the instinctive recognition of life is limited by the range of our senses and does not work for things smaller or larger than we can see".[31]

This says much more about the Gaia concept than Lovelock realizes. He is wrong when he says that our "instinctive recognition of life" fails to include "things smaller or larger than we can see". The evidence presented in this book clearly shows that individuals in all human societies have a very strong instinct about the strategic *logos* – the dynamic life-system that provides their survival and prosperity – despite being unable to see it or to understand it with the conscious mind. The bewildering forms of religion bear witness to that reality. Religion is the ultimate expression of our instinct regarding the dangers facing the strategic *logos*. This is the very reverse of the situation claimed by Lovelock for Gaia: we respond to the dangers facing the hidden *logos* instinctively rather than intellectually, whereas Lovelock claims we respond to the dangers facing Gaia intellectually rather than instinctively. Why do we have no instinct regarding Gaia? The most obvious answer is that Gaia is no more than a figment of the imaginations of the priestly philosophers of the new Green religion. We should always question ideas that are not a response to desires.

Lovelock's predictions about the future state of both the Earth and human society are wrong. Why? Because of his failure to develop a general dynamic theory of Gaia. Accordingly, he assumes that the existing technological paradigm will persist into the future until the breakdown of both Gaia and human society. He fails to understand the system of technological paradigm shifts at the center of the dynamic-strategy theory. Lovelock is trapped within the present technological paradigm and falls back on the discredited approach of naive historicism – of extrapolating past trends into the future, rather than employing a realist general dynamic theory for scientific prediction. As discussed in part III, by using the dynamic-strategy theory I was, in the mid-1990s, able to predict that a new technological paradigm shift – the Solar Revolution – will replace the currently exhausting industrial paradigm during the second half of the twenty-first century. This, as discussed in detail in my new book entitled *The Coming Eclipse* (Snooks 2010), will solve the current problem of global warming. And it will provide the technological potential to enable mankind to journey to other planets and solar systems as our sun expands and wipes out the planet of our origin.

Why Gaia and Daisyworld are works of fiction

The central flaw in Daisyworld is the supposed direct relationship between the assumed life forms (various types of daises) and the growing luminosity of the sun. Lovelock assumes that these life forms respond *directly* to solar rays and either reflect or absorb their heat. Consequently, the various types of daisies and their environment expand and prosper, or retreat and die.

What this scenario totally ignores is the role played by the strategic *logos*. Instead of being a collection of interacting individuals, life on Earth consists of a collection of interacting strategic *logoi* in which individuals either wax or wane. The strategic *logos* is the life-system in which individuals in a particular species/society attempt to satisfy their strategic desires by employing the heat of the sun, and the fuel produced from it, to maintain their metabolic systems. The strategic *logos*, therefore, is an open dynamic life-system that operates relatively independently of the wider physical environment. Accordingly, the individuals operating within their strategic *logos* have only an *indirect* relationship with their physical surroundings. The *logos* is a protective entity that ensures the survival and prosperity of individuals. Accordingly, individual life forms do not wax and wane directly in response to long-term changes in global or regional temperature. What responds and adjusts is the strategic *logos*. In human society, falling global temperatures are accommodated via the strategic *logos* by changing forms of economic activity, changing dynamic strategies, technological change, the construction of warmer buildings, the development of new heating systems; while increasing global temperatures similarly result in new strategies, housing, cooking systems, clothing, innovations, etc. The existing location and pattern of population change may persist, because of the accommodating transformation of the strategic *logos*. It is the strategic *logos* and not Gaia that operates to protect and enhance life.

The strategic *logos*, therefore, is the key to combating changes in the physical environment, even that of a steadily increasing luminosity. Even 1,000 myrs from now, when the sun becomes too hot for even the human *logos* to continue to exist on Earth[32], the scientific and technological advances it will have generated will enable mankind to transfer its operations to other solar systems. Too far fetched? As science and technology are advancing at an exponential rate, and as we have come this far in just over 200 years, the possibilities in the next 1,000 myrs – longer by a factor of five million – are boundless.

The strategic *logos* is also the key to understanding the development of the biosphere. The *logos*, which is a dynamic living system operating within the physical environment provided by the Earth, derives its energy from the sun, extracts strategic inputs – minerals and chemicals – from the Earth's crust, and returns strategic byproducts to both the crust and the atmosphere. Contrary to Lovelock's claim that life is an "inseparable" part of Gaia, the *logos* is an independent life-system driven from within by strategic desire and transformed continuously according to its own strategic laws. The strategic *logos* is a selfcreating – or autogenous – dynamic life-system. The Earth, on the other hand, is driven by a dynamic of its own. Primarily, this is the impact of its gradually cooling core on its dynamic system of tectonic plates and on volcanic action.[33] And the atmospheric region above the Earth is dominated by a variety of weather and climatic systems. Hence the biosphere – what Lovelock calls Gaia – is the outcome of the interaction between a number of very different and independent dynamic systems – the *logos* and the evolving physical/climatic character of the Earth. This is why Lovelock has no general dynamic theory for Gaia – it does not exist in its own right. The fact that the Earth has provided a relatively favorable environment for life is a fortuitous fact exploited by a range of flexible and innovative strategic *logoi*.

We need to consider Lovelock's claim that the animate and inanimate aspects of Gaia are "inseparable". In *Ages of Gaia* (1990) he claims that "the evolution of the species and the evolution of their environment are tightly coupled together as *a single inseparable process*"; and in *Revenge of Gaia* (2006) he writes that "we are part of, and *not separate from Gaia*".[34] But these assertions are just not true. Even though it is possible – indeed highly likely – that life emerged on Earth (as opposed to being transported here by meteorites), the strategic *logos* is of such a nature that it definitely is theoretically separable from the Earth. All that is required is the development of a way of transporting the *logos* of man to another suitable planet from which suitable minerals and chemicals can be extracted and sunlight exploited. Even today we appear to be on the brink of visiting other planets (such as Mars) in our solar system and investigating the possibility of changing the chemical composition of their atmospheres and exploiting frozen water supplies. This will enable the establishment of human colonies, which would form the basis of a new strategic *logos* entirely separate from that on Earth. If successful, mankind will be able to leave the Earth entirely when our old physical environment ceases to provide the strategic inputs we require. In this way the *logos* of man will continue to survive and prosper, while the Earth and, eventually, the solar system, will die. Gaia, therefore, is *not* one indivisible whole as Lovelock mistakenly believes.

Here we can conclude that Gaia – "the living Earth" – is a figment of Lovelock's fertile imagination. There is no single dynamic system consisting of inseparable animate and inanimate components – a system that is supposed to embody the goal of providing an environment that favors the dominant living dynasty; a system that exercises "revenge" against this dynasty when it acts in a dangerously reckless manner. As we have seen, there are a number of very different and independent living and physical systems that interact with each other. While the strategic *logos* has a goal – to survive and prosper – and is driven by strategic desire, the Earth and its atmosphere have no goals and are driven purely by inanimate forces. The indisputable fact that these two systems have interacted in a way beneficial to life over the past 4,000 myrs is a happy coincidence for man and his strategic *logos*. It is definitely not something that has been willed in any way by Gaia as Lovelock claims. Eventually the strategic *logos* of mankind will leave the Earth behind to suffer its inevitable fate, alone.

Gaia and God

Lovelock claims that, as a scientist, he finds it difficult to believe in a Biblical God. Yet he is able to believe in Gaia as the most immortal living entity in our world. Gaia's status as the source and sustainer of all life should, according to Lovelock, engender in us an attitude of reverence rather than the more common one of exploitation. But if we continue to abuse the Earth for our own selfish ends – if we continue to place humanity before Gaia – then, like an avenging angel, She will wipe us from the face of the planet. Before that happens, we have the choice of living in the "heavenly garden" of the countryside, or in the "hell" of urban life.

This religious attitude is reflected in the following representative passages from his books. On the religious response to Gaia in the late 1980s, Lovelock wrote:

> Thinking of the Earth as alive makes it seem, on happy days, in the right places, as if the whole planet were celebrating a sacred ceremony. Being on the Earth [in contrast to viewing it from space] brings that same special feeling of comfort that attaches to the celebration of any religion when it is seemly and when one is fit to receive.[35]

He even details the reasons for this religious attitude, including Gaia's longevity and her roles as creator and sustainer of life and humanity. And he attempts to justify this reverential attitude on the grounds that it is based on a scientific approach. For Lovelock, the cult of Gaia is a religion of science. We are told:

> Any living organism a quarter as old as the Universe itself and still full of vigor is as near to immortal as we ever need to know. She is of this Universe and, conceivably, a part of God. On Earth she is the source of life everlasting and is alive now; she gave birth to humankind and we are a part of her.
>
> This is why for me, Gaia is a religious as well as a scientific concept ... Theology is also a science ... Belief in God is an act of faith and will remain so. In the same way, it is otiose to try to prove that Gaia is alive. Instead, Gaia should be a way to view the Earth, ourselves, and our relationship with living things.
>
> The life of a scientist who is a natural philosopher can be deeply religious. Curiosity is an intimate part of the process of loving. Being curious and getting to know the natural world leads to a loving relationship with it. It can be so deep it cannot be articulated, but it is nonetheless good science.[36]

It is hardly surprising that Gaia has since been adopted by "New Agers" as a "mythic goddess". While admitting that this has not helped the scientific acceptability of the Gaia hypothesis, Lovelock appears to believe that the New Agers are more imaginative than the scientists – that religion is more important than science perhaps. In 2006, Lovelock wrote:

> In a way, however harmful this has been to the acceptance of the theory in science, the New Agers were more prescient than the scientists. We now see that the great Earth system, Gaia, behaves like the other mythic goddesses, Khali and Nemesis; she acts as a mother who is nurturing but ruthlessly cruel towards transgressors, even when they are her progeny.[37]

Lovelock's faith in the new religion of science is clear. He states quite openly, if inconsistently:

> I am a scientist and think in terms of probabilities not certainties and so I am an agnostic. But there is a deep need in all of us for trust in something larger than ourselves, and I put my trust in Gaia, and declared it in my autobiography, *Homage to Gaia*, in 2000.[38]

Lovelock's deification of "the living Earth" is probably the most influential example of the emergence of a religion of science in an era when science has displaced the old religion as the strategic ideology of the world's leading nations. It arose from Lovelock's frustration with the encroachment of "agribusiness" – ironically an instrument of the capitalist urban society that provides his not inconsiderable fortune – on the countryside of England in which he has been wealthy enough to live for much of his life.

BIOCOSM – THE SUPERMIND AS GOD

The Biocosm hypothesis proposed by James Gardner in his recent book – *Biocosm. The new scientific theory of evolution: intelligent life is the architect of the Universe (2003)* – is a straight-forward, if mystical, extension of the Lovelockian thesis. Gaia is a story about the "living" Earth, while Biocosm is a myth about the "living" Universe. Gardner claims that the Universe "is literally in the process of transforming itself from inanimate to animate matter".[39] If Gaia is a superorganism, then Biocosm is a super-superorganism. Not surprisingly the underlying methodology is similar, as both hypotheses employ Darwinian natural selection and complexity theory. And both hypotheses lead their authors, and presumably their followers, to equate these superorganisms with God. Both, therefore, provide the foundation for a new religion of science – a religion to replace the obsolete strategic ideologies of monotheism. Dead god rising.

Despite these basic similarities – namely "that the natural forces of evolution, emergence, and self-organisation inexorably propel biotic systems, wherever they may exist, to even higher levels of complexity and integration" – Gardner claims that these hypotheses have different origins:

> It is interesting that two theories that developed from very different starting points – the Gaia hypothesis arose from an effort to explain the far-from-equilibrium status of the Earth's atmosphere, while the Selfish Biocosm hypothesis is an attempt to account for the oddly life-friendly laws of physics that prevail in our cosmos – should coincide on this key point.[40]

Possibly. But it is clear that Lovelock's much earlier "Gaia" is Gardner's model for the construction of "Biocosm". The main difference, of course, is that while Lovelock predicts the collapse of civilization, Gardner optimistically believes in continued progress that will ultimately lead to the emergence of a cosmic supermind. It is also clear that the Selfish Biocosm is a synthesis of the wilder speculations made by a larger number of astronomers and cosmologists, many of whom occasionally stray into the borderlands between science and science fiction.

Despite Gardner's dogged attempt to convince his readers that the Selfish Biocosm hypothesis is "scientific" – falsifiable in the Popperian sense – he falls far short of being convincing. Essentially, this is an exercise in mythmaking, in the grand tradition of all strategic societies in which the priestly philosophers attempt to transform strategic ideologies into religions. Like other members of this intellectual priesthood, Gardner is concerned to identify the deity – in this case the cosmological "supermind" – responsible for shaping the cyclical development, or eternal recurrence, of the cosmos.

What is the Selfish Biocosm?

Gardner claims we need a theory about the dynamics of the cosmos in order to explain the "profound mystery" of a "strangely life-friendly or 'anthropic'"

Universe. There is nothing new here, at least. It is an old philosophical issue that has worried metaphysicians throughout human civilization. To explain this starting point, Gardner refers to a book by Martin Rees, former Astronomer Royal in Britain, entitled *Just Six Numbers*. We are told that Ree's book

> is an extended reflection on the astonishing fact that every aspect of the evolution of the universe – from the birth of galaxies to the origin of life on Earth – is sensitively dependent on the precise values of seemingly arbitrary constants of nature like the strength of gravity, the number of extended spatial dimensions in our universe, and the initial expansion speed of the cosmos following the Big Bang. If any of these physical constants had been even slightly different, life as we know it would have been impossible.[41]

Gardner concludes that "so fine-tuned are the laws of physics to favor life that it almost seems as if the universe and the life forms that inhabit it have coevolved, like earthly creatures and the ecosystems they populate".[42] He *believes* that such a finely tuned cosmos could not possibly be due to chance. There has to be cosmic designer. It is to identify and explain this cosmic designer, which could only be a God, that Gardner develops the Selfish Biocosm hypothesis.

Gardner is aware of the similarity between this cosmic-designer argument and the divine-designer arguments of religious writers of the intelligent design variety. Indeed, he is keen to be seen as someone able to provide a proper "scientific" foundation for this theological tradition. He is also aware of the arguments of more skeptical scientists who, like myself, argue that although the existence of such a "life-friendly" Universe may be highly improbable – possibly of the order of one in 10^{220} – the very fact that we are discussing this issue suggests that improbable outcomes do occur and, in the absence of any evidence to the contrary, it is probably due to chance. Our Universe may be just one in an incredibly large number of parallel universes; all with different constants of nature; virtually all devoid of life.

Some intellectuals are unable to accept the idea that life is merely an accident of nature. Gardner is one of those. His Selfish Biocosm hypothesis is an attempt to provide a meaningful reason for the existence of life in the cosmos. Gardner summarizes his hypothesis as follows:

> The basic idea is that the anthropic, or life-friendly, qualities that our universe exhibits are logical and predictable consequences of a cosmic reproduction cycle in which a cosmologically extended biosphere, developed and evolved over billions of years to unimaginable levels of sophistication, serves as a device by which our cosmos duplicates itself and propagates one or more 'baby universes' ... Under the Selfish Biocosm theory, the cosmos is 'selfishly' focused upon the overarching objective of assuring its own replication.[43]

By "selfish" he has in mind "the same metaphorical sense that Richard Dawkins proposed that genes are 'selfish'". And, as we shall see, it is metaphor rather than theory in both cases that drives these fantastical concepts – these exercises in science fiction.

What is the Selfish Biocosm? Essentially it is the cosmos interpreted as a superorganism, which is the supposed outcome of an emergent supermind capable of creating new universes endowed with life-friendly laws and constants of nature. Gardner claims that this supermind emerged from the operation of two, currently fashionable, dynamic mechanisms, namely Darwinian natural selection and self-organization. He explains:

> The Selfish Biocosm hypothesis does not purport to supplant or overthrow Darwin's great theory but rather to *subsume* it to a more encompassing explanation of 'what happened'. Under the proffered scenario, terrestrial evolution is reconceptualized as a subroutine in an inconceivably vast ontogenetic process through which the universe gives birth to life and intelligence and, through the mechanism of highly evolved versions of those intermediaries, is able to reproduce itself. The scenario offers a more encompassing explanation than Darwin's theory because it attempts to explain the essential qualities of inanimate as well as animate matter and to link those explanations.[44]

Darwin, Gardner graciously acknowledges, was right about the dynamic mechanism of natural selection, just that he applied it on the miniscule scale of life on Earth. Similarly, no doubt, he would regard Lovelock's extension of Darwinism to include inanimate as well as animate components of Gaia to be on the right track, just limited in scope. Gardner wants to lift our sights to the entire cosmos.

Complexity theory is also accorded an honored place in Gardner's cosmic schema. For it is complexity theory that shows how "a fitness environment that emerged from a relentless struggle for survival and that rewarded the fittest organisms with the ultimate prize of reproductive success [could] somehow metamorphose into a metasystem that was essentially benign and favorable to the continued existence of all competitors."[45] He goes on to assert that:

> A serious effort is now underway, using the latest software tools of artificial life research, to attempt to model the emergence of a global homeostatic system – the metabolism of Gaia, if you will – from the *interactions* of constituent biotic subsystems. If it succeeds, this effort will not only triumphantly vindicate the Gaia hypothesis but provide strong support for a key premise of the Selfish Biocosm hypothesis: that the natural forces of evolution, emergence, and self-organization *inexorably* propel biotic systems, wherever they may exist, to ever higher levels of complexity and integration.[46]

How is the Selfish Biocosm able to replicate itself? This is where Gardner's *speculation* reaches truly cosmic proportions. He argues, under the influence of John von Neumann, that for a "parent universe" to transmit "heritable" traits to its offspring – or "baby" universes – it must possess "four key elements": a "blueprint" for the construction of offspring; a "factory" to undertake this construction; a "controller" to ensure the plan is properly executed; and a "duplicating machine" to transmit a copy of the blueprint to the offspring universes. This, he tells us, is a form of "cosmos-logical natural selection".[47]

The "blueprint" is the scientific understanding of the laws and constants of nature; the "factory" is the workshop in which black holes, the alleged sources of "baby" universes, are created; the "controller" is the "natural process of emergence hypothesized by evolution and complexity theory"; and the cosmic "duplicating machine" is the "highly evolved life and intelligence … in the far distant future".[48] Gardner claims to have found "strong support in the theoretical *speculations* of a number of prominent scientists … that sufficiently evolved life and intelligence could conceivably exert a global effect on the overall state of the cosmos, much as life has reshaped the atmosphere of the Earth over the eons".[49]

But how will this "sufficiently evolved life and intelligence" – this supermind consisting of a global network of biological and cybernetic intelligence – actually achieve the momentous trick of cosmic self-replication? How, in his jargon, could the supermind function as a von Neumann "duplicator"? Surely this would be a work of magic to make even the ancient Egyptian priest-magicians, who could suspend and manipulate the laws of nature, tremble at the prospect. With the aplomb of the ancients, Gardner introduces his magical concept of the "eschaton" – "a neologism I selected because of its relationship to the word *eschatology*, a *theological* doctrine dealing with the topic of last or final things". This newly invented eschaton is "that hypothesised final cosmic state" that exhibits "maximal computational capability". It is a state in which the "ultimate computer" – "a computing device as powerful as the laws of physics allow" – could turn all its matter into energy. This energy could then be used to "exert a global effect on the entire physical cosmos and indeed enable the cosmos to reproduce". Gardner's cosmic reproduction would occur at "the theoretical point of transition from the contraction phase of the universe [the Big Crunch] to a new expansion phase [a new Big Bang] … a nonsingular condition characterized by extremely high temperature and density …"[50]

But would there be sufficient time for the cosmos to employ this computing power to reproduce itself? Here Gardner falls back on Einstein's theory of relativity "which predicts that the dimension of time will expand toward infinity as the final singularity [Big Crunch] is approached". Then, we are told, "the instant of the eschaton will be perhaps the closest that mortals can come to experiencing eternity – the oceanic sense of a vast expanse of time, extending without perceptible limit to the temporal horizon of the universe". This neat Einsteinian solution will provide the cosmic supermind with all the time it needs to create the baby universes that will enable the cosmos to replicate itself. There is just one small complication for the Selfish Biocosm – for the cosmic supermind – it will be unable to pass through the eschaton to be with, or communicate with, its siblings. The only things that can make it through the Big Crunch are the life-friendly laws and constants of nature, which are embodied in the "baby" Universe.[51]

The argument that a life-friendly Universe exists because the appropriate laws and constants of nature have been determined by a supermind in a former parent Universe, raises the age-old philosophical problem of infinite regress. The problem is, in other words, if *our* Universe had a parent Universe, who was the parent of the parent? *Ad infinitum.* By postulating an uncreated creator, the ancient Egyptians (and Greeks) were able to sidestep the problem of who created the creator. The modern equivalent of this ancient sleight-of-hand is the idea of "closed timelike curves" (CTCs), which are justified by reference to Einstein's theory of general relativity. Gardner explains that CTCs are:

> hypothetical configurations of space and time where gravity is sufficiently strong to bend the space-time continuum into a looping configuration that allows future events to influence the past ... [In the absence of] some rule like the chronology protection conjecture proposed by Stephen Hawking (which states that the laws of physics conspire to forbid the actual manifestation of CTCs, at least at the macroscopic scale), the 'Universe can be its own mother'.[52]

How silly of the Egyptians (and Greeks) not to have thought of this roundabout way of sidestepping infinite regress in metaphysical arguments!

Evaluating the Selfish Biocosm hypothesis

Throughout his book, Gardner insists his Selfish Biocosm hypothesis is scientific, in the senses that it is a synthesis of ideas held by cosmologists and astronomers, and that it is potentially falsifiable. What should we make of these claims for scientific status? First, the ideas Gardner finds in the work of others that are sympathetic with his hypothesis are usually the wilder *speculations* of scientific writers who have stepped out of the mainstream of their disciplines. Essentially, Gardner's hypothesis consists of *speculations based on the speculations of others*. Hardly a scientific methodology. Second, the "scientific" tests he proposes for his hypothesis are not at all persuasive. Usually they are neither critical nor exclusive tests of his ideas.

Gardner suggests two main tests. One concerns his claims that the "emergence of life and intelligence are not meaningless accidents ... but at the very heart of the vast machinery of creation, cosmological evolution, and cosmic replication"[53], which, we are told, can be tested by SETI predictions coming true, the emergence of intelligence in other species (such as dolphins), the evolution of artificial intelligence, and the emergence of transhuman machine intelligence. Clearly, these so-called tests of falsifiability are either truistic or they can only be undertaken at some impossibly distant time in the future. When Popper developed his falsifiability concept, it was to be paid for in the currency of our own time not that of some future time which neither we nor even our distant kin would ever experience. Even theologians could make the same claim for scientific status, because at the end of time God will reveal all his plans! This comparison is particularly applicable to Gardner's second test concerning the claim that "life and intelligence could, in the far distant future, evolve to a point of such power and sophistication that it could exert a global effect on the entire physical cosmos and indeed enable the cosmos to reproduce".[54] In turn, this momentous event would depend upon the ability and desire of the cosmological supermind investing the totality of the Universe's resources in the "ultimate computer". Needless to say, the only way to test these ideas would be to wait for tens of billions of years until the Big Crunch approached to see if it were true or not. This is not science, but science fiction pretending to be science.

Gardner has no understanding of the *real* dynamics of life. Accordingly, the theoretical structure of the Selfish Biocosm hypothesis is faulty. It is faulty because it relies on the obsolete Darwinian and complexity theories, which have been refuted in *The Collapse of Darwinism* (2003) and a series of articles in the scientific journals *Complexity* (2008) and *Advances in Space Research* (2005).[55] In particular, the suggested link between natural selection and complexity (or "emergence") theory is very weak and highly superficial. Gardner believes that the mind – the focus of his interest in evolution – is an "emergence" phenomenon that doesn't require any real explanation. Therefore he doesn't see the necessity of explaining how "the next great leap upward in the ongoing ascendancy of mind" – in which computing will "take charge of its own evolution" – will actually occur.[56] And he doesn't realize that the dynamics of all living systems is a selfcreating process, with **strategic exchange** (rather than individual interaction) and **strategic selection** (rather than natural selection) at its core (see the Appendix).

The Selfish Biocosm hypothesis is also unsoundly based on the idea that the Universe will be empowered and replicated by the emergence of a supermind. This cosmological phenomenon will, Gardner claims, result from the networking of highly advanced biological and cybernetic systems of intelligence. What Gardner fails to understand in this context is that desires drive and ideas merely facilitate. Where is the strategic desire, which drives all living systems, in his schema? Without it, ideas will wither and his entire system will collapse. As I show in *The Selfcreating Mind* (2006), mind is a product of material desire. No body, no mind. Intelligence is merely a strategic instrument that responds to **logosian demand** not to the physical laws of the cosmos. The idea of a disembodied supermind is the stuff of science fiction.

There are a host of additional objections that can be made to Gardner's hypothesis. First, is the Selfish Biocosm real or merely metaphor? If merely metaphor, the whole schema is meaningless. As we saw in the case of Lovelocks' Gaia, metaphor can only be scientifically used to illustrate theory, not as a substitute for theory. Second, why would a supermind – assuming for a split second that it actually existed – wish to generate "baby" universes which it would not be able to join or communicate with. Indeed, as our supermind would not survive the Big Crunch, how would it even know it had been successful in creating new universes? And, of course, the baby universes would never remember or know their parents. What incentive could there possibly be to spend the critical "eschaton" using all the resources of the cosmos to build an ultimate computer for replication purposes, when it had absolutely nothing to gain personally from this incredibly expensive undertaking. This would be a denial, and a reversal, of the very incentive system that had brought it to this stage over tens of billions of years. Indeed, had this inter-Universe altruism been embodied in the cosmos from the very beginning – as Gardner's discussion of CTCs implies that it is – then the entire enterprise would have broken down at the very beginning, because altruism is neither sustainable nor capable of acting as a driving force. This is the type of problem we always encounter in metaphysical systems that abstract from strategic desire. It is the type of trap that intellectuals – peddlers of ideas, usually someone else's – regularly fall into. A trap that never ensnares the decision-making strategists who, motivated by strategic desire, are responsible for driving the development of human civilization.

Finally, Gardner, like Lovelock, sees life in general and humanity in particular as instruments of "higher" entities such as Gaia or the cosmos. In the hands of metaphysicians – the priestly philosophers – humanity always ends up being the plaything of the gods, even the gods of science.

God of the cosmos – the supermind

Gardner believes the cosmic supermind – which is evolving from intelligent life forms and is responsible for the "progress" and replication of the Universe – can be equated with God. In a section of his book entitled "The Mind of Man → The Mind of God", he paraphrases, with approval, the arguments of a number of intellectuals on this subject. For example, Gardner writes:

> Freeman Dyson has famously written that the idea of sufficiently evolved mind is indistinguishable from the mind of God. The Selfish Biocosm hypothesis takes Dyson's assertion of equivalence one step further by suggesting that there is a discernable and comprehensible evolutionary ladder by means of which mortal minds will one day ascend into the intellectual stratosphere that will be the domain of superminds – what Dyson would call the realm of God.
>
> To use Hawking's terminology, the hypothesis implies that the mind of God is the natural culmination of the evolution of the mind of humans and other intelligent creatures throughout the universe, whose collective efforts conspire, admittedly without deliberate intention, to effect a transformation of the cosmos from lifeless dust to vital, living matter capable of the ultimate feat of life-mediated cosmic reproduction. This act of transformation and replication, should it eventually succeed, will surely prove to be the defining conquest of ignorance by intelligence, the consummate victory of life over nonlife, the final triumph of mind over matter, and the ultimate revelation of the meaning of the cosmos.[57]

Here we have a clear, if triumphal, statement of hope, that at the end of time, supermind will not only overcome desire and materialism but will be transformed into God. This is a completely metaphysical and teleological, rather than a scientific, hypothesis.

Gardner, however, would not be particularly concerned by this type of criticism, because he believes that an interaction between science, religion, and philosophy is both unavoidable and "fruitful". He tells us that

> Far from being separate 'nonoverlapping magisteria' that should be contemplated in isolation and separated by rigid *cordon sanitaire* (as Stephen Gould has implausibly suggested), the overlapping domains of science, religion, and philosophy should be regarded as virtual rain forests of cross-pollinating ideas ... The messy science/religion/philosophy interface should be treasured as an incredibly fruitful cornucopia of creative ideas ...[58]

Hence, for Gardner and his ilk, the accusation that his work is metaphysical and teleological would – in contrast to that of a real scientist – *not* move him. This helps to explain the unrestrained speculation in his work.

Gardner is even willing to agree with the British philosopher Alfred Whitehead that the reason for the unique event of the West's invention of science was due to the cultural attainment of medieval Christianity – a issue we explored in Chapter 5. He quotes with approval from Whitehead's 1925 Lowell lectures at Harvard that: "the faith in the possibility of science, generated antecedently to the development of modern scientific theory, is an unconscious derivative from medieval theology".[59] In reality, modern science emerged in Western Europe in response to the strategic demand generated by the unfolding strategic sequence of commerce and technological change. As always, desires drive and ideas merely facilitate. While a philosopher, whose stock-in-trade is ideas isolated from reality, might be forgiven such a grievous error, someone like Gardner, who claims to understand the evolution of the cosmos, cannot be excused so easily. Indeed, he compounds his error by asserting:

> Whitehead's analysis suggests that the historical interplay of these three great Western systems of thought – Judeo-Christian religion, Greek philosophy, and Western science – can be viewed as a uniquely portentous instance of cultural coevolution and emergence that has powerfully shaped the path of intellectual history.[60]

This "cultural coevolution", according to Gardner, led to "the curious fact that European civilization alone had yielded the cultural phenomenon we know as scientific enquiry".[61]

The belief in the primacy of ideas and matters intellectual underlies Gardner's entire analysis. He views the disembodied supermind not only as the driving force in life, but the embodiment of cosmic meaning and, ultimately, the expression of divinity. Just as the great monotheistic religions have done. Gardner promises that at the end of time all will be revealed by the Mind of God – by the cosmic supermind. At this time truth (ideas) will triumph over untruth (desires and materialism), mind will finally dominate all matter, the inanimate will become animate. The Persian prophet Zarathustra would have felt comfortable with these metaphysical ideas.

This typical supply-side explanation, which ignores the roles of strategic desire and strategic demand, is both intellectually vacuous and positively dangerous. Vacuous because it explains nothing, and dangerous because it attempts to explain the emergence of ideas (particularly science) solely in cultural terms. The danger in arguing that science is an outcome of cultural differences between Western Europe and the rest of the world is that it begs the deeper question: how do we account for cultural differences? And, in the absence of a demand-side theory of dynamics – such as the dynamic-strategy theory – the only answer to the question is one based on race. Like most other cultural relativists, however, Gardner innocently fails to realize this.

CONCLUSIONS

Owing to the exhaustion of the neolithic technological paradigm in the mid-eighteenth century and the subsequent rise of the industrial technological paradigm, the old strategic ideology of monotheism was replaced by the new strategic ideology of scientism. The old Judeo-Christian-Islamic God was displaced by the new deity of science. A number of attempts have been made to give shape to this new deity, owing to the failure of their authors to recognize, let alone understand, the dynamic life-system – the strategic *logos* – responsible for the survival and prosperity of human civilization. Instead they have associated the deity of science with either the "living" planet, or Gaia, or the "living" cosmos, or Biocosm. These new guardians attract reverence and ritual attendance from their true believers. What we now need to do is to explode these modern myths by exploring, for the first time, the nature of the strategic *logos* – the hidden universal life-system.

PART III
THE
UNIVERSAL
LIFE-SYSTEM

Chapter 10
Life's Great Odyssey

Over the past 3,800 million years (myrs), carbon-based life forms have flourished on this planet, despite its difficult environment. In the course of this great odyssey, life has been transformed from very simple organic forms into highly complex and intelligent structures. While life as a whole has been extremely successful, individual species, populations, societies, and dynasties have emerged, flourished for a brief season, and then suddenly disappeared. Until recently we have been unable to explain the rise and fall of major life forms. This has generated in our species a profound anxiety about the future, which, I have argued, is responsible for the creation of mankind's many myths and religions.

Our concern in part III is to reveal in full the universal life-system, or strategic *logos*, that is responsible for the remarkable, if ephemeral, success of life in general and human society in particular. In this chapter the patterns of change generated by life are explored; in Chapter 11, a general theory to explain these patterns of life and to provide a basis for the reconstruction of the hidden life-system is outlined; and the strategic *logos* is presented in Chapter 12. It is the conclusion of this final part of the book that the remarkable success of life's odyssey is a testament to the effectiveness of the strategic *logos* as the great vehicle of life. Yet, while the *logos* remains hidden, our future remains obscure.

THE PATHWAY OF LIFE
The pathway of life over the past 3,800 myrs possesses three sets of characteristics. First, there is the rate of acceleration of life, which I call the **logological constant**; second, there are the very long-run fluctuations by which this development occurs, called here the **great waves of life**; and finally, there are the biological and technological paradigm shifts, which make the entire odyssey of life possible. It was by observing, recording, and analyzing these pathway patterns that I was able to construct a general dynamic theory capable of explaining and predicting the fluctuating progress of life.

The logological constant
The remarkable aspect of life is its ability to thrive in an extremely difficult physical world – a world dominated by entropy, or increasing disorder (explained by the second law of thermodynamics), and subject to random physical shocks. This has only been possible because of the entropy-defying, shock-resisting life-system that I have called the strategic *logos*. It is the *logos* – a dynamic system of interaction between a community of organisms and their societal system – that protects and sustains life. Without the *logos*, biological/

technological transformation would be impossible, and individual life forms, even if they managed to emerge, would be swept away by a hostile physical world.

Second only to the ability of life to thrive in a hostile physical world, is its capacity to develop at a constant exponential rate. My research in the early 1990s revealed that each major biological transformation during the history of life on Earth (see Figures 10.2 to 10.4) took only one-third of the time taken by its predecessor.[1] It was also discovered that the geometrically declining duration of these paradigmatic transformations was accompanied by an approximately proportional increase in biomass (species population multiplied by average weight).[2] This geometric increase in biomass is the outcome of greater access by organisms to the planet's natural resources made possible by either, or both, genetic change and technological change.

The relationship between global biomass and time in my book *The Dynamic Society* was expressed as:

$$y = a\ (3^{t-1}) \tag{i}$$

where y is global biomass generated by genetic and technological change over the past 3,800 myrs and t is time. This has been called the Snooksian algorithm.[3] What this algorithm tells us is that the biomass generated by nature and human society is accelerating at a constant rate. In 1996, these results were also plotted on both arithmetic and logarithmic scales and are reproduced as Figure 10.1. While the growth of Earth's biomass over 3,800 myrs is exponential – thereby approaching the vertical on the right-hand side of the arithmetic curve – it is also log-linear – in this case an approximately 45° straight line in the logarithmic box.

What can be called the **coefficient of acceleration of life** is approximately 3.0. As mentioned earli er, this means that each great wave of biological/ technological progress – and its underlying technological paradigm shift – occurs in just one-third of the time take by its predecessor (Figures 10.2 and 10.4). In other words, while the dynamic process of life generates an increasingly larger quantity of global biomass per unit of time, its compound (or geometric) rate of growth is constant. This is true under both the "genetic option", which prevailed before 2 myrs BP (before present), and the "technology option", which prevailed thereafter (Figures 10.3 and 10.4).

This constant rate of biological transformation, as measured by the coefficient of acceleration, is what I have called the **logological constant**. It is the great constant of life generated in a hostile physical world by the strategic *logos* (hence the name). This constant of nature is the outcome of what I have elsewhere called the Law of Cumulative Biological/Technological Change, which states that the relationship between a series of genetic/technological paradigm shifts is geometric owing to the cumulative effect generated when the "technological" (either genetic or industrial) output of one paradigm becomes the input of the next.[4] A parallel concept in the physical world is the "cosmological constant" governing the expansion of the Universe.

Figure 10.1 **The logological constant of life**

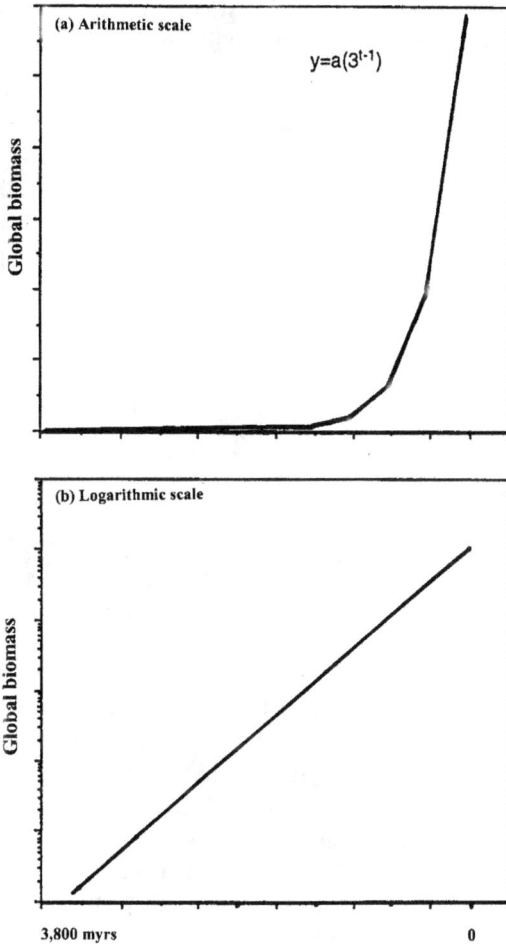

(a) Arithmetic scale

$$y=a(3^{t-1})$$

Global biomass

(b) Logarithmic scale

Global biomass

3,800 myrs   0

Source: Snooks 1996: 80

The logological constant is a measure not only of biological/technological transformation, but also of the effectiveness of the strategic *logos* in generating the great odyssey of life. The strategic *logos*, which operates according to its own laws (see Chapter 12), is, therefore, able to provide life with a degree of independence from the laws of physics. Consequently, the expansion of life can be understood not in terms of physical laws but only in terms of the laws of life and history. These laws have been isolated, presented, and discussed in my book *The Collapse of Darwinism*.[5]

The great waves of life

The great odyssey of life over the past 3,800 myrs has occurred in a fluctuating but systematic manner. Figure 10.2, which is based on the discoveries of paleontologists concerning the fluctuating diversity of the Earth's flora and fauna, shows that life has proceeded by what I have elsewhere called the **great waves of life**. With the progression of time, those great waves have experienced a geometric reduction in duration and expansion in amplitude.

Figure 10.2 **The great waves of life – the past 3,800 myrs**

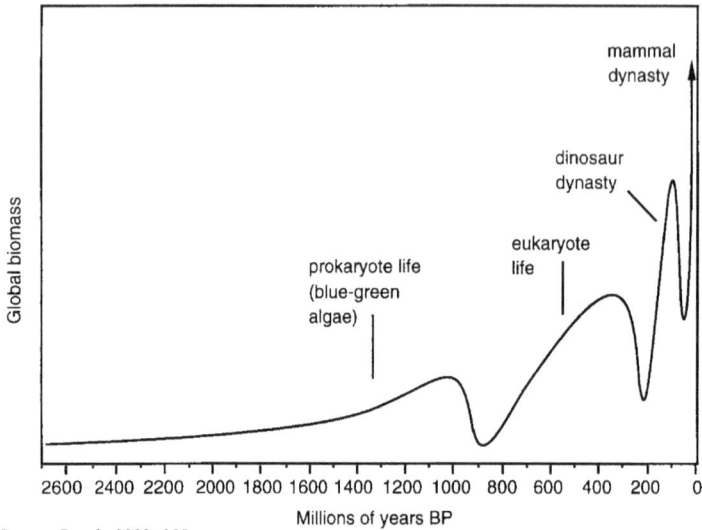

Source: Snooks 2003: 155

The dynamic **timescape** presented in Figure 10.2 shows a series of four great waves of biological activity: the first is about 2,000 myrs in duration; the second about 600 myrs; the third about 180 myrs; and the fourth, which is by no means complete, about 60 myrs. While it is not possible to provide a precise vertical scale, the available evidence suggests that the reduction in duration – each great wave is about one-third as long as the one that preceded it – is matched by a proportional increase in global biomass. There can be little doubt, therefore, that the momentum of life on Earth is accelerating, owing to the increasing access to natural resources made possible initially by genetic change (under the **genetic option**) and more recently by technological change (under the **technology option**).

Either this systematic relationship between the great waves is purely coincidental or it is powerful evidence that it is endogenously determined, rather than being exogenously and randomly driven by natural catastrophes or fortuitous genetic occurrences. Elsewhere I have argued that this systematic pattern is not coincidental but that it is driven by a powerful endogenous mechanism embedded in the strategic *logos*. The endogenous mechanism is discussed in Chapter 11, and the strategic *logos* in Chapter 12.

To understand the great waves, we need to identify the main turning points in life, when one major dynasty of life gave way to another. These transformations include the shift from prokaryotic life (blue-green algae) to eukaryotic life (plant and animal organisms) at about 900 myrs BP; the shift from ectothermic life (cold-blooded reptiles) to endothermic life (warm-blooded protomammals) at about 245 myrs BP; and the replacement of dinosaurs with mammals at about 65 myrs BP. Other setbacks, such as the widespread extinctions around 435 myrs, 370 myrs and 215 myrs BP constitute major fluctuations within the great waves, just as more minor fluctuations can be detected within the major fluctuations, and so on. It is a system of waves within waves, all generated by an endogenous dynamic mechanism. Exogenous shocks were only responsible for minor distortions to this pattern. These biological transformations have been discussed at length in my *The Collapse of Darwinism*.

LIFE'S DYNAMIC MECHANISMS

There are two important dynamic mechanisms that help to explain the odyssey of life over the past 3,800 myrs. They are the great steps of life – the great genetic and technological paradigm shifts – and the great wheel of life. One leads to biological and economic progress, and the other to the eternal recurrence. Both play a central role in life's dynamics.

The great steps of life

The dynamic structure of life – reflected in Figures 10.3 and 10.4 – is defined by a series of genetic and technological paradigm shifts, which I call the **great steps of life**. These great steps, which outline the genetic/technological potential for biological/economic development, are driven by the major genetic/technological revolutions that I have examined in detail in *The Dynamic Society* and *The Collapse of Darwinism*. Owing to the logological constant discussed above, these great steps have been changing exponentially in two dimensions: increasing in height while reducing in depth. What this reflects is the accelerating dynamics of both life and human society over the past 3,800 myrs. Each great step, in other words, is not only larger, but is taken more quickly than its predecessor. In this sense, history is speeding up.

There have been three genetic paradigm shifts and three technological paradigm shifts since life began on Earth. And they are involved in a systematic geometric relationship. This pattern of change suggests that a new technological paradigm shift will occur soon – sometime in the middle decades of the twenty-first century – and that it will be completed rapidly probably within a generation. This prediction is supported by evidence concerning paradigmatic exhaustion that is marshalled in my recent book *The Coming Eclipse* (Snooks 2010). I first discussed the probablility of this future development in *The Dynamic Society* (1996: ch. 13).

The genetic paradigm shifts are part of what I call the genetic option and the technological paradigm shifts are part of the technology option. Each "option" has dominated the progress of life on Earth. With each paradigm shift, the capacity of the genetic option was progressively exploited by life forms until it was finally exhausted around the time the dinosaurs were in their prime about 80 myrs ago. The technology option, however, only displaced the defunct genetic option when the intellectual capabilities of the hominids enabled them to employ the technological strategy, sometime before 2.4 myrs ago. During the almost 80 myrs between these major events, nature was dominated by the **great wheel of life** discussed below.

Figure 10.3 **The great steps of life – the past 3,800 myrs**

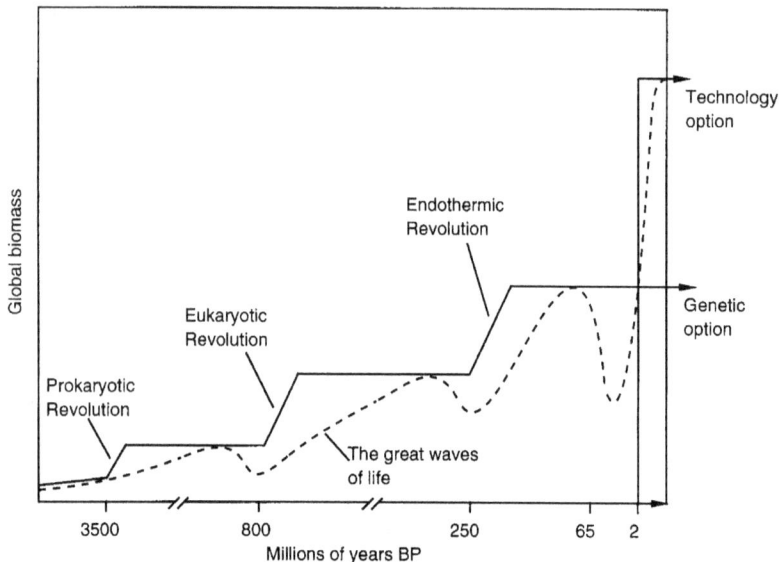

Source: Snooks 2003: 252

Figure 10.4 **The great steps of life – the past 80,000 years**

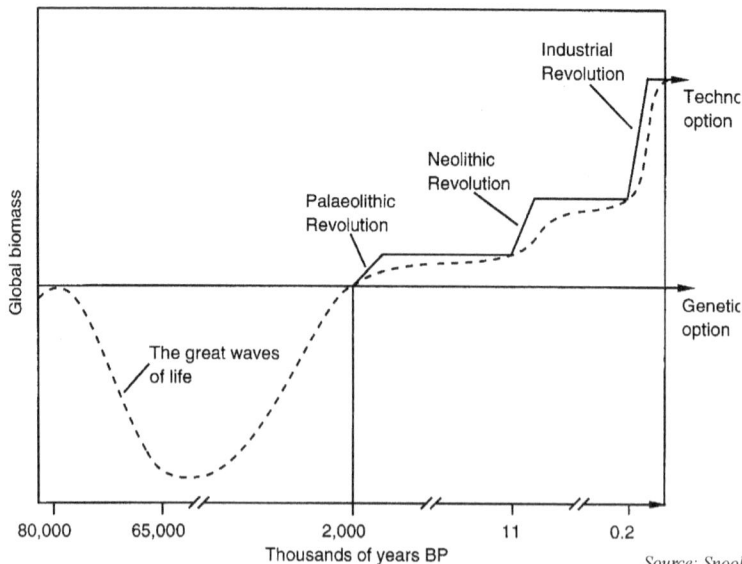

Source: Snooks 2003: 253

As suggested earlier, the great paradigm shifts were generated by a series of genetic and, later, technological revolutions. The genetic revolutions included:

- the Prokaryote Revolution – development of a metabolic system based on photosynthesis – by blue-green algae from 3,500 myrs BP;

- the Eukaryote Revolution – development of complex, integrated biological organisms – by plants and animals (beginning with cold-blooded types) from 900 myrs BP;

- the Endothermic Revolution – biological systems for the internal generation of body heat – by warm-blooded animals and associated plants from 250 myrs BP; and

- the Intelligence Revolution by the hominids from 2.4 myrs to 150,000 years BP.

The last of these genetic revolutions led not to a genetic paradigm shift but rather to a series of technological paradigm shifts. At this time, genetic change by itself was unable to provide more intense access to natural resources, only the ability to create and employ technology to do so instead. As shown earlier, these technological revolutions (Figures 10.2 and 10.3) include:

- the Paleolithic (hunting) Revolution from 2 myrs BP;

- the Neolithic (agricultural) Revolution from 10,600 years BP;

- the Modern (Industrial) Revolution from AD 1780; and

- the future revolution – the Solar Revolution – which can be expected from middle decades of the twenty-first century.

As shown earlier, these technological paradigm shifts had a major impact on strategic ideology/religious ideas both through the new strategic demand they generated for ideological support and by the increases in surpluses available to fund ideological and religious institutions. The Neolithic Revolution was responsible for transforming simple views about supportive strategic guardians into elaborate theologies about creator gods; while the Modern Revolution replaced the old strategic gods with science and technology – of monotheism with scientism. As shown in Chapter 11, the potential for material progress created by each technological paradigm shift was taken up gradually through the pursuit of one or other to the four dynamic strategies. Following the Paleolithic Revolution this involved the family-multiplication strategy (of procreation and migration); following the Neolithic Revolution it involved the conquest and commerce strategies; and following the Industrial Revolution it involved the technological strategy. When, in Figure 10.4, the "actual" pressed against the "potential", there was great economic pressure for a new technological paradigm shift.

What the great steps of life represent is the step-like progress that has taken place in biological and economic activity throughout the history of life on Earth.

Each giant step forward, which was facilitated by a genetic or technological revolution, made possible more intensive access to natural resources. In turn this enabled a higher level of biological/economic activity – or life "output" – to be achieved. In the pre-human era, this meant a growing number of more complex organisms that contributed to a higher level of global biomass. And in the human era, it resulted in not only a rapid increase in human and domesticated animal and plant populations, but also an exponential increase in human living standards, particularly concerning the consumption of services and nonperishable commodities. In brief there has been an exponential increase in the complexity of life on Earth. What of the future? For as long as we are confined to this planet, human progress will be measured in terms of increases in living standards rather than population. But, once we break out into the solar system and beyond, as we undoubtedly will, population expansion will become important again.

The reason for the step-like profile of global biomass/real GDP per capita is that with each genetic/technological revolution there was a quantum leap in *potential* access to natural resources owing to the occurrence of a major innovation or cluster of innovations. The *actual* utilization of this potential, however, is a gradual and wave-like process driven by the **strategic desire** of materialist organisms (including man) in pursuit of their non-genetic or non-technological strategies. But in order to achieve this potential, it was usually necessary to develop add-on genetic/technological devices, such as those employed by blue-green algae to combat the adverse effects of their waste product oxygen, or newly conceived war machines to further Rome's conquest strategy. The relationship between potential and actual outcomes is represented diagrammatically in Figures 10.2 to 10.4

In Figures 10.2 and 10.3, the *actual* curves represent the biological development path that I have called the great waves of life (measured in terms of global biomass); and in Figure 10.4 the *actual* curve represents the development path of global economic activity (measured by real GDP per capita). Once a particular genetic or technological paradigm has been exhausted (where the potential is fully realized), the *actual* curve presses persistently against the *potential* curve. Under the genetic option the resulting overpopulation leads to the collapse and extinction of the prevailing dynasty (such as the dinosaurs), due to the inevitability of outbreak of "world war". Only once the intense competition for scarce resources has been eliminated – through dynastic collapse – is it possible to bring the slow-acting genetic strategy into play. In contrast, under the technology option, paradigmatic exhaustion leads to the adoption of a new technological revolution by the same, not a replacement, dynasty, owing to the much greater rapidity with which it can be introduced – a generation or less, compared with millions of years. Global conquest and collapse – possibly even extinction – could theoretically occur in human society if we were to eliminate growth-inducing technological change in the mistaken belief that this will save the environment. This scenario is discussed in 1996 in my *The Dynamic Society* (ch. 13) and in 2010 in my *The Coming Eclipse*.

The interplay between genetic and technological change in the critical period between *Homo habilis* and *Homo sapiens* – between 2.4 myrs and 150,000 years BP – is fascinating. And it is a real test of any general dynamic theory. This period experienced what I call the **Intelligence Revolution**. The strategic demand generated by the hominid family-multiplication strategy led to a *relatively* sudden increase in brain size in order to create and employ the non-biological tools that were required to change their diet from nuts and tubers to meat and marrow so as to enable the great global diaspora of mankind.

The Intelligence Revolution, therefore, led to a more intensive use of natural resources through the employment of better strategic instruments of a technological rather than a genetic nature. Genetic change was employed only until technology could take over, after which it was abandoned because technological instruments are more direct, precise, and quick-acting – in short, more economical. This, together with the much earlier exhaustion of the genetic option, is why the Intelligence Revolution led to a technological rather than a genetic paradigm shift.

As can be seen in Figure 10.3, the genetic paradigm profile continues as a horizontal line from the time the dinosaurs were at their peak, whereas the technological paradigm takes off vertically from about 2 myrs ago, thereafter tracing out the familiar step-like pattern, except that it occurs in a greatly accelerated fashion. Even in the future when genetic engineering will, no doubt, be undertaken on a large scale, it will lead to paradigm shifts not of a genetic but of a technological nature. Genetic engineering will merely serve the dominant technological strategy. The technology option has permanently replaced the genetic option.

The great wheel of life

The conventional wisdom is that the emergence of intelligence on Earth, once life had firmly established itself, was merely a function of "evolutionary" time. This wisdom is ill-founded. As I show in *The Collapse of Darwinism*, there was nothing inevitable about the rise of intelligent life on Earth, or anywhere else in the Universe. It was merely a matter of chance. Had we the ability to rerun the dynamics of life on Earth repeatedly, the chances that intelligent life would ever appear again are very remote. Or, to put it another way, even assuming that life is commonplace throughout the Universe, the probability that it would generate an intelligent species is very low. Why? Because the emergence of intelligent life was the outcome of a long chain of improbable and *unsought* happenings.

This is not to say, however, that the dynamics of life is unsystematic, just that it can take many different pathways. In fact, as I show in *The Collapse of Darwinism*, species and dynasties rise and fall in a predictable cycle, even though the detailed manner in which they do so cannot be known in advance.

This suggests that there is a dynamic mechanism in life that could account for the regular rise and fall of dynasties without the emergence of intelligence, even until the solar system itself expired. Indeed, what I have argued is that such a dynamic mechanism should be regarded as the normal process for any mature system of life anywhere in the Universe. Intelligent life is the very rare exception, not the rule in our cosmos.

This dynamic mechanism, which I call the **great wheel of life**, comes into operation in a mature life-system when the genetic option has been exhausted. That occurs when it is no longer possible to gain further access to natural resources through the use of genetic instruments – when all conceivable habitats or niches have been occupied as fully as possible through biological adaptation. At this stage, genetic change can no longer be employed to increase the global level of the biomass of life. This is not to say that minor variations in global "output" will not occur as the physical environment makes marginal adjustments (such as the rise or fall of sea levels), just that the available natural resources cannot be used any more intensively through genetic adjustment alone.

The exhaustion of the genetic option on Earth appears, as suggested earlier, to have occurred by the time the dinosaurs were at their peak about 80 myrs ago. Evidence for this comes from a comparison of the metabolic systems of the four great endothermic dynasties: the protomammals (therapsids), the archosaurs, the dinosaurs, and modern mammals. While advanced dinosaurs possessed more sophisticated metabolic systems – higher body temperatures, higher calorie intakes, faster reactions and speed – than the protomammals, they were similar to those of modern mammals.[6] What this implies is that the dinosaurs took the Endothermic Revolution, which had been initiated by the protomammals and carried forward by the archosaurs, a further and final step. Hence, they were able to employ the Earth's resources more intensively than all preceding dynasties. Modern mammals, whose great radiation was based not on any genetic innovation, do not appear to have advanced beyond the dinosaurs in this key resource-accessing ability. Indeed, while the dinosaurs existed on Earth, the mammals were only marginal players in life, unable to move to center stage.

Some readers, who are aware that the mammals have been able to generate a greater range of species than were the dinosaurs, might claim this as a sign of greater effectiveness in accessing natural resources. This is not so. In life there exists a three-way trade-off between the number of species, the size of individuals, and the number of individuals that can exist at a particular time with a given supply of natural resources. If members of a dynasty "opt" – as a result of the "style" of their dynamic strategies – for large individual size and large numbers of individuals, then they will be limited to a lesser number of species. But if they opt for greater diversity – a larger number of species – together with a similar number of individuals, then the size of those individuals will be smaller. My argument in *The Collapse of Darwinism* is that the dinosaurs opted for size and numbers rather than diversity and numbers, whereas modern mammals did the reverse. The mammals were able to do so even though they were operating in the same genetic paradigm and at the same level of **genetic competence** as the dinosaurs.

We need to consider why and how the dinosaurs and mammals were able to opt for different degrees of diversity. This can best be done in terms of the "force versus finesse" argument developed in *The Collapse of Darwinism*.[7] Briefly, a dynasty, such as the dinosaurs, that favors force rather than finesse – because, for a successful species in the early stage of its development, force is more economical – will opt for size and numbers rather than diversity. Large size and numbers are essential for any dynasty that is accustomed to pursuing their dynamic strategies with brute strength. This was the case for all land dynasties before the era of modern mammals, and particularly for dinosaurs. Dinosaur herbivores reached sizes of 40,000 kg and carnivores attained sizes of 3,000 kg; whereas mammal herbivores (excluding the unsuccessful mega fauna) reached only 5,000 kg and their carnivores little more than 200 kg. Instead, mammals, which in the Mesozoic period (250–65 myrs BP) had been forced to live by their wits on the margins of life for 150 myrs by the aggressive dinosaurs, favored finesse rather than force. Hence they opted for diversity rather than sheer size. And greater diversity, which requires more regular genetic innovation, needs greater intelligence to control the mechanism of **strategic selection** (to be discussed in Chapter 12). The need for greater finesse and greater diversity is why mammal brains were relatively larger than dinosaur brains, and why their brains continued to grow.

From the time that the genetic option was exhausted – somewhere between the times of the protomammals and the dinosaurs (275–65 myrs BP) – the **great wheel of life** displaced the great steps of life as the dominant dynamic mechanism underlying macrobiological activity. And while the great wheel rotated slowly in space-time, no progress could be made in terms of intensity (or productivity) of resource use, or of increase in global biomass. From this time, new dynasties only able to resort to genetic (and not technological) change would merely replace old dynasties without gaining forward strategic traction. From this time, each great wave of life would be forced to peak at about the same level of biological activity as the early "endotherms". This is the **eternal recurrence** of life.

The great wheel of life is represented diagrammatically in Figure 10.5. When examining this diagram we should be aware of the different but related types of motion: the rotation of a point on the circumference of the wheel around its axis **I**; and the forward movement of the wheel from **I** to **II** over a very long period of time, say 100 myrs. Like any wheel traveling along a plane, the rotation leads to directional movement. In other words, the rotation of the wheel cannot lead to a reversal of time as would be implied by a fixed axis. Also, it should be noted that, as the genetic option has been exhausted, the plane along which the wheel travels through time is horizontal rather than upwardly inclined. This implies that there can be no "progress", in terms of biological outputs or productivity between this non-innovating dynasty and its predecessor.

The above argument can be cast in terms of the great-wheel diagram as follows:

- A new postgenetic-option dynasty begins its adventure in life at **a**, when competition is minimal and resources are abundant. Individuals are faced with the size/numbers/diversity issue, which they resolve unconsciously by pursuing the dynamic strategy of genetic change, with varying degrees of "preference" for force/finesse. This causes the great wheel to rotate upward, increasing biological output and moving forward in time along a horizontal plane.

- Once they arrive at **b** the genetic strategy will be exhausted and the maximum level of "productivity" (or output per unit of input) in the use of energy and other resources will be achieved. Any further rotation of the wheel and, hence, forward movement through time will require the pursuit of the family-multiplication and commerce (symbiosis) strategies to drive their **genetic styles** (species) around the globe. As the wheel turns from **b** to **c**, global biomass (or biological output) will increase, but productivity remains the same, because the wheel is still traveling along the horizontal plane dictated by the exhausted genetic option.

- When the great wheel reaches **c** the family-multiplication strategy and the genetic paradigm for the dynasty as whole will have been exhausted. The only option for individuals in this *Darwinian world* of intense competition and scarce resources is to pursue the *non-Darwinian strategy* of conquest (the Darwinian strategy is genetic change). While this leads to gains for winners, it is at the expense of a growing loss of life, a *reduction* in diversity (Darwin predicts an *increase* in diversity), a decline in global biomass, and a severe deterioration in the environment. Hence, the wheel rotates slowly but inevitably from **c** to **d**, at which point conquest gives way to terminal chaos.

- Between **d** and **a** the wheel accelerates downwards as the entire dynasty begins to collapse. By the time **a** is reached, the dynasty has gone extinct. During the time taken to complete one revolution of the wheel of life – say 100 myrs in the case of this postgenetic-option dynasty – its forward motion has been along the horizontal plane **I-II**. In other words, there has been little or no progress in terms of biological output or productivity beyond that achieved by the former dynasty (except for some minor fine-tuning). Progress would require traction along an upward-sloping plane of the type that existed prior to exhaustion of the genetic option.

- With dynastic extinction, the opportunity is presented to the surviving species, previously on the margins of life, to take over center stage where competition is now minimal and resources are abundant. As they do so – slowly, as the global environment has been severely damaged by "world war" – the great wheel begins to rotate around the same horizontally constrained axis once more. Hence, the cast of characters in the vehicle of life will have changed, but the play and its ending remains the same for a dynasty (including protomammals, archosaurs, and dinosaurs) trapped by an exhausted genetic option. The great wheel of life, therefore, leads to the **eternal recurrence**, which should be regarded as the normal condition of mature forms of life throughout the Universe. Only by adopting the technology option *before* the great wheel begins its inevitable downward descent is it possible for a new dynasty to gain more intensive access to resources once all possible habitats have been saturated through genetic change. Only technical ideas under the driving force of strategic demand are able to transcend these acute biological limitations. And technical ideas depend on the emergence of an Intelligence Revolution.

Figure 10.5 **The great wheel of life – the rise and fall of a non-innovating dynasty**

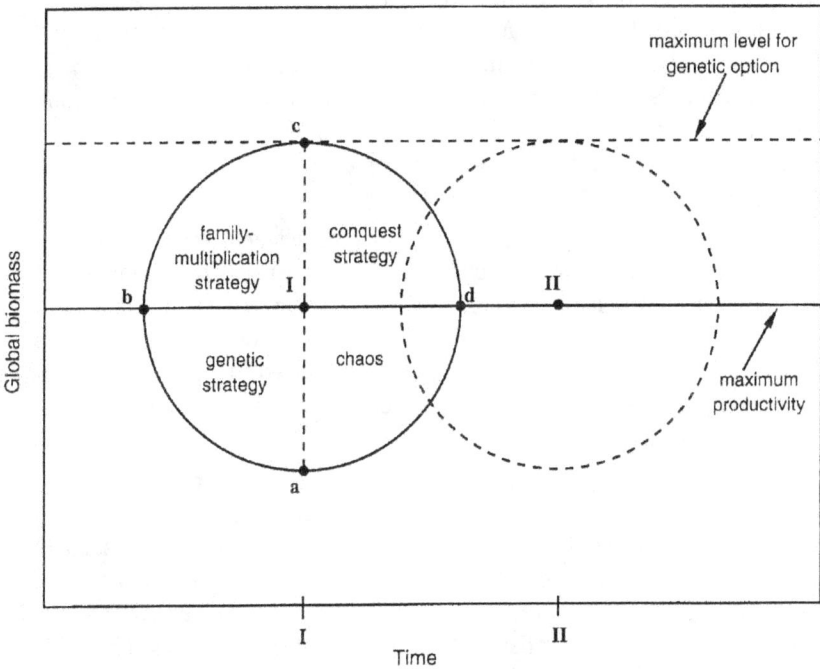

Source: Snooks: 2003: 259

It is sobering to realize that the technology option is the outcome of blind chance. The central reason is that this option does not bestow any advantage on the *individual* decision maker – the **dynamic strategist** – only on the species as a whole. And species do *not* make strategic decisions. In reality it is only something that can be recognized and valued in retrospect. And, so far, only by our species and only in this work. Why is this so? Why doesn't the individual see the technology option as being in his best interest? The answer is that all individuals die, irrespective of whether one species (mankind) stumbles on the secret of perpetuating its own existence. This is what I call the **organism/ species paradox**. Even had the apemen – or the mammal species that gave rise to them – recognized the very long-run implications of adopting the technological strategy, would one of its members have traded even a day's supply of food for the remote possibility that the species replacing theirs would, some 2.4 myrs later, break out of the eternal recurrence? The answer, of course, is no. The dynamic strategist is concerned only with his own immediate survival and prosperity or, at most, that of close family members. Hence the technology option is merely the unintended consequence – and a highly unlikely one at that – of the individual struggle for a more secure and better life. And as it was unintended and unsought, the Intelligence Revolution was a matter of blind chance. Only those who believe in some sort of divine purpose – such as the creationists and advocates of scientism like James Lovelock and James Gardner – could conclude otherwise. The organism/species paradox is the reason that James Gardner's argument about the cosmic supermind cerating offspring universes with which it cannot communicate is flawed.

What then is required to enable the inadvertent substitution of the technology option for the exhausted genetic option? What is required to break out of the eternal recurrence? Here are a number of essential, but not necessarily exhaustive, conditions.

- Life forms need to develop central nervous systems. This eliminates all non-vertebrate life forms such as bacteria, viruses, soft-bodied marine organisms, as well as the extensive plant kingdom. Hence, the vast majority of life forms that have ever existed on Earth must be disqualified from the race. As far as the technology option is concerned, the development paths "chosen" by these life forms were all dead ends. Yet these highly successful life forms neither know nor care.

- For vertebrates to develop the large brains required to stumble on the technology option, they needed to develop endothermic (warm-blooded) systems, so as to control body temperature and keep it at a constant level. Just a slight change of body temperature in either direction renders large and complex brains inoperative. This requirement rules out all ectothermic (cold-blooded) animals such as fish, amphibians, reptiles and insects. The ability to generate the technology option now depends on a few eccentric dynasties: the protomammals (or therapsids) that emerged as recently as 240 myrs ago; the archosaurs from 225 myrs BP; and the dinosaurs from 190 myrs BP. But most species in these dynasties failed the following additional test.

- It is also essential that warm-blooded vertebrates opt for finesse rather than force in their strategic pursuit. Without this vital ingredient there will be no pressure to increase brain size from the minimum required to effectively pursue the four-fold dynamic strategies (see Chapter 11). This eliminates the archosaurs and dinosaurs completely (actually they, with the exception of birds, eliminated themselves!) and all but one small and insignificant (at the time) branch of the protomammals.

- Having barely survived the "world war" of the dinosaurs, a small shrew-like descendent of the protomammals needed not only to engage in the strategic pursuit with finesse rather than force just to survive on the margins of the dinosaur world, but to do so at a pace that enabled the technology option to be stumbled upon *before* the family-multiplication strategy of their extensive mammal family was exhausted and the terminal conquest strategy embarked upon. But none of these "decision makers" knew that time was running out; and had they know they would not have given a damn.

- In retrospect it is clear that only one small branch of the extensive mammalian family that had generally employed finesse rather than force in the strategic pursuit had the necessary intellectual potential. This small and insignificant branch was occupied by the primates. And among the primates only the hominids seemed to be keeping to a feasible time schedule; and among the hominids only *Homo* looked like getting across the finishing line, provided they got a move on! Had we all taken the path chosen by the apeman *Australopithecus robustus*, who pursued the more specialized substrategy (of the family-multiplication strategy) of nut-and-tuber eating rather than meat-and-marrow eating (which enabled the great global diaspora), then this race of blind man's buff would have been lost. Larger brains were needed to pursue this global version of the family-multiplication strategy, as explained in my book *The Collapse of Darwinism* (2003: ch. 12).

- And it was a race barely completed by man – who had no realization of his victory – because there are signs that the family-multiplication strategy for the entire mammalian dynasty was approaching global exhaustion. Indeed, the heroic attempt made by mankind to generalize their version of this strategy and to break out of their restricted and highly specialized environment (that trapped the apemen) reflects an obviously exhausting strategy. Had they not succeeded against all the odds, or had a modest catastrophe wiped out their very small (not more than a few thousand individuals some 3–2 myrs ago) and concentrated (in a few restricted regions of one continent, Africa) numbers, the great wheel of life would have continued to turn unwittingly and relentlessly in endless time without gaining any upward traction. Life on Earth only broke out of the eternal recurrence through the agency of one small, insignificant, and deviant species from the vast numbers that had existed over the previous 3,800 myrs.

Owing to these extremely stringent requirements, we can reasonably conclude that the probability of the technology option ever being "discovered" was extremely, extremely low. It was merely the fortuitous outcome of a long chain of highly unlikely, unforeseen, and unsought events. The implication, therefore, is that intelligence is not only the scarcest resource on Earth but also its likelihood of occurring or existing anywhere else in the Universe is very, very low. Most likely we are alone in the Universe and that any life elsewhere – which undoubtedly exists – is dominated by the "great wheel". This makes nonsense of scientism's argument that the entire purpose of the Universe is to give birth to a supermind. In the highly unlikely event that intelligent life does emerge elsewhere, the probability is that it will lag considerably behind that on Earth owing to the remarkably fortuitous causal chain that we have experienced.

CONCLUSIONS

This chapter provides an outline of life's great odyssey over the past 3,800 myrs. It shows that this journey has been characterized by exponential growth in biological/GDP output governed by the logological constant; by the great waves of life of growing intensity; by the great biological and technological paradigm shifts; and by the great wheel of life. It has been argued that the mammalian break out from the eternal recurrence was a matter of blind chance and that, accordingly, intelligent life is the most scarce resource in the Universe. This puts paid to the current idea in scientism that a superintelligence or supermind is shaping the destiny of the cosmos. Further, these are the characteristics, or patterns, of life that require explanation in this final part of the book. For this reason, a general dynamic theory is presented in the next chapter.

Chapter 11
Selfcreation – A Realist Theory of Life

With the main characteristics of the great odyssey of life outlined in Chapter 10, a general dynamic theory that can explain these patterns of time is required. Accordingly, an outline of the dynamic-strategy theory – first presented in *The Dynamic Society* (1996) and developed further in *The Collapse of Darwinism* (2003) – is provided in this chapter. The dynamic-strategy theory has shown itself to be highly successful in explaining the dynamics of both life and human society. It is a realist theory about the process of selfcreation, which can be contrasted with metaphysical theories of self-organization and complexity. Quite unexpectedly, the construction of the dynamic-strategy theory revealed the hidden vehicle of life, which I have called the strategic *logos* and have examined in Chapter 12.

What are the characteristics of a truly dynamic theory of life? Unlike the Darwinian algorithm of natural selection – the only universally accepted scientific theory of life – a general dynamic theory must focus on *processes* or mechanisms, as well as *outcomes*. These processes will involve the interactions between individual organisms and their social and physical environments, the **dynamic strategies** they adopt to survive and prosper, the manner in which these strategies operate at the micro- and macro-biological levels, as well as the impacts these strategies have upon the physical and social worlds.

An endogenous dynamic theory will be self-starting and self-sustaining – in a word, "selfcreating" – subject only to *passive* inputs (sunlight and various chemical substances) from the physical world. And the dynamic life-system will respond positively and creatively, rather than passively and reactively, to external shocks. Exogenous shocks are likely to be of two main types: those emanating from the physical world, including shifting tectonic plates, changing climates, and changing sea levels; and those generated by other life forms, such as disease and invasion. Such a theory must be relevant to both the natural and humans worlds because, as I show in Chapter 10, both share the same dynamic characteristics. The theory, therefore, is outlined here at its most general level, despite our focus on religious institutions in human society.

THE DYNAMIC-STRATEGY THEORY – A BRIEF OUTLINE

The dynamic-strategy theory consists of four interrelated elements and one random force, as outlined below and shown graphically in Figure 12.1:

1. The competitive driving force of individual organisms to survive and prosper – the concept of strategic desire – provides the theory with its self-starting and self-sustaining nature.

2. The dynamic strategies – including genetic/technological change, family multiplication, commerce (symbiosis), and conquest – are employed by individual organisms through the process of strategic selection, to achieve their objectives.

3. The strategic struggle is the main "political" instrument by which established individuals/species (old strategists) attempt to maintain their control over the sources of their prosperity, and by which emerging individuals/species (new strategists) attempt to usurp such control.

4. The constraining force operating on the dynamics of a species/dynasty is the eventual exhaustion of the dominant dynamic strategy/paradigm pursued by its members, which leads to the emergence of internal/external conflict and to collapse.

5. Exogenous shocks, both physical (continental drift, volcanic action, weather events, asteroid impact) and biological (disease and invasion), impact randomly, distortingly, but marginally, on this endogenously driven dynamic system. Since the 1970s, scientists claim that climate has been shaped in part by human activity.

In the dynamic-strategy theory, therefore, the very long-run driving force arises from the universal motivation of all living organisms – to survive and prosper at any cost. And the wave-like process of biological/economic activity by which this is achieved is generated by the creative exploitation and exhaustion of the dynamic strategies aimed at accessing natural resources. The ultimate constraints on life, therefore, arise from the very sources of its expansion and growth. Both are internal to the theory, and they are strategic not physical. Exogenous forces, on the other hand, in the form of physical and organic shocks, do *not* drive or systematically shape the dynamic process of life, but they do occasionally distort the systematic pattern in a largely random manner. Importantly, the internal dynamic always rapidly asserts itself following any such shock, which, at most, temporarily impacts upon the endogenous dynamic pathway. The reason for this, as shown in Chapter 12, is the robust nature of the strategic *logos*.

The dynamic-strategy theory is a theory about selfcreation. And the essence of selfcreation is found in the creative exchange between purposeful agents and their society's unfolding dynamic strategy. It is this **strategic exchange** that lies at the very heart of the self-sustaining dynamics of living systems. Social agents are self-motivated and self-driven, and they generate complexity and order in a *creative* response to a continuously changing **strategic demand**. It is this *creative exchange* between the demand and supply sides of a dynamic living system (or strategic *logos*) that generates changing genetic structures, technologies, ideas of all types, institutions and organizations. By attempting to meet this constantly changing strategic demand, both the agents and their society are transformed in the long run. The creative process of exchange by which this takes place constitutes the "life-system" for the group of social agents in whom we are interested. Living systems, therefore, are **autogenous** – or **selfcreating** – systems.[1]

The driving force

The endogenous force in life is the **strategic desire** of all individual organisms to survive and prosper. Basically, this is the need for living organisms, no matter how simple or how complex, to obtain sufficient fuel to feed their metabolic processes. Without fuel, the constituent cells in a living organism begin to break down and die. A systematic examination of the history of life and human society – presented in my books *The Dynamic Society* (1996), *The Ephemeral Civilization* (1997), *Laws of History* (1998) and *The Collapse of Darwinism* (2003) – shows that organisms attempt at all costs to survive *and*, having survived, to prosper. This can be characterized as the **materialist organism** and **materialist man**. It is the essence (and definition) of life, which has shaped our genetic and technological structure from the very beginning. Organisms that fail to embody strategic desire strongly, overwhelmingly, are eliminated from the gene pool.

To achieve this fundamental objective, organisms adopt the particular dynamic strategy that is expected to maximize their probability of survival and prosperity. This trial-and-error procedure (*not* a cost-benefit calculation) is strongly influenced by the prevailing degree of external competition. In *The Collapse of Darwinism* (2003) I show that, contrary to Darwinian convention, intense competition leads to the adoption of the conquest strategy and to death and extinction; whereas minimal competition leads to the genetic strategy and to prolific speciation; and more "normal" competition generates the family-multiplication and commerce strategies that in turn lead to rapid population growth and diaspora. This is not a haphazard affair. In each case a dynamic strategy is "chosen" because it is the most effective one available in the prevailing physical and social environments.

But how do individuals from the lowest to highest life forms make these choices? There are two existing extremist answers to this question provided by the neo-Darwinists and the neoliberal (economic rationalist) economists. The neo-Darwinists insist it is our genes that decide behavior, while the neoliberal economists insist it is our rational faculties or ideas.[2] Some readers might be tempted to say that the neo-Darwinists are right about animals and the neoliberals are right about humans. This, however, would only maintain the unsupportable dualism in our attitude to life – a dualism that Darwin and, particularly, Wallace tried unsuccessfully to eliminate more than a century ago.

Neither the neo-Darwinists nor the rationalists are correct in this matter for *any* life form, high or low. Essentially the same process of decision making is employed by all life forms, and that is determined *neither* by genes *nor* by ideas. Instead it is determined by strategic desire – the desire to survive and prosper. Both genes and ideas, combined in varying proportions by different life forms, merely facilitate desires. They encode and translate the methods by which desires are successfully achieved.

As genes and ideas do not drive animal society but merely facilitate the desires of its members, we need to replace both the neo-Darwinist genetic model and the neoliberal rationalist model with a realist theory of decision making. Through the inductive method employed in my earlier books it has been possible to derive a theory of "decision making" relevant to both low and high life forms and, thereby, finally eliminate the present dualism. I call it the **strategic-imitation** model of decision making. [3]

In reality, decision making is based on the need to economize on nature's scarcest resource – intelligence. This is clearly the case with lower life forms, and it is one of the reasons that neo-Darwinists have opted for the "genetic leash" argument (the other is that they are professional geneticists of one sort or another, and have a vested interest in claiming that genes rule life). But what of our own species? The neoliberal rationalists have adopted a totally unrealistic view of human decision making involving: the construction of mental models about the way the world works; the collection of vast quantities of economic cost-benefit information; and the possession of rapid and accurate intellectual processing abilities.

The strategic-imitation theory rejects both the anti-intellectual view of the neo-Darwinists and the supraintellectual view of the neoliberal rationalists. In the real world, in contrast to the fantasy worlds of these game-playing deductionists, individuals do make choices. But rather than acting like computers the great majority of animals, including humans, merely imitate those individuals and those activities that are conspicuously successful. This means that the only information sought by the vast majority of decision makers is that needed to answer the simple, but key, question: who is successful and why? In this way the many follow the successful few.

The "few" are the strategic pioneers and the "many" are the strategic followers. This is how and why religions emerge and flourish so readily. The only information decision makers require is the relatively costless **imitative information**, not the prohibitively expensive cost-benefit information; and the only intellectual faculty needed is that required to determine that some of one's peers are more successful than others. Even the strategic pioneers do not employ rationalist techniques when seeking new ways of exploiting strategic opportunities. Rather than using sophisticated techniques to calculate the "best" solution from the large number available, the pioneers believe that their intuitively chosen solutions *are* the best. Only a few will have their universally optimistic expectations vindicated, but it is the "fewest of the few" who are slavishly imitated by the many. While the tendency for animals to imitate each other has received widespread recognition, the strategic-imitation model is the first to employ this act as part of a general dynamic theory – as in my books *The Dynamic Society* (1996) and *The Collapse of Darwinism* (2003).

But what of life forms without any intellectual capacity at all? Organisms in pursuit of survival and prosperity control their dynamic strategies through a number of **strategic instruments**, including brains in organisms that possess them and special genes in those that do not. In *The Collapse of Darwinism* and *The Selfcreating Mind* I call these instruments the **strategic cerebrum** and the **strategic gene**. Early life forms were able to pursue the full range of dynamic strategies without the use of central nervous systems or brains.[4] Simple life forms possess a gene or genes that switch dynamic strategies on and off according to the availability of nutrients and the degree of competition. Considerable scientific research has been conducted on this topic.[5] The only matter in dispute is who is in control of this process, the selfish gene or the selfish organism.

There is a sound empirical and theoretical basis for my view that it is the selfish organism that controls its dynamic strategies through the strategic gene. Even genetic structures are shaped by the choices made by organisms in the strategic pursuit. The reason that organisms eventually developed central nervous systems and quickly substituted the strategic cerebrum for the strategic gene was to more effectively supervise their dynamic strategies as they became more complex. The brain is a far more flexible and imaginative instrument of strategic control than the strategic gene. Accordingly the strategic gene was abandoned by more advanced organisms. There can be no doubt where the real power over life lay. This argument was originally presented in *The Collapse of Darwinism* (2003, ch. 12) and developed more fully in *The Selfcreating Mind* (2006: part III).

The dynamic mechanism

Strategic desire is a self-starting and self-sustaining force that drives a dynamic mechanism centered on the strategic pursuit. It is a process involving the adoption and exploitation of the most effective available dynamic strategy (or substrategy) by the **materialist organism** – or **materialist man** – to achieve its objective of survival and prosperity. A dynamic strategy begins as an individual or a family activity which, if successful, is adopted by successively wider social groups, at first local, then regional and, finally, global. This aggregation process, which involves a progression from the micro- to macro-biological/economic levels, takes place via the strategic-imitation mechanism by which conspicuous success is rapidly copied. In this way, a successful dynamic strategy becomes widespread throughout a population, a species, even a dynasty.

The sequence of dynamic strategies

The choice of dynamic strategy – from four possibilities including genetic/ technological change, family multiplication, commerce (symbiosis), and conquest – depends on the underlying material and social conditions, such as the relative abundance of natural resources and the degree of external competition. It is important to realize that organisms "invest" energy and resources in each of these dynamic strategies at different times and under different conditions to achieve the same universal objective – survival and prosperity.

Typically, organisms in a given species will pursue a sequence of strategies from the time they begin to diverge from the parent species or society until they finally go extinct. The **strategic sequence** prior to the emergence of human society 2 myrs ago was typically genetic change $\rightarrow$ family multiplication (or commerce) $\rightarrow$ conquest. Each dynamic strategy is continuously exploited until it is exhausted, which leads to a temporary crisis until a new strategy can be developed and employed in the species' strategic pursuit. If, in a normally competitive environment, a new strategy cannot be found to replace an old, exhausted strategy, that species will collapse and go extinct prematurely. Accordingly, this strategic sequence leads not to a linear development path but – as shown in Chapter 10 – to a series of biological/economic waves, which describe the phases of expansion, stagnation, crisis, decline and, with a lapse in time, renewed expansion.

Imagine a non-Darwinian world characterized by minimal competition and abundant resources that emerges following the dramatic extinction of an earlier animal dynasty. Contrary to the predictions of Darwin's theory of natural selection, this is precisely the time when surviving organisms invest energy in the **genetic strategy**, because they have both the time and opportunity to exploit abundant resources. By creating a new **genetic style** (or species) they are able to gain more intensive access to employed resources and/or new access to unused resources. The resulting increase in biomass per input of resources is equivalent to economic growth generated by technological change in human society.

How, we need to ask, are organisms able to manipulate genetic change and turn it to the advantage of themselves and their families? Basically it involves the new concept of **strategic selection** that is a response to strategic demand. While only a brief outline can be given here, strategic selection is discussed in detail in *The Collapse of Darwinism* (2003: ch. 12). A beneficial mutation that improves an organism's access to resources will attract the attention of those with similar abilities or aspirations. These individuals will cooperate and/or mate with each other, thereby improving the prospects of the existing generation as well as the genetic characteristics of the next. Selection by the organism at the phenotypic level, therefore, shapes the genotype. This is what I mean by strategic selection. It is a form of self-selection – or selfcreation – that replaces the "divine selection" of the creationists and the "natural selection" of the Darwinists. Over very long periods of time this key principle is responsible for the upsurge in speciation that always follows a major extinction – an outcome that Darwinian natural selection cannot explain.

Strategic selection is also the answer to the question that has always been a great embarrassment to the neo-Darwinists: why sex? They are unable to satisfactorily explain the "popularity" of sex as a means of replication, because their central dogma about "reproductive success" – that organisms attempt to maximize copies of their genes in the gene pool – requires that asexual reproduction, which enables individuals to pass on copies of *all* their genes rather than just half of them, should be the norm. Clearly this is not the case with sexual reproduction.

The dynamic-strategy argument about sex is that it provides individuals with greater control over their dynamic strategies. This is the concept of **selective sexual reproduction**. In the first place, reproduction through sex enables individuals to choose partners that display characteristics, both physical and instinctual, most needed in the particular dynamic strategy they are pursuing. For genetic change one requires characteristics that can provide better access to natural resources; for family multiplication, those that provide greater fertility and mobility; for commerce (symbiosis), those that enable the monopolization and exchange of strategic resources; and for conquest, those that enable "military" success and territorial domination. Organisms are able to pursue and change dynamic strategies more effectively by being able to choose between the different physical and instinctual characteristics embodied in potential mates. Second, sexual reproduction increases the rate of mutation and genetic variety in the family, both of which are the primary material for the dynamic strategy of genetic change and for the diversity of family abilities required to maximize strategic opportunities more generally. And third, sexual reproduction provides the basis for specialization and division of labor along gender lines in family groups, thereby increasing both strategic efficiency and the probability of strategic success. Essentially, all these matters provide organisms with greater control over life's strategic pursuit.

Once a new genetic style (or species) has fully emerged, the dynamic strategy of genetic change will have exhausted itself. It will, therefore, be more cost-effective in terms of metabolic energy use for an organism to switch investment from the genetic to the **family-multiplication strategy**. A higher cost-effectiveness in energy use is translated into a higher probability of survival and prosperity. The new dynamic strategy will lead to an exclusive focus by organisms on the procreation and migration needed to fully exploit the new genetic style. In this way the members of our new species can outflank their parent and sibling species by rapidly increasing their populations and spreading throughout the accessible world. All the great diasporas in life have been based on the family-multiplication strategy. It is a strategy that leads to "expansion" (more resources accessed by larger numbers of organisms at the same degree of intensity) rather than "growth" (more intensive resource use), and it occurs during periods of "normal" competition – competition that is neither minimal nor extreme. Indeed, individuals and families are able to escape extreme competition by migrating to unoccupied or underoccupied regions.

This expansion phase is characterized in some species by the individual's pursuit of the more specialized **dynamic strategy of commerce** or symbiosis. It is a strategy that involves the interaction between individuals in two different species (or societies), each specializing in access to different resources and "trading" with the other for mutual gain. These "commercial" relationships exist between organisms in different species of plants, different animals and plants, and different species of animals. Examples include: algae and coral polyps; algae and fungi (lichens); acacias that house and feed ant colonies in return for protection; ants that culture fungi for food; bacteria in the digestive systems of many animal species – to name just a few. Similarly mutually beneficial relationships also characterize human societies. The great commerce societies of the past – as seen in earlier chapters – have included the Egyptians, Phoenicians, Greeks, Carthaginians, Venetians, Dutch, and British.

In both the family-multiplication and commerce strategies, the choice of, and cooperation between, associates and sexual partners is based not on the ability to exploit existing resources more intensively but on the ability either to procreate and migrate, or to monopolize and trade scarce resources/commodities. In other words, through the operation of "strategic selection", benign mutations in the expansion phase will be ignored (by the selective sexual reproduction mechanism) unless they assist in promoting the family-multiplication or commerce strategies. It is for this reason alone that the genetic profile of a species will approximate what has been misleadingly called "punctuated equilibria" by Niles Eldredge and Stephen Gould.[6]

By the time a genetic style has been exhausted through procreation and migration, resources available to individuals in this species will be scarce, resulting in intense competition for them. This produces a crisis, because the earlier family-multiplication and commerce strategies will have generated levels of population and consumption that can only be maintained by a continuous inflow of natural resources. To prevent going under during such a crisis, individuals search for a new dynamic strategy to replace the old exhausted one. The only possibility in these circumstances of constrained time and resources is the **conquest strategy**. As usual, this new strategy starts at the individual level and, if successful, progresses to the regional, national and global levels through the strategic-imitation mechanism.

With the exhaustion of any given genetic style (once the family-multiplication strategy has come to an end) individuals in that species will battle fiercely with each other for the diminishing supply of resources as overpopulation damages their ecosystem. In the process, they will turn upon each other to take control of key resources. This type of conquest strategy, which can be likened to civil war, renders a species vulnerable to a takeover of their ecosystem by a closely competing species or to any adverse change in their physical environment. Extinction of the species in these circumstances is highly probably. The fossil record shows that extinction also happens under these conditions in closely interacting groups of species, when the exhaustion of their genetic styles coincides.

When the wider **genetic paradigm** (see Figure 10.1) of an era is exhausted, the entire dynasty resorts to the conquest strategy and is plunged into "world war", which ultimately leads to the extinction of the entire dynasty. But as this world war is waged over a period of hundreds of thousands of years, many species employ genetic change to support their conquest strategies by developing offensive and defensive biological weapons.[7] This add-on "technology" is a response to changing **strategic demand** as the conquest strategy unfolds. Organisms do not have the time or resources to effect a complete genetic transformation.

Hence the Darwinian world of scarce natural resources and intense competition leads not to "evolution" through natural selection but to conquest and, ultimately, the extinction of the entire dynasty. Only once the old *non-*Darwinian world of minimal competition and resource abundance has been ushered in does directional genetic change and speciation occur once more. While Darwinism has collapsed just as surely as the dinosaurs, most scientists pretend not to have noticed.

The reason that the conquest strategy in human society did not lead to the extinction of humanity, was the role played by technological change – an option not open to other species. Conquest in human society is a neolithic dynamic strategy, and its systematic pursuit by a succession of civilizations – such as Assyria, Babylon, Persia, Macedonia, Rome, Parthia, and medieval Europe – is the mechanism by which the neolithic technological paradigm was eventually exhausted (Figure 10.4), opening the way for the Industrial Revolution and the introduction of the technological strategy. It was the technological strategy that prevented conquest from eventually destroying mankind and his natural environment. Wars in the industrial technological era by leading nations are self-defeating and short term, because they are not as materially rewarding as the technological strategy. Without the technology option, mankind would have gone the same way as the dinosaurs.

The dynamic strategies employed in human society are the same as those discussed above for all pre-human dynasties. The main difference is the historical sequence in which these strategies have been utilized. The old sequence, as we have seen, was genetic change → family multiplication or commerce → conquest; and it was determined by the eternal recurrence of the great wheel of life – of the cyclical process of genetic rise and fall. With the substitution of the new technology option for the old genetic option, a new strategic sequence was introduced. Instead of being cyclical it was progressive, and was advanced by the technological paradigm shifts discussed in Chapter 10. Hence, the earliest human dynamic strategy, which was associated with the paleolithic technological paradigm, was the family-multiplication strategy. The pursuit of this strategy –

leading to the great diaspora of mankind –eventually exhausted the paleolithic paradigm (about 10,600 years BP) and opened the way for the Neolithic Revolution of agriculture. During the era of the neolithic technological paradigm the dynamic strategies of conquest and commerce were employed to raise material living standards above the level that could be generated by agricultural productivity. In earlier chapters we have seen how successful conquest (Rome) and commerce (Egypt) societies were in achieving this objective. The pursuit of conquest and commerce eventually exhausted the neolithic technological paradigm (by the mid-eighteenth century), and opened the way for the Industrial Revolution and the industrial technological strategy. But while the strategic sequence of humanity is different to that of non-human species, the objective and basic operation of these strategies is very similar. Even the strategic cerebrum plays only a facilitating role in the strategic pursuit of mankind.

A dynamic form for the new theory

As individual organisms seek to exploit their physical and social environments, which sets in train a mass movement orchestrated through strategic imitation, the dominant dynamic strategy unfolds. By this I mean that the materialist opportunities inherent in the strategy are progressively exploited and, finally, exhausted. This unfolding process generates a great wave of biological/ economic output, as discussed in Chapter 10 and illustrated in Figure 10.1. It is important to realize, however, that there is nothing automatic, inevitable, or teleological about this unfolding process, which is merely the outcome of dynamic strategists exploring and investing in existing strategic opportunities. Herein lies a stark contrast with the metaphysical and teleological theories of Gaia and the Biocosm discussed in Chapter 9.

But why and how does the expansion of a species/society lead ultimately to strategic exhaustion? As I show in *The Dynamic Society* (1996: ch. 12) and *The Collapse of Darwinism* (2003: ch. 15), strategic exhaustion is the outcome of the "law of diminishing strategic returns". A stage is reached in the expansionary phase of a species/society when each additional unit of metabolic energy/total resources invested by individuals in the dominant dynamic strategy leads to a decline in additional units of resources accessed. Eventually, the extra or marginal unit of energy/resource cost will be driven down to equality with marginal resource returns. At this point in time the dynamic strategy is exhausted and it will be abandoned, because any further expenditure of energy/ resources would fail to pay for itself. No life form can afford to expend more energy/resources than it is able to access through its dynamic strategies. Thereafter, stagnation of the species/society sets in, followed by a general decline as many individuals are unable to obtain sufficient resources to satisfy basic requirements.

The rise and fall of a dynamic strategy pursued by individuals in a species/ society, or even a dynasty, traces out a distinctive strategic pathway in terms of biomass/GDP, which can be seen in the fossil and historical record. This strategic process has been discussed in my books *The Ephemeral Civilization* (1997) and *The Collapse of Darwinism* (2003). Because our evidence for human society is more complete than for the rest of life, the nature of our theory's dynamic form can best be illustrated by selecting a country for which reliable long-run data can be obtained. The best-documented country for the past millennium is England. The strategic sequence of conquest → commerce → technological change can be seen reflected quite clearly in the case of England over the past millennium in Figure 5.4. Here we can see the three great waves of economic change for England: the first generated by conquest; the second by commerce; and the third by technological change. While the evidence is less complete, similar great waves corresponding to a sequence of dynamic strategies can be seen driving all viable societies. The same is true of non-human societies.

What the evidence suggests, therefore, is that the dynamic-strategy theory expresses itself through a series of biological/economic waves within waves. The great waves of life (of geometrically declining duration), shown in Figure 10.1, generated by the rise and fall of biological dynasties, encompasses the long waves (of about 30 myrs) generated by the rise and fall of groups of species, which in turn contain the shorter waves (of up to 6 myrs or so) generated by the rise and fall of significant individual species. In human society, as we have seen, there are the great economic waves of about 300 years, which contain long waves of about 40 to 60 years, and short waves of about 5 to 20 years. At all levels in both life and society, these waves are generated by the exploitation, exhaustion, and replacement of dynamic strategies, genetic/technological styles, and genetic/technological paradigms. This pattern of waves within waves, therefore, constitutes the dynamic form of our theory and models. Owing to historical contingency and exogenous influences, the duration of these waves can never be precisely predicted, but they can be identified in a rough and ready way.

Strategic demand and strategic confidence
The unfolding dynamic strategy, driven by the competitive energy of materialist organism/man, plays a central role in our theory. Not only does it provide a realistic dynamic form, but it also gives rise to the two important concepts of **strategic demand** and **strategic confidence**. These concepts are important in explaining not only the investment of energy/resources by organisms in the four-fold dynamic strategies, but also the impetus for the fundamental process of strategic selection.

Strategic confidence, which rises and falls with the dominant dynamic strategy, is the cement that binds society together. It is responsible for the dynamic order that underlies the trust and cooperation between individuals in any social group. Rather than having trust in each other – which neither sociobiologists nor economic rationalists are able to convincingly explain –

individuals have confidence in their successful joint dynamic strategy, owing to the stream of resources and income it provides. It is this *strategic* confidence that gives rise to the decisions made by organisms to invest energy/resources in the dominant dynamic strategy. In contrast, when a dynamic strategy is exhausted, the evaporating strategic confidence contributes to the emerging crisis in the species/society by fracturing the orderly relationship between individuals. Only when a new strategy arises does strategic confidence, and hence order, stability and trust, return. As I show in *The Ephemeral Civilization*, fundamental strategic confidence – rather than ephemeral consumer confidence favored by orthodox economists – is the key to understanding the process of depression and recovery in human society.[8]

Strategic demand, which is *the* core concept in the dynamic-strategy theory, also rises and falls as the dynamic strategy unfolds. It comprises the dynamic demand generated by the **strategists**, or individual decision makers, for a range of inputs required in the strategic pursuit as a continuum through time. To exploit strategic opportunities, individuals need to invest in infrastructure (the fabric of shelters, burrows, nests, beaver dams, farms, cities, transport and communications, organizations) and "ideas" (both genetic and technological); to pass on acquired knowledge to the younger generation; and to develop and enforce social conventions, organizational relationships, and strategic ideologies. As far as this book on strategic ideology and religion is concerned, it is strategic demand that accounts for the origin and change in religious ideas, rites, and institutions. While local cultural and social influences (which are the outcome of earlier strategic demand) influence the superficial characteristics of society, it is strategic demand that determines the more fundamental aspects of strategic ideology/religion. Societies at the same stage in a technological paradigm, pursuing the same dynamic strategy, will have, at the fundamental level, very similar strategic ideologies/religions.

Strategic demand, therefore, is the central active principle in life. And it is the formal recognition of this critically important fact that makes the dynamic-strategy theory unique in an intellectual world of supply-side theories. Naturally, the supply response in terms of population change, infrastructure, construction, and genetic/technological change – which in turn is influenced by the relative scarcity of these factors reflected in "relative factor prices" – will contribute to the way in which strategic opportunities are exploited. But they do so passively. It is strategic demand that creates its own supply, *not* the other way around as most scientists, both natural and social believe. At the center of this strategic demand-supply response is **strategic inflation**. As I show in *Longrun Dynamics* (1998), in human society, *strategic* inflation is *essential* for long-run economic growth. This is why inflation targeting is economically untenable and socially unacceptable (Snooks 2008b; 2008c). The only problem with strategic inflation is the orthodox attempt – based on a fear of societal change – to deflate the economy to eliminate it. No strategic inflation, no long-run economic growth.

This is reflected in my discovery of the growth-inflation curve. *Nonstrategic* inflation – the outcome of poor monetary policy and exogenous price shocks – however, should be controlled.

In non-monetized human society and animal society, "strategic inflation" takes a non-price form. Yet the role is just the same. Those resources that are much in demand for reasons of survival are highly "valued" and competition for them is intense. Where these resources are embodied in certain individuals or groups of individuals, these individuals are highly sought after so that their status in their group and their feelings of self-worth are enhanced. This greater "value", "sense of self-worth", and "status" in non-monetarized societies, whether human or non-human, operates to the same end as strategic inflation in more sophisticated societies. It provides an indication of the urgent requirement of the dynamic strategy being pursued by society. The equivalent of inflation targeting in non-monetarized societies would be to suppress the status and sense of self-worth of individuals urgently required by a society's dynamic strategy. Herein lies its irrationality.

The strategic struggle

A mechanism central to the "politics" of life is the **strategic struggle**. It is entered into by individuals attempting to maintain or take control of their "society", and by groups, populations, and species attempting to replace old genetic or technological styles/paradigms with new ones. To do so, these individuals and groups employ the dynamic tactics of order and chaos. The tactics of order, which are used by insiders to maintain and exploit the status quo, include the threat of punishment or ostracism, and the enforcement of customary "rules". And the tactics of chaos, which are used by outsiders to disrupt the existing order, include attempts to undermine the authority of the existing leader, or even to challenge him to combat (or, in modern political parties, to a leadership challenge in the party room). In each case, the aim is to either maintain or usurp control of the dominant dynamic strategy. Why? Because it is the source of society's ability to survive and prosper and therefore of great personal wealth and power for the strategic leader.

The common occurrence in many species of intimidation and conflict between males is not, as the neo-Darwinists claim, primarily about sex. Males battle for supremacy, we are told with mind-numbing frequency, to maximize the presence of their genes in the gene pool by mating with as many females as possible. But in reality, males battle with each other to gain control over the sources of their society's dynamic strategy, which in the animal world involve territories that provide access to food and shelter. They battle, in other words, to become the leading strategist in their group. Their conflict is part of the struggle for "political" control of their "society". Having won this battle and maintained/ hijacked strategic control, which ensures his survival, the **strategic leader** is in a good position to maximize his prosperity, which involves the consumption of food, sex and, for the time being, leisure. While procreation assumes greater significance when it is a response to the strategic demand generated by the dynamic strategy of family multiplication, even then it is merely a means to a more important end.

The strategic struggle also plays a central role in the rise and fall of genetic/technological styles and paradigms. With the exhaustion of a genetic style, for example, individuals within a species battle with each other for control over the depleting sources of their dynamic strategy. Like warlords in a world of conquest, they attempt to assume strategic leadership to improve their prospects of survival and prosperity at the expense of others in their species. More significant, however, is the strategic struggle that emerges when an entire genetic paradigm approaches exhaustion. In these circumstances, the struggle takes place between the old strategists – the leaders of the old dominant dynasty – and the new strategists – the leaders of the newly emergent or resurgent dynasty. Because the old strategists have been weakened by the exhaustion of their genetic paradigm, the strategic struggle eventually favors the new strategists, such as the triumph of the archosaurs (protodinosaurs) over the therapsids (protomammals).[9] But, as we have seen, this may involve many regional battles throughout the accessible world over tens, even hundreds, of thousands of years. In these battles, the old strategists employ the dynamic tactics of order, while the new strategists employ those of chaos.

As is well known, similar struggles occur in human society during critical times, when technological strategies and paradigms are exhausted. Whenever a human dynamic strategy approaches exhaustion, the old and new strategists struggle for the leadership of their society, as it provides control over the diminishing sources of their wealth. An example is the struggle between the old gentrified commerce leaders and the new industrialists in Britain in the first half of the nineteenth century.[10] More serious, however, is the strategic struggle in societies that have exhausted their entire strategic sequence – such as Rome after 190 AD – because it involves a terminal conflict between groups of strategist within and without its borders.[11] Finally, there is the struggle for global supremacy between leading societies when the prevailing technological paradigm is finally exhausted. The most recent example is the exhaustion of the neolithic technological paradigm in the mid-eighteenth century. This precipitated a struggle for technological supremacy between the leading powers of Western Europe, which ultimately led to the disastrous consequences of the First World War, 1914–1918. Will there be a similar outcome when the industrial paradigm exhausts itself later in the twenty-first century? Only if we fail to learn the lessons, not of the past, but of dynamic-strategy theory.

Strategic exhaustion

The force constraining life is not the limited supply of natural resources but rather the limitations of society's dynamic strategies. Many readers will have difficulties with this concept. To their minds, natural resources are finite, so that, once a species (including mankind) or a dynasty has "used up" its resources, its ecosystem will crash. This is the flawed thinking behind the currently popular concept of "sustainable development". Fortunately this type of thinking is not correct, otherwise life would have stagnated, or even collapsed, about 3,500 myrs ago when heterotrophic life forms (which are unable to use photosynthesis to manufacture their own food supply) exhausted the supply of free-floating organic molecules to create the world's first "energy crisis". Life was able to continue owing to genetic innovation – owing to the creation of new life forms that could employ existing resources more effectively.

The entire history of life on Earth is a story about organisms employing dynamic strategies to gain access to natural resources. This access occurs in two ways: a more intensive and a more extensive use of resources. To gain more intensive access to a given stock of resources, organisms employ either the genetic or the technological dynamic strategy. This requires the creation of new genetic or technological styles and, at the wider level, of new genetic or technological skills. Organisms can extract a greater stream of services from existing resources, thereby increasing output per unit of input or productivity. An obvious example in human society is the application of machinery and fertilizers to agricultural land to increase crop yields; while in the early stages of life on Earth, cyanobacteria (or blue-green algae) by breaking down water to gain hydrogen were six times more efficient than sulphur (or green and purple) bacteria, which obtained hydrogen by breaking down hydrogen sulphide.

To gain more extensive access to the Earth's natural resources, organisms have taken their new genetic or technological styles to previously inaccessible areas by the pursuit of the family-multiplication, commerce, or conquest strategies. For example, before the emergence of mankind, dispersion was made possible by the Endothermic Revolution whereby newly emerged warm-blooded animals could, for the first time, migrate to the planet's colder regions. And in human society, the invention of windmills, for example, enabled the extension of agricultural lands through the draining of marshes. Hence, the supply of natural resources is limited only by the effectiveness of our dynamic strategies. In other words, the supply of resources can only be defined relatively (rather than absolutely) in terms of the dynamic strategies available to exploit them.

Strategic exhaustion operates at a number of levels. The first of these is at the level of the species or individual genetic style. A new genetic style, which provides improved access to natural resources, is exploited by individuals in that species until its potential is exhausted. With exhaustion, a crisis occurs as population presses heavily upon natural resources. The response by individuals in the species is to opt for the "internalized" conquest strategy (civil war), which is a short-run, zero-sum game that ultimately leads to the collapse of the genetic style or species. This accounts for the so-called "background extinctions" within a dynasty.

In human society, the exhaustion of comparable technological styles (or substrategies) and even the larger dynamic strategies, are usually negotiated through a relatively peaceful strategic struggle in which the casualties are measured in terms of economic loss. But occasionally it does lead to civil war. Here are two examples, discussed in my *The Ephemeral Civilization* (1997): the English civil war of the 1640s, which was a clash between remnants of the old conquest strategists led by the recalcitrant Stuarts and the new commerce strategists led by the Parliamentarians (Oliver Cromwell); and the American civil war, which was a clash between the northern states pursuing an industrial technological strategy (wanting a protected mega-market for its output) and the southern states pursuing a commerce strategy (wanting free trade with Europe).

A more encompassing type of strategic exhaustion occurs at the levels of the dynasty and even the genetic paradigm. A new dynasty, or collection of closely related species – such as the Permian reptiles, or the protomammals, or dinosaurs, or modern mammals – exploit their joint strategic opportunities until they are finally exhausted. Approaching dynastic exhaustion is reflected in a growing rate of "background extinction" as groups of species exhaust their genetic styles, and in an increasingly depressed "origination" rate as unaccessed global resources decline. The outcome of this process is a growing dominance of the prevailing dynasty by one or two species, which is a sure sign that the dynasty is approaching exhaustion. And the outcome of dynastic exhaustion is the pursuit of conquest, the outbreak of "world war", followed by ecological crisis, collapse and, finally, dynastic extinction. While this is a terribly destructive process, it clears the way for the emergence of a new dynasty that, in its turn, will create a range of entirely new genetic styles to improve its access to natural resources. It may take the rise and fall of a number of dynasties before an old genetic paradigm (such as the ectothermic) is exhausted and a new genetic paradigm (such as the endothermic) emerges to take its place. *The meaning of life, therefore, is all about unlocking a growing stream of services from the natural resources that were inherited when the Earth was formed some 4,500 myrs ago.*

The same, of course, is true of the meaning of human society. It is sometimes harder to see this in our own lives owing to the greater complexity of our own dominant dynasty and the highly subjective manner in which we usually view it. But there is a major difference. And this concerns the outcome of the exhaustion of a technological paradigm. As suggested above, while exhausting technological paradigms – the paleolithic (10,600 BP), the neolithic (mid-eighteenth century) and the modern (mid twenty-first century) – can lead to major wars, such as the Napoleonic, First and Second World Wars, they have obviously never resulted in the collapse of our dynasty. And the reason is that technological change provides an escape from a continuous cycle of world war.

Social organization and transformation

Sociobiologists attempt to explain the social interactions between related and unrelated individuals by employing the genetically based kin-selection model. Even if we assume, just for the sake of argument, that their model is correct, sociobiologists are still unable to "explain" social interactions beyond the extended family. In particular they have failed to explain the structure of human society or the way it changes over time. And, as I show in *The Collapse of Darwinism* (2003: ch. 7), they are in fact unable to explain social relationships even in the extended family. Even those sociobiologists who favor coevolution theory are left empty handed. In the coevolution model, as we discovered in Chapter 8, human nature and action is seen as the outcome of "epigenetic" rules controlled by genes under the influence of natural selection. In this way individuals are held on a "genetic leash" – an explanation that many find offensive as well as unpersuasive – and social institutions are merely extruded from the human mind.[12] It is just another failed supply-side theory.

Institutionalists of both the old (Veblen and Commons) and new (Hayek and North) varieties have advanced our knowledge little further than the sociobiologists. Both groups view institutions (social rules) as central to the dynamics of human society and focus on "Darwinian" evolutionary-like processes. Despite the long history of this tradition, institutionalism has yet to provide a convincing dynamic theory. The primary reason is that it treats institutional change as a central self-contained mechanism rather than as a response to strategic demand generated by society's unfolding dynamic strategy. Because of their supply-side, evolutionary nature, these models are unable to explain the reversals that commonly occur in the process of sociopolitical change. Democracy, for example, is *not* an evolutionary process, as in the past it has undergone dramatic and systematic reversals, as I show in *The Ephemeral Civilization* (1997: ch. 4). Like sociobiology, institutionalism is a supply-side theory in a demand-side world.

Figure 11.1 **The concentric spheres model of decisionmaking**

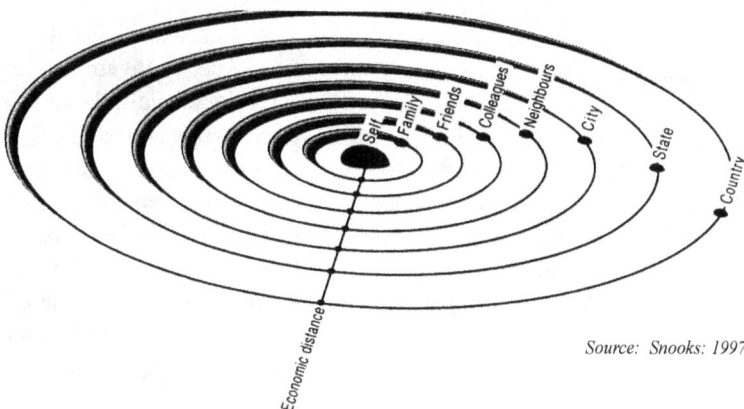

Source: Snooks: 1997: 30

How then do we account for the coherence of society in both the animal and human spheres? The dynamic-strategy theory contains a model of individual interaction that I've called the **concentric-spheres model**.[13] It is based on the notion of genetically determined desires, but allows for varying degrees of individual choice and action. It shows that the way the self relates to other individuals and groups depends on their potential contribution to maximizing the probability of the self's survival and prosperity. This potential contribution is measured in the concentric spheres model (Figure 11.1) by the **economic distance** between the self and all other individuals and groups who occupy different positions on a set of concentric spheres that radiate outwards.

Underlying the dynamics of this model are two balancing sets of forces, one centrifugal and the other centripetal. The centrifugal force is the innate desire of the self to survive and prosper, which leads typical individuals to persistently pursue their self interests. This is the life-energizing force of strategic desire, which continually threatens to disrupt social relations. In contrast, the centripetal force, which can be thought of as the economic gravity holding animal society (from the highest to lowest forms) together, is generated by the self's need to cooperate with other individuals and groups in order to achieve its own objectives through the joint pursuit of a common dynamic strategy. While this model was developed primarily to explain animal (including human) behavior, it can also be applied to plant and earlier life forms (bacteria and viruses).

It is through the interaction of competition and cooperation that individuals maximize the probability of their survival and prosperity. And it is in this way that their societies progress towards higher living standards and greater complexity. But it is important to realize that the underlying condition for the "trust" required for cooperation is not "altruism", genetic or otherwise, as argued by sociobiologists and institutionalists. Rather it is, as argued earlier, strategic confidence. This is the confidence that arises from the conspicuous success of the dynamic strategy being jointly pursued by these cooperative but highly self-interested individuals. And the cooperative actions undertaken by these individuals are shaped by strategic demand – a relationship I've recently called the process of **strategic exchange**.[14]

Because Darwin's theory of natural selection – or "survival of the fittest" – does not allow for cooperation, neo-Darwinists were forced to invent a fanciful hypothesis about a genetic-based "altruism" to "explain" social relationships. This concept is discussed and refuted in *The Collapse of Darwinism* (2003: chs 7 and 8). Social scientists who have adopted this concept run into difficulties similar to those facing sociobiologists in explaining the real world.

In contrast, the dynamic-strategy theory is able to completely explain the dynamics of social organization. In my theory, systematic changes in strategic demand provide the incentives, opportunities, and imperatives for the changing structure of animal and human society. The strategic cycle of adoption, exploitation, exhaustion, stagnation, and decline – the complete unfolding process of a dominant dynamic strategy – has a characteristic impact on the organizational and institutional structure of society. Unlike evolutionary theory, the dynamic-strategy theory can explain institutional reversal in terms of the traditional reversal of the strategic sequence – expressed, for example, as: conquest → commerce → conquest, which was the typical sequence in the pre-modern world. This is discussed in detail in both *The Ephemeral Civilization* (1997) and *The Collapse of Darwinism* (2003).

Institutional change, despite the claims of sociobiologists and evolutionary institutionalists, has no life of its own. Nor is it the outcome of the independent action of genes plotting from within their "lumbering robots", "survival machines", or – as you and I recognize them – individual organisms. Institutional change, including religious change, is reactive, not proactive. It has no "evolutionary" logic of its own. Animal society, whether simple or complex, is merely a vehicle for achieving the basic desire of life forms to survive and prosper – a vehicle I call the strategic *logos*. While the dynamic process is eternal, the sociopolitical institutions and organizations of life are ephemeral.

CONCLUSIONS

Life has an observable pattern and an existential meaning. The rise and fall of species, dynasties, societies, empires, and civilizations; the great genetic and technological revolutions; the great diasporas, civil wars, world wars, and extinctions – all are a part of an intelligible whole. These patterns, outlined in Chapter 10, are the outcome of individual organisms struggling to gain access to nature's resources, through the pursuit of a four-fold set of dynamic strategies, in order to survive and prosper. It is a pattern and meaning that can be understood from within life itself – rather than by approaching supernatural beings – through the dynamic-strategy theory. As we have seen in this chapter, this is a theory about the selfcreating nature of living systems.

We are now in a position to travel into completely unknown territory. Life also has an unobservable pattern and a hidden meaning. This invisible pattern – like the unseen forces determining the structure and dynamics of the physical world – can only be detected indirectly. The indirect method is the dynamic-strategy theory itself. This invisible pattern, which is generated by the unseen but powerful interactions between organisms and their society, is the universal life-system or, more succinctly, the **strategic *logos***. And it is the strategic *logos* that provides the true meaning of life – a hidden but essentially materialistic meaning. The strategic *logos* is the subject of the final chapter.

Chapter 12
The Strategic *Logos*

Life is the most profound mystery in the Universe. It is the mystery of mysteries. Although scholars take great pride in their major scientific achievements, they don't really understand how life emerged on our planet, how it was able to generate complex genetic and institutional forms, how it was able to sustain itself over the past 3,800 myrs, what the future might bring, or whether intelligent life exists on worlds other than our own. The fundamental reason for these critical uncertainties in human knowledge is that the underlying life-system is a hidden system, which, until recently, has eluded the objective methods of science. Accordingly, the life-system has, over many thousands of years, become the subject of much speculation, myth, and religion. It is the objective of the present chapter to dispel the mystery of millennia by exposing the hidden life-system. This is done by introducing the materialist strategic *logos*, which provides the key to understanding not only life and human society, but also the origin, role, and dynamics of mythmaking and religion.

THE VEHICLE OF LIFE
Some natural scientists are fond of telling us that we inhabit a peculiarly "life-friendly" Universe. By this they meant that the laws of physics and the values of the "fundamental constants of nature" – including the cosmological constant, gravity, the velocity of light – are just what is required to enable the emergence of carbon-based life in the Universe.[1] As shown in Chapter 9, these scientists usually have some sort of teleological theory – either the "Mind of God" or the superintelligence – that they are promoting. In contrast, those scholars studying life-systems in either the natural or human domains are keenly aware that the physical world is extremely hostile to life.

Because the Universe is so hostile to life, all its forms are dominated by the overriding desire to survive and prosper. For example, life forms only exist because they have found ways to defy the second law of thermodynamics. This law tells us that while heat flows *spontaneously* from hot to cold bodies, this inevitable process cannot be reversed, at least not *spontaneously*. The upshot of this law is that all *closed* physical systems are trapped in a one-way trip towards the final state of thermodynamic equilibrium, or "heat death". Stated in slightly different terms, this equilibrium is the outcome of increasing entropy. Hence, all closed systems are moving inevitably from a state of order to state of disorder.

Entropy is a variable rather than a constant, and the change in entropy (ds), which measures the change in disorder, is related to temperature (T) and heat (dtQ). Hence, an infinitesimal amount of heat absorbed by any system leads to a change in the entropy (disorder) of that system according to the formula:

$$dtQ = Tds \text{ or } ds = dt/T$$

Of course, while the entire physical system may be closed – such as the Universe as a whole – any part of it may find ways to decrease its entropy (or increase its order) by absorbing heat released by other parts of the larger system. This, in physical terms, is how order and complexity can be achieved by open biological systems, without violating the laws of physics. It happens when ways and means are found to convert energy from a body like the sun (or from the molten core of a planet in the ocean depths) into work – a less than fully efficient process that loses energy to the environment in the form of heat.

While all of this sounds straightforward in physical terms, the trick, and it is not an easy one to master as far as life forms are concerned, is to develop techniques that provide continuous access to energy supplies. These techniques, as discussed in Chapter 11, can be both biological and technological, which are generated by investment of time and energy in new "ideas". Much of my work – generated by metabolic energy derived both directly and indirectly from the sun – over the past few decades has been devoted to showing how this has been undertaken. What should be realized is that biological and technological "ideas" do not just emerge spontaneously in a way similar to the flow of heat from hot to cold bodies. While *disorder* is a spontaneous physical process, the creation of *order* requires considerable energy, effort, and creative impulse to be achieved. In other words, life forms need energy not only to survive and prosper, but also to develop a continuous supply of techniques to gain long-term access to sources of energy. But the survival "trick" requires more than this. Energy is needed to develop "dynamic life-systems" in order to protect and sustain this extremely difficult process of survival and prosperity in a hostile world that is continuously running down. This protective life-system – which I call the **strategic** *logos* – has to be dynamic because it is necessary to continuously reinvent ways of gaining access to sources of energy. A static system would quickly perish in a world running down.

Once established, a strategic *logos* operates according not to the laws of physics but to its own internal laws – the laws of life and history. The laws of physics merely provide the background against which agents of the strategic *logos* play out the game of life. While the laws of physics make it possible to play the game of life, it is the players – the individual organisms driven by strategic desire – who decide whether or not to play the game and, if so, how it should be played. And we play this exacting game in the self-contained world of the strategic *logos*; a world which defies the hostilities, difficulties, and mindlessness of the physical world. Because the strategic *logos* operates according to its own internalized rules, scientists are unable to employ the laws of physics to explain life. This is why self-organizational and complexity theory – the usual supply-side models – which emerged from the natural sciences, are not capable of conveying an understanding of life and human society.[2] To understand these amazing things we must first understand the strategic *logos* and the internal laws by which it operates.

Once a viable strategic *logos* – or dynamic life-system – has been established, it is necessary to defend it against a wide range of external threats. These threats come from both the physical and organic worlds. Physical threats include asteroid attack, volcanic eruptions, earthquakes, tsunamis, floods, typhoons, droughts, fires, and other climatic extremes. Most viable strategic *logoi* are able to withstand these physical threats, although they may force a dynamic life-system into a temporary decline, with recovery taking time, energy, and the employment of accumulated wealth. These random events temporarily distort the more cyclical pattern that has been detected (as discussed in Chapter 10) in human and other life-systems. In contradiction of the claims of most natural scientists and environmentalists interested in this issue, the strategic *logoi* of life and human society are remarkably resilient to the onslaught of random physical shocks. Massive volcanic eruptions can tear holes in a society – such as the Roman city Pompeii in AD 79 – but viable societies just repair these holes and continue on with life; major changes in climate – such as those in Egypt from the prehistoric to the Old Kingdom – can provoke viable societies to respond creatively through the introduction of new technologies (irrigation systems) and the adoption of new economic activities (agriculture in place of hunting), but they are not responsible for the collapse of those societies. This is merely a myth propagated by natural scientists and their Green followers, who have not constructed the dynamic theory required to analyze complex living systems. As I have shown in *The Dynamic Society* (1996), *The Ephemeral Civilization* (1997) and *The Collapse of Darwinism* (2003), the collapse of dominant species, societies, and dynasties is the outcome not of random physical shocks, but of the exhaustion of dynamic strategies and of biological and technological paradigms. The same will be true of human-induced climate change, as discussed in *The Coming Eclipse* (Snooks 2010).

More problematical are the threats posed by other life-systems. These more serious threats arise from other strategic *logoi* within the same species and from other species. In our own species, the greatest threat comes from competing strategic *logoi*, particularly those pursuing the dynamic strategy of conquest. For example, Phoenicia was swept away by Alexander the Great; Carthage was finally completely destroyed by Rome; Egypt was seriously challenged by Assyria, Persia, and Macedonia, and finally extinguished by Rome; Venice was challenged by the Ottomans and eventually fell to Napoleon. Ironically, even the victorious societies in these conflicts eventually collapsed owing to their very success – ultimately they exhausted their dynamic strategies of conquest. And an exhausted, irreplacable strategic *logos* does not survive for long, as shown by the fall of Rome the greatest of all conquest societies.

Less challenging for the human strategic *logos* are the attacks of other species. Wild animals are annoying because they take human life and generate minor economic loss, but microbiological life forms have had a greater impact. In the past, diseases like bubonic plague, which eliminated between one-third and one-half of the populations of viable societies have been devastating. But the fascinating thing is that these societies continued as if nothing had happened. In Europe during the mid-fourteenth century, the Hundred Years' War between England and France hardly missed a beat even when bubonic plague first struck Western Europe.[3] The point is that the strategic *logos* is a very effective mechanism for throwing off even large-scale effects of exogenous shocks. It was the same in the case of the international influenza epidemic immediately following the First World War; as will be any future large-scale outbreak of bird flu that medical scientists are currently threatening us with. Individuals are highly vulnerable to the attack of virulent new diseases, but the strategic *logos* is remarkably resilient. It has to be if life is to survive in a hostile world.

The resilience and success of the strategic *logos* is reflected in the **logological constant** of life discussed in Chapter 10. What it measures is just as remarkable and unchanging as the fundamental constants of the physical world. As we have seen, it shows that over the past 3,800 myrs the global biomass/GDP has not only increased at an exponential rate, but that in geometric (or compound growth-rate) terms it is a constant with a coefficient value of approximately 3.0. This suggests that each biological/technological transformation (taken as a whole) occurs in one-third of the time taken by the previous one. This fundamental constant of life is ample proof of the resilience and effectiveness of the strategic *logos* in the face of both the second law of thermodynamics and the hostile physical and biological world. Hence, it is the strategic *logos* rather than the brute physical facts of the Universe that is "life-friendly". It is the strategic *logos* that confounds the gloomy predictions of the crisis exaggerators.

DEFINING THE STRATEGIC *LOGOS*

In view of its fundamental and critical importance, we need to formally address the question: what is the strategic *logos*? It is, as suggested above, the dynamic life-system that is essential to our individual and group survival and prosperity. Without the *logos* we would all perish; without the *logos* life would never have gained a foothold on this planet; and without the *logos* life certainly would not have flourished. The strategic *logos* is an entropy-defying, shock-absorbing mechanism. Yet despite its absolutely essential role in our very existence, the *logos* is still a great mystery to the science community, which is incapable of exploring its hidden forces. Instead, scientists think they see complex systems arising spontaneously – like entropy – from the mere interaction of decision-making agents. Life is seen as a form of social physics.[4] This response is no more sophisticated than the mythmaking of the priestly philosophers of the pre-modern world.

Previous usage of the term "logos"

The Greek word *Logos* (λόγου) has a long history. While this history has in no way influenced the content of my concept of the "strategic *logos*" – the concept was complete before this history was even known to me – it can be usefully surveyed here.[5] In Homer (ninth century BC), meanings of the word *logo* include: "to gather", "to count", "to enumerate", "to enter on a list", "to narrate" and "to say". There was also a sense of wholeness or comprehensiveness about any such enumeration or narration. Likewise the noun *logos* — the plural of which is *logoi* — had, for Homer, the meanings of "collection", "gathering", "assemblage", "list", "calculation", "account", "reckoning", "narrative" and "speech". Soon after Homer's time, the meaning of *logos* became restricted to rationally established and constructed speech.

Heraclitus (around 500 BC), from my reading of his collected fragments[6], employed the term *logos* to denote a mysterious, possibly divine, "system", which had a controlling influence over human society. Its usage implies that our world has unity, coherence, and meaning, which is established through ever present change or flux. Heraclitus was the expert of the ancient world on the dynamics of life and human society, which is why I am so interested in his work, as fragmentary as it is:

Heraclitus tells us:

> For wisdom, listen
> not to me but to the *logos*
> and know that all is one.

The *logos* is also the entity "from which all things follow". Yet he appears exasperated that:

> The *logos* proves
> those first hearing it
> as numb to understanding
> as the ones who have not heard.

(No doubt the same will be true regarding the reception of the strategic *logos* in this book.) Instead, he tells us, the people and their leaders prefer the shallow explanations of "specialists" or experts:

> Although we need the *logos*
> to keep things known in common,
> people still treat specialists
> as if their nonsense
> were a form of wisdom.

He could, of course, be commenting on our own times – particularly regarding the public "treatment" of market economists and climate mitigationists – rather than those of 2,500 years ago. Heraclitus even tells us that these "specialists", deluded by their popularity with the people, attack those who seek to discover and explain the *logos*:

Dogs, by this same logic,
bark at what they cannot understand.

After the time of Heraclitus, the word *Logos* was employed by Christian theologians – St John the Divine and Philo, for example – to refer to the revelation of Christ. In this context, *Logos* is usually translated into English as "Word", meaning the spiritual aspect of Jesus Christ that has the power to create and sustain life. And in Western philosophy today, *Logos* is taken to refer to the rational principle that governs and develops the Universe; in theology it refers to the divine Word of God made known by Jesus Christ; and in one interesting but eccentric work in sociology (Roy Rapport) it is construed as the "rational order uniting nature, society, individual humans and divinity into 'a great cosmos'", which is established through religious ritual.[7] My use of the term strategic *logos*, as shall be seen, is very different to all these, although in sentiment it comes closest to what we can detect in the fragmented writings (quoted in other ancient works) of Heraclitus.

While the strategic *logos* is invisible and its meaning hidden, all ancient societies have been aware of its shadowy presence, and based their mythologies and religions on it. They referred to it as: harmony, order, stability, cosmic balance, security, truth, law of the Universe, unity of nature, "sacred circle" (Sioux).They saw this shadowy reality as the changelessness beneath the superficial flux of everyday life. And they personified the various perceived characteristics of this underlying reality as gods. We can even see the longing for order, balance and stability today in the inflation-targeting policies of central banks, and the climate-mitigation policies of environmentalists.

Some ancient and pre-modern societies even had names for this hidden system of order, balance and stability. As we have seen, the Greeks called it *logos*; but, in addition, this mystery of mysteries was called *maat* by the Egyptians, Asha by the Persians, Rta by the Vedic Indians, Nelli by the Toltecs, and Wakan-Tanka (or "Great Mystery") by the Sioux.[8] All these societies, as well as those who had no special name for this mysterious system underlying life, were extremely concerned to sustain it together with all its life-giving powers. They were convinced that their life-system would be disrupted by inappropriate behavior, either of omission or commission, and the result would be disorder and chaos. Without understanding the scientific concept of entropy, they had a strong sense of the world running down. Hence, it was essential in their eyes to undertake the appropriate sacrifice and ritual, and to live according to the laws of the *logos*. In this, as we have seen in earlier chapters, they looked to their wisemen and their kings. This was the real origin and purpose of religion.

A WORKING MODEL OF THE STRATEGIC *LOGOS*

The strategic *logos* is a dynamic mechanism that generates a largely invisible process of interaction between human agents and their society. It is a self-generating and self-sustaining life-system that not only protects its members from a hostile world but enables them to progress both technologically and culturally. In the absence of overwhelming external shocks – such as the invasions of the New World in the early sixteenth century and of the Great South Land in the late eighteenth century – the strategic *logos* continues to flourish until its entire sequence of dynamic strategies is completely exhausted. In the case of the world's most successful societies, such as ancient Egypt or Rome, this can last anywhere from one to three millennia. During this time, the *logos* is driven and shaped by its own internal laws – the laws of history – which are independent of the laws of physics.[9] Ultimately, however, the laws of history run their course, the strategically exhausted society enters into terminal crisis, and the strategic *logos* collapses. The heart of this particular human society throbs no more.

The strategic *logos*, therefore, is ephemeral rather than eternal. It exists only as long as the society that gave it birth. While a *logos* accounts for the rise and fall of a particular society, it is in fact the creation of that society – or, at least, of the collectivity of individuals in that society, who are integrated by their common strategic pursuit. The strategic *logos*, as will be demonstrated, is both the outcome of and reason for the creative interaction between the people and their society, which I have called the **strategic exchange**.[10] Hence, the *logos* is born with the emergence of a particular society and the *logos*, together with its guardians, dies with that society. It is this close and essential relationship that has led human societies to worship the unknown strategic *logos* and to call its guardian God. As each society unknowingly creates its own strategic *logos* – and in turn is created by it – many *logoi* exist at any point in time. It was for this reason, as discussed in earlier chapters, that human societies in both the Old and New Worlds had their own home-grown gods. Each society created its own god or gods in order to protect and sustain its own strategic *logos*.

A simple two-dimensional model

In an effort to make visible what has for many thousands of years remained invisible, a diagrammatic model of the strategic *logos* is presented in Figure 12.1. This model is based on the dynamic-strategy theory (Chapter 11), which in turn was constructed inductively from the close and systematic observation of living systems in both the human and non-human worlds (Chapter 10). Needless to say, this figure is merely a simple, two-dimensional representation of a complex, three-dimensional process. What Figure 12.1 clearly shows, however, is the fundamental circular nature of interaction between man and society – the selfcreating process of strategic exchange – which lies at the heart of the strategic *logos*. This pattern of concentric circles – this complex mandala – bears a close resemblance to the dominant role that circles and concentric circles played in the sacred art of the paleolithic era. As shown in Chapter 2, these concentric circles represented the life-system of early hunting societies.

The circular process of strategic exchange occurs at four main levels. These include: **I** the **dynamic strategy** pursued by society; **II** the **strategic demand** that this unfolding process generates for a wide range of strategic inputs; **III** the individual and collective response to strategic demand; and **IV** the resulting strategic vehicle that carries society forward in its **strategic pursuit**. These forces also generate the laws of history (and of life).

The strategic *logos* is driven by **strategic desire**, which, as shown in Chapter 11, is the motive force that powers the dynamic circle, or mandala, of life. It is the center of life's pulsating heart, and it provides this dynamic engine with its self-starting and self-sustaining character. Strategic desire, which is fed both directly and indirectly with energy from the sun, operates primarily by driving both the dynamic strategy being pursued by society together with its **strategic response**. In both cases this activity is facilitated by the supervisory and planning role played by the **strategic cerebrum**.

The great *directing* force in human society is strategic demand, which continually changes as the dominant dynamic strategy unfolds. This directing force provokes a necessary response from the people, thereby providing the institutional, organizational, and cultural vehicle required to engage successfully in the strategic pursuit. This societal vehicle also provides the medium for natural-resource exploitation, as well as for economic growth and the structural change required to meet the people's strategic objective of survival and prosperity.

Just as the laws of physics are derived from observing physical relationships in the cosmos, so the laws of history have been derived from observing societal relationships in the strategic *logos*. These laws shape and regulate the dynamics of human society and civilization. In *Laws of History* (1998), I derived eight general and universal laws from the operation of the strategic *logos*. These "primary" laws, which are listed but not explained here, include:

- The law of human motivation
- The law of competitive intensity
- The law of strategic optimization
- The law of strategic imitation
- The law of strategic struggle
- The law of diminishing strategic returns
- The law of strategic crisis
- The law of societal collapse.

These laws define the entropy-defying nature of the strategic *logos*. Other laws – "secondary" (five of these) and "tertiary (nine) – applicable to the major historical eras, have been derived from these eight primary laws by introducing different initial conditions from these eras.

Figure 12.1 **The strategic *logos* – the meaning of life**

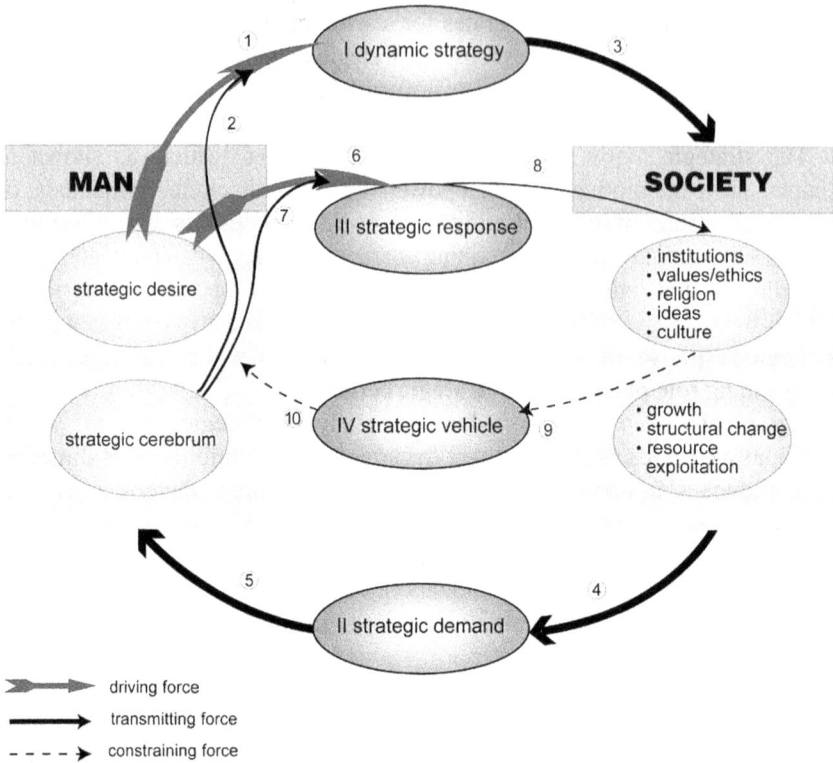

With this overview in mind, we can investigate the operation of the strategic *logos* in Figure 12.1. We begin with "Man" in the left-had box. Man is dualistic in his strategic nature. Not only driven by strategic desire to achieve his fundamental joint objective of survival and prosperity, Man also possesses a highly sophisticated instrument – the strategic cerebrum – employed to plan and supervise the strategic pursuit. This was achieved, as we saw in Chapter 11, through the adoption and exploitation of one of a quartet of dynamic strategies – family multiplication, conquest, commerce, technological change – available to that society. As the chosen dynamic strategy unfolds, society increases its access to natural resources, grows economically, and changes structurally. In the process, the "Society" generates strategic demand for an extensive range of strategic inputs, including land, labor, capital, ideas (technological, strategic, other), institutions (societal rules), organizations (societal networks), values, ethics, religion, and culture. The nature of these inputs bears the stamp of the particular dynamic strategy being pursued. All human values, in other words, are initiated outside man by the strategic *logos*, not purely from the mind of man as most scholars claim.

The drive behind the strategic response to **logosian demand** is, once again, provided by strategic desire, and is facilitated by the strategic cerebrum. A major outcome of this strategic response is the creation of an institutional, ethical, religious, cultural vehicle capable of carrying the strategic pursuit forward and, thereby, delivering the material success that meets the needs of strategic desire, which initiated the entire process. The completion of this circular interaction, however, doesn't lead to equilibrium, because strategic desire is never satisfied. Accordingly, the circular interaction becomes an upward spiral that continues until the strategic *logos* collapses, sending the whole process into reverse.

While this diagrammatic model of the strategic *logos* provides a convenient two-dimensional sketch of a complex dynamic engine of society, its limitations are obvious. First, Figure 12.1 is merely a cross-section of the entire circular process of strategic exchange. The missing third dimension is time, which is needed to show how the *logos* allows a society not only to exploit the founding dynamic strategy, but also how its exhaustion, which threatens the continuing viability of the *logos*, opens the way for the adoption and exploitation of a further dynamic strategy from its four-fold armory.

By adding time, a three-dimensional model would demonstrate the strategic sequence, which would burrow into the surface of the page at level I. Such a sequence would show how a changing strategic demand impacts on the strategic vehicle we call civilization. One need only reflect, for example, on how different was Greek civilization under the conquest strategy (400–100 BC) compared with that under the commerce strategy (800–500 BC). Of particular interest in this example, is how the strategic sequence of conquest → commerce → conquest led ancient Greece to advance toward and, later, retreat from democratic ecosociopolitical forms, as discussed in my book *The Ephemeral Civilization* (1997: ch. 8). This unfolding strategic sequence was presided over by the Greek *logos*, which was recognized but misinterpreted as the divine *Logos* by Heraclitus around 500 BC.

Secondly, the strategic *logos* should not be thought of as being confined by fixed dimensions as Figure 12.1 probably suggests. By adding the missing variable of time, the *logos*, as a dynamic engine, grows larger (or smaller, if in decline), more complex (representing a spiral rather than an ellipse), and it generates greater (or lesser) levels of population, GPD and GDP per capita. In a more partial and ad hoc manner, these issues can be dealt with by employing conventional **timescapes** that show changes in the variables by which the success (or failure) of societies and civilization are usually measured. What is important to note here is that these performance variables feed back into the decisions made by agents through strategic confidence. Also we need to remember that all three outcomes are generated by the strategic *logos*, which is not to be simplistically confused with the crude representations of it made in Figure 12.1.

Finally, it is important to realize that in life, dynamics – or, in the words of Heraclitus, "flux" – is deep and abiding, not superficial and intermittent.

Not only is life in constant flux, but the system of life that generates this flux is also dynamic in itself. In other words, the dynamic engine that is the strategic *logos* acts upon itself as well as on life and society. The *logos* is not absolute, eternal, and changeless in the way that gods are supposed to be, but rather it is ephemeral and in a state of continuous change. The strategic *logos* changes as its dynamic strategy unfolds; and it is transformed as the global genetic/technological paradigm shifts occur. Both the mover and the moved are dynamic. This reality is in stark contrast to the theological idea that arose to explain this mystery of mysteries – the fanciful idea of the unmoved mover.

The strategic *logos* depicted in Figure 12.1 can be generalized to embrace all "societies" in life. They would differ largely in terms of degree of sophistication of the strategic cerebrum (or, in its absence, the **strategic gene**), of complexity of the strategic vehicle, or of the type and magnitude of material outcomes. As discussed in *The Collapse of Darwinism* (2003), even simple, single-cellular life adopts and pursues the generalized quartet of dynamic strategies available to human society. Hence, the strategic *logos* accounts for the origin and growing complexity of the entire "society" of life. The *logos* is, in other words, the dynamic machine responsible for the selfcreating – or autogenous – process that can be detected in all species of life.

Historical reality and ultimate reality

What are we to make of the strategic *logos*? There are, in my philosophy of life, two forms of reality. First, there is **historical reality**, which consists of *objects* and physical relationships between objects that can be perceived through the senses over time. And, second, there is **ultimate reality**, or the strategic *logos*, that is the outcome of a complex set of invisible relationships between *forces* – such as strategic desire and strategic demand – that cannot be perceived through the senses, despite having materialist origins. Only the agents (**strategists**) and outcomes (institutions, organizations, infrastructure, and material wealth) generated by these invisible forces can be detected by the senses.

The invisible pattern of forces described in the diagrammatical representation (Figure 12.1) of the strategic *logos* can only be comprehended by developing a general dynamic theory (Chapter 11) that can explain and predict the recurring visible patterns in historical reality. This type of relationship between invisible forces and visible objects (people, organizations, wealth), which gives rise to observable patterns, is similar to that in the physical world explored by physicists, as discussed in Chapter 7.[11] Ultimate reality in life, therefore, is the dynamic system responsible for generating life together with all its vehicles of change.

Interestingly, the dynamic-strategy theory outlined in Chapter 11 was developed not in pursuit of the strategic *logos*, the existence of which I had not initially considered, but rather to explain and predict the recurring patterns found in historical reality. Only once this theory had been constructed was it possible to detect the existence of the *logos*, precisely because it is not directly accessible to the senses. Hence, it is historical reality that leads the way to life's ultimate reality; and it is the dynamic-strategy theory that provides the link between them.

This theoretical link between levels of reality should be Janus-like – it should work in both directions. Here it might help to play a mind game that has nothing to do with reality. If one could apprehend only ultimate reality – the strategic *logos* – it would still be possible to develop the underlying dynamic-strategy theory (and the laws of history) by analyzing the relationships between strategic forces. In turn this dynamic theory could be used to discover the patterns in historical reality (had they been unknown to us). Of course, we would have to be very different beings to work in this way. Remember, this exercise is only a game, but a game with a serious point to make: which is that historical reality and ultimate reality are linked through the exercise of **strategic thinking**, whereby observable patterns are identified and employed as the basis for inductive theory making. The nature and role of strategic thinking, which is contrasted with deductive thinking, has been discussed at length in *The Selfcreating Mind* (2006). The implication of this argument is that the strategic *logos* could not have been discovered in any other way – such as by deductive thinking – by beings like us. The history of philosophy over the past 3,000 years attests to this.

GUARDIANS OF THE *LOGOS*

The strategic *logos* is the only source of hope for life in a hostile world. This existential fact clearly has been understood by all societies in the past for which evidence is available. All societies, as seen in earlier chapters, have been only too aware of their precarious circumstances in this world. The ruins of former, once flourishing, societies and civilizations are there for all to see. In Mesoamerica for example, the Aztecs saw their life-system as the Fifth Sun, as they were acutely aware that four other life-systems, or "Suns", together with their gods, had flourished in their world for a time, and then collapsed. And in Egypt, every night was a time of potential crisis, as the sun god Re and his divine retinue passed through the underworld, for the ancient Egyptians believed that as their ordered world (*maat*) had emerged from a watery chaos (*nun*) so it would end in a watery chaos. Today there is a widespread fear that climate change will irreparably harm our own life-system. Such concern can be appreciated, because, if our strategic *logos* were irrepairably damaged, there would be no hope for societal progress or individual survival.

All societies, therefore, are very keen, even desperate, to discover the best way to protect and sustain the unknown system that provides them with life and material pleasure. The problem facing us all is: if we cannot see and understand the hidden life-system – this mystery of mysteries – how can we hope to sustain it. It is fascinating that all societies faced with this dilemma have come to the same conclusion – that it is necessary to gain access to beings greater than man who can understand this mystery. Someone must understand this mystery of life, as some societies are clearly more successful than others; and that someone would have to be a supernatural being – a being greater than man. Such supernatural beings are prime candidates for the critical role of guardians of the strategic *logos*.

Having come to this conclusion, the universal problem has been how to enter into the presence of potential guardians in order to persuade them to adopt the cause of the supplicants. And the solution has been just as universal. Wisemen schooled in the arts of creating trance-like states and of performing rituals of sacred song and dance, claimed to be able to enter into the presence of the guardians who dwell either in the heavens or the underworld. By cultivating the correct attitude to the guardians, by following appropriate ritual, and by offering proper sacrifices of humans, animals, and/or wealth, these wisemen claimed to be able to persuade the guardians to protect the strategic *logos* of their society. It was, however, an art rather than a science, because this approach to the guardians did not always work, perhaps owing to an art lost, a ritual forgotten, the failure to live properly, or even the fickleness of the guardian itself. And, in the absence of the guardian, the society collapsed or was taken over by a competitor. With time, these guardians became gods, and the wisemen became great and wealthy priests. Once we discovered science and technology, we replaced the old gods of religion with the new gods of scientism. We have continued the cycle of dead god rising.

Epilogue
Dead Gods Also Rise

Old gods exhaust themselves in the service of mankind, and then they die. New gods always take their place. We have seen this happen innumerable times during the course of human history. History is a great story about the death and rebirth of the gods. But in the future, will dead gods also rise? There is little doubt that they will. The dynamic strategies of mankind need their guardians, and the priestly philosophers need to transform these into metaphysical beings to render the stark materialism of life both bearable and meaningful.

Yet one big question about life has been left unanswered in this book so far. What does the discovery of the strategic *logos* tell us about the existence of a Creator God? The discovery of the strategic *logos* has finally revealed the true nature of the God of human experience. It is a revelation that throws light on the God of the Jews (YHWH), the God of the Christians (Jesus Christ), the God of the Muslims (Allah), together with the tens or hundreds of thousands of gods that have ever existed in the mind of man. All these gods, without exception, are fictional strategic guardians of the human *logos*. They have been called upon by the priestly philosophers of all societies to protect, sustain, and advance their particular *logos*. God is the personification of – or metaphor for – the universal life-system of mankind.

But what does this imply for those seeking to establish the existence of a Creator God? What it implies is that as every god ever imagined by man is a fictional strategic guardian, none of them – not YHWH, not Christ, not Allah, not Ahura Mazda, not even Amun Re – qualifies for the position of Creator God. If, however, a Creator God did exist, it would be unlike any god that man has ever imagined. Even the word "god" would have to be discarded, as it was devised for the guardian of the unknown strategic *logos*.

Where does this leave us? What this book has done is to dramatically reduce the conceptual space available for a creator "god" to inhabit. If such a "god" does exist, it has never bothered to make any form of contact with mankind or to leave any evidence of its presence in the Universe that we have been able to discover. Prior to the rise of science, all the holy scriptures ever written; all the relics ever crafted; all the temples and churches ever built; all the priests ever trained; all were created to ensure the continued survival and success of the strategic *logos*. Hence, none of this strategic construction can be counted as evidence for a true creator "god". It is "merely" the response of anxious strategists to **logosian demand**.

If "God" exists it must be regarded as the *unknown* "god". We are unable to even speculate about the nature of the unknown "god", other than to say that the traditional idea of "god" as intellect is highly suspect. My study of the strategic *logos* suggests that a mind – or intellect – without a body is something beyond the experience of this Universe. Which is why I have rejected the hypothesis of scientism that the cosmos is being shaped by a "supermind". While there can be desire (or will) without intellect – as there are organisms without minds – there cannot be intellect without desire — mind without body. God as the manifestation of pure intellect doesn't seem possible.

While it is not possible finally to say that the Creator "God" doesn't exist, the probability of that existence has declined dramatically with the discoveries in this book. Agnosticism would appear to triumph over both belief (theism) and non-belief (atheism). But, of course, agnosticism is a form of procrastination, and this life demands practical commitment. Hence, the only logical way to proceed is to assume that "god" doesn't exist, and just get on with life. To be, in other words, agnostic in theory but atheistic in practice. "God" appears totally irrelevant to this life.

Mankind, as we have discovered, is anything but logical. We are driven by desires, not reason. Accordingly, many still find life more bearable through the adoption of an irrational faith in some sort of divine being, which they insist on dressing up in traditional (strategic) mythical form. And this, despite the fact that "god" is no longer required to sustain the strategic *logos*. Science can deliver in that arena, something that the strategic gods never could.

In the end we are all left to deal with any residual existential anxiety as best we can. For this simple reason, even in modern human society, dead gods also rise.

Appendix
Self-organization or Selfcreation?

As shown in this book, a number of the writers discussed have made hopeful references to self-organization and complexity theory to explain their views about life. For this reason, a brief evaluation of these concepts is required. More in-depth discussions can be found in my recent articles in *Complexity* (Snooks 2008a), the journal of the Santa Fe Institute, and *Social Evolution & History* (Snooks 2007).

The theory of self-organization has arisen from the use of statistical physics to explain the emergence of complexity and order in living systems. The history of this currently fashionable concept has taken two paths. First, some physicists have attempted to develop a physics of society – literally to explain the complexity of living systems in terms of the laws of physics. These are the hard-line intellectual warriors, who prefer to see people as particles. Second, there are others, mainly computer-oriented economists and political scientists, who are attempting to combine the structure of the physics model with the decision-making characteristics of living agents. While abandoning the laws of physics, these agent-based theorists heroically assume, under the influence of physics, that complexity is the outcome of supply-side interactions between agents subject to bounded rationality.

"Self-organization" is a misnomer, because, as a theoretical construct, it does not embody a self-organizing mechanism. Rather, it relies on either an exogenous driving force (physics model) or an exogenous rule-setter (agent-based model). Only the process of **selfcreation** transcends these limitations. Even more significantly, the concept of self-organization is unable to account for the dynamics of life or human society. A physics of society, therefore, is totally out of the question.

SELF-ORGANIZATION – A THEORY OF INANIMATE INTERACTION

The basic idea behind the physics model of living systems is that their observed order and complexity is an outcome of interactions between large numbers of agents. These interactions are said to obey a few simple rules. It is an idea that arises from an analogy with the order that emerges spontaneously in inanimate systems owing to the laws of motion, gravity, and friction. In an open physical system, the interactions between its inanimate members are generated by the imposition of an external source of energy. Although it is not possible to calculate with any degree of precision the pattern of numerous colliding objects, the outcome is known to be ordered and complex. The so-called sand-pile model, developed by Per Bak (1997), is a favorite analogy with those attempting to persuade us of the relevance of self-organization theory to human society. The issue usually emphasized in discussion of the sand-pile model is the contrasting states of a sand-pile in equilibrium on a tabletop, and the same sand-pile augmented by a flow of sand grains from above. This simple model gave rise to the concept of self-organized criticality (SOC), a far-from-equilibrium state created by a flow of energy from outside the system – a state that leads to unpredictable outcomes. These unpredictable outcomes are said to obey a "power law" – the law of large numbers – which governs the probability of fluctuations of a given size (Newman 2005). The contentious issue is whether this approach can be applied to living systems.

Complexity theory clearly has a number of useful applications in the physical world. One popularizer of this approach has enthusiastically said:

> Scientists are beginning to realize [assert?] that the theoretical framework that underpins contemporary physics can be adapted to describe social structures and behaviour, ranging from how traffic flows to how the economy fluctuates and how businesses are organized. (Ball 2004: 13)

Self-organized criticality has been employed by some to explain the size-distribution of earthquakes, volcanic activity, forest fires, solar flares, and "starquakes" (Bak 1997). This may well be reasonable in the case of these inanimate systems. Self-organization theory is also being used by young avant-garde architectural designers to create innovative urban structures (R.W. Snooks 2008). Yet, much less convincingly, there have been attempts to apply this form of statistical physics to living systems: to the origin of life (Kauffman 1993; 1995); to the extinction of species (Bak 1997); to various extreme situations in human society (Axelrod 1984; Axelrod and Bennett 1993); to the transformations of human civilization; and to the emergence of a cosmological "supermind" (Gardner 2003). Recently, there has also been a push, called agent-based modeling (ABM), to formalize this concept in the social sciences in general and economics in particular (Epstein and Axtell 1996; Epstein 1999; Tesfatsion and Judd 2006). To justify this inflation of complexity theory, the science writer Philip Ball (2004: 135, my emphasis) says: 'To develop a physics of society, we must take a bold step that some might regard as a leap of faith and others as a preposterous idealization ... [in which] *particles will become people'*. It certainly is both bold and preposterous, but more significantly it is totally unable to encapsulate the dynamics of life.

The central deficiency of complexity theory is that it does not constitute an endogenous general dynamic theory of life and human society. It does not, in other words, embrace a self-starting, self-sustaining system driven by self-motivated agents capable of participating in a **creative exchange** with their society's constantly changing parameters. It postulates either a system of interacting particles driven by an exogenous force or, more recently, a system of "heterogenous autonomous actors with bounded information and computing capacity" (Epstein 1999: 56). In both cases the structure of the theory is essentially the same. Hence, complexity theory is unable to explain or predict the group dynamics of living systems. Without these abilities, a physics of society, or of life, is impossible. The best case that can be made for the theory of self-organization is that its conclusions are not entirely inconsistent with the outcomes – rather than the processes – of living agents *caught up in extreme or arbitrary situations over which they have no control*. These situations include traffic jams, flight from burning buildings, and the like. Also the focus in these attempts to model living systems is usually on the mechanical way life forms travel over physical terrain.

Many of the studies in question focus on the physical pathways of life forms (bacteria), including our own (cities). Why? Because physical laws are clearly involved in the way life forms traverse the physical terrain of this planet. The flaw in this approach, however, is that our movement on the Earth's surface is the outcome of a more profound dynamic process, driven by laws of its own. This geographical expansion of human society can take the form of urban development that is the outcome of either the commerce strategy of the pre-modern era, or the technological strategy of the our own era; or of the occupation of new productive lands, trading bases, or fortified towns as the outcome of the family-multiplication, commerce, or conquest strategies respectively. While physical constraints must be overcome in any type of geographical expansion, the underlying dynamic processes are not physical but strategic.

Complexity theory, therefore, is completely unable to explain the fundamental dynamic processes of life. Accordingly it has focused instead on the trivial outcomes of those processes, such as the fractal patterns of growing bacteria, the way crowds of people react to crisis in constrained conditions, and the reaction of car drivers in traffic jams. Even if it could be demonstrated that the laws of physics can explain these dynamically marginal and nonstrategic happenings, this would still be a very long way from building the fanciful citadel of "social physics". The problem for would-be social physicists is that even in highly physically constrained situations, self-motivated "people" can and do respond in ways that "particles" cannot and will never do. This is why the statistical results of human interactions never conform entirely to what is expected of particles obeying power laws. Instead, the so-called mechanical interactions on the part of individuals caught up in extreme situations are a form of **strategic interaction** – of following those individuals who, or rules that, give promise of success (called **strategic imitation**) – which is shaped by the more fundamental **strategic exchange**. Even in extreme situations, human behavior can best be explained using my dynamic-strategy theory.

Some complexity theorists, however, are not satisfied with examining the physics of crowd behavior. They appear to believe that an all-embracing physics of society really is possible. Accordingly they are determined to apply their theory to less trivial – in a dynamic sense – aspects of human society. These issues include the history of civilization, "economic" fluctuations, income distribution, the size and growth of firms, the role of government, cooperation, the world wide web, voting, crime and punishment, and marriage. Elsewhere (Snooks 2007), I evaluate these claims in the negative.

LOCAL INTERACTION OR STRATEGIC EXCHANGE?

To some, statistical physics continues to offer a degree of hope and universality in an apparently chaotic and fragmented world. We are, for example, encouraged to respond

> with a certain wonder at the universality that organizes many aspects of society in the same way as it directs the properties of atoms. We need not turn this into a 'religion of science' … We can simply celebrate the fact that there are indeed 'laws of large numbers', and that they let us divine order and regularity in an otherwise terrifying diversity. (Ball 2004: 310)

Of course, a "terrifying diversity" is the fate facing those who possess no realist general dynamic theory to explain the world in which we live – a terrifying diversity that causes many to clutch at the straws of an entirely deficient complexity theory and, worse, to develop a "religion of science". As has been shown in this book, life's fundamental uncertainty is the source of all religions.

Neither physics nor ABM – as I show elsewhere (Snooks 2007; 2008a) – has much to tell us about the choices made by living agents. And choice is central to the process of **strategic exchange** that drives all living systems. Complexity in human culture is not simply extruded from the supply side of human society through "local interaction" but rather is the outcome of a creative response to the strategic demand generated by an unfolding dynamic strategy, as shown in Chapter 11 above. Similarly, complexity is not the isolated outcome of individual psychology as many behaviorists would claim. That too is an unhelpful supply-side approach, as shown in *The Selfcreating Mind* (Snooks 2006a). To understand the real "global state" of human society, we need to adopt a realist general dynamic theory from within the social sciences, not a statistical theory from the physical sciences.

The essence of the theory of selfcreation is to be found in the creative exchange between purposeful agents and their society's unfolding dynamic strategy. It is this strategic exchange that lies at the very heart of the self-sustaining dynamics of living systems. Social agents are self-motivated and self-driven, and they generate complexity and order in a *creative* response to a continuously changing **strategic demand**. It is this creative *exchange* between the demand and supply sides of a dynamic living system that generates changing genetic structures, technologies, ideas of all types, institutions, organizations, and religions. By attempting to meet this constantly changing strategic demand, both the agents and their society are transformed in the long run. The creative process of exchange by which this takes place constitutes the life-system, or

strategic *logos,* for the group of social agents in whom we are interested. Living systems, therefore, are autogenous – or selfcreative – systems.

Selfcreation, as discussed in Chapters 11 and 12, is an entirely new concept. In the selfcreation model, strategic exchange determines all other relationships in society, including the interaction between its constituent members. Strategic exchange is the core dynamic process, whereas agent interaction is a derived and, hence, secondary process. What this implies is that cooperation is central to the pursuit of survival and prosperity, while competition between agents is an attempt at the margin to improve individual strategic advantage. And cooperation is the outcome not of reiterative interactions between agents, as claimed by game theorists, but of the need to ensure the success of their joint strategic pursuit. The point here, of course, is that a society's strategic success is immeasurably more important to every individual than marginal changes in the individual pecking order. This key issue is completely lost on the theorists of self-organization.

Notes

Chapter 1 The Mystery of Mysteries

1. Armstrong (2005: 4, 7).
2. Hornung (1996: 17).
3. For a discussion of, and theory about, the ephemerality of human society, see Snooks (1997a).
4. From the early Anglo-Saxon poem "The Wanderer", translated by S.A.J. Bradley (1982).
5. Why is inflation-targeting irrational? See Snooks (1998b; 1999; 2000; 2008b; 2008c; 2008d).
6. For a discussion of existential schizophrenia, see Snooks (1996; 2006a).
7. The progression from existential schizophrenia to pathological schizophrenia – see Snooks (2006a: 202–207).
8. Strategic frustration leading to social neurosis was introduced in Snooks (2006a: 220–22), and is discussed in Chapters 4 and 5 above.

Chapter 2 Birth of the Gods

1. An account of the earliest discoveries of art materials can be found in Flood (1997: 138).
2. The earliest used and striated pigment evidence is discussed in Marshack (1981) and Flood (1997: 138).
3. For evidence on art in Neanderthal sites, see White (2003: 67–68), Aldhouse-Green (2005: 19–23), and Flood (1997: 138–39).
4. The earliest European art is discussed by White (2003: 132–33).
5. On early art and shamanism, see White (2003: ch. 3).
6. Early North American art is shamanic in origin – see White (2003: 203–206).
7. On the common features of paleolithic art – see Flood (1997: 136–39).
8. White (2003: 64).
9. For a discussion of "worked" objects in the Pech de l'Aze caves, see Mithen (2006: 230).
10. On Australian Aboriginal sand "paintings" – see Strehlow (1964).
11. The Berekhat Ram figurine is discussed by Marshack (1997) and D'Errico and Nowell (2000).
12. The Divjc Babe bone "flute" is discussed by Turk (1997) and Kunej and Turk (2000).
13. The incised and pierced objects at Bilzingsleben are noted in Maria (1988) and Davies and Underdown (2006).
14. For other representation objects, see Bednarik (1995).
15. A major anti-Neanderthalist is Mithen (2006).
16. White (2003: 68). My emphasis.
17. Mithen (2006: 232).

18. The relative brain sizes of Cro-Magnons and Neanderthals is discussed by Davies and Underdown (2006: 147).

19. For a comparison of physical characteristics of Cro-Magnons and Neanderthals, see ibid.

20. The encaphalization quotient (EQ) for hominids – see Kappelman (1996).

21. Kappelman (1996: 270–71) on the relationship between brain size, body mass, and cognitive ability.

22. For an account of the relationship between nutrition and human stature, see Floud et al (1990), and Komlos and Baten (2004).

23. The type of animals hunted can be reconstructed from diet studies – see Bocherens et al (2005).

24. See Moncel et al (2005) on Neanderthal technology.

25. Mithen (2006: 231).

26. Niewochner et al (2003) show that Neanderthals were as technologically advanced as modern humans.

27. The Neanderthal denigrators include Gamble (1999), Mellars (1996), and Mithen (2006).

28. On Neanderthal burials, see Aldhouse-Green (2005: 29).

29. Found objects in Neanderthals graves — see White (2003: 64).

30. On preparation of Neanderthal dead for admission into presence of ancestors, see Aldhouse-Green (2005: 26).

31. Ibid: 29.

32. Mithen (2006: 221).

33. Ibid: 226.

34. Ibid: 227–28. My emphasis.

35. Snooks (2006a: 133–43).

36. While too specialized for the text, we need to consider how a supply-side theorist like Mithen attempts to explain the Neanderthal "paradox" of his own making. The answer is that he falls back on the discredited theories of evolutionary psychology – which in turn owes much to the highly flawed theory of sociobiology – by arguing that the hominid brain consists of a large number of Darwinian modules, which "evolved" to perform specific adaptive functions. In my recent book *The Selfcreating Mind* (2006), I have attempted to demonstrate the fatal empirical and logical flaws in this ultra-Darwinist argument, and have developed a replacement dynamic-strategy theory of the mind. And in my earlier book *The Collapse of Darwinism* (2003), I have critically evaluated sociobiology, together with other forms of neo-Darwinism, and have proposed a realist theory of life.

   Mithen's contribution to this ultra-Darwinist literature is the argument that while all hominid brains consist of a large number of adaptive modules – "domain specific neural circuits" – only the brain of modern man has a module for making connections between all other modules (Mithen 2006: 232–33). He chooses two examples to illustrate this ultra-Darwinist concept of the Neanderthal mind. First, although the Neanderthals possessed the skills both to produce tools as sophisticated as "any modern human" and to develop complex social relationship, "they were unable to use their technical skills to make artefacts to mediate those social relationships, in the way that we do all the time by choosing what clothes or jewellry to wear, and as do all modern hunter-gatherers through their choice of beads and pendants". Second, although the Neanderthals had "an extensive and detailed knowledge of animal behavior, they were unable to design specialized hunting weapons because they could not bring their technical and natural history intelligence together into a single 'thought'".

This is hardly a persuasive argument – indeed it makes Neanderthal man out to be some sort of Frankenstein's monster. No attempt has been made, nor could be made, by Mithen to explain why Neanderthal man lacked an integrative module – "two bob short of a quid" as we used to say in Australia – or why modern man possessed one. Such a distorted view of a highly successful hominid could only be held by those who accept the equally unrealistic idea that the brain of modern man consists of a large number of independent modules. A domain-specific, or modular, brain would be a very inflexible instrument, completely unable to respond to unpredictable changes in the real world. It could only do what it had "evolved" through natural selection to do – to solve *pre-existing* problems. It could certainly not cope with something as totally unprecedented as civilization, as there would be no "civilization module" in a brain that had "evolved" 150,000 years ago on the east African savannah. As we have seen, even the guru of sociobiology, Edward Wilson (1998: 48), has admitted that, as the Darwinian brain cannot anticipate future needs that were not part of the evolutionary process, it could not prepare humans for civilized living: "That [i.e. anticipating civilization] is the great mystery of human evolution: how to account for calculus and Mozart".

In contrast, the dynamic-strategy theory, which views the hominid brain – the "selfcreating mind" (Snooks 2006a) – as a general and flexible instrument that is able to respond to any unpredictable situation, has no difficulty accounting for the fact and nature of civilization. Modern man is not unique in this respect. All hominids possessed brains that acted as general, flexible instruments; otherwise they would have been completely unable to participate in the dynamics of life. It is just that as the hominid brain transformed itself (in response to changes in strategic demand) from *Australopithecus afrarensis* (4 to 3 myrs BP) to *A. garhi* (3 to 2.5 myrs BP) to *Homo ergaster* (2 to 1 myrs BP) to *H. neaderthalensis* and *H. sapiens*, this general, flexible instrument became more powerful and sophisticated. Owing to the close similarities between the Neanderthals and modern humans it is hard to believe that the former did not employ symbolic thought and symbolic language. This is the strategic reality that contrasts with the ultra-Darwinist fantasy.

37. If language is the driving force in societal dynamics, how would Mithen account for the dynamics of other species?

38. Mithen (2006: 229).

39. Ibid: 230–31.

40. d'Errico (1998; 2003), views Neanderthals, prior to the arrival of modern man, as innovative.

41. Ibid (2003).

42. White (2003: 68).

43. Ibid. My emphasis.

44. Ibid: 97.

45. Ibid: 97, 98.

46. Ibid: 116.

47. Ibid: 119.

48. Aldhouse-Green (2005: 7–8).

49. White (2003: 121–22).

50. Aldhouse-Green (2005: 11–12). Also see Eliade (1989: 9–10).

51. Aldhouse-Green (2005: 17).

52. Eliade (1989: 4).

53. For a discussion of the symbolism of the shaman's costume and drum, and the descent into the underworld, see Eliade (1989: chs V and VI).

54. Aldhouse-Green (2005: 13).

55. Ibid: 12.

56. Beaton (1983), on phases of Aboriginal population growth.

57. Flood (1997: 223–24) on Aboriginal settlement.

58. On art around 60,000 BP, see Roberts and Jones (1994).

59. On rock paintings: around 40,000 BP, see O'Connor (1995); and around 35,000–30,000 BP, see Cole and Watchman (1992; 1993).

60. Flood (1997: 24).

61. Ibid.

62. On Aboriginal "proto-sculpture", see Gallus (1971).

63. Flood (1997: 93).

64. For the controversy concerning the "Panaramitee style", see Maynard (1979), Rosenfeld (1991), and Bedmarik (1995b).

65. Clegg (1995) prefers to call the "Panaramitee style" the Australian "track and line genre", which he views as part of an international style.

66. White (2003).

67. For composition of "track and line genre", see Flood (1997: 125–26).

68. Ibid: 133–34.

69. Ibid: 155–59.

70. Ibid: 150–52.

71. *Macquarie Dictionary* (1991).

72. Berndt and Berndt (1999: 230). My emphasis.

73. Ibid: 415. My emphasis.

74. Flood (1997: 194).

75. Maynard (1979).

76. Flood (1997: 299). My emphasis.

77. Ibid: 302–03.

78. Ibid: 307.

79. Berndt and Berndt (1999: 272–73).

80. Ibid: 291–92.

81. Ibid: 271.

82. Ibid: 273.

83. Ibid: 240–41.

84. For a discussion of strategic participation in different types of societies, see Snooks (1997a: ch. 3).

85. Berndt and Berndt (1999: 246, 308–10.

86. Ibid: 312.

87. Ibid: 331. My emphasis.

88. Ibid: 478.

89. Aldhouse-Green (2005: 40) on European stone-age burials.

90. Bahn and Vertut (1988).

91. For a general discussion and refutation of the Darwinian brain-module concept, see Snooks (2006a: 171–74, 242–47); and in relation to Neanderthal man, see note 36 for Chapter 2 above.

92. Flood (1997: 143–44).

93. Ibid: 323–25.

94. Ibid: 323.

95. For a discussion of the Aboriginal dynamic equilibrium, see Snooks (1996: ch. 8), and Snooks (2006b: 7–12).

Chapter 3 **The Gods Transformed**

1. The neolithic technological paradigm shift was first analyzed theoretically in Snooks (1996: ch. 12).

2. For an analysis of the shaping influence of strategic demand on institutions and organizations, see Snooks (1997a).

3. The differences between strategic and deductive thinking are discussed in Snooks (2006a: ch. 8).

4. On the emergence of the first farmers in the Middle East, see Fagan (2004: 91–2) and Haywood (2005: 22–3).

5. The emergence of the dynamic strategies of commerce and conquest in the Middle East is analyzed in Snooks (1996: 54–6, 396).

6. The dynamic strategy being pursued shapes a society's religious outlook – see Snooks (1997a: chs 6–9).

7. On the Mesopotamian afterlife, see Woolf (2005: 92).

8. On the role of the gods in the fluctuating fortunes of Agade, capital of Akkad, see Leick (2002: 103–08).

9. Ibid: 139.

10. Ibid: 131.

11. Ibid: 265.

12. Inana, Mesopotamian (Ur) goddess of "primal drive" – see Leick (2002: 133).

13. Seidlmayer (2004a: 9–10) on the stone-age climate of Egypt.

14. The "funnel of transformation" was coined in Snooks (1996: 225–27, 434).

15. Bongioanni and Croce (2003: 270).

16. For a general discussion of the great-wave pattern in the ancient and modern worlds, see Snooks (1996: 382–88).

17. Manley (1996: 23).

18. Seidlmayer (2004a: 36).

19. Kessler (2004a: 45).

20. Silverman (2003: 48).

21. Romer (2007: 460).

22. Ibid: 74–6.

23. Ibid: 118, 197, 451.

24. For an analysis of the exploitation and exhaustion of the commerce strategy, see Snooks (1996: ch. 11).

25. Quoted by Manley (1996: 30).

26. Kessler (2004b: 105).

27. On the role of commerce as patron of the arts, see Snooks (1997).

28. Kessler (2004b: 107).

29. Manley (1996: 65).

30. Kessler (2004c: 143).

31. Some scholars have argued, unconvincingly, that Akhenaten initiated a religious revolution as part of a struggle against the powerful priests of Amun – see Reeves (2005). As Tyldesley (2005: 74) comments, there is no evidence for such a struggle. I have suggested that a modern equivalent to the cult of Akhenaten is that of Mao Tse-Tung – see Chang and Halliday (2005) on the latter.

32. Bongioanni and Croce (2003: 136).

33. Tyldesley (2005: 180).

34. Ibid.

35. Reeves and Wilkinson (2002: 205).

36. For an account of the rediscovery of the once great Egyptian gods of commerce, see Reeves and Wilkinson (2002).

37. Ibid: 203.

38. Fagan (2004) outlines major Egyptian inventions and technology.

39. Pinch (2002: 160).

40. Hornung (1996: 215–16).

41. Franfort (1948: 15).

42. Bongioanni and Croce (2003: 181). My emphasis.

43. Wilson (1951: 45).

44. Hornung (1996: ch. 1).

45. Ibid: 258, 256, 257.

46. Ibid: 201. Here Hornung is quoting J. Spiegel *ASAE* 40 (1940): 258 II.5–6 (Twentieth Dynasty).

47. Hornung (1996: 143).

48. Ibid: 160.

49. Ibid: 161.

50. From the Faulkner (1998: plate 29b) edition of *The Egyptian Book of the Dead*.

51. For a discussion of strategic versus metaphysical thinking, see Snooks (2006a: 139–42).

52. Burkard (2004: 447).

53. Goelet (1998: 168b).

54. My diagrammatic representation of the strategic *logos* in Figure 12.1, predates this book. It emerged from an earlier book of mine – *The Death of Zarathustra. Notes on Truth for the Risktaker* – that examines the nature and role of truth in human society. The typescript of this book was completed in July 2004, but withheld temporarily from publication. I have long made a practice of publishing books in order not of completion but of logical presentation.

55. Pinch (2002: 173).

56. Ibid: 71.

57. Ibid: 84–5.

58. Ibid: 9. For an excellent but more pragmatic account of the building of the Great Pyramid, see Romer (2007).

59. Tyldesley (2005: 67).

60. The interpretation of Akhenaten as an antistrategist is novel, and is at odds with those – such as by Reeves (2005) – concerning the king's adoption of the cult of Aten as a way of breaking the power of the priests of Amun.

61. Tyldesley (2005: 69).

62. The Papyrus of Ani – see Faulkner (1998).

Chapter 4 **Triumph of the One God: I Zoroastrianism and Judaism**

1. I first investigated the problem of strategic frustration in detail – having introduced it in Snooks (2000) – in my recent book *The Selfcreating Mind* (Snooks 2006a: 209–10). This is what I wrote (in part) there:

> While psychotic disorders are an outcome of the malfunctioning mechanisms of human nature – namely loss of strategic integration [of coordination between strategist and strategic instrument, body and conscious mind, desire and reason] – neurotic disorders are largely an outcome of **strategic frustration**. By strategic frustration I mean the psychological response of individuals and groups of individuals to persistent barriers raised against their participation in the strategic pursuit. This frustration leads to distressing mood disorders, which are strategy-challenging rather than strategy-terminating. It is the opposite of **strategic satisfaction**, which is the balanced state of mind attained by individuals and groups of individuals when they are able to participate successfully in the strategic pursuit.

> Strategic frustration arises from problems that can affect entire societies, social groups, and individuals. I first encountered this issue at the societal level, where a significant gap can sometimes emerge between the strategic expectations of individuals throughout society on the one hand, and the ability of its leaders to meet these expectations on the other ... This is likely to lead ... to **societal neurosis** ... and ... to mood disorders in individuals suffering economic difficulties.

When I wrote this, I was under the impression that it was a modern phenomenon, occurring in otherwise successful strategic societies owing to a failure of strategic leadership. Since undertaking research for this book, I now realize that it also occurred in those pre-modern societies that experienced severe episodes of strategic failure. The most persistent and severe episodes – lasting for millennia – of strategic failure were experienced by small societies on the borderlands between competing superpowers, namely Palestine and Arabia throughout the history of the Jewish, other Canaanite, and Arab societies. It was this caldron of strategic failure and strategic frustration that led to the strategic ideologies of these peoples being transformed into metaphysical mythologies or religions. These religions are Judaism, Christianity, and Islam.

2. There is considerable uncertainty about Zarathustra's time in history. The most commonly accepted dates for his birth and death are 628 and 551 BC. Some – Boyce (1975; 1982) – have suggested much earlier dates, somewhere in the range 1700 to 1400 BC. If the latter were correct (which is probably unlikely), Zarathustra's monotheism would have been even earlier than Akhenaten's (1340 BC).

3. de Menasce (1974: 197).

4. Ibid: 189.

5. For a brief account of ancient Iranian empires, see Brosius (2006).

6. de Menasce (1974: 199).

7. On deciphering the Egyptian hieroglyphic script, see Reeves and Wilkinson (2002: 64–6).

8. The archaeological evidence for the first Israelites is discussed by Finkelstein and Silberman (2002).

9. Ibid: 115.

10. Ibid: 118. My emphasis.

11. Ibid: 119–20.

12. Ibid: 154.

13. Ibid: 159.

14. For an estimate of Egypt's population in the mid-third millennium BC, see Romer (2007: 76).

15. Finkelstein and Silberman (2002: ch. 7).

16. Ibid: 193–94.

17. On Israel's breeding of horses for export, see ibid: 211.

18. On the imposition of direct Assyrian rule in Palestine in the mid-eighth century BC, see Haywood (2005: 46).

19. For estimates of Israelites deported by the Assyrians in the mid-eighth century BC, see Haywood (2005: 46) and Finkelstein and Silberman (2002: 216).

20. Estimated numbers of Israelites deported in the later-eighth century BC – see Finkelstein and Silberman (2002: 221).

21. Graphical accounts of the changing balance of power between Egypt and Assyria are contained in Manley (2002: 118–19, 120–21) and McEvedy (1983: 42–49).

22. For graphical sketches of the final struggles of Assyria with Egypt before falling to the Babylonians, see Manley (2002: 122–23) and Haywood (2005: 46–47).

23. Finkelstein and Silberman (2002: 283).

24. Egyptian population estimates for late seventh century BC can be found in Romer (2007: 76).

25. Finkelstein and Silberman (2002: 277).

26. Ibid.

27. Naaman (1991).

28. Finkelstein and Silberman (2002: 295).

29. Aramaic is a semitic language closely related to Hebrew. The same script – derived from the Phoenician – is employed for both languages, which have "approximately the same phonological characteristics, including the position of the stress" (Douglas 1962: 713).

30. The invention of the alphabet is discussed in Fagan (2004: 229).

31. Caquot (1974: 86).

32. Britannica (2005).

33. Caquot (1974: 87). My emphasis.

34. Jordan (2002).

35. Ibid: 167.

36. On the tribal origins of YHWH – see Armstrong (1999: 29).

37. Bible (Revised Standard Version).

38. This account of the *origin* and *history* of the Hebrew Bible draws heavily on Finkelstein and Silberman's (2002) persuasive analysis. However, my conclusions concerning the Bible's *purpose* differs markedly from theirs. I employ a strategic interpretation.

39. Armstrong (1999: 19–20) and Finkelstein and Silberman (2002: 11–13).

40. Finkelstein and Silberman (2002: 45).

41. Ibid: ch. 2.

42. Ibid: 66–71.

43. Ibid: 72. See also Darnell and Manassa (2007).

44. The Armarna tablets are discussed by Tyldesley (2005) and Darnell and Manassa (2007).

45. The Sea Peoples and the "invasion" of Canaan – see Manley (1996: 96–97).

46. Finkelstein and Silberman (2002: 90–92).

47. Ibid: 95.

48. Ibid: 96. My emphasis.

49. Ibid: 50. My emphasis.

50. The "minimalists" include Thompson (1999), Lemche (1994), and Davies (1992).

51. On the insignificance of Judah in the time of David and Solomon, see Finkelstein and Silberman (2002: 132–34, 143).

52. Ibid: 144.

53. Ibid: 194–95.

54. For evidence of pagan worship in ninth and eight century BC Judah, see ibid: 241.

55. Ibid: 301–02.

56. Neusner (2006: 593).

57. Ibid: 594.

58. Ibid: 588.

Chapter 5 **Triumph of the One God: II Christianity and Islam**

1. For a discussion of Greek and Roman strategic guardians, see Snooks (1997a: chs 6 and 8).

2. For a comparison of rates of expansion of Rome, UK, and the world over periods of five to seven centuries, see Snooks (1993: 247; 1997a: 137).

3. The best way to visualize the changing face of medieval Europe is by consulting a series of political maps. See McEvedy (1980).

4. The changing distribution of Western Europe's population from 0–1000 AD has been calculated from Maddison (2001; 2003).

5. For a detailed analysis of the strategic-sequence mechanism in England, 1000 to date, see Snooks (1997a: ch. 10).

6. Mack (1994: 21).

7. Ibid: 22.

8. On the discovery of the Gospel of Thomas, see Meyer (1992).

9. Mack (1994: 37).

10. Ibid: 111–12.

11. On the influence of the Cynic school of philosophy on Jesus of Nazareth, see Mack (1994) and Crossan (1995). Crossan is more cautious in this than Mack, with – as we will see – good reason.

12. Mack (1994: 115).

13. Ibid: 120.

14. Book of Q: Qs 20.

15. Quoted in Crossan (1995: 117).

16. Ibid: 118–19.

17. Ibid: 93.

18. Ibid: 101.

19. Ibid: 68.

20. Ibid: 82.

21. Mack (1994: 134). My emphasis.

22. Ibid: 173–74.

23. Ibid: 178.

24. The story about the Gospel of Judas is told by Kronsey (2006). The 1,500-year-old manuscript of the Judas Gospel was discovered during the second half of the 1970s in the Nile Valley just north of El Minya. It was not repaired, translated, and published until 2006. In this work, originally written about AD 150, Judas the betrayer becomes Judas the confidante of Jesus – indeed the only disciple who truly understands Jesus' mission and is able to help facilitate it. The other disciples are left in ignorance.

25. See Mack (1994: 187) for an account of Luke's interest in the history of Christianity.

26. On the apostolic mythology concocted by Luke see ibid: 234.

27. Balling (2003: 76).

28. Ibid: 78.
29. Chadwick (2002: 47).
30. Balling (2003: 81).
31. For orthodox explanations of the survival of the early Church in the face of Roman persecutions, see ibid: 81.
32. On Christian martyrs and terrorists, see Chadwick (2002: 48–49).
33. Ibid: 51.
34. There are many leaders today who could learn from the orderly succession of Roman leadership in the early fourth century AD!
35. Balling (2003: 82).
36. The collapse of the western half of the Roman empire is analyzed strategically in Snooks (1997a: ch. 6).
37. Chadwick (2002: 68).
38. Ware (2002: 133).
39. Ibid: 134.
40. Ibid: 139–40.
41. Ibid: 142–43.
42. Balling (2003: 118).
43. Mayr-Harting (2002: 106).
44. Balling (2003: 115).
45. Mayr-Harting (2002: 110).
46. Ibid: 111.
47. Sociopolitical characteristics are shaped by the type of dynamic strategy pursued, and the stage reached in the strategic unfolding process. See Snooks (1997a: chs 3, 6, 10).
48. Morris (2002: 231).
49. Balling (2003: 146).
50. Ibid.
51. Ibid: 148.
52. Ibid.
53. Ibid: 155.
54. Ibid: 135.
55. Collinson (2002: 248).
56. Ibid.
57. Ibid: 249.
58. Balling (2003: 188–90).
59. For a detailed strategic analysis of the emergence of protestantism in England, see Snooks (1997a: ch. 10).
60. "Capitalism" is a vague, unscientific, and unhelpful term. *All* societies (including those in the ancient world) are capitalist in the sense that they mobilize surpluses to invest heavily in the infrastructure of their dynamic strategy so as to generate high rates of return. Modern market societies are not unique in this respect.

61. Armstrong (2001: 3). See also Lapidus (2007: 24–26).

62 Ibid: 6–7.

63. Kennedy (2007: 44). For a helpful visual overview of the fluctuating fortunes of the various Islamic empires, see McEvedy (1980).

64. Kennedy (2007: 46).

65. Quran (4: 74).

66. Quran (8: 45).

67. Kennedy (2007: 65). This confirms the message of my first strategic-pursuit book, *The Dynamic Society* (Snooks 1996: 430): "The end of the Dynamic Society? There is no end towards which it is inexorably progressing. There is no final destination. Only continuous journeying." The failure to do so leads to crisis and collapse.

68. Kennedy (2007: 71).

69. Armstrong (2001: 25).

70. Kennedy (2007: 135).

71. Ibid: 62.

72. Lapidus (2007: 31–106, 299–333, 337–397); Smith (1999: 305–45).

73. Lapidus (2007: 815).

74. Ibid: 226–44.

75. Ibid: 226–29.

76. Ibid: 248–94; Lapidus (1999: 347–93).

77. Armstrong (2001: 40).

78. Ibn Khaldun (1967).

79. Armstrong (2001: 87).

80. Ibid: 88.

81. In his encyclopedia of gods, Jordan (2002) lists some 2,500 deities, yet "makes no claim to be exhaustive" (p. vii). He explicitly excludes "demi-gods, demons or mythical heros". Jordan also notes that the Hittites alone were said to have had "in excess of 10,000" gods, and that both Japanese Shintoism and Chinese religion had at least that number. Also see Bowker (2002) and Hind (2004). Clearly the gods of some 2,000 years ago must have numbered in the hundreds of thousands.

Chapter 6 **Death of the Old God**

1. Nietzsche first announced the death of God in *The Gay Science* (1882: Bk 3: 108, 125).

2. Nietzsche, *Zarathustra* (1883: Part I, # 2&3).

3. Balling (2003: 238–39).

4. A lack of preconditions: As shown in *The Collapse of Darwinism* (Snooks 2006a), the reason for the failure of the supply-side evolutionary theory of neo-Darwinism to explain the emergence of civilization is that natural selection is a blind and artificial mechanism that cannot anticipate future needs. Even the high priest of sociobiology, Edward Wilson (1998: 48) is forced to confess this reality.

5. For discussions of the persecution and/or intimidation of scientists and intellectuals by the Catholic Church from the sixteenth to the twentieth centuries, see Bald (1998) and Gribbin (2002).

6. Material progress is the outcome of a blind striving to survive and prosper – see Snooks (1996; 1997a; 1998a).

7. Balling (2003: 242).

8. For an account of Charles Lyell and his new geology, see Oldroyd (2006).

9. Darwin's astonishment at the impact of the earthquake in Concepción on the local cathedral is recorded in his Beagle *Diary*, 5th March 1835.

10. Darwin's Beagle voyage is discussed by Desmond and Moore (1991: 101–82).

11. Darwin's analysis can be found in Darwin (1859; 1868; 1871). For a biographical account see Desmond and Moore (1991); and for a critical account — *The Collapse of Darwinism* — see Snooks (2006a: chs 2–4).

12. On the nineteenth-century struggle between professional scientists and parson-naturalists, see McGrath (2005).

13. Desmond and Moore (1991: 465).

14. The new social scientists, who emphasized historical laws rather than divine laws, are discussed in Snooks (1998a: chs 4–5).

15. Comte (1896: 1–2).

16. On J.S. Mill's flirtation with Comte and the method of induction, but his eventual recidivism, see Snooks (1998a: 96–105).

17. Buckle (1894: vol. I, p. 335).

18. A more detailed discussion of Buckle's ideas can be found in Snooks (1998a: 105–14).

19. For an account of Heraclitus, Hegel and Marx, see Snooks (1998a: ch. 3).

20. On the metaphysical nature of Marx's theories, see Snooks (1998a: 49–55).

21. On Darwin's letter to Spencer, see Carneiro (1974: lx–lvii).

22. On Spencer's evolutionary theory, see Snooks (1998a: 59–62).

23. The fundamental shortcomings of the grand Victorian theories of Marx, Darwin, and Freud are discussed in Snooks (1998a; 2003; 2006), respectively.

24. Balling (2003: 249).

25. On the ecumenical movement, see Chadwick (2002: 381–82).

26. On the world distribution of Christianity from 1780 to 2000, see Taylor (2002: 652).

27. On increasing membership in major world religions from 1920 to 2000, see ibid: 649.

28. On America as a "covenanted nation", see Marty (2002: 403).

29. Esposito (1999a: 643).

30. Ibid: 656.

31. On the Islamic modernist movement, see Lapidus (2007: 817–18, 453–68) and Esposito (1999: 643–90).

32. Esposito (1999: 648) discusses al-Afghani's distinction between Islam as religion and as civilization.

33. Ibid: 656.

Chapter 7 **Dead God Rising**

1. The discussion of the technological-paradigm-shift mechanism is based on Snooks (1996; 1997; 1998a).

2. The Snooks-Panov algorithm is discussed in Nazaretyan (2005a; 2006b) and Snooks (2005: 229–31), and Chapter 10 above.

3. For the first formal discussion of the future technological paradigm shift, see Snooks (1996: ch. 13). It is discussed in further detail — together with the implications for climate mitigation — in *The Coming Eclipse* (Snooks 2010).

4. On the future "Solar Revolution", see Snooks (1996: 429–30; 2003: 262–63) and Snooks (2009).

5. For a graphic account of the most important inventions of the ancient world, see Fagan (2004).

6. The technological strategy was not an economic option until the exhaustion of the neolithic technological paradigm in the mid-eighteenth century. This is why every ancient society returned to conquest once its commerce strategy had been exhausted.

7. For a discussion of the Greek **strategic sequence** and its societal impact, see Snooks (1997a: ch. 8).

8. In this book, Greek science is of greater interest than Greek religion because it is the former rather than the latter that impacted on Western civilization as the facilitator of the industrial technological paradigm shift.

9. For an outline of the outcomes of Egyptian science, see Fagan (2004).

10. The British Industrial Revolution is analyzed in Snooks (1994b; 1997a: ch. 10).

11. "Emerging from the dark" – Gribbin (2002: 3–4).

12. Galileo's story is well told by Gribbin (2002: ch. 3) and Sobel (1999). Also see Bald (1998).

13. On scientific developments in the eighteenth century, see Gribbin (2002: ch. 8).

14. Quoted in Isaacson (2007: 90).

15. Williams in Britannica (2005): "The 20th-century revolution", p. 1.

16. Isaacson (2007: 94–101).

17. Ibid: 335, 460–61.

18. Ibid: 463.

19. Could a strategically irrational ecological dictator derail the scientific revolution? See Snooks (1996: ch. 13) and Snooks (2010: ch. 5).

20. Williams (2005: 2).

21. Shermer (2002). My emphasis.

22. The flawed nature of sociobiology is discussed in Snooks (2006a: chs 7 and 8), and Chapter 8 above.

23. The limitations of social physics are outlined in Snooks (2007; 2008a), and the Appendix above.

24. For my discovery of the growth-inflation curve, see Snooks (1997b; 1998: ch. 11); and for applications, see Snooks (2008b; 2008c).

Chapter 8 **A Science of Religion?**

1. Wilson (1999: 290) – my emphasis. It should be noted that over time I have used two different printings of *Consilience*: the initial 1998 volume and the later 1999 reprint that has different pagination.
2. Ibid: 262.
3. Wilson (1998: 164) – the initial volume.
4. Ibid: 137.
5. Ibid: 165.
6. Ibid: 165–66.
7. Ibid: 151.
8. Wilson (1975: 4).
9. Wilson (1978: 167). My emphasis.
10. Other critics of sociobiology include Gould and Lewontin (1979), Eldredge (1995), and Rose (2001).
11. Jones (1999: xxxvi).
12. Wilson (1998: 158).
13. Ibid: 143.
14. For geneticists who disagree with Wilson's "tight genetic leash" interpretation, see Snooks (2003: 132–33).
15. Wilson (1998: 154).
16. On the "myth of coevolution", see Snooks (2003: 134–39).
17. Wilson (1998: 127).
18. Ibid: 128.
19. Ibid: 130.
20. Ibid: 136.
21. Ibid: 223.
22. The psychological fantasies of neo-Darwinists like Wilson are exposed in Snooks (2006a; 242–47).
23. The developing brain is a response not to epigenetic rules but to strategic demand – see Snooks (2006a: chs 8 and 9).
24. Wilson (1999: 270).
25. Ibid: 276–78.
26. Ibid: 277.
27. Ibid: 280.
28. Exploding the myth of religions "evolution" – see Snooks (1997a: ch. 1).
29. Wilson (1999: 281).
30. Ibid: 281–82.
31. Ibid: 282 and 286. My emphasis.
32. Ibid: 281.

33. Contrary to the publisher's puffery for Richard Dawkins' *The God Delusion*, the book is *not* "brilliantly argued"; it does *not* exhibit "clarity and elegance"; it is *not* "well written"; it is *not* an "elegant book"; it is *not* "a heroic and life changing book". Rather, it is a tired, pompous, short-tempered, forced, entirely misjudged, poorly written, crude, and exceedingly dull book. But worst of all, it is completely wrong in its analysis and conclusions. It is hard to believe that the author of *The God Delusion* is the same person responsible for the brilliantly written and witty – although equally intellectually flawed (and for the same reasons) – book *The Selfish Gene* of some thirty years earlier.

34. Dawkins (2006: 71).

35. Ibid: 31.

36. Ibid.

37. For a discussion of the new concept of selfcreation, see Snooks (2003: ch. 12; 2006a: ch. 3) and the Appendix above.

38. Dawkins (2006: 282).

39. Ibid.

40. The critics of the "ultra-Darwinism" of Dawkins and his mates include Gould and Lewontin (1979) and Eldredge (1995).

41. For a discussion of the methods employed by Dawkins, see Snooks (2003: ch. 6).

42. Dawkins (2006: 283).

43. Ibid: 120.

44. In *The God Delusion*, Dawkins states his faith in natural selection as the only workable alternative to chance on at least six occasions: namely, pp. 114, 120, 121, 150–51, 155–56, and 158.

45. My work – particularly Snooks (1996; 1997a; 1998a; 2003; 2006a) – has been the subject of many discussions on a website ("Internet Infidels"), which Dawkins includes in an appendix (p. 376) to *The God Delusion* with the title "A partial list of friendly addresses for individuals needing support in escaping from religion". Yet Dawkins chooses to ignore one of his own favored sources. Also I emailed him a copy of my 2005 article, "The origins of life on Earth", published in *Advances in Space Research*. This paper has been one of *ASR*'s most downloaded articles. Since then I have published a major article – "A general theory of complex living systems" – in the widely-read and influential science journal *Complexity* (the journal of the Santa Fe Institute) in 2008. Dawkins continues to ignore this new alternative to Darwinism.

46. Dawkins (2006: 215–16).

47. Ibid: 219–20.

48. On "Darwinian mistakes", see Dawkins (2006: 221).

49. Ibid: 223.

50. On the absurdity of the selfish-gene concept and flaws in natural selection, see Snooks (1996: 143–50; 2003: part I).

51. Dawkins (2006: 140–41).

52. Ibid: 164–65.

53. Ibid: 169.

54. Ibid: 172–74.

55. Ibid: 174–76.

56. Ibid: 179.

57. Ibid: 188.

58. Ibid.

59. The flaws in the "meme" concept are exposed in Snooks (1996).

60. Dawkins (2006: 199).

61. Ibid: 1–2.

62. Ibid: 304.

63. Ibid: 306.

64. Ibid: 312–13.

65. Ibid: 319.

66. Ibid: 341.

67. No attempt has been made to review the creationist literature here because their use of metaphysical mythology to provide a "scientific" and "rational" explanation of the origin of the cosmos and of life is misdirected and pointless. Those interested in this futile attempt could consult Numbers (2006). Also, for a theological response to Dawkins, see McGrath (2004; 2005).

68. Hamer (2004: 142).

69. Ibid: 213.

70. Ibid: 28.

71. Ibid: 11.

72. Ibid: 73–74.

73. Ibid: 75–76.

74. Ibid: 11.

75. Ibid: 139.

76. Ibid: 12.

77. Ibid: 159.

78. Ibid: 15–16.

79. Ibid: 13.

80. Ibid: 162.

81. Ibid: 214.

82. Neo-Darwinist camp-followers include Boyer (2001), Atran (2002), and Dennett (2006). The group-selectionist "heretic" is David Wilson (2002).

83. Dennett (2006: 35).

84. Ibid: 39.

85. Ibid: 37.

86. Ibid: 116, 123.

87. Ibid: 114. My emphasis.

Chapter 9 **A Religion of Science**

1. Davies (1993: 148–49). My emphasis.
2. Ibid: 20.
3. Ibid: 21.
4. Ibid: 93.
5. Ibid: 108–109.
6. Ibid: 152.
7. Wilson (1998: 48).
8. Ibid: 232. My emphasis.
9. On the deficiencies of social physics and complexity theory, see Snooks (2007; 2008a), and the Appendix above.
10. Lovelock (1990: xvi; 2006).
11. Lovelock (2006: 15).
12. Lovelock (1990: 31).
13. Lovelock (2006: 15–16).
14. Ibid: 17. My emphasis.
15. Ibid: 21. My emphasis.
16. Ibid: 35–36.
17. Ibid: 38.
18. Lovelock (1990: 42).
19. Lovelock (2006: 17). My emphasis.
20. Lovelock (1990: 39).
21. Lovelock (1990: 57, 60–61) suggests a self-regulating "climate control system" as an analogy for the way Gaia is supposed to work.
22. Lovelock (1990: 31, 33).
23. Ibid: 45.
24. Ibid: 59.
25. Ibid: 60.
26. Ibid: 232.
27. Ibid: 158. My emphasis.
28. Ibid: 158–59.
29. Lovelock (2006: 44–45).
30. Ibid: 45. My emphasis.
31. Ibid: 135, 136.
32. Recent (March 2008) calculations by Robert Smith and his team at the University of Sussex suggest that the Earth will be engulfed by the sun in about 7,600 myrs. Life, however, will disappear long before then.
33. For a fascinating discussion of plate tectonics as a general theory of dynamics of the Earth's physical system, see Cloud (1988: 117–216). See also Snooks (1996: 28–30), and Oldroyd (2006).

34. Lovelock (1990: 12; 2006; 145). My emphasis.
35. Lovelock (1990: 205).
36. Ibid: 206–07.
37. Lovelock (2006: 147).
38. Ibid: 148.
39. Gardner (2003: 9).
40. Ibid: 205.
41. Ibid: 25.
42. Ibid: 15.
43. Ibid: 119.
44. Ibid: 126.
45. Ibid: 204.
46. Ibid: 204–05. My emphasis.
47. Ibid: 177.
48. Ibid: 178.
49. Ibid. My emphasis.
50. Ibid: 143–49. My emphasis.
51. Ibid: 149–51.
52. Ibid: 163.
53. Ibid: 136.
54. Ibid: 148.
55. For a critical analysis of Darwinian and complexity theories, see Snooks (2003; 2005; 2007; 2008a).
56. Gardner (2006: 207–10).
57. Ibid: 228.
58. Ibid: 225–26.
59. Whitehead is quoted in ibid: 226.
60. Gardner (2006: 228).
61 Ibid: 226.

Chapter 10 **Life's Great Odyssey**

1. The research underlying the "Snooks algorithm", which describes the exponential growth of life and human society over the past 3,800 myrs, can be found in Snooks (1996: 79–82, 92–95, 402–05).
2. The geometric increase in biomass is discussed in Snooks (1996: 74–95) and Snooks (2003: chs 9 and 13).
3. The Snooksian algorithm: Some seven years after my discovery of this algorithm, the Russian physicist A.D. Panov (2005) independently developed an algorithm with a very similar coefficient of acceleration – 2.67 ± 0.15 compared with my 3.0 (see Narazatyan 2005a; 2005b). This combined research outcome is called the "Snooks-Panov vertical" in the literature.

4. The "Law of Cumulative Biological/Technological Change" was first presented in Snooks (2003: 287–88).

5. A discussion of the laws of both life and human society can be found in Snooks (1998a; 2003: ch. 5).

6. For an account of metabolic systems, see Bakker (1978: 137–40).

7. The "finesse versus force" argument can be found in Snooks (2003: 182–95).

Chapter 11 Selfcreation – A Realist Theory of Life

1. A detailed discussion of the new concept selfcreation – and its contrasting nature compared with self-organization – can be found in Snooks (2003; 2007; 2008a). Also see the Appendix above.

2. Neo-Darwinist decision-making is discussed in Snooks (2003: chs 6 and 7), while rationalist decision making is evaluated in Snooks (1997a: chs 4 and 5).

3. For the development over time of my strategic-imitation decision model, see sequentially Snooks (1996; 1997a; 1998b; 1999; 2003; 2006a).

4. Early life forms could pursue a full range of dynamic strategies – see Snooks (2003: chs 9 and 12).

5. For pioneering research on the use of special genes in simple life forms to direct, what I call, dynamic strategies, see Cairns et al (1988), Hall, (1988), and Foster (1999).

6. The confused "punctuated equilibria" concept was introduced by Eldredge and Gould (1972).

7. For the employment of genetic change in the development of biological weapons during a dynastic (e.g. dinosaur) conquest strategy, see Snooks (2003: ch. 9).

8. The role of strategic confidence in depression and recovery in history is discussed in Snooks (1997: 415–16), and in contemporary society in Snooks (2008d).

9. For a discussion of the strategic struggle between the protodynosaurs and the protomammals, see Snooks (2003: 169–73).

10. The struggle between the leaders of commerce and of industry for control of Britain's dynamic strategy in the first half of the nineteenth century is discussed in Snooks (1997a: ch. 9).

11. The terminal struggle for control of Rome, once its conquest strategy was exhausted, is analyzed in Snooks (1997a: ch. 6).

12. For a discussion of coevolution and the "genetic leash" argument see Chapter 8 above, and Snooks (2003: ch. 8; 2006a: ch. 13).

13. For an overview of the development of the concentric-spheres concept in my work, see Snooks (1994; 1997a; 1998b; 1999; 2003; 2006a).

14. The concept of "strategic exchange" was first suggested in Snooks (2007) and developed in Snooks (2008a).

Chapter 12 The Strategic *Logos*

1. For a brief discussion of the "universal constants of nature" – including Newton's gravitational constant, Boltzmann's constant, Avogadro's constant, the velocity of light, Planck's constant, the electron charge, electron mass, proton mass, W-particle

mass, cosmological constant – see Bais (2005). What scientists have overlooked is the "logological constant" introduced in chapter 10.

2. For an evaluation of self-organization and complexity theory see Snooks (2007; 2008a) and the Appendix above.

3. A discussion of the impact of the bubonic plague on the Hundred Year's War can be found in Snooks (1997a: ch. 10).

4. Social physics and complexity theory are discussed from the dynamic-strategy theory standpoint in Snooks (2007, 2008a), and, briefly, in the Appendix above.

5. This survey of what I call the universal life-system (or strategic *logos*) owes much to Roy Rappaport, although it should be noted that I didn't read (October 2005) his eccentric *Ritual and Religion* (2002) until after the typescript of my as yet unpublished book on truth – in which the concept of the strategic *logos* was first outlined in detail – had been completed (July 2004). The book on truth – *The Death of Zarathustra. Notes on Truth for the Risktaker* – will not be published until after *Dead God Rising* has appeared, owning to my desire to provide a more orderly sequence for my books in the "strategic pursuit" project.

6. The edition of Heraclitus consulted is Haxton (2001).

7. The eccentric, but engaging, Roy Rapport (2002: ch. 11).

8. For the various names given to the mystery of mysteries in the ancient and premodern world, see Rapport (2002: 353–70), Grimal (1974: 190–93), Redford (2003: 189–91), and Spence (2004).

9. The laws of the strategic *logos* – or the laws of history and of life – are identified and discussed in Snooks (1998a; 2003: ch. 15).

10. The concept of "strategic exchange" is introduced and discussed in Snooks (2007; 2008a); and it is contrasted with the flawed supply-side concept of "emergence".

11. Curiously, while physicists have been able to observe patterns in the cosmos and thereby construct physical laws, they have been unable to develop a general dynamic theory of the Universe that incorporates these laws together with the observable constants of nature. Instead they have focused on simple mathematical descriptions of all known laws at both the micro (quantum theory) and the macro (relativity theory) levels. Mathematics can limit as well as advance the development of science.

Glossary of new terms and concepts

This glossary includes the new terms and concepts arising from the dynamic-strategy theory and employed in this book. When a new term or concept is first mentioned in any of the above chapters it appears in bold type. Italics in the glossary indicate that additional concepts are defined here.

Antistrategists are individuals who attempt to undermine the strategic pursuit for their own nefarious purposes by engaging in rent-seeking activities. Under normal conditions, antistrategists are a source of irritation and constitute a manageable cost to human society, but if they gain positions of dictatorial authority they will attempt to oppress the *strategists* and divert the former strategic surplus to their own devious ends. Examples of the latter include Akhenaten (the "criminal of Akhetaten"), Mao Tse-Tung, Stalin, Hitler, and Pol Pot. Terrorists are also antistrategists who can impose considerable costs on human society. A regime dominated by climate mitigationists would also be antistrategic.

Autogenous – see *selfcreation.*

Coefficient of acceleration of life is the geometric rate of change in the growth of global biomass (see Figure 10.1). The Snooks-Panov algorithm suggests that this coefficient has the constant value 3.0. I have called this the *logological constant.*

Commerce strategy. The dynamic strategy of commerce, or symbiosis, is a more specialized means of achieving prosperity, practiced by a variety of plants, bacteria, viruses, insects, and other animals, and, most spectacularly, by some human societies. It can be thought of in nature as an alternative *dynamic strategy* to *family multiplication* and in human society as an alternative to *conquest.* Under this strategy an organism/society that manages to gain a monopoly over an important resource or location may exchange it for a resource or locational access held by a different organism/society. This exchange is to their mutual, even if unequal, advantage.

Concentric-spheres model of behavior. In the concentric-spheres model represented in Figure 11.1 – originally developed to explain human society – the self is at the center of a set of concentric spheres that define the varying strength of cooperative relationships between it and all other individuals and groups in society. The strength of the social relationships between the self and others – which can be measured by the *economic distance* between them – will depend on how essential they are to maximizing the probability of the self's survival and prosperity. As the economic distance – a measure of materialistic rather than genetic relatedness – between the center and each sphere increases, the degree of cooperation (*not* "altruism") between them diminishes. It is because economic forces transcend biological forces that the concentric-spheres model can explain what the kin-selection model cannot – the varying cooperative relationships between any given individual and all others in society. The concentric-spheres model, therefore, involves two sets of forces, one centrifugal and the other centripetal in nature. The centrifugal force is the incessant *strategic desire* of the self to survive and prosper – a desire that leads, on average, to the individual placing itself above all others. It is the driving force in life. The centripetal force – the economic gravity holding society together – is the need to cooperate with other individuals and groups in order to pursue the dominant *dynamic strategy* more effectively. It is through both competition and cooperation that the *materialist organism* maximizes the probability of its survival and prosperity. See also *strategic exchange*.

Conquest strategy. This has played a major role in the dynamics of both life and human society. In life, conquest has been responsible for the elimination – the extinction – of those species and dynasties that had exhausted their *genetic styles* and/or *genetic paradigms*. By doing so they provided other species and potential dynasties with the opportunity to show what they could do. If the dinosaurs, for example, had not eliminated themselves through their "world wars", the mammals would never have had the chance to show what their passion for the intellect could do on life's stage. And in human society, conquest was responsible for taking the agricultural revolution around the world – at first the Old World and then the New World – thereby ultimately exhausting the neolithic technological paradigm (by the mid-eighteenth century in the Old World) and making way for the Industrial Revolution (1780 to 1830). This transforming role could only be identified in retrospect. In prospect, conquest has always been adopted because, once a species' *family-multiplication strategy* had been exhausted, it was the only way that organisms could hope to survive and prosper in a competitive world.

Dynamic strategies. To achieve its objective of survival and prosperity, the *materialist organism* must find a way to gain consistent, long-term access to the resources required for generating metabolic energy and for providing shelter. It must pursue a dynamic strategy that will deliver a reliable return on the energy it expends in its participation in life. The most appropriate dynamic strategy will depend on the physical environment – on the availability of natural resources – and on the degree of competition with other organisms in their own and neighboring species. The dynamic strategies of life are four-fold: *genetic/technological change, family multiplication, commerce* (symbiosis), and *conquest*. These strategies are "dynamic" because they are employed by organisms (including man) to maximize the probability of survival and prosperity over the lifetime of the individual, and because, when successful, they lead to the transmutation of species, to population increase, to geographic expansion of the species or dynasty, and to biological or economic growth (an increase in "output" per unit of input).

Dynamic strategist – see *strategist*.

Dynamic-strategy theory is a general dynamic theory that transcends the specialist preoccupations of both the biologist and the social scientist. It can explain and predict the dynamics of both life and human society together with the origin and role of the conscious mind. Without it we cannot understand or survive future climate change. It has also led to the discovery of the *strategic logos* and, hence, to an understanding of the nature of God and the role of religion. This theory, which is the only successful demand-side dynamic theory, was first proposed in Snooks (1996). See also *strategic demand-response mechanism*.

Economic distance is the measure of the strength of material relationships between the self and all other individuals and groups in society. Economic distance is inversely related to the importance of other individuals and groups in maximizing the material objectives of the self. Hence family and close associates occupy the spheres nearest to the self, and strangers are to be found on the most distant spheres. It is an important component of the *concentric-spheres model of behavior*. This model replaces the flawed neo-Darwinist theory of kin selection.

Eternal recurrence in reality is the ultimate outcome of the exhaustion of the resource-accessing capacity of life's *genetic option*. Subsequent biological activity involves the rise and fall of life's dynasties without any improvement in their access to Earth's resources. This is the *great wheel of life* (see Figure 10.5). The only way to break out of this eternal recurrence is through the replacement of the genetic option with the *technology option*. In Nietzsche's philosophy this existential eternal recurrence is given a metaphysical interpretation.

Existential schizophrenia is a non-pathological condition required to resolve the problem of "strategic dualism" in man (Snooks 2006a). It involves the need to divide our lives into mutually exclusive compartments – what we do and what we pretend we do – to enable our minds to coexist with our bodies. When this mechanism breaks down, psychotic mental disorders emerge in susceptible individuals. This concept was first introduced in Snooks (1996) and developed in Snooks (2006a).

Family-multiplication strategy involves the exploitation of unused resources through procreation and migration to new regions. By increasing the size of the extended family and gaining greater control over natural resources, the family head is able to achieve the universal objectives of survival and the maximization of material advantage. This is the force that drove the primitive dynamic, which has been called here the "great dispersion". Family multiplication is a strategy pursued by plants as well as animals and humans.

Funnel of transformation is a physical environmental factor that helped to determine where the Neolithic Revolution would occur once the paleolithic technological paradigm was approaching exhaustion. In the Old World this was the Fertile Crescent, and in the New World it was the Mesoamerican isthmus. During the Paleolithic Revolution the Rift Valley of East Africa played a similar role; as did the Anglo-Dutch lake (the North Sea) and surrounding territories during the Industrial Revolution. These were corridors of greater population density, heightened competition, appropriate resources, and exchange of ideas through which people passed on a regular basis. They were primary sites of technological change and springboards for its transfer to the rest of the known world.

Genetic competence is the effectiveness with which a dynasty is able to exploit life's *genetic option* in order to gain access to the Earth's resources.

Genetic option. In the history of life, organisms have been able to improve their access to the Earth's resources through the genetic option – the use of the dynamic strategy of *genetic change* – and, when it was totally exhausted, the *technology option*. With each *genetic paradigm shift* the capacity of the genetic option was progressively exploited until it was finally exhausted by the time the dinosaurs were in their prime (80 myrs ago). The technology option, however, only displaced the defunct genetic option when the intellectual capability of the hominids enabled them to employ the *technological strategy* (2.4 myrs ago). During the almost 80 myrs between these events, nature was dominated by the *great wheel of life*. If life had relied only on the genetic option it would never have escaped the *eternal recurrence,* and humanity would never have emerged.

Genetic paradigm. This is the genetic basis on which an entire dynasty of life gains access to the Earth's resources. Each paradigm consists of a series of *genetic styles* – more commonly known as species – which employ specialized genetic techniques to survive and prosper.

Genetic strategy. Possibly the most controversial feature of the *dynamic-strategy theory* is its treatment of genetic change. Rather than viewing the emergence of species as the outcome of either "divine selection" or "natural selection", it is seen as the result of *strategic selection*, or self-selection writ large. Genetic change in other words is a *dynamic strategy* that is deliberately pursued by organisms – similar to the role of technological change in human society – when the circumstances are favorable. Organisms select those mutations that assist their dominant dynamic strategy and they ignore the rest. They do this by cooperating and mating with those individuals who have an edge in accessing natural resources as demonstrated by their material success. This occurs not just when pursuing genetic change as a dominant dynamic strategy, but also sometimes under the non-genetic strategies in response to the strategic demand that they generate for military weapons (*conquest*) and fertility/mobility aids (*family multiplication*). Accordingly, the concept of strategic selection is far more general in its application than Charles Darwin's concept of natural selection, to which he was forced to add "sexual selection" as a separate and puzzling process (Snooks 2003). This is why the dynamic-strategy theory, in contrast to Darwinian evolution, is a *general* dynamic theory.

Genetic style. Within any *genetic paradigm* there is a series of genetic styles that are the outcome of species pursuing the dynamic strategy of *genetic change* in order to gain access to the Earth's resources and hence to survive and prosper. See also *technological styles*.

Great steps of life. The dynamic structure of life is defined by a series of *genetic* and *technological paradigm shifts*, which I have called the great steps of life (Figures 10.3 & 10.4). These great steps, which outline the genetic/technological potential for biological/economic development, are driven by major genetic/technological revolutions. Owing to the nature of the dynamics of life, these great steps have been changing exponentially in two dimensions: increasing in height while reducing in depth. What this implies is that the dynamics of both life and human society have been accelerating over the past 3,500 myrs – see *coefficient of acceleration of life*. There have been three genetic paradigm shifts and three technological paradigm shifts over that vast period of time, and they are involved in a systematic geometric relationship – see *logological constant*.

Great waves of economic change, which are of about 300 years in duration, are responsible for transmitting economic progress in human society. These waves are driven by the dynamic strategies of conquest, commerce, or technological change.

Great waves of life (of geometrically declining duration) are generated by the rise and fall of dynasties and encompass the long waves (of about 30 myrs) generated by the rise and fall of groups of species, which in turn contain the shorter waves (of up to 6 myrs or so) generated by the rise and fall of individual species (Figure 10.2). At all levels these waves are generated by the expansion, exhaustion, and replacement of *dynamic strategies, genetic/technological styles*, or *genetic/technological paradigms*. This pattern of waves within waves, therefore, constitutes the dynamic form of the *dynamic-strategy model*.

Great wheel of life. This is the mechanism of the *eternal recurrence* (Figure 10.5). It is the process of biological baton-passing whereby a dynasty emerges to exploit a *genetic paradigm*, exhausts their version of it, collapses and is followed in the same way by a new dynasty operating within the same paradigm. The great wheel of life rotates without gaining traction, without being able to generate a new paradigm shift to replace the old exhausted paradigm. Without gaining more intensive access to the Earth's natural resources. The great wheel of life comes into operation in a mature life system when the *genetic option* has been exhausted. At this point in time it is no longer possible through genetic change to increase the global level of the biomass of life. The only way to break out of this eternal recurrence is through the replacement of the genetic option with the *technology option*.

Imitative information is sought and processed by the strategic cerebrum to achieve long-term survival and prosperity. Essentially, this constitutes data about who and what is successful and why. The objective is to imitate conspicuous success. It is the basis of *strategic imitation* by which the successful strategies of the few are copied by the many. See also *pattern-recognition information*.

Intelligence Revolution. This revolution was the outcome of mammals – in contrast to dinosaurs – following the strategic pursuit with finesse rather than force. It enabled one line of mammals – *Homo sapiens* – to escape the *eternal recurrence* as represented by the *great wheel of life*.

Logological constant reflects the resilience and success of the *strategic logos*. I have discovered that over the past 3,000 myrs the global biomass/GDP has not only increased at an exponential rate, but also at a constant geometric rate, with a value of approximately 3.0. This suggests that each biological/technological transformation (taken as a whole) occurs in one-third of the time taken by the previous one. This fundamental constant of life is ample proof of the resilience and effectiveness of the *strategic logos* in the face of both the second law of thermodynamics and the hostile physical and biological world. What the "logological constant" measures is at least as remarkable and unchanging as the fundamental constants of the physical world (particularly the cosmological constant). The logological constant is our guarantee against the ravages of climate change.

Logosian – see *strategic logos* and *strategic demand*.

Materialist man, a subset of the *materialist organism*, is a central concept in longrun dynamics. Materialist man should be contrasted to the neoclassical concept of *homo economicus*. Rational economic man is not a dynamic force in society, but rather an abstract collection of preferences and rational choices concerning consumption and production – a set of optimizing conditions. Economic theorists have divorced these behavioral outcomes from more fundamental human motivational impulses. Economic man is no more than a mathematical convenience. Materialist man on the other hand is a real-world decision-maker who attempts to survive and, with survival, to maximize material advantage over his lifetime. This does not require perfect knowledge or sophisticated abilities to rapidly calculate the costs and benefits of a variety of possible decision-making alternatives, just an ability to recognize and imitate success — see *strategic imitation.*

Materialist organism. A systematic examination of the history of life undertaken in the dynamic-strategy project (Snooks, 1996; 1997; 1998a; 2003; 2006a) suggests that organisms attempt at all costs to survive *and*, having survived, to prosper – to maximize their consumption subject to the prevailing physical, social, and genetic/technological constraints. This is the dynamic concept of the materialist organism. It is the all-important driving force in the dynamic system, striving at all times, irrespective of the degree of competition, to increase its access to natural resources. It is this most basic force in life – here called *strategic desire* – that accounts for the *dynamic-strategy theory's* self-starting and self-sustaining nature. More intense competition merely raises the stakes of the strategic pursuit. Also see *materialist man.*

Neolithic technological paradigm shift is the great agricultural revolution that occurred in the Fertile Crescent about 10,600 years ago and in the Mesoamerican isthmus about 7,000 years ago. It was an outcome of the exhaustion of the age-old paleolithic (hunting) technological paradigm, and it ushered in the unprecedented era of human civilization.

Nonstrategists are those individuals and groups in society unable to invest freely in or profit directly from the prevailing dynamic strategy. They are controlled and manipulated by the *strategists* or *antistrategists,* who exercise a monopoly over society's resources and wealth. They are subject to *strategic frustration* and are fertile ground for charismatic sages – such as Jesus, Buddah, Mahammed, Zoroastra – who are concerned to build nonstrategic (or "religious") communities within oppressed societies.

Organism/species paradox lies at the heart of the *eternal recurrence,* which is the process by which animal dynasties rise and fall without life as a whole progressing toward the intelligence revolution. The underlying reason is that the intelligence revolution, while making it possible for the enabling species (man) to perpetuate its own existence rather than going extinct like the dinosaurs, is of no interest to individual decision makers, who are preoccupied solely with survival on a daily basis. Because of the organism/species paradox, the intelligence revolution was merely an outcome of chance – but chance operating within a systematic materialist process.

Pattern-recognition information. There are broadly two types of information processed by the strategic brain: information required for pattern recognition, and information required for *strategic imitation.* Pattern-recognition data, supplied by the senses, are employed both to undertake daily activities (short-term survival) by all organisms, and to explore new strategic opportunities by a few exceptional individuals (long-term survival). Also see *imitative information.*

Priestly philosophers are the metaphysicians in any society, who are interested in a virtual world of their own imagining rather that the real world of experience that can only be explored by the senses. In contrast to the *strategic thinkers,* who employ an inductive approach, they are committed to deductivism. They have been responsible for transforming the strategic guardians into gods, and strategic ideologies (including science) into religions. See also *scientism.*

Scientism is the strategic ideology of advanced, twenty-first century societies – societies that have passed through the Industrial Revolution and cast off the old, obsolete strategic ideology of monotheism. It is an ideology that rationalizes and supports the belief in science as the guardian of the modern *strategic logos.*

Selective sexual reproduction is based on those perceived characteristics in other individuals that will improve the prospect of survival and prosperity of the selecting individual. If this perception turns out to be correct, those physical and instinctual characteristics will also be passed on to the individual's offspring. Mate choice is an important technique for implementing all four *dynamic strategies,* not just of *genetic change.* Selective sexual reproduction provides individuals with greater control over their dynamic strategies, which is the reason for the emergence of sex some 1,000–600 myrs ago.

Selfcreating system. This is a living system that is both self-starting and self-sustaining. In a word, it is an "autogenous" system. The selfcreating system is the outcome of a circular flow of forces (see Figure 12.1) driven by *strategic desire,* transmitted by *strategic demand,* and facilitated by the pursuit of a sequence of *dynamic strategies.* This system, which has been described by the dynamic-strategy theory, is the core of the *strategic logos,* which provides for the survival and prosperity of constituent organisms in a world hostile to life.

Strategic cerebrum. Organisms in pursuit of survival and prosperity control their dynamic strategies through *strategic instruments.* These strategic instruments include brains in organisms that possess them and special genes in those that do not. These instruments are the strategic cerebrum and the *strategic gene.* A watershed occurred in life, some 500 myrs ago, when some organisms were able to replace the strategic gene with the strategic cerebrum in response to *strategic demand.*

Strategic confidence, which is the outcome of a successful *dynamic strategy,* is the force that keeps animal (including human) society together. A successful dynamic strategy leads to an effective network of competitive/cooperative relationships, together with all the necessary "rules" and "organizations". In societal transactions, individuals relate directly to the successful strategy and only indirectly to each other. It is not a matter of mutual "trust" as such – of having confidence in the nature of other individuals – but rather having confidence in the wider dynamic strategy in which they are all involved and on which they all depend. What we know as "trust" is derived from strategic confidence. Once the dynamic strategy has been exhausted and cannot be replaced, strategic confidence declines and, in extreme cases, disappears. And as strategic confidence declines, so too does "trust" and cooperation. Strategic confidence is communicated directly to individuals in both animal and human society by the rise and fall in material standards of living.

Strategic demand is the central concept in the dynamic-strategy theory of both life and human society. It is an outcome of the unfolding dynamic strategy that is driven by strategic agents exploring their strategic opportunities, and exerts a longrun influence over the employment of resources, the institutional and organizational structure of animal and human society, the genetic and technological structure of organisms and human societies, and the nature of the human mind. It operates through *strategic inflation*. Shifts in strategic demand occur as the dominant dynamic strategy unfolds and as one dynamic strategy replaces another. These shifts elicit changes in the way organisms employ resources and interact with each other.

Strategic demand-response mechanism. This mechanism, which operates through *strategic inflation,* lies at the heart of the *strategic logos*. It is the way in which *strategic desire* is translated into reality through an unfolding *dynamic strategy*. It is the reason the *dynamic-strategy theory* is described as a demand-side theory.

Strategic desire. The attribute that first separated living from non-living cells some 4,000 myrs ago was not the ability to reproduce systematically but the intense need to obtain organic material to fuel their internal metabolic systems. This need to meet "metabolic demand" is called strategic desire. It is the driving force in life. Replication (or *family multiplication*), which is merely one of the *dynamic strategies* employed by organisms to survive and prosper, is secondary to strategic desire. Without strategic desire, life would not exist.

Strategic exchange describes the key interaction between individuals in the *strategic logos*. It is a creative interaction between those demanding and those supplying inputs for the unfolding *dynamic strategy*. It is the process underlying the reality of *strategic demand* creating its own supply. This supply response, mediated through *strategic inflation,* is always forthcoming because it is an innovative reaction based on *strategic desire* – the desire to survive and prosper.

Strategic failure occurs when the *dynamic strategy* through which a society attempts to survive and prosper breaks down, usually as the result of unequal competition with more powerful societies. Strategic failure plays an important role in this book's story, as it leads to the generation of *strategic frustration,* which provides a powerful incentive to transform strategic ideology into religion. Strategic frustration in Palestine and Arabia – regions in the borderlands of the surrounding superpowers – led to the emergence of the monotheistic religions of Judaism, Christianity, and Islam.

Strategic frustration, which is the outcome of barriers raised to the *strategic pursuit*, operates at both the societal and individual levels. At the societal level, governments unable or unwilling to provide adequate *strategic leadership,* or governments unable to provide protection from neighboring superpowers, provoke strategic frustration – a type of *societal neurosis* – amongst the population, who then turn to radical groups or charismatic individuals to find relief. This has been the source of new religions. At the individual level, strategic frustration emerges when persistent barriers are raised against their participation in the strategic pursuit. This frustration leads to distressing mood disorders, such as manic depression. *Strategic satisfaction* is the opposite of strategic frustration.

Strategic gene. Organisms in pursuit of survival and prosperity control their *dynamic strategies* through what I call *strategic instruments*. These strategic instruments include brains in organisms that possess them and special genes in those that do not. These instruments are the *strategic cerebrum* and the strategic gene. Strategic genes are used by organisms to respond to changing physical and social environments — which determine the availability of nutrients and presence of competitors — and to activate the most appropriate dynamic strategy. As such, strategic genes do not drive life, they merely facilitate it. They do not have an independent existence or any driving ambitions of their own as claimed by the neo-Darwinists. See Snooks (2003; 2006a).

Strategic guardians are those mythical supernatural beings that paleolithic society sought out to sustain their hidden life-system, or *strategic logos.* It was the responsibility of the shamans – the first *priestly philosophers* – to make contact with, gain the confidence of, and manipulate the strategic guardians. These strategic guardians are the origins of the gods of neolithic society.

Strategic ideology is a mythological explanation and rationalization of the mystery of mysteries – the hidden life-system or *strategic logos.* It was employed to increase *strategic confidence* and to reduce the fear of *strategic failure.* In those regions of endemic strategic failure – the borderlands between the ancient superpowers – these ideologies became the source of modern monotheistic religions at the hands of the *priestly philosophers.*

Strategic imitation. It is in the process of strategic imitation, by which the vast majority of organisms emulate the action and values of successful "strategic pioneers", that societal "rules" are created and employed. Institutions are needed to economize not on benefit–cost information, as the economic institutionalists or rationalists argue, but on intelligence. This is true not only in animal society where intelligence is particularly scarce, but also in human society where most individuals find intellectual activity difficult and unhelpful. Intelligence is the scarcest resource on Earth, and probably non-existent in the rest of the Universe. The rule-makers, therefore, are the "strategic followers", who demand guidance in their strategic pursuit; while the rule-breakers are the "strategic pioneers", who attempt to break out of the restrictions of institutional conventions as they follow their new visions. As the "followers" constitute the vast majority of organisms in life, "rules" are essential to the dynamics of both animal and human society even though they are purely a response to it.

Strategic inflation. In the dynamic-strategy theory the role of prices is central to the interaction between *strategic demand* and the strategic response – the *strategic demand-response mechanism*. The unfolding *dynamic strategy* generates an increase in strategic demand that places pressure on existing resources, technologies, and institutions thereby leading to an increase in prices and profits. This provides incentives for the strategic response. It is the systematic increase in prices arising from the dynamic process that constitutes strategic inflation. This must be distinguished from nonstrategic inflation, which arises from errors in monetary and fiscal policy, monopoly actions, and external price hikes. Strategic inflation has its equivalent in the natural world, in terms of the higher value and status placed on certain individuals much in demand by their society. Policies aimed at repressing strategic inflation (or status/values) inevitably lead to the repression of innovation, ecomomic growth, and societal progress. This concept was first developed in Snooks (1998b).

Strategic instruments are agents or values employed by organisms (including man) to supervise or facilitate their *strategic pursuit*. The agents include the *strategic gene* in primitive life forms and the *strategic cerebrum* in more advanced life forms. The values, such as truth, honesty, generosity and justice, are not innate characteristics of man, but rather generalized forms of societal rules required to make civilization work. Values economize on impossibly long and complex lists of rules. Values are a response to *strategic demand* and, hence, are external to man.

Strategic insurance is the expenditure societies make on their *strategic ideology* in an attempt to reduce the risk of *strategic failure.* In leading strategic societies in both the past and present, this form of insurance has amounted to about 8–10 percent of GDP. In pre-modern society this expenditure took the form of investment in the infrastructure of religious institutions, whereas in modern industrial society it takes the form of investment in the infrastructure of knowledge, science, and technology. The aim in both modern and premodern society was and is to sustain the *strategic logos.*

Strategic leadership helps to facilitate the successful unfolding of a society's dominant *dynamic strategy* and in maintaining the viability of the *strategic* *logos.* Strategic leaders, who work with *strategists* rather than against them (as in antistrategic societies or in strategic societies dominated by interventionists), have traditionally taken a central role in generating an effective *strategic ideology* in order to sustain the confidence of the people in the face of adversity and to gain the support of the strategic guardians or gods.

Strategic *logos* is the great creative system of life – the great pulsating heart of each and every living system. This entropy-defying, shock-absorbing system is a largely invisible circular process of interaction between man and his society (see Figure 12.1). It is a complex *strategic demand-response mechanism*. It is also a self-starting and self-sustaining process that continues to pulsate until the entire sequence of dynamic strategies available to a given society is completely exhausted. In the case of the world's most successful societies, such as ancient Egypt or ancient Rome, this can last for between one and three millennia. Eventually, however, the strategic society collapses because its *logos* finally exhausts itself. It is the strategic *logos* that generates all culture, religion, values, institutions, progress, liberty, and even man and God. It is from the strategic *logos* that "all things follow". See also *strategic exhaustion.*

Strategic pursuit. All life is dedicated to the strategic pursuit, in which the pioneering *strategists* explore the material potential of the most effective *dynamic strategy* and its substrategies. It is important to focus on the strategic pursuit rather than the means (*family multiplication, conquest, commerce, genetic/technological change*) by which this driving force is translated into a material surplus. In the life sciences both the neo-Darwinists and the neoliberal economists have focused on static physical structures rather than the dynamics of the strategic pursuit. In doing so they have failed to develop general dynamic theories.

Strategic selection is a central concept in this work. It is a dynamic process in which organisms are themselves responsible for selecting or rejecting benign (non-lethal) mutations. It operates through the *strategic imitation* process. If an individual experiences a beneficial mutation that enables better access to natural resources – within the context of the *dynamic strategy* it is pursuing – that individual will increase its prospects of survival and prosperity. This success will attract the attention of others. Those with similar abilities will cooperate with each other to improve their joint prospects. The point of strategic selection is that individual organisms – rather than gods, genes, or blind chance – are responsible for selecting comrades, mates, and siblings that have the necessary physical and instinctual characteristics to successfully pursue the prevailing dynamic strategy. It is important to realize that strategic selection operates under varying degrees of competition, not just under intense Darwinian competition, and that it responds to each of the four dynamic strategies, not just the *genetic strategy*. Also it is associated with the welfare of the self and not that of future generations. Strategic selection is a form of self-selection at the "societal" level that replaces the "divine selection" of the creationists and the "natural selection" of the Darwinists.

Strategic sequence. Typically, organisms in a species will pursue a sequence of strategies from the time they begin to diverge from the parent species until their species finally goes extinct. The sequence prior to the emergence of human society 2 myrs ago was typically *genetic change, family multiplication* or *commerce (symbiosis)*, and *conquest*. Each *dynamic strategy* is exploited until it is exhausted, which leads to a temporary crisis until a new strategy can be employed in their *strategic pursuit*. If, in a normally competitive environment, a new strategy is not adopted by a species following the exhaustion of an old strategy, that species will collapse and go extinct prematurely. Human societies also generate strategic sequences – usually in the order of family multiplication, conquest, commerce, technological change – with similar outcomes. Accordingly this strategic sequence leads not to a linear development path but to a series of waves consisting of phases of expansion, stagnation, crisis, decline, and renewed expansion.

Strategic struggle is the main "political" instrument by which established individuals/species (old *strategists*) attempt to maintain their control over the sources of their prosperity, and by which emerging individuals/species (new strategists) attempt to usurp such control. Although it employs "political" instruments it is fundamentally an "economic" struggle – a struggle for survival and prosperity in the face of scarce resources. In the process these individuals/species employ the dynamic tactics of order and chaos. See *strategic leadership*.

Strategic success is the outcome of successful attempts to sustain the *strategic logos*. This involves effectively negotiating a sequence of *dynamic strategies* that leads to survival and prosperity. See also *strategic failure*.

Strategic thinking is the type of thinking that comes naturally to the *strategic cerebrum* that emerged about 500 myrs ago in order to supervise the *strategic pursuit* of the *unconscious organism* in an increasingly sophisticated social environment. It is an inductive form of thinking that employs *pattern-recognition information*. It is to be contrasted with rationalist thinking based on benefit–cost information, which emerged with human civilization a mere 6,000 years ago. See Snooks (2006a: 139–42).

Strategists comprise the dynamic group in animal and human society that invests time and resources in pursuing and profiting from one of the four *dynamic strategies*. The strategists are a diverse group. We must distinguish between the "strategic pioneers" (the more ambitious and less risk-averse) and the "strategic followers"; between the old strategists (supporters of the traditional strategy) and the new strategists (supporters of the emerging strategy); and between the surplus-creating strategists and the surplus-consuming strategists. While there is synergy between the pioneers and the followers and the surplus-creators and surplus-consumers, the old and new strategists are generally involved during predictable critical periods in a struggle against each other for control of society's dominant dynamic strategy. See *strategic struggle*.

Technology option. The emergence of intelligence enabled the most intellectually advanced line of the dynasty of mammals to replace the *genetic option* with the technology option, which was to spawn a series of *technological paradigm shifts* and, within each of these, a series of *technological styles*. This released life from the *eternal recurrence*.

Timescapes are those portraits of reality provided by a visual representation of longrun quantitative and qualitative data. These portraits emerge from the statistical record of the course taken by life and human society over vast expanses of time. They show us the nature of real-world relationships, such as the great waves of life and of economic change. They provide a glimpse of dynamic processes operating in life and in society, and constitute the building blocks of existential models. As fact is stranger than fiction they provide a breadth of vision required to build realist dynamic models that is missing in the deductive approach.

Ultimate reality is a complex set of invisible relationships between forces (rather than objects) – such as *strategic desire* and *strategic demand* – that cannot be perceived through the senses. I call this ultimate reality the *strategic logos*. This invisible pattern of forces (see Figure 12.1) can only be apprehended by developing a general dynamic theory that can explain and predict the recurring patterns in everyday reality that are detected by the senses.

Unconscious organism. The dynamic-strategy theory embodies the concept of strategic dualism, based on the biological fact that human beings are a fusion of the unconscious organism that can trace its origins back to the beginning of life some 4,000 myrs ago, and the strategic cerebrum that first emerged only 500 myrs ago. The unconscious organism, which is driven by *strategic desire,* attempts to survive and prosper through the adoption of a quartet of *dynamic strategies*. This was first achieved by the *strategic gene,* but in some species, more recently, by the *strategic cerebrum,* which is just a *strategic instrument* developed through *strategic selection* to facilitate the *strategic pursuit*.

References

Abdel Haleem, M.A.S., trans (2005). *The Qur'an*. Oxford: Oxford University Press.

Aldhouse-Green, M. and Aldhouse-Green, S. (2005). *The quest for the shaman. Shape-shifters, sorcerers and spirit-healers of ancient Europe*. London: Thames & Hudson.

Altenmüller, H. (2004). "Daily life in eternity – the mastabas and rock-cut tombs of officials". Pp 78–93 in *Egypt. The world of the pharaohs*, edited by R. Schulz and M. Seidel. Königswinter: Könemann.

Armstrong, K. (1999). *A history of God. From Abraham to the present: the 4000-year quest for God*. London: Vintage.

Armstrong, K. (2002). Islam. *A short history*. London: Phoenix Press.

Armstrong, K. (2005). *A short history of myth*. Edinburgh: Canongate.

Arsuga, J.-L. de (2003). *The Neanderthal necklace: in search of the first thinkers*. Chichester: Wiley.

Atran, S. (2002). *In gods we trust: the evolutionary landscape of religion*. Oxford: Oxford University Press.

Axelrod, R. (1984). *The evolution of cooperation*. New York: Basic Books.

Axelrod, R. and Bennett, D.S. (1993). "A landscape theory of aggregation". *British Journal of Political Science* 23: 211–233.

Bahn, P.G. ed. (2003). *Atlas of world archaeology*. London: B.T. Batsford.

Bahn, P.G. and Vertut, J. (1988). *Images of the ice age*. New York and Oxford: Facts on File.

Bais, S. (2005). *The equations: icons of knowledge*. Cambridge, MA: Harvard University Press.

Bak, P. (1997). *How nature works*. New York: Oxford University Press.

Bakker, R.T. (1978). "Dinosaur renaissance". In *Evolution and the fossil record: readings from Scientific American*, edited by L.F. Laporte. San Francisco: W.H. Freeman & Co.

Bald, M. (1998). *Banned books: literature suppressed on religious grounds*. New York: Facts on File Inc.

Ball, P. (2004). *Critical mass*. London: Arrow Books.

Ballhatchet, K. and Ballhatchet, H. (2002). "Asia". Pp. 508–38 in *The Oxford history of Christianity*, edited by J. McManners. Oxford: Oxford University Press.

Balling, J. (2003). *The story of Christianity from birth to global presence*. Grand Rapids, Michigan & Cambridge, UK: W.B. Eerdmans Pub. Co.

Beaton, J.M. (1983). "Does intensification account for changes in the Australian holocene archaeological record?" *Archaeology in Oceania* 18: 94–7.

Bednarik, R. (1995a). "Concept-mediated marking in the lower paleolithic". *Current Anthropology* 36: 605–32.

Bednarik, R. (1995b). "Taking the style out of the Panaramitee style". *AURA Newsletter* 12: 1–5.

Berger, T.D. and Trinkaus, E. (1995). "Patterns of trauma among the Neanderthals". *Journal of Archaeological Science* 22: 841–52.

Berndt, R.M. and Berndt, C.H. (1999). *The world of the first Australians. Aboriginal traditional life: past and present*. Canberra: Aboriginal Studies Press.

Bible. Revised standard version.

Blades, B. (1999). "Aurignacian settlement patterns". *Current Anthropology* 40: 712–18.

Bocherens, H. et al (2005). "Isotopic evidence for diet and subsistence pattern of the Saint-Césaire I Neanderthal: review and use of a multi-source mixing model". *Journal of Human Evolution* 49:71–87.

Bongioanni, A. and Croce, M.S. (2003). *The treasures of ancient Egypt from the Egyptian Museum in Cairo*, translated by C.T.M. Milan. New York: Universe Publishing.

Bowker, J. (2002). *God. A brief history*. New York: DK Publishing.

Boyce, N.E.M. (1979). *A history of Zoroastrianism, Vol. 1*. Leiden: Brill.

Boyce, N.E.M. (1985). *A History of Zoroastrianism, Vol. 2*. Leiden: Brill.

Boyer, P. (2001). *Religion explained: the evolutionary origins of religious thought*. New York: Basic Books.

Boyle, K.V. (2000). "Reconstructing middle paleolithic subsistence strategies in the south of France". *International Journal of Osteorarchaeology* 10:336–56.

Bradley, S.A.J. (1982). *Anglo-Saxon poetry: an anthology of old English poems in prose translation*. London: Dent.

Brosius, M. (2006). *The Persians. An introduction*. London & New York: Routledge.

Buchanan, M. (2000). *Ubiquity*. London: Weidenfeld & Nicolson.

Buckle, H. (1894). *History of civilization in England*, 3 vols. London: Longmans, Green & Co.

Burkard, G. (2004). "Conceptions of the cosmos – the universe". Pp. 444–49 in *Egypt. The world of the pharaohs*, edited by R. Schulz and M. Seidel. Königswinter: Könemann.

Byrne, J.M. (1997). *Religion and the enlightenment. From Descartes to Kant*. Louisville, Kentucky: Westminster John Knox Press.

Cairns, J. et al (1988). "The origin of mutants". *Nature* 335(6186), September: 142–45.

Campbell, J. (1975). *The hero with a thousand faces*. London: Abacus.

Caquot, A. (1974). "Western Semetic lands: the idea of the supreme god". Pp. 85–96 in *World mythology*, edited by P. Grimal. London: Hamlyn.

Carneiro, R.L. (1974). "Editor's introduction". *The evolution of society: selections from Herbert Spencer's principles of sociology*. H. Spencer. Chicago: Chicago University Press.

Casson, L. (2001). *Libraries in the ancient world*. New Haven & London: Yale University Press.

Casti, J.L. (2001). *Paradigms regain. Unraveling the mysteries of modern science*. London: Abacus.

Chadwick, H. (2002). "The early Christian community". Pp. 21–69 in *The Oxford history of Christianity*, edited by J. McManners. Oxford: Oxford University Press.

Chadwick, O. (2002). "Great Britain and Europe". Pp. 349–95 in *The Oxford history of Christianity*, edited by J. McManners. Oxford: Oxford University Press.

Chang, J. and Halliday, J. (2005). *Mao: the unknown story*. New York: Knopf.

Chappell, J. (1994). "Upper quaternary sea levels, coral terraces, oxygen isotopes and deep-sea temperatures". *Journal of Geography,* 103: 828–40.

Chase, P.G. and Nowell, A. (1998). "Taphonomy of a suggested middle paleolithic bone flute from Slovenia". *Current Anthropology* 39: 549–53.

Clegg, J. (1995). "Tracks and lines". *Proceedings of NEWS 95*, International Rock Art Congress, Turin, September.

Cole, N. and Watchman, A. (1992). "Painting with plants: investigating fibres in Aboriginal rock paintings at Laura, north Queensland". *Rock Art Research* 9: 27–36.

Cole,N. and Watchman, A. (1993). "Accelerator radiocarbon dating of plant-fibre binders from northeastern Australia". *Antiquity* 67: 355–58.

Collier, M. and Manley, B. (1998). *How to read Egyptian hieroglyphs*. Berkeley and Los Angeles: University of California Press.

Collinson, P. (2002). "The late medieval church and its reformation (1400–1600)". Pp. 243–76 in *The Oxford history of Christianity*, edited by J. McManners. Oxford: Oxford University Press.

Comte, A. (1896). *The positive philosophy*, 3 vols. London: Bell.

Crossan, J.D. (1995). *Jesus. A revolutionary biography*. New York: HarperSanFrancisco.

Darnell, J.C. and Manassa, C. (2007). *Tutankhamun's armies: Battle and conquest during ancient Egypt's late 18ᵗʰ dynasty.* Hoboken, NJ: John Wiley & Sons.

Darwin, C. (1859). *On the origin of species by means of natural selection or the preservation of favoured races in the struggle for life*. London: John Murray.

Davies, P. (1993). *The mind of God. Science and the search for ultimate meaning*. London: Penguin Books.

Davies, P.R. (1992). *In search of ancient Israel*. Sheffield: JSOT Press.

Davies, R. and Underdown, S. (2006). "The Neanderthals: a social synthesis". *Cambridge Archaeological Journal* 16(2): 145–64.

Dawkins, R. (1976). *The selfish gene*. Oxford: Oxford University Press.

Dawkins, R. (1982). *The extended phenotype. The gene as the unit of selection*. Oxford: Freeman.

Dawkins, R. (2006). *The God delusion*. London: Bantam Press.

de Menasce, J. (1974). "Persia: cosmic dualism". *World mythology*, edited by P. Grinal. London: Hamlyn.

Dennett, D.C. (2006). *Breaking the spell. Religion as a natural phenomenon.* New York: Viking.

d'Errico, F., Zilhão, J., Julien, M., Baffiet, D. and Pelegrin, J. (1998). "Neanderthal acculturation in western Europe?" *Current Anthropology* 39: 31–44.

d'Errico, F. and Nowell, A. (2000). "A new look at the Berekhat Ram figurine: implications for the origins of symbolism". *Cambridge Archaeological Journal* 10: 123–67.

d'Errico, F. and Sanchez Goni, M.F. (2003). "Neanderthal estimation and the millennial scale climatic variability of OIS 3". *Quaternary Science Reviews* 22: 769–88.

Derricourt, R. (2005). "Getting 'out of Africa': sea crossings, land crossings and culture in the Hominin migrations". *Journal of World Prehistory* 19: 199–132.

Desmond, A. and Moore, J. (1991). *Darwin.* London: Michael Jospeh.

Doniger, W. ed. (2006). *Britannica encyclopedia of world religions.* New York: Encyclopedia Britannica.

Donner, F.M. (1999). "Muhammad and the caliphate. Political history of the Islamic empire up to the Mongol conquest". Pp. 1–61 in *The Oxford history of Islam*, edited by J.L. Esposito. New York: Oxford University Press.

Douglas, J.D. (1962). *The new bible dictionary.* London: Inter-Varsity Fellowship.

Drell, J.R. (2000). "Neanderthals: a history of interpretation". *Oxford Journal of Archaeology* 19: 1–24.

Eldredge, N. (1995). *Reinventing Darwin: the great debate at the high table of evolutionary theory.* New York: Wiley.

Eldredge, N. and Gould, J. (1972). "Punctuated equilibria: an alternative tophyletic gradualism". Pp. 82–115 in *Models of paleobiology*, edited by T.J.M. Schopt. San Francisco: Freeman, Cooper.

Eliade, M. (1989). *Shamanism. Archaic techniques of ecstasy.* London: Arkana Penguin Books.

Epstein, J.M. (1999). "Agent-based computational models and generative social science". *Complexity* 4: 41–60.

Epstein, J.M. and Axtell, R. (1996). *Growing artificial societies: social science from the bottom up.* Washington, DC: Brookings Institution.

Esposito, J.L. ed. (1999a). *The Oxford history of Islam*. New York: Oxford University Press.

Esposito, J.L. (1999b). "Contemporary Islam". Pp. 643–90 in *The Oxford history of Islam*, edited by J.L. Esposito. New York: Oxford University Press.

Everitt, N. (2004). *The non-existence of God*. London & New York: Routledge.

Fagan, B.M. (2004). *The seventy great innovations of the ancient world*. London: Thames & Hudson.

Faulkner, R.O. trans (1998). *The Egyptian book of the dead. The book of going forth by day. Being the papyrus of Ani. Written and illustrated c. 1250 BCE*. San Francisco: Chronicle Books.

Finkelstein, I. and Silberman, N.A. (2002). *The bible unearthed. Archaeology's new vision of ancient Israel and the origin of its sacred tents*. New York: Simon & Schuster (Touchstone Books).

Finlayson, C. (2004). *Neanderthals and modern humans: an ecological and evolutionary perspective*. Cambridge: Cambridge University Press.

Finlayson, C. (2006). "Late survival of Neanderthals at southern most extreme of Europe". *Nature* 443:850–53.

Finlayson, C. and Carrión, J.S. (2007). "Rapid ecological turnover and its impact on Neanderthal and other human populations". *Trends in Ecology and Evolution* 22:213–22.

Flood, J. (1997). *Rock art of the Dreamtime. Images of ancient Australia*. Sydney: Angus & Robertson.

Floud, R. et al (1990). *Height, health and history: nutritional studies in the UK, 1750–1980*. Cambridge: Cambridge University Press.

Forty, S. (2003). *Symbols*. San Diego: Thunder Bay Press.

Foster, P.L. (1999). "Mechanisms of stationary phase mutation: a decade of adaptive mutation". *Annual Review of Genetics* 33: 57–88.

Franfort, H. (1948). *Kinship and the gods*. Chicago: University of Chicago Press.

Gallus, A. (1971). "Results of the exploration of Koonalda Cave, 1956–68". Pp. 87–133 in *Archaeology of the Gallus site, Koonalda Cave*, edited by R.V.S. Wright. Canberra: Australian Institute of Aboriginal Studies.

Gamble, C. (1993). *Timewalkers: the prehistory of global colonization*. Strand: Sutton.

Gamble, C. (1999). The paleolithic societies of Europe. Cambridge: Cambridge University Press.

Gardner, J.N. (2003). *Biocosm. The new scientific theory of evolution: intelligent life is the architect of the universe.* Makawao, Maui, HI: Inner Ocean.

Garrett, B. (2006). *What is this thing called metaphysics?* London & New York: Routledge.

Goelet, O. (1998). "Commentary". Pp. 137–70 in *The Egyptian book of the dead.* R.O. Faulkner. San Francisco: Chronicle Books.

Görg, M. (2004). "Gods and deities". Pp 432–43 in *Egypt. The world of the pharaohs*, edited by R. Schulz and M. Seidel. Königswinter: Könemann.

Gould, S.J. and Lewontin, R.C. (1979). "The spandrels of San Marco and the Panglossian paradigm: a critique of the adaptionist programme". *Proceedings of the Royal Society of London* B205: 281–88.

Gribbin, J. (2002). *Science: a history, 1543–2001.* London: Allen Lane.

Gribbin, J. (2005). *Deep simplicity: chaos, complexity and the emergence of life.* London: Penguin Books.

Grimal, P. ed. (1974). *World mythology.* London: Hamlyn.

Grollenberg, L.H. (1961). *Shorter atlas of the bible.* London & Edinburgh: Elsevier/Nelson.

Gutgesell, M. (2004a). "The military". Pp. 364–69 in *Egypt. The world of the pharaohs*, edited by R. Schulz and M. Seidel. Königswinter: Könemann.

Gutgesell, M. (2004b). "Economy and trade". Pp. 370–75 in *Egypt. The world of the pharaohs*, edited by R. Schulz and M. Seidel. Königswinter: Könemann.

Hackel, S. (2002). "The orthodox churches of eastern Europe". Pp. 539–67 in *The Oxford history of Christianity*, edited by J. McManners. Oxford: Oxford University Press.

Haddad, Y.Y. (1999). "The globalization of Islam. The return of Mulims to the west". Pp. 601–41 in *The Oxford history of Islam*, edited by J.L. Esposito. New York: Oxford University Press.

Hall, B.G. (1988). "Adaptive evolution that requires multiple spontaneous mutations". *Genetics* 120 (December): 887–97.

Hamer, D. (2004). *The god gene. How faith is hardwired into our genes.* New York: Doubleday.

Harris, R.L. (1995). *The world of the Bible*. London: Thames and Hudson.

Harvati, K. (2003). "The Neanderthal taxonomic position: models of intra- and inter-specific craniofacial variation". *Journal of Human Evolution* 44: 107–32.

Haywood, J. (2005). *Historical atlas of ancient civilizations*. London: Penguin Books.

Hegel, G.W.F. (1888). *Lectures on the philosophy of history*. London: G. Bell.

Heraclitus (2001). *Fragments: the collected wisdom of Heraclitus*. Translated by Brooks Haxton. New York: Viking.

Hinchcliff, P. (2002). "Africa". Pp. 474–507 in *The Oxford history of Christianity*, edited by J. McManners. Oxford: Oxford University Press.

Hind, R. (2004). *One thousand faces of God*. London: Carlton Books.

Hinnells, J.R. ed. (1984). *The Penguin dictionary of religions*. London: Penguin Books.

Horgan, J. (1996). *The end of science*. New York: Broadway Books.

Hornung, E. (1996). *Conceptions of God in ancient Egypt. The one and the many*. Translated by J. Baines. Ithaca, NY: Cornell University Press.

Houghton, P. (1993). "Neanderthal supralaryngeal vocal tract". *American Journal of Physical Anthropology* 90: 139–46.

Ibin Khaldun, Abd al-Rahman (1967). *The Mugaddimah: an introduction to history*. Edited by N.J. Dawood and translated by Franz Rosenthal. Bollingen Series. Princeton: Princeton University Press.

Isaacson, W. (2007). *Einstein: his life and universe*. New York: Simon & Schuster.

Johns, J. (2002). "Christianity and Islam". Pp. 167–204 in *The Oxford history of Christianity*, edited by J. McManners. Oxford: Oxford University Press.

Johnson, C. (2006). *Australia's mammal extinctions. A 50,000 year history*. Cambridge: Cambridge University Press.

Jones, S. (1999). *Almost like a whale. The origin of species updated*. London: Doubleday.

Jordan, M. (2002). *Encyclopedia of gods. Over 2,500 deities of the world*. London: Kyle Cathie Ltd.

Kamff-Segfried, F. (2004). "The Valley of the Queens". Pp. 244–47 in *Egypt. The world of the pharaohs*, edited by R. Schulz and M. Seidel. Königswinter: Könemann.

Kappelman, J. (1996). "The evolution of body mass and relative brain size in fossil hominids". *Journal of Human Evolution* 30: 243–76.

Kauffman, S. (1993). *The origins of order*. New York: Oxford University Press.

Kauffman, S. (1995). *At home in the universe*. New York: Oxford University Press.

Kennedy, H. (2007). *The great Arab conquests. How the spread of Islam changed the world we live in*. London: Weidenfeld & Nicolson.

Kenny. A. (2004). *The unknown god: agnostic essays*. London & New York: Continuum.

Kessler, D. (2004a). "The political history of the Third to English Dynasties". Pp. 40–45 in *Egypt. The world of the pharaohs*, edited by R. Schulz and M. Seidel. Königswinter: Könemann.

Kessler, D. (2004b). "The political history from the Ninth to the Seventeenth Dynasties". Pp. 104–08 in *Egypt. The world of the pharaohs*, edited by R. Schulz and M. Seidel. Königswinter: Könemann.

Kessler, D. (2004c). "The political history of the Eighteenth to the Twentieth Dynasties". Pp. 142–51 in *Egypt. The world of the pharaohs*, edited by R. Schulz and M. Seidel. Königswinter: Könemann.

Kessler, D. (2004d). "Tanis and Thebes – the political history of the Twenty-first to Thirtieth Dynasties". Pp. 270–75 in *Egypt. The world of the pharaohs*, edited by R. Schulz and M. Seidel. Königswinter: Könemann.

Kirk, J.T.O. (2007). *Science and certainty*. Collingwood, Australia: CSIRO Publishing.

Klein, R.G. (2003). "Whither the Neanderthals?" *Science* 299: 1525–27.

Komlos, J. and Baten, J. (2004). *Recent research in anthropometric history. Special issue of Social Science History* 28(2).

Kriwaczek, P. (2003). *In search of Zarathustra. The first prophet and the ideas that changed the world*. London: Phoenix Paperbacks.

Krosney, H. (2006). *The lost gospel. The quest for the gospel of Judas Iscariot*. Washington, DC: National Geographic.

Kunej, D. and Turk, I. (2000). "New perspectives on the beginnings of music: archaeological musicological analysis of a middle palelotihic bone 'flute'". Pp. 235–68 in *The origins of music*. Edited by N.L. Wallin, B. Merker and S. Brown. Cambridge MA: MIT Press.

Lapidus, I.M. (1999). "sultanates and gunpowder empires. The Middle East". Pp. 347–93 in *The Oxford history of Islam*, edited by J.L. Esposito. New York: Oxford University Press.

Lapidus, I.M. (2007). *A history of Islamic societies*, 2nd edition. Cambridge: Cambridge University Press.

Leakey, (1958).

Leeming, D. (2003). *From Olympus to Camelot. The world of European mythology*. New York: Oxford University Press.

Leick, G. (2002). *Mesopotamia. The invention of the city*. London: Penguin Books.

Lemche, N.P. (1994). "Is it still possible to write a history of ancient Israel?" *Scandinavian Journal of Old Testament* 8: 165–90.

Lieberman, P. (1992). "On Neanderthal speech and Neanderthal extinction". *Current Anthropology* 33: 409–10.

Lieberman, D.E. and Shea, J.J. (1994). "Behavioral differences between archaic and modern humans in the Levantine Mousterian". *American Anthropologist* 96: 300–332.

Lovelock, J. (1990). *The ages of Gaia. A biography of our living Earth*. Oxford: Oxford University Press.

Lovelock, J. (2006). *The revenge of Gaia. Why the Earth is fighting back – and how we can still save humanity*. Camberwell, Victoria: Allen Lane.

Lucas, P.C. and Robbins, T. eds (2004). *New religious movements in the twenty-firt century. Legal, political and social challenges in global perspective*. New York & London: Routledge.

Luft, U. (2004). "A different world – religious conceptions". Pp. 416–31 in *Egypt. The world of the pharaohs*, edited by R. Schulz and M. Seidel. Königswinter: Könemann.

McEvedy, C. (1980). *The Penguin atlas of medieval history*. London: Penguin Books.

McEvedy, C. (1983). *The Penguin atlas of ancient history*. London: Penguin Books.

McGrath, A. (2004). *The twilight of atheism. The rise and fall of disbelief in the modern world.* London: Rider Books.

McGrath, A. (2005). *Dawkins' God. Genes, memes and the meaning of life.* Malden, MA: Blackwell.

Mack, B.L. (1994). *The lost gospel. The book of Q and Christian origins.* New York: HarperSanFrancisco.

McManners, J. ed. (2002). *The Oxford history of Christianity.* Oxford: Oxford University Press.

McManners, J. (2002a). "the expansion of Christianity (1500–1800)". Pp. 310–45 in *The Oxford history of Christianity*, edited by J. McManners. Oxford: Oxford University Press.

Maddison, A. (2001). *The world economy: a millennial perspective.* Paris: OECD.

Maddison, A. (2003). *The world economy: historical statistics.* Paris: OECD.

Mania, D. and Mania, U. (1988). "Deliberate engravings on bone artefacts of *Homo eructus*". *Rock Art Research* 5: 91–107.

Manley, B. (1996). *The Penguin historical atlas of ancient Egypt.* London: Penguin Books.

Manley, G.T. ed. (1960). *The new bible handbook.* London: Inter-Varsity Fellowship.

Markus, R.A. (2002). "From Rome to the Barbarian Kngdom (330–700)". Pp. 70–100 in *The Oxford history of Christianity*, edited by J. McManners. Oxford: Oxford University Press.

Marshack, A. (1981). "On paleolithic ochre and the early uses of color and symbol". *Current Anthropology* 22: 274–82.

Marshack, A. (1997). "The Berekhat Ram figurine: a late Acheulian carving from the Middle East". *Antiquity* 71: 327–37.

Marty, M. (2002). "North America". Pp. 396–436 in *The Oxford history of Christianity*, edited by J. McManners. Oxford: Oxford University Press.

Marx, K. (1947). *Capital: a critical analysis of capitalist production*, vol. I. Moscow: Progress Publishers.

Mathers, S.L.M. trans (1991). *The Kabbalah unveiled.* London: Arkana Penguin Books.

Maynard, L. (1979). "The archaeology of Australian Aboriginal art". Pp. 83–110 in *Exploring the visual art of Oceania*, edited by S.M. Mead. Honolulu: University of Hawaii Press.

Mayr-Harting, H. (2002). "The west: the age of conversion (700–1050)". Pp. 101–30 in *The Oxford history of Christianity*, edited by J. McManners. Oxford: Oxford University Press.

Mellars, P. (1996). *The Neanderthal legacy: an archaeological perspective from western Europe*. Princeton, NJ: Princeton University Press.

Meyer, M. trans (1992). *The gospel of Thomas. The hidden sayings of Jesus*. New York: HarperSanFrancisco.

Mills, A. ed. (2005). *Mythology. Myths, legends, and fantasies*. Sydney: Hodder Headline.

Mitchell, B. (2002). "The Christian conscience". Pp. 618–43 in *The Oxford history of Christianity*, edited by J. McManners. Oxford: Oxford University Press.

Mithen, S. (2006). *The singing Neanderthals: the origins of music, language, mind and body*. London: Phoenix.

Moncel, M-H. (2005). "Pre-Neanderthal behaviour during isotopic stage 9 and the beginning of stage 8 …". *Journal of Archaeological Science* 32: 1283–1301.

Morenz, S. (1992). *Egyptian religion*. Translated by A.E. Keep. Ithaca, NY: Cornell University Press.

Morris, C. (2002). "Christian civilization (1050–1400)". Pp. 205–42 in *The Oxford history of Christianity*, edited by J. McManners. Oxford: Oxford University Press.

Naaman, N. (1991). "The kingdom of Judah under Josiah". *Tel Aviv* 18: 3–71.

Nasr, S.V.R. (1999). "European colonialism and the emergence of modern Muslim states". Pp. 549–99 in *The Oxford history of Islam*, edited by J.L. Esposito. New York: Oxford University Press.

Nazaretyan, A.P. (2005a). "Snooks-Panov vertical". *The global studies dictionary*. Edited by I.I. Mazow and A.N. Chumakov. Moscow/Amhert, NY: Dialog Raduga Publishers/Prometheus Books.

Nazaretyan, A.P. (2005b). "Big (universal) history paradigm: versions and approaches". *Social Evolution and History* 4: 61–86.

Neusner, J. (2006). "Judaism". Pp. 585–621 in *Britannica encyclopedia of world religions*. Edited by W. Doniger. New York: Encyclopedia Britannica.

Newman, M.E.J. (2005). "Power laws, Pareto distributions and Zipf's law". *Contemporary Physics* 46: 323–51.

Nietzsche, F. (1882). *The gay science*. Translated by W. Kaufmann (1974). New York: Vintage Books.

Nietzsche, F. (1883). *Thus spoke Zarathustra*. Translated by A. Del Caro. Cambridge University Press.

Niewoehner, W.A., Bergstrom, A., Eichele, D., Zuroff, M. and Clark, J.T. (2003). "Manual dexterity in Neanderthals". *Nature* 22: 395.

Numbers, R.L. (2006). *The creationists. From scientific creationism to intelligent design*. Cambridge, MA & London: Harvard University Press.

O'Connor, S. (1995). "Carpenter's Gap rockshelter 1: 40,000 years of Aboriginal occupation in the Napier Rangers, Kimberley, WA". *Australian Archaeology* 40: 58–59.

OECD (2003). *OECD science, technology and industry scoreboard.* Paris: OECD.

Oldroyd, D. (2006). *Earth cycles: a historical perspective*. Westport, CT: Greenwood Press.

Otte, M. (2000). "On the suggested bone flute from Slovenia". *Current Anthropology* 41: 271–72.

Panov, A.D. (2005). "Scaling law of biological evolution and the hypothesis of the self-consistent galaxy origin of life". *Advances in Space Research* 36: 220–25.

Pardey, E. (2004). "The royal administration and its organization". Pp. 356–63 in *Egypt. The world of the pharaohs*, edited by R. Schulz and M. Seidel. Königswinter: Könemann.

Patou-Mathis, M. (2000). "Neanderthal subsistence behaviors in Europe". *International Journal of Osteoarchaeology* 10: 379–95.

Pettitt, P.B. (1999). "Disappearing from the world: an archaeological perspective on Neanderthal extinction". *Oxford Journal of Archaeology* 18: 217–40.

Pike, F. (2004). "Latin America". Pp. 437–73 in *The Oxford history of Christianity*, edited by J. McManners. Oxford: Oxford University Press.

Pinch, G. (2002). *Egyptian mythology. A guide to the gods, goddesses, and traditions of ancient Egypt*. Oxford: Oxford University Press.

Price, S. and Kearns, E. (2003). *The Oxford dictionary of classical myth and religion*. Oxford: Oxford University Press.

Quirke, S. (2001). *The cult of Ra. Sun-worship in ancient Egypt*. New York: Thames & Hudson.

Quran, The. Translated by M. A.S. Abdel Haleem. Oxford and New York: Oxford University Press, 2005.

Rappaport, R.A. (2002). *Ritual and religion in the making of humanity*. Cambridge: Cambridge University Press.

Redford, D.B. (2003). *The Oxford essential guide to Egyptian mythology*. New York: Berkley Books.

Reeves, N. and Wilkinson, R.H. (2002). *The complete Valley of the Kings. Tombs and treasures of Egypt's greatest pharaohs*. London: Thames & Hudson.

Reeves, N. (2005). *Akhenaten. Egypt's false prophet*. London. Thames & Hudson.

Rice, M. (2002). *Who's who in ancient Egypt*. London & New York: Routledge.

Roberts, R.G. and Jones, R. (1994). "Luminescence dating of sediments: new light on the human colonisation of Australia". *Australian Aboriginal Studies* 2: 2–17.

Romer, J. (2007). *The great pyramid. Ancient Egypt revisited*. Cambridge: Cambridge University Press

Rose, H. and Rose, S. (2001). *Alas poor Darwin. Arguments against evolutionary psychology*. London: Vintage.

Rosenfeld, A. (1991). "Panaramitee: dead or alive?" pp. 136–44 in *Rock Art and Prehistory*. Edited by P. Bahn and A. Rosenfeld. Oxford: Oxbow.

Roux, G. (1992). *Ancient Iraq*, 3rd edition. London: Penguin Books.

Schepartz, L.A. (1993). "Language and modern human origins". *Yearbook of Physical Anthropology* 36: 91–126.

Schneider, T. (2004). "Sacred kingship". Pp. 322–29 in *Egypt. The world of the pharaohs*, edited by R. Schulz and M. Seidel. Königswinter: Könemann.

Schulz, R. (2004). "Between heaven and Earth – temples to the gods in the middle kingdom". Pp. 132–41 in *Egypt. The world of the pharaohs*, edited by R. Schulz and M. Seidel. Königswinter: Könemann.

Schulz, R. and Seidel, M. eds (2004). *Egypt. The world of the pharaohs*. Königswinter: Könemann.

Schulz, R. and Sourouzian, H. (2004). "The temples – royal gods and divine kings". Pp. 152–215 in *Egypt. The world of the pharaohs*, edited by R. Schulz and M. Seidel. Königswinter: Könemann.

Seidel, M. (2004). "The Valley of the Kings", pp. 216–43 in *Egypt. The world of the pharaohs*, edited by R. Schulz and M. Seidel. Königswinter: Könemann.

Seidel, M. and Schulz, R. (2005). *Egypt: art and architecture*. Königswinter: Könemann.

Seidlmayer, S. (2004a). "Egypt's path to advanced civilization". Pp. 8–23 in *Egypt. The world of the pharaohs*, edited by R. Schulz and M. Seidel. Königswinter: Könemann.

Seidlmayer, S. (2004b). "The rise of the state to the Second Dynasty". Pp. 24–39 in *Egypt. The world of the pharaohs*, edited by R. Schulz and M. Seidel. Königswinter: Könemann.

Shaw, I. ed. (2003). *The Oxford history of ancient Egypt*. New York: Oxford University Press.

Shermer, M. (2002). "The shamans of scientism". *Scientific American* May 13th.

Silverman, D.P. ed. (2003). *Ancient Egypt*. London: Duncan Baird Publishers.

Smith, J.I. (1999). "Islam and Christendom. Historical, cultural and religious interaction from the seventh to the fifteenth centuries". Pp. 305–45 in *The Oxford history of Islam*, edited by J.L. Esposito. New York: Oxford University Press.

Snooks, G.D. (1993). *Economics without time. A science blind to the forces of historical change.* London: Macmillan/Ann Arbor: University of Michigan Press.

Snooks, G.D. (1996). *The dynamic society: exploring the sources of global change.* London & New York: Routledge.

Snooks, G.D. (1997a). *The ephemeral civilization. Exploding the myth of social evolution.* London & New York: Routledge.

Snooks, G.D. (1997b). "Strategic demand and the growth-inflation curve: new theoretical and empirical concepts in economics". ANU Working Papers in Economic History, no. 195 (July). Canberra: Australian National University. [See **InstituteGDS** website.]

Snooks, G.D. (1998a). *The laws of history*. London & New York: Routledge.

Snooks, G.D. (1998b). *Longrun dynamics. A general economic and political theory.* New York/London: St Martins Press/Macmillan.

Snooks, G.D. (1999). *Global transition. A general theory of economic development*. New York/London: St Martins Press/Macmillan.

Snooks, G.D. (2000). *The global crisis makers. An end to progress and liberty?* New York/London: St Martins Press/Macmillan.

Snooks, G.D. (2002). "Uncovering the laws of global history". *Social Evolution and History* 1: 25–53.

Snooks, G.D. (2003). *The collapse of Darwinism, or the rise of a realist theory of life*. Lanham, MD & Oxford: Lexington Books, Rowman & Littlefield.

Snooks, G.D. (2005). "The origin of life on earth: a new general dynamic theory". *Advances in Space Research* 36: 226–34.

Snooks, G.D. (2006a). *The selfcreating mind*. Lanham, MD & Oxford: University Press of America, Rowman & Littlefield.

Snooks, G.D. (2006b). "Dynamics downunder: Australian economic strategy and performance from the paleolithic to the twenty-first century". Centre for Economic Policy Research *Discussion Paper* no. 539 (December). Canberra: Australian National University. [See **CEPR** webpage.]

Snooks, G.D. (2007). "Self-organisation or selfcreation? From social physics to realist dynamics". *Social Evolution and History* 6: 118–44.

Snooks, G.D. (2008a). "A general theory of complex living systems: exploring the demand side of dynamics". *Complexity* 13(6): 12–20.

Snooks, G.D. (2008b). "The irrational 'war on inflation': why inflation targeting is both socially unacceptable and economically untenable". Global Dynamic Systems Centre *Working Papers*, no. 1 (March). Canberra: Australian National University. [See **InstituteGDS** website.]

Snooks, G.D. (2008c). "Australia's long-run economic strategy, performance and policy: a new dynamic perspective". *Economic Papers* 27: 208–32. [Also see **InstituteGDS** website.]

Snooks, G.D. (2008d). "Recession, depression, and financial crisis: Everything economists want to know but are afraid to ask". Global Dynamic Systems Centre *Working Papers,* no. 7 (October). Canberra: Australian National University. [See **InstituteGDS** website.]

Snooks, G.D. (2009). *Climate mitigation or technological revolution? A critical choice of futures.* Global Dynamic Systems Centre *Working Papers* No. 10 (February). Canberra: Australian National University. [See **InstituteGDS** website.]

Snooks, G.D. (2010). *The Coming Eclipse, or The Triumph of Climate Mitigation Over Solar Revolution.* Canberra: IGDS Books. [See **InstituteGDS** website.]

Snooks, R.W. (2008). "Observations on the algorithmic emergence of character". E. Abruzzo, E. Ellingson and J.D. Solomon, eds, *Models: 306090 Books* 11: 92–102.

Sobel, D. (1999). *Galileo's daughter. A drama of science, faith and love.* London: Fourth Estate.

Sobel, D. trans (2001). *To father. The letters of Sister Maria Celeste to Galileo, 1623–1633.* London: Fourth Estate.

Spence, L. (2004). *Myths and legends of the North American Indians.* London: CRW Publishing.

Spencer, H. (1969). Principles of Sociology. Hamden, Comm: Archon Books.

Speth, J.D. (2004). "News flash: negative evidence convicts Neanderthals of gross mental incompetence". *World Archaeology* 36: 519–26.

Stadelmann, R. (2004). "Royal tombs from the age of the pyramids". Pp. 46–77 in *Egypt. The world of the pharaohs*, edited by R. Schulz and M. Seidel. Königswinter: Könemann.

Stanford, C.B. and Bunn, H.T. eds (2001). *Meat eating and human evolution.* Oxford: Oxford University Press.

Strehlow, T.G.H. (1964). "The art of circle, line, and square". *Australian Aboriginal art*, edited by R.M. Berndt. Sydney: Ure Smith

Strehlow, T.G.H. (1993). *Central Australian religion.* Alice Springs: Northern Territory Government Printer.

Stringer, C.B. and Mellars, P. eds (1989). *The human revolution: behavioural and biological perspectives on the origins of modern humans.* Edinburgh: Edinburgh University Press.

Stringer, C.B. and Gamble, C. (1993). *In search of the Neanderthals: solving the puzzle of human origins.* London: Thames & Hudson.

Stringer, C.B. (2002). "New perspectives on the Neanderthals". *Evolutionary Anthropology* suppl. 1: 58–59.

Strudwick, N. and Strudwick, H. (1999). *Thebes in Egypt. A guide to the tombs and temples of ancient Luxor.* Ithaca, NY: Cornell University Press.

Taylor, J. (2002). "The future of Christianity". Pp. 644–83 in *The Oxford history of Christianity*, edited by J. McManners. Oxford: Oxford University Press.

Tesfatsion, L and Judd, K.L. (2006). *Handbook of computational economics, Vol. 2: Agent-based computational economics*. Amsterdam: Elsevier/North-Holland.

Thiselton, A.C. (2002). *A concise encyclopedia of the philosophy of religion*. Oxford: Oneworld Publications.

Thompson, T.L. (1999). *The mythic past: Biblical archaeology and the myth of Israel*. New York: Basic Books.

Trinkaus, E. and Shipman, P. (1994). *The Neanderthals: changing the image of mankind*. London: Cape.

Turk, I. ed. (1997). *Mousterian 'bone flute' and other finds from Divje Babe I cave site in Slovenia*. Ijubljana: Založba ZRC.

Tyldesley, J. (2005). *Nefertiti. Unlocking the mystery surrounding Egypt's most famous and beautiful queen*. London: Penguin Books.

Vermes, G. (1998). *The complete Dead Sea scrolls in English*. London: Penguin Books.

Voll, J.O. (1999). "Foundations for renewal and reform". Pp. 509–47 in *The Oxford history of Islam*, edited by J.L. Esposito. New York: Oxford University Press.

Ware, K. (2002). "Eastern Christendom" pp. 131–66 in *The Oxford history of Christianity*, edited by J. McManners. Oxford: Oxford University Press.

White, R. (2003). *Prehistoric art: the symbolic journey of humankind*. New York: Harry N. Abrams.

Wiles, M. (2002). "What Christians believe". Pp. 571–86 in *The Oxford history of Christianity*, edited by J. McManners. Oxford: Oxford University Press.

Willeitner, J. (2004). "Royal and divine festivals". Pp. 450–57 in *Egypt. The world of the pharaohs*, edited by R. Schulz and M. Seidel. Königswinter: Könemann.

Wilson, A.N. (1999). *God's funeral*. New York & London: Norton.

Wilson, B. (2002). "New images of Christian community". Pp. 587–617 in *The Oxford history of Christianity*, edited by J. McManners. Oxford: Oxford University Press.

Wilson, D.S. (2002). *Darwin's cathedral: evolution, religion and the nature of society*. Chicago: University of Chicago Press.

Wilson, E.O. (1975). *Sociobiology: the new synthesis.* Cambridge, MA: Belknap Press of Harvard University Press.

Wilson, E.O. (1978). *On human nature.* Cambridge, MA: Harvard University Press.

Wilson, E.O. (1998). *Consilience: the unity of knowledge.* New York: Knopf.

Wilson, E.O. (1999). *Consilience: the unity of knowledge.* New York: Vintage Books.

Wilson, E.O. (2002). *The future of life.* London: Little Brown.

Wilson, J.A. (1951). *The culture of ancient Egypt.* Chicago: University of Chicago Press.

Wrathall, M.A. (2003). *Religion after metaphysics.* Cambridge: Cambridge University Press.

Woolf, G. ed. (2005). *Ancient civilizations. The illustrated guide to belief, mythology and art.* London: Duncan Baird Publishers.

Yoder, J.H. (2003). *The Jewish–Christian schism revisited.* Edited by M.G. Cartwright and P. Ochs. Grand Rapids, Michigan & Cambridge, UK: W.B. Eerdmans Pub. Co.

Yong, J. (2003). *The death of God and the meaning life.* London & New York: Routledge.

ABOUT THE AUTHOR

Graeme Donald Snooks is the Executive Director of the Institute of Global Dynamic Systems (IGDS) in Canberra. For twenty-one years between 1989 and 2010 he was the foundation Coghlan Research Professor in the Institute of Advanced Studies at the Australian National University. More than two decades ago he embarked on an ambitious research program to develop a realist dynamic theory of the changing fortunes of human society and life from their beginnings. This has given rise to the widely acclaimed dynamic-strategy theory (recently published in *Advances in Space research* and in *Complexity* the journal of the Santa Fe Institute), which Professor Snooks is employing to rethink all aspects of the life sciences. This is the first general dynamic theory in the history of human thought to employ an effective demand-side approach. The significance of this is that all supply-side theories are fundamentally flawed.

The results of this research have been published in a number of well-received trilogies, including the global history trilogy (*The Dynamic Society, The Ephemeral Civilization,* and *The Laws of History*), the social dynamics trilogy (*Longrun Dynamics, Global Transition,* and *The Global Crisis Makers*), and the dynamics of life trilogy (*The Collapse of Darwinism, The Selfcreating Mind,* and *Dead God Rising*). Future volumes will explore the dynamic nature of human values and will provide an overview of the entire research program. The core discovery of this work is the universal life system, analyzed for the first time in *Dead God Rising*.

I G D S

ABOUT IGDS BOOKS

IGDS Books is the imprint of the publishing activities of the Institute of Global Dynamic Systems in Canberra. It is the mission of IGDS Books to publish innovative work that pushes beyond the existing frontiers of knowledge – a challenge that major scholarly publishers have abandoned in this electronic era. As executive director of the institute, Professor Graeme Snooks oversees the activities of IGDS Books.

For information about the Institute or **IGDS Books,** see the Institute's website, or contact Professor Snooks at seouenaca@gmail.com.

Other **IGDS Books** include:

G.D. Snooks, *The Coming Eclipse – or The Triumph of Climate Mitigation Over Solar Revolution* (August 2010)

G.D. Snooks, *Ark of the Sun. The Improbable Voyage of Life* (forthcoming 2011)

G.D. Snooks, *The Death of Zarathustra. Notes on Truth for the Risk-taker* (forthcoming 2011).

For information about and orders for the Institute's publications – books and working papers – please contact the Institute Administrator at institutegds@gmail.com.

www.ingramcontent.com/pod-product-compliance
Lightning Source LLC
Chambersburg PA
CBHW070539270326
41926CB00013B/2145